A HISTORY OF IRISH AUTOBIOGRAPHY

A History of Irish Autobiography is the first critical survey of autobiographical self-representation in Ireland from its recoverable beginnings to the twenty-first century. The book draws on a wealth of original scholarship by leading experts to provide an authoritative examination of life-writing in the English and Irish languages. Beginning with a comprehensive overview of autobiography theory and criticism in Ireland, this *History* guides the reader through seventeen centuries of Irish achievement in autobiography, a category that incorporates diverse literary forms, from religious tracts and travelogues to memoirs, diaries and digital narratives. Chapters are structured around key subgenres, themes, texts and practitioners, and each features a guide to recommended further reading. The volume's extensive coverage is complemented by a chronology of Irish autobiographical writing from the fifth century to the contemporary era, the first of its kind to be published.

LIAM HARTE is the author or editor of ten books, among them *Reading the Contemporary Irish Novel 1987–2007* (2014), *The Literature of the Irish in Britain: Autobiography and Memoir, 1725–2001* (2009) and *Modern Irish Autobiography: Self, Nation and Society* (2007), the last two of which are widely recognized as pioneering publications in the field of modern Irish life-writing. He is Senior Lecturer in Irish and Modern Literature at the University of Manchester.

A HISTORY OF IRISH AUTOBIOGRAPHY

EDITED BY

LIAM HARTE

University of Manchester

CAMBRIDGE
UNIVERSITY PRESS

CAMBRIDGE
UNIVERSITY PRESS

University Printing House, Cambridge CB2 8BS, United Kingdom

One Liberty Plaza, 20th Floor, New York, NY 10006, USA

477 Williamstown Road, Port Melbourne, VIC 3207, Australia

314–321, 3rd Floor, Plot 3, Splendor Forum, Jasola District Centre,
New Delhi – 110025, India

79 Anson Road, #06–04/06, Singapore 079906

Cambridge University Press is part of the University of Cambridge.

It furthers the University's mission by disseminating knowledge in the pursuit of
education, learning, and research at the highest international levels of excellence.

www.cambridge.org
Information on this title: www.cambridge.org/9781107131446
DOI: 10.1017/9781316443279

© Cambridge University Press 2018

First published 2018

Printed in the United States of America by Sheridan Books, Inc.

A catalogue record for this publication is available from the British Library.

Library of Congress Cataloging-in-Publication Data
NAMES: Harte, Liam, editor.
TITLE: A history of Irish autobiography / edited by Liam Harte, University of Manchester.
DESCRIPTION: Cambridge ; New York : Cambridge University Press, 2017. | Includes index.
IDENTIFIERS: LCCN 2017025813 | ISBN 9781107131446
SUBJECTS: LCSH: Autobiography – Irish authors – History and criticism.
CLASSIFICATION: LCC CT34.I735 H57 2017 | DDC 920.041709–dc23
LC record available at https://lccn.loc.gov/2017025813

ISBN 978-1-107-13144-6 Hardback

Contents

Contributors

NICHOLAS ALLEN is Franklin Professor of English and Director of the Willson Center of Humanities and Arts at the University of Georgia.

JONATHAN BOLTON is Professor of English at Auburn University. He specializes in modern British and Irish literature. He is the author of *'Blighted Beginnings': Coming of Age in Independent Ireland* (2010) and *Personal Landscapes: British Poets in Egypt* (1997). His essays have appeared in such journals as *Modern Drama, New Hibernia Review, Journal of Modern Literature, Contemporary Literature* and *South Atlantic Review*.

PATRICK BUCKRIDGE is Adjunct Professor of Literary Studies at Griffith University, Brisbane. He has published widely on the history of reading, particularly in Australia, on literary biography, and on the Irish and Scottish presences in Australian literature. He contributed a chapter to the fifth volume of *The Oxford History of the Irish Book* (2011), was a contributing editor to *By the Book: A Literary History of Queensland* (2007) and is the author of several articles in the *Australian Dictionary of Biography*.

MARIE-LOUISE COOLAHAN is Professor of English at the National University of Ireland, Galway. She is the author of *Women, Writing, and Language in Early Modern Ireland* (2010), as well as articles and book chapters engaged with questions of gender, authorship and textual transmission. She is currently principal investigator of the ERC-funded research project 'RECIRC: The Reception and Circulation of Early Modern Women's Writing, 1550–1700' and co-investigator of the Leverhulme-funded project 'Women's Poetry in Ireland, Scotland and Wales, 1400–1800', which is led by Sarah Prescott at Aberystwyth University.

MICHAEL CRONIN holds a Personal Chair in the School of Applied Language and Intercultural Studies at Dublin City University. He has published widely on questions of language, mobility and identity. He is the author of *Across the Lines: Travel, Language, Translation* (2000) and *The Expanding World: Towards a Politics of Microspection* (2012), and co-editor of *Tourism in Ireland: A Critical Analysis* (1993) and *Irish Tourism: Image, Culture, Identity* (2003). He is a member of the Royal Irish Academy and the Academia Europeae.

KELLY FITZGERALD lectures in Irish Folklore and Celtic Civilisation at University College Dublin. Her work has focused on the development of folkloristics and folklore studies in Ireland, as well as on the creative process behind the verbal arts. She is a director of the National Folklore Collection and director of the Irish Association of Professional Historians. She also works as an ethnographer and oral historian for Anu Productions, of which she is one of its company directors.

LOUISE FULLER is an associate fellow of the Department of History at Maynooth University. She is author of *Irish Catholicism since 1950: The Undoing of a Culture* (2002) and co-editor with Eamon Maher and John Littleton of *Irish and Catholic? Towards an Understanding of Identity* (2006).

ELIZABETH GRUBGELD is Professor of English at Oklahoma State University. She is the author of *George Moore and the Autogenous Self: The Autobiography and Fiction* (1994) and *Anglo-Irish Autobiography: Class, Gender, and the Forms of Narrative* (2004), as well as many articles on Irish literature, life-writing and disability studies. She is currently completing a book entitled *Disability and Life Writing in Post-Independence Ireland.*

GLENN HOOPER lectures in Tourism at Glasgow Caledonian University. He has held previous positions at St Mary's University College, Belfast, the University of Aberdeen and the Open University. As well as publishing widely on travel and tourism, he has organized several international symposia on these topics and is the co-founder of the international Borders and Crossings conference series. He is the author of *Travel Writing and Ireland, 1760–1860* (2005) and editor of *Landscape and Empire, 1770–2000* (2005) and *The Tourist's Gaze: Travellers to Ireland, 1800–2000* (2001).

LAURA P. Z. IZARRA is Associate Professor of English and Irish Literatures at the University of São Paulo. She has published widely on the Irish diaspora in South America, including the first Portuguese translation of

The Amazon Journal of Roger Casement (2016). Her books include *Narrativas de la diáspora irlandesa bajo la Cruz del Sur* (2010), *Mirrors and Holographic Labyrinths: The Process of a New Aesthetic Synthesis in the Novels of John Banville* (1999) and, as co-editor with Munira Mutran, *Kaleidoscopic Views of Ireland* (2003). She has co-edited *ABEI Journal: The Brazilian Journal of Irish Studies* since 1999 and *Lectures* since 2010.

MATTHEW KELLY is Professor of History at Northumbria University. He has written extensively about the history of Irish nationalism, including articles in *Past and Present* and *Journal of British Studies* and thematic accounts for recent edited volumes published by Cambridge, Oxford and Princeton university presses. He also works on the environmental history of modern Britain and is the author of *Quartz and Feldspar. Dartmoor: A British Landscape in Modern Times* (2015).

MARIA LUDDY is Professor of Modern Irish History at the University of Warwick. She has written extensively on the history of women in Ireland and is co-author with Mary O'Dowd of a forthcoming study entitled *A History of Marriage in Ireland, 1660–1925*.

CLAIRE LYNCH received her doctorate from the University of Oxford and is now Senior Lecturer at Brunel University London. She is the author of *Irish Autobiography: Stories of Self in the Narrative of a Nation* (2009) and several articles and chapters on Irish fiction and life-writing. Her latest book, *Cyber Ireland: Text, Image, Culture* (2014), explores the presence and significance of cyberculture in Irish literature. She serves as Secretary of the British Association of Irish Studies.

MOIRA J. MAGUIRE holds a PhD in History from American University and is the author of *Precarious Childhood in Post-Independence Ireland* (2009) and numerous articles and book reviews. For twelve years she was an associate professor of History at the University of Arkansas, Little Rock. She is currently Dean of Liberal Arts at Schenectady County Community College in New York.

CHRISTINA HUNT MAHONY is a senior research fellow in the School of English at Trinity College Dublin and a former director of the graduate Center for Irish Studies at the Catholic University of America in Washington, DC. Her publications include *Contemporary Irish Literature: Transforming Tradition* (1998), *Out of History: Essays on Selected Writings of Sebastian Barry* (2006) and *The Future of Irish Studies: Report of the Irish Forum* (2006).

ANTHONY P. MCINTYRE is an associate lecturer at University College Dublin. He has published chapters and articles in numerous scholarly collections and journals and is currently finishing a monograph entitled *Millennial Tensions*, which examines the cultural and affective interplay of generational cohorts, screen cultures and politics. He is co-editor of *The Aesthetics and Affects of Cuteness* (2017) and managing editor of the journal *Television and New Media*.

MARY MULDOWNEY is an independent Dublin-based scholar who uses oral history as the primary source for much of her research, which has been published in the form of monographs, book chapters and journal articles. She is director of the Alternative Visions Oral History Group and a former director of the Oral History Network of Ireland. Mary also designs and delivers training courses for community and trade union activists.

DIANE NEGRA is Professor of Film Studies and Screen Culture and Head of Film Studies at University College Dublin. A member of the Royal Irish Academy, she is the author, editor or co-editor of ten books and serves as co-editor of the journal *Television and New Media*.

MÁIRE NÍ MHAONAIGH is Professor of Celtic and Medieval Studies at the University of Cambridge. She has published much on medieval Irish literature and history, with a particular focus on Ireland's place in the wider world. She is the author of *Brian Boru: Ireland's Greatest King?* (2006), co-editor, with Howard Clarke and Raghnall Ó Floinn, of *Ireland and Scandinavia in the Early Viking Age* (1999) and co-editor, with Roy Flechner, of *The Introduction of Christianity into the Early Medieval Insular World* (2016).

BRÍONA NIC DHIARMADA is the Thomas J. and Kathleen M. O'Donnell Professor of Irish Studies and Concurrent Professor of Film, Television and Theatre at the University of Notre Dame. Among her many publications is *Téacs Baineann, Téacs Mná* (2005), a full-length study of the poetry of Nuala Ní Dhomhnaill, as well as numerous articles on Irish-language literature and culture. Her most recent book, *The 1916 Irish Rebellion* (2016), is a companion to the RTÉ and PBS documentary series that she also wrote and produced.

GEORGE O'BRIEN was born in Enniscorthy and reared in Lismore, Co. Waterford. His publications include an autobiographical trilogy, *The Village of Longing* (1987), *Dancehall Days* (1988) and *Out of Our Minds*

(1994). He is Professor Emeritus of English at Georgetown University, Washington, DC.

MARGARET O'CALLAGHAN is a historian and political analyst at the School of Politics, International Studies and Philosophy at Queen's University, Belfast. A former Laski Research Scholar at St John's College, Cambridge and fellow of Sidney Sussex College, she has taught at the universities of Cambridge and Notre Dame. She is the author of numerous works on aspects of British high politics and the state apparatus in Ireland from the late nineteenth century to the revolutionary period. She has also published on the Royal Irish Constabulary the Royal Ulster Constabulary, and the careers of Richard Pigott, Roger Casement and Tom Kettle. She is co-editor, with Mary E. Daly, of *1916 in 1966: Commemorating the Easter Rising* (2007).

EMMET O'CONNOR was born in Dublin and raised in Waterford. On leaving school he worked as a shipping clerk in Waterford Glass before studying at the National University of Ireland, Galway and St John's College, Cambridge. He is currently a senior lecturer in the Department of History at Ulster University. An honorary president of the Irish Labour History Society, he has published widely on labour history, most recently *Big Jim Larkin: Hero or Wrecker?* (2015).

EOIN O'MALLEY is Senior Lecturer in Political Science in the School of Law and Government at Dublin City University. His research is mainly focused on Irish politics and government. In addition to thirty peer-reviewed articles, he is the author of a textbook, *Contemporary Ireland* (2011), and co-editor of two volumes, *Irish Political Studies: Key Contributions* (2008), with Conor McGrath, and *Governing Ireland: From Cabinet Government to Delegated Governance* (2012), with Muiris MacCarthaigh. He is currently working on a monograph on political leadership in modern Ireland and a co-edited book on the Fianna Fáil party.

KEVIN RAFTER is Professor of Political Communications in the School of Communications at Dublin City University. He is a former political journalist with roles including assistant editor of the *Sunday Tribune* newspaper in Dublin and editor of *Magill* magazine. He is the author of histories of several Irish political parties, including *Road to Power: How Fine Gael Made History* (2011), *Sinn Féin 1905–2006: In the Shadow of Gunmen* (2005) and *The Clann: The Story of Clann na Poblachta* (1996), as well as biographies of Neil Blaney and Martin Mansergh.

JAMES SILAS ROGERS is editor of *New Hibernia Review/Iris Éireannach Nua* and former Director of the Center for Irish Studies at the University of St Thomas, Minnesota. His scholarly publications on Irish-American literature include two edited volumes, *Extended Family: Essays on Being Irish American from 'New Hibernia Review'* (2013) and *After the Flood: Irish America 1945–1960* (2009), and a monograph, *Irish-American Autobiography: The Divided Hearts of Athletes, Priests, Pilgrims, and More* (2017). He is a past president of the American Conference for Irish Studies.

BARRY SLOAN is Emeritus Professor of English at the University of Southampton. His publications include *Writers and Protestantism in the North of Ireland* (2000) and chapters on Irish life-writing in *Children, Childhood and Irish Society* (2014), edited by Maria Luddy and James M. Smith, and *Modern Irish Autobiography: Self, Nation and Society* (2007), edited by Liam Harte. He is co-editor, with Mary Hammond, of *Rural-Urban Relationships in the Nineteenth Century: Uneasy Neighbours?* (2016).

ROBERT TOBIN is Chaplain and Tutor in Theology at Oriel College, Oxford. A Fulbright Scholar, he studied at Harvard, Trinity College Dublin, Oxford and Cambridge. His monograph, *The Minority Voice: Hubert Butler and Southern Irish Protestantism, 1900–91*, was published in 2012. He is currently writing a book on identity and activism in the American Episcopal church since 1945.

Acknowledgements

I would like to express my sincere gratitude to Dr Ray Ryan, Senior Commissioning Editor at Cambridge University Press, for inviting me to take on this project and for his wise and patient stewardship of it from start to finish. It has been a pleasure to work with Ray and with the design and production teams at Cambridge University Press, particularly Dr Sharon McCann, who provided expert assistance during the book's final stages. My thanks also go to the six anonymous readers who offered perceptive feedback on my initial prospectus. The twenty-eight contributors to this *History* have been co-operative, patient and responsive throughout the book's gestation; I thank them all sincerely for their excellent scholarship and diligent commitment. As always, my deepest thanks go to my wife Yvonne and children, Oisín and Síofra, for their love and support.

Select Chronology

Autobiographical works that announce themselves as fiction are indicated with an asterisk.

c. 450	St Patrick, *Confessio*
c. 700	*Immram Brain maic Febail* ('Voyage of Bran son of Febal'); *Immram Curaig Máele Dúin* ('Voyage of the Curragh of Máel Dúin'); *Navigatio Sancti Brendani Abbatis* ('Voyage of St Brendan')
c. 800–900	*Caillech Bérri* ('Old Woman of Beare'); *Messe ocus Pangur Bán* ('White Pangur and I')
c. 1200–50	Muireadhach Ó Dálaigh, *M'anam do sgar riomsa a-raoir* ('My soul parted from me last night')
1553	John Bale, *The Vocacyon of Johan Bale to the Bishoprick of Ossorie in Ireland*
1607–08	Tadhg Ó Cianáin, *Imeacht na nIarlaí* ('The Earls' Departure')
1621–24	Bernard O'Brien, 'Bernard O'Brien's Account of Irish Activities in the Amazon, 1621–1624'
1623	Richard Boyle, 'True Remembrances: An Account of the Life of Richard Boyle, Earl of Cork'
c. 1629	John Cusack, 'Irelands Comfort'
1641	Establishment of parliamentary commission to take depositions (eyewitness testimonies) on the 1641 rising.
1641–47	Tarlach Ó Mealláin, *Cín Lae Uí Mhealláin* ('Friar O Meallan Journal')
1653	John Rogers, *Ohel, or, Beth-shemesh*
1671–73	Mary Rich, 'Some Specialties in the Life of M. Warwicke' (written; published 1848)
1671–1714	Elizabeth Freke, *The Remembrances of Elizabeth Freke, 1671–1714* (written; published 1913)

1940	John Lavery, *The Life of a Painter*; Seosamh Mac Grianna, *Mo Bhealach Féin* (*My Own Way*); Sean O'Faolain, *An Irish Journey*; Conchúr Ó Síocháin, *Seanchas Chléire* (*The Man from Cape Clear*); Forrest Reid, *Private Road*
1941	Kate O'Brien, *The Land of Spices**; Enid Starkie, *A Lady's Child*
1942	Elizabeth Bowen, *Bowen's Court* and *Seven Winters*; Sean O'Casey, *Pictures in the Hallway*; Seamus Ó Grianna, *Nuair a Bhí Mé Óg* (*When I Was Young*); Nesca A. Robb, *An Ulsterwoman in England, 1924–1941*
1943	Kathleen Coyle, *The Magical Realm*; Charles B. Driscoll, *Kansas Irish*; Colm Ó Gaora, *Mise* (*Myself*)
1944	Annie M. P. Smithson, *Myself – and Others*
1945	Sean O'Casey, *Drums Under the Window*; Mark F. Ryan, *Fenian Memories*
1946	Micheál Mac Liammóir, *All for Hecuba*; Kathleen Nevin, *You'll Never Go Back**; Cathal O'Byrne, *As I Roved Out*
1947	Bureau of Military History established Mary Colum, *Life and the Dream*
1949	Tom Barry, *Guerrilla Days in Ireland*; James Duhig, *Crowded Years*; Sean O'Casey, *Inishfallen, Fare Thee Well*; George Bernard Shaw, *Sixteen Self Sketches*
1950	James H. Cousins and Margaret E. Cousins, *We Two Together*; Monk Gibbon, *Swiss Enchantment*; Seamus Murphy, *Stone Mad*
1951	Paul Henry, *An Irish Portrait*; Liam Ó Briain, *Cuimhní Cinn* (*Memoirs*)
1952	Sean O'Casey, *Rose and Crown*; Sheila Wingfield, *Real People*
1953	Denis Johnston, *Nine Rivers from Jordan*; Micheál Ó Guiheen, *Is Truagh ná Fannan an Óige* (*A Pity Youth Does Not Last*); Frank Pakenham, *Born to Believe*
1954	Christy Brown, *My Left Foot*; Sean O'Casey, *Sunset and Evening Star*
1955	Elizabeth Gurley Flynn, *I Speak My Own Piece*; C. S. Lewis, *Surprised by Joy*; Máire Nic Shiubhlaigh, *The Splendid Years*; W. B. Yeats, *Autobiographies*
1956	Sean O'Casey, *Mirror in My House*, 2 vols.

1957   Ernest Blythe, *Trasna na Bóinne* (*Across the Boyne*);
        Ninette de Valois, *Come Dance with Me*; Mary
        McCarthy, *Memories of a Catholic Girlhood*; John
        O'Donoghue, *In a Quiet Land*

1958   Brendan Behan, *Borstal Boy*; John O'Donoghue, *In a
        Strange Land*; Séamas Ó Maoileoin, *B'Fhiú an Braon
        Fola* (*It was Worth the Spilling of Blood*)

1959   Mící Mac Gabhann, *Rotha Mór an tSaoil* (*The Hard Road
        to Klondike*); Peter Tyrrell, *Founded on Fear* (written;
        published 2006)

1960   Cecil Day-Lewis, *The Buried Day*; Robert Harbinson, *No
        Surrender* and *Song of Erne*; Dónall Mac Amhlaigh,
        Dialann Deoraí (*An Irish Navvy*); Edna O'Brien, *The
        Country Girls**

1961   Robert Harbinson, *Up Spake the Cabin Boy*; Frank
        O'Connor, *An Only Child*

1962   Austin Clarke, *Twice Round the Black Church*; Kildare
        Dobbs, *Running to Paradise*; Brian Inglis, *West Briton*

1963   Eamonn Andrews, *This Is My Life*; Robert Harbinson,
        The Protégé; Kate O'Brien, *Presentation Parlour*

1964   Patrick Kavanagh, *Self Portrait*; John B. Keane, *Self-
        Portrait*; Janet McNeill, *The Maiden Dinosaur**; Sean
        O'Faolain, *Vive Moi!*

1965   Louis MacNeice, *The Strings Are False*; John
        McGahern, *The Dark**; Brian Moore, *The Emperor of
        Ice Cream**

1966   Aidan Higgins, *Langrishe, Go Down**; Florence Mary
        McDowell, *Other Days Around Me*

1967   Patrick Peyton, *All for Her*

1968   Christabel Bielenberg, *The Past is Myself*; Bulmer
        Hobson, *Ireland Yesterday and Tomorrow*; Frank
        O'Connor, *My Father's Son*

1969   Bernadette Devlin, *The Price of My Soul*; William
        O'Brien, *Forth the Banners Go*; Seán Ó Criomhthain,
        Lá dár Saol (*A Day in Our Life*)

1970   Christy Brown, *Down All the Days**; Anne Gregory, *Me
        and Nu*; Julia O'Faolain, *Godded and Codded**

1971   Hanna Greally, *Bird's Nest Soup*; Francis Stuart, *Black
        List, Section H**

McCafferty, *Nell*; Graham Norton, *So Me*; Maureen O'Hara, *'Tis Herself*

2005   Nick Laird, *Utterly Monkey**; Frank McCourt, *Teacher Man*; Barry McCrea, *The First Verse**; John McGahern, *Memoir*; Kathy O'Beirne, *Kathy's Story*; Kathleen O'Malley, *Childhood Interrupted*

2006   Ireland Life-Writing Archive established at University College Dublin

Lucy Caldwell, *Where They Were Missed**; Brian D'Arcy, *A Different Journey*; Geraldine Plunkett Dillon, *All in the Blood*; Hugo Hamilton, *The Sailor in the Wardrobe*

2007   David Andrews, *Kingstown Republican*; Patricia Craig, *Asking for Trouble*; John Montague, *The Pear is Ripe*

2008   Leland Bardwell, *A Restless Life*; Gerald Dawe, *My Mother-City*; Denis O'Driscoll, *Stepping Stones*; Gerry Ryan, *Would the Real Gerry Ryan Please Stand Up*

2009   Publication of *Dictionary of Irish Biography*, 9 vols.

Dónal Óg Cusack, *Come What May*; Jennifer Johnston, *Truth or Fiction**; Coleen Nolan, *Upfront and Personal*; Colm O'Gorman, *Beyond Belief*; Cathal Ó Searcaigh, *Light on Distant Hills*; Joe Queenan, *Closing Time*

2010   The 1641 depositions published in print and online

Launch of the Peace Process Layers of Meaning Project

Bertie Ahern, *The Autobiography*; Charles Fanning, *Mapping Norwood*; Nuala Fennell, *Political Woman*; Eamon Gilmore, *Leading Lights*; Albert Reynolds, *My Autobiography*

2011   Oral History Network of Ireland established

Launch of the *Irish Times* 'Generation Emigration' online forum

Sister Stanislaus Kennedy, *The Road Home*; Patrick McGinley, *That Unearthly Valley*

2012   Launch of the @Ireland Twitter account

Substantial part of Bureau of Military History collection published online

David Norris, *A Kick Against the Pricks*; Edna O'Brien, *Country Girl*; Mary O'Rourke, *Just Mary*; Mary Robinson, *Everybody Matters*; Katie Taylor, *My Olympic Dream*; Monica Wood, *When We Were the Kennedys*

CHAPTER I

Introduction
Autobiography Theory and Criticism in Ireland

Liam Harte

To say that a history of autobiographical self-representation in Ireland is long overdue is to make a grand understatement.[1] Despite the immense proliferation of variant forms of first-person narratives in Irish culture since medieval times, autobiography, memoir and life-writing have long been little more than marginal presences in the authoritative histories of the nation's literature.[2] Why this is so is open to speculation, though the very fact that autobiography in Ireland is such an ancient and widespread practice, which has attracted a broad spectrum of writers (obscure as well as renowned, marginally literate as well as educationally privileged) and given rise to a highly diverse miscellany of texts (spoken as well as written, obliquely self-revelatory as well as purposefully confessional), presents a formidable obstacle to systematic investigation. The sheer prevalence of autobiographical writing may even obscure awareness of a coherent tradition, even though there is broad agreement in practice about which texts make up the core canon.

No less daunting is the challenge of demarcating the boundaries of this messily multifarious corpus of writing, much of which has fallen into oblivion. Not only could vast tracts of Irish literature legitimately be characterized as autobiographical in some degree, but the genre of autobiography itself is notorious for being 'fundamentally unstable and hence unclassifiable, a shifting, borderless locale'.[3] Scepticism about the essential unity of such 'an unruly

---

[1] For practical as much as philosophical reasons, this *History*'s coverage does not extend to autobiographical work in the genres of poetry, drama, film or the visual arts.

[2] As is well known, there is no consensus among scholars about the terminology used to describe the practice of autobiographical self-representation. Although there are important distinctions among the key terms – 'autobiography', 'auto/biography', 'memoir', 'life narrative', 'life-writing' and 'self-writing' (the last two of which are often spelled without the hyphen) – the lines of demarcation between them, when not opaque, are contested, evolving and often hard to maintain in practice. So while the title of this commissioned *History* clearly privileges the first of these terms, as editor I have allowed each contributor to use their preferred terminology and critical vocabulary.

[3] Paul John Eakin, *How Our Lives Become Stories* (Ithaca: Cornell University Press, 1999), 2.

and even slightly disreputable field'[4] may therefore be a factor in the critical undervaluation of this body of literature; so too may the tendency to regard autobiography as a secondary endeavour, a discursive supplement to historiography or a 'textual accessory, either to its author's extra-textual life, which is the text's seductive but otherwise inaccessible ground, or else to his published oeuvre'.[5] Or perhaps the root cause lies in the traditional reluctance of critics to engage with a genre that encompasses a high proportion of 'non-literary', mass-marketed and tabloid-styled texts, the legitimization of which as objects of study is a relatively recent, and still contested, phenomenon. Whatever its causes, this critical neglect has deprived scholars and students of a thorough evaluative survey of Irish autobiographical writing and left the literary historian without that essential research tool, a bibliographical guide, there being no Irish equivalents to the descriptive bibliographies that have aided the study of autobiography in Britain and the United States of America, for example.[6] In fact, no detailed chronology, let alone taxonomy, of this centuries-old tradition has yet been published; the select chronology compiled for this volume is offered as a first step in that direction.

Although the historiography of Irish autobiography may not be very copious, it has produced several perceptive and, in differing degrees, engaging studies of particular periods, traditions, authors and individual works nevertheless. The primary focus of most of these studies has been twentieth-century Irish literary autobiography, particularly the highly imaginative, formally restless renditions of personal and historical experience produced by the three most eminent autobiographers associated with the Irish Literary Revival (c. 1890–1930): William Butler Yeats, George Moore and Sean O'Casey. Despite significant differences between them, all three writers were compulsive self-interrogators whose mastery of the multi-volume autobiography established the importance of life-writing within the larger project of Irish cultural nationalism, Yeats being convinced that 'the power of our epoch on Ireland in the next generation will greatly depend on the way its personal

[4] Linda Anderson, *Autobiography* (London: Routledge, 2001), 2.
[5] John Sturrock, 'Theory versus Autobiography', in Robert Folkenflik, ed., *The Culture of Autobiography* (Stanford: Stanford University Press, 1993), 23.
[6] See, for example, William Matthews, *British Autobiographies: An Annotated Bibliography of British Autobiographies Published or Written Before 1951* (Berkeley: University of California Press, 1955); Louis Kaplan, *A Bibliography of American Autobiographies* (Madison: University of Madison Press, 1961); John Burnett, David Vincent and David Mayall, eds., *The Autobiography of the Working Class: An Annotated Critical Bibliography* (Brighton: Harvester Press, 1984–89), 3 vols.

history is written'.[7] But just as these writers' complex relations with cultural nationalism did not prevent them from being ardent internationalists, their approaches to life-writing were not constrained by national preoccupations. To the contrary, the innovative modes of self-inquiry developed by Yeats, Moore and O'Casey make them pivotal figures in the canon of modernist autobiography, in which context their self-mythologizing texts are exemplary of the attempt to break free of inherited forms of apprehending and representing identity and lived experience. These writers' serial acts of self-portraiture emanate from an understanding of autobiography as process, as performative act – a continually renewed attempt to create the self at the time of writing.

Of the three, Yeats has commanded the most critical and theoretical attention; indeed, no Irish autobiographer's work has been more extensively studied than his. The first journal article on his autobiographical prose appeared in 1942, a mere three years after his death, and the following decades saw the publication of several book-length studies, chiefly by North American scholars, devoted to his sophisticated art of literary self-portraiture.[8] What unites these studies is their elucidation of the diverse components of Yeats's manipulation of the autobiographical form and the expressive strategies engendered by his determinedly dialectical conception of selfhood. Guided by the doctrine of the mask or anti-self – 'the Image which is the opposite of all that I am in my daily life, and all that my country is' – Yeats recognized that his insistent quest for an integrated 'personality' and a harmonizing 'Unity of Being' and culture could only ever be realized in symbol, myth and art.[9] Thus, as David G. Wright notes: 'Yeats's writing constantly juxtaposes a desire for definition and completeness with the realisation that life prohibits such finality.'[10] Furthermore, because his 'urge to build a coherent mythology

---

[7] W. B. Yeats, *The Letters of W. B. Yeats*, ed. Allan Wade (London: Rupert Hart-Davis, 1954), 586. Cited in R. F. Foster, *W. B. Yeats: A Life, I: The Apprentice Mage 1865–1914* (Oxford: Oxford University Press, 1998), 492.

[8] See Shirley Neuman, *Some One Myth: Yeats's Autobiographical Prose* (Portlaoise: Dolmen Press in association with Humanities Press Inc., 1982); Daniel T. O'Hara, *Tragic Knowledge: Yeats's Autobiography and Hermeneutics* (New York: Columbia University Press, 1981); Joseph Ronsley, *Yeats's Autobiography: Life as Symbolic Pattern* (Cambridge, MA: Harvard University Press, 1968); Gail C. Schricker, *A New Species of Man: The Poetic Persona of W. B. Yeats* (Lewisburg: Bucknell University Press, 1982); David G. Wright, *Yeats's Myth of Self: A Study of the Autobiographical Prose* (Dublin: Gill and Macmillan, 1987).

[9] W. B. Yeats, *The Collected Works of W. B. Yeats III: Autobiographies*, ed. William H. O'Donnell and Douglas N. Archibald (New York: Scribner, 1999), 218, 342, 164.

[10] Wright, *Yeats's Myth of Self*, 98.

of self[11] was in ceaseless dialogue with his vision of the self as a masquerading performer, Yeats the autobiographer, in the words of Shirley Neuman, 'stage-manages his own life, and directs, in retrospect, an actor who is his earlier self'.[12] Her theatrical analogy can be readily transposed to the technically complex modes of self-projection that shape the polyvocal autobiographies of Moore and O'Casey, both of whom resisted the straitjacket of generic precedent in order to dramatize autobiographical subjectivities that are protean and infinitely modifiable.[13]

It was not until the 1980s that critical and theoretical attempts were made to place the work of these and other Irish literary autobiographers within a distinct and coherent national tradition of life-writing. First into the field was Kevin P. Reilly, who in a 1981 article examined the work of six male autobiographers – Moore, Yeats, O'Casey, William Carleton, Frank O'Connor and Patrick Kavanagh – with reference to the long-standing cultural tradition of personifying Ireland as mother, maiden or mistress.[14] Using a psychoanalytical compass, Reilly posited a direct link between these writers' persistent but ultimately 'unfulfillable desire'[15] for intimacy with an archetypal national goddess and the images they present in their autobiographies of the actual women in their lives. 'Because autobiography affirms identity', he asserted, 'the genre provides these Irish writers, determined to revive their cultural identity, with the distinct opportunity to affirm their individual identities as sons and lovers of Ireland.'[16] Reilly went on to draw attention to the interpersonal relationship between the

---

[11] Ibid., 99.

[12] Neuman, *Some One Myth*, 56. For insightful commentary on Yeats's strategies of self-definition, see Neal Alexander, 'Dialogues of Self and Soul: The Autobiographies of W. B. Yeats and R. S. Thomas', *Almanac: A Yearbook of Welsh Writing in English*, 12 (2007–08), 1–31; Eamonn Hughes, '"You Need Not Fear That I Am Not Amiable": Reading Yeats (Reading) Autobiographies', *Yeats Annual*, 12 (1996), 84–116; Rónán McDonald, 'The "Fascination of What I Loathed": Science and Self in W. B. Yeats's *Autobiographies*', in Maria DiBattista and Emily O. Wittman, eds., *Modernism and Autobiography* (New York: Cambridge University Press, 2014), 18–30.

[13] The definitive study of George Moore's representations of the self in autobiography and fiction is Elizabeth Grubgeld's *George Moore and the Autogenous Self: The Autobiography and Fiction* (Syracuse: Syracuse University Press, 1994). Michael Kenneally's *Portraying the Self: Sean O'Casey and the Art of Autobiography* (Gerrards Cross: Colin Smythe, 1988) is the most comprehensive analysis of O'Casey's autobiographical methods. See also Ronald Ayling, ed., *Sean O'Casey: Modern Judgements* (London: Macmillan, 1969); Peter James Harris, *Sean O'Casey's Letters and Autobiographies: Reflections of a Radical Ambivalence* (Trier: Wissenschaftlicher Verlag Trier, 2004); Robert G. Lowery, ed., *Essays on Sean O'Casey's Autobiographies* (London: Macmillan, 1981).

[14] Kevin P. Reilly, 'Irish Literary Autobiography: The Goddesses That Poets Dream Of', *Éire-Ireland*, 16:3 (1981), 57–80.

[15] Ibid., 75.   [16] Ibid., 77.

writer and 'the remote yet intimate reader'[17] in whose imaginative presence this process of identity affirmation takes place, thus anticipating the debates about relationality and alterity that emerged in critical work on Irish auto-biography in the 1990s and beyond. Four years after Reilly's intervention, Terence Brown provided a literary-historical overview of many of the same texts, in which he highlighted the writers' contrasting portrayals and inter-pretations of the Revival and its prime architect, Yeats, whose life, as James Olney observed in a 1993 essay collection devoted in part to modern Irish autobiography, became 'the great reference for the lives of the other auto-biographers, and his voice, as heard by each of the others, echoes through their books in an endless string of anecdotes'.[18]

It was Michael Kenneally, however, who in 1989 injected fresh critical rigour into these discussions with a theoretically informed analysis of Irish literary autobiography, which paid careful attention to the underlying structuring principles and stylistic features of the genre.[19] Kenneally hypothesized that since most of the leading literary autobiographers of the Revival and counter-Revival periods were shaped by their involvement in revolutionary nationalism, their self-portraits share common structural patterns, the most notable of which is a narrative arc that propels the (male) protagonist from an idealism fuelled by the rhetoric of romantic nationalism, through varying degrees of doubt and disappointment with the politics of liberation, to eventual alienation from, or partial accom-modation with, the unheroic actualities of state and society after inde-pendence. The 'perception of a special relationship between self and nation, the tendency to explore and define oneself in terms of patriotic values and national goals, to equate one's development with national destiny'[20] – these features, Kenneally persuasively argued, combine to provide the governing metaphor of twentieth-century Irish literary auto-biography. The fullest examination of this phenomenon is contained in a much-consulted unpublished doctoral dissertation on the autobiographies of Kavanagh, O'Connor, Sean O'Faolain and Francis Stuart by Eamonn Hughes, in which he postulates that 'to understand Irish autobiography it is necessary to understand Irish nationalism as a phenomenon which both

---

[17] Ibid., 80.

[18] James Olney, 'On the Nature of Autobiography', in James Noonan, ed., *Biography and Autobiography: Essays on Irish and Canadian History and Literature* (Ottawa: Carleton University Press, 1993), 117.

[19] Michael Kenneally, 'The Autobiographical Imagination and Irish Literary Autobiographies', in Michael Allen and Angela Wilcox, eds., *Critical Approaches to Anglo-Irish Literature* (Gerrards Cross: Colin Smythe, 1989), 111–31.

[20] Ibid., 123.

underwrites the specific problematics of self-definition in Ireland and provides the overarching framework within which Irish autobiographers define themselves'.[21]

What Kenneally left unsaid in his analysis is that this habit of mapping individual life stories onto a communal national story was first formed in the autobiographies of nineteenth-century Irish nationalists, particularly those associated with the Young Ireland movement of the 1840s. It was they, observed David Lloyd in *Nationalism and Minor Literature: James Clarence Mangan and the Emergence of Irish Cultural Nationalism* (1987), who 'inaugurated a cultural tradition that conceives the responsibility of literature, and of other cultural forms, to be the production and mediation of a sense of national identity'.[22] The literary model that emerged at this time placed an onerous responsibility on the autobiographer to make textual amends for political and historical deficiencies by imagining an inspirational synchrony between personal biography and nationalist aspiration:

> The biography of the national hero is, in the first instance, a repetition of the history of the nation. Through conscious identification with the nation, the individual transcends in himself the actual disintegration of the nation by coming to prefigure the nation's destiny: the total identification of the individual with the spirit of the nation is a figuration of the total unity of the political nation that is the goal of the nationalist's labors.[23]

What makes this a flawed aesthetic politics in Lloyd's view is its dependence on imperialist models of cultural development. In demanding that autobiographers produce representative protagonists whose autonomy and identity can only be realized through absolute identification with the stateless nation, Irish nationalist life-writing of the Victorian period replicates the bourgeois ideology of the colonial power and consequently works to conceal the fissures and dislocations of colonized subjectivities. Thus, John Mitchel's attempt to reconstitute the continuity of his personal identity in *Jail Journal* (1854) merely heightens his awareness of his own – and nationalism's – internal contradictions, while James Clarence Mangan 'registers the radical non-identity of the colonized subject'[24] by his refusal to present a stable, integrated subjectivity in his unfinished

---

[21] Eamonn Hughes, 'Nation and Self: A Study of Four Modern Irish Literary Autobiographies' (PhD diss., University of Leicester, 1990), 2.

[22] David Lloyd, *Nationalism and Minor Literature: James Clarence Mangan and the Emergence of Irish Cultural Nationalism* (Berkeley: University of California Press, 1987), xi.

[23] Ibid., 160.   [24] Ibid., xi.

autobiography of 1848. Sean Ryder provided a necessary addendum to Lloyd's critique of the limits and contradictions of nineteenth-century nationalist life-writing when he pointed out that the 'symbolic grammar' of Mitchel and Mangan's autobiographies is gendered in ways that 'make nationality conditional upon masculinity, and deny the possibility of an authentic female subjectivity'.[25]

The colonial and postcolonial theorizing that informs these readings of cultural nationalist autobiography was further developed by Seamus Deane in his short but highly influential introduction to the section entitled 'Autobiography and Memoirs 1890–1988' in *The Field Day Anthology of Irish Writing* (1991).[26] For Deane, Irish subjectivities are always already estranged from the concept of a unitary selfhood, always in a dialogical relationship with that which is not-the-self. This is because the material histories of colonialism in Ireland have rendered the articulation of autonomous agency and psychologically integrated subjectivity untenable. The same historical conditions make it impossible to disaggregate the personal and the political components of selfhood or separate self-definition from matters of power, domination and hierarchy. Irish autobiographical identities are therefore axiomatically relational in Deane's view, being 'concerned with the "other", the person or persons, events or places, that have helped to give the self definition', and necessarily oppositional: 'An idea of Ireland has to be fashioned, discovered, recreated over and against that which threatens to disallow it.'[27] The 'struggle between the sense of the "other" and the wish to find a way of including the other in some unified version both of self and culture' produces self-narratives that are constituted around conflict, inversion and an irredeemable 'sense of a missing feature or energy', such that the search for subjective authenticity 'is reaffirmed through its cancellation'.[28] What emerges from Deane's reading of modern Irish autobiography through the lens of the self/other binarism is a conception of subjectivity that is at once powerfully constrained and seemingly open-ended. By insisting upon the generative force of tension and contradiction in Irish autobiographical discourse, and by

[25] Sean Ryder, 'Male Autobiography and Cultural Nationalism: John Mitchel and James Clarence Mangan', *Irish Review*, 13 (1992/1993), 71. See also his '"With a Heroic Life and a Governing Mind": Nineteenth-Century Irish Nationalist Autobiography', in Liam Harte, ed., *Modern Irish Autobiography: Self, Nation and Society* (Basingstoke: Palgrave Macmillan, 2007), 14–31.

[26] Seamus Deane, 'Autobiography and Memoirs 1890–1988', in Seamus Deane, gen. ed., *The Field Day Anthology of Irish Writing* (Derry: Field Day, 1991), vol. 3, 380–83. The inclusion of a section devoted to autobiographical writing in this landmark publication was a key milestone in the critical recognition of the genre in Irish literary criticism.

[27] Ibid., 380.   [28] Ibid., 382–83.

foregrounding the interplay of identity and difference, his analysis draws attention to the potential for extremes to meet, for polarities to interpenetrate each other and for 'radical privation'[29] to produce gains as well as losses.

As much as Deane's postcolonial metanarrative provided an expanded conceptual framework for Irish autobiographical writing and a fresh critical language in which to discuss the emerging canon, its suasive force was blunted by myopic lapses. The most conspicuous of these were his implicit understanding of the self as masculine and his marginalization of lifewritings by women, both of which sparked controversy and debate. Interestingly, the temporal parameters of Deane's selection and its distinct bias towards works of literary autobiography proved less contentious, even though these aspects buttress the perception of Irish life-writing as a modern, post-Romantic endeavour that is mostly practised by a politically *engagé* intellectual elite. It was not until the early twenty-first century that these blind spots were remedied and the field reframed in ways that allowed for a much fuller appreciation of its rich variousness. Fittingly, the most potent revisionist intervention came in the form of the much-heralded fourth and fifth volumes of the *Field Day Anthology*, published in 2002, which were exclusively devoted to writings by and about women.[30] The editors' feminist scholarship and flexible understanding of the category of 'writing' helped them to excavate and evaluate a vast collection of texts spanning fourteen centuries; the result is a richly expansive historicization of Irish women's writing that illuminates a complex history of discursivity.

From a life-writing perspective, two of the most noteworthy aspects of these volumes are how relatively few of the anthologized extracts originate in autobiographies as conventionally conceived and how many complicate our understanding of the practice of self-referential writing by women in Ireland. Strikingly, women's autobiographical impulses are as readily traceable in historical and legal records, religious tracts, petitions, travelogues, political pamphlets, manuals, journalism, cultural commentary, songs, oral tales, personal letters and diaries as they are in printed life stories. By capturing in their wide net such a plurality of autobiographical acts, many of them in non-written form, *Field Day* IV and V reveal the heterogeneous array of subject positions around which Irish female

---

[29] Ibid., 383.
[30] Angela Bourke, Siobhán Kilfeather, Maria Luddy, Margaret MacCurtain, Gerardine Meaney, Máirín Ní Dhonnchadha, Mary O'Dowd and Clair Wills, eds., *The Field Day Anthology of Irish Writing, Volumes IV and V: Irish Women's Writings and Traditions* (Cork: Cork University Press in association with Field Day, 2002).

autobiographical identities have been constituted. In the process, the volumes provide a radically expanded groundwork for further critical inquiry into the history, forms, themes and tropes of autobiographical storytelling in Ireland.

At the same time as the *Field Day* editors were remapping the landscape of Irish women's writing *en tout*, Taura Napier was training her analytical lens on the ground occupied by six modern female autobiographers. In *Seeking a Country: Literary Autobiographies of Twentieth-Century Irishwomen* (2001), Napier examines the ways in which Augusta Gregory, Katharine Tynan, Mary Colum, Elizabeth Bowen, Kate O'Brien and Eavan Boland 'discovered methods of self-narrative that merged their artistic devices as writers and experiences as educated women in a proscriptive intellectual milieu'.[31] Deploying the theoretical model of the deflected autobiography, she argues that the 'autobiographical "I" of Irishwomen characteristically takes precautions against accusations of arrogance and self-centeredness', which means that 'essential aspects of the self are disseminated throughout the *dramatis personae* among whom the autobiographer moves and by whom she is surrounded'.[32] Napier distinguishes the actual women these authors depict from the allegorical muses of their male compatriots, as discussed by Reilly, and from the 'external agency'[33] that Deane insists is the creative provocation for much Irish autobiography after 1890. Napier also challenges the contention that the nation is a key axis of self-identification for women autobiographers. Responding directly to Hughes's doctoral thesis, she asserts that 'the concept of nation tends to limit severely, rather than complete, women's apprehension of a full identity', and argues that 'female Irish literary autobiographers take particular care to separate the ideas of nation and self'.[34]

Hughes himself, meanwhile, in a 2003 article reassessed the problematics of subjectivity in autobiography written during and shortly after the Literary Revival.[35] Acknowledging the fraught relationship between subject and nation for those marginalized by gender, class position and material circumstance, he highlights the extent to which women autobiographers' capacity to inhabit a subjectivity of their own choosing was compromised by 'the paradigmatic narrative of the dissolution of self

---

[31] Taura Napier, *Seeking a Country: Literary Autobiographies of Twentieth-Century Irishwomen* (Lanham: University Press of America, 2001), 7.
[32] Ibid., 10.   [33] Deane, 'Autobiography and Memoirs 1890–1988', 381.
[34] Napier, *Seeking a Country*, 160.
[35] Eamonn Hughes, '"The Fact of Me-ness": Autobiographical Writing in the Revival Period', *Irish University Review*, 33:1 (2003), 28–45.

into nation', leaving them with an invidious choice between being co-opted by the nation-self narrative and 'finding an, at best, ambivalent mode of self-expression'.[36] A broader historical perspective on the tension between the individual's desire to authorize a form of authentic selfhood and the ideologically driven demands of national subjectivity is provided by the essays in my edited volume, *Modern Irish Autobiography: Self, Nation and Society* (2007). The eleven contributors explore autobiographers' story-telling strategies in different kinds of life narrative composed between the mid-1800s and the early 2000s, and present a range of views on such topics as the problematics of memory, autobiography's relationship with fiction and history and autobiographers' recurring struggle for self-definition within a web of competing narratives of identity, history and belonging.

The revisionist scholarship represented by the work of Hughes, Napier and others constitutes the most vigorous and fertile strain of recent histor-iography on Irish autobiography, central to which is the desire to expand the generic and historical boundaries of this heterogeneous field and diversify understandings of autobiographical subjectivity as determined by forces other than political nationalism. No sooner, indeed, had Hughes noted the need for criticism to address 'other forms of identity such as gender and class', so as to 'challenge or even strategically suspend the predominance of the national as the principal domain of identity formation',[37] than Elizabeth Grubgeld's erudite *Anglo-Irish Autobiography: Class, Gender, and the Forms of Narrative* (2004) appeared, one of the arguments of which is that the autobiographies of this particular segment of the Irish population resist nationalized confinement.[38] Grubgeld analyses the organizational and gen-eric features that make Anglo-Irish life-writing distinctive, with reference to a wide range of late nineteenth- and early twentieth-century texts. In addi-tion to examining spiritual, comic and satiric autobiographical modes, she evaluates the constricting effects of Anglo-Ireland's 'obsession with family history, patronym, and inherited property' on female autobiographers, arguing that they had to 'adopt, adapt, and sometimes abjure culturally assigned identities' in order represent and interpret their life stories.[39] Grubgeld's gendered reading of this subgenre provides further evidence of

[36] Ibid., 39, 36.   [37] Ibid., 30.
[38] Elizabeth Grubgeld, *Anglo-Irish Autobiography: Class, Gender, and the Forms of Narrative* (Syracuse: Syracuse University Press, 2004), xviii. The quality of Grubgeld's assiduous scholarship is magnified by the shortcomings of a contemporary study that covers some of the same ground, Johannes Wally's *Selected Twentieth Century Anglo-Irish Autobiographies: Theory and Patterns of Self-Representation* (Bern and Oxford: Peter Lang, 2004).
[39] Ibid., xviii, 34.

the ways in which women autobiographers in Ireland were forced to tell their stories differently when confronted by male-centred schema. Her subjects, she observes, 'both wrote and rewrote masculinist narratives to create for themselves a dynamic place within a story that would otherwise render them ciphers'.[40]

Claire Lynch, in her insightful monograph, *Irish Autobiography: Stories of Self in the Narrative of a Nation* (2009), reaches a similar conclusion about two contemporary Irish autobiographers, Nell McCafferty and the late Nuala O'Faolain, who lived and wrote in contexts far removed from those of Grubgeld's subjects. What distinguishes these writers' autobiographical practice, Lynch claims, is not their treatment of the evolving interpretations of Irishness in relation to their own lives so much as their readiness to challenge the proprieties of self-writing in Ireland and breach the gendered prohibitions on autobiographical disclosure. She argues that the textual and extra-textual relationship between these two high-profile feminist journalists, who also lived together as a couple for many years, 'can be viewed as a microcosm of the change which occurred in late twentieth-century Irish autobiography, in which the reader, whether personally connected to the author or otherwise, took an increasingly significant, even active role in the writing of a life'.[41] Certainly, the disarming candour of O'Faolain's *Are You Somebody? The Accidental Memoir of a Dublin Woman* (1996), which became an international bestseller, triggered a remarkable outpouring of personal responses from readers, which O'Faolain reflects upon in her sequel, *Almost There: The Onward Journey of a Dublin Woman* (2003). The fact that so many readers came to recognize their own vulnerabilities in her frank inscription of personal pain, anger, loneliness, confusion and inner hunger suggested that O'Faolain was telling a new kind of story that resonated deeply with a community's consciousness. At the same time, however, her emphasis on her lack of self-worth and self-knowledge – 'I have only the most tentative explanations for anything I ever did or didn't do. And this unfinished understanding of myself leaves room for the reader to join me, to project something of themselves'[42] – makes hers an exemplary Irish life story, one that underlines the critical consensus that Irish autobiographical subjectivities are mostly constituted around deficiency, deprivation and loss. As Eibhlín Evans cogently argues, *Are You Somebody?* is 'an

---

[40] Ibid., xviii.
[41] Claire Lynch, *Irish Autobiography: Stories of Self in the Narrative of a Nation* (Bern and Oxford: Peter Lang, 2009), 172.
[42] Nuala O'Faolain, *Almost There: The Onward Journey of a Dublin Woman* (London: Michael Joseph, 2003), 140.

exposition of a shared history by a very singular individual', one that can be read as emblematic of 'a generation's psychological journey, a generation often bullied, denied, neglected and repressed, but most of all a generation left ripe for seduction, ready to relieve the paucity of its present realities and buy into myths which ultimately leave the individual ever more profoundly bereft'.[43]

Studies of other subfields of Irish autobiography reveal that women were not alone in chafing against inherited literary forms or in reconfiguring the male-defined convention whereby 'autobiography in Ireland becomes, in effect, the autobiography of Ireland'.[44] There is in fact a constellation of autobiographical subjects of both genders whose relation to the norms of the nation narrative, and to the linguistic and stylistic conventions of middle-class autobiography in general, is complicated by multiple, sometimes competing, factors. The working-class socialist, the Gaelic-speaking islander, the Traveller, the economic migrant, the non-white Irish citizen, the Northern Irish Protestant, the person with a disability, the survivor of childhood abuse, the LGBTQ person – each of these categories of autobiographer presents us with alternative personal and collective histories, many of which were hitherto (self-)repressed or rendered culturally unspeakable, which contest hegemonic representation and contribute to a more complex, ambivalent narrative of 'nationness'.[45] Some of these autobiographers explore the terms of their cultural identities in ways that unsettle the regulatory norms and homogenizing discourse of who 'we' are as a people and, like Nuala O'Faolain, connect with an invisible republic of readers. Disabled author Christopher Nolan is one such example: the linguistic inventiveness of his third-person autobiography, *Under the Eye of the Clock* (1987), has been read as a 'refusal to fit into the language sanctioned by dominant discourse, a refusal that finds its origins in the experience of the disabled body'.[46] Gay hurling star Dónal Óg Cusack is another, as Anne Mulhall demonstrates in her incisive appraisal of his landmark coming-out autobiography *Come*

---

[43] Eibhlín Evans, 'Letters after the Fact: Responses to Nuala O'Faolain's *Are You Somebody?*', *Critical Survey*, 14:3 (2002), 53, 62.

[44] Declan Kiberd, *Inventing Ireland: The Literature of the Modern Nation* (London: Jonathan Cape, 1995), 119.

[45] Benedict Anderson, *Imagined Communities: Reflections on the Origin and Spread of Nationalism*, revised edn. (London: Verso, 1991), 4.

[46] Tom Coogan, '"Brilliant, Bright, Boiling Words": Literary Disability, Language, and the Writing Body in the Work of Christopher Nolan', *Disability and Society*, 27:2 (2012), 288.

What May (2009), which was applauded for challenging entrenched stereotypes of Irish masculinity.[47]

Other autobiographers narrate stories of difference and outsiderness
using 'vocabularies of the self'[48] that bear little relation to the familiar
scripts of literary or middle-class autobiography, in part because the
authors' storytelling styles originate in subcultures that have traditionally
been oral. This applies to those few Irish Travellers who have published
their 'quasi-oral'[49] life stories and to the rather more prolific emigrant
labourers whose works have long been assigned subliterary status. Bernard
Canavan's pioneering survey of the personal accounts of Irish migrant
workers in Victorian and modern Britain helpfully contextualizes the
formal challenges that confronted those who sought to turn their life
histories into written narratives.[50] Moving from rural communities
where a centuries-old indigenous tradition of storytelling still existed, to
a culture in which literary models of autobiography predominated, these
worker-writers 'had to abandon the story-telling tradition with its local
defensiveness and unreflective qualities in favour of the more explicit and
personalized tone of the literary tradition'.[51] Canavan also notes those
autobiographers 'who had abandoned commitment, and for whom
Ireland held no romantic attractions or memories',[52] thus anticipating
John McGahern's observation in *Memoir* (2005) that in Irish emigrant
communities in postwar England 'the local and the individual were more
powerful than any national identity'.[53] In *The Literature of the Irish in
Britain: Autobiography and Memoir, 1725–2001* (2009), I investigate this
subterranean autobiographical tradition in more detail, using an interdisciplinary methodology to examine the various ways in which autobiographers from different social, cultural and religious backgrounds negotiated

[47] Anne Mulhall, '"What's Eating Victor Cusack?" *Come What May*, Queer Embodiment, and the
Regulation of Hetero-Masculinity', *Éire-Ireland*, 48:1–2 (2013), 282–308. See also Glen O'Brien, ed.,
Coming Out: Irish Gay Experiences (Dublin: Currach Press, 2003).

[48] Diane Bjorklund, *Interpreting the Self: Two Hundred Years of American Autobiography* (Chicago:
University of Chicago Press, 1998), xii.

[49] Paul Delaney, 'Stories from Below: Sean Maher and Nan Joyce', *Studies: An Irish Quarterly Review*,
93:372 (2004), 464. See also José Lanters, '"We Are a Different People": Life Writing,
Representation, and the Travellers', *New Hibernia Review*, 9:2 (2005), 25–41; Martin Shaw,
'Warning Signs: Violence and Flexibility in the Story of Irish Traveller Nan Joyce's Arrest,'
Nordic Irish Studies, 10 (2011), 79–96; Christine Walsh, *Postcolonial Borderlands: Orality and Irish
Traveller Writing* (Newcastle upon Tyne: Cambridge Scholars, 2008).

[50] Bernard Canavan, 'Story-Tellers and Writers: Irish Identity in Emigrant Labourers' Autobiographies,
1870–1970', in Patrick O'Sullivan, ed., *The Irish World Wide: History, Heritage, Identity. Volume 3: The
Creative Migrant* (Leicester: Leicester University Press, 1994), 154–69.

[51] Ibid., 155.   [52] Ibid., 161.

[53] John McGahern, *Memoir* (London: Faber and Faber, 2005), 211.

their complex positioning within and outwith the national imaginary of the nation state.[54]

Those autobiographers who stayed put in their impoverished communities faced their own particular 'struggle of self-making'[55] when they chose to take writing in their own hands. One highly localized community that achieved 'an extraordinary quality of utterance'[56] in autobiography was that of the Blasket Islands in the south-west of Ireland, three of whose members – Tomás O'Crohan, Maurice O'Sullivan and Peig Sayers – established an enduringly influential genre of Gaelic or Gaeltacht autobiography in the 1920s and 1930s. A substantial body of criticism has grown up around the enormously popular writings of these islanders, each of whom has a distinctive narrative voice and presence. The most probing commentary moves beyond discussions of their writings' anthropological value to provide theoretically informed accounts of how the Blasket canon in general, and O'Crohan's *An tOileánach* (*The Islandman*) (1929) in particular, were appropriated for a nationalist agenda by the decolonizing nation state, often against the grain of the texts themselves.[57] In her study of O'Crohan's masterpiece, Irene Lucchitti scrutinizes the anxieties that led to the book's cultural canonization by ideologues keen to promote an edifying version of authentic Irishness, cleansed of colonial impurities. She also argues that conventional readings that subordinate O'Crohan's identity as an autobiographer to his iconic status as 'a pure, essential man, pitting himself against the elements, untainted by learning or knowledge of the wider world' obscure his achievements

---

[54] Liam Harte, ed., *The Literature of the Irish in Britain: Autobiography and Memoir, 1725–2001* (Basingstoke: Palgrave Macmillan, 2009). Individual and collective experiences of Irish migration have been illuminated by studies that make excellent use of disparate autobiographical materials, including personal letters, memoirs and oral interviews. See David Fitzpatrick, *Oceans of Consolation: Personal Accounts of Irish Migration to Australia* (Ithaca: Cornell University Press, 1994); Angela McCarthy, *Personal Narratives of Irish and Scottish Migration, 1921–65* (Manchester: Manchester University Press, 2007); Kerby A. Miller, Arnold Schrier, Bruce D. Boling and David N. Doyle, *Irish Immigrants in the Land of Canaan: Letters and Memoirs from Colonial and Revolutionary America, 1675–1815* (New York: Oxford University Press, 2003); Johanne Devlin Trew, *Leaving the North: Migration and Memory, Northern Ireland 1921–2011* (Liverpool: Liverpool University Press, 2013).

[55] Grubgeld, *Anglo-Irish Autobiography*, xi.

[56] Declan Kiberd, *Irish Classics* (London: Granta, 2000), 520.

[57] See John Eastlake, 'Orality and Agency: Reading an Irish Autobiography from the Great Blasket Island', *Oral Tradition*, 24:1 (2009), 125–41; Mark Quigley, 'Modernity's Edge: Speaking Silence on the Blasket Islands', *Interventions*, 5:3 (2003), 382–406; Ciaran Ross, 'Blasket Island Autobiographies: The Myth and Mystique of the Untranslated and the Untranslatable', *Translation and Literature*, 12:1 (2003), 114–43.

as a 'highly skilled and dexterous literary craftsman'.[58] Such revisionist appraisals of O'Crohan have benefitted from the scholarship of Seán Ó Coileáin and others, which led to the publication of the definitive edition of *An tOileánach* in 2002, the reinstated material in which illuminates the nature and extent of the cultural puritanism that shaped the original 1929 edition.[59]

According to Sidonie Smith and Julia Watson, autobiographical story-telling by individuals who have endured a history of suffering or loss often 'make an urgent, immediate, and direct bid for attention and call the reader/listener to an ethical response through their affective appeals for recognition'.[60] This thesis is borne out by many of the personal narratives that have been published since the late 1980s by those whose lives were blighted by physical, sexual or emotional maltreatment in twentieth-century Ireland, whether within families or in one of the many religious- and state-run institutions in whose care children and young people from impoverished or dysfunctional backgrounds were placed. The proliferation of such works is emblematic of the shattering of the culture of silence and wilful amnesia that allowed violence against children to flourish with impunity in such institutions over many decades. Although frequently disparaged as 'misery memoirs', to homogenize these texts in such reductionist terms is to downplay their interventionist role in debates and campaigns that have helped shift the axes of religious and political power in contemporary Ireland and reconfigured the relation between citizen, community and nation from the perspective of the psychically bruised. It is also to overlook the role of these memoirists in authorizing the experiences of the hurt child as a subject of Irish autobiographical discourse. Better-informed analyses explicate these works' political, ethical, representational and historiographical importance. Thus, Kate Douglas reads Irish abuse survival memoirs as part of a pervasive trend within Western societies, whereby 'the autobiographical child has become a socio-cultural, even political, construct upon which memory struggles are contested'[61]; Emilie Pine views them as part of an 'anti-nostalgia' Irish remembrance

---

[58] Irene Lucchitti, *The Islandman: The Hidden Life of Tomás O'Crohan* (Bern and Oxford: Peter Lang, 2009), 35, 163.

[59] Ibid., 128–9. See also Thomas F. Shea, 'The Islander: A More Provocative Tomás O'Crohan', *New Hibernia Review*, 18:3 (2014), 93–109. A new, unabridged English-language edition of *The Islandman*, translated by Gary Bannister and David Sowby, was published in 2012.

[60] Sidonie Smith and Julia Watson, *Reading Autobiography: A Guide for Interpreting Life Narratives*, 2nd edn. (Minneapolis: University of Minneapolis Press, 2010), 133.

[61] Kate Douglas, *Contesting Childhood: Autobiography, Trauma, and Memory* (New Brunswick: Rutgers University Press, 2010), 43.

culture, the effect of which is 'to break open the representation of childhood as a space of innocence and security and to almost inextricably link
the idea of Irish childhood, and the Irish past, with trauma'[62]; and
Diarmaid Ferriter claims that the value of these autobiographical works
'lies not only in the articulation of personal experience, but also the light
they shed on key themes of modern Irish history'.[63] Appraisals of these
memoirists' narrative techniques remain scarce, however. Those few critics
who have examined their aesthetic features tend to consider texts that
announce themselves as autobiography alongside fictional accounts of
traumatic childhoods, with a consequent dilution of focus on the
specific strategies autobiographers employ to represent subjectivity
through the act of remembering.[64]

The most (in)famous Irish misery memoir of all – indeed, the one
accused of proliferating the subgenre[65] – is also one of the most garlanded
autobiographies of recent decades. Such was the magnitude of the commercial success and cultural impact of *Angela's Ashes* (1996), Frank
McCourt's recreation of his abjectly poor upbringing in interwar
Limerick, that it became 'the exemplary Irish autobiography of the period',[66] one that resonated with primed readerships on both sides of the
Atlantic, as Declan Kiberd explains:

> It appealed through the late 1990s to two very different constituencies –
> *internationally* to those WASP readers who wished, in spite of the Celtic
> Tiger, to read a book which showed them an Ireland as colourfully desperate
> as ever; and *nationally* to a confident, even brash people keen for some
> measure of how fully they had transcended the old world of failed fathers,
> smug priests, harassed mothers and so on.[67]

Yet while a multitude of readers found *Angela's Ashes* 'compellingly
endearing', there were also those who regarded it as 'repulsively

[62] Emilie Pine, *The Politics of Irish Memory: Performing Remembrance in Contemporary Irish Culture*
(Basingstoke: Palgrave Macmillan, 2011), 45.
[63] Diarmaid Ferriter, 'Suffer Little Children? The Historical Validity of Memoirs of Irish Childhood',
in Joseph Dunne and James Kelly, eds., *Childhood and Its Discontents* (Dublin: Liffey Press,
2002), 70.
[64] See Peter Guy, 'Black Habits and White Collars: Representations of the Irish Industrial Schools',
Études Irlandaises, 36:1 (2012), 59–72; Michael R. Molino, 'The "House of a Hundred Windows":
Industrial Schools in Irish Writing', *New Hibernia Review*, 5:1 (2001), 33–52.
[65] See Kathryn Holmquist, 'Mammy, I'm Poignant', *Irish Times Weekend*, 20 February 1999, 4.
[66] Lynch, *Irish Autobiography*, 147.
[67] Declan Kiberd, *The Irish Writer and the World* (Cambridge: Cambridge University Press, 2005),
277. Original emphasis.

manipulative'.[68] The hornets' nest of debate that the book stirred up showed how volatile and discomfiting the memoir genre can be, particularly when the truth status of autobiographical disclosure is at stake. Autobiography theorists may confidently proclaim that 'of the three defining terms of autobiography – the self, the life, the writing – only the writing has survived the poststructuralist and postmodern housecleaning of antiquated beliefs',[69] but readers from other disciplines beg to differ. One of the most acerbic critiques of *Angela's Ashes* came from historian Roy Foster, who bristled at McCourt's seductive brand of embellished biography: 'The conventions of magical realism and post-structuralist flannel have had a decisive effect on the genre of autobiography: while this can be presented as a liberation from the tyranny of the ascertainable fact, it makes for some confusion as far as the reader is concerned.'[70] Foster's devastating itemization of McCourt's stylistic shortcomings is ancillary to his central complaint, which is that in conforming to 'the comfortable old straitjackets of the stories that have gone before' and peddling 'a version of Irish childhood which does duty for a more comfortable and ambiguous reality', *Angela's Ashes* gave succour to an outmoded and clichéd interpretation of Irishness.[71] While McCourt had his defenders,[72] other critics weighed in with indictments of different aspects of his autobiographical method, critiquing his unself-reflexive narrative style,[73] his 'reduction of individuality to commonality'[74] and his reinstatement of 'the "old autobiographical 'I'"', that stable subject so many avant-garde literary experiments of the twentieth century sought to do away with entirely'.[75]

Whereas the arraignment of *Angela's Ashes* makes it an exemplary Irish autobiography in a negative sense, critics' effusive embrace of Hugo Hamilton's *The Speckled People* (2003) positions it as a positive foil to McCourt's Pulitzer prizewinner. As with the publication of *Angela's Ashes*, timing was an important factor in the book's popular and critical

---

[68] James B. Mitchell, 'Popular Autobiography as Historiography: The Reality Effect of Frank McCourt's *Angela's Ashes*', *Biography*, 26:4 (2003), 617.

[69] Nancy K. Miller, 'Facts, Pacts, Acts', *Profession* (1992), 10.

[70] R. F. Foster, *The Irish Story: Telling Tales and Making It Up in Ireland* (London: Allen Lane/ Penguin, 2001), 166.

[71] Ibid., 174, 175.

[72] See Edward A. Hagan, 'Really an Alley Cat? *Angela's Ashes* and Critical Orthodoxy', *New Hibernia Review*, 4:4 (2000), 39–52.

[73] George O'Brien, 'The Last Word: Reflections on *Angela's Ashes*', in Charles Fanning, ed., *New Perspectives on the Irish Diaspora* (Carbondale: Southern Illinois University Press, 2000), 238ff.

[74] Eric P. Levy, 'The Predicament of Individuality in *Angela's Ashes*', *Irish University Review*, 32:2 (2002), 260.

[75] Mitchell, 'Popular Autobiography as Historiography', 612.

reception. The recurrence of the approving adjective 'timely' in appraisals of Hamilton's evocation of his emotionally wrenching 1950s Irish-German childhood, which broadens out into a compelling endorsement of nation-hood and identity as open and multifaceted, reflects the fact that the economically rejuvenated Ireland of the early 2000s was home to many recently arrived immigrants and their families, whose contested status as the 'new Irish' brought to the fore issues that *The Speckled People* thema-tizes: the challenges of living with transnational cultural differences, multi-lingual entanglements and overlapping national affiliations. This backdrop of emergent multiculturalism and globalization made Hamilton's a much more palatable narrative of troubled childhood than McCourt's, particu-larly to those 'who wish to see, not only Irish writing, but Irish life, interpreted in a much more radical way than the time-warped comfort zone of Anglo-centric familiarities and introverted two-way stereotypes'.[76] The book's avid reception even led to Hamilton being envisioned as 'the embodiment of a culturally diverse, inclusive, modern Ireland' and popu-larized the metaphor of the 'speckled people' as 'a shorthand for an Irish multicultural self-image'.[77]

The Speckled People, then, ranks high in the emergent canon of twenty-first-century Irish autobiography, valued for the piquancy of its progressive polyethnic vision as much as for the sophistication of its formal methods. Eamonn Hughes groups it with a dozen other autobiographies and mem-oirs published since 1990, most of them by writers and academics, which he argues are unified by 'their mix of memoir (with a strong emphasis on childhood) with social history and cultural analysis: the tendency, that is to say, is towards a representation of the self *in its very uniqueness* as representative, a representative quality brought about more often than not by the formative deficiencies of upbringing'.[78] Hughes goes on to extra-polate the extent to which this characteristic signifies a decisive change in the way the self is conceptualized and represented in contemporary Irish autobiography:

[76] Gerald Dawe, 'Speckled People: Breaking the Closed Shop of Irish Writing', *Irish Pages*, 2:2 (2004), 272.
[77] Jason King, 'Irish Multicultural Epiphanies: Modernity and the Recuperation of Migrant Memory in the Writings of Hugo Hamilton', in Pilar Villar-Argáiz, ed., *Literary Visions of Multicultural Ireland: The Immigrant in Contemporary Irish Culture* (Manchester: Manchester University Press, 2014), 176.
[78] Eamonn Hughes, '"Stories That You Have to Write Down are Different": Hugo Hamilton's *The Speckled People* and Contemporary Autobiography', *Irish Review*, 44 (2012), 127. Original emphasis.

This could be regarded as a shift from thinking of oneself in the supposedly homogenous framework of the nation to a representation of the self as a citizen of a necessarily heterogeneous society. In other words, this is a generation of Irish autobiographers who have finally broken with the idea that the method of and motive for writing autobiography in Ireland is inextricably linked to the nation story: that to say 'I' in an autobiography is also somehow to tell the story of Ireland.[79]

This view is supported by Stephen Regan, who asserts that the 'unsettling of traditional autobiographical modes has tended to bring with it a strong sense of identity held in abeyance, painfully thwarted, strangely suspended'.[80]

These conclusions lead us fruitfully back to Yeats, the autobiographer who, despite being so heavily implicated in the tradition of making individual and national identities cohere and reinforce each other, understood that self and nation can never be homologous, any more than they can be seamlessly identical with themselves. The evidence suggests that Yeats's insights are not lost on his latter-day heirs. They, like him, recognize that there is no simple formula for understanding the evolving dynamics of autobiographical memory, experience, subjectivity and identification. The relations between the three Greek words that make up the term 'autobiography' – *autos* (self), *bios* (life), *graphe* (writing) – are always in flux. 'Life', as G. Thomas Couser reminds us, 'inevitably far exceeds the capacity of writing to contain it.'[81] In our time as in Yeats's, the constructive essence of the autobiographer's task is to find a language, a literary form and an artistic structure – 'logical process',[82] in Yeats's terms – that will accommodate the never fully finished process of giving a narrative account of oneself.

A History of Irish Autobiography examines the diverse and complex ways in which Irish autobiographers have negotiated this process, from the earliest times to the contemporary era. As the first comprehensive critical introduction to Irish autobiographical writing as seen in context, this volume

---

[79] Ibid.

[80] Stephen Regan, '"Sacred Spaces": Writing Home in Recent Irish Memoirs and Autobiographies (John McGahern's *Memoir*, Hugo Hamilton's *The Speckled People*, Seamus Deane's *Reading in the Dark* and John Walsh's *The Falling Angels*)', in Scott Brewster and Michael Parker, eds., *Irish Literature since 1990: Diverse Voices* (Manchester: Manchester University Press, 2009), 248. See also Pine, *The Politics of Irish Memory*, chapter two, for a reading of the ways in which six recent autobiographies 'represent a dislocation between the present and the past, and thus contribute to the anti-nostalgia of contemporary Irish remembrance culture' (54).

[81] G. Thomas Couser, *Memoir: An Introduction* (Oxford: Oxford University Press, 2012), 22.

[82] Yeats, *The Collected Works of W. B. Yeats III*, 341.

significantly expands the historical, geographical and generic parameters for the study of this vast and incorrigibly enigmatic topic. In keeping with its heterogeneous subject matter, the authorship of the *History* is multi-disciplinary and international in its reach. The collection draws on the best new work of leading scholars of medieval, early modern, modern and contemporary Irish literature, history and society, each of whom sheds valuable light on their chosen topics in their distinct ways. While the contributors' perspectives on this evolving literary form are necessarily plural, there is a common emphasis on self-representation in Ireland as a historically situated practice and a shared recognition that all autobiographies are, in the words of Regenia Gagnier, 'rhetorical projects embedded in concrete material situations'.[83] The essays are also connected by an awareness of the determining influence of pre-existing narrative modes on the way people present their lives in print, and of the impact of the changing availability of these modes on autobiographers' self-conception.

From these shared bases, the essayists map out the great variety of Irish autobiographical practices and survey the diverse needs, motives, uses and goals of autobiographical self-expression. Appraisals of the value of auto-biography to social and cultural history sit alongside explorations of auto-biographical identities as literary constructs and measured readings of the inventive endeavours of particular writers. If the significance of place, embodiment and belonging for how Irish identities are shaped and remembered is a governing theme of these essays, so too is the centrality of public events, especially those moments of great political and social upheaval that call for, and call forth, a re-reckoning and rearticulation of what is means to belong to this island nation. And because this island's history has produced so many examples of the instrumental use of autobiography for polemical ends, there is a pervasive critical alertness in this volume to the politics of remembering in Irish life-writing – the implications of what is recollected and what is obscured – and an engagement with the ways in which the materials of the past are shaped to serve the needs of the present. Repeatedly, the history of Irish auto-biography reflects the truth of Nuala O'Faolain's dictum that 'A memoir may be retrospective, but the past is not where its action takes place.'[84]

The design of this book is both chronological and thematic in nature. The twenty-four chapters that follow this Introduction range across

[83] Regenia Gagnier, *Subjectivities: A History of Self-Representation in Britain, 1832–1920* (Oxford: Oxford University Press, 1991), 40.
[84] O'Faolain, *Almost There*, 52.

seventeen centuries of Irish achievement in autobiography, with essays structured around key subgenres, themes, texts and practitioners. Within and across chapters, the contributors analyse the determining influence of a rich tapestry of attributes, events, experiences, behaviours and beliefs on the production of autobiography on the island of Ireland and in certain key parts of its global diaspora. While the focus is on written autobiography, oral and digital life narratives are also given attention, with a chapter devoted to each of these topics. Mindful of the traditional bias shown towards aesthetically accomplished life-writing, this *History* strives to moderate this by affording attention to 'low' as well as to 'high' cultural forms. In the same democratic spirit, the volume's breadth of coverage is underpinned by an adaptable and expansive approach to the category of autobiography. While every definition of the genre is subject to contestation and debate, those that veer towards the prescriptive, such as Phillip Lejeune's influential definition of autobiography as 'the respective narrative in prose that someone makes of his own existence when he puts the principal accent upon his life, especially upon the story of his own personality',[85] are less critically enabling in an Irish context than more inclusive formulations, such as that of Harold Rosen: 'Autobiographical discourse embraces all those verbal acts, whether they be whole texts or parts of texts, whether they be spoken or written, in which individual speakers or writers or two or more collaborators attempt to represent their lives through a construction of past events and experiences.'[86]

The aims of this *History*, then, are fivefold: to provide an evaluative historical guide to the practice of Irish autobiography as it has developed in the English and Irish languages, from the coming of Christianity to the contemporary era; to increase awareness of the reach and diversity of this underexplored and undervalued literary tradition, thereby expanding the canon in different directions; to elucidate the main social, economic, political, religious and intellectual contexts that have informed and nourished the different forms of Irish life-writing from one period to the next; to provide authoritative assessments of the significance of individual autobiographers' achievements and their contribution to the wider tradition; and to offer productive pointers for future research.

In seeking to meet these aims, this volume hopes to stimulate readers to deeper understandings of the particular Irish articulation of autobiography and provoke fresh perceptions of how, in this national context,

---

[85] Quoted in Smith and Watson, *Reading Autobiography*, 1.
[86] Harold Rosen, *Speaking from Memory: A Guide to Autobiographical Acts and Practices* (Stoke on Trent: Trentham Books, 1998), 12.

autobiographers have configured their life stories and narrated their identities in relation to larger collectivities. Ireland's comparatively small size
and its distinctive history have given autobiography a wider social and
political significance in the country, one that transcends mere entertainment or even aesthetics. As a consequence, the study of Irish autobiography
is more than the study of specific writers, forms and texts. As the chapters
here demonstrate, it can equally provide a condensed arena in which to
examine how private experiences emerge from, and merge back into,
communal histories, and to analyse the ways in which individual and
society, self and other, sincerity and artifice and memory and imagination
interact. Just as no autobiography can ever tell the whole story, no history
of autobiography can cover every writer or topic worthy of consideration,
or provide the last word on this perennially fascinating and complex
subject. *A History of Irish Autobiography* will serve its purpose if, in addition
to enlightening its readers, it opens up possibilities of reading and initiates
further explorations of a field of study that is ripe for enrichment and
development.

CHAPTER 2

Writing in Medieval Ireland in the First-Person Voice

Máire Ní Mhaonaigh

Ego Patricius ('I am Patrick'): thus begins one of the earliest extant documents from medieval Ireland, the fifth-century *Confessio* of St Patrick, an account written in old age looking back on his life. In his own words, Patrick relates something of his experience of being taken prisoner and brought to Ireland as a boy, as well as of the later vision which brought him back to Ireland as a missionary. His purpose is not to provide a narrative of his life, however, but to defend his activity, explaining it with reference to the support he was given by God. While valuable insights can be gleaned from it and his earlier writing, *Epistola*, these texts provide few facts.[1] Patrick employs biblical citations freely in his works. In addition, he is indebted to Augustine of Hippo, a church father, whose earlier *Confessiones* (c. 397–400) had combined acknowledgement of his earlier youthful failings with praise of God. As a text concerned with conversion, this highly influential work was one on which Patrick might well have drawn.

Discovering the 'individual'

Augustine's composition is often deemed autobiographical, but its author's main aim, like that of Patrick after him, was to worship God.[2] Yet Augustine himself is a dominant presence in his narrative, as is Patrick in his writings, which were composed less than a century after Augustine of Hippo's work. Both men speak in a first-person voice, but they are not primarily concerned with relating the events of their own lives. If autobiography is first and foremost an individual's own narrated story, the heart of which is the

---

[1] For both texts and translations, see www.confessio.ie (accessed 3 March 2016).
[2] See Paul Lehmann, 'Autobiographies of the Middle Ages', *Transactions of the Royal Historical Society*, 3 (1953), 41–52 and John Freccero, 'Autobiography and Narrative', in Thomas C. Heller, Morto Sosna and David E. Wellbery, eds., *Reconstructing Individualism: Autonomy, Individuality and the Self in Western Thought* (Stanford: Stanford University Press, 1986), 16–29.

presentation of a sense of self, then neither Augustine, much less Patrick, created such a text. Nor should we expect them to have done. As a specific concept, the 'individual' first became prominent in Western Europe during the eleventh and twelfth centuries and this era of reform and renewal has been characterized as witnessing the discovery of the self.[3] This development was both complex and subtle, and intimately connected with other significant changes of this period.[4] Its precise manifestation is difficult to determine, not least because of our very different present-day notions of personality and ego.[5] The individuality which came into view in the eleventh and twelfth centuries had none of the hallmarks of autonomous non-conformity associated with individualism in modern times.[6] It was above all contextual, the sense of self being defined in relation to an other, as well as communities, and being configured in imitation of earlier models.[7] And in the Christian, intellectual context in which such changes were occurring, the primary role model was Christ.

Imitatio Christi ('Imitation of Christ'), therefore, was a key concept, God being frequently asked for assistance in its application. Drawing on his personal experiences and writing in his own vernacular (Bairisch), an eleventh-century monk, Othlo of St Emmeram in Regensburg, requested God to help him in following a Christian way of life.[8] In both form and content, this Bavarian poem, *Othlos Gebet* ('Othlo's Prayer'), bears general comparison with an Irish composition of about the same date in which a skilful poet bemoans the manner in which his thoughts stray from him as he is trying to study the psalms, and he calls on God to help him focus his mind. In the Irish poem *Is mebul dom imrádud* ('Shame to my thoughts!'), it is the possessor of the thoughts who is centre stage, looking on apparently

[3] See, for example, John F. Benton, 'Consciousness of Self and Perceptions of Individuality', in Robert L. Benson and Giles Constable with Carol D. Lanham, eds., *Renaissance and Renewal in the Twelfth Century* (Cambridge, MA: Harvard University Press, 1982), 263–98.

[4] See, for example, Thomas F. X. Noble and John van Engen, eds., *European Transformations: The Long Twelfth Century* (Notre Dame: University of Notre Dame Press, 2012).

[5] See R. N. Swanson, *The Twelfth-Century Renaissance* (Manchester: Manchester University Press, 1999), 141–51.

[6] See John V. Fleming, 'Medieval European Autobiography', in Maria DiBattista and Emily O. Wittman, eds., *The Cambridge Companion to Autobiography* (Cambridge: Cambridge University Press, 2014), 35–48 and Heller et al., eds., *Reconstructing Individualism*.

[7] See, for example, Caroline Walker Bynum, 'Did the Twelfth Century Discover the Individual?', *Journal of Ecclesiastical History*, 31:1 (1980), 1–17 and Colin Morris, 'Individualism in Twelfth-Century Religion: Some Further Reflections', *Journal of Ecclesiastical History*, 31:2 (1980), 195–206.

[8] Marion E. Gibbs and Sidney M. Johnson, eds., *Medieval German Literature* (London: Routledge, 2002), 49.

helplessly as his mind wanders in whichever direction it pleases.[9] The lengthy description of the recalcitrant mind-waves functions as extended metaphor for the author's own intellect, as Elizabeth Boyle has noted, drawing attention to parallels in a contemporary Latin poem, *Mentis in excessu* ('In ecstasy of mind'), attributed to an eleventh-century bishop of Dublin, Patrick, who died in 1084.[10] Life situations may underlie the works to the extent that the intellectual endeavours of these poets provide their starting point. Their learned audiences were invited to uncover their deeper meaning, however, and interpreted them in more abstract ways.

In search of salvation

Metaphorical poetry in the first person was a feature of Irish writing at an earlier period also. *Messe ocus Pangur Bán* ('White Pangur and I'), a well-known poem from the ninth century, draws a complex comparison between a studious narrator and his feline companion. The cat's persistent hunting and ultimate success in catching mice functions as an elaborate metaphor for the poet's diligent pursuit of knowledge. The cat's joy at killing his prey – *hi nglen luch inna gērchrub* ('when a mouse sticks in his sharp claw') – is equated with the happiness experienced by the poet when he understands *ceist doraid dil* ('a dearly loved difficult problem'). Both apply their minds (*menma*) with the same assiduity to their specific art (*saindán*).[11] In personifying the cat in this manner, the author produces a nature poem exulting in God's creation, as explored by Gregory Toner. His inspiration may have been the emphasis on God's wondrous works prevalent in the Bible and patristic writings, study of which was paramount in medieval Irish – and European – ecclesiastical schools.[12] Observation of feline behaviour may, of course, have informed the poem, but this sophisticated work is far from being (merely) an autobiographical account of a scholar and his cat.

Nonetheless, the use of the first person throughout the poem is striking, as signalled by the emphatic first-person subject pronoun *messe* ('me myself'),

[9] Gerard Murphy, ed. and trans., *Early Irish Lyrics: Eighth to Twelfth Century* (Oxford: Oxford University Press, 1956), 38–42.

[10] Elizabeth Boyle, 'Allegory, the *Aes Dána* and the Liberal Arts in Medieval Irish Literature', in Deborah Hayden and Paul Russell, eds., *Grammatica, Gramadach and Gramadeg: Vernacular Grammar and Grammarians in Medieval Ireland and Wales* (Amsterdam: John Benjamins Publishing Company, 2016), 11–34.

[11] Murphy, *Early Irish Lyrics*, 2–3.

[12] Gregory Toner, '"Messe ocus Pangur Bán": Structure and Cosmology', *Cambrian Medieval Celtic Studies*, 57 (2009), 1–22.

with which it opens and, in accordance with strict metrical rules, closes as well.[13] First-person verbal forms, together with first-person possessive and reflexive pronouns, are then scattered throughout the poem from beginning to end. This ego-centred approach is present too in other ninth-century poems, including a skilfully executed work of two stanzas, beginning *Domfharcai fidbaide fál* ('A hedge of trees overlooks me'), in which a first-person form is found in seven of its eight lines.[14] Preserved on the margins of a manuscript page, the subject matter of which is Latin pronouns, it is tempting to speculate, with Patrick Ford, that the abundance therein of that specific grammatical feature provided a deliberate vibrant illustration of the matter in hand.[15] Ultimately, however, this poem too celebrates God's creation expressed through what is presented as the narrator's direct engagement with the natural world.[16] That it should be preserved as part of a codex concerned with Latin grammar underlines the educational context in which these first-person poems took form.

Praise of God was paramount, rather than a realistic portrayal of a pleasant natural scene. Specifically, the idyllic workplace depicted by the poet in which writing was undertaken *fo roída ross* ('beneath a forest of woodland') scarcely rings true, considering the paraphernalia required for scribal activity, as observed by Donnchadh Ó Corráin.[17] These are constructed vignettes in which the poet-narrator dons a particular persona to pray to God. They may have had a pedagogical purpose, demonstrating effective engagement with an all-powerful creator, to whom every Christian hoped to return. That journey involved avoiding temptation, as Daniél Ua Líathati, abbot of Lismore, Co. Waterford, is alleged to have done according to a poem put into his mouth in which he rebukes a woman whose mind was set on profitless folly. Proclaiming that he will not

---

[13] *Dúnad* ('closure') is the formal term applied to the ending of a poem echoing its opening phrase.

[14] Murphy, *Early Irish Lyrics*, 4–5.

[15] Patrick Ford, 'Blackbirds, Cuckoos and Infixed Pronouns: Another Context for Early Irish Nature Poetry', in Ronald Black, William Gillies and Roibeard Ó Maolalaigh, eds., *Celtic Connections: Proceedings of the Tenth International Congress of Celtic Studies, I, Language, Literature, History, Culture* (East Linton: Tuckwell Press, 1999), 162–70.

[16] See Daniel F. Melia, 'A Poetic Klein Bottle', in A. T. E. Matonis and Daniel F. Melia, eds., *Celtic Language, Celtic Culture: A Festschrift for Eric P. Hamp* (Belmont: Ford and Bailie, 1990), 187–96 and his 'On the Form and Function of the "Old-Irish Verse" in the *Thesaurus Palaeohibernicus*: How Patrick Ford Opened My Eyes to an Important Aspect of Early Irish Poetry and Some Conclusions I Have Come to as a Result', in Joseph F. Nagy and Leslie E. Jones, eds., *Heroic Poets and Poetic Heroes in Celtic Tradition: A Festschrift for Patrick F. Ford. Celtic Studies Association of North America Yearbook, 3/4* (Dublin: Four Courts Press, 2005), 283–90.

[17] Donnchadh Ó Corráin, 'Early Irish Hermit Poetry?', in Donnchadh Ó Corráin, Liam Breatnach and Kim McCone, eds., *Sages, Saints and Storytellers: Celtic Studies in Honour of Professor James Carney* (Maynooth: An Sagart, 1989), 251–67.

sell heaven for sin, he advises the woman to act in like manner, since should they persecute God in this life, they will rue it in the next.[18] The anonymous author-speaker of another verse does not even countenance such a thought: on hearing 'a melodious bell' (*clocán binn*) he claims 'to prefer to tryst with it to trysting with a wanton woman' (*ba ferr lim dul ina dáil / indás i ndáil mná baíthe*).[19] His example should undoubtedly be followed, and the way mapped out is easier when presented by one who has already allegedly trodden the self-same road. It is Christ whom one should ultimately emulate, but human intermediaries who appear to have succeeded leave clear steps to trace.

At the journey's end lay salvation, bringing with it everlasting happiness in an eternal 'Seventh Age'. In recalling what was presented as their own immanent temporal experience, exemplary fellow Christian travellers inspired imitation. When interpreted symbolically, their first-hand words were associated with an ideal to which one could perhaps more easily aspire, communicated as it was in a tangible voice. That voice was frequently anonymous, yet also common was the adoption of a particular persona, either fictional or historical, through whom the words were deliberately expressed. In donning a poetic mask, as Maria Tymoczko has described it,[20] the author accorded his work greater influence and prestige, and its exemplary, educative effect may have been all the greater as a result.

One of the most striking literary poses assumed by an author is that of the *caillech Bérri* ('Old Woman of Beare') into whose mouth a commentary on ageing and a retrospective account of a life well lived are placed.[21] A complex and composite poem, the original composition of 'The Lament of the Old Woman of Beare' may date to around the same time as the writing of *Dom-fharcai fidbaide fál* and *Messe ocus Pangur Bán*, but it was revised and augmented at a later period. On a literal level, the speaker looks back on her life and explores the process of growing old. She acknowledges her stage of life – 'old age is upon me I myself recognize it' (*do-fil áes dam / at-gén féin*) – as well as its universality: 'winter of age which overwhelms everyone, its first days have come to me' (*gaim aís báides cech duine, / domm-ánic a fhochmuine*).[22] Her

[18] Murphy, *Early Irish Lyrics*, 6–9.   [19] Ibid., 4–5 (poem 3).

[20] Maria Tymoczko, 'Poetry of Masks: The Poet's Persona in Early Celtic Poetry', in Kathryn A. Klar, Eve E. Sweetser and Claire Thomas, eds., *A Celtic Florilegium: Studies in Memory of Brendan O Hehir* (Lawrence: Celtic Studies Publications, 1996), 187–209.

[21] Donncha Ó hAodha, ed. and trans., 'The Lament of the Old Woman of Beare', in Ó Corráin et al., eds., *Sages, Saints and Storytellers*, 308–31.

[22] Ibid., 313, 316.

feelings, when indicated, are mixed: she regrets 'being in the darkness of an oratory' 'after feasting by bright candles', while recognizing that 'every acorn is doomed to decay' (*Aminecán morúar dam / – cach dercoin is erchraide – / íar feis fri condlib sorchaib / bith i ndorchaib derrthaige*).[23] Indeed, since her hair has gone grey 'it is no bad thing that there is an ugly veil covering it' (*ní líach drochcaille tarais*).[24] She shows disdain for a younger generation – 'it is riches you love, and not people' (*It moíni / charthar lib, nídat doíni*) – noting that 'although they bestow little, great is the extent to which they boast of it' (*cíasu bec do-n-idnaiget, / is mór a mét no-moídet*).[25] Envy is reserved for natural features that are rejuvenated: ebb-tide may come to her as to the sea (*Aithbe damsa bés mara*), but while the ocean will once more be in flood, everything for her is ebbing (*atá uile for aithbe*).[26]

Notwithstanding the finality of this, the closing sentiment of the poem as it survives, a note of optimism runs throughout.[27] Her body has been loaned to her by God and 'when the son of God deems it time, let him come to carry off his deposit' (*tan bas mithig la mac nDé / do-té do breith a aithni*).[28] Moreover, in the course of the spiritual journey outlined in the composition, Jesus redeems what he had left with her, so that she can confidently state 'I am not sad up to ebb' (*conám toirsech co aithbe*).[29] The liberality she practised in all aspects of her life is proclaimed as a Christian virtue.[30] Her place in heaven is reserved, since, in a deliberate biblical allusion, she reveals that both her right and left eyes have been taken to make her claim to that land more secure.[31] Embracing her varied past life and the inevitability of its earthly end, the *caillech Bérri* too can serve as a role model, since her generosity, humility and charity will ensure that she is granted eternal life. In that way, the secularity of the poem's imagery acquires particular significance, as the path the *caillech* has followed is accessible to the royalty and nobility with whom she associated in her

---

[23] Ibid. On the biblical significance of the acorn, see John Carey, 'Transmutations of Mortality in "The Lament of the Old Woman of Beare"', *Celtica*, 23 (1999), 36.

[24] Ó hAodha, 'Lament', 312, 316.   [25] Ibid., 311, 315.

[26] Ibid., 311, 315, 317. These are the opening and closing stanzas of the poem, as it has come down to us, closure (*dúnad*) being indicated by the key concept *aithbe* meaning 'ebbing'.

[27] There is a repeated *dúnad* in the last three stanzas of the poem (33–35); originally, it may have ended at stanza 33 with the *caillech*'s positive statement that she is 'not sad up to ebb'. Stanzas 34 and 35, with their emphasis on the finality of ebbing, introduce a pessimistic note that is in marked contrast to the optimism that has been deliberately built up throughout the poem.

[28] Ó hAodha, 'Lament', 311, 315. This image too is biblical; see Carey, 'Transmutations of Mortality', 36.

[29] Ó hAodha, 'Lament', 315, 317.   [30] Ibid., 316, 317.

[31] Ibid., 314, 316; the reference is to Matthew 18:9.

youth. In this context, the ambiguity of her title – *caillech*, meaning 'veiled one', referring to a married or widowed woman, as well as to a nun – is surely deliberate.[32] The *drochcaille* ('ugly veil'), which has the dubious advantage of covering her grey hair, will be replaced by *caille finn* ('a fair veil') which, with its familiar Christian connotations, is specifically welcomed by the speaker.[33] This alternative veil is the equivalent of the ever-yellow covering (*barr*) of the plain of Femen, Co. Tipperary, mentioned in the very next stanza. Similarly, as God prepares 'a green cloak' (*brat úaine*) for another place, Drummain, he may provide her with a garment to replace her own *brat*, which is far from new. This reading is underlined by the juxtaposition of the two stanzas. The implication, therefore, is that the tangible symbols of this world can be customized by God as preparation for the next life. As an exponent of a Christian royal secular existence, the *caillech Bérri* could serve as an example for others living a full and lengthy lay life.

It may have been her strong association with sovereignty that led to her functioning in this role, if we can assume that as a persona the *caillech Bérri* had a prior literary life.[34] This poem, commencing *Aithbe damsa bés mara*, however, is the earliest extant text in which she occurs.[35] By the eleventh or twelfth century, it had been prefaced by a prose introduction, in which her fame as royal ancestor figure was highlighted – one who was converted by having a blessed veil placed on her head.[36] The reference therein to the 'seven periods of her youth' (*secht n-aís n-aíted*) alludes to the common parallelism between the seven ages of the world in Christian chronology and the ages of man.[37] According to this prevalent scheme, the development of the world was mapped onto that of a human. Thus, the 'age and infirmity' (*áes ocus lobrae*) of the *caillech Bérri* became a measure of the passing of time of the Christian world. This serves as an indication that the life of the *caillech Bérri* may well have been subject to allegorical interpretation, as other aspects of her character which later become popular were being formed.

---

[32] See Máirín Ní Dhonnchadha, 'Caillech and Other Terms for Veiled Women in Medieval Irish Texts', *Éigse*, 26 (1994–95), 71–96.

[33] Ó hAodha, 'Lament', 312, 316.

[34] See Tomás Ó Cathasaigh, 'The Eponym of Cnogba', *Éigse*, 23 (1989), 27–38 and Carey, 'Transmutations of Mortality'.

[35] What survives as a tale title, *Serc Caillige Berre do Fhothud Chanand*, preserves her name. See Proinsias Mac Cana, *The Learned Tales of Medieval Ireland* (Dublin: Dublin Institute for Advanced Studies, 1980), 48.

[36] Ó hAodha, 'Lament', 309.

[37] See Máire Ní Mhaonaigh, '"The Metaphorical Hector": The Literary Portrayal of Murchad mac Bríain', in Ralph O'Connor, ed., *Classical Literature and Learning in Medieval Irish Narrative* (Cambridge: D. S. Brewer, 2014), 144–45.

The cult of personality

Notwithstanding the universal and readily identifiable feelings concerning ageing communicated by the poem through its narrator, the *caillech Bérri*, 'The Lament of the Old Woman of Beare' is a composition conveying various meanings, some of which remain opaque. It is noteworthy, however, that the author deemed it most effective to present such complex thoughts in a first-person voice. The adoption of a literary persona, whether newly constructed or already established, ensured immediacy and intimacy, while also creating distance between an anonymous author and his (or her) words.[38] Above all, it allowed for expression by an 'expert' and so accorded authority to the poem. Influence was more easily achieved through the words of a recognized figure, thereby according a text greater prestige. This approach is particularly prevalent in the areas of royal instruction and legal pronouncements, which are frequently ascribed to an idealized king or mythical jurist, rendering the knowledge imparted or judgement arrived at more secure.[39] 'Cormac's Precepts' (*Tecosca Cormaic*), for example, is a ninth-century kingship-manual put into the mouth of the legendary king of Ireland, Cormac son of Art. Couched as a series of extended answers to brief questions asked by Cormac's son, Cairpre, this alliterative poem constitutes a handbook for successful rule, setting out a leader's rights and desired qualities, and urging balance and moderation in every respect, as befits a Christian king.[40] Cormac may be associated with a pagan past, but he is made to advocate the importance of 'worshipping great God' (*adrad Dé móir*), and it is the Lord who bestows upon a king the necessary attributes, in his view.[41] As a king famed for justice, Cormac is also cited as an authority in legal tracts. Poet-jurists are similarly accorded that role and it is in their words that verdicts, adjudications and important maxims are often expressed.[42] Once again, the alleged wisdom of the past is invoked to enhance the authority of what are contemporary Christian laws.

Christian saints themselves also function as vessels of authority, most notably the late sixth-century northern Irish saint Columba (Colm Cille), to whom a varied body of later poetry has been attributed. Exile forms a

---

[38] On the author's gender, see Thomas Clancy, 'Women Poets in Early Medieval Ireland', in Christine E. Meek and M. Katharine Simms, eds., *'The Fragility of Her Sex?' Medieval Irish Women in Their European Context* (Dublin: Four Courts Press, 1996), 43–72.

[39] See Robin Chapman Stacey, *Dark Speech: The Performance of Law in Early Ireland* (Philadelphia: University of Pennsylvania Press, 2007).

[40] Kuno Meyer, ed. and trans., *The Instructions of King Cormac Mac Airt* (Dublin: Royal Irish Academy, 1909), 44–45.

[41] Ibid., 2–3, 4–5.   [42] Stacey, *Dark Speech*, 73–74.

dominant thematic strand in this material, building on his reputation as founder of a monastery – Iona – overseas. As Máire Herbert has observed, however, the regretful tone ascribed to the saint longing for his idyllic homeland is at some remove from the testimony of the seventh-century *Vita Columbae* ('Life of Columba'), which presents the departure of the holy man from Ireland in conventional hagiographical terms, 'wishing to be a pilgrim for Christ' (*pro Christo pereginari volens*). Moreover, in Columba's own time and for some considerable period thereafter, Iona could scarcely have been regarded as exilic, forming part of an extended Gaelic cultural world.[43] Such was the nature of the saint's continued links with his home territory that he would not have imagined that 'never more shall it [his blue eye] see the men of Ireland nor its women' (*noco n-aceba íarmo-thá / fíru Érenn nách a mná*).[44] The Columba of these eleventh- and twelfth-century compositions, therefore, is as much a constructed persona as the *caillech* of Beare, and his intense musings concerning his original locality a creative vehicle for powerful poetry of place.

The inspiration for this poetry may have been derived in part from Ovid's characterization of exile, as Herbert has argued, noting that access to popular Ovidian texts could have been provided by the many Irish scholars who were active in continental centres of learning and royal courts.[45] One of these, Sedulius Scotus, a ninth-century author based for a time at Liège, refers to exile himself in his copious Latin writings, though the extent to which his own experience informs this is difficult to determine. According to his own playful, poetic account, he combined learned activities with carousing: 'I read and write and teach, philosophy peruse. I eat and freely drink, with rhymes invoke the muse' (*Aut lego vel scribo, doceo scrutorve sophiam: / ... Vescor, poto libens, rithmizans invoco Musas*). And while this may in broad outline be true, the poem is scarcely autobiographical as such, and ends with a humorous appeal: 'Christ and Mary, pity this miserable man!' (*Parcite vos misero, Christe Maria, viro*).[46]

Love of books

Among those who followed Sedulius Scotus and others to the Continent in later centuries was Máel Brigte, alias Marianus Scotus, an eleventh-century

[43] Máire Herbert, 'Becoming an Exile: Colum Cille in Middle-Irish Poetry', in Nagy and Jones, eds., *Heroic Poets*, 132–33, 135.

[44] Murphy, *Early Irish Lyrics*, 64–65 (poem 29).   [45] Herbert, "Becoming an Exile", 134–38.

[46] James Carney, ed. and trans., *Medieval Irish Lyrics* (Portlaoise: Dolmen Press, 1967), 62–63 (poem XXIV).

scholar whose name change coincided with a move from the north of Ireland to Germany in the 1050s. He achieved some fame as a chronicler and a world history he composed was drawn on widely as a source for historical writing after his death. A part-autograph manuscript of this *Chronicon* has survived, Codex Palatino-Vaticanus 830, on the margins of which contemporary jottings provide some insight into Marianus' learned life.[47] He inserts himself into his historical composition in another way, by means of a somewhat opaque Latin verse. Within it, the reader is directed to pick out the 'opening letter' (*littera anterior*), and when enumerated the author comes into being (*existat ... auctor*). When taken together, the initial letters of a series of words at this point in the poem do indeed unmask the author, spelling out the phrase *Moel Brigte clausenair rom tinol* ('Máel Brigte the hermit compiled me').[48] In this way, the manuscript itself is made to reveal the scribe's identity, though only to observant readers. As in the adoption of a persona, the use of an acrostic enabled the author to maintain a certain distance from his work. On deciphering the device, however, Máel Brigte's ownership of his history and embracing of his book is disclosed.

Another book, a psalm-book, may have been embraced, equally cryptically, by a poet writing in Irish at about the same time. A verse addressed to a woman, Crínóc, has been interpreted in this way, ingeniously and anthropomorphically, by James Carney.[49] Her name, literally 'dear old one', could well have been chosen deliberately to conjure up the image of the well-worn vellum of a cherished book. The clerical narrator-author, although his flesh burns with love for her, is free from fault. She too is 'guiltless of any sin with man' (*glan cen pheccad fri fer*), despite her apparent promiscuity, four having lain where he had lain. Her real form becomes apparent when the poet rejoices in the fact that she brings the Scriptures to everyone; following her poetic art (*dán*) daily leads one to God. He has allowed himself to be directed by her: 'beautiful your course, across

---

[47] See Bartholomew McCarthy, *The Codex Palatino-Vaticanus No. 830* (Dublin: Royal Irish Academy, 1892) and Brian Ó Cuív, 'The Irish Marginalia in Codex Palatino-Vaticanus No. 830', *Éigse*, 24 (1990), 45–67.

[48] The acrostic has been illuminated by Michael Clarke, upon whose work I draw here with gratitude: 'Medieval Ireland in the Wider World: New Perspectives from the Manuscripts', in Joe Fenwick, ed., *Lost and Found: Discovering Ireland's Past*, vol. 3 (Dublin: Wordwell, forthcoming).

[49] James Carney, 'A Chrínóc, cubaid do cheól', *Éigse*, 4:4 (1945), 280–83. See also Tomás Ó Broin, 'The Genesis of "An Chrínóc"', *Éigse*, 9:1 (1958), 1–3 and Máirín Ní Dhonnchadha, 'A Chrínóc, cubaid do cheól (To an Old Psalm-Book)', in Angela Bourke et al., eds., *The Field Day Anthology of Irish Writing, Volume IV: Irish Women's Writings and Traditions* (Cork: Cork University Press in association with Field Day, 2002), 127–29.

every ocean' (*adbal do rith tar cach rían*).[50] The contrast with the inattentive poet whom we have already encountered, and who was writing at about the same time, is marked: that clerical narrator-author's course, he claims, is not one of great wisdom (*ní rith rogaíse*), and when studying the psalms in particular his thoughts wander down a stray path.[51] A reader encountering both allegorical compositions would be encouraged to bestow affection on his or her own book of psalms.

Fictionalized figures

The address to the anthropomorphized Crínóc was considered by Carney to have been the work of an Armagh ecclesiastic, Máel Ísu Ua Brolcháin, although the evidence for his authorship is not secure. This acclaimed poet, who was described as 'eminent sage of Ireland' (*ardsuí na Herend*) on his death in Munster in 1086,[52] concerned himself with religious themes.[53] Written in a first-person voice, his compositions call on God for assistance and protection and beseech him for a place in heaven, revealing little of the man within. If a prayer for forgiveness attributed to him reflects reality, he transgressed when 'a tender youth' (*móethóclach*) and 'offered fair women of gleaming teeth lascivious lips' (*ba lainn lemm mo bóethphócad / do mnáib détgelaib dilib*).[54] This is likely to be rhetorical, however, the formulaic retrospective of one who presents himself as an old man approaching death.[55] A predilection for transgression is intimated in a *lorica* or breastplate poem, in which he requests that God shield his various limbs and organs and thus prevent them from committing sin. Yet this too is conventional, as is the litany of prospective body parts, comprising eyes, ears, tongue, heart, stomach, hands and feet.[56]

Lust-avoidance is included among his wish list and God is called on to protect his penis too: 'Guard my male organ in the matter of pure chastity' (*Coimét mo ball ferda / im genus co nglaine*).[57] Celibacy forms the central theme of a verse composition written a century or so later in the voice of a ninth-century king-bishop of Cashel, Cormac mac Cuilennáin, whose career is

---

[50] For the text and a free translation, see Carney, *Medieval Irish Lyrics*, 74–79; for comment, see xxvii–xxviii.

[51] Murphy, *Early Irish Lyrics*, 38–43.

[52] Seán Mac Airt, ed. and trans., *The Annals of Inisfallen (MS. Rawlinson B. 503)* (Dublin: Dublin Institute for Advanced Studies, 1951), 238–39.

[53] See Murphy, *Early Irish Lyrics*, 52–59 (poems 22–25).

[54] Carney, *Medieval Irish Lyrics*, 78–79 (poem XXXI).   [55] Ibid., 80–81.

[56] Murphy, *Early Irish Lyrics*, 54–59 (poem 24).   [57] Ibid., 56–57.

outlined in other sources.[58] The poem is addressed to another historical personage, Gormlaith, daughter of an Ua Néill king, Flann Sinna, with whom Cormac is associated in other literary texts.[59] Whatever the precise nature of their relationship, Gormlaith now has a powerful rival – the church: 'the woman who torments me is the church of God for whom poetry is made' (*As í bean atá 'com chrádh | ecclas Dé dá ndéntar dán*).[60] In his desire to remain faithful to his new love, he cites the example of a series of saints who refused beautiful women for 'love of God' (*grádh Dé*).[61] Like them, he too has given his virginity to God (*tucas m'óighe do Día*),[62] repudiating Gormlaith as a result. In the contemporary context of religious reform, the poem had a specific resonance, since an increased emphasis on celibate clergy was a feature of the changes the church underwent in the eleventh and twelfth centuries. To present his view of what was an important issue, an anonymous author chose to cast himself as Cormac, whose dual role as secular ruler and ecclesiastic could be perceived as giving him a superior perspective. In choosing the Munster king as persona, however, the author was undoubtedly influenced by his fame as a literary figure and poet in his own right. Expressed through Cormac, the writer's own consideration of celibacy, whether based on his own experiences or not, carried greater weight.

Cormac's literary consort, Gormlaith, notwithstanding her role in this poem as silent (and unnamed) addressee, was accorded a poetic voice in her own right.[63] The corpus of material put into her mouth belongs to the later medieval period and thus to an era in which the individual, emerging as a concept in the eleventh and twelfth centuries, as has been noted, was very differently perceived. The genre of medieval romance which blossomed in this and later periods reflected the changing attitude towards personality.[64] Why things happened are analysed to a greater degree; states of mind are scrutinized; feelings are explored. As a result of these developments, intimate stories of a different kind could be created, constituting a continuous narration of an

---

[58] See Máire Ní Mhaonaigh, 'Cormac mac Cuilennáin: King, Bishop and "Wondrous Sage"', *Zeitschrift für Celtische Philologie*, 58 (2011), 109–28.

[59] See Máire Ní Mhaonaigh, 'Tales of Three Gormlaiths in Medieval Irish Literature', *Ériu*, 52 (2002), 1–24.

[60] Máirín Ní Dhonnchadha, 'On Gormfhlaith Daughter of Flann Sinna and the Lure of the Sovereignty Goddess', in Alfred P. Smyth, ed., *Seanchas: Studies in Early and Medieval Irish Archaeology, History and Literature in Honour of Francis J. Byrne* (Dublin: Four Courts Press, 2000), 234.

[61] Ibid., 235.   [62] Ibid., 237.

[63] Osborn Bergin, ed. and trans., *Irish Bardic Poetry* (Dublin: Dublin Institute for Advanced Studies, 1970), 202–15, 308–15. See also Anne O'Sullivan, 'Triamhuin Ghormlaithe', *Ériu*, 16 (1952), 189–99.

[64] Classics of the genre include Benoît de Sainte-Maure's *Roman de Troie* and Chaucer's *Troilus and Criseyde*.

individual's experience, concentrating on a single person as an object of love.[65] It is in this context that the later poetry ascribed to Gormlaith should be placed. The sequence of poems is concerned for the most part with her emotional state after the death of her lover, another historical ruler and contemporary of Cormac, Níall Glúndub, son of the northern ruler, Áed Finnlíath. Reference is made in passing to Cormac and another partner, Cerball mac Muirecáin.[66] She is adamant, however, that 'dearer to me Niall than either' (*annsa leam Níall no gach fear*); all that remains for her to do is to go 'to the grave of Niall' (*go húaidh Néill*) and lie down close beside him.[67]

The collection of eleven poems contains much which is conventional. Niall's generosity was boundless: he gave Gormlaith thrice what she had got from other kings,[68] and she claims that 'if I should speak well of Niall, the poets would speak far better' (*dā n-abruinnsi maith ré Níall / adēradh an chlíar maith badh ró*).[69] Nonetheless, the voice of one who is depicted as a bereaved woman is to the fore: 'alas my separation from my beauty' (*uchagān, mo scaradh réim sgéimh*).[70] She forsook all her previous lovers for Niall, wishing to do his will.[71] The poems acquired some popularity and are referred to by the seventeenth-century annalist Conall Mac Eochagáin, who is mindful of 'pittifull and learned dittyes in Irish' composed by Gormlaith. The tone of his brief account of her life as widow, begging 'from doore to doore, forsaken of all her friends and allies', also accords with that of the extant verse. Moreover, reference to a dream in which the ghost of Niall appeared to his former wife is preserved in both the annalistic compilation and in one of the poems.[72]

Thus, Gormlaith's literary life is enduring and a wealth of material attributed to her survives. As a recognizable persona she becomes a vehicle for emotional expression. The sentiments ascribed to this tenth-century queen are far from (auto)biographical, however, as the preceding discussion will have made clear. The feelings described in the late medieval poems linked with her may mask those of a poet or poets for whom Gormlaith's story provided echoes of their own. If so, those real lives remain hidden from view. In the case of other poems of this bardic genre, emotions may be more

---

[65] See Sverre Bagge, 'The Autobiography of Abelard and Medieval Individualism', *Journal of Medieval History*, 19 (1993), 327–50.
[66] See Ní Mhaonaigh, 'Tales of Three Gormlaiths', 7–11.
[67] Bergin, *Irish Bardic Poetry*, 206, 309 (poem III).   [68] Ibid., 215, 315 (poem XI).
[69] Ibid., 214, 314 (poem X).   [70] Ibid., 208, 310 (poem VI).
[71] Ibid., 212, 313 (poem X, stanzas 1 and 2).   [72] See Ní Mhaonaigh, 'Tales of Three Gormlaiths', 7.

easily associated with specific individuals. An earlier spousal elegy, ascribed to the thirteenth-century poet Muireadhach Ó Dálaigh and written to mourn his wife, Maol Mheadha, is likely to express genuine grief. His soul departed from him with her passing; he is 'a body in two pieces since the lovely bright and gentle one is gone' (*corp idir dá aisil inn / ar dtocht don fhinn mhaisigh mhoill*). Scarcely written for recompense from a patron, this lament is for a woman who bore the poet eleven children and with whom he spent twenty years. Notwithstanding this, it is her youth and untimely death which is emphasized: 'her departure from her husband while fresh and young' (*a héag ó a fior go húr óg*).[73]

This poem is all the more remarkable since it provides a personal insight into the life of one of the most skilful professional poets of his day. Muireadhach Ó Dálaigh too acquired a literary persona, which is portrayed most vividly in the Annals of the Four Masters.[74] Yet the evidence of the poems, which in all likelihood were composed by him, show a master craftsman writing for a range of chieftains, both Gaelic and Anglo-Norman, in Ireland and in Scotland alike.[75] His association with Scotland acquired him the soubriquet *Albanach* ('Scottish'), and he may also have journeyed further afield to the Mediterranean, if he is indeed the author of the work beginning 'Help from Cruachain is far off across the wave-bordered Mediterranean sea' (*Fada in chabair a Cruacain / tar muir Torr(i)an tonnburachaig*).[76] The art of bardic poetry, however, was to eulogize a patron in return for a reward, and for that reason an expert artist gave voice to a chieftain's desired sentiments for the most part, rather than insert his own life into his poems. There are metrical exceptions, as the lament for his wife by Muireadhach Ó Dálaigh and the material put into the mouth of the Gormlaith character prove. Moreover, these were written throughout the period of four hundred years or so associated with the genre, since Ó Dálaigh was among the early practitioners of the bardic craft and the verse ascribed to Gormlaith dates from the later part of the era during which this poetry was composed. However, the genre in general is far from autobiographical; it constitutes life-writing of a different kind.

---

[73] Bergin, *Irish Bardic Poetry*, 101–03, 257–58 (poem XXII).

[74] See Brian Ó Cuív, 'Eachtra Mhuireadhaigh Í Dhálaigh', *Studia Hibernica*, 1 (1961), 56–69.

[75] See Katharine Simms, 'Bardic Poetry as a Historical Source', in Tom Dunne, ed., *The Writer as Witness* (Cork: Cork University Press, 1987), 59–60.

[76] Gerard Murphy, 'Two Irish Poems Written from the Mediterranean in the Thirteenth Century', *Éigse*, 7:2 (1953–55), 74–79.

Conclusion

Variety is the hallmark of the extensive, vibrant writing that survives from medieval Ireland in various languages in the first-person voice. In surveying a rich literary landscape of well over a thousand years, this chapter has drawn attention to but a few textual examples and highlighted no more than a number of dominant themes. Hovering around the twelfth century, which marks a significant development in the understanding of self, as a result of which the individual is differently presented and perceived, we have journeyed backwards, encountering allegory and anthropomorphy, and forwards to experience a more personal tone. Religion and education provide the intellectual framework within which these voices must be interpreted; a prevailing concern is the production of an authoritative expression. In their concern with lasting influence, authors frequently adopted personae, whose association with the work enhanced its prestige. Even when expressed through the creator's own being, however, first-person narrator and author are in some sense never one. While the well-nigh autobiographer Augustine of Hippo admits to various transgressions, the sinful figure he presents in his *Confessiones* is a construct to which other would-be converts can relate. The *ego* ('I') with which Patrick's similarly and deliberately named *Confessio* (and with it medieval Irish writing) commences is far from identical with the evasive and elusive saint.

Further reading

Aird, William. 'Life-Writing and the Anglo-Saxons', in David Roffe, ed., *The English and Their Legacy, 900–1200: Essays in Honour of Ann Williams*. Woodbridge: Boydell Press, 2012: 5–16.

Misch, Georg. *Geschichte der Autobiographie*. 3rd revised edn. Frankfurt: Schulte-Bulmke, 1949–69. 5 vols.

Rubenstein, Jay. 'Biography and Autobiography in the Middle Ages', in Nancy Partner, ed., *Writing Medieval History*. London: Bloomsbury Academic, 2005: 22–41.

Spearing, A. C. *Medieval Autographies: The 'I' of the Text*. Notre Dame: University of Notre Dame Press, 2012.

Stock, Brian. 'The Self and Literary Experience in Late Antiquity and the Middle Ages', *New Literary History*, 25:4 (1994), 839–52.

Zumthor, Paul. 'Autobiographie au Moyen Age?', in Paul Zumthor, ed., *Langue, Texte, Énigme*. Paris: Seuil, 1975: 165–80.

CHAPTER 3

Early Modern Irish Autobiography

Marie-Louise Coolahan

In his classic study of autobiography in seventeenth-century Britain, Paul Delany defined the genre of autobiography as 'a coherent account of the author's life, or of an extensive period or series of events in his life ... composed after a period of reflection'.[1] Influenced by modern autobiographical practice and developments in autobiography theory, this is a view that has come under intense scrutiny since the late 1980s. Scholars now regard this conception of autobiography – the coherent, unitary, retrospective account of the individual's life – as merely one form of early modern life-writing, and a form that is elusive at that in this period. Traditionally, the emergence of autobiography has been located in the impetus to self-examination that was prompted by Protestant religious practices. For example, the Independent 'gathered' churches of the mid-seventeenth century, which advocated non-episcopal forms of church government, encouraged admission testimonies or conversion narratives – accounts of the individual's journey towards religious conversion and spiritual rebirth – as conditions for membership. This stimulus to self-reflection and the articulation of personal experience according to a narrative paradigm that encompassed one's life engendered a shift towards spiritual autobiography, a development that reached fruition in such canonical works as John Bunyan's *Grace Abounding to the Chief of Sinners* (1666) and informed early eighteenth-century fiction such as Defoe's *Robinson Crusoe* (1719).[2] While this traditional model for the emergence of autobiography retains its value, attesting to real developments in literary evolution, recent scholarship has expanded our frames for understanding representations of early modern lives.

---

[1] Paul Delany, *British Autobiography in the Seventeenth Century* (London: Routledge and Kegan Paul, 1969), 1.

[2] See, for example, J. Paul Hunter, *Before Novels: The Cultural Contexts of Eighteenth-Century English Fiction* (New York: Norton, 1990).

Scholars of early modern women's writing, in recuperating the full range of texts that were authored by women, turned to autobiographical writing. The landmark 1989 anthology, *Her Own Life*, drew attention to the wealth and breadth of such material, introducing twelve writers whose accounts of their lives emerged in diaries, meditative verse, radical religious tracts and polemical pamphlets, as well as in the more familiar form of the retrospective first-person account.[3] This interest in the diverse forms of women's literary production led to an expansion of the genres under consideration as autobiography and a concomitant recalibration of the field as life-writing or self-writing.[4] This critical shift has embraced autobiographical forms produced by non-elite men as well as women of all social classes. The most recent scholarship has further extended the kinds of texts in which articulations of selfhood by men and women can be found. Adam Smyth, for example, analyses print almanacs, financial accounts, commonplace books and parish registers as part of a 'culture of innovation and adaptation' in which 'individuals seeking to produce textual records of their lives experimented and improvised with other available forms'.[5] Meredith Anne Skura has challenged the temporal boundaries of autobiography's emergence as a genre by reaching back into the sixteenth century. She defines autobiography as an author 'writing about his or her experience ... looking back over the experience and organizing it into a narrative of some sort', and finds it in court documents, printed poetry, allegory, fiction and non-fiction.[6]

At stake in these debates are questions about the nature of subjectivity in the early modern period more broadly, including the question of when

[3] Elspeth Graham, Hilary Hinds, Elaine Hobby and Helen Wilcox, eds., *Her Own Life: Autobiographical Writings by Seventeenth-Century Englishwomen* (London: Routledge, 1989).

[4] Michelle M. Dowd and Julie A. Eckerle, eds., *Genre and Women's Life Writing in Early Modern England* (Aldershot: Ashgate, 2007) and 'Recent Studies in Early Modern English Life Writing', *English Literary Renaissance*, 40 (2010), 132–62. The dominance of scholarship on women's writing over this field is clear from the latter's Section III, 'Studies of Individual Authors' (142–58), in which twenty-one of twenty-seven authors are women. See also Elspeth Graham, 'Women's Writing and the Self', in Helen Wilcox, ed., *Women and Literature in Britain, 1500–1700* (Cambridge: Cambridge University Press, 1996), 209–33; Elizabeth Clarke, 'Diaries', in Michael Hattaway, ed., *A Companion to English Renaissance Literature and Culture* (Oxford: Blackwell, 2003), 609–14; David Booy, *Autobiographical Writings by Early Quaker Women* (Aldershot: Ashgate, 2004); Sharon Cadman Seelig, *Autobiography and Gender in Early Modern Literature: Reading Women's Lives, 1600–1680* (Cambridge: Cambridge University Press, 2006); Ramona Wray, 'Autobiography', in Laura Lunger Knoppers, ed., *The Cambridge Companion to Early Modern Women's Writing* (Cambridge: Cambridge University Press, 2009), 194–207.

[5] Adam Smyth, *Autobiography in Early Modern England* (Cambridge: Cambridge University Press, 2010), 2.

[6] Meredith Anne Skura, *Tudor Autobiography: Listening for Inwardness* (Chicago: University of Chicago Press, 2008), 2.

a coherent sense of self develops. The Burckhardtian view of the Renaissance as being characterized by the emergence of individual self-consciousness and self-determination has been disputed and modified in the face of the range of genres – letters, diaries, journals, memoirs, poems, spiritual confessions, trial records, almanacs, account-books, petitions, legal depositions – that facilitated representations of the self.[7] More importantly, this diversity of genres points us to the various ways in which the self was articulated, often partially and refracted through other expressive functions. Henk Dragstra's study of execution ballads as sites for semi-oral autobiography memorably illustrates the possibilities that have opened up.[8] Equally at issue are the parameters of genre, which determine the version of the self that is articulated. That self is always a constructed persona and its shape is fashioned by the requirements of the specific kind of life-writing chosen to narrate it.

Moreover, historical events drove the emergence of these forms of life-writing. This is particularly the case in early modern Ireland, where reiterated cycles of warfare and migration mitigated against the measured composition of a life story from the perspective of comfortable distance but nevertheless compelled many, from all walks of life, to present themselves and their situations in autobiographical modes. As this chapter will show, those who came to articulate narratives of their own lives in Ireland in this period were doing so in response to social turmoil and instability, often with the explicit aim of securing support, assistance or survival. Those who authored autobiography, in its various forms, tended to be Anglophone, from the Old English or New English communities – the former descended from the Normans who had arrived and assimilated four centuries previously, the latter, recent arrivals as part of the Tudor entrenchment of crown jurisdiction. The native, or Gaelic, Irish were driven to represent themselves mainly in other languages as a result of clashes with English authorities and the concomitant changes in the support structures of Gaelic culture (although the latter led to some personal experience emerging in the later bardic poetry of writers such as Dáibhí Ó Bruadair). Since

---

[7] Jacob Burckhardt, *The Civilization of the Renaissance in Italy* (New York: Harper, 1958), 2 vols. See in particular David Aers's critique, 'A Whisper in the Ear of Early Modernists; or, Reflections on Literary Critics Writing the "History of the Subject"', in David Aers, ed., *Culture and History, 1350–1600: Essays on English Communities, Identities, and Writing* (Detroit: Wayne State University Press, 1992), 177–202 and Michael Mascuch, *Origins of the Individualist Self: Autobiography and Self-Identity in England, 1591–1791* (Cambridge: Polity Press, 1997).

[8] Henk Dragstra, 'Last Farewell to the World: Semi-Oral Autobiography in Seventeenth-Century Broadside Ballads', in Henk Dragstra, Sheila Ottway and Helen Wilcox, eds., *Betraying Our Selves: Forms of Self-Representation in Early Modern English Texts* (Basingstoke: Macmillan, 2000), 166–82.

genre as well as circumstance mediated and moulded the versions of the self that were presented, this chapter will focus on the key genres of early modern life-writing in Ireland: petitions, depositions, letters, conversion narratives, autobiographies and autobiographical fragments. Conceived expansively, the autobiographical territory of Anglophone Ireland is rich and under-researched. What's more, not only the content but the various modes of composition in themselves are illuminating of the island's culture during this period.

Petitions

A petition is a formal request for the granting of a particular suit. Whether directed at securing advantage for oneself or one's kin, a successful petition demands familiarity with petitionary etiquette and protocols, the rhetoric of persuasion, the formulation of argument and techniques of self-representation. Moreover, the deference entailed in any successful suit required that the author deploy simultaneously the languages of supplication and self-assertion. Many Irish petitioners addressed the English or Spanish crown in pursuit of protection, maintenance or acknowledgement of rights, and many such texts survive in the state archives of Britain and Spain. Their composition demanded not only command of the petitionary conventions but also recruitment of amanuenses and even interpreters, as in the case of Shane O'Neill, who pressed his claims to the Tyrone earldom through a series of petitions between 1559 and 1566. These petitions are not in O'Neill's native tongue but in Latin and English, a signal of the collaborative process involved. They pitch the chieftain's life narrative in different ways, always aiming to present him in terms that will win over the monarch – a goal that required fluid invention as O'Neill took up arms in Ulster.[9] For example, his petition of 8 February 1561 narrates his paternity and his election to the title Ó Néill according to Gaelic tradition. It offers his version of recent military clashes and argues for his good management of the territory as grounds for both peace and the English title of earl. His petition also includes an offer of marriage to a noble Englishwoman of the queen's choosing and proposes a visit to London 'to declare not onely what state I found my country when I was Elected to Rule. What state it is nowe in. what gowernement I vse what Iustice I show vniu*er*sally to eu*ery* man*n*.'[10]

---

[9] See Patricia Palmer, *Language and Conquest in Early Modern Ireland: English Renaissance Literature and Elizabethan Imperial Expansion* (Cambridge: Cambridge University Press, 2001).

[10] National Archives, London, SP 63/3, fol. 31r.

Perhaps the most infamous petition is that made in 1593 by Gráinne Ní Mháille (Grace O'Malley), the 'pirate queen' of legend, to Queen Elizabeth I in London. This text, also dependent on a translator/scribe, is testament to the exploitation and subversion of petitionary conventions. Composing the petition in order to justify her military resistance of the queen's governor of Connacht, Richard Bingham, and to secure the monarch's approbation of her own property rights as well as those of her offspring and kin, Ní Mháille spoke as '*your* Loyall and faithfull subiect', presenting her life and past actions in a sympathetic light in order to secure the queen's support. Hence, her past use of arms and force is attributed to the 'continuall discord sturres [stirs] and dissention'[11] that surrounded her and her people, while the shift to Elizabethan taxation mechanisms is presented as compelling her to continue in arms for the maintenance of herself and her community. Every persuasive tool is incorporated into the petitionary arsenal. Not only these historical causes, but the petitioner's gender and perceived vulnerability of widowhood and old age are marshalled to support the case she is making. Self-representation here is coloured by the means to an end; this is not a transparent account of Ní Mháille's life but a representation calculated to make her sympathetic to her intended reader. Astonishingly, this petition concludes by requesting 'free liberty ... to invade *with* sword and fire all *your* highnes enemyes',[12] that is, permission to continue in arms, although now allegedly on behalf of the crown and in defence of the realm.

The flood of refugees from Gaelic Ireland to Catholic Spain generated a different form of petitionary life-writing.[13] The Spanish award of *entretenimiento* or state pension to Irish men and women who could establish their noble lineage and service to the Counter-Reformation cause engendered a cascade of petitions in which emigrants' lives were framed to conform exactly with these conditions. Again, gender provided for additional rhetorical tools of persuasion. For example, Cecilia Fitzgerald, who addressed a petition to King

---

[11] National Archives, London, SP 63/170, fol. 204 (64). For a modern edition, see Helen Ostovich and Elizabeth Sauer, eds., *Reading Early Modern Women: An Anthology of Texts in Manuscript and Print, 1550–1700* (New York: Routledge, 2003), 198–201.

[12] Ibid.

[13] For the experiences of Irish refugees abroad, see 'The Irish in Europe' series: Thomas O'Connor, ed., *The Irish in Europe, 1580–1815* (Dublin: Four Courts Press, 2001); Thomas O'Connor and Mary Ann Lyons, eds., *Irish Migrants in Europe after Kinsale* (Dublin: Four Courts Press, 2003); *Irish Communities in Early Modern Europe* (Dublin: Four Courts Press, 2006); *Strangers to Citizens: The Irish in Europe, 1600–1800* (Dublin: Four Courts Press, 2008); and *The Ulster Earls and Baroque Europe: Refashioning Irish Identities, 1600–1800* (Dublin: Four Courts Press, 2010); Raymond Gillespie and Ruairí Ó hUiginn, eds., *Irish Europe, 1600–1650: Writing and Learning* (Dublin: Four Courts Press, 2013).

Philip IV of Spain on 20 May 1623, carefully formulated her suit according to the terms of eligibility. Her Gaelic nobility and losses in Ireland, as well as her husband and son's military and naval service in the royal Spanish army, are outlined. But her petition concludes with the sucker punch of gendered destitution: 'thus leaving her helpless, poor, in sorrow and burdened with two orphaned maiden daughters, without any hope other than the help that Your Majesty may wish to give her'.[14] Through such documents of impoverishment we find not only the (translated) life stories of Gaelic Irish refugees but the responses of others who felt deserving but squeezed out, such as the elite bardic poet Fearghal Óg Mac an Bhaird, who complained in verse of the injustice attending his own poverty in the face of Spanish support for *daoine dáora* ('base folk').[15]

The 1641 depositions

Following the outbreak of the 1641 rising, a royal commission was ordered to establish what had occurred and to record the losses experienced by English Protestant settlers with a view to future reparations. The terms of the commission shaped the life narratives that were recorded. The commissioners were instructed to ask specific questions of deponents: name, place of abode and status; details of robberies or spoils committed on themselves or others, and the identities of those responsible; reports of the speech and actions of rebels; and any information on murders, deaths resulting from privation or conversions to papistry. This resulted in a rich cache of material. While some deponents adhered in minimalist fashion to the questions posed, many others, such as Robert Maxwell and Elizabeth Price, developed extended life narratives. Maxwell had been rector of the parish of Tinon, Co. Armagh. He was captured by the leader of the rebels in Ulster, Sir Phelim O'Neill, which afforded him privileged access to O'Neill and his followers. His deposition recounts this period of captivity, during which he kept a diary. He reports conversations he had with the rebels (many of these self-incriminating) as well as their conversations among themselves, which he translates from Irish into English.[16]

---

[14] Archivo General de Simancas, Spain, Estado, Neg. de España, Legajo 2752; my translation from the original Spanish. See also Micheline Walsh, 'Some Notes Towards a History of the Womenfolk of the Wild Geese' and 'Further Notes Towards a History of the Womenfolk of the Wild Geese', *The Irish Sword*, 5 (1961–62), 98–106, 133–45.

[15] Osborn Bergin, *Irish Bardic Poetry* (Dublin: Dublin Institute for Advanced Studies, 1970), 41, 227–28.

[16] Trinity College Dublin, MS 809, fols. 5r-12v; TCD, 1641 Depositions Project, http://1641.tcd .ie/deposition.php?depID<?php echo 809005r002?> (accessed 22 January 2016).

Elizabeth Price had also been a resident of Armagh and witnessed one of the most violent episodes of the rising, the massacre of Protestants at Portadown Bridge in November 1641 in which five of her children were killed. Price's narrative details that event and her struggles to survive in its aftermath. There is some degree of compensatory narrative satisfaction in her account of the supernatural female apparition that appeared in the river Bann on multiple occasions thereafter, proclaiming revenge and scaring off the Irish who sought to repopulate the land.[17]

Moreover, the act of deposing could also lead to the authoring of a more traditional autobiographical account, as in the case of Elizabeth Dowdall, whose deposition of 3 October 1642 itemizes financial and property losses. This text contrasts with the far fuller and self-centred account of her military command that was composed by Dowdall only three days following her deposition, entitled 'A true note of my several services done in county of Limerick'.[18] Hence, the act of framing a life according to the predetermined deposition structure resulted in the composition of an autobiographical narrative that represented a high degree of self-determination, unencumbered by legal conventions.

Letters

Letters are another form which allowed for expressions of the self and narratives of life in Ireland. Where an individual letter may represent only an ephemeral moment in time, multiple letters offer the broader perspective of a life more readily associated with autobiography. Nine surviving letters written by Susan Montgomery, wife of the bishop of Derry, from Ulster to her sister and brother-in-law in Somerset recount the peaks and troughs of her experiences as a planter, all the while urging them to visit and settle in Ireland themselves. Running from 1606 to 1613, this collection of letters, if read in sequence, could be seen as a kind of epistolary autobiography.[19] That the epistolary form could be strategically exploited

---

[17] Trinity College Dublin, MS 836, fols. 101r-105v; TCD, 1641 Depositions Project, http://1641.tcd.ie/de position.php?depID<?php echo 836101r054?> (accessed 22 January 2016).

[18] Trinity College Dublin, MS 829, fols. 138r-139v; TCD, 1641 Depositions Project, http://1641.tcd.ie/de position.php?depID<?php echo 829138r082?> (accessed 22 January 2016). British Library, Sloane MS 1008, fols. 66r-69r; also in Angela Bourke et al., eds., *The Field Day Anthology of Irish Writing, Volume V: Irish Women's Writings and Traditions* (Cork: Cork University Press in association with Field Day, 2002), 22–24; first published in J. T. Gilbert, ed., *History of the Irish Confederation and the War in Ireland, 1641–1649* (Dublin, 1882–91), 7 vols., vol. 2, 69–73.

[19] See Marie-Louise Coolahan, 'Ideal Communities and Planter Women's Writing in Seventeenth-Century Ireland', *Parergon*, 29 (2012), 69–91.

in order to justify one's actions during wartime is illustrated by one Mrs Briver, wife of the mayor of Waterford during that city's siege at the hands of Confederate forces in 1641. Briver composed two versions of events in order to exonerate herself and her husband from accusations of conspiring with the besiegers: a continuous narrative and a series of four letters, both addressed to one Captain Evelings, an officer at the nearby English garrison at Duncannon.[20] As with Elizabeth Dowdall, here we can see the different genres of life-writing bleeding into each other.

John Dunton's *The Dublin Scuffle* (1699) exploited the epistolary form, which was soon to become the mainstay of eighteenth-century fiction, by mixing fact, fiction, life-writing and plagiarism. Recounting the London bookseller's efforts to insert himself into the book auction trade in Dublin, his attempted seduction at the hands of a citizen's wife, and a travel account of his time in Ireland, its tripartite narrative is rendered entirely in letters. The first section comprises twelve letters from Dunton to a bookseller friend in London, with the friend's letters ('Remarks') in reply; the second contains the seduction letter of 'Dorinda' with Dunton's three letters repelling her and the London friend's epistolary reply; the third, a single letter addressed to 'an Honourable Lady' (whom his recent editor takes to be a real person) with her letter in response. Notwithstanding its epistolary frame, its real subject, Andrew Carpenter argues, is Dunton himself, its structure lending it the quality of self-therapy: 'One way of making sense of the apparent excesses of Dunton's book is . . . to see it as an elaborate structure of dialogue with the less welcome sides of his own personality.'[21]

Conversion narratives

Cromwellian Ireland was hospitable to the modes of autobiography more readily associated with the genre's Anglophone trajectory. John Rogers's Independent congregation was based at Christ Church in Dublin in the early 1650s. His publication of thirty-seven conversion narratives composed by members of this congregation at the centre of his treatise, *Ohel, or, Beth-shemesh* (1653), drew attention to the godly advances being made under the regime, performing a political and colonial function as well as attesting to the stimulation of puritan autobiographical culture in Ireland.

---

[20] See Naomi McAreavey, 'An Epistolary Account of the Irish Rising of 1641 by the Wife of the Mayor of Waterford', *English Literary Renaissance*, 42 (2012), 90–118.
[21] John Dunton, *The Dublin Scuffle*, ed. Andrew Carpenter (Dublin: Four Courts Press, 2000), xv.

Moreover, this particular stimulus to life-writing, grounded in the radic-alism of the Independent churches, allowed for a high degree of gender balance: twenty of these testimonies are attributed to men, seventeen to women. Rogers is open about his editorial work in preparing these accounts for print publication, reminding us that all such narratives are constructed and mediated: 'although in the choicest and most extraordin-ary ones, I shall gather the stalk longer, least I hurt the beauty and hide the excellency of those flowers; yet without hurt to the rest, in those which are ordinary, I shall be very short'.[22]

Typically, conversion narratives followed a formula that tracked the proofs of election and salvation as a process over time. Hence, the life recounted would involve sin, then awakening and some signs of election, then self-doubt and 'backsliding' prior to eventual assurance of salvation and spiritual rebirth.[23] Notwithstanding the conventional teleology of the form, conversion narratives often incorporated individuated experience, and those of Rogers's congregation adopted Irish inflections. For example, Thomas Huggins, a fellow preacher, recounted his struggles to commit to his ministry, including his period of study at Trinity College Dublin. Others were soldiers in Cromwell's army, stationed in Ireland a few years earlier. Frances Curtis told the church of having 'lived wantonly in my youth', her efforts to amend her behaviour, and subsequent struggles. For her, the impact of the events of 1641 cast a long shadow that challenged her powers of providential interpretation. 'In these wars', she says,

> I was stripped by the Rebels (being abroad) and came home so, thorough sad tempests ... A while after, I heard my Husband was killed by the Rebels, which I feared was by my sins, and so my troubles were renewed; and then the enemies came upon us, the Cannon-bullets flew over my head; and in few days I was turned out of doors, with my childe in my arms.[24]

Ultimately, however, her family's survival enabled her to construe her experiences as signs of God's grace: 'I cannot express what God hath done for me, in saving my life, and my Husbands, in hearing my prayers and tears; and now in satisfying my soul with himself.'[25] The religious imperative decreed that the life should be understood wholly in terms of one's relationship and standing with God.

---

[22] John Rogers, *Ohel, or, Beth-shemesh: A Tabernacle for the Sun, or, Irenicum Evangelicum* (London, 1653), 392 (sig. Ddd4v).

[23] See Nigel Smith, *Perfection Proclaimed: Language and Literature in English Radical Religion, 1640–1660* (Oxford: Clarendon Press, 1989); Tom Webster, 'Writing to Redundancy: Approaches to Spiritual Journals and Early Modern Spirituality', *Historical Journal*, 39 (1996), 33–56.

[24] Rogers, *Ohel*, 10–11 (sigs. ggg3v–ggg4r).   [25] Ibid.

Diaries and autobiography

Protestants of all kinds responded similarly to the call for interiority and self-examination. We could point to *The Vocacyon of Johan Bale to the Bishoprick of Ossorie in Ireland* (1553) as the earliest autobiography focused on Irish experience. Appointed bishop of Ossory in 1552, John Bale struggled to embed the new religion and suffered from being in the wrong place at the wrong time; when the Catholic Mary Tudor was declared queen of England and Ireland in July 1553, Bale and his household were targeted in an ambush. He escaped to the Continent and published a first-hand account of his brief and turbulent time in Ireland the following year.[26] As Anne Fogarty has observed, this work is 'a fusion of saint's life, historical chronicle and spiritual diary'[27] that anticipates the spiritual autobiographies of the seventeenth century. Bale's Irish experiences are immersed in Reformation polemic and the struggle against papistry. His account is overtly modelled on St Paul's travels, with his successful flight depicted as providential deliverance, mirroring that of Paul from Damascus. It is enlivened by his contemptuous reports of idolatrous and corrupt priests and bishops and his thankless efforts to institute ecclesiastical reforms, as well as the hostility – or persecution, in Bale's eyes – they provoked.

Ireland was also a land of opportunity for ambitious secular Protestants and these too turned to autobiographical modes. Richard Boyle, the 'great' Earl of Cork, exemplifies the self-aggrandizement that could ensue. His autobiographical memoir, 'True Remembrances: An Account of the Life of Richard Boyle, Earl of Cork', of which two versions survive, one made in 1623 and the other in 1632, conforms to more modern expectations. It recounts his rise from penniless but opportunistic Protestant settler to richest man in Ireland. His diaries, which cover the years from 1611 through to 1643, detail his rise up the social and political ladder and record land transactions, payments and rents, as well as births, deaths, marriages, preferments and the impact of events such as the 1641 rising.[28] His youngest daughter, Mary Rich, later Countess of Warwick, is a prime example of the spilling-over of conversion narrative to

---

[26] Peter Happé and John N. King, eds., *The Vocacyon of Johan Bale* (Binghamton, NY: Medieval and Renaissance Texts Society, 1990). See also Skura, *Tudor Autobiography*, 49–72.

[27] Anne Fogarty, 'Literature in English, 1550–1690', in Margaret Kelleher and Philip O'Leary, eds., *The Cambridge History of Irish Literature* (Cambridge: Cambridge University Press, 2006), 2 vols., vol. I, 144.

[28] Alexander Grosart, ed., *The Lismore Papers: viz. Autobiographical Notes, Remembrances and Diaries of Sir Richard Boyle, First and 'Great' Earl of Cork* (London: printed for private circulation, 1886), 5 vols. For the autobiography, see vol. 2, 100–17 and Thomas Birch, ed., *The Works of Robert Boyle* (London, 1774), 5 vols., vol. I, vii-xi.

spiritual autobiography. She wrote her own autobiography, 'Some Specialties in the Life of M. Warwicke', later in life between 1671 and 1673, in England. Structured as a conversion narrative, this work includes an account of her childhood in Ireland viewed through a providential interpretative frame, in which her defiance of her father (in marrying Charles Rich, younger son of the Earl of Warwick) is vindicated through her introduction to a pious family and journey towards grace, assurance and salvation. Again, however, the particular circumstances and constructedness of early modern autobiography are laid bare; Rich's diaries reveal a very different account of a fractious marriage, in tandem with the spiritual accounting of daily religious life that abounded in puritan culture.[29] Similarly, the four versions of her own life authored by Yorkshire-born Alice Thornton, daughter of Christopher Wandesford, lord deputy of Ireland in 1640, incorporate her childhood in Ireland, recast as providential vindication of the self, when her reputation was under threat later in life.[30]

The experience of imminent shipwreck off the coast of Cork prompted the publication of pamphlets by the regicide John Cook, who had worked in Thomas Wentworth's Irish administration in the mid-1630s and led the prosecution of King Charles I in 1649, and his wife Frances in 1650. Composed in the immediate aftermath of the storm, the experience stimulated the couple to interpret their deliverance as a sign of God's approbation of their life choices and, more particularly, of their political allegiance. The Cooks had sailed from Wexford, a soldiers' garrison and site of Cromwell's famous assault a few months previously. John Cook's account of the storm at sea narrates a prophetic dream, in which Christ directed his understanding, revealing the event as 'an extraordinary Tempest raised by Satan (by Gods permission) to destroy those which were coming to fight against his Servants'.[31] Satan, of course, was foiled. Frances's narrative is less overtly framed as political vindication; rather, it is an articulation of religious epiphany and salvation that serves to justify the

---

[29] For the autobiography, see British Library, Add. MS 27,357; for the diaries, British Library, Add. MSS 27,351–5. Both were edited in the nineteenth century: the diary extracts and religious writings in *Memoirs of Lady Warwick: Also Her Diary, from A.D. 1666 to 1672* (London: Religious Tract Society, 1847) and the autobiography in *Autobiography of Mary Countess of Warwick*, ed. Thomas Crofton Croker (London: Percy Society, 1848). For the discrepancies between autobiography and diaries, see Ramona Wray, '[Re]constructing the Past: The Diametric Lives of Mary Rich', in Dragstra et al., eds., *Betraying Our Selves*, 148–65.

[30] See Raymond Anselment, '"My First Booke of My Life": The Apology of a Seventeenth-Century Gentry Woman', *Prose Studies*, 24 (2001), 1–14 and 'Seventeenth-Century Manuscript Sources of Alice Thornton's Life', *Studies in English Literature 1500–1900*, 45 (2005), 135–55.

[31] John Cook, *A True Relation of Mr. Iohn Cook's Passage by Sea from Wexford to Kinsale in that Great Storm* (Cork and London, 1650), sig. Bv.

act of writing, inspiring her to compose autobiographical verse in the mode of the Psalms.[32] Together, these 'husband-and-wife' texts turn self-writing to the wider cause of puritan republicanism. The providential paradigm – so often deployed in life-writing of this period – serves to justify spiritual and worldly actions.

By contrast, the autobiography of Ann Fanshawe, written in 1676, is not presented as self-writing at all; rather, this animated, anecdotal first-person account of her travels across Ireland and Europe is composed as a biography of her husband, the royalist diplomat Sir Richard, for their son. The Fanshawes arrived in Ireland in April 1649 to meet Prince Rupert, whose fleet was then at Kinsale. Their year in Ireland involved six months in Cork, concluded by a quick exit when the English revolted in the city, and a peripatetic journey north through Macroom and Limerick, then a memorable encounter with a *bean sí* ('fairy woman') at the home of Honora O'Brien in Co. Clare, and finally a sojourn in Galway, whence they fled Cromwell's advancing forces for Spain. As chief protagonist and eyewitness to their travels in Ireland, Portugal and Spain, Fanshawe's biography is equally autobiography – although its self-denying presentation is a salutary reminder of the proscriptions pertaining to secular self-assertion as well as to female authorship.[33] This returns us to the ways in which autobiography can emerge in the unlikeliest of places, even where the conventions of genre ostensibly forbid it.

Marginal autobiography

The importance, through the early modern period, of justifying self- and life-writing according to moral and religious imperatives can also be seen through the obverse. Where Protestant religious practice sanctioned a particular form of life-writing, Catholic doctrine rather deterred nuns and priests from seeking personal recognition and credit. While obituary writing was commonplace among the religious orders, the first-person narrative voice emerges only in the interstices, usually as verification of testimony, as in the writings of Mother Mary Bonaventure Browne of the Poor Clares and the Dominican John O'Heyne. Both authors composed histories, or chronicles, of their religious orders. The writing self was necessarily sidelined in such accounts but the credibility of the eyewitness

---

[32] Frances Cook, *Mris. Cookes Meditations* (Cork and London, 1650).
[33] John Loftis, ed., *The Memoirs of Anne, Lady Halkett and Ann, Lady Fanshawe* (Oxford: Clarendon Press, 1979).

testimony necessitated its insertion at strategic narrative points.[34] Hence, the final kind of life-writing to be discussed in this chapter is marginal autobiography, so termed to describe the autobiographical fragments that emerge from texts apparently written for entirely different purposes.

'Irelands Comfort' is one of two works composed by John Cusack about 1629 (the other, 'The Kingedoms crye', is not known to survive). A legal treatise dedicated to King Charles I, its main purpose is to effect a reformation of the common laws. In the course of twenty chapters, Cusack – a member of the Old English community who claims loyalty to the crown and accepts Ireland's colonial status – set out the limits of the English and Irish jurisdictions, and most particularly the extent to which an Irishman or Englishman, both free denizens, should be considered liable to the laws of the other country. Notable for its careful carving out of a position of independence for Irish colonial subjects, the work demonstrates how closely entwined autobiography could be with other genres; in this case, the legal treatise. The dedication to the king explains Cusack's motive in writing, in the process revealing his life experiences. It emerges that the author was orphaned at a young age. His father's goods having been allegedly embezzled, the embezzler's heir (an unnamed female executrix) has stymied all his efforts at recovering his inheritance, as also his claims to the legacy of his great-uncle, Sir Thomas Cusack, who was at one time lord chancellor of Ireland. Cusack's experience of the courts is extensive and represents 'twenty years opression'.[35] A seven-year chancery suit against the embezzler's executrix entailed a prolonged battle with Sir Edward Coke, who served as chief justice of the court of common pleas and of the king's bench during the period concerned. Coke is alleged to have opposed King James's judgement in Cusack's favour because it would have established 'a precedent of opressed orfancy'. More disastrously for Cusack, Coke's triumph

> imbouldened one of the bastard intruders on my sayd inherytance in the darke, & muddy waters of Common lawe, to laie his snare for me with impunity, by his practice, & combination with a corrupt Judge, & a cruell goaylor, for the diuertinge of my suite against him by my imprysonment of allmost twelue years.[36]

---

[34] John O'Heyne, *Epilogus Chronologicus exponens succincte Conventus et Fundationes Sacri Ordinis Praedicatorum in regno Hyberniae* (Louvain, 1706), trans. and ed. Ambrose Coleman, *The Irish Dominicans of the Seventeenth Century* (Dundalk: William Tempest, 1902); 'Chronicle of Mother Mary Bonaventure Browne', MS, Galway Monastery of the Poor Clares, ed. Celsus O'Brien, *Recollections of an Irish Poor Clare in the Seventeenth Century* (Galway: Connacht Tribune, 1993). Browne composed her chronicle history between 1668 and 1671.
[35] Folger Shakespeare Library, MS G.a.10, fol. 1v.   [36] Ibid., fol. 6v.

The combination of seven years in court and twelve in prison fuelled the author's determination. His entire legal polemic is framed from the outset in colourfully autobiographical terms. Moreover, it is the autobiography that drives the writing; Cusack's personal experience compels him to think in wider terms about the legal system at the same time as it justifies his original decision to write, both to the king and on this topic.

Mary Trye's *Medicatrix, or the Woman-Physician* (1675) is primarily a defence of her father, the medical chemist Thomas O'Dowde, against attacks by a rival, Henry Stubbe, and of her own medical practice and treatments. A second-generation Irish migrant and medical practitioner who lived in England, Trye was trained by her father, a royalist who left Ireland during the wars of the 1640s. Her own autobiographical account is relegated to the paratextual margins. Her dedication to one Lady Fisher, a former acquaintance, narrates her apprenticeship with her father and her continuing vocation, urged on by his deathbed injunction: 'I should never suffer them [his medicines] to fall to the ground, or to dye and be buryed in oblivion, nor never to stop my Ears from the cry of the Poor, languishing for want of such Medicines.'[37] Paternal legacy and tribute combine in her proud continuation of his practice, 'to the succour of many Hundreds, more out of Charity then my private Interest, to the bright Glory of these Chymical, and not to be paralel'd Medicines'.[38] Self-promotion, here, is veiled behind filial obligation. Self-writing is enmeshed in altruistic, disputatious, familial, scientific and business motives.

An earlier generation of Elizabethan colonial administrators utilized the Irish dimensions of their lives in order to position their writings. Lodowick Bryskett's humanist dialogue *A Discourse of Ciuill Life*, translated from Giambattista Giraldi Cinthio's Italian original, was composed in Dublin during the 1580s. Its preface paints a picture of the author at the centre of a civilized Renaissance gathering of the great and the good: Edmund Spenser, the archbishop of Armagh, eminent undertakers of the Munster plantation, army captains and administrators.[39] The genesis of his translation is therefore pitched as a product of this milieu, implicitly opposed to the barbarity of the Irish frontier. This symbolic value has raised question marks over its autobiographical truthfulness.[40] But more important is its

---

[37] Mary Trye, *Medicatrix, or the Woman-Physician* (London, 1675), sig. A3.   [38] Ibid.

[39] Lodowick Bryskett, *A Discourse of Ciuill Life containing the Ethike Part of Morall Philosophie* (London, 1606), 5–6.

[40] See Andrew Carpenter, *Verse in English from Tudor and Stuart Ireland* (Cork: Cork University Press, 2003), 20–21; Fogarty, 'Literature in English', 150; Andrew Hadfield, *Edmund Spenser: A Life* (Oxford: Oxford University Press, 2012), 179–80.

demonstration of the richness, even pliability, of autobiographical dis-course in early modern Ireland as a seam to be mined in response to circumstance, as a means of persuasion, as a source of credibility and as a mode of literary self-fashioning. Bryskett's prefatory narrative attributes to Spenser an account of *The Faerie Queene*'s creation; we might look to another of his poems, *Colin Clouts Come Home Againe*, written in December 1591, in pursuit of early modern Irish autobiography. Safeguarded by its poetic form against reductive biographical readings, the poem plays with the possibilities of autobiography. Allegory combines with life to convey the challenges of having two homes – Cynthia's court and the shepherds' nation – and the degrees of ambivalence towards each that are explored and expressed in the poem. From the perspective of poetry, the caveats around autobiographical reading may seem self-evident. Their very vis-ibility should remind us of the constructedness of the self and its media-tion through the conventions and functions of genre, which pertains to all autobiographical modes of the period.

Conclusion

The forms of life-writing discussed in this chapter shape the lives they narrate. Rather than enjoying a subjectivity or coherent sense of self that demands to be expressed, the life-writer of early modern Ireland was usually compelled by circumstance (privation, assertion of legal claims, defence of reputation, admission to church, spiritual accounting, main-tenance of social ties) to represent the self. The process and form of self-representation determined which version of the self was constructed. The parameters of genre determine the shape and interpretation of the life narrative. Whether petition, deposition, letter, conversion narrative, spiri-tual autobiography, diary, marginal autobiography or verse, the genre of self-representation imposed its own conventions on the life narrative, as did the goal of the author who composed it. Furthermore, these texts were not necessarily written down by their authors; the early modern autobio-graphical voice was mediated not only through genre and circumstance but often also through scribes, amanuenses, interpreters and witnesses. The orality, contingency and sheer variety of autobiographical writing in early modern Ireland offer abundant and fertile grounds for understanding this tumultuous period and the ways in which it was experienced by those who lived through it.

Further reading

Coolahan, Marie-Louise. *Women, Writing, and Language in Early Modern Ireland.* Oxford: Oxford University Press, 2010.

Dowd, Michelle M., and Julie A. Eckerle, eds. *Genre and Women's Life Writing in Early Modern England.* Aldershot: Ashgate, 2007.

Dragstra, Henk, Sheila Ottway and Helen Wilcox, eds. *Betraying Our Selves: Forms of Self-Representation in Early Modern English Texts.* Basingstoke: Macmillan, 2000.

Skura, Meredith Anne. *Tudor Autobiography: Listening for Inwardness.* Chicago: University of Chicago Press, 2008.

Smyth, Adam. *Autobiography in Early Modern England.* Cambridge: Cambridge University Press, 2010.

Webster, Tom. 'Writing to Redundancy: Approaches to Spiritual Journals and Early Modern Spirituality', *Historical Journal*, 39 (1996), 33–56.

CHAPTER 4

Irish Protestant Life-Writing in the Eighteenth and Nineteenth Centuries

Elizabeth Grubgeld

Life-writing in the eighteenth and nineteenth centuries encompasses the literary autobiography, the collaborative or as-told-to autobiography, travel writing, autobiographical fiction, diaries, letters, religious narratives, court testimony, military memoirs and various private or family writings such as genealogies, cookbooks and records of gardening and farming. For reasons of space, my discussion will be confined to a selection of full-length narratives primarily concerned with the individual experiences of their authors. Because of limitations in literacy and access to publication, few of the Irish Protestant autobiographers of this period could be described as working class.[1] Some are from the upper classes – landowners, holders of professional positions, military officers or women within families of social and economic privilege – but many also originate in the more precarious world of the minor gentry and the lower bourgeoisie: the clergyman, lawyer, journalist, land agent, governess, teacher, independent farmer or small manufacturer. Still other writers document a decline into penury or menial labour consequent upon a series of unpredictable calamities, as well as the changeability of a woman's status following the loss of a husband or as a result of her own misfortunes.

The life-writing of Irish Protestants from the late 1880s through the decades following independence demonstrates a preoccupation with an ambiguous identity in a radically changed world, but earlier works evince less concern with nativist claims to a legitimate presence in Ireland or avowals of one's ongoing cultural relevance. Neither large-scale land reform nor the modern Catholic nation state were yet imminent, and thus the perspective of the earlier writings is considerably less elegiac than that of later texts. Nor does eighteenth- and early nineteenth-century life-writing engage the later tropes of

---

[1] Five such works are listed in John Burnett, David Vincent and David Mayall, eds., *The Autobiography of the Working Class: An Annotated Critical Bibliography* (Brighton: Harvester Press, 1984–89), 3 vols.

nostalgia for an idealized childhood or for a house endowed with the anthropomorphic qualities of a family member. Few demonstrate the genealogical and patrilineal preoccupations of later writers. However, these earlier works all reflect an uneasy and sometimes openly hostile relation with the Catholic majority, especially in times of political or socio-economic instability. They also anticipate in varying degrees other traits of Protestant autobiography after the 1880s, including a sectarian affiliation more sociological than theological; unapologetic criticism of the status of women, particularly in relation to property; frequent travel back and forth between Ireland and England; and a tendency to view one's life ironically through a lens of satiric comedy.

The libraries of Anglo-Irish houses tended to be rich in four kinds of narratives: religious testaments, travel writing, picaresque novels and epistolary novels. Even among autobiographers with limited access to books, those modes dominate the shape of the life-writings through which they record their travels and travails. Autobiographies of the period often developed from the raw materials of the diary, which records details of events in their immediacy as well as the writer's perspective on those events at the time. Those events are then reshaped into a teleological narrative about the formation of a self. However, even within a retrospective story of self-development, many texts replicate the picaresque nature of the diary, as well as structural features like dated entries. In some cases, the retrospective frame seems little more than an afterthought that invokes the language of the repentant sinner or beleaguered sufferer.

One of the earliest of these diaristic texts, *The Remembrances of Elizabeth Freke, 1671–1714*, derives from two archival manuscripts originally published in 1913 and recently re-edited. Amidst her financial records and catalogues of recipes and cures, Freke inserted 'some few remembrances of my misfortuns [that] have attended me in my unhappy life since I were marrryed'.[2] Although these dated entries are episodic rather than emplotted, Freke attempts a narrative arc of ever-increasing sufferings, suggesting that the 'most dreadfull raynie day' of her wedding was 'a presage of all my sorrows and misfortunes to mee'.[3] She establishes a consistent tension between her identity as the beloved daughter of an English father and her obligations as the wife of a landowner with estates in Cork. Her vehement resentment of the way her husband, Percy, managed the money and lands given to her by her father underscores the powerlessness of married women in matters that

---

[2] Elizabeth Freke, *The Remembrances of Elizabeth Freke, 1671–1714*, ed. Raymond A. Anselment (Cambridge: Cambridge University Press, 2001), 37.
[3] Ibid., 211.

affected their security. Even a small gift from her father could not truly belong to her. She reports, for example, that 'My deer father sent mee into Ireland a hundred pounds for a New Years guiftt ... and ordered mee thatt iff Mr Frek medled with itt itt should be lost ... Butt Mr Frek took itt from me.'[4] In 1684, the Frekes decided to live with her father after 'the dreadfull hard winter' in Ireland, but the man to whom they leased their Irish house arrived three weeks early and demanded that they and their goods be immediately removed: 'nothing could prevaile butt they must bee immediattly thrown out of doors and I with them', while the country came to witness the spectacle.[5] To her satisfaction, God's vengeance against the man arrived when the forces of King James II seized the house and transferred its ownership to a Catholic Jacobite. Although the Williamite victory restored ownership of the estate to the Frekes, they found the 'greatt house att Rathbary burntt downe by the Irish'[6] during their absence. While Percy busied himself in Dublin as a member of the Irish parliament, Elizabeth stayed ill and confined to her room within a half-destroyed house. Her husband's 'beloved Ireland'[7] was never Elizabeth Freke's, and correspondingly she expresses none of the topophilia associated with a Coole Park or Bowen's Court. Ireland remains an unreliable source of erratic income and a temptation to her husband's fiscally dangerous attempts to enhance his holdings, as well as a place of humiliation and isolation from the Catholic majority. Although Freke never discusses religion except to ask and thank God for acts of revenge upon her enemies and blessings upon those she cared for, her Protestantism was a social and class identity she clung to through the vicissitudes of her life.

Neither religion nor nation features centrally in *The Life and Entertaining Adventures of Mrs. Christian Davies* (1740); nor do domestic affairs, the familial house, nor any concerns about her place in Irish society. 'Taken from her own mouth when a pensioner of Chelsea-Hospital, And known to be true by Many',[8] this tale of a woman who lived for many years disguised as a male soldier presents a narrator who defied every category of identity in her quest for adventure. Although taught to read and do needlework, she confesses that she had always

> too much Mercury in me, to like a sedentary Life ... I was always at the
> Farm to assist my Mother; this I did as much thro' Inclination as Duty,

[4] Ibid., 50.   [5] Ibid., 50, 51.   [6] Ibid., 227.   [7] Ibid., 316.

[8] Mrs. Christian Davies, *Life and Entertaining Adventures of Mrs. Christian Davies, Commonly Called Mother Ross* (London: C. Welch, 1740), no pagination. Eighteenth Century Collections Online (ESTC 19153). I have modernized the orthography for ease of reading.

being delighted with a Country Life, it indulging to my Love of ramping, and the Pleasure I took, in manly Employments; for I was never better pleased than when I was following the Plough, or had a Rake, Flail, or Pitchfork in my hand, which implements I could handle with as much Strength and Dexterity, if not more, than any of my Mother's Servants.[9]

As war broke out, her father joined the army of King James to 'support his lawful Sovereign, notwithstanding his being of a different Religion, which he thought not Reason sufficient to affect his Loyalty'.[10] Despite being Protestant Jacobites, the family was repeatedly menaced by their Catholic neighbours and her father soon died, she reports, of a heart broken by the 'villainous ingratitude from a man who he had always treated with great humanity', 'one Kelly, an Irish papist who served him' and then stole his horses when he was wounded.[11] Having wed a young man who disappeared into the war against France, Davies took the guise of a soldier and set off to find him. After numerous campaigns, she discovered him involved with another woman, but the couple agreed to pass as brothers; when her gender was finally exposed following an injury, she remained with the army as his acknowledged wife and provisioner. After her husband's death, she married twice again, retiring finally to Dublin and, as a widow for a third and last time, to England.

Although Davies's story was originally thought to be the invention of Daniel Defoe, its authorship, like its veracity, remains uncertain. Recent research has suggested that some of the events recounted, as well as its humorous and jaunty tone, derive from the traditions of popular balladry and that the story may have been embellished as an entertainment for the families of military men and an enticement for those considering a military career.[12] But the facticity of Davies's text is less significant than its wide appeal among readers who enjoyed the narratives of pirates and explorers, and who were titillated by tales of criminals and the memoirs of women who lived outside the bonds of propriety. Although not openly salacious like the infamous memoir of Mrs Leeson, the Dublin madam, the story includes molestation, various attempted (and actual) rapes, the tale of the prostitute who alleges that Davies 'fathered' her child, and the narrator's efforts to hide her gender by courting a woman. If there is anything characteristically Irish about Davies's account beyond the first chapters, it is the constant peregrinations between Ireland and England. Like other

---

[9] Ibid., 2.   [10] Ibid., 4.   [11] Ibid., 9.
[12] Scarlett Bowen provides useful summaries of these arguments, as well as debates as to whether the text reifies or challenges gender conventions, in *The Politics of Custom in Eighteenth-Century British Fiction* (New York: Palgrave Macmillan, 2010), 79–102.

eighteenth-century autobiographers, Davies moved frequently and without any sense of dissonance between the two countries in efforts to fulfil familial obligations and tend to financial concerns. When her third husband drank away the profits from their Dublin tavern, she moved to Chelsea to sell pies as if she were relocating to a nearby city, rather than migrating between countries distinct in all but political sovereignty.

Laetitia Pilkington's *Memoirs*, published in three volumes between 1748 and 1754, reveal a similar fluidity of locale and identity. Also like Davies, Pilkington plays upon popular appetites for the scandalous while documenting the dangers for a woman too well brought up to make a living soldiering or selling pies but, as a divorcée, too much of a pariah to marry again into respectable society. Without property of her own or an annuity from her former husband to keep her from poverty, she made her way by means of her beauty, charm and wit. Brought up in the prosperous east end of Dublin, Laetitia van Lewen married an Anglican clergyman, Matthew Pilkington, in 1725 and shone in the literary and intellectual circles of the city until the discovery of mutual adulteries led to a divorce in 1738. Pilkington lost her children and her position in society; consequently, she fled the small world of Dublin for London, where she wrote verses for gentlemen to use in their romantic conquests, composed an opera and worked her way into the world of Grub Street. Encouraged to write her memoirs by Colley Cibber, she created a lively and suspenseful narrative full of entertaining dialogue, gossip and richly drawn comic portraits of her society. Her characterizations of herself and others satirize social pretensions and hypocrisy and convey the ongoing irony of her situation as an intelligent and well-read woman in a world that favoured neither trait in a woman raised among the upper middle classes but reduced to shabby lodgings, a mother of children who could not speak of them, and a vivacious and beautiful woman whose talents and appearance kept her alive and, at the same time, precariously close to supporting herself by 'vile Means'.[13]

Pilkington's text is almost indistinguishable from comparable books by English women, but one disagreeable and potentially dangerous reminder of her origin occurs when, on her own in London and without funds, she is arrested for non-payment of a small debt. A 'Couple of ill-favoured Fellows', sent to roust her from her lodgings into debtor's prison, shout: 'Get up, you Irish Papist bitch . . . Ay, the Irish Whore, here is something

[13] Laetitia Pilkington, *Memoirs of Laetitia Pilkington*, ed. A. C. Elias Jr. (Athens: University of Georgia Press, 1997), vol. I, 180.

about some Roman Father, that's the Pope, and be damn'd to you, is it?"[14] Her Irishness is here unpleasantly confounded with Catholicism as a double mark of her outsider status in England. On one hand, her narrative follows that frequent pattern of Irish Protestant life-writing in which 'Ireland is left like the shell of the egg out of which the chicken emerged.'[15] On the other, her Irish origin never fully disappears, as it can be wielded against her when expedient. Additionally, her memoir participates in an Anglo-Irish tradition of satiric self-portraiture, a mode that would continue to be employed well into the twentieth century as a way to address the ambiguities and ironies of this community's place in a nation that was both alien and home.

The last eighteenth-century woman here considered presents yet another variant of life-writing. In the narrative she titled *Retrospections of an Outcast or the Life of Dorothea Herbert*, composed in 1806, Dorothea Herbert recast the diaries of youth into a melodramatic account of her early days as an Anglican clergyman's daughter and her unrequited passion for the son of a neighbouring family. Barbara Hughes's invaluable study of this work highlights its contribution to a historical understanding of life among the lower gentry during the period, its insights into gender relations and representation, the story's debt to popular fiction and the complicated relationship between its self-portraiture and mental illness as understood during the period.[16] Citing Herbert's notations of her frequent attacks of 'nerves' and increasingly strange behaviour towards the end of her book, Hughes speculates that Herbert suffered from 'paranoid schizophrenia'.[17] However, we have no evidence of such a severe state of delusion beyond the narrator's own declaration of her mental decline. Is her story of being beaten and confined by her relatives factual, the product of hallucination, or a metaphoric projection of her isolation and sexual frustration? Alternatively, could it originate in the gothic tendencies of her chosen genre? Perhaps, as Hughes suggests, the rhetoric of madness enabled Herbert to declare her identity as 'Mrs John Roe' and in so doing the unmarried middle-aged recluse could imagine herself with authority sufficient to write an autobiography.[18]

Whatever the veracity of her 'retrospections', Herbert places her story within a context of both personal and social disorder. Even in the first volume, 'sweet remembrances' are juxtaposed with terrifying accounts of

---

[14] Ibid., 202.   [15] Terence de Vere White, *The Anglo-Irish* (London: Victor Gollancz, 1972), 168.
[16] See Barbara Hughes, *Between Literature and History: The Diaries and Memoirs of Mary Leadbeater and Dorothea Herbert* (Bern and Oxford: Peter Lang, 2010).
[17] Ibid., 123.   [18] Ibid., 114–15.

attacks upon her family by the White Boys during the anti-tithe campaign of the 1780s, attacks that send her mother into 'one of her old violent Nervous Fevers which lasted a long time'.[19] In chapters with titles like 'A Review: Odd Characters and Ludicrous Incidents', Herbert recounts scenes of mental disturbance: 'a lunatic wanderer'[20] of indeterminate gender, an exceedingly foppish cousin who cannot keep his money, an uncle whose bizarre behaviours (which include wearing newspapers wrapped around his head) humiliate his wife and numerous women who take to their beds in hysteria. Male relatives compulsively engage in duels and actions that might now lead to arrest and imprisonment; these are recounted as 'pranks' and 'madcaps', as if it were customary to set fire to the room in which one's disabled music teacher is trapped. The narrator's ever-increasing loneliness and sense of persecution are cast as gothic melodrama, a genre so ubiquitous and excessive that Jane Austen was to mock it in *Northanger Abbey* (1817) just over a decade after Herbert finished her *Retrospections*. At the same time, her focus on the abnormal among her family and relatives draws from British political satire and novels like *Tristram Shandy* (1759–67), as well as from an emerging Anglo-Irish cultural discourse focused on instability, incongruity and verbal vehemence.[21]

   This discourse is also part of the legend of Thomas 'Buck' Whaley, whose life was so notorious that he needed no published confession of his sins and follies for street ballads to chronicle his exploits. Although he finished his *Memoirs* in 1797 on the Isle of Man, where he had fled his many creditors and tried for a short while to live quietly, his family suppressed the manuscript for more than a century. The son of 'Burn-Chapel Whaley', so named because he amused himself by setting fire to Catholic churches and dwellings, Buck Whaley lived a dissipated life of alcoholism and vice, openly selling his votes during his time in the Irish parliament and rapidly spending by his own admission over £400,000 on gambling, prostitutes and alcohol, then later contracting some £30,000 more in gambling debts. Although his manuscript is framed by repentant

---

[19] Dorothea Herbert, *Retrospections of Dorothea Herbert 1770–1806* (Dublin: Townhouse, 1988), 87.

[20] Ibid., 59.

[21] For further discussion, see 'Comic Autobiography and the Satiric Tradition', in Elizabeth Grubgeld, *Anglo-Irish Autobiography: Class, Gender, and the Forms of Narrative* (Syracuse: Syracuse University Press, 2004), 126–59. Lady Morgan (Sydney Owenson) records her English mother's shock at first hearing the humorous and often ribald conversation that was part of late eighteenth-century Dublin society and notes: 'The tendency to wit, or to its substitute – fun, had been a fashion in Ireland since the time of Charles the Second.' Lady Morgan, *Lady Morgan's Memoirs: Autobiographies, Diaries and Correspondence* (London: W. H. Allen, 1862), vol. 1, 70.

breast-beating and admonitions to youth not to follow in his path, Whaley also proclaimed himself the kind of bold figure who would later appear in the poetry of Bryon and the fiction of Mary Shelley. He asserts:

> I was born with strong passions, a lively imagination, and a spirit that could brook no restraint. I possessed a restlessness and an activity of mind that directed me to the most extravagant pursuits and the ardour of my disposition never abated till satiety had weakened the power of enjoyment; till my health was impaired and my fortune destroyed.[22]

Such a remorseful framing statement is little more than that; the rest of the book relates those 'extravagant pursuits' with relish. Most vivid is the long narrative of his travels to Jerusalem, a journey undertaken to meet a £15,000 wager with his gambling acquaintances. In addition to landscapes, Whaley offers salacious descriptions of concubinage, erotic dancing boys and sexual slavery in the Arab and Turkish world. His narrative also relates his own purchase of a thirteen-year-old slave girl and his abduction of a French woman on his return home. Other portions of the text are burdened by clichéd phrasings and generalities, but the story of 'the Jerusalem wager' offers the best portrait of its author, in that those very aspects of foreign life that are for Whaley most intriguing also form a mirror image of his own preoccupations and interactions with the world at home and abroad.

Whaley's masculine version of the scandalous memoir parallels to some degree Jonah Barrington's *Personal Sketches of his Own Times*, published in three volumes between 1827 and 1832. Barrington's portrait of Anglo-Irish society at the turn of the nineteenth century reflects a great deal of drinking and aimless activity but lacks the viciousness and sexual exploitation of Whaley's text. Still, the vivacity of Barrington as a narrator derives from his stories of outlandish behaviour. Barrington blames his failure to find a profession and consequent lack of direction on his youthful excesses of carousing, dancing, cock-fighting and midnight feasts with plenty of 'cherry-bounce (brandy)'.[23] But the story of his life serves mostly as the structural apparatus for a travel narrative through his own country, one that points out its famous people, politics, customs and eccentrics. Partly gossip, partly a memoir of his ancestry and place (although he expresses no fondness for the family home, calling it an 'uncouth mass, warring with

[22] Thomas Whaley, *Buck Whaley's Memoirs*, ed. Edward Sullivan (London: Alexander Moring, 1906), 335.
[23] Jonah Barrington, *Personal Sketches of His Own Times* (London: H. Colburn and R. Bentley, 1830), vol. I, 68.

every rule of symmetry in architecture'[24]) and primarily a satiric portraiture of the foibles of others, it too participates in the tradition of comic reductionism.

Richard Lovell Edgeworth began his memoirs in 1808 but died before he was able to take the story beyond 1780, leaving his daughter Maria to complete the story of his life as a third-person retrospective account. His book is essentially an eighteenth-century text, not only because of the period it describes but because of its clear debt to Rousseau's stories of education, its preoccupation with mechanical science and its forays into humour. That he chose to raise his eldest son following the method prescribed in *Emile* (1762) is well known, and his memoir resembles both *Emile* and Rousseau's own experiment in life-writing. Distinguishing his project from stories of travel and adventure, he declares that his experience in educating his large family (four wives and twenty-two children) renders him particularly adept at tracing a story of education. Thus, he describes scenes of childhood and youth and simultaneously evaluates them as to their efficacy as educational experiences. Like Rousseau, Edgeworth expresses some regret for poor decisions but also takes pains to explain and defend his actions, especially those that drew censure from his contemporaries. For example, although he confesses his rash judgement in making a hasty youthful marriage, he blames his upbringing and makes no effort to hide the contempt in which he held his first wife, who died giving birth to their fifth child while he stayed away in France in order to resist the temptation of another English woman whom he married shortly afterwards. Expressing no love of place, no sense of nationality beyond a childhood confusion over his accent or even much engagement with the political events of his day, the *Memoirs* concern themselves with his various inventions, his sentiments and love affairs and his strong attachment to his friend Thomas Day. Day's impulsive and peculiar behaviour draws Edgeworth's fascination and admiration, which even extended to Day's social experiment of adopting two orphan girls with the intention of raising a wife for himself, then escaping to France to avoid the gossip that ensued and to ensure that the girls might grow up uncorrupted by any influence beyond his own. Day's follies, like those of Edgeworth himself, are either left unacknowledged, very gently mocked or rationalized. The sentimental cult of 'feeling' valorizes the actions of both Day and Edgeworth on the basis of their emotional intensity.

---

[24] Ibid., 2.

The life-writing of the early nineteenth century differs entirely in approach, as its authors focus less on the inner life of the self and more on the tumultuous circumstances of the 1798 rebellion, the Tithe War of the early 1830s and the onset of famine. As Melesina Trench sardonically observes in her diary regarding her husband's relations in Enniscorthy:

> I find Rebellion is the prominent object in the minds of his family, as it is, more or less, of most who have passed through it. It is their principal epoch, and seems to have divided time into two grand divisions, unmarked by any lesser periods; before, and after, the Rebellion. The first of these seems to resemble Paradise before the Fall. They had then good servants, fine flowers, fine fruit, fine horses, good beer, and plenty of barm – that indispensable requisite in rural economy. Since that period of perfect felicity, the servants have been unmanageable, the horses restive, the beer sour, the barm uncome-at-able, and all things scarce and dear.[25]

Most of the memoirists of the period, however, would not agree with Trench. Many express sympathy for the rebellion, even those who suffered from its violence. Some write from the perspective of their religious faith; others are directly involved in the nationalist movement. The texts included in John D. Beatty's *Protestant Women's Narratives of the Irish Rebellion of 1798* (2001) represent but a fraction of those extant in manuscript, while many Irish Quakers, both male and female, wrote memoirs of their lives, encouraged to do so by the emphasis on individual experience and social equality within the Society of Friends. Dinah Goff's *Divine Protection through Extraordinary Dangers experienced during the Irish Rebellion of 1798* (1856) is a single example of what are estimated to be more than a thousand such Quaker writings housed in archives.[26] Unusually vivid in its particulars, Goff's narrative proves especially valuable to studies of Irish women's lives in offering a detailed picture of Protestant women's interactions with rebels and soldiers.

Another Quaker, Mary Leadbeater, moderated some of her sympathies for the rebels of 1798 as she transferred materials from her diaries into *The Annals of Ballitore* (1862), published decades after her death in 1826. The *Annals* is one of the few women's memoirs of the uprising to be published and read outside of denominational circles, even eliciting a favourable review in the *Dublin University Magazine* shortly after its appearance.[27]

---

[25] Melesina Trench, *The Remains of the Late Mrs. Richard Trench: Being Selections from Her Journals, Letters, and Other Papers*, ed. St. George Trench (London: Parker, Son, and Bourn, 1862), 129.

[26] Helen E. Hatton, *The Largest Amount of Good: Quaker Relief in Ireland, 1654–1921* (Montreal: McGill-Queens University Press, 1993), 39.

[27] Hughes, *Between Literature and History*, 195.

It contains the extended narrative she developed from the journals she kept between 1776 and 1824. Like Dinah Goff, Leadbeater depicts acts of mercy and cruelty on both sides of the conflict and acknowledges having been terrified by the pervasive violence. Perhaps because the tenor of the Society of Friends had shifted from the fervency of the seventeenth century to a period of quietism, Leadbeater's tone is consistently subdued. Those who have worked on her manuscript diaries note that in the writing she intended for publication – and the *Annals* were presumably so intended – she muted her observations of the domestic brutality of everyday village life, her attraction to the rebel cause and the emotional turmoil in which she found herself prior to her marriage.[28] Instead, public events take the forefront, as in most of the autobiographies of the era.

The nationalist life-writing of this period includes that of public figures like Wolfe Tone, Thomas Russell and John Mitchel, whose work is discussed in Chapter 7. The widely read and much-discussed novelist Lady Morgan (Sydney Owenson) was not a revolutionist but in the autobiography she dictated as an elderly woman she speaks from the same position of cultural nationalism from which she had written her fiction. Stating her purpose to be no more than 'to speak a few true and final words of herself' after a lifetime of approbation and condemnation, she humorously eschews the more predictable motives for a woman's autobiography when she observes:

> *Memoires pour servir* generally mean either 'serving out' one's friends and enemies, or feeding a morbid appetite for secret slander. I can promise no scandal, neither can I open a biographical ledger, after the fashion of Miss Betsy Thoughtless and others, with an 'I was born, &c., &c.,' or 'the villain who deceived me was quartered in the town where my father lived;' nor yet can I pretend to give a description of the 'scene of rural innocence where first I saw the light'.[29]

Morgan presents her life from its beginnings as a paradigm of an Irish history she claimed as her own. Celebrations drawn from a Gaelic old order attend her birth on Christmas Day, and her confirmation takes place with a dinner 'according to the law and custom of Ireland from the days of St. Patrick'.[30] As a lover of music, she delighted in Carolan's compositions and Moore's *Irish Melodies* (1807–34). Neither her Anglicanism nor her partly English parentage inhibits her proclamation of an Irish identity. *Lady*

---

[28] Hughes sees Leadbeater's refusal to include the darker side of rural life in her published works as a response to the anti-pastoral tendency in the writings of contemporaries such as Oliver Goldsmith and George Crabbe.

[29] Morgan, *Lady Morgan's Memoirs*, vol. 1, 2.   [30] Ibid., 11.

Morgan's Memoirs, like her novels, narrates the adventures of a heroine with romantic nationalism at her core.

Lady Morgan died before completing her life story, which breaks off suddenly in 1801, but her assistant added to the memoir for which she had acted as scribe a number of letters that reveal the author's ambivalence between a desire to be respected as a woman of letters and a desire to be admired according to more conventional notions of femininity. In an 1803 letter to a friend, she distinguishes herself from 'some women [who], in attaining that intellectual acquisition which excites admiration and even reverence, forfeit their (oh! how much more valuable) claims on the affections of the heart'.[31] To avoid being 'less the woman',[32] she admits that she refrained from the study of chemistry or classics and from pursuing music and drawing as serious arts. Frances Power Cobbe, born in 1822, had no such inhibitions and threw herself into the study of science and philosophy as a young woman educated in a home full of books that she was free to read as she desired. Her feminism is less compromised than Lady Morgan's and she had no need to cloak her intelligence in wit and raillery, as did Laetitia Pilkington. By the time of her death in 1904, she had authored more than forty books and pamphlets on moral philosophy, science, workhouse reform and women's rights. She was antagonistic to nationalist aspirations, and the portion of her memoir entitled 'Ireland in the Forties' is for the most part impersonal and comprises set pieces describing the foolishness of various rural types. According to her biographer Sally Mitchell, Cobbe extracted these patronizing and unsympathetic portraits verbatim from an anti-Fenian article she had published in 1865, almost thirty years before. Autobiographies of the period, especially those by women, often included correspondence, testimonials, juvenilia and other documents as companions to the retrospective prose narrative; however, as Mitchell points out, the racialized bigotry of 'Ireland in the Forties' is inconsistent with the reformist agenda that occupied Cobbe's adult life. Perhaps, as Mitchell suggests, this section 'seems to reflect both a fading memory of the famine's horror and an unrecognized anxiety, at the century's end, for some means of Anglo-Irish self-justification in the face of growing Irish nationalism'.[33]

It is women's rights rather than a national or sectarian identity that shapes Cobbe's memoir. Her intentions, she states, were to reflect 'the true

---

[31] Ibid., 229–30.   [32] Ibid., 230.

[33] Sally Mitchell, 'Frances Power Cobbe's *Life* and the Rules for Women's Autobiography', *English Literature in Transition, 1880–1920*, 50:2 (2007), 145.

and complete history of a woman's existence *as seen from within*; a real LIFE which he who reads may take as representing fairly the joys, sorrow and interest, the powers and limitations, of one of my sex and class in the era which is now drawing to a close'.[34] But neither of her two volumes presents much of an interior view of the author's life. Constrained by her times from writing about the woman to whom she was married in all but law, Cobbe maintains a composed tone throughout and presents little entry into her inner life. The one exception to this rule occurs in her ardent expressions of love for her mother, who fostered her education and surrounded her with affection and encouragement. Considering how frequently the mother is either absent or demonized within the Anglo-Irish autobiography, Cobbe's expression of such deep affection speaks powerfully to the centrality of women in her life, even while the woman who meant most to her could not enter the *Life* as text.

As much as the 1798 rebellion preoccupied earlier autobiographers, so do other writers at the end of the nineteenth century respond to the devastation of the Great Famine and the social and political changes that accompanied wide-scale land reform later in the century. Two works, Sir William Gregory's *An Autobiography* (1894) and Emily Lawless's *A Garden Diary: September 1899–September 1900* (1901), look back on the century and also anticipate many of the features of Irish Protestant autobiography in the post-independence era. However, unlike twentieth-century autobiographers, neither expresses a sense of guilt at having been part of a colonial enterprise, nor do they admit to a feeling of relief at the relinquishment of an increasingly unsustainable burden of family property and history. Gregory's narrative is primarily a record of his public life in parliament, as landowner in Co. Galway and as the chief administrator of the British colony of Ceylon. Never for a moment does he express doubt concerning the justice of British rule over its colonies, nor the supremacy of the European Protestant male. Yet his story – scrupulously edited to remove personal matter or statements his widow judged might offend the living – presents a striking portrayal of the profound ambivalence within a man whose status and custom demanded political positions that were contrary to his humane instincts and belief in religious liberty. Throughout, Gregory openly regrets having advocated policies that, while more generous than those in place at the time, were susceptible to manipulation by the

---

[34] Frances Power Cobbe, *The Life of Frances Power Cobbe* (London: R. Bentley, 1894), vol. 1, iv–v. Original emphasis.

unscrupulous. Recounting the sale of some of his properties and its unanticipated effects on the tenants, he recalls:

> I was so occupied with other matters that I quite forgot their danger. Indeed it never crossed my mind, for I had then heard of no particular instances of rapacity on the part of new purchasers; but I very soon had a terrible account of my remissness in not securing these poor folk.[35]

The new landlord raises rents so drastically as to ruin the tenants, and Gregory remarks: 'it was such proceedings, which I found were too common elsewhere, which made me a tenant righter, and the advocate of measures which, in a different state of society, I should have opposed'.[36] Similarly, his memories of the Famine register the shock he experienced at coming back to Galway unprepared for the sight of mass starvation and disease, as well as his sense of helplessness in its face and his condemnation of British policies whose detrimental effects he had not recognized previously.

After some discussion of boyhood, Sir William Gregory displaces his life story into a narrative about public history. The poet and novelist Emily Lawless writes about herself by writing about the activity of gardening, and *A Garden Diary* provides a fitting conclusion to this selective survey of eighteenth- and nineteenth-century Protestant autobiography. Ostensibly a book about gardening, it is actually a passionate, homesick lament for the west of Ireland, where Lawless grew to adulthood until relegated by circumstance to England. As her title suggests, land itself becomes subject to narrative time and, in her view, historical time was eroding her past, the life she knew in Co. Clare and the very rocks and shoreline she adored. Like Lady Morgan, Lawless felt a personal identification with the heroine of her own best-known national tale, *Grania: The Story of an Island* (1892), but believed herself to be a disinherited exile who would die in a dull London suburb dreaming of the Atlantic storms that took the life of her fictional character. Although she locates the following sentiments in her youth, the rest of *A Garden Diary* reinforces the sense that they speak for the present as well:

> There was a time when nothing short of an entire ocean, none of your petty babbling channels, but the whole thundering Atlantic, sufficed for my ambition. In those days only upon the largest combination of sea, sky, mountain; sea-scape, land-scape, cloud-scape, did it seem possible adequately to exist. As for a mere rustic landscape, as for a confined one, as

---

[35] Sir William Gregory, *An Autobiography* (London: John Murray, 1894), 159.   [36] Ibid.

for a humdrum English one, above all as for a landscape within fifty miles of London, why the mention of such things merely moved my commiseration! Those were the days when to be called upon to leave what is sometimes uncivilly called the ruder island, and to repair, even temporarily, to the more prosperous one, seemed a fall and a degradation hardly to be measured by words. When the contraction of the horizon seemed like a contraction of all life, and of all that made life worth having.[37]

The intensity of Lawless's topophilia, her sense of exile, her belief in the formative relationship between the landscape and her own consciousness, her attribution of anthropomorphic feeling to the topography that appears throughout *A Garden Diary* – all of these elements foreshadow the writings of Elizabeth Bowen, T. R. Henn, Maud Wynne, Augusta Gregory and other Irish Protestants of the rural landed and professional class who struggled to understand their place in post-independence Ireland, and whose work is the subject of Chapter 17. These characteristics, conjoined with a continuing fondness for familial satire, a love of incongruity and oddity and the abiding conviction that one's life is inextricably intertwined with public history, produce a distinct national and cultural tradition in life-writing from the eighteenth century and beyond.

Further reading

Akenson, Donald. *Small Differences: Irish Catholics and Irish Protestants, 1815–1922*. Montreal: McGill-Queens University Press, 1988.

Claydon, Tony and Ian McBride, eds. *Protestantism and National Identity: Britain and Ireland, c. 1650–1850*. Cambridge: Cambridge University Press, 1998.

Connolly, S. J. *Religion, Law and Power: The Making of Protestant Ireland 1660–1760*. Oxford: Oxford University Press, 1992.

Cook, Daniel and Amy Culley, eds. *Women's Life Writing, 1700–1850: Gender, Genre, Authorship*. New York: Palgrave Macmillan, 2012.

Grubgeld, Elizabeth. *Anglo-Irish Autobiography: Class, Gender, and the Forms of Narrative*. Syracuse: Syracuse University Press, 2004.

Ryder, Sean. '"With a Heroic Life and a Governing Mind": Nineteenth-Century Irish Nationalist Autobiography', in Liam Harte, ed., *Modern Irish Autobiography: Self, Nation and Society*. New York: Palgrave Macmillan, 2007: 14–31.

---

[37] Emily Lawless, *A Garden Diary: September 1899–September 1900* (London: Methuen, 1901), 8–9.

CHAPTER 5

Irish Women's Spiritual and Religious Life-Writing in the Late Eighteenth and Nineteenth Centuries

Maria Luddy

One of the most profound influences on women's lives in the eighteenth and nineteenth centuries, and for much of the twentieth, was religion. Religious teaching regarding women, whether Catholic or Protestant, emphasized the repression of sexuality, placed an emphasis on domestic virtues and generally taught that women should be humble, virtuous and obedient. To a certain extent women, of whatever religious persuasion, were receiving the same messages but they interpreted these in different ways in the different denominations. Within Catholicism, for instance, religious teaching was one of a number of powerful influences restricting women to a domestic role, whereas among Protestant women religion provided inspiration to enlarge their sphere of action and enabled them to enter the public domain. Religion shaped women's perception of themselves as spiritual beings and led many to introspective reflection on their lives. For many, religious activism, whether it was in establishing a devout community, organizing a philanthropic enterprise or simply visiting the poor, gave public expression to their beliefs and value systems.

We still have scant knowledge of the extent of Irish women's spiritual and religious writings over the centuries, little of which has been studied or published.[1] There is not much in this chapter that is directly autobiographical, and the sources used, in particular diaries and letters, suggest that it

---

[1] The starting point for the exploration of women's religious writings is Angela Bourke et al., eds., *The Field Day Anthology of Irish Writing, Volume IV: Irish Women's Writings and Traditions* (Cork: Cork University Press in association with Field Day, 2002), 459–749. See also the valuable studies of Marie-Louise Coolahan, including *Women, Writing, and Language in Early Modern Ireland* (Oxford: Oxford University Press, 2010), which offers a superb study of the varieties and complexities of women's writing, and Gerardine Meaney, Mary O'Dowd and Bernadette Whelan, *Reading the Irish Woman: Studies in Cultural Encounter and Exchange, 1714–1960* (Liverpool: Liverpool University Press, 2013), chapters one and two. For the diaries of Quaker men and women, see O. C. Goodbody, *Guide to Irish Quaker Records* (Dublin: Irish Manuscripts Commission, 1967).

is more valuable to utilize terms such as 'self-writing' or 'life-writing' when
trying to understand women's religious experiences of this period. While
diaries are available in a number of repositories, there is no inventory of
women's manuscript diaries or other forms of unpublished writings. The
most extensive published work, relating directly to the religious experiences of
women in Ireland, concerns Methodist women. Yet when we examine this
work we find that most of it has been compiled or edited by men, often by
husbands or other family members. For example, the Reverend Edward
Smyth compiled the letters and hymns of Margaret Davidson (published in
1782); Thomas Bennis edited the letters of his mother, Eliza (1809); Reverend
Adam Averell the memoirs of Mrs Dorothea Johnson (1818); John James
M'Gregor the memoir of Alice Cambridge (1832); and the Reverend George
Alley the memoir of Grace Hunter (1896). Anne Lutton was unusual in
having Jane Hicks Westcott edit her work, though Westcott hid her gender
by using only her initials.[2] Charles Henry Crookshank, in his *Memorable
Women of Irish Methodism in the Last Century* (1882), provides short biographical studies of eighteen women, his purpose being to 'lead some of our
sisters in the present day to renewed and complete consecration to the services
of Christ'.[3] As this suggests, such works were essentially published for the
spiritual and moral edification of female readers. In the absence of the original
papers on which these works were based, however, it is difficult to know what
was left out or changed in the editing.

   Some of the writers explored in this chapter kept diaries and were
therefore not consciously writing their life story or expecting anyone else
to read their work. Within the sphere of religious writing it is important to
explore the manuscripts left by nuns, which include letters, convent annals
and personal writings, all of which provide unique access to the spiritual
lives of their authors. These kinds of texts not only reveal a great deal about
the personality, values and experiences of the writers; for nuns, such
writings were also a means through which their particular religious community was formed, shaped and maintained. The variety of female religious communities in Ireland – a phenomenon that developed in the
nineteenth century – suggests the importance of letter writing in particular
in shaping spiritual communities. The purpose of this chapter is to explore
the varieties of spiritual and religious reflection available in Irish women's

[2] J. H. W, ed., *Memorials of a Consecrated Life Compiled from the Autobiography, Letters and Diaries of
    Anne Lutton of Moira Co. Down, Ireland and of Cotham, Bristol* (London: T. Woolmer, 1882).
[3] C. H. Crookshank, *Memorable Women of Irish Methodism in the Last Century* (London: Wesleyan-
    Methodist Book Room, 1882), 3.

life-writing of this period and to examine some of the factors that shaped first-person accounts of religious experience.

Before examining the range of spiritual and religious life-writing by women in the nineteenth century it is important to take account of contextual factors such as denominational affiliation, social class and education and literacy levels, all of which must shape our approach to this subject. Throughout the 1800s, the denominational attachment of the Irish population was unevenly divided between three major religions. In 1834, Catholics made up 80.9 per cent of the population, 10.7 per cent adhered to the Church of Ireland and 8.1 per cent were committed to Presbyterianism. In 1861, the figures were, respectively, 77.7 per cent, 12 per cent and 9 per cent. By 1901, 74.2 per cent were Catholic, 13 per cent Church of Ireland and 9.9 per cent Presbyterian. Smaller communities, such as Jews, Methodists, Quakers and Congregationalists, made up the remainder. These various denominations were unevenly distributed across the country. Catholics were in a minority in four Ulster counties (Antrim, Armagh, Down and Londonderry) and in the towns of Belfast and Carrickfergus, and they constituted only slightly more than half the population of Fermanagh and Tyrone. Elsewhere, Catholics were in the substantial majority, comprising 86 per cent of the population of Leinster and more than 90 per cent in Munster and Connaught, while 96 per cent of Presbyterians lived in Ulster. There were also important social distinctions among the various denominations. Anglicans were over-represented among the landowning class and made up a great majority of substantial landowners. They were also over-represented in the professions, at the upper levels of financial and commercial life and in government posts. In Ulster, Anglicans constituted the majority of landowners but Presbyterians tended to dominate in the middle classes. Throughout Ireland, Catholics tended to be at the bottom of the social scale but from the late 1700s onwards there was a growing Catholic middle class and by the end of the 1800s a great number of Catholic farmers owned their own land. Differential literacy levels among the various denominations were also telling. In 1861, 46 per cent of Catholics aged five years and over were unable to read and write compared with 16 per cent of Anglicans and 11 per cent of Presbyterians.

Protestant evangelical life-writing

From the eighteenth century onwards, evangelical ideas spread among the Protestant community in Ireland. Women played an important part in the expansion of evangelical Protestantism and also played significant roles in Quakerism and Methodism, partly because their forms of worship prioritized inner truth over received dogma and emphasized emotion and experience over tradition and formality. Women were encouraged not only to read the Bible but to know it intimately and to feel that they had an important and rightful place in the world, which carried with it responsibilities towards society. Women thus had divine duties outside the purely domestic sphere. Methodist women were encouraged to keep journals and diaries, and it is no surprise that much of what we currently know of women's religious and spiritual feelings comes from these sources. As noted above, the published material available on these women has, in most cases, been written by men, or the women's words have been edited, mostly by men. This body of work is nevertheless important for the insights it provides into an otherwise hidden dimension of life-writing in pre-1900 Ireland.

There were a number of well-known female preachers of Methodism operating in Ulster in the late eighteenth and early nineteenth centuries. Alice Cambridge, for instance, was said to have attracted eight to ten thousand people during a tour of Ulster at the beginning of the 1800s. The diaries and journals kept by Methodist women were not intended to record daily events faithfully but rather to act as a means of spiritual self-examination, the aim of which was to achieve a deeper communion with Christ. A notable feature of these journals is the relentless self-denigration they record, the corollary of which is an intense level of religious commitment, often stemming from the moment of conversion, which opened a new window onto the world. Cambridge recounted that

> on the gallery of the old preaching house in Bandon ... Mrs Strickett was telling her experience of the gracious dealings of God towards her, and while she was thus speaking delightfully good of His name, He lifted upon me the light of His countenance; my mourning was turned into joy; I felt a change, which until that glad moment I had been a stranger to, and I rejoiced with joy unspeakable and full of glory.[4]

Similarly, Mrs Agnes Smyth noted in her diary that her conversion to Methodism allowed her to be 'filled with comfort; my spirit rejoices in God my Saviour. My joy is unspeakable, and I have a peace this world cannot give.'[5] Theodosia Blanchford, at nineteen, experienced what she regarded as a spiritual awakening, although like many women she struggled to overcome what she saw as her faults. As a result of her conversion to Methodism, however, she found that

[4] Bourke et al., eds., *The Field Day Anthology of Irish Writing, Volume IV*, 541.
[5] Crookshank, *Memorable Women*, 135.

that violence of temper which, in the commencement of it was my besetting sin, and had daily effects on my conduct, as well as my peace, has been in a great measure subdued and it so often mocked my strength and repeated resolutions, that I should be very unbelieving not to attribute this to the power of God ... on the whole I bless God, for the comparative tranquility of my spirit and find happy fruits of it in all my avocations.[6]

Angel Anna Slack's journal record of her conversion is couched in an even more ecstatic register. Born into a Church of Ireland family in 1748, she married at seventeen and later became ill on a visit to Dublin. While recovering, she overheard two Methodist men praying and singing; so taken was she by the sound of their prayers that she asked them to take her to a Methodist meeting. The preacher evoked a powerful physical reaction in Slack, as she noted in her journal: 'My heart throbbed and I was obliged to press myself against the seat where I knelt to prevent my sobs from being taken notice of, but when I found others as much affected as myself, I gave an unconfined scope to my tears.'[7] The embodied character of her conversion is further underlined by her description of her emotional state after she had prayed with a Methodist minister: 'when I arose from my knees I found all my fears were gone, that condemnation vanished and that I could tread as light as if I mounted on air – a pleasing inward warmth diffused through my heart, I felt peace indeed'.[8] Such visceral emotionalism is the hallmark of these accounts of female religious awakening, and while similar conversion narratives can be found in the writings of women who established Catholic communities of nuns, this note of intense, embodied spirituality is absent. For such women, the conversion is represented as a spur to social action rather than as a catalyst for a more intense form of religious belief. A prime example is Nano Nagle, who founded the Presentation Sisters in Cork in 1775. Prior to this, Nagle had entered a convent in France for a time, believing there was nothing she could do for the poor in Ireland. It was during her stay in the convent that she understood 'the will of heaven' and returned to Ireland to begin the work of educating the poor.[9]

---

[6] The Wicklow Papers, MS 4810, National Library of Ireland (NLI). See also Rosemary Raughter, 'Eighteenth-Century Catholic and Protestant Women', in Bourke et al., eds., *The Field Day Anthology of Irish Writing, Volume IV*, 490–516.

[7] Angel Anna Slack, 'The Journal of Angel Anna Slack', Cavan County Library, no pagination. See also Mary O'Dowd, *A History of Women in Ireland, 1500–1800* (Harlow: Pearson, 2005), 189–92.

[8] Slack, 'The Journal of Angel Anna Slack', no pagination.

[9] Mother Clare Callaghan to Bishop Coppinger, 'Letter xxvii', in T. J. Walsh, *Nano Nagle and the Presentation Sisters* (Dublin: M.H. Gill and Sons, 1959), 382. For conversion narratives, see Michael Brown, 'Conversion Narratives in Eighteenth-Century Ireland', in Michael Brown, Charles I.

Narratives of Catholic nationalist conversion

Conversion narratives generally represent powerful instances of identification with a religious community, and this is certainly the case with the
Methodist women discussed above. However, for a number of other women
in the late nineteenth and early twentieth centuries their political conversion
to Irish nationalism involved an equally intense emotional dimension. These
women's conversion tales allow for a recreation of the self within the context
of a revitalizing Irish identity, whereby the self is brought into a spiritual
connection with what is viewed as one of the essences of Irishness,
Catholicism, and this binds the individual to the nation. When these
women write about religion and spirituality, therefore, they do so primarily
as nationalists. One such woman was Charlotte Elizabeth (Lily) MacManus,
the daughter of a Mayo landowning family, for whom life began at forty-one
when, already a published author, she went into a lending library in
Worthing in Sussex and started to browse two of George Stokes's ecclesiastical histories, *Ireland and the Celtic Church* (1886) and *Ireland and the Anglo
Norman Church* (1889). 'I remember', she wrote in her autobiography *White
Light and Flame* (1929), 'a sudden wonder, an interest, a feeling that those
books and I should be acquainted, that we had been acquainted, somehow,
somewhere, and that I, in the South Saxon land was in spirit with them and
their story, though what that story was I did not know'.[10]

MacManus was firm friends with the staunchly Catholic Mary Butler
(Máire de Buitléir), the daughter of a Co. Clare landowner, whose sister, a
nun, wrote her biography and said of her conversion to nationalism that

> it happened to Mary as it happened to many another. The writings of
> Standish O'Grady, Douglas Hyde, AE, W. B. Yeats and others of the
> Literary and Language Revival, though dealing directly with Ireland's
> right to spiritual independence, made her think of a really free Ireland.
> She said herself that she 'was beginning to get glimmerings of light' – by this
> she meant light to see that Ireland is ours to have and to hold.[11]

MacManus depicted Butler's conversion in her own autobiography, noting
that, when visiting a priest friend, Butler spotted John Mitchel's *Jail*

McGrath and Thomas P. Power, eds., *Converts and Conversion in Ireland, 1650–1850* (Dublin: Four
  Courts Press, 2005), 237–74. Brown's focus is on male narratives; women are mentioned only in
  passing.
[10] Lily MacManus, *White Light and Flame: Memories of the Irish Literary Revival and the Anglo-Irish
  War* (Dublin: Talbot Press, 1929), 3.
[11] Mere Columba Butler, 'Mary: Life of Mary E. L. Butler', Butler MS 7321, NLI, no pagination. See
  also Máiréad Ní Chinnéide, *Máire de Buitléir: Bean Athbheochana* (Dublin: Comhar Teoranta,
  1993).

Journal (1854) on his shelves and subsequently borrowed it, 'and when she had finished the last page she turned her back on Dublin Castle for ever'.[12] Butler herself argued that religion 'evokes the deepest and most authentic note in the racial genius',[13] such that for her the true Irish person was intensely Catholic. In her unpublished novel *The Price*, she has a character visit a contemplative order, where she reflects that 'the mystical beauty of her faith to which she belonged had never seemed so sublime to her as it did at that moment. She felt how immeasurably exalted it is above the pseudo-mysticism of a school illuminated by supernatural life, and of minds bounded by finite reason.'[14] In the same text, Butler suggests that a convent community offers a model for government, noting that 'in this remote Western convent there was afforded proof of the fact that the Catholic Church is the only body which has solved the problem of a genuine democracy and a true aristocracy combined ... the Church is not an organisation but an organism ... a living force'.[15]

Annie M. P. Smithson, author of *Myself – And Others* (1944), underwent a double conversion, to Catholicism and to Irish nationalism. Born in 1873 into a middle-class Dublin Protestant family that fell into penury, she trained as a nurse in London and subsequently worked in several locations in Britain and Ireland, including Edinburgh, Dublin and Portadown. The emotional legacies of an unhappy childhood, coupled with the distress of a doomed affair with a married man, inclined her towards Catholicism, a move that was quickened by her attending a Redemptorist mission in Glasgow in 1906. Like many other women, Smithson's conversion brought a degree of certainty to her life and ended a period of spiritual torment and anxiety. Soon, her commitment to nationalism was as staunch as her Catholic allegiance. 'I do not remember when I first became an Irish Irelander, it seemed to have just come naturally to me',[16] she recalls, before going on to confess her excitement on learning that her father was a Fenian who took part in the abortive 1867 rising. Smithson joined Cumann na mBan in 1920 and rejected the Anglo-Irish Treaty of the following year. Her novels, which were very popular, fuse romantic nationalism and intense Catholicism to create such heightened narrative tension as to cause fellow novelist Eimar O'Duffy to remark that 'Miss Smithson's

---

[12] Ibid., 18.
[13] Máire de Buitléir, 'Some Traits of the Catholic Gael', *Catholic Bulletin*, 6 (February 1916), 99.
[14] Mary Butler, transcript of *The Price*, Mary Butler Papers, MS 8323 (2), NLI, 182.
[15] Ibid., 230–31.
[16] Annie M. P. Smithson, *Myself – And Others: An Autobiography* (Dublin: Talbot Press, 1944), 227–28.

naïve pages are thronged with people who live in a state of chronic patriotic hysteria.'[17]

Diaries, journals and letters

Keeping religious diaries and journals gave women a space in which to vent their frustrations, record their inner torments and come to some degree of self-awareness or a level of reconciliation with their feelings. Lady Anne Jocelyn, who was born into a wealthy evangelical Church of Ireland family in 1795, is a case in point. She kept a diary that reveals an intense personal piety, filled with self-reproach and gloomy introspection. For example, in July 1822 she recorded:

> Up late, horrible thoughts in the night, I trust rather a grief to me – reading bad I grieve to say, and prayers rather dead and cold. I tried a little to conquer my love of dress and please God will try more, but failed completely this morning. Having to try on a gown I was excessively ill-tempered in my heart, and showed it. ... I read a little after breakfast to myself in Matthew, I found I got a good deal more good that way in prayers after-wards ... this whole evening I have felt melancholy and deserted and this whole day I have been so happy in being near the Lord ... but Blessed Be His Name, He did shine a little on me since I have come to my room and has showed me a glimpse of my past vileness.[18]

Not all women were sanguine about the value of keeping a diary, however. When forty-eight-year-old Mary Mathew decided to keep a journal for 1772, she did so believing 'I shall by that only see how unprofitably I spend my time god grant it may be a means of my doing better another year.'[19] By the end of the year, she had decided to abandon the journal, observing that 'my time past in so trifling a manner tis not worth recording so here I end'.[20] Sarah Jane Potts was inspired by religious feeling to keep her diary. After a number of abortive attempts, she finally managed to maintain one when she moved to Dublin from her Armagh home. Like Mathew, she hoped that the task of recording her ideas, feelings and occupations would help her to develop into a better person. She

---

[17] Eimar O'Duffy, review of Annie M. P. Smithson's *The Walk of a Queen*, *Irish Review*, 1 (1923), 70. See also James Maguire and James Quinn, eds., *Dictionary of Irish Biography: From the Earliest Times to the Year 2002* (Cambridge: Cambridge University Press, 2009), 9 vols., vol. 8, 1035–36.

[18] Lady Anne Jocelyn, 'Diary of Lady Anne Jocelyn', MS 18430, NLI, no pagination.

[19] Mary Mathew, *The Diary of Mary Mathew*, ed. Maria Luddy (Thurles: Tipperary Historical Society, 1991), 1.

[20] Ibid., 46.

constantly notes her failings and records her training as a teacher and her involvement in Bible classes and Sunday school.[21] Similarly, the diaries of Mary Barron, the daughter of a Presbyterian minister, record her philanthropic and teaching work. After considerable editing, they were published in 1915 by her husband, the Reverend Robert Barron, along with his own copious notes about his 'beloved late wife'.[22]

For many women their religious beliefs and spiritual connections helped them to meet with challenges in their lives. Caroline Wyndham married the second Earl of Dunraven in 1810 at the age of twenty. Her numerous diaries survive but the letters she wrote and received offer a deeper insight into her emotional world. Wyndham too had been influenced by the evangelical revival of the time and one of the interesting themes to emerge from her letters and diaries is her attitude to death.[23] Having lost two grandchildren within a very short space of time, she found it difficult to submit to the will of God. She described how her daughter, Anna Maria, had through her faith accepted the death of her child. Her calmness, she noted, 'never forsook her, she felt that the Almighty had taken the child to himself, that he was eternally happy and not a murmur escaped her'.[24] Wyndham herself, however, struggled to reconcile herself to the loss: 'with the life of this darling ended all my hopes of having grandchildren this year & I trust I may be enabled to bow under the chastisement with the submission which I am preaching to my poor afflicted children'.[25]

The Quaker Mary Leadbeater kept a diary from 1769, when she was eleven years old, until 1826, shortly before her death.[26] The diaries mark her transition from adolescence to adulthood and recount the ordinary events of her life, including her marriage, the birth of her children and her social and religious worlds. Her Quakerism gave her a way of looking at and experiencing the world; it was also, at times, a source of tension

---

[21] Diary and correspondence of Sarah Jane Potts, 1870–1914. T. 1848, Public Record Office of Northern Ireland, Belfast.

[22] Robert Barron, *Mary Barron: A Biography* (Belfast: Sabbath School Society for Ireland, 1915).

[23] The Earl of Dunraven Papers, Special Collection, D/3196, Glucksman Library, University of Limerick. See also Odette Clarke, 'Divine Providence and Resignation: The Role of Religion in the Management of the Emotions of the Anglo-Irish Countess of Dunraven, Caroline Wyndham-Quin (1790–1870)', in Willemijn Ruberg and Kristine Steenbergh, eds., *Sexed Sentiments: Interdisciplinary Perspectives on Gender and Emotion* (Amsterdam: Rodopi, 2011), 71–91.

[24] Dunraven Papers, 1845, ULSC, D/3196/E/2/48/60.

[25] Dunraven Papers, 1837, ULSC, D/3196/E/2/40/68.

[26] There are fifty-four diaries in total and these are housed in the National Library of Ireland in Dublin.

between how she wanted to live and what was expected of her as a believer.[27] Although her diaries are not as explicitly religious as those of some of the evangelical women noted above, the beliefs that shaped her own spiritual life and that of her community are nevertheless present throughout.[28] As a published author, Leadbeater often wrote 'improving' texts, writings that were meant to be of practical use to her readers. She offered advice on household matters and the conduct of peasant lives, advocating a way of life that would bring material benefits and promote social cohesion. Another Quaker woman, Elisabeth Clibborn, also kept a journal, which covers the years from 1808 to 1817, wherein she recorded a range of family events and her reactions to them. As the mother of fifteen children, anxieties about giving birth and the responsibilities of parenthood are particular themes of hers. In January 1814, for example, she recorded that she was 'very low & poorly, dear M. Fayle's decease has made a strong impression [and] increased many apprehensions respecting my approaching confinement'.[29] In contrast, Jane Abell, who was also a Quaker, kept a spiritual diary that is uninterrupted by details of life events and which she never intended for publication.[30] These women, like many others, operated in a social world where public and familial interactions were often shaped by private and intense spiritual reflections that were confided to the pages of personal diaries and journals.

Diaries, journals or autobiographies in which Catholic women talk explicitly about their spiritual and religious lives appear to be rare. Mary Colum and Katharine Tynan, for example, note the influence of a convent education in their published memoirs, yet neither woman was overtly spiritual in their writing careers.[31] We do, however, have autobiographical insights into the lives of those who founded and ran convents from the eighteenth century onwards, thanks to the growth of scholarship on the work of female religious communities in Ireland.[32] Whatever the spiritual

[27] See Mary O'Dowd, 'Mary Leadbeater: Modern Woman and Irish Quaker', in D. W. Hayton and Andrew Holmes, eds., *Ourselves Alone? Religion, Society and Politics in Eighteenth- and Nineteenth-Century Ireland* (Dublin: Four Courts Press, 2016), 137–53.

[28] Mary Leadbeater, *The Leadbeater Papers* (London: Bell and Daldy, 1862), 2 vols., vol. 1, 103–04.

[29] Elizabeth Clibborn, 'Journal of Elizabeth Clibborn (1780–1861)', 59. Friends Library, Dublin.

[30] Jane Abell, 'Extracts from the Private Memoranda of Jane Abell'. Friends Library, Dublin.

[31] Mary Colum, *Life and the Dream: Memories of a Literary Life in Europe and America* (London: Macmillan, 1947); Katharine Tynan, *Twenty-Five Years: Reminiscences* (London: Smith, Elder and Company, 1913).

[32] See, for example, Caitriona Clear, *Nuns in Nineteenth-Century Ireland* (Dublin: Gill and Macmillan, 1987); Tony Fahey, 'Nuns and the Catholic Church in Ireland in the Nineteenth Century', in Mary Cullen, ed., *Girls Don't Do Honours: Irish Women in Education in the 19th and 20th Centuries* (Dublin: Women's Education Bureau, 1987), 1–24; Maria Luddy, *Women and Philanthropy in Nineteenth-Century Ireland* (Cambridge: Cambridge University Press, 1995); Margaret MacCurtain, 'Late in the Field: Catholic Sisters in Twentieth-Century Ireland and the New

and social motivations were in joining religious communities, it is clear that the majority of women found happiness and fulfilment there. As noted by Mary Peckham Magray, loyalty and love were evident in the relationships that existed within these religious communities and had a profound effect on the way convents were managed, even to the extent of determining the success or otherwise of a particular community.[33] It was these emotions, together with adherence to the religious ideals of the community, that bound the sisters together in their work. Evidence of the ties of friendship can be found in the numerous letters written by community members, and it is through such letters that we can come to a better understanding the personal beliefs and values of female religious in Ireland.

Exploring the letters of nuns offers fresh insights into the spiritual and religious lives of women who had considerable social and religious presence but who rarely appear before us as actual women. Through their letters these women were forming and consolidating friendships and relationships, forging bonds and loyalties, and shaping how the self could be represented in a religious collective. What is evident is that female religious founders such as Nano Nagle, Mary Aikenhead and Catherine McAuley understood the importance of using correspondence to create political alliances with the male hierarchy. More pertinent to our purposes, they also knew of its importance in expressing the promise of spirituality to create happy and contented communities. Some letters were carefully drafted formal narratives that sought assistance from benefactors or members of the Catholic hierarchy. Others offered less formal encouragements to sisters in branch convents or expressed sympathy about the difficulties they were experiencing. Many were humorous and full of convent news. Always they held some form of exhortation to spiritual awareness. These letters were essentially affective texts that enabled the correspondents to maintain a degree of sociability across distance and nurture emotional bonds that supported and enhanced the work of religious orders. Through these letters we witness the significance of religion and spirituality in these women's lives and how they shaped their identities and communities.[34]

Religious History', *Journal of Women's History*, 6/7 (1995), 49–63; Mary Peckham Magray, *The Transforming Power of the Nuns: Women, Religion, and Cultural Change in Ireland, 1750–1900* (New York: Oxford University Press, 1998); Rosemary Raughter, ed., *Religious Women and Their History: Breaking the Silence* (Dublin: Irish Academic Press, 2005); Yvonne McKenna, *Made Holy: Irish Women Religious at Home and Abroad* (Dublin: Irish Academic Press, 2006).

[33] See Magray, *The Transforming Power of the Nuns*, chapter four.

[34] There are numerous published collections of letters relating to Irish nuns. For the most interesting, see Mary C. Sullivan, ed., *The Correspondence of Catherine McAuley, 1818–1841* (Dublin: Four Courts

The letters and conversations that were most significant to nuns were those that came to them via their own religious superiors. That was where the 'spirit' of the community lay. Writing to Sister M. Cecilia at the Convent of Mercy in Birr, Co. Offaly in 1841, Catherine McAuley, whose letters were often playful and full of warmth, stated: 'I am almost infatuated with the darling heavenly Sr. Margaret D[wyer]. I never met in this great world a sweeter little dove, all animation, candor and real good sense. I declared she should be Queen of the Order in General.'[35] Another pioneering figure, Mary Aikenhead, founder of the Sisters of Charity, had a close friendship with Mother Magdalen McCarthy, who worked with her in managing the congregation and became its second superior general after Aikenhead's death in 1858. Sometimes, however, such loyalty could mask deeper reasons for entering a community. Writing to the archbishop of Dublin in 1860, one nun described her reasons for wishing to be dispensed of her vows:

> I feel I have no vocation nor never had, I really think I came into the convent in a fit of fervour, I was only a few months home from school I was to have returned there again only I came into the convent. I was really only a month thinking of it seriously and did not mention it to my confessor.[36]

This sister drew encouragement from speaking to her confessor for a second time but later realized, after living in the community for six years, that much of the attraction of convent life resulted from her being

> very much attached to my superior which I fear was a great inducement to me to remain in religious [life], I thought I never could be happy away from her, I was under her care for the entire of my religious life with the exception of the last 2 years. I have never known what it was really to subdue myself till lately. I feel I never will be a good nun.[37]

Another sister, wishing to be dispensed of her vows after four years in a community, simply stated that she had 'no vocation' and had entered the convent very much against her will.[38] Through such letters we glimpse

---

Press, 2004); P. M. MacSweeney, ed., *Letters of Mary Aikenhead* (Dublin: M.H. Gill and Son, 1914). Many letters of various founders remain unpublished in convent archives.

[35] Mother Catherine McAuley to Sister M. Cecilia Marmion, St John's Convent, Birr, 22 March 1841, in Sister M. Ignatia Neumann, ed., *Letters of Catherine McAuley* (Baltimore: Helicon Press, 1969), 317–18.

[36] Unnamed sister to Archbishop Cullen, 16 July 1860. Cullen Papers, Section 333/6/8, File II: Sisters of Mercy 1860, Dublin Diocesan Archives.

[37] Ibid.

[38] Sister Catherine Callaghan, Carmel, Blackrock to Cardinal Cullen, 18 May 1876. Cullen Papers, Nuns 1876, File 322/6/25, Dublin Diocesan Archives.

women's understanding of the meaning and practical implications of a vocation, and their ability or inability to accept one. Excessive human emotions that might cause disruption to a community were to be guarded against. On the issue of jealousy, Aikenhead wrote that 'we ought not to allow that natural little jealousy, which most communities unfortunately yield to, to influence us; at least we ought to mortify every exterior expression of it'.[39]

It was through the creation of rules of conduct and behaviour that founders managed community life and brought the community closer together. While many nuns maintained strong links with their families and wrote letters and received visits from them, such communication was expected to be limited. Letters could only be sent or received after they were read by a sister appointed by the community.[40] While visits from families were not discouraged, it was noted that it was better for sisters to avoid 'secular intercourse', even with members of their own family, as 'relatives too often expect a religious to enter into and fill her mind with all that regards them – even to their minute domestic details – and sometimes to share their aversions and identify herself with their interests, as if she had never renounced the world'.[41] Care therefore had to be taken about the nature of any conversation engaged in by visitors to the convent. 'Should', it was ruled, 'conversation unsuitable to our state be introduced, where the rank, age, etc., of the visitor renders censure indiscreet, the Sister should endeavour to turn the conversation, or by her silence or manner check it, as prudence may direct'.[42] Within all female religious communities limitations were placed on physical contact. The rules of the Sisters of Charity stated: 'In order that the gravity and modesty becoming religious persons be observed, no one is to touch others, even by way of jest, unless embracing in token of charity, when any one is returning from or going to a distance.'[43] Similarly, it was a rule that

> no one must enter the chamber of another without the general or particular leave of the Superior; and if anyone be within, she who is on the outside must not open the door till she has knocked, and been

[39] Mother Mary Aikenhead to Mother Mary de Chantal, 20 February 1836, in MacSweeney, ed., *Letters of Mary Aikenhead*, 67.
[40] Sisters of Charity, *Rules of the Religious Sisters of Charity* (Dublin: Mount St Anne's Milltown, 1941), 35–36.
[41] Sisters of Mercy, *Guide for the Religious Called Sisters of Mercy* (Birmingham: Sisters of Mercy, 1867), 97.
[42] Ibid., 99.   [43] Sisters of Charity, *Rules*, 64–65.

subsequently desired to enter, and the door must remain open whilst they remain together.[44]

The cell was perhaps the most personal space utilized by nuns, though they did not have a right to ownership of it. Individually, nuns owned little, nor could they buy, sell or exchange anything.[45] Choir nuns brought dowries with them, which often consisted of substantial amounts of money, over which they had no direct control within the community. In terms of property ownership, the Mercy rule book observed that 'to promote order certain things are allotted to the use of each Sister; on these, she may, with permission, put the mark assigned to her in the Community, but not her name; yet she must not forget that even these things are not hers'.[46] Thus, nuns had to be willing at all times to relinquish anything that had been assigned to them, so that 'exchanging them or being deprived of them will cause no pain or surprise'.[47] Again, it was noted that to ensure this 'disengagement of heart',[48] sisters could at any point be asked to exchange their cells or any other items by the Superior or anyone appointed by her. It was also suggested that terms denoting ownership, such as 'mine' and 'yours', be replaced by 'for my use', 'for your use' or 'ours'. Such regulations provided the space for women to be contemplative and reflective about their own spirituality. What rules and founders' letters did for communities was to provide stability and cohesion so that the internal and external practice of religious belief and spirituality could continue, unfettered by the distractions of the material world.

Conclusion

For the period covered by this chapter, the variety of religious experience and spiritual reflection engaged in by Irish women is broad. The experience of religious conversion finds expression in language of great emotion and intensity in first-person narratives that testify to the achievement of equanimity and inner peace. That conversion might also link one to a national cause seemed to confer even greater authority on a particular religion; in Ireland's case, that religion was Catholicism. However, religious introspection by women could also lead to anxiety, self-denigration and unhappiness. Distinctions existed around denominations, social status, education and community. It appears that a strong denominational identity, such as that provided by Quakerism and Methodism, and that supported by

[44] Ibid., 64.   [45] Sisters of Mercy, *Guide*, 78.   [46] Ibid., 77.   [47] Ibid., 75.   [48] Ibid., 77.

Catholic convents, gave women an opportunity for spiritual reflection that could add significant meaning to their lives. For lay women, spaces for religious and spiritual reflection were to be found in journals, diaries and letters as much as in meeting houses, chapels and churches. For female religious, the physical space of the convent allowed them to reflect on their spiritual lives in personal and communal settings, while the affective letters of superiors helped to bind them more firmly together. These letters also form part of the spiritual legacies of convent founders and have been retained in the archives of many communities as moral guides and spiritual touchstones. If such letters have individual meanings for their authors and communal significance for their foundations, they also allow the modern reader intimate access to the lives of 'ordinary' women who lived together as nuns, and reveal the shaping power of religion and spirituality on thought, word and deed.

Further reading

Bourke, Angela, et al., eds. *The Field Day Anthology of Irish Writing, Volumes IV and V: Irish Women's Writings and Traditions*. Cork: Cork University Press in association with Field Day, 2002.

Coolahan, Marie-Louise. *Women, Writing, and Language in Early Modern Ireland*. Oxford: Oxford University Press, 2010.

Hempton, David and Hill, Myrtle. *Evangelical Protestantism in Ulster Society 1740–1890*. London: Routledge, 1992.

Magray, Mary Peckham. *The Transforming Power of the Nuns: Women, Religion, and Cultural Change in Ireland, 1750–1900*. New York: Oxford University Press, 1998.

Raughter, Rosemary, ed. *The Journal of Elizabeth Bennis 1749–1779*. Dublin: Columba Press, 2007.

Sullivan, Mary C., ed. *The Correspondence of Catherine McAuley, 1818–1841*. Dublin: Four Courts Press, 2004.

CHAPTER 6

Spiritual and Religious Life-Writing in Ireland since 1900

Louise Fuller

The Augustinian model of religious doubt, questioning, struggle and ultimate intellectual conversion is the classic touchstone of spiritual life-writing. Until the late twentieth century, religion and spirituality tended to be conflated, so that conceptualizations of the spiritual typically pertained to membership of a church or organized religion, to how one saw oneself in relation to the divine and to a belief in a supernatural life. Against this background, it is not surprising that professional religious or ex-religious people have been primarily, though not exclusively, drawn to this genre. However, sociological, philosophical and attitudinal changes have brought about more nuanced and expansive definitions of spirituality, which has led in turn to a marked expansion of the generic parameters of spiritual autobiography. For many, including ex-religious people, spirituality is no longer necessarily understood in terms of a congregational faith or a collectivist morality; rather, it is equated with an individualistic quest for meaning, the ultimate goal of which is self-fulfilment or self-realization. Thus, the increasing secularization of Irish society in the period since the 1960s has witnessed a proliferation of life-writing in which the search for inner meaning has replaced the desire for intimacy with the divine, a trend that reflects the emergence of a new religious or humanist individualism, one sign of which is the preference of many people to identify themselves as spiritual rather than religious. Although struggle remains central to such narratives, the emphasis is often on journeys that diverge from the traditional paths to fulfilment offered by institutional religion.

This chapter deals primarily with autobiographers from the Irish Catholic tradition, including priests, ex-priests, nuns and a bishop. It also features memoirs by members of the Church of Ireland and Jewish faiths. Only ten of the autobiographies cited here pre-date 1990; most of the remainder were published after 2000. Not all of these life stories can be considered spiritual autobiography in the traditional sense but are included on the basis of their specific associations with religion and/or spirituality. Catholic convert Dorothy Day described the business of the autobiographer as 'giving yourself away';[1] Belfast-born C. S. Lewis regarded his hugely popular *Surprised by Joy: The Shape of My Early Life* (1955) as a 'suffocatingly subjective' work that 'gets less like a general autobiography as it goes on'.[2] Both of these characteristics are among those that differentiate spiritual autobiography from other forms of the genre, so that the works considered here arguably become 'spiritual' only when the writer plumbs those deeper levels of consciousness that equate to their innermost being or 'soul', a process that may or may not be linked to institutional forms of religion.

For most of the 1900s, those Irish Catholic clerics who wrote their life stories tended to be involved in extra-clerical activities, such as those associated with a social or political cause, a sport or a community development project, and it was often within such contexts that they framed their lives. One of the earliest twentieth-century examples of Irish religious life-writing, *Mo Sgéal Féin* (*My Own Story*) (1915) by Father Peadar Ó Laoghaire (Peter O'Leary), conforms to this type. Land reform, education, national sovereignty and the revival of the Irish language were defining concerns of late nineteenth- and early twentieth-century Irish society, and religious affiliation was central to many people's sense of identity. Against this backdrop, and with Catholicism in the ascendant, Ó Laoghaire was, in the words of his translator Sheila O'Sullivan, 'a thorough clergyman, a keen social and educational worker, a Land League priest, and the Father O'Leary of the Gaelic Revival'.[3] For such a cleric, there was evidently little necessity to interrogate matters of faith, doubt and spirituality, at least not in an autobiography. There were others, however, who did not fit the template laid down by Ó Laoghaire and who, in Augustinian fashion, turned to writing in an attempt to resolve their doubts and crises of faith.

One such was Gerald O'Donovan, author of the autobiographical novel *Father Ralph* (1913). O'Donovan trained for the priesthood at St Patrick's College, Maynooth from 1889 to 1895, after which he was appointed to the parish of Loughrea in the diocese of Clonfert. He too was active in local politics, in his case in the co-operative movement, and was highly respected by Horace Plunkett, a leading force in the development of co-operativism in Ireland. In the theological sphere, O'Donovan was influenced by the

---

[1] Dorothy Day, *The Long Loneliness* (New York: Harper, 1952), 10.
[2] C. S. Lewis, *Surprised by Joy: The Shape of My Early Life* (London: Fontana, 1976), 7.
[3] An tAthair Peadar Ó Laoghaire, *My Own Story*, trans. Sheila O'Sullivan (Dublin: Gill and Macmillan, 1973), xii.

ideas of the Catholic modernist movement that developed in continental Europe in the late nineteenth and early twentieth centuries. Scholastic theology demanded conformity to laws that were impervious to cultural change; modernism questioned traditional Catholic teaching and sought to reinterpret it in light of advances in scientific and philosophical thought. *Father Ralph* chronicles, in the guise of fiction, the serious difficulties O'Donovan was having with the church, both locally and at a theological level, which ultimately caused him to leave the priesthood in 1904. His is a valuable life story, as his spiritual struggle, his questioning of authority and the way he resolved his issues display an independence of mind and spirit not encouraged in the Roman Catholic church at that time, least of all in Ireland.

An important memoir published in the mid-1920s corroborated O'Donovan's reflections on the stale intellectual ethos of Ireland's national seminary in the decades before independence. Kilkenny-born Walter McDonald was professor of theology in Maynooth from 1881 until his death in 1920. His *Reminiscences of a Maynooth Professor* (1925), which was published posthumously under the direction of Denis Gwynn, chronicles McDonald's early life, his time as a student, his professorial career and his role as founding-editor of the *Irish Theological Quarterly*. His autobiography also deals with the conflicts and controversies he was involved in with the college authorities and with Rome as a result of his criticism of autocratic church governance and calls for reform. McDonald creates a picture of an Irish church very cut off from influential currents of thought in science and philosophy, which were presenting challenges to traditional Catholic theology at that time. He writes of doubts he was experiencing about the foundations of his faith and is openly critical of his narrow theological formation:

> I say now, very solemnly, that the conservatism in which I was trained very nearly drove me out of the Church on many occasions, or into a mad-house, and that the good, easy men who, for the honour of God would in the interest of religion, insist on these traditional views – making dogmas of what are but school traditions – are tormenting souls and driving them out of the Church.[4]

In the preface, Gwynn quotes McDonald as saying that 'my whole life has been one long protest, which will be continued while breath is left to me'.[5]

---

[4] Walter McDonald, *Reminiscences of a Maynooth Professor*, ed., Denis Gwynn (Cork: Mercier Press, 1967), 93.
[5] Ibid., 41.

Written over a considerable period of time, *Reminiscences* bears witness to a spiritual and intellectual struggle that defined McDonald's life and which he was determined would transcend his mortality.

Catholic theological formation throughout most of the twentieth century did not encourage questioning, which partly explains the paucity of material in this genre until the end of the century. From the time of the Reformation, the Catholic church was concerned to protect its followers from dissenting or heterodox views which were considered hazardous to faith and morals, and this censorious culture remained in place until the Second Vatican Council (1962–65). It is therefore not surprising that doubt, questioning and spiritual struggle did not loom large in the writings of clergy who committed their lives to the page. Their struggles were primarily practical and political, as can be seen in some of the more notable examples. For instance, *All for Her* (1967), the autobiography of Irish-American priest Father Patrick Peyton, focuses on his worldwide crusade to promote the family rosary; Father James McDyer recorded his work in developing local industries in his native Donegal in *Fr McDyer of Glencolumbkille* (1982); maverick priest Joseph Dunn chronicled his pioneering career in broadcasting and the first twenty-five years of the RTÉ television documentary series *Radharc* in *No Tigers in Africa* (1986); and Monsignor James Horan outlined his develop-ment of Knock shrine as a site of Catholic pilgrimage and his campaign to build Ireland West Airport in *Monsignor James Horan: Memoirs 1911–1986* (1992), which was posthumously edited for publication by Micheál MacGréil S.J. Born in the earlier years of the twentieth century, these men were products of an era in which Catholicism was deeply embedded in the fabric of Irish society, when loyalty to the church was axiomatic and when clerics were regarded with deference and respect. All four of these priests were idealistic, dynamic, community-oriented clerics and the causes they espoused proceeded from an activist Christian philosophy. The fact that they focus on their career-defining endeavours at the expense of sustained inner reflection or engagement with questions of faith is an understandable, if regrettable, feature of their autobiographical writings.

For the classic Irish spiritual autobiography of the twentieth century we must turn to C. S. Lewis's *Surprised by Joy*. Lewis was born into the Anglican tradition in Belfast and claimed that what he called 'my deep-seated hatred of authority, my monstrous individualism, my lawlessness'[6] caused him to have no truck with religion for much of his early manhood. In spiritual life-writing, the protagonist often structures the narrative

---

[6] Lewis, *Surprised by Joy*, 139.

around pivotal moments of experience, either positive or negative, that assume profound significance. Tensions in parental relations also often feature. The death of a parent, particularly when one is young, can be a climacteric event; it can raise the most fundamental of existential questions and force the bereaved to contemplate mortality at a time when their psychological and spiritual resources are still developing. In Lewis's case, his mother's death from cancer in 1908 was one such event:

> With my mother's death all settled happiness, all that was tranquil and reliable, disappeared from my life. There was to be much fun, many pleasures, many stabs of Joy; but no more of the old security. It was sea and islands now; the great continent had sunk like Atlantis.[7]

Lewis's marine image finds an echo in a poem by fellow deracinated Ulster Anglican Louis MacNeice, whose poetry is haunted by the loss of his mother after a prolonged illness when he was seven years old. In 'Last before America', MacNeice casts himself as one of those 'who despise charts but find their dream's endorsement / In certain long low islets snouting towards the west / Like cubs that have lost their mother.'[8] Although both writers followed a similar path into the British intelligentsia – English public school followed by the study of classics at Oxford – their spiritual journeys diverged markedly. Religious affiliation can provide answers to life's uncertainties, but on the basis of allegiance to a power and authority beyond the self. Lewis rebelled against this trade-off and maintained a defiantly atheistic stance for many years until God eventually 'closed in on' him and led him first to Theism and thence to Christianity, the last phase of this transition occurring rather bathetically in Bedfordshire: 'I know very well when, but hardly how, the final step was taken. I was driven to Whipsnade one sunny morning. When we set out I did not believe that Jesus Christ is the Son of God, and when we reached the zoo I did.'[9] MacNeice's act of rebellion had an added, intimate dimension, since his father was a Church of Ireland rector who came to embody religion's forbidding, all-pervasive childhood presence. He recalls in *The Strings Are False: An Unfinished Autobiography* (1965): 'what my father did by himself was frightening. When I was in bed I could hear his voice below in the study … intoning away, communing with God. And because of his conspiracy with God I was afraid of him.'[10] Unlike Lewis,

---

[7] Ibid., 23.
[8] Louis MacNeice, *Collected Poems*, ed. Peter McDonald (London: Faber and Faber, 2007), 264.
[9] Lewis, *Surprised by Joy*, 179, 189.
[10] Louis MacNeice, *The Strings Are False: An Unfinished Autobiography* (London: Faber and Faber, 1982), 38.

however, who eventually reconciled himself to Christianity's 'transcendental Interferer',[11] MacNeice rejected 'self-abnegation' and remained, in the words of his friend John Hilton, 'Questingly agnostic'.[12]

Questions of faith are not easily set aside and often force themselves on people's consciousness at traumatic times in life. In the case of Anglican-born Frank Pakenham, the seventh Earl of Longford, the catalyst was a bout of deep depression. In his autobiography *Born to Believe* (1953), he relates how, as a young man, he was suddenly overwhelmed by the 'full awfulness' of the possibility 'that there is not an after-life after all' and 'that there is no such person as God'.[13] Pakenham remained in the church and prayed that his faith would return before eventually turning to a Jesuit friend for help, a decision he describes as 'the greatest in my life'.[14] After many months spent weighing the arguments for and against Catholicism, he converted to the faith. No such resolution was possible for David Marcus, however, who grew up Jewish in Cork in the 1930s and 1940s, and whose *Oughtobiography: Leaves from the Diary of a Hyphenated Jew* (2001) provides a rare outsider perspective on the hegemonic Catholic culture of that time. In it, Marcus explains how his inability 'to say a categorical "yea" or "nay"'[15] to God as a teenager left him in a state of limbo for much of his life, without faith yet lacking the courage to embrace atheism. The 'moment of illumination', when it eventually arrived, led not to religious conviction but to a distinctly idiosyncratic spiritual outlook: 'Since my inner revelation . . . I have followed the way of my own God, the God in me, and can only hope that if there is a God in heaven, it will have found acceptance in His eyes.'[16]

The autobiography of Sister de Lourdes Stack, a Presentation nun, betrays no such ambivalence or uncertainty. Born in 1905, she spent her life teaching in Cahirciveen, Co. Kerry. Her *As We Lived It* (1981) is a valuable chronicle of religious life as lived in the early twentieth century. The self-abnegation rejected by Louis MacNeice was a cornerstone of convent life. Individualism, self-expression and questioning were actively discouraged. As a novice, Stack became accustomed to ritualistic behaviour such as observing silence during meals and practising the spiritual

---

[11] Lewis, *Surprised by Joy*, 139.
[12] John Hilton, 'Louis MacNeice at Marlborough and Oxford', in MacNeice, *The Strings Are False*, 282.
[13] Frank Pakenham, *Born to Believe: An Autobiography* (London: Jonathan Cape, 1953), 94.
[14] Ibid., 96.
[15] David Marcus, *Oughtobiography: Leaves from the Diary of a Hyphenated Jew* (Dublin: Gill and Macmillan, 2001), 193.
[16] Ibid., 193, 195–96.

discipline known as custody of the eyes, which entailed not making eye contact with others and directing one's gaze downwards when walking; she also recalls a penance exercise for those who transgressed, whereby a nun would, in the presence of the other sisters, bend low and kiss the floor in order to 'strike a blow at the lurking pride within'.[17] In the pre-Vatican II era, the church emphasized the idea that this life was a 'valley of tears' and that true happiness was only attainable in heaven. Suffering therefore had to be accepted as part of life, and self-denial and mortification were virtues to be cultivated. But such concepts found little resonance in the culture of the 1960s and after, which eulogized freedom, fulfilment and, above all, self-realization. Vatican II, in attempting to respond to changing cultural trends, itself brought about revolutionary change, which meant that convent life, as described by Stack, was utterly transformed. This caused a crisis for many religious, male and female. Vocations declined from the late 1960s onwards and defections from the religious life became routine, having hitherto been a cause of considerable social stigma. The rancorous reaction of many practising Catholics to Pope Paul VI's 1968 encyclical *Humanae Vitae*, which decreed that the use of artificial contraception was a mortal sin, was a tipping point. In addition, the emergence of second-wave feminism and the explosion of media and pop culture provided new cultural contexts in which the principles of freedom of conscience and individual choice trumped those of selflessness and deference to institutional authority, thereby providing many counter-narratives within which people began to define their identity.

John O'Donohue and John Moriarty were two late twentieth-century spiritual thinkers who each caught the prevailing mood of a culture in which old certainties were crumbling fast and irrevocably. Clare-born O'Donohue was ordained in 1982 and left the priesthood eighteen years later. His first book, *Anam Cara: Spiritual Wisdom from the Celtic World* (1997), became an international bestseller and catapulted him towards unexpected celebrity status. Moriarty's first book, *Dreamtime*, was published in 1994 and the first volume of his autobiography, *Nostos*, appeared in 2001. These writers witnessed traditional Catholic religious allegiance in Ireland come under enormous pressure over a long period. From the 1970s there were ongoing tensions between the Catholic hierarchy and the laity in relation to moral and sexual issues. These were compounded by a litany of clerical abuse scandals that broke from the early 1990s onwards and which further eroded the church's influence. At a time when the gospel

---

[17] Sister de Lourdes Stack, *As We Lived It* (Tralee: The Kerryman, 1981), 36.

message was, for many, severely compromised by these developments, when the first significant decline in Catholic religious practice was being registered and when analysis was more reactive than incisive, the spiritual reflections of O'Donohue and Moriarty struck a chord. They did so in part because they were distilled from sustained philosophical engagements with the mystical traditions of Christianity, refracted through the authors' own life experiences. So while the ideas of O'Donohue and Moriarty were developed within a Catholic framework, they resonated with readers whose needs were no longer being addressed by traditional religion for a variety of complex reasons. Their work was also countercultural and as such became a touchstone for those who felt alienated by many aspects of postmodern culture in general, and for those who recoiled from the excesses of the Irish economic boom of the late 1990s and early 2000s. In a more secular, depersonalized age, O'Donohue and Moriarty each championed the quest for communion with the deeper inner self, which they asserted could only be found in contemplation and silence, and by stripping away the distractions of modernity. Arguably, the writings of O'Donohue and Moriarty represent a paradigmatic shift in Irish spiritual autobiography because the themes and ideas they address continue to preoccupy twenty-first-century practitioners of this genre.

Seán Dunne's *The Road to Silence* (1994) is an early example of this new departure. Published in the same year that the term 'Celtic Tiger' entered Irish public discourse, Dunne's work has elements of the classical Augustinian conversion story, the most notable of which is the motif of the narrator's circuitous journey from faith to doubt and back again.[18] As a child, Dunne saw the world through a religious optic. Every situation was framed by rules and warnings that one could be damned by one's actions. Yet the church's pageantry appealed to him 'because somewhere in the centre of it, there was a sense that life had another element' – there was 'a sense of the spiritual'.[19] But for Dunne, as for many others of his generation, the negative version of Catholicism prevailed and was rejected in time. After the age of sixteen he 'lost all sense of Catholicism as a positive thing' and entered 'a void full of questions and doubts'[20] from which the weekly sermons and rituals could not rescue him. In *Nostos*, Moriarty characterizes a similar experience as falling 'out of my story' and feeling 'bereft' because 'there was no God that I could appeal to'.[21] In Dunne's

---

[18] See David J. Leigh, *Circuitous Journeys: Modern Spiritual Autobiography* (New York: Fordham University Press, 2000).

[19] Seán Dunne, *The Road to Silence: An Irish Spiritual Odyssey* (Dublin: New Island Books, 1994), 12.

[20] Ibid., 15, 16.   [21] John Moriarty, *Nostos: An Autobiography* (Dublin: Lilliput Press, 2001), 21.

case, this was happening some years after the riots in the Sorbonne and Berkeley that signalled tectonic sociocultural shifts. In spite of the Vatican II reforms, the model of Catholicism that he and other late twentieth-century Irish spiritual autobiographers describe could not withstand the fundamental philosophical, social and attitudinal changes that character-ized the culture of the 1960s and beyond.

Cardinal Cahal B. Daly's *Steps on My Pilgrim Journey* (1998) provides a clerical perspective on these developments, from a theologian who served as archbishop of Armagh and primate of all Ireland from 1990 to 1996. One of Daly's themes is the search for deeper spiritual meaning in the midst of an affluent, desacralized society in which religious alienation has become increasingly common. As a teacher of philosophy, he was aware of the more sceptical and questioning outlook of a better-educated laity and the need to respond to such developments with a theology commensurate with 'the interiority and mystery in the depths of the human heart'.[22] Yet the church's challenge to convince people 'that Christ is the ultimate answer to all their questioning and to all human searching'[23] was clearly a formid-able one, as Dunne's autobiography attests. Dunne's search for answers led him to the Cistercian monastery of Mount Melleray in Co. Waterford, where he found reassurance in conversation with some of the monks there, as they had also known doubt. Like many of the spiritual autobiographers discussed here, Dunne took inspiration from mentors and eventually found a route back to religious belief via poetry, fiction and Zen Buddhism. Daly, who spent time studying in France, recalls the smugness and superiority that marked his early reactions to the problems of the French church in the postwar era. He and many Irish clergy at the time saw Ireland as a model Catholic country, untroubled by conflicts between traditionalists and liberals. Churches were full and dissent was little in evidence, but this did not last. Writing in the late 1990s, it was clear to Daly that there would be 'more Seán Dunnes in the future'.[24]

In his autobiography *Mark of Protest* (1993), Dean Victor Griffin points out that the institutional church in the Irish Protestant tradition did not have 'the same exalted standing as in Roman Catholicism', which meant that orthodoxies, whether religious or political, were 'subject to continuous critical examination in the Protestant consciousness'.[25] While the examples of Lewis, MacNeice and Pakenham would tend to bear this out, this was not

---

[22] Cardinal Cahal B. Daly, *Steps on My Pilgrim Journey: Memories and Reflections* (Dublin: Veritas, 1998), 114.

[23] Ibid.   [24] Ibid., 227.

[25] Victor Griffin, *Mark of Protest: An Autobiography* (Dublin: Gill and Macmillan, 1993), 219.

the experience of Patrick Semple, born into a Church of Ireland family in 1940. He began ordination studies in Trinity College Dublin in October 1962 – the inaugural moment of the Second Vatican Council – at a time when Catholics were still banned by their church from entering Trinity, in the interests of safeguarding their faith and morals. In *Believe It or Not* (2002), Semple records his frustration at not finding much questioning among his confreres and 'little support for my own sceptical approach to matters of belief'.[26] After three years in ministry he took time out to re-evaluate his faith and to travel to the United States, where new experiences and further theological studies developed in him the confidence to confront the issues that troubled him, without necessarily quelling the 'restless nature'[27] of his belief.

A nun whose life straddles the period before and after the Second Vatican Council, and who testifies to the 'monumental changes'[28] it engendered, is Sister Stanislaus Kennedy, affectionately known as Sister Stan. As its title implies, her *The Road Home* (2011) is quite typical of classic spiritual auto-biography in which much weight is attached to the journey and to the pivotal experiences it engenders. Kerry-born Kennedy became a Sister of Charity in 1958. She remembers hearing the dawn chorus when she was about twelve and feeling that she was 'in the presence of something very special, something beyond sacred'.[29] This she characterizes as one of the most significant moments of her life, 'a spiritual moment … which drew me into a stillness that has remained with me'.[30] Of her early years she recalls full churches on Sundays, queues for confession on Saturdays and thronged annual parish missions. At that time there was an overriding emphasis on following clearly defined rules and on the avoidance of sin. But subsequent developments – particularly the emergence of the liberation theology movement in Latin America, with its focus on addressing systemic poverty and social injustice in the here-and-now – broadened understandings of what a Christian life should entail and emphasized Catholics' responsibility for the welfare of their fellow humans. Kennedy's lifelong social activism on behalf of the underprivileged exemplifies these fundamental shifts. She too points to the importance of discovering one's authentic inner self and her spiritual journey also involves struggle, but she is sustained by prayer, meditation and scripture. Her story combines the activism of priests like McDyer and Horan with the reflectiveness of philosopher-theologians such as O'Donohue.

---

[26] Patrick Semple, *Believe It or Not: A Memoir* (Dublin: Columba Press, 2002), 74.   [27] Ibid., 128.
[28] Sister Stanislaus Kennedy, *The Road Home: My Journey* (London: Transworld Ireland, 2011), 19.
[29] Ibid., 16.   [30] Ibid., 16–17.

The changing emphases within Catholic theology are also reflected in the life story of a contemporary of Kennedy's, Father Harry Bohan. In the introduction to *Swimming Upstream* (2013), he explains that he is not 'interested in writing a memoir "ego trip"' but wishes rather to explore 'the issues and the implemented initiatives that define me in a priesthood of fifty years'.[31] Like McDyer and Horan before him, Bohan was the driving force behind several practical projects aimed at strengthening his rural community in Co. Clare. Ordained in 1963, he witnessed in the space of a mere forty years periods of economic stagnation and acceleration and the sociocultural changes they heralded, most notably, the collapse of the influence and authority of the Catholic church in Ireland. In his experience, economic progress did not always go hand in hand with spiritual wellbeing. He reflects that 'a growing number of people were searching for meaning, but the Church did not seem able to respond effectively',[32] which caused many to gravitate towards non-Christian forms of contemplative practice, such as yoga and Buddhism. Like Kennedy, Bohan is aware of the importance of nourishing the contemplative aspect of Catholic belief and sees the spiritual dimension of Irish life as having been seriously eroded during the Celtic Tiger era.

The more questioning approach to matters religious found in the writings of Dunne and Semple has continued to be a trend in postmillennial Irish spiritual life-writing. This can be seen in the autobiographies of John F. Deane, born in Achill Island, Co. Mayo in 1943, and Brian D'Arcy, born in Fermanagh in 1945. Both men commenced training for the priesthood in the landmark year of 1962, the same year that Semple began his theological studies. In *Give Dust a Tongue* (2015), Deane explains that there was no epiphany behind his decision to become a priest (in this he echoes Kennedy, who describes how she 'stumbled into the religious life'[33]), as such life-defining decisions did not need much deliberation in the socioreligious climate of the time. It was simply a matter of embracing a set of 'rules and regulations that, if followed to the letter, would lead a soul through the valley of tears to the safe haven of a vaguely wonderful heaven, avoiding the dreadful pits of Hell with their fires perpetual'.[34] Instead of encouraging him to be a critical thinker, Deane's philosophical training consisted of 'a treasure chest of received and unquestioned tenets and teachings' that had been 'predetermined over the ages, to be shared out

---

[31] Harry Bohan, *Swimming Upstream: Finding Positives in a Negative Ireland* (Dublin: Columba Press, 2013), 17.

[32] Ibid., 98.   [33] Kennedy, *The Road Home*, 23.

[34] John F. Deane, *Give Dust a Tongue* (Dublin: Columba Press, 2015), 40.

unchanged until the end of time'.[35] D'Arcy's experience of monastic life, as recounted in *A Different Journey* (2006), is remarkably similar. He writes of being trained to walk with head bent and eyes cast to the ground, and of having to mortify the eyes and confess in public the slightest infringement, thus echoing the experience of Sister de Lourdes Stack two generations earlier. Novices were, in D'Arcy's view, 'formed in a spiritual wasteland'.[36] It seemed that little had changed in Catholic theological formation since McDonald and O'Donovan voiced their criticisms in the 1910s and 1920s.

Gradually, Deane began to realize that the deity he believed in was 'a God of negatives'.[37] On reading Teilhard de Chardin, a new conception of faith began to take root, hastened by the death of his grandmother. The stigma of leaving the seminary is poignantly captured. Mid-morning, while his fellow trainees were at lauds, Deane crept away home, a 'spoiled priest'.[38] He subsequently married, but the death of his wife in 1980 was a low point and his faith became precarious. When he encountered the work of the Augustinian priest-poet Pádraig J. Daly, the idea of working out his faith problems through poetry took hold. Like O'Donohue and Moriarty, Deane too came to realize that 'life is truest in the honesty and integrity that can be found within the self, if that self can be got at'.[39] With this in mind, he went on pilgrimage to Croagh Patrick in his home county and, on reaching the summit, 'heard, suddenly, somewhere deep inside me, Christ's question put to me, personally: Who do you say that I am?'[40] When he decides to trust poetry to lead him to the answer, he senses that 'the God who is hidden had drawn very near' and that he 'was working towards a newfound and uplifting faith in Christ'.[41]

By the time Brian D'Arcy reached the silver jubilee of his ordination in 1994, he was not sure that he wanted to remain a priest. He persisted nonetheless, but continued to find much to criticize in the church, which ultimately led to his being formally censured by the Vatican in 2010 for expressing views that were at variance with church orthodoxy. As with other autobiographers discussed here, spiritual reading sustained him – he cites Thomas Merton in particular – yet his journey also has its distinctive aspects because of his high media profile in Ireland. In the 1960s, D'Arcy assumed the role of unofficial chaplain to many of the popular showbands of the day and later became one of Ireland's best-known clerics as a result of his journalism and broadcasting. Although his

---

[35] Ibid., 122.   [36] Brian D'Arcy, *A Different Journey* (Dublin: Sliabh Bán Productions, 2006), 66.
[37] Deane, *Give Dust a Tongue*, 123.   [38] Ibid., 137.   [39] Ibid., 170.   [40] Ibid., 188.
[41] Ibid., 189.

popular profile afforded him a degree of freedom that would have been impossible a generation earlier, D'Arcy was shaken by Rome's censure nevertheless. His description of the episode as 'the most devastating faith-crisis of my life'[42] suggests that his struggles with his priestly life and ministry are far from resolved.

As we have already seen, both self-revelation and critique are rare commodities in pre-1960s Irish spiritual autobiography. To express dissenting views or grievances was to risk accusations of disloyalty or worse. In more recent times, however, the imperative to uphold at all costs the flawless public image of a monolithic Catholic church is no longer a constraint. Images of perfection have been shattered and censorship of ideas is not as effective as in the past. That said, the modern emphasis on the importance of self-realization can be difficult to reconcile with the conformity to doctrinal principles which is demanded in religious life. Although he has not written an autobiography as such, the Redemptorist priest Tony Flannery has charted his spiritual path in a number of books, including *The Death of Religious Life* (1997), *From the Inside* (1999) and *Keeping the Faith* (2005). In 2012, Flannery was suspended from public ministry by the Vatican for his liberal views on women priests, homosexuality and contraception. He gives a detailed account of his spiritual struggle and his interactions with his superior and the authorities in Rome in *A Question of Conscience* (2013), an exposé of a very personal episode in Flannery's life which he says has made him feel less at home in the church in which he has ministered all his life.

In the postconciliar era, one of the foremost concerns of many in religious life has been the quest to recover an authentic subjectivity that was suppressed, if not obliterated, by years of self-denial. Michael Harding's *Staring at Lakes* (2013) powerfully exemplifies this quest. Harding was ordained a priest in 1980, at a time when Catholic culture seemed to be taking on a less dogmatic, more relaxed aspect. But this was also the beginning of Pope John Paul II's pontificate, which was marked by his determination to reassert papal authority over a laity that was vulnerable to secularizing forces. Against this backdrop, Harding's journey was one of turmoil and doubt, which led eventually to his decision to 'walk in the wilderness' and 'make sense of my life in a different way' by leaving the priesthood.[43] After a few years of marriage, however, he missed the

---

[42] Brian D'Arcy, *Food for the Soul* (Dublin: Columba Press, 2013), 9.
[43] Michael Harding, *Staring at Lakes: A Memoir of Love, Melancholy and Magical Thinking* (Dublin: Hachette Books Ireland, 2013), 100.

consolations of faith and embarked upon his own pilgrimage, taking refuge in Buddhism and visits to Japan, India and Mongolia. He found peace temporarily but then lapsed into depression and became obsessed with exploring his own identity. Revealingly, Bob Dylan's 'It Ain't Me, Babe' resonated with him; as an expression of the 1960s zeitgeist, the song represents the antithesis of the spirit of self-sacrifice and deference inculcated by the religious life. In keeping with the times, Harding signed up with a therapist 'to talk out the knotted weave of all that hidden past which makes us human',[44] and at his journey's end proclaims himself no longer a believer in anything. So whereas Kennedy's soul searching culminates in the conviction that 'the spiritual journey is finding all things in God, and God in all things',[45] Harding arrives at a desacralized place, having found 'a deeper mother in the world and in all its loveliness'.[46]

What unites most of these writers is their quest to find the essential meaning of life and to ascertain if there is something that transcends human existence. In recent years, this search has led many to look beyond Western Christianity to other traditions, Michael Harding being a case in point. Two other autobiographers whose spiritual journeys took them on a path through Buddhism are Maura 'Soshin' O'Halloran and William Johnston S.J. O'Halloran was born in Boston to an Irish father and an American mother and spent most of her adult life in Ireland. In 1979, she went to Japan and began rigorous training in Zen at the Toshoji Temple, thus becoming the first Western woman to be accepted among the ranks of Japanese Buddhist monks. After three years she was recognized as a Zen master, but tragically lost her life six months later in a road accident in Thailand. O'Halloran left a diary, which her mother and siblings published as *Pure Heart, Enlightened Mind* (2007). Having reached enlightenment at the age of twenty-six, she writes that 'there is nothing else to strive after' and so wants live her life 'for other people'.[47] Like Kennedy and Bohan, O'Halloran senses that civic activism is necessary to create 'a society that fosters more spiritual, more human, values',[48] with the proviso that individuals must also cultivate a deeper spirituality in themselves through meditation. Her journey is presented as a search for liberation from a system based on 'desire for money and commodities',[49] her critique of which is common to many spiritual autobiographers of the contemporary era.

---

[44] Ibid., 226.   [45] Kennedy, *The Road Home*, 199.   [46] Harding, *Staring at Lakes*, 290.
[47] Maura O'Halloran, *Pure Heart, Enlightened Mind: The Life and Letters of an Irish Zen Saint* (Boston: Wisdom Publications, 2007), 165.
[48] Ibid.   [49] Ibid.

Johnston's *Mystical Journey* (2006) is a very revealing account of his
spiritual odyssey from his birth in Belfast to his life and work as a Jesuit
priest in Japan, to where he was posted in 1951. His encounter with Eastern
spirituality and the practice of Zen led him to reappraise the mystical
traditions of Christianity and transform his religious practice, thus paving
the way for his pioneering work on interfaith dialogue between Buddhism
and Christianity. Yet, like many of the memoirists discussed here, he too
experiences spiritual conflict and inner struggle. Looking back, he singled
out an 'earth-shaking retreat' he undertook 'as one of the blessings of my
life',[50] since it helped him to reconcile the Christian and Buddhist strands
of his spirituality.

In the more traditional society that existed in Ireland until the 1960s,
institutional religion provided satisfactory answers to many of the spiritual
questions pertaining to the meaning of life and to what, if anything, lies
beyond this worldly existence. A simple faith nourished by religious rituals
was cultivated in a climate where deference was instilled and individualism
was regarded as dishonouring God and capitulating to the sin of pride.
Viewed in this context, it is understandable that the earlier autobiographers
discussed in this chapter were scarcely exercised by fundamental issues of
faith and doubt, or if they were they did not see fit to write about them. The
growth of more secular mindsets, combined with the collapse of belief in the
authority of institutional religion, especially Catholicism, has meant that
recent generations of Irish spiritual autobiographers have been writing in
radically changed circumstances. Paradoxically, however, the rise of religious
scepticism seems to have fuelled rather than quenched a desire for spiritual
wholeness and self-knowledge, and led many to seek answers in Eastern
religions and in the practice of meditation, as evidenced by several of the
autobiographies discussed above. If in these works self-exploration becomes
the central preoccupation of the narrative, taking the protagonists to various
destinations via circuitous routes, it also reveals that Irish spiritual autobiographers' search for ultimate truths is no longer necessarily premised on a
relationship with a divine being or a belief in the hereafter.

Further reading

Barbour, John. D. 'Spiritual Autobiography', in Margaretta Jolly, ed., *The
Encyclopedia of Life Writing: Autobiographical and Biographical Forms*.
London: Fitzroy Dearborn, 2001. Vol. 2: 835–37.

[50] William Johnston, *Mystical Journey: An Autobiography* (New York: Orbis Books, 2006), 140.

Fuller, Louise. *Irish Catholicism since 1950: The Undoing of a Culture.* Dublin: Gill and Macmillan, 2002.

Grubgeld, Elizabeth. *Anglo-Irish Autobiography: Class, Gender, and the Forms of Narrative.* Syracuse: Syracuse University Press, 2004.

Harte, Liam, ed. *Modern Irish Autobiography: Self, Nation and Society.* Basingstoke: Palgrave Macmillan, 2007.

Hutch, Richard A. *The Meaning of Lives: Biography, Autobiography, and the Spiritual Quest.* London: Cassell, 1997.

Kort, Wesley A. *Textual Intimacy: Autobiography and Religious Identities.* Charlottesville: University of Virginia Press, 2012.

CHAPTER 7

Irish Political Autobiography from Wolfe Tone to Ernie O'Malley

Matthew Kelly

If Irish nationalist autobiography written under the Union had a genesis, it would be the posthumous publication of Theobald Wolfe Tone's memoir by his son William in 1826. Written in Paris and dated 7 August 1796, Tone's prompt to write was the decision of the revolutionary government of France to send a fleet under General Hoche to aid a United Irish rising. With death or imprisonment likely, Tone took the opportunity 'to throw on paper a few memorandums relative to myself and my family, which may amuse my boys, for whom I write them, in case they should hereafter fall into their hands'.[1] Writing surely helped to fill the anxious time before departure – one purpose of his memoir – and his nervousness perhaps accounts for his relentless *joie de vivre* and frank approach to the less commendable aspects of his past. On this occasion, however, he escaped a nasty end, bad weather ensuring the fleet made an ignominious return to France. As his voluminous journals show, Tone's continued lobbying helped to ensure the mission was repeated in 1798, this time with more success, but his memoir was to be denied a straightforwardly heroic addendum.

Tone's memoir eschewed a simple conversion narrative and emphasized his temperament and the 'spirit of adventure' characteristic of his family; his 'dash of coxcombry' and 'the true vagrant turn of the family' were made of a piece with his attempt to sail with the East India Company or become a Whig member of parliament.[2] All were preferable to studying law and pursuing a career at the bar. Dallying with the Whigs, though, taught Tone that 'the influence of England was the radical vice of our government', and an argument about their merit established his friendship with Thomas Russell, a man he loved 'as a brother' and his

---

[1] Theobald Wolfe Tone, *Life of Theobald Wolfe Tone*, ed. Thomas Bartlett (Dublin: Lilliput Press, 1998), 11.
[2] Ibid., 14.

closest comrade in the United Irishmen.[3] Despite this, in the summer of 1790 they were most preoccupied by their plan for the colonization of the Sandwich Islands, which they presented to Lord Grenville, secretary of state for foreign affairs. Tone apparently saw no contradiction between this scheme and his developing republican separatism, though he admitted the absence of ministerial encouragement prompted his decisive swing towards radical politics.

Pique, then, can be instrumental, but so too can friendship, and by tracing the evolution of the band of brothers that eventually cohered as the United Irish leadership, Tone produced a text fashioned according to eighteenth-century tropes of sentiment and sociability. This growing fraternity was catalysed by the French Revolution, the source of its idealism, which Tone argued was made meaningful in Ireland by the 'controversy'[4] between Edmund Burke and Thomas Paine over the relationship between the individual and the state. Henceforth Ireland, awakened from its 'lethargy', was divided 'into two great parties, the Aristocrats and the Democrats'.[5] Political activism – as distinct from the routines of conventional politics – was now a viable occupation for a principled young man seeking purpose but unable to overcome his congenital allergy to conventional bourgeois life. Faced with the concomitant rise of a radical Catholic politics, Tone's charisma and wider abilities saw him win through as the salaried agent of the United Irishmen; his memoir can therefore be read as an account of the challenges Ireland posed a Presbyterian man of talent alienated from the Anglican establishment.

Much nationalist autobiographical writing traced a comparable realization of purpose, though it tended to be written in the aftermath of an event and sometimes functioned as a reckoning for one of the parties involved. For example, after the failed 1848 rebellion of the Young Irelanders, John Mitchel and Charles Gavan Duffy used autobiographical writing to attribute responsibility and address fundamental questions of political principle and morality. Moreover, the Toneite notion that Ireland's state of political wakefulness determined the prospects of the individual found its cognate in later texts – not that political purpose was necessarily found through the revolutionary sublime. T. P. O'Connor described the satisfaction he derived from steady work as a Home Rule MP at Westminster; Duffy eventually found the same, though in Australia rather than London. If this contrast suggests much about changing political contexts, their respective autobiographical writings are also a warning against reductive

[3] Ibid., 30, 32.   [4] Ibid., 39.   [5] Ibid.

or strongly structural explanations. Personality and temperament matter too. Where Duffy found that the rigour of parliamentary life exposed his frailty, O'Connor discovered unknown reserves of strength and stamina.

By sparing nineteenth-century readers the salacious detail that gives Tone's memoir its racy riskiness, William Tone produced a less opportunistic account of his father's political awakening. Later nationalists were more pious still, originating their nationalist commitments in genealogy and upbringing and linking them to a sense of place and belonging. Decisive roles are often projected onto a charismatic elderly relative or family friend who taught the subject to see the Irish landscape as the locus of the appropriation and dispossession of Catholic Ireland by Protestant England. Others encountered the Irish landscape from a position of privileged externality, bringing either a romantic or an ethnographic perspective to bear on it. How the subject situated himself (the genre is male-dominated) in relation to 'the people' of Ireland and their geographies says much about how social class shaped perceptions of the national community. What follows, then, is a broadly chronological encounter with some key autobiographical writings by Irish nationalists during the long nineteenth century. It is by no means a complete anatomy, but by elaborating on the themes touched on in this introduction, this chapter explores some of the ways in which nationalists represented themselves in a literary form that is often gesturally self-effacing but purposefully egocentric. A wariness of the siren call of the textual self, with its apparent order and stability, should be maintained, therefore, just as the fictitious quality of autobiographical writing should not be mistaken for fiction.

Michael Donaghy, John Mitchel and Charles Gavan Duffy

In his preface to the 1914 edition of Michael Doheny's *The Felon's Track* (1849), Arthur Griffith described the book as having 'morals deducible for all manner of Irishmen, and one for those English statesmen who comfort themselves with the illusion that Irish Nationalism, like Jacobitism, is a platonic sentiment'.[6] Doheny was a middle-aged barrister of humble background whose 'social anchorages were deep-cast'.[7] Under the influence of Thomas Davis he rejected O'Connellism, became a Young Irelander and was roused to rebellion by John Mitchel's short-lived but

---

[6] Michael Doheny, *The Felon's Track or History of the Attempted Outbreak in Ireland Embracing the Leading Events in the Irish Struggle from the year 1843 to the close of 1848* (Dublin: M. H. Gill and Son, 1914), vii.

[7] Ibid.

highly combustible weekly newspaper, the *United Irishman*. To Griffith, the lesson Doheny taught the British was clear enough. The Irish, including the beneficiaries of the status quo, would not remain supine forever. Doheny did indeed find Mitchel the avatar of the age, giving voice to the 'fire' that burned 'at the bases of man's social hopes throughout Europe',[8] but the trigger for action came not from within the Young Ireland movement but the government's suspension of Habeas Corpus in July 1848. As Doheny later told it, his overnight journey to join the political leadership in Carrick-on-Suir, Co. Tipperary proved transformative, granting his life a singular purpose: concentrated in the revolutionary action to come was an absolute response to centuries of English tyranny.[9] Romantic reverie soon gave way to a reality of disorder and confusion; the inspiring courage of the rebels was no match for the restraining influence of the priests and the gathered crowds soon dispersed. Blaming the priests was *de rigueur* for radical nationalist memoir. Doheny's account of being on the run with Fenian leader James Stephens now becomes fully fledged romance, emphasizing the felt liberty brought by free movement through the landscape.

In this way, Doheny comes to know Ireland and his text develops into a prosy display of topographical description that emphasizes the solace found in natural beauty. If tension and exhaustion heighten Doheny's sensibilities, he is also aware of how his engagement with rural Ireland is part of a broader cultural phenomenon. Posing as travellers 'engaged in sketching the enchanting views in the neighbourhood',[10] the two fugitives go out of their way to see famously beautiful sites and take their cues from fashionable poetry. Above all, Doheny the fugitive experiences a novel sense of freedom. The proximity of police barracks prevents him from kissing the Blarney Stone or feeling entirely at ease while exploring Killarney's lakes, but the elemental need to survive and the uncertainty of the future means that he lives free of the usual constraints. Experiencing with Stephens 'these picturesque scenes in intense delight; the more so because there seemed no limit to our journey, and no definite aim to which our efforts led', Doheny concludes that 'we have learned to lose all consciousness of our own fate in contemplating lines of beauty'.[11]

Sensibility did not, however, preclude sense, and Doheny thought the vast bog between Killarney and Kenmare seemed 'quite susceptible of reclamation and improvement'.[12] This is a striking observation, for despite the Mitchelite inflection of Doheny's politics, the Famine barely impinges

---

[8] Ibid., 127.   [9] Ibid., 159–60.   [10] Ibid., 222.   [11] Ibid., 231, 241.   [12] Ibid., 246.

on his account of the journey. Skibbereen is a 'doomed district' and a scathing reference is made to the 'heartless experiments' of the Board of Works, but the author's unawareness of the suffering around him is revealed by his noting the 'kindest attention' they received everywhere, 'frequently finding a rude mountain cabin furnished with excellent beds and every delicacy'.[13] The distancing mechanisms of Doheny's romanticism are thrown into sharp relief when, en route to France disguised as a priest, he grumbles about having to travel in a third-class railway carriage.[14]

If *The Felon's Track*, to follow Wordsworth, describes 'emotion recollected in tranquillity', John Mitchel's iconic *Jail Journal; or, Five Years in British Prisons* (1854) is immediate and abrasive. His experience as a convicted treason-felon is shaped both by his class status and the special kind of freedom he felt at being honestly situated in relation to British power. Kept away from the common criminals also facing transportation, Mitchel writes exultantly of his first night in his cockroach-infested cabin on board the HMS Scourge: 'Here goes, then, for my first swing in the hammock – and I feel myself a freer man to-night than any Irishman living at large, tranquilly in his native land, making believe that he fancies himself a respectable member of society.'[15] *Jail Journal*, with its shifting moods and tangents, is the product of a restless mind, but whereas Doheny's writing is derivative, Mitchel's, despite its Carlylean cadences, retains its individuality. The hallucinogenic energy that drives the dialogue between Ego and Doppelgänger, exploring the arguments for and against revolution, remains compelling, while the range of allusion and reference points to wide reading. But it is as *the* seminal intervention in the Young Ireland 'autobiography wars' and, in particular, as an assault on the character and integrity of Charles Gavan Duffy, that *Jail Journal* will be read here. Duffy had an extraordinarily successful career, as his own autobiography would make clear, but in the 1880s and 1890s Mitchel's criticisms still stung.

Jail Journal suggests that Mitchel witnessed Duffy's brief imprisonment, trial and rehabilitation through newspapers that occasionally came his way. In this mediated way, his former friend's good fortune undermined the phlegmatic attitude he took towards his own captivity and increased the animus he felt for the *Nation* and what he now saw as its innate conservatism. He felt the 'Lefayette-Lamartinists' had represented 'me and the like of me' as 'wild montagnards',[16] and he was particularly

---

[13] Ibid., 231, 258, 252, 256.   [14] Ibid., 274.
[15] John Mitchel, *Jail Journal; or, Five Years in British Prisons* (New York: W. H. Tinson, 1854), 63.
[16] Ibid., 31.

enraged by Duffy's condescension and riled by his apparent incapacity to recognize the influence at his disposal and overcome his need to be thought respectable. Believing the trial was an opportunity to summon the Irish people to action, Mitchel found Duffy's appeal for clemency, his attempt to distance himself from the *Nation*'s most radical journalism and the emphasis placed on his good character by high-profile witnesses a betrayal of the wider political movement. 'The cause is not desperate', raged Mitchel, 'and it is both base and impudent to say, to mean, to think, or to hint that it is.'[17] Duffy's post-Famine *Nation* was thus condemned for advocating the growth of 'individually independent, energetic, and truthful men (under British rule)', who in time, 'after stern self-examination', would decide they were 'fit to manage their own affairs' and then 'dissolve the Union'.[18]

Duffy's bourgeois individualism meant that he did not believe Ireland had a right to self-determination, but would become self-governing when Ireland had been re-made in the image of himself. That was Mitchel's view. Duffy, by contrast, pitched his attempt to revivify Irish nationalist politics through a reformist parliamentary agenda as a pragmatic response to the realities of post-Famine politics. Despite Mitchel's notorious condemnation of the Famine as an act of English genocide, he did not witness its devastating consequences for the Irish public sphere. Duffy thought there could be no effective Irish nationalism until Irish public opinion was regenerated and he found absurd Mitchel's Carlylean belief that revolutions were essentially spontaneous responses to the peculiar alchemy of a given moment.

Duffy explained his political decisions, critiquing Mitchel along the way, in *My Life in Two Hemispheres* (1898), the most formidable autobiography written by an Irish nationalist during the nineteenth century. It adheres closely to the conventions of the genre, beginning with a description of his family's origins and offering a chronological account of its protagonist's activities up until his retirement. A chief theme is the principled consistency of Duffy's behaviour from his time as editor of the *Nation* in the 1840s to his retirement from active politics in 1880. He explains that he had aspired 'to be a statesman, and ... it would be strangely unjust to reproach me with not being a demagogue, a career which was odious and impossible for me'.[19] Mitchel's critique was thus based on a fundamental misreading of Duffy's political purposes. Duffy

---

[17] Ibid., 163. [18] Ibid., 221.
[19] Charles Gavan Duffy, *My Life in Two Hemispheres* (London: T. Fisher Unwin, 1898), vol. I, 245.

came from a propertied Catholic family in largely Protestant Monaghan. He writes of his 'ardent'[20] youth, the nationalist sentiment he picked up at home, and his experience as the only Catholic boy in a classical academy, where he was soon accepted by the other boys and befriended Terence Bellew MacManus. His was an upbringing in which Orange Order processions 'forbade us to forget the past',[21] survivors of the 1798 rebellion filled his head with stories and a Quaker neighbour and a Catholic curate taught him to think of the Irish question as less a matter of kings and governments than of land and the fundamental fact of Catholic dispossession. Entering the world of Dublin journalism aged twenty, Duffy was disillusioned to discover that 'public life was a stage play, where a man gesticulated and perorated according as his *rôle* was cast by his stage manager'.[22] He found Daniel O'Connell, whom he was 'ready to venerate and obey',[23] disappointing, which primed him for a fateful encounter with Thomas Davis and the offer of the editorship of the *Nation*.

Duffy attributed Mitchel's radicalization to the influence of James Fintan Lalor's radical agrarianism, but his fate to his untrammelled egoism; whereas Lalor 'had singularly sound judgement',[24] Mitchel was too arrogant to take advice. Delineating the contours of their dispute, Duffy presented his case for a politics based on fixed principles and a carefully worked out policy. In particular, he argued that parliamentary politics provided the only available platform from which the Irish case would be heard by the whole of Europe. Writing in the 1890s, with the parliamentary agitation of the Home Rule Party in mind, Duffy felt vindicated, arguing that his experience of the present justified his position in the past. Still, he conceded that the French Revolution of 1848 left the Irish Confederation with 'no honourable choice'[25] but to seek Irish unity and fight. Despite this, Duffy insisted that the *Nation* had been 'a National, not a Jacobin journal'[26] that aimed to bring about Irish liberty rather than – *pace* Lalor – foment class war.

Thus, Duffy used the autobiographical form to establish the ideological coherence and consistency of his position in a period of rapid political change. By this reading, the moderate stance of the post-Famine *Nation* represented not a break with the past but the adaptation of long-established principles to unpropitious circumstances. The failure of the Independent Irish Party at Westminster in the 1850s and the infamy of John Sadleir and William Keogh are well known, and Duffy left Ireland for Australia in 1856

[20] Ibid., 5.   [21] Ibid., 13.   [22] Ibid., 27.   [23] Ibid., 29.   [24] Ibid., 247.   [25] Ibid., 258.
[26] Ibid., 272.

because, he explained, it had become unendurable now he 'could no longer promise the suffering people relief, and to witness injustice without curb and wrong without remedy would render life too painful'.[27] Australia was appealing because 'the reformers of Victoria had won for their colony'[28] self-government, although Duffy insisted he emigrated with the intention of pursuing a career at the bar rather than in politics. That resolve, he wrote, was undermined by the enthusiastic welcome he received from the political opposition and the hopes its members had placed in him. At a public banquet held in his honour Duffy insisted that he remained an Irish rebel but was ready to work as an Australian citizen, this being a country 'where no nationality need stand on the defensive, for there was fair play for all'.[29] His autobiography turns on this speech, signalling the transition of a life from insecurity and disorder to one of focus and sustained application.

The remainder of *My Life in Two Hemispheres* traces Duffy's gradual elevation to the position of prime minister of Victoria and his legitimate exercise of executive power within the confines of the constitution. This served to expose the qualitative difference between the politics of the agitator, whether as a journalist, activist or parliamentarian, and what a man of talent and determination could achieve within liberal political structures that allowed him to exercise his abilities according to their merit. For Duffy, leaving Ireland was akin to escaping the disorder of a dysfunctional family. When the time came to retire, he could do so with a sense of achievement and yet with little sentimental attachment to his adopted country. It cannot have been gratifying to return to an Ireland where he was still defined by decisions made during a few fraught months in 1848.

The recollections of Fenians and Home Rulers

Autobiography wars were not so characteristic of the glut of Fenian memoirs published around the turn of the twentieth century. New advanced nationalist newspapers and publishing enterprises created fresh opportunities for the expression of personal and political views, while young activists, disillusioned by the politics of Home Rule, provided a new readership. Autobiographical writing that we read in book form today often began life as newspaper serial instalments. Examples

---

[27] Charles Gavan Duffy, *My Life in Two Hemispheres* (London: T. Fisher Unwin, 1898), vol. II, 106.
[28] Ibid., 132–33.   [29] Ibid., 133.

include the autobiographies of John Daly and Tom Clarke, both of whom
wrote for *Irish Freedom*, the newspaper of the revived Irish Republican
Brotherhood. John O'Leary's *Recollections of Fenians and Fenianism* (1896)
and Jeremiah O'Donovan Rossa's *Recollections: 1838–1898* (1898), both
published at a time when the divided Home Rule Party was losing political
traction, were particularly prominent examples of the genre. The fact that
Rossa's memoirs, which were serialized in Griffith's *United Irishman*, do
not cover his prison experiences between 1865 and 1871 – for these, the
reader must consult his *Six Years in English Prisons* (1874) – gives the
Recollections a somewhat sanitized quality; the reputation of the work
probably owes more to Patrick Pearse's famous graveside oration of 1913
than to the text itself. By contrast, the reputation of O'Leary's autobiography, the tone of which is indebted to that of Wolfe Tone, has never
recovered from the faint praise offered by W. B. Yeats, who expected a
seminal text of the Irish Literary Revival but instead found something 'dry,
abstract, and confused'.[30] O'Leary's prose style was indeed convoluted, but
it was his deflating mien that made his textual self distinct.

Land is the dominant preoccupation in Rossa's *Recollections* and he
reverts repeatedly to Catholic genealogies, the historic dispossession of
Catholic landholders and the consequent dispersal of families. In Rossa's
Ireland, the English had undermined the fundamental link between people, place and culture, which weakened the Irish language and strained to
breaking point the links of kith and kin. These narratives of forcible
dispossession and migration are thrown into sharp relief by his account
of his rural upbringing in Co. Cork, which offers an idyllic portrait of
rootedness in a dairy farm, of family life conducted through the Irish
language and of the power of the oral storytelling tradition to nurture
national identity. In what can be read as a metaphor for attachment, Rossa
writes with frank intimacy of how he was breastfed until he was three and
was unhappy to be weaned, of how his tongue carried 'the Irish language
without any strain' and of how the battle of New Ross in 1798 'was a
fireside story in every home around me when I was a boy'.[31] Although there
are parallels here with Duffy's account of his childhood, Rossa's politics
were Mitchelite: there had been no Famine in Ireland but the 'plunder of
the Irish people by the English Government of Ireland'.[32]

---

[30] W. B. Yeats, *Autobiographies* (London: Macmillan, 1955), 212.
[31] Jeremiah O'Donovan Rossa, *Rossa's Recollections: 1838–1898* (New York: Mariner's Harbor, 1898), 9,
   10, 46.
[32] Ibid., 36.

Most remarkable is Rossa's acute sense of Ireland as an appropriated space. For example, he draws our attention to the walls that surrounded the estates and homes of the Anglo-Irish Ascendancy, built after 'the English came into Ireland', and to the deliberate destruction of the Irish language, 'because wherever the language is spoken it gives the name and ownership of the castle to the old Irish owner of it'.[33] Jumping from the politics of his youth to the politics of the present, he argues that there could be no Home Rule without the comprehensive overthrow of this English landlordism. Thus, Rossa contextualizes his role as the sponsor of a grassroots revolutionary politics that was at odds with Duffy's rigorous constitutionalism, but which he believed would achieve what Duffy's methods could not. Fenianism killed the 'spirit of faction-fighting', unified the lower-class men of Ireland and reanimated a nation 'stricken by a kind of tromluighe – a kind of "heavy-sleep" that came upon it after the failure of '48'.[34] Yet despite its sombre subject, Rossa's is also a knowingly playful text. He jokes about the vanity of revolutionaries who thought they were as fitted to free Ireland as they were irresistible to women and mischievously blames English 'tyranny' for the extermination of the fairies, as well as the people, of Ireland.[35]

O'Leary attributes his political awakening to the writings of Thomas Davis; by the 1890s he could only vaguely remember his previously 'unregenerate state'.[36] Although 'Davis was the *Nation* and the *Nation* was Davis', O'Leary nonetheless describes himself as a 'Mitchelite before Mitchel', which somewhat contradicts his more Duffyite reflection that 'Irishmen ... found words far too readily, and were too often not sufficiently careful to lay any foundation of facts or ideas at the bottom of the words'.[37] As an editor of the *Irish People*, O'Leary developed an unforgiving approach to the nationalist doggerel submitted for publication, an attitude that is consistent with his characteristically deflationary remarks on the minor role he played in 1848: 'Here I have to relate what I may call my first escapade, and no doubt a very foolish escapade it must seem to the present preternaturally practical race of Irish politicians.'[38] Despite the tonal difference, O'Leary, like Mitchel, does not apologize for his youthful ardour, though there is more weariness than stridency in his description of his '"storm and stress" period': 'my whole mental and moral nature had been shaken from its very depths, and such thoughts and feelings awakened

---

[33] Ibid., 75.   [34] Ibid., 207, 147.   [35] Ibid., 14–15.
[36] John O'Leary, *Recollections of Fenians and Fenianism* (London: Downey and Co., 1896), vol. I, 3.
[37] Ibid., 4–6.   [38] Ibid., 18.

in me as have never slept since, and are little likely to slumber now until they and I find final rest which soon or late comes to all'.[39] So his autobiography continues over two querulous volumes.

Although Rossa complained that almost every Fenian became a Parnellite, he did not offer a satisfactory account of the transition, attributing it to the manipulative politics of 'the Gladstones', generic liberals to whom the Irish were ruinously susceptible. In this regard, A. M. Sullivan's *New Ireland* (1877), an account of post-Famine Irish politics, is more suggestive, both as a history and as an indirect exercise in autobiography. Sullivan sought to chronicle, 'chiefly from personal observations', a period of 'startling transformations', which begins with a sentimental account of the customs and the people of his childhood on Ireland's western seaboard.[40] If Rossa saw in the passing of the old ways the destruction of rooted communities, Sullivan's account of Irish emigration prefaces a more Whiggish tale of progress, which culminates in the prospect of a dynamic Home Rule movement resolving the dialectical tensions within Irish nationalism. His sense that Ireland stands on the brink of seismic change reflects how his seminal political experiences were less the failures of revolution than the gradual dismantling of the Anglo-Irish Ascendancy through progressive Liberal legislation and the opening up of the political sphere to upwardly mobile Catholics like himself.

The Home Rule campaign generated a strong biographical tradition, most notably exemplified by R. Barry O'Brien's *Life of Parnell* (1898) and Stephen Gwynn's *John Redmond's Last Years* (1919), but there was also some significant autobiographical writing. Michael Davitt's *The Fall of Feudalism in Ireland* (1906) and Anna Parnell's *The Tale of a Great Sham* (written in 1907 but not published until 1986) offered personal accounts of the Home Rule Party's edgy relationship with radicalism, particularly radical agrarianism and the conflict over how the Land War was brought to an end in 1882. This might have developed into an autobiography war had Parnell found a publisher and Davitt not died in 1907. Also notable were William O'Brien's extensive personal-historical accounts of political campaigns he orchestrated – his *Recollections* (1905) was followed by a 'continuation' volume, *Evening Memories*, in 1920 – and the manuscript autobiography, since published in an abridged form, by Alfred Webb, the Quaker Home Ruler.[41] T. P. O'Connor's avuncular *Memoirs of an Old*

[39] Ibid., 44.
[40] A. M. Sullivan, *New Ireland* (London: Sampson Low, Marston, Searle and Rivington, 1877), iii, 1.
[41] Alfred Webb, *Alfred Webb: The Autobiography of a Quaker Nationalist*, ed., Marie-Louise Legg (Cork: Cork University Press, 1999).

Parliamentarian (1929), the most substantial of these writings, opens with the caveat that it is 'not an autobiography' but an account of the 'personalities and incidents' of his parliamentary life.[42] Key sections are nonetheless concerned with his own psychology and inner life; he describes, for example, how he unexpectedly overcame his 'lack of push, initiative and self-confidence', which reflected the 'inferiority complex' that 'is part of the inner temperament' of every Irishman.[43] O'Connor was selected to contend Galway Borough and then, in 1885, Liverpool Scotland, the only British constituency likely to return a Home Rule MP. He sat in the House of Commons for forty-nine years, eventually becoming father of the House. Here too another talented Irishman found purpose.

Maud Gonne MacBride and Margaret Skinnider

For the most prominent woman nationalist activist of her generation, the challenge was less to find purpose than to find a place in an overwhelmingly male tradition of revolutionary endeavour. Maud Gonne MacBride's *A Servant to the Queen* (1938) offers an ebullient, if somewhat egomaniacal, account of this challenge. In it, she took her story to the beginning of her disastrous marriage to John MacBride in 1903, a narrative decision that marks the consummation of a trajectory that began with Gonne's break with her Anglo-Irish background, her fervent embrace of separatist nationalism and Catholicism and her instrumental role in the foundation of Inghinidhe na hÉireann ('Daughters of Ireland'). Hers is a busy telling of the story, a ricocheting between accounts of life as a debutant, an agrarian activist, an occultist, a fund-raising lecturer in the USA and an advanced nationalist activist in Dublin, as well as recollections of semi-domesticity in London and France. This was not a milieu restricted by rigid political boundaries, or at least not for a woman of Gonne's compelling personality and class status. In the politically fluid 1890s and early 1900s, separatists, Home Rulers and agrarian activists alike were happy to have her on their platform. Timothy Harrington, the Dublin Home Rule MP, plays a notably large role in her story, as do the Catholic priests who acted as her guides in the west of Ireland, exposing her to the harrowing eviction scenes that provided the moral foundation of her activist interventions in Dublin.

---

[42] T. P. O'Connor, *Memoirs of an Old Parliamentarian* (London: Ernest Benn, 1929), vol. 1, 1.
[43] Ibid., 3, 6–7.

Her moral suasion swung an election for the Home Rulers and won a victory for the tenants in a nasty agrarian struggle, or so she claimed. She thought her striking appearance – a combination of height and beauty – helped to cow male officials, endear her to the crowd and transform her into an almost mythic figure to the peasantry (in one instance she was taken to fulfil a prophecy of deliverance). Yet her account, which could be characterized as feminist but not forcefully so, is also peppered with references to the various organizations that excluded her because she was a woman. Her retort on being refused membership of the National League – '"How strange," . . . "Surely Ireland needs all her children"'[44] – probably recalls not an actual conversation but rather intentionally invokes the 1916 Proclamation.

Yeats complained that Gonne's autobiography revealed a 'remarkable intellect at the service of the will, no will at the service of the intellect'.[45] She herself confessed that she had 'never indulged in self-analysis' and was prone to focus obsessively on a single activity, which at times meant she lost a 'sense of proportion'.[46] Friends and enemies might have agreed. Yeats, who was in her eyes 'terribly introspective', failed to persuade her to be more so, but Gonne airily says she relied on 'the spiritual force of Ireland' to guide her actions, thereby neatly bypassing any need for personal or moral responsibility.[47] 'I never willingly discouraged either a Dynamiter or a constitutionalist, a realist or a lyrical writer', she writes. 'My chief preoccupation was how their work could help forward the Irish Separatist movement.'[48] Given how central Gonne was to Yeats's telling of his own story, particularly in the 1890s, it is striking just how marginal he is to hers. O'Leary, Harrington, Lucien Millevoye (her lover, father of her daughter and French rightist) and several others are all more prominent, not least Griffith, with whom she seemingly enjoyed a strong mutual affinity. This self-definitional urge comes into particular focus when she is recalling her theological discussions with Canon Dissard, a Bonapartist French nationalist who eased her path into the Catholic church and approved of her decision to marry MacBride. Dissard was external to her Dublin world and the recitation of their discussions provides the only calm and intellectually focused passage in the book. Her conversion complete, she presents her decision to marry MacBride as a joyful moment of defiance and the fulfilment of

---

[44] Maud Gonne MacBride, *A Servant of the Queen* (Gerrards Cross: Colin Smythe, 1994), 95.
[45] R. F. Foster, *W. B. Yeats: A Life, II: The Arch-Poet 1915–1939* (Oxford: Oxford University Press, 2003), 640.
[46] Gonne MacBride, *A Servant of the Queen*, 287.   [47] Ibid.   [48] Ibid., 178.

her duty to Cathleen ni Houlihan, the queen she served. Gonne and MacBride had an acrimonious separation and he faced the firing squad in 1916, but for all that was said and done, Gonne kept faith with the political symbolism of that moment.

Margaret Skinnider's *Doing My Bit for Ireland* (1917) is a hastily written account of her role in the 1916 Easter Rising. Written for an Irish-American audience, she too blends the personal and the political, describing in particular the activism of Constance Markievicz and James Connolly, the development of the Irish Citizen Army and Fianna Éireann (the republican boy scout movement) and her wounding during the Rising. British atrocities in Ireland feature prominently in her narrative and are judged to be worse than the German atrocities in Belgium that were used to mobilize Irish support for the war effort. Skinnider's activities were less wide-ranging than Gonne's, but her account is similarly frenetic – revolution was something of a lark – and conveys a callous attitude towards shooting the enemy or, indeed, a Dublin worker: 'One drayman refused his cart and persisted in his refusal, not believing it when our men told him this was war. He was shot.'[49] She goes on to admit she was more affected by the death of a military horse than that of a British soldier.[50]

Skinnider's brusque attitude towards the necessity of killing might be read as an over-compensation for the wariness with which women were accepted as nationalist fighters. She was conscious of the unique status afforded Markievicz within the Irish Citizen Army and she convinced commandant Michael Mallin that the 1916 Proclamation proved women 'had the same right to risk'[51] their lives as the men. Her reward was the most serious injury suffered by a woman during the rebellion. Gender inflects Skinnider's text in other ways too. If Gonne's status as a woman brought her attention and influence, Skinnider's allowed her a useful anonymity, particularly as a messenger, a contemporaneous photograph confirming that she could pass as a boy and could play the part 'even if it came to wrestling or whistling'.[52] The significance of such gender mimicry is perhaps undermined by the emphasis Skinnider places on the military bearing of the men, but her text nonetheless suggests revolutionary activism was attractive to some women because it permitted unorthodox modes of behaviour.

---

[49] Margaret Skinnider, *Doing My Bit for Ireland* (New York: The Century Co., 1917), 105.
[50] Ibid., 109.   [51] Ibid., 143.   [52] Ibid., 120.

Ernie O'Malley

Wolfe Tone committed suicide in his cell in November 1798, whereas all the other autobiographers discussed in this chapter died of natural causes. The same was true of Ernie O'Malley, an IRA activist in the War of Independence and an Irregular during the Irish Civil War. During his long post-revolutionary life, O'Malley remained preoccupied by his formative experiences, collecting the testimony of his former comrades and writing his own autobiographies. The most notable of these is *On Another Man's Wound* (1936), a chronicle of his revolutionary experiences and a work of conscious literary ambition. It is divided into three parts. 'Flamboyant' tells of O'Malley's conversion to advanced nationalism in response to the Easter Rising; 'Gothic' details his role as a senior IRA officer organizing forces in rural Ireland; and 'Romanesque' recounts his experiences as a prisoner of the British in the latter months of the Irish revolution.

The Rising provoked in O'Malley contradictory feelings. As a middle-class youth, he felt 'irritation at those fellows for doing the unexpected'[53] – these were men and women his upbringing had taught him to underestimate – but this feeling soon gave way to anger that the British were fighting his fellow Irishmen on the streets of Dublin. Focused purpose only came after 1919 when he joined the IRA and was tasked with travelling throughout the country to organize volunteers, teach the rudiments of military planning and dodge arrest. O'Malley thus came to know the landscapes and people of Ireland from the saddle of his bicycle. He found the country 'strange', realizing how 'very sheltered' his home life had been, but he soon came to know individuals who were almost always poorer, less educated and less refined than himself.[54] This most cerebral and bookish of revolutionaries remained most at ease with men and women of his own class, such that *On Another Man's Wound* is in some respects closer to an ethnographical text like J. M. Synge's *The Aran Islands* (1906) than to populist autobiographical accounts of the revolution, such as Dan Breen's *My Fight for Irish Freedom* (1924) and Tom Barry's *Guerrilla Days in Ireland* (1949). O'Malley represents his revolutionary experience as shaped by instinctive kindnesses, transnational class affinities, ethnicized loyalties and hatreds and the intimacies of physical violence. A characteristic insight is his claim that the IRA depended 'on personality, understanding and intimate or intuitive knowledge', whereas the British were

---

[53] Ernie O'Malley, *On Another Man's Wound* (Dublin: Anvil Books, 2002), 39, 43.   [54] Ibid., 134.

'an automaton which spoke a regulation voice and was dehumanized'.[55] Confronted with 'a movement of the people' which they could not 'hit at with organized force', the British 'mask of assurance and arrogance'[56] began to slip. As the revolutionaries found purpose, so the British seemed to lose theirs.

As O'Malley came to know the Irish people, so he came to know Ireland. His writing expresses an environmental determinism – the country's varying topography has shaped the characters of its inhabitants – and he found the landscape to be a palimpsest inscribed with Ireland's pasts. When 'despondent' he 'mucked through', knowing his path was that 'of many another trying to do what I was attempting'.[57] But more than this, O'Malley's ability to integrate a sense of place and purpose gives his autobiographical treatment of the Irish revolution its particular emotional and lyrical heft. In the bravura passages in chapter ten that form the centrepiece of *On Another Man's Wound*, O'Malley's deftly cinematic account of his journeying by bicycle through a countryside of changing seasons becomes a virtuoso exercise in impressionistic nature writing. O'Malley, however, was not locked into a solitary battle with nature; rather, he was deeply imbricated in the anthropic violence of the revolution:

> October with its lash in the air, the snap of frost made one feel extra strength and take deep virile breaths. On hardy nights I often fell from the bicycle trying to guide myself and look up at the crackling stars. Wet days when soft, gentle rain fell unnoticed until one realized that clothes had become sodden; stinging rain that whipped the face and stung, teeming on the land, but with a taut challenge that one accepted. Hands became blue on the handlebars, and it was hard to draw a gun quickly, gloves were in the way of a grip.[58]

Detonating this recollection reawakens the reader to O'Malley's revolutionary purpose. The affective detail takes us somewhere extra-textual, as good autobiographical writing, whatever its politics, always threatens to do.

Further reading

Comerford, R. V. *The Fenians in Context: Irish Politics and Society 1848–82*. Dublin: Wolfhound Press, 1998.

---

[55] Ibid., 287.   [56] Ibid.   [57] Ibid., 156.   [58] Ibid.

Elliott, Marianne. *Wolfe Tone*. Liverpool: Liverpool University Press, 2012, 2nd edn.

Flanagan, Frances. *Remembering the Irish Revolution: Dissent, Culture, and Nationalism in the Irish Free State*. Oxford: Oxford University Press, 2015.

Kelly, M. J. *The Fenian Ideal and Irish Nationalism, 1882–1916*. Woodbridge: Boydell Press, 2006.

Kinealy, Christine. *Repeal and Revolution: 1848 in Ireland*. Manchester: Manchester University Press, 2009.

Pašeta, Senia. *Irish Nationalist Women, 1800–1918*. Cambridge: Cambridge University Press, 2013.

CHAPTER 8

The Memoirs of Male Politicians in Independent Ireland

Eoin O'Malley and Kevin Rafter

The central goal of most autobiographies is to tell the story of a private life, thereby making it public. Political autobiographies differ in that readers are usually being invited to view what are essentially public lives from the inside. Political memoirists also differ from other autobiographers in that, at least in democratic societies, they are or have been elected public officials entrusted with the responsibility of making decisions on behalf of others, whether on a local, national or international level. Anyone who thinks themselves suited to such a role is likely to have an unusually elevated sense of their own judgement and worth, a factor that must be borne in mind when analysing political memoirs. Paradoxically, however, such egoism does not always translate into autobiographical candour. Indeed, the paucity of self-reflection in some so-called political autobiographies places a question mark over their generic status. George Egerton reminds us of the usefulness of Roy Pascal's distinction between autobiography, the focus of which is 'primarily inward, on the development of the self',[1] and memoir, which is oriented towards other people and external events. Judged by this measure, the life stories of many modern politicians are more accurately characterized as works of memoir rather than autobiography. But since the distinction is not watertight, and since most politicians describe their self-narratives as autobiographies, both terms will be used in the following discussion.

In most parts of Europe and North America, the writing of political memoir is a fairly commonplace activity. The importance of political life-writing as a public record is certainly recognized in Ireland's nearest cultural equivalent, the United Kingdom, where members of parliament are in agreement that 'there is a strong public interest in the publication of

---

[1] George Egerton, 'The Anatomy of Political Memoir: Findings and Conclusions', in George Egerton, ed., *Political Memoir: Essays on the Politics of Memory* (London: Frank Cass, 1994), 346.

political memoirs and diaries'.[2] This view is primarily influenced by a belief that these publications provide uniquely valuable insights into the operation of governmental systems, the lessons of political leadership, the processes of decision-making and the principles of statecraft. In Ireland, however, it is more commonplace to complain about the dearth of political memoirs. A number of reasons may explain the historical aversion of Irish politicians to autobiographical disclosure. First, given that the post-independence generation of leaders rarely elaborated in detail on their personal involvement in the violence that transformed Ireland after 1916, memoir writing would have been incompatible with their preference for self-imposed silence. Second, the principle of cabinet confidentiality may have influenced habits of secrecy that extended to memoir writing and caused some political actors to keep their counsel indefinitely so that government could continue to function effectively. Interestingly, in the British context, a 2006 Public Administration Select Committee report included the observation that

> There has to be a degree of confidentiality within government even in the relationship between politicians. Cabinet government would not be improved if those around the table were aware that any one or more of them was intending to publish their own account of Cabinet the moment the meeting had ended.[3]

Happily for our purposes, autobiographical reticence has not been universal among Irish politicians. In this chapter, we include in the category of political memoir not only works by elected public representatives but also those by officials and advisers in the political sphere. We can identify few such publications in the early years of the Irish state, though those that do exist were widely read, focusing as they do on the turbulent events that led to Ireland's independence in 1922. Among the most notable of these are Dan Breen's *My Fight for Irish Freedom* (1924), Ernie O'Malley's *On Another Man's Wound* (1936), Tom Barry's *Guerrilla Days in Ireland* (1949) and C. S. 'Todd' Andrews's *Dublin Made Me* (1979), all of which became bestsellers in their time. Joseph Connolly, in his posthumously published *The Memoirs of Senator Joseph Connolly* (1996), also wrote about the events of 1916, the War of Independence and the Civil War, as well as his membership of Fianna Fáil cabinets in the 1930s. Like

---

[2] House of Commons Public Administration Select Committee, *Whitehall Confidential? The Publication of Political Memoirs*, HC 689-I (London: HMSO, 2006). Available at www.publications.parliament.uk/pa/cm200506/cmselect/cmpubadm/689/68906.htm (accessed 15 April 2016).
[3] Ibid.

Andrews, Connolly provides a sense of the scale of the state-building challenges that confronted the first generation of independent politicians, though neither man was a senior government figure. It is striking that no member of the Cumann na nGaedheal governments of 1923–32 wrote an autobiography, nor did epoch-defining Fianna Fáil leaders Éamon de Valera or Seán Lemass or any of their senior ministers, though de Valera did commission an authorized biography, published in 1970. The closest Jack Lynch, Lemass's successor as Fianna Fáil leader and taoiseach (prime minister), got to a memoir was a 1979 magazine article.[4] Lynch's successor, Charles Haughey, considered writing an autobiography but later changed his mind, citing by way of justification Benjamin Disraeli's dictum, 'Never complain. Never explain.' All of which meant that we had to wait a full seven decades after independence for the first former taoiseach, Fine Gael's Garret FitzGerald, to publish a memoir, *All in a Life*, in 1991. Since then two other former prime ministers, Bertie Ahern and Albert Reynolds, have followed suit, and FitzGerald produced a second volume of recollections, *Just Garret*, in 2010.

There is, of course, no necessary correlation between political rank and literary quality. One of the best-written and most entertaining of Irish political memoirs (in part because the author never submitted to any urge to censor himself) is Noël Browne's *Against the Tide* (1986). This was possibly the first autobiography by an Irish politician to address the author's period in ministerial office, which in Browne's case covered the years from 1948 and 1951, when he served as minister for health in a coalition government led by John A. Costello. Browne was also unusual in that he was writing at a significant temporal remove from his tenure as minister and therefore from events historians had already formed opinions on, most particularly the so-called Mother and Child scheme, his highly contentious plans for subsidized state-funded medical care for mothers and their families. In his autobiography, Browne engages with the verdicts of commentators and historians and frequently rebuts their assertions, albeit by relying more on argument than evidence.

Later ministerial office-holders who have followed Browne's example include Ruairi Quinn and Desmond O'Malley, authors of *Straight Left* (2005) and *Conduct Unbecoming* (2014) respectively. Their books were accompanied into print by those of others who served as cabinet ministers in the late twentieth century, notably Conor Cruise O'Brien's *Memoir* (1998), Barry Desmond's *Finally and in Conclusion* (2000), Pádraig

---

[4] Jack Lynch, 'My Life and Times', *Magill*, November 1979, 33–51.

Faulkner's *As I Saw It* (2005) and Ivan Yates's *Full On* (2014). Recent years have also seen portraits of government appear in the form of Dan Boyle's *Without Power or Glory* (2012) and Eamon Gilmore's *Leading Lights* (2010) and *Inside the Room* (2015). A small corpus of memoirs by political advisers has also emerged: Seán Duignan's *One Spin on the Merry-Go-Round* (1996), Fergus Finlay's *Snakes and Ladders* (1998), Frank Dunlop's *Yes, Taoiseach* (2004) and John Walshe's *An Education* (2014). Even relatively obscure figures have begun to break silence, such as long-serving backbench Fianna Fáil TD John O'Leary, author of *On the Doorsteps* (2015), and party activist Johnny Fallon, whose *Party Time* (2006) narrates his upbringing in a politically active family. These works add to our understanding of the motivations and priorities of public representatives and advisers of varying political persuasions, abilities and achievements. What remains rare, however, is the perspective of the public official. We do have the testimonies of three civil servants who each headed a government department – T. K. Whitaker's *Interests* (1983), León Ó Broin's *Just Like Yesterday* (1986) and Kevin Cardiff's *Recap: Inside Ireland's Financial Crisis* (2016) – and the account of a junior diplomat – Eamon Delaney's *An Accidental Diplomat* (2001) – but these works vary in their level of analysis and personal insight.

While we sometimes complain that memoirists omit key events, their choice of what to include tells its own story. Political memoirs tend to follow a familiar narrative trajectory, which begins with the subject's family background and childhood recollections, then moves on to their entry into political life and experience of electoral politics, and culminates in their ministerial elevation and reflections on the challenges of holding governmental office. Policy formation and analysis rarely attract commensurate attention, probably because of the assumption that these topics would not interest readers. Most memoirs by politicians in the Republic have been penned by office holders and the overwhelming majority cover political careers since the 1960s, which means that certain themes recur, such as economic expansion and contraction, the Northern Ireland conflict and relations with the European Union. These memoirists tend to focus on their departmental duties and responsibilities, often to the detriment of wider political issues, even when the latter may have been more important to the overall governmental process. This narrow focus is evident from the earliest ministerial memoirs to the most recent. For example, Joseph Connolly provides a detailed recollection of his period in the Department of Lands and Forestry but has relatively little to say about other policies adopted by Fianna Fáil when it came to power in 1932. Similarly, Ivan Yates, who was minister for agriculture from 1994 to 1997, concentrates on developments in his portfolio, with only passing reference to the broader government agenda. Strikingly, neither Yates nor Ruairi Quinn devote any significant space to consideration of the situation in Northern Ireland after the Provisional IRA ceasefire ended in early 1996. These works illustrate one of the common features of the political memoir, the privileging of subjective perception over historical perspective.

If these post-1960 memoirists are not discussing wider government business, neither are they greatly concerned with happenings in the Dáil. That parochial concerns and internal party spats are afforded much more prominence than parliamentary affairs is exemplified by John O'Leary, whose memoir contains long accounts of candidate-selection conventions and internal Fianna Fáil power struggles in his Kerry constituency, as well as insights into the strategic thinking that informed his cultivation of a local power base, such as the following:

> I quickly realised that it was very important to get to know a key person in every parish in the constituency – the local postman. If they were Fianna Fáil members or supporters, the postmen would be of great benefit for feeding me local news and information from their areas ... [He] would know the handwriting and would be able to tell me if [a political rival] was writing to someone in particular.[5]

As one of the few autobiographies by a backbench Irish politician, O'Leary's work has the merit of illuminating issues that those at the centre cannot or will not acknowledge. His grassroots perspective provides a welcome contrast to that of the so-called 'big beasts' of the political jungle, not least because he harbours fewer illusions about his importance and, as a non-office holder, has less of a stake in presenting particular policies in a positive light. O'Leary's memoir also exemplifies the point that the analyses of political leaders offered by their lieutenants are often more incisive than the self-reflections of the leaders themselves.

Memoir, memory and motivation

A criticism that can reasonably be levelled at Irish political memoirs is that many comprise little more than a litany of events and personal anecdotes. Certainly, few match the scope and depth of some of the great British

---

[5] John O'Leary, *On the Doorsteps: Memoirs of a Long-Serving TD* (Killarney: Irish Political Memoirs, 2015), 127.

autobiographies of recent decades, such as those by Roy Jenkins, Denis Healy and Douglas Hurd. Only Garret FitzGerald and Conor Cruise O'Brien subject their lives in public politics to sustained, in-depth analysis. Most other memoirists tend to avoid personal introspection, rarely reveal details that are not already in the public domain and provide few references to source materials. In the main, Irish political autobiographies tended to be centred on the public persona and activities of the author, although this may be changing.[6] Their breezy style and informal tone may make them easy to read but these same features limit their usefulness as guides to sociopolitical realities.

These characteristics may be explained in part by the fact that Irish politicians tend not to maintain personal papers or keep diaries. Even FitzGerald, arguably the most comprehensive of the modern generation, acknowledges that he only briefly kept a diary, although he does draw on other documentary sources. Dan Boyle's account of Green Party involvement with Fianna Fáil in the 2007–11 coalition government is a rare example of a memoir that uses internal party minutes to recreate the behind-the-scenes developments that led to the administration's collapse. Thus, we hear Green Party leader John Gormley tell his colleagues on 17 November 2010: 'It's so hard to get to the truth; very difficult to get a clear picture at Cabinet.'[7] A day later he admits: 'I know why we're leaving. We can't work with them any more.'[8] Boyle's portrait, written shortly after the events it describes, sacrifices mature reflection in order to recreate the immediacy of an unfolding political drama, using contemporaneous evidence. By contrast, most other memoirists rely mainly or solely on personal memory. Joseph Connolly, for example, explains that his life story is 'a simple record of what I knew, saw and experienced during an eventful period of our history',[9] and Pádraig Faulkner writes that his autobiography is based on 'memories of events as I saw them'.[10] The emphasis in almost

---

[6] Some recent political autobiographers seem more willing to expose their personal lives to scrutiny, a trend that may be driven in part by a desire to boost sales by means of headline-grabbing titbits. The personal revelations of Ivan Yates in *Full On* are an example of this nascent trend, though his openness might have more to do with his career change from politics to broadcasting.

[7] Dan Boyle, *Without Power or Glory: The Greens in Government* (Dublin: New Island Books, 2012), 217.

[8] Ibid., 220.

[9] Joseph Connolly, *The Memoirs of Senator Joseph Connolly: A Founder of Modern Ireland*, ed. J. Anthony Gaughan (Dublin: Irish Academic Press, 1996), 432.

[10] Pádraig Faulkner, *As I Saw It: Reviewing Over 30 Years of Fianna Fáil and Irish Politics* (Dublin: Wolfhound Press, 2005), x.

all cases is on subjective opinion and personal recollection. Aspirations towards objective evaluation are few and far between.

A reliance on memory can, of course, be a problem in recounting past events. While political memoirists probably do not set out to lie, selective recollection is difficult to guard against and, as Ben Pimlott observes, 'even the most ascetic of . . . truth-seekers deceive themselves'.[11] Political antagonisms also play a part. Conor Cruise O'Brien's long-standing antipathy to Charles Haughey reveals itself autobiographically in his claim that Fianna Fáil's controversial 1977 election manifesto 'bore all the marks of the mind of CJ Haughey',[12] even though the testimonies of others who were closer to events tell us that Haughey had nothing to do with it and was possibly sceptical of the programme. A further difficulty emerges when the writer sidesteps or simply ignores controversial episodes in their political career. We see this in Gilmore's *Leading Lights*, which glosses over contentious aspects of his membership of the Workers' Party at a time in the late 1980s and early 1990s when allegations of criminality engulfed the movement.

For these and other reasons the genre of political memoir is not without its critics, particularly from within the academic community. Egerton recalls the sceptical reaction of political scientists and historians to the news that former US President Ronald Reagan intended to write his memoirs, and the lack of expectation that truthful disclosure or penetrating insight would result.[13] Such scepticism is often directed towards the 'self-serving perspective'[14] of many political memoirs, wherein events are framed to suit the needs of the author. This brings us to the core issue of a politician's motivations for writing a memoir in the first place. One obvious motive is money, though the size of the Irish market dictates that the sums involved are relatively modest. Another common driver, the desire to settle old political scores, does not appear to be uppermost in the minds of Irish politicians. Many salacious stories have been suppressed and the sharp edges of opinions smoothed. Though many complain that memoirs in general have become top-heavy with invective to facilitate sales, in Ireland, little if any personal vindictiveness appears on the page. Noël Browne's portraits of his cabinet colleagues are biting but, in truth, they are a rarity in Irish political memoir, though this did not prevent *Against the*

[11] Ben Pimlott, 'The Future of Political Biography', *The Political Quarterly*, 61:2 (1990), 215.
[12] Conor Cruise O'Brien, *Memoir: My Life and Themes* (London: Profile Books, 1998), 357.
[13] George Egerton, 'The Politics of Memory: Form and Function in the History of Political Memoir from Antiquity to Modernity', in Egerton, ed., *Political Memoir*, 2.
[14] Conor McGrath, 'Policy Making in Political Memoirs: The Case of the Poll Tax', *Journal of Public Affairs*, 2:2 (2002), 71.

Tide meeting with sharp criticism from Conor Cruise O'Brien and Barry Desmond. O'Brien admitted that after the 1969 general election, when he and Browne shared an office in Leinster House for a number of weeks, he came to regard him as 'half-mad and dangerous to know',[15] while Desmond described Browne's memoir as 'grossly offensive', 'ill-judged' and a 'poisonous denigration of some 90 persons he came across in his career'.[16] More representative is Eamon Gilmore's portrait of his time in government in *Inside the Room*. Having resigned as leader of the Labour Party in 2014 in advance of an expected challenge led by deputy leader Joan Burton, Gilmore evidently harboured hopes of retaining a cabinet position. Far from dwelling on the disappointment of such hopes, however, he merely says of his meeting with Burton that 'the entire exchange took two, maybe three minutes'.[17] Such reticence may well be influenced by the village atmosphere of Irish politics, where antagonists know that their paths will inevitably cross again. This club mentality is also evident in the treatment of public officials; unless offering praise, Irish political memoirists tend to adhere to a shared convention of not naming individual civil servants.

A third motive of the political memoirist is to offer his or her own assessment of events by setting down 'a first history of [an] episode based on both unique remembrance and privileged documentation',[18] so as to pre-empt and influence subsequent interpretations. The precedent here is Winston Churchill, who famously noted that history would be kind to him 'as I propose to write that history myself'.[19] If Enoch Powell is right in asserting that 'all political lives ... end in failure',[20] then autobiography provides an opportunity for the subject to promote achievements and reframe failures, thus becoming a kind of self-propagandist. That this can be done subtly is shown by FitzGerald when he acknowledges criticisms of his high-spending government but argues that imposing early budget cuts might have delivered a terminal shock to the economy. He also points out the difficulty that belt-tightening would have caused his coalition partners in the Labour Party, while simultaneously accepting that at

---

[15] O'Brien, *Memoir*, 323.
[16] Barry Desmond, *Finally and in Conclusion: A Political Memoir* (Dublin: New Island Books, 2000), 118.
[17] Eamon Gilmore, *Inside the Room: The Untold Story of Ireland's Crisis Government* (Sallins: Merrion Press, 2015), 291.
[18] Egerton, 'The Anatomy of Political Memoir', 348.
[19] Winston Churchill, speech in the House of Commons, 23 January 1948.
[20] Enoch Powell, *Joseph Chamberlain* (London: Thames and Hudson, 1977), 151.

times he was too conscious of Labour's position, to the detriment of his own parliamentary party.

Such willingness to accept or at least acknowledge criticism makes FitzGerald's self-justificatory passages more plausible. The reverse is also true: the crass refusal of memoirists to acknowledge their mistakes undermines their history-framing projects. The title of the penultimate chapter of Albert Reynolds's autobiography illustrates this approach: 'If mistakes were made, they were made elsewhere.'[21] Reynolds places himself centre stage in his account of the efforts to convince the British authorities that Sinn Féin was ready to change its political strategy in late 1980s, thereby making himself the author of the Northern Ireland peace process. That he was one of the key figures in the nascent initiative, whom historians are likely to treat kindly, is not in doubt; but Charles Haughey might reasonably claim to have started the process of engaging Sinn Féin in democratic politics before Reynolds's premiership. On other topics, such as the collapse of the two governments he led, Reynolds appears to be either lying or self-deluded. In each instance, he evidently convinced himself that the two parties he entered into coalition with in the early 1990s, the Progressive Democrats and Labour respectively, had already decided that they wanted to pull out of government and that there was nothing he could have done to prevent this happening. What he fails to see is the importance of his actions in their desire to withdraw. Writing in a similar vein, Bertie Ahern's evasion of uncomfortable issues that will be important to historical assessments of his political career, especially those concerning money he accepted from supporters, detracts from the credibility of his recollections. For example, he distances himself from Haughey, claiming he was never part of his clique in the way that former minister Pádraig Flynn once was, a claim that seems barely credible. Instead, Ahern tries to portray himself as an honest broker between the warring sides during the heaves against Haughey, though he does admit that his 1997 party conference speech, which indirectly criticized the ex-taoiseach, was difficult to deliver because 'the old reflexes for Haughey remained'.[22]

A related common autobiographical motivation is to make the subject feel good about themselves, often by placing themselves at the centre of events, an approach famously parodied in the title of Spike Milligan's *Adolf Hitler: My Part in His Downfall* (1971). For example, on reading Faulkner's *As I Saw It* and John O'Connell's *Doctor John* (1989), one

---

[21] Albert Reynolds, *My Autobiography* (London: Transworld Ireland, 2010), 406.
[22] Bertie Ahern, *The Autobiography* (London: Arrow Books, 2010), 134.

could be forgiven for concluding that the office of ceann comhairle (chairperson of Dáil Éireann) is one of great importance, when in reality the position carries little power. The contradictory testimony of Paddy Harte in *Young Tigers and Mongrel Foxes* (2005) also falls under this category – on the one hand, he claims he was ignored by successive Fine Gael leaders; on the other, that he had some influence over their attitude towards Northern Irish Protestants. Such egoism can mislead readers and, by feeding the impression that politicians are masters of their destinies, obscure the roles played by political structures, historical circumstances and sheer luck. These forces tend to be acknowledged only in cases where the policy failures are too obvious to deny, or where the subject's agency is compromised by developments beyond their control, one example of which is Ahern's blaming the post-2008 Irish economic crisis on international events.

A fifth and final motivation worth noting is the still-active politician's use of autobiography as a campaigning tool. There are many instances of senior politicians publishing a memoir in advance of an election or when seeking a party nomination, their purpose being to position themselves as a hero in waiting, poised to solve the problems facing their country. Indeed, US and French presidential aspirants tend to see the publication of a memoir as an important step in the electoral process. Not so in Ireland, where memoirs tend to be produced when political careers have reached their end. Recently, however, a number of serving politicians have penned autobiographies, though these are rarely linked directly to electoral campaigns, with the possible exception of Gerry Adams, a prolific memoirist whose books relate exclusively to his promotion of an irredentist nationalism. That is not to say that these works are without political agenda, however. In *The House Always Wins* (2010), Fianna Fáil TD John McGuinness focuses on his time as a junior minister at the Department of Enterprise, Trade, and Employment (2007–09), the predominant theme of which is his critical view of the civil service. By identifying himself with a national issue, his memoir can be read as an attempt to mark himself out as a potential future party leader. By contrast, Gilmore's *Inside the Room* may be said to be more concerned with matters of posterity. In it, he justifies Labour's decision to enter government, defends its record while there and recounts cabinet battles, thus bidding to frame his legacy not only in historians' eyes but also in the eyes of contemporary commentators.

Memoir, memory and truth

Reading Gilmore's first-hand account of being in government, one is tempted to conclude that self-justification is an inseparable part of the political memoirist's stock-in-trade. But if no single testimony can lead us to the truth behind any given episode or event, might consulting multiple memoirs yield a more profitable outcome? Or, to put it another way, can the examination of a particular political episode from a diversity of auto-biographical perspectives provide us with clarification, insight or even enlightenment? To answer this question we wish to devote the final part of this chapter to the examination of a case study. The example we have chosen is the tax amnesty introduced in 1993 by the then Fianna Fáil-Labour coalition, an episode that is referenced in several memoirs by political figures from the period. Here, we make use of those by Albert Reynolds (the then taoiseach), Bertie Ahern and David Andrews (Fianna Fáil cabinet ministers), John O'Leary (Fianna Fáil TD), Fergus Finlay (political adviser to the Labour Party) and Seán Duignan (government press secretary).

The amnesty itself was a significant policy initiative by the Reynolds-led coalition government, which held power between 1992 and 1994. It was also, according to Andrews, the source of the 'most significant'[23] disagreement between the coalition partners. The proposal was apparently pushed through cabinet more quickly than expected, despite considerable differences of opinion, not just between the two coalition parties but also between the taoiseach and his finance minister, Ahern. A previous amnesty had been introduced in 1988 to allow those with undeclared income to regularize their affairs with the revenue commissioners. At the time, it was presented as a one-off measure, which meant that many were taken aback when a second amnesty was proposed five years later. The 1993 amnesty included favourable terms for those who came clean about their tax liabilities, including a 15 per cent tax rate, no additional penalties and a secrecy clause that prevented the commissioners from cross-checking information included in amnesty declarations with other tax records.

Tellingly, no unified account of the circumstances in which the amnesty was proposed and progressed through the government policy formation process emerges from an analysis of the relevant autobiographical narratives. Reynolds is widely considered the project's main champion, the then taoiseach seeing the amnesty as a means to bring in 'a significant level of

---

[23] David Andrews, *Kingstown Republican: A Political Memoir* (Dublin: New Island Books, 2007), 231.

much-needed revenue'[24] for capital and investment projects. However, in his autobiography Ahern traces the origins of the proposal to lobbying by Fianna Fáil backbenchers, although the source of this lobbying is not identified.[25] Several of the previously mentioned characteristics of Irish political memoir emerge from reading the different recollections of the various protagonists. First, none of these accounts make use of official papers or other documentation; all are reliant upon subjective memory and recall. Second, although the views of the Department of Finance and the revenue commissioners are mentioned, none of the writers identify individual civil or public servants by name. Third, we find evidence of a narrowing of focus influenced by the writer's vantage point. For example, Andrews, despite recognizing the seriousness of internal disagreements about the amnesty, admits: 'I have to confess to not having expressed a strong view one way or another at the time; I allowed it to happen, as it were.'[26] Fourth, not every writer refers to this political flashpoint in their autobiography. There is no mention of the episode in Ruairi Quinn's memoir despite his position as a senior Labour minister in the coalition government. Fifth, several memoirists offer their own assessment of this controversy with the clear objective of influencing how the historical record will be written. Thus, the authors tend to stress the correctness of their own stance and the misguided positions of those on the other side of the argument. Overall, then, these political memoirs offer widely differing assessments of the tax amnesty episode, making the task of locating the truth of the matter all the more challenging, a point further underlined by a closer comparative analysis of the narrative accounts provided by these politicians.

We know that the amnesty proposal emerged in early 1993. According to Reynolds's version, the idea was a component of pre-budget discussions, a claim rejected by Finlay. The opening salvoes in Reynolds's telling of the story coincide with his being on holiday in Cyprus. Having become aware of the proposal, the tánaiste (deputy prime minister) and Labour Party leader, Dick Spring, faxed Reynolds, indicating that Labour 'could not countenance the new "amnesty" tax as it served to benefit the super-rich'.[27] According to Reynolds, the threat of a general election was made if the amnesty plan proceeded. Duignan, in a diary reference quoted in his memoir, records that Reynolds was warned that if he pressed ahead, he would lose a vote at cabinet by thirteen votes to two, to which the taoiseach

---

[24] Reynolds, *My Autobiography*, 260.   [25] Ahern, *The Autobiography*, 152.
[26] Andrews, *Kingstown Republican*, 231–32.   [27] Reynolds, *My Autobiography*, 260.

responded by insisting that he could 'carry the cabinet if I want'.[28] Central to the conflict of views about this specific policy is the role of Bertie Ahern. The memoirs of the other protagonists contain contrasting interpretations of Ahern's attitude to the amnesty and of his actions as the measure proceeded through the Dáil. There is agreement that he was opposed to the idea prior to its reaching the cabinet table for approval. Reynolds maintains that Spring had received support for his oppositional stance from Ahern, who also 'agreed to drop the current discussions on the "amnesty tax" or to postpone it until the autumn'.[29] In Finlay's recollection, Ahern 'argued consistently and strongly against the amnesty from the start'.[30] In fact, such was his hostility that Labour did not even need 'to expend political capital on a confrontation with the Taoiseach',[31] since a majority of cabinet members were in the opposition camp. These views are borne out by Ahern's own testimony, in which he unambiguously says that he 'hated'[32] the amnesty. It is interesting to note, however, that while Andrews concedes that the taoiseach favoured the amnesty and Labour were 'extremely uneasy'[33] about it, he makes no mention of the attitude of the minister for finance.

On the eve of the proposal being brought to cabinet in March 1993, then, the taoiseach did not have the backing of his coalition partners and neither, apparently, did he have the support of his minister for finance. Ahern was in contact with Labour advisors in the hours before the cabinet meeting to ensure they would oppose the measure. We know more about this cabinet decision than most others because of a subsequent parliamentary inquiry into the administration of the Irish tax system in the 1980s and 1990s. However, we do not know what was said at the meeting. The ministerial memoirs do not assist us in this regard as none reproduce discussion from the meeting or, indeed, given any real flavour of the atmosphere in the room. According to the Labour version, as recounted by Finlay, Reynolds used his position as chair to force the measure through cabinet, Ahern reneged on his pre-meeting commitment to oppose the measure and the Labour ministers were so shocked by this *volte face* that they did not contribute at this point in the discussions. Reynolds in his autobiography says that he spoke in favour of the amnesty at the cabinet table or, as he puts it, 'when it finally came up at a meeting'.[34] Contrary to

[28] Seán Duignan, *One Spin on the Merry-Go-Round* (Dublin: Blackwater Press, 1996), 91.
[29] Reynolds, *My Autobiography*, 261.
[30] Fergus Finlay, *Snakes and Ladders* (Dublin: New Island Books, 1998), 171.   [31] Ibid.
[32] Ahern, *The Autobiography*, 153.   [33] Andrews, *Kingstown Republican*, 231.
[34] Reynolds, *My Autobiography*, 261.

the claims of others, he says Ahern also lent his support to the measure. In Ahern's version, however, he was the sole ministerial voice of opposition to the amnesty and points out that the Labour ministers 'just sat on their hands looking sheepish'.[35] Ahern speculates that Reynolds and Spring had done a pre-meeting deal, although it is not clear what political benefit Labour would have derived from accepting the amnesty. The party had been highly critical of the 1988 measure and had made considerable electoral gains on the back of ongoing criticism of Fianna Fáil's approach to financial ethics and its association with so-called 'golden circles' of favoured business people.

Reynolds gives no indication of any deal being brokered with Spring. In fact, at one point he identifies the amnesty as an issue that could have collapsed the coalition, such was the strength of Labour opposition. In evidence to the 1999–2001 parliamentary inquiry into the administration of deposit interest retention tax (DIRT), Reynolds suggested Labour were in fact outmanoeuvred by Ahern, although he does not revisit this claim in his memoir. Ahern, as minister for finance, could probably have blocked or at least delayed the proposal if he had forced the issue at cabinet. As the sponsoring minister for the tax amnesty proposal, he ultimately had two options following the cabinet meeting of March 1993: accept the decision or resign. Rejecting the latter option, a 'furious'[36] Ahern proceeded to support the measure in public. But here again the autobiographical sources diverge. By Ahern's own admission, his lack of enthusiasm for the amnesty was evident to the media: 'They could see straight through that. They knew I had opposed it.'[37] Not so his Fianna Fáil colleague John O'Leary, who reveals in his memoir that his initial opposition to the amnesty changed after he heard Ahern's arguments about the revenue windfall it would generate.[38]

Finally, it is worth noting the differing views of the impact of the tax amnesty debacle on relations in the Fianna Fáil-Labour government. Andrews bluntly asserts that 'by any reckoning, the tax amnesty must be considered a public relations disaster as far as the government was concerned'.[39] The Labour Party's failure to prevent its introduction provoked a senior adviser to tender his resignation (later withdrawn) and Duignan recalls another Labour adviser making it clear to him that 'Labour felt deeply aggrieved at being "forced" to cave into Fianna Fáil on the issue.'[40]

---

[35] Ahern, *The Autobiography*, 153.   [36] Ibid.   [37] Ibid., 154.
[38] John O'Leary, *On the Doorsteps*, 271.   [39] Andrews, *Kingstown Republican*, 232.
[40] Duignan, *One Spin on the Merry-Go-Round*, 91.

Yet, according to Finlay, 'at the end of the day, . . . it has to be said that the tax amnesty did not sour relations between the parties'.[41]

What conclusions, then, about the relation between memory, memoir and truthfulness are we to draw from this comparative analysis of the autobiographical accounts of the 1993 tax amnesty episode? If it is naïve to expect clarification or consensus from the autobiographical testimony of the various political actors, it would also be wrong to leap to judgement about their motives. Conflicts and contradictions in the autobiographical evidence do not necessarily mean that those involved are guilty of manipulating the historical record or deliberately telling untruths. As we know all too well, memory can be unreliable and can change over time. Yet neither should we absolve the memoirists of all self-serving intent, since tendentiousness and special pleading surely come with the territory. As Egerton observes, 'the urge "to neaten things up," to exaggerate intentionality in treating past success, to rationalize failures, and particularly to find a unity and pattern in the disorder of the past political strife – all present seductive attractions'[42] for the political memoirist.

If this case study illustrates anything, surely it is the danger of relying on memoirs and autobiographies as sole sources of scholarly inquiry. Their very real value as records of political events by those who were present at the time is strengthened when they are utilized alongside other documentary sources, such as official records, press reports, contemporaneous notes and private diaries. Not that documentary evidence will necessarily cast full light on a contested episode such as the one discussed above. The release of cabinet papers from the 1993 period may not provide any greater assistance to the political scientist or historian who wishes to determine the actual sequence of events and identify where the truth lies. Memoir aids our understanding of political personalities, behaviours, cultures, struggles and events, more by highlighting their complexity than by imposing order and coherence on them.

Further reading

Egerton, George, ed. *Political Memoir: Essays on the Politics of Memory*. London: Frank Cass, 1994.
Hopkins, Stephen. *The Politics of Memoir and the Northern Ireland Conflict*. Liverpool: Liverpool University Press, 2013.

---

[41] Finlay, *Snakes and Ladders*, 173.   [42] Egerton, 'The Anatomy of Political Memoir', 347.

McGrath, Conor. 'Policy Making in Political Memoirs: The Case of the Poll Tax', *Journal of Public Affairs*, 2:2 (2002): 71–84.

Neville-Shepard, Ryan and Kirsten Theye. 'Writing a Candidacy: Campaign Memoirs and the 2012 Republican Primacy', *American Behavioral Scientist*, 57:12 (2013): 1704–15.

Pimlott, Ben. 'The Future of Political Biography', *The Political Quarterly*, 61:2 (1990): 214–24.

Rafter, Kevin. '"Never Justify. Never Explain": Some Thoughts on Irish Political Memoirs', in Kevin Rafter and Mark O'Brien, eds., *The State in Transition: Essays in Honour of John Horgan*. Dublin: New Island Books, 2015: 284–310.

CHAPTER 9

Women's Political Autobiography in Independent Ireland

Margaret O'Callaghan

Any account of political autobiography by Irish women in the near-century since 1922 must begin with an acknowledgement of the apparent dearth of material. In the period since the establishment of the Irish Free State, few female politicians have written autobiographies. This is unsurprising as there were few women in Dáil Éireann or in the Seanad up until the 1980s.[1] The historical reasons for female political under-representation are similar to those elsewhere in Europe and North America, but are also shaped by factors specific to Ireland. From the 1920s, the post-independence political sphere consigned most women to the domestic and non-public realms, despite the key role of women in the struggle for national self-governance. Conservative male rhetoric represented revolutionary women as dangerous viragoes, saboteurs of the family, of themselves and of the image of Ireland that the new state wished to project. The solution lay in seeking to relegate women to their 'appropriate' place within the family and the home, as was confirmed by the 1937 Constitution. The enshrining of the Catholic moral code in the law of the state, combined with the matriarchal nature of the Irish Catholic family and the simultaneously enabling and disabling cult of the Virgin Mary, had profound consequences for women's public and private lives, as evidenced by the banning of contraception, the control of Catholic teaching hospitals and the illiberal social attitudes engendered by doctrinaire Catholicism. Agitation for change did not come about until the emergence of a liberal-feminist agenda and movement in the early 1970s, which had at their core the desire to dismantle the prevailing legal and constitutional regulation of female capacity and sexuality. Since then, campaigners have sought to reduce, if not eradicate, the influence of the

---

[1] For analyses of women in Irish politics, see Yvonne Galligan, *Women and Politics in Contemporary Ireland: From the Margins to the Mainstream* (London: Pinter, 1998), Rosemary Cullen Owens, *A Social History of Women in Ireland* (Dublin: Gill and Macmillan, 2005) and Myrtle Hill, *Women in Ireland: A Century of Change* (Belfast; Blackstaff Press, 2003).

Catholic moral code on Irish law and public policy, and give women control over their own bodies. Feminism has been at the heart of the secularizing process in modern Ireland.

The relationship between 'woman' and the Irish state is in the process of being incrementally reassessed and rewritten.[2] Conventional archives yield new stories only when new questions are asked of them. Political studies of the post-independence period have documented the ways in which women were excluded from power, jury service, legal personality and paid work after marriage. To date, however, there has been an underuse of political autobiography in examining these processes and their tangible and affective impact on women. That said, the concept of political autobiography requires expansion and modification if it is to have meaning for works written by women in independent Ireland. Traditionally, political autobiography has been a restrictive and gendered category. Narrowly defined around the concept of the 'great man' memoir that had its high point in the Victorian era, political life-writing was for long underpinned by the belief that the lives of notable men can reveal transferrable truths about history, culture and society. In this chapter, I will expand the usual reach of this genre beyond the works of professional politicians to include the life-writings of socially and civically active women, which can be read as political in the broadest sense. In the process, I will build on arguments I have made elsewhere about the need to reconsider and redefine the political in twentieth-century Ireland.[3]

To write about female political autobiography in twentieth- and twenty-first-century Ireland is to demand that the political be read as personal, sexual, gendered and class-based. As Maya Angelou's autobiographical writings have redefined the political meanings of the African American experience for the contemporary generation, so too can the recovery of occluded female self-narratives change our view of what constitutes women's lives and the political in independent Ireland. This process of redefinition is still ongoing, as can be seen from the testimonies given to the recent public inquiries into the Magdalene laundries and clerical sexual abuse, and from the accounts submitted by women to the commission of investigation into mother and baby homes and selected county homes in the Republic. What women can or are prepared to present as formal

---

[2] See Angela Bourke et al., eds., *The Field Day Anthology of Irish Writing, Volume V: Irish Women's Writings and Traditions* (Cork: Cork University Press in association with Field Day, 2002) for an overview of important work in this area.

[3] See Margaret O'Callaghan, 'Women and Politics in Independent Ireland, 1921–68', in Bourke et al., eds., *The Field Day Anthology of Irish Writing, Volume V*, 120–34.

autobiography is at least partially culturally determined. Confessional writing that revealed the story of Irish female subjectivity as anything other than a virtuous one could have socially ruinous consequences for its authors in twentieth-century Ireland, at least until the 1980s. Pioneering or courageous women like Leland Bardwell could admit to eccentricities or to living outside of social norms, but the fact that most Irish women, unless they were protected by a prior exceptionalism, could not write about the self except in the most restricted or disguised of terms is in itself a political and cultural story.[4] The social elevation of the ideal of respectability, which was primarily measured by an exaggerated emphasis on female sexual probity, reached its high point during the late 1940s and 1950s and remained relatively intact into the 1970s, during which time it rendered female political autobiography, as a formal genre, virtually non-existent. A core premise of this chapter, therefore, is that we need to revise our understanding of what constitutes female political autobiography and adopt parameters that are hospitable to an eclectic range of women's writings.

The revolutionary generation

The revolutionary generation of nationalist Irish women, born in the late nineteenth century, produced a disparate body of autobiography, as well other forms of life-writing such as letters and diaries.[5] This corpus includes works such as Máire Nic Shiubhlaigh's *The Splendid Years* (1955), Lil Conlon's *Cumann na mBan and the Women of Ireland 1913–25* (1969), Kathleen Keys McDonnell's *There Is a Bridge at Bandon* (1972) and Sydney Gifford Czira's *The Years Flew By* (1974). Many of these texts have not fared well critically or historiographically. Maud Gonne MacBride's *A Servant of the Queen* (1938) is often dismissed by historians; Anna Parnell's version of events in *The Tale of a Great Sham* (1986) was traduced and buried, and remained unpublished in book form in her lifetime; and

---

[4] Unionist women were even more circumspect autobiographically, though their private communications remain unexplored.

[5] For an innovative use of letters as a source, see Lindsay Earner-Byrne, "'Should I Take Myself and Family to Another Religion[?]": Irish Catholic Women, Protest, and Conformity, 1920–1970', in Christina S. Brophy and Cara Delay, eds., *Women, Reform, and Resistance in Ireland, 1850–1950* (Basingstoke: Palgrave Macmillan, 2015), 77–100. See also Leanne Lane, *Rosamond Jacob: Third Person Singular* (Dublin: UCD Press, 2010) for a particularly revealing analysis of female life-writing from this period and Lucy McDiarmid, *At Home in the Revolution: What Women Said and Did in 1916* (Dublin: Royal Irish Academy, 2015) for a good bibliographical overview.

Katharine O'Shea's involuntarily autobiographical two-volume memoir of her husband, *Charles Stewart Parnell: His Love Story and Political Life* (1914), has been ridiculed. Writing in the 1930s, Gonne had more formidable protections against calumny than Parnell's sister or wife. Her wealth, beauty and lack of living parents gave her a freedom to live as she pleased, at least until she married John MacBride. *A Servant of the Queen* demonstrates that she took herself seriously – a prerequisite for conventional political auto-biography – yet successive analysts mock and berate her self-importance. The autobiographical writings of Augusta Persse, Lady Gregory, a cultural as well as a political actor, have received more nuanced critical attention, especially her *Seventy Years, 1852–1922* (1974).[6] The work of Enid Starkie, the distinguished literary scholar of Rimbaud and Baudelaire, remains neglected, even though *A Lady's Child* (1941) contains fascinating insights into the author's formation in the unionist Killiney of her youth.

Kathleen Clarke's edited autobiography, *Revolutionary Woman: Kathleen Clarke 1878–1972* (1991), is the most interesting of the first-person accounts by the 1916 generation in revealing the convictions that shaped a political activist. As a young Limerick woman running a successful dress-making business with her sister, she first met the Fenian Tom Clarke when he came to stay with her intensely nationalist family. Independent-minded, determined and in love, she acted against her family's wishes in following him to New York and marrying him there. Because theirs was a happy and passionate marriage, Kathleen was reluctant to return to Ireland where she knew Clarke would be involved in fomenting revolution. She was as political as he was, however, and went along with his plans because she understood what drove him. Devastated by his death in 1916 and that of her only brother, Edward Daly, in her autobiography she recalls her last night with her husband in prison before his execution, during which she decided not to tell him that she was pregnant. She writes of her later miscarriage and describes hearing his voice and that of their extraordinarily close friend Sean MacDiarmada, after which she felt as though she had returned from a near-death experience. Kathleen later became an active member of Fianna Fáil and was the first woman lord mayor of Dublin in 1939. Despite this, she recalls that she was seen as marginal by her male colleagues, including Éamon de Valera, who was unwilling to give her credit for proposing new tactics for Sinn Féin from 1924, and who

---

[6] See Taura S. Napier, 'Pilgrimage to the Self: Autobiographies of Twentieth-Century Irish Women', in Liam Harte, ed., *Modern Irish Autobiography: Self, Nation and Society* (Basingstoke: Palgrave Macmillan, 2007), 70–90. Napier's chapter also considers works by Katherine Tynan, Kate O'Brien, Elizabeth Bowen and Eavan Boland, all of whose autobiographies can be read as political texts.

attempted to persuade her to withdraw from the Senate elections to make way for Mrs Pearse, mother of republican icon, Patrick.

Clarke's autobiography was not published until 1991. *All in the Blood*, the edited memoirs of Geraldine Plunkett Dillon, activist and sister of another executed 1916 republican, did not appear until 2006, twenty years after her death. These and other delayed autobiographies by nationalist women are proof that 'women's stories' simply did not interest a male-dominated publishing industry. We would have even fewer autobiographical writings by political women of this generation were it not for the pioneering work of Uinseann MacEoin, whose *Survivors: The Story of Ireland's Struggle as Told Through Some of Her Outstanding Living People* (1980) brought together personal statements from anti-state republicans in the 1970s, among whom were Cumann na mBan members Máire Comerford and Síghle Humphreys. So while Maud Gonne retained the status and profile to publish an autobiography in the 1930s, she was the exception that proved the rule. Few of the republican women with whom she mixed were as successful in getting into print, least of all Alice Milligan who, with Ethna Carbery, was perhaps the finest female political writer of that political generation, yet who remained, as she herself saw it, interned by the border and silenced on the northern side of it by her radical nationalist politics.

Published book-length memoirs by this generation are few, then, but this dearth is partially redeemed by the existence of an extraordinary repository that contains first-hand accounts by female republican activists that would not have been preserved but for a government-led initiative of the 1940s. The Bureau of Military History (BMH) collection includes personal statements, of varying length, collected from over 1,700 people who took part in political events that occurred between 1913 and 1921. The collection was closed to the public until 2003, and a substantial part of it was published online in March 2012. Included among these witness statements are over one hundred testimonies by women, all of which are now available online.[7] Taken together, these constitute a unique collection of female narratives of revolutionary engagement through which we can examine the constitution and narration of gendered selfhood in specific historical circumstances.

Both the material itself and the conditions of its collection raise complex questions about what constitutes the autobiographical. Many of

---

[7] See www.bureauofmilitaryhistory.ie/ (accessed 1 July 2016). See also Eve Morrison, 'The Bureau of Military History and Female Republican Activism, 1913–1923', in Maryann Gialanella Valiulis, ed., *Gender and Power in Irish History* (Dublin: Irish Academic Press, 2009), 59–83.

the women who submitted statements to the BMH did not attempt to write or publish an autobiography, as conventionally understood. Their testimonies were written or dictated by invitation, on the assurance that what each witness disclosed would not be revealed until after the death of the last person to make a statement, a promise that was kept. Is it accurate, then, to describe these statements as autobiographical? And how do we assess the impact of the circumstances of their creation and collection on what was written or recorded? I think that we must accord these statements autobiographical status and respect the integrity of these women's voices, whatever the conditions of their production, however fragmentary and partial they may be and however great the gap between the event and the recollection of it.[8] The vivid testimonies in the BMH constitute a radically transformative autobiographical source that enables us to examine the ways in which politically active women represented themselves and their actions.

Whereas a minority of BMH statements are by women such as Gonne, who had the self-assurance to put themselves at the centre of their narratives, as they would in a crafted autobiography, most women produced statements that are closer to reportage than literature.[9] The crucial point, however, is that the vocabulary, grammar and speech rhythms of these women are largely their own, as a sampling of the statements makes clear. Alice Barry of Upper Pembroke Street in Dublin testified to the BMH in 1952. She writes that in October 1920 she was asked by Michael Collins to 'publicly dissociate ourselves with Sinn Féin public politics and keep our house as a refuge for dangerously wounded I.R.A. men'.[10] Her six-page statement, which is full of dramatic incident involving Collins, Dan Breen and Ernie O'Malley, offers few clues to her personal motives, but is emphatically a previously unheard, vibrant political voice. The statement of Dulcibella Barton, on the other hand, is more obviously autobiographical.[11] Dulcibella, a sister of Robert, one of the signatories of the Anglo-Irish Treaty, recorded her testimony in 1954, by which time she had been bed-ridden with arthritis for twelve years. Enlivened by dialogue and incidental detail, her twelve-page statement conveys a powerful sense of her view of her life as having being shaped by political choices made as a very young girl. As a reflection on her own life and a disturbing insight into an

---

[8] Lucy McDiarmid explores a selection of these statements to tell a particular story of the 1916 Rising in *At Home in the Revolution*.
[9] Interestingly, Gonne used her statement, given in 1949, to correct errors in her published autobiography and to critique what she regarded as the misrepresentation of her close friend, Constance Markiewicz, by Sean O'Faolain and Sean O'Casey. See BMH, WS 317.
[10] BMH, WS 723, 1.   [11] BMH, WS 936, 1.

extended family scarred by different twentieth-century wars, Barton's testimony represents a fragment of a life story whose wider contours will never be known. Like a wealth of other statements by women in this archive, it shines fleeting light on experiences that would otherwise have been unwritten and are now to be read.

The post-revolutionary generation

Among the women who gave statements to the BMH was Margaret Browne, wife of the Fianna Fáil government minister, Sean MacEntee. One of her daughters, Máire Mhac an tSaoi, went on to become a poet, diplomat, wife of the writer-politician Conor Cruise O'Brien and, as Máire Cruise O'Brien, author of an important autobiography. *The Same Age as the State* (2003) is an epoch-defining work in which is manifest the self-comprehension of many of O'Brien's generation, for whom the narratives of self and state were often closely aligned. The text, which carries reso-nances of earlier Irish-language self-narratives, reveals a new kind of woman forged in the intellectual ferment of the post-independence dec-ades, bound to tradition but also reshaping it. Intensely political, O'Brien embodies in her exceptional voice a particular Irish female world, which is captured in the way her subjectivity is shaped around ancestors, places and heritage, and an internationalism which is reflected in chapter titles such as 'Widening Horizons' and 'Into Africa'. Her first chapter, 'My Mother's People', introduces us to the idea of *mo dhaoine* ('my people') as central to one's self-definition in the Ireland of her time. She begins her account with a vignette of her maternal grandmother, Kate Browne, who was a daughter of the strong farmer class that benefitted from the Land War of the 1880s: 'I remember her from the waist down. We went together to feed the hens at the back of her house in the village of Grangemockler, County Tipperary, at the foot of Slievenamon in the Decies ... God rest her! Her story has been part of my consciousness from the beginning.'[12] Here and elsewhere in the book, O'Brien gives us a powerful sense of how subjectivity is constituted through thinking through the generations; the self is consti-tuted out of one's genealogy and is not merely the story of an individual life. O'Brien's idea of who she is is informed by her knowledge of the history of her mother's family that has been passed on to her and by her familiarity with their ground and place of origin. The Irish language revival

---

[12] Máire Cruise O'Brien, *The Same Age as the State* (Dublin: O'Brien Press, 2003), 13. An esteemed Irish-language poet, O'Brien publishes her poetry under her own name, Máire Mhac an tSaoi.

project of the state is echoed in her deep fluency in Irish, abandoned by her ancestors or forced from them, but reanimated in her through time spent in the holiday home of her uncle in Dún Chaoin in the Kerry Gaeltacht.

Catholic bishops, in their public pronouncements in support of the Treaty in the 1920s, indicated that the 'name of Ireland' was a particular concern and that as a concept it depended on the purity of women, thus confirming that female sexuality was the site on which the religious and moral ideology of the new state was to be built.[13] Many women born in the 1920s were suffocatingly imbued with what the writer Kate O'Brien captured in the title of her 1963 memoir, *Presentation Parlour*: a decorous respectability of almost surreal virtuousness. Nuns were central to the dissemination of this ideology, with a woman's class background dictating the kind of nuns who sought to shape her as a woman.[14] For good or ill, from the convents of the Catholic elite to the orphanages of the abandoned poor and the Magdalene laundries of 'fallen' women, religious faith inculcated by nuns formed most Irish Catholic women for most of the twentieth century. These religious women rarely controlled doctrine or power, however, and few wrote autobiographies. Their most powerful legacy was possibly their stoic Catholic work ethic. The latter-day demonization of all nuns for the cruelty of some is as unjust as it is popular.

The voices of poor urban and rural women, and those who emigrated in their tens of thousands after 1922, are rarely found in autobiographical form. Some first-person sources can be tracked down through female self-descriptions in government reports, sexual abuse inquiries and other testimonies.[15] Other women used the essay form for confessional purposes, among them the historian Miriam Daly, who was born in 1928. It is clear from her reflections on her Dublin upbringing and struggles with Catholicism that feminism was not important to her. Instead, she was passionately drawn to civil rights activism and republican politics in 1970s Northern Ireland, where she was murdered in 1980.[16] Women marginalized by extreme republican politics, and the poverty which usually accompanied

---

[13] See Margaret O'Callaghan, 'Religion and Identity: The Church and Irish Independence', *The Crane Bag*, 7:2 (1983), 65–76.

[14] For an exploration of a mother's extraordinary hidden past as an Irish Catholic nun, see John Lanchester's *Family Romance: A Memoir* (London: Faber and Faber, 2007).

[15] Some recent autobiographical accounts try to reconstruct the story of pregnancy, fear and adoption. See, for example, Caitríona Palmer, *An Affair with my Mother: A Story of Adoption, Secrecy and Love* (Dublin: Penguin Ireland, 2016).

[16] See Miriam Daly, 'Believing Today', *The Furrow*, 18:10 (1967), 555–64. See also her 'Evolution of the Modern Irish State (Irish Democracy)', *Christus Rex: Journal of Sociology*, 24:2 (1970), 85–92. I would like to thank Patrick Maume for bringing Daly's intellectualized life-writings to my attention.

them, sometimes expressed their voices through letters to the newspapers. Máire Comerford's short autobiographical text in MacEoin's *Survivors* at least protected her from anonymity. In her public presence, she linked the pre-revolutionary generation of the historian Alice Stopford Green, whose secretary she was until they assumed opposite sides on the Treaty, to the generation of the 1970s, in which decade she still retained a public voice.

Irish feminist autobiography

The new generation of political activists and feminists that created the Irish Women's Liberation Movement (IWLM) in 1970 met initially in Dublin cafes and restaurants and later in each other's flats and houses. In addition to figures such as Scottish feminist Margaret Gaj, doctor Máire Woods, writers Clare Boylan and Eavan Boland and future political actors Nuala Fennell and Máirin Johnston, the group included some of the most important campaigning journalists of their generation – June Levine, Nell McCafferty, Mary Kenny, Mary Maher, Rosita Sweetman, Fionnuala O'Connor – several of whom have written autobiographical or semi-autobiographical works. Arguably the most important of these is Levine's *Sisters: The Personal Story of an Irish Feminist* (1982). Despite its subtitle, the book is both a solo autobiography and a group biography, a chronicle of the feminist remaking of a divorced Jewish Dubliner interwoven with a cultural history of the Irish women's movement in the 1960s and 1970s.[17]

Sisters begins with an arresting passage in which Levine conjures up the first and most intimate of her 'sisters', her former self with whom she has a conflicted relationship:

> She's like a sister to me now, that female that was me, exasperating when she edges me aside, and interferes with the way I want to be now, stirring up old habits born of the old rules, tricks to pull me down, leave nothing gained. Still, I understand and accept her; after all, sisterhood is powerful. I'm quite fond of the woman who was me. God, she was hard to live with, hard to know, hard to convince, but she was young, beautiful, vivacious, believing that those assets would fulfil the myth of womanhood prized . . .[18]

[17] *Sisters* can be read in conjunction with Levine's contribution to the fifth volume of *The Field Day Anthology of Irish Writing*, entitled 'The Women's Movement in the Republic of Ireland, 1968–80', 177–228.
[18] June Levine, *Sisters: The Personal Story of an Irish Feminist* (Dublin: Ward River Press, 1982), 9.

Levine's use of a bifurcated persona powerfully captures the deep-rooted chronic effects of the contradictory signals and behaviours that shaped her self-development from early childhood, since when she was 'Conditioned as a female to blame myself for everything, for not fitting in and doing as I was expected'[19] by a patriarchal society. She goes on to chart her painful, fitful journey from a 'hollow state' of marital entrapment in Canada through a fog of 'madness' to 'the dawn of consciousness' on joining the women's movement in 1960s Dublin.[20] Levine chronicles her involvement in the consciousness-raising radical feminist side of the movement but also reflects wryly on how others pursued more liberal-feminist goals that included joining the political system. She shows how the latter grouping later gravitated to the Women's Political Association, which became a training ground for future women politicians, though this was not the politics that radical feminists embraced at the time. Levine powerfully exemplifies in her self-understanding and expression how, in the mantra of that generation of politicized women, 'the personal' was 'political'.

Levine's contemporary, Derry-born Nell McCafferty, was also prominent in the 1970s women's movement, though she was later shunned by many Dublin-based feminists after her apparent identification with the republican women in Armagh prison during the 'dirty protests' of the early 1980s. Labelled a tacit supporter of the IRA, McCafferty's refusal to condemn the organization was emblematic of the profound localism that conditioned her loyalties and ties. Who are the IRA's members, she asked, but her neighbours' sons in Derry's Bogside? Her stance proved unacceptable to the feminist bohemian circle in which she made her spiritual home after moving to Dublin and becoming a staff journalist with the *Irish Times*. This tension also highlights how, in her person and in her career, Nell epitomized what linked and divided Ireland, north and south, particularly during the Troubles. Exaggeratedly devoted to her powerfully hospitable mother, whose virtues she proclaimed, her confessional writings – most notably *Nell: A Disorderly Woman* (2004), her autobiography proper – chart a life and outlook revolutionized by the nightly rioting and shootings before and after Bloody Sunday in Derry in 1972. For McCafferty, the northern side of the border would always be a place of revolution and turmoil, whereas the south was about potential feminist liberation. Yet when two of her northern friends, Bernadette Devlin and Mary Holland, became pregnant outside of convention, McCafferty did not really bring her feminist principles to bear on her analysis of their situations. Devlin, the most brilliant Northern Irish

[19] Ibid., 80.   [20] Ibid., 48, 52, 79.

woman politician of her generation and author of *The Price of My Soul* (1969), has walk-on parts in *Nell* but is never accorded the status granted to others, and she eventually fades from a narrative that becomes increasingly focused on Nell's life and times in Dublin.

The evolutionary stages of the Irish women's movement are powerfully conveyed in *Nell* by an essentially social being who revels in interaction with the world. Yet McCafferty's sociable disposition and strong identification with her working-class roots did not protect her from a destructive self-loathing as a lesbian in a society where the word could scarcely be spoken. Pigeonholed past a certain point as a 'butch' lesbian, her sensitivity and nervousness about how to perform being a woman set her up for torment and abuse by those with whom she became intimate. The grand passion of her life was political journalist Nuala O'Faolain, who later undermined the extent to which her fifteen-year relationship with Nell was a sexual passion. In addition to illuminating the personal relations between influential feminists, *Nell* also provides insights into the world of the Dublin media and the many feminist campaigns of the 1970s and 1980s. McCafferty captures the exuberant fun and intimate friendships of these campaigning women, but also their intimate betrayals and compromises. As a subjective portrait of a generation of feminist activists who were deeply connected to one another, *Nell* is rivalled only by Levine's *Sisters*. More significantly, perhaps, as a searing examination of what it meant to be at odds with the heteronormative conventions of Irish society, *Nell* is Ireland's first true autobiography by a gay woman.

Other works take their place alongside *Nell* and *Sisters* in this mini-canon of Irish feminist life-writing. For example, Mary Kenny's *Something of Myself and Others* (2014) casts a sceptical eye over the IWLM; Maura Richards's *Single Issue* (1998) recalls the experience of unmarried motherhood in 1970s Ireland and details her struggle to establish Cherish, a self-help group for single mothers; and Rosita Sweetman's *On Our Backs: Sexual Attitudes in a Changing Ireland* (1979) gathers autobiographical accounts from a multiplicity of women who speak confessionally about the confrontation between public morality and private desires. The harrowing interview testimony Sweetman elicits from a Dublin prostitute prefigures June Levine's painful *Lyn: A Story of Prostitution* (1987), co-written with Lyn Madden. Originally serialized in *Magill* magazine in 1983, this account of sexual exploitation and abuse in modern Dublin exposed a hidden Ireland that was wilfully ignored by many in society, including elected politicians. Madden herself wrote a sequel, *Lyn's Escape* (2007), in which she describes her life after prostitution and her attempts to care for her heroin-addicted son.

Barrister Mary Robinson acted in many of the legal cases brought forward by the IWLM, including Máirín de Búrca and Mary Anderson's successful challenge to laws that effectively prevented women from sitting on juries. As a Labour Party politician, a pioneering lawyer and later Ireland's first female president, Robinson was in many ways the apotheosis, if not always the intimate, of this generation of activist women. Yet her autobiography, *Everybody Matters* (2012), co-written with her daughter Tessa, is revealing for how it chooses to present the self. Despite being the most successful female politician of her generation, Robinson's choice of title seeks to draw attention away from her exceptionalism by embedding her life story in a narrative of equality with, and devotion to, others. She moulds her self-narration in the style of a deflected autobiography, as if to guard against accusations of vanity or self-importance, qualities still seen as unbecoming in a woman of her generation and cultural background. Her promotion of the notion that 'everybody matters' as a way of telling her life story illustrates the austere work of self-presentation required of a gifted, ambitious woman in late twentieth-century Ireland. To succeed in this society one had to present as almost perfect; there are therefore no tales of indiscreet behaviour or sexual rebellion. What resistance there is is family-centred. Robinson presents herself as the product of her struggle against the social ambition of her mother, who is depicted as a *nouveau* entrant into the English-educated Bourke family, with its ancestral links to Protestantism and British imperial service. Throughout, Robinson primarily identifies with the natural dignity of her father, who refused grandeur for a life as a country doctor in Co. Mayo. Yet even though Robinson rejects her mother's insistence on the family's socially elevated status, she recognizes that it shaped her nonetheless and gave her a certainty and a certain aloofness that protected her from the self-doubt that hampered other women.

From Mount Anville secondary school to Trinity College Dublin, *Everybody Matters* reveals how the privilege, propriety and wholesomeness of Robinson's Ballina upbringing with four brothers give her a sense of purpose, direction and confidence. Her narrative of moving from the high religiosity of her very Catholic home to a more secular early adulthood is a powerful one, and is shared by many women of her generation. So too is her regard for ancestral nuns who, as entrepreneurs and social activists, provided her with a genealogy of female achievement. Her own achievements – admission to Harvard Law School, appointment as Reid Professor of Law at Trinity, election to the Irish Seanad at the age of twenty-five – are narrated in a manner that indicates how her disciplined, trained and careful disposition enabled her to negotiate a path through male-dominated cultures at home and abroad. If being the only girl in a family of boys made Robinson feel more valued and less dispensable than many women of that era, her close relationships with women such as Ann Lane and Bride Rosney are shown to be important in sustaining and carrying her forward. Yet *Everybody Matters* reveals little of these women except insofar as they shaped her progress. Her marriage to the Church of Ireland lawyer and scholar Nick Robinson, which initially upset her parents, can be read emblematically as another step on Ireland's journey towards maturity and independence. In many ways, Mary Robinson's story, like that of Máire Cruise O'Brien, resembles a 'national tale' in which she and the nation grow and improve together.

The autobiography of Nuala O'Faolain expresses an altogether more unruly feminist sensibility, that of a woman in whose work many of the aspirations, tensions and frustrations of the 1960s cohort of activists are played out. The provocative title of her bestselling 1996 memoir, *Are You Somebody?*, encapsulates a core conundrum of life-writing: to embark upon an autobiography one has to believe that one's life story has inherent value, yet the act of self-writing subjects that belief to interrogation. There is a courageous frankness to O'Faolain's reflections on her own struggle to feel entitled to write an autobiography and her quest for a voice in which to do so. Like Levine's *Sisters, Are You Somebody?* embodies not just an individual's uncertain subjectivity but a generation's sense of itself by laying bare the familial, social, religious and political forces that formed O'Faolain and many of her contemporaries. Towards the end, O'Faolain reflects:

> I've been trying here to understand the way things have worked out in my life. And though what I've written is personal, part of my predicament is general. The challenges of middle-age, and the challenges of loneliness – which I know exist even within relationships – confront many more people than me ... My problems are banal only because so many people share them.[21]

Yet *Are You Somebody?* also represents something new in Irish female political autobiography, in that it is a work in which a woman is prepared to shape herself through revelation in a society devoted to concealment, particularly female concealment. O'Faolain was the first Irish woman to

---

[21] Nuala O'Faolain, *Are You Somebody? The Accidental Memoir of a Dublin Woman* (Dublin: New Island Books, 1996), 190–91.

write an autobiography that relates the politics of poverty and class to a mother's endless pregnancies and connects a daughter's emotional and sexual formation to her growing alcoholism. Chaotically reared yet academically brilliant, O'Faolain did not do what even liberated Irish women of her generation were trained to do: hide the mess. Although she identifies with her dapper, boozing, philandering father, *Are You Somebody?* also lets the reader see the denied pull of her clever but overwhelmed mother, who was all that a woman in conservative 1950s Ireland ought not to have been. The pain of a family gone awry through poverty, addiction and unharnessed talent is the stuff of fiction. The dilemma of how to live up to feminine ideals in such a family, and in such a political and religious culture, is one of the governing themes of the memoir, and it is further illuminated by O'Faolain's sharp-witted depiction of the challenges faced by those few women who inhabited bohemian Dublin of the 1950s and early 1960s. Here, she incisively notes, 'in the circles where academia and journalism and literature met, women either had to make no demands, and be liked, or be much larger than life, and feared'.[22]

Cabinet memoirs by female politicians

I wish to conclude this chapter by examining some of the few autobiographies by elected female politicians in the Republic. The first of these, *At the Cutting Edge* (1990), the cabinet diaries of Fine Gael's Gemma Hussey, who served as minister for education from 1982 to 1986, cannot really be seen as autobiographical. As if to compensate for her exposed position as one of the very few women in the cabinet, Hussey avoids the personal and the reflective except in her introductory chapter, and even here her tone is cautious and restrained. Taoiseach Garret FitzGerald's commitment to hold a constitutional referendum to copper-fasten the illegality of abortion during her period in office opened up a chasm between pro-choice feminists and more conservative feminists like Hussey and her Fine Gael colleague Nuala Fennell, who was appointed the Republic's first junior minister for women's affairs and family law reform in 1982. In her memoir *Political Woman* (2010), Fennell writes about her generation's awareness of the works of Betty Friedan, Germaine Greer and Simone de Beauvoir, and also provides a critical overview of the differences within the IWLM and an account of why she broke with the movement. She recalls how she was at first entranced by Mary Kenny and describes the sense of desertion felt by many in the women's movement when Kenny seemed to abandon feminist activism following her marriage to the conservative, if maverick, English journalist Richard West. Read in conjunction with the memoirs discussed above, *Political Woman* offers a more contested history of the women's movement in Ireland. It also conveys better than other accounts the full range of legal disabilities under which Irish women laboured, which Fennell was proud to have had the opportunity to highlight and address at a governmental level.

Both Gemma Hussey and Nuala Fennell can be seen as feminists whose election and appointment to cabinet positions gave momentum to the drive for gender equality in Irish politics, even though such women were few and far between in the 1980s. Their entry into politics was highly exceptional in a political system and clientelist culture shaped and dominated by conservative-minded men. The foundation of the Progressive Democrats and the prominence of Mary Harney and Liz O'Donnell in that party from the mid-1980s, combined with the role of journalist Geraldine Kennedy as chronicler and participant, appeared to normalize the presence of women in Irish politics. Yet until the adoption of candidate gender quotas in 2012, the percentage of women TDs has never exceeded 20 per cent, which means that all women politicians in Ireland operate at a considerable disadvantage compared with their male counterparts.

Fianna Fáil's first female minister, appointed in 1979, was Máire Geoghegan-Quinn. Her rise heralded the promotion to cabinet of other women in the party, notably Síle de Valera, Mary Hanafin and Mary Coughlan, the last of whom served as tánaiste from 2008 to 2011. To date, the only female member of a Fianna Fáil government to write an autobiography is Mary O'Rourke, who was herself the daughter of an elected politician. In *Just Mary* (2012), she shows how she was politicized by the daily actuality of politics as a child and provides a unique insight into the atmosphere, protocols and modes of political life in the Athlone of her youth. Fearless, cutting, indomitable and independent-minded, O'Rourke reveals herself to be an intuitive feminist who rejects special measures to increase the number of women in politics, yet seems in denial about the advantages her own family background gave her. Objectionably labelled 'mammy' by media satirists, O'Rourke is in fact resistant to stereotypes and comes across as being remarkably well-adjusted to the combative nature of Irish politics. As one of the few Irish women to have held cabinet office, she embodies the apparent normalization of women's voices in the public sphere.

Conclusion

Female political autobiography in Ireland is a new field of study. The changing narrative of how politicized women represented and shaped their personal and public journeys since the 1920s is itself a compelling political story, one that cannot be confined to works by those few women who stepped into what was for most of the past century a man's world. To uncover through autobiography the cultural, social and political history of the mentalities of twentieth- and twenty-first-century Irish women we must widen our definitional and analytical lenses and read anew all that they have written across a diversity of genres. As we move forwards, it is likely that as more women enter the Dáil and Seanad, more of them will write autobiographical accounts of their lives in politics. Yet it is also likely that for many women in Irish public and political life the self-exposure that the genre of autobiography demands will continue to present difficult challenges, both in terms of production and, more crucially, reception.

Further reading

Bureau of Military History Witness Statements, www.bureauofmilitaryhistory.ie/
Maguire, James and James Quinn, eds. *Dictionary of Irish Biography: From the Earliest Times to the Year 2002*. Cambridge: Cambridge University Press, 2009. 9 vols.
McDiarmid, Lucy. *At Home in the Revolution: What Women Said and Did in 1916*. Dublin: Royal Irish Academy, 2015.
Napier, Taura S. 'Pilgrimage to the Self: Autobiographies of Twentieth-Century Irish Women', in Liam Harte, ed., *Modern Irish Autobiography: Self, Nation and Society*. Basingstoke: Palgrave Macmillan, 2007: 70–90.
O'Callaghan, Margaret. 'Women and Politics in Independent Ireland, 1921–68', in Angela Bourke et al., eds., *The Field Day Anthology of Irish Writing, Volume V: Irish Women's Writings and Traditions*. Cork: Cork University Press in association with Field Day, 2002: 120–34.
Pašeta, Senia. *Irish Nationalist Women, 1900–1918*. Cambridge: Cambridge University Press, 2013.

CHAPTER 10

Autobiography and the Irish Literary Revival

Nicholas Allen

The art of autobiography and the invention of the Irish Literary Revival share an intimate cultural history. The coming to consciousness of an individual as a register of the vitality of the national imagination requires a particular set of aesthetic, political and historical conditions to enact.[1] These conditions can generate other genres that are not autobiographical, even if they borrow heavily from the idea of a life lived in fiction. The border between the *Bildungsroman* and the memoir is, like the boundary between nation and empire, porous, indeterminate and generative of more questions than answers.[2] Autobiography is less a revelation of the true self than the archaeology of other selves uncovered by the textual arrangement of circumstance and social expectation, of which literature makes its own demands in the shape of genre, style and the close attendance of the reader. Revelation was the Revival's key mode and autobiography a central form of its aesthetic. The fact that the story of Ireland's cultural transformation was written as, and sometimes before, it happened might alert the reader to the slipperiness of autobiography as a vehicle for the rendition of remembered pasts.

The Irish Literary Revival was not conceived of as a movement so much as a mode of aesthetic renewal in a national context, which began in the 1890s and lingered into the 1920s. It was partly for this reason that the writers of the Revival were so dismissive of the complex cultural creativity that preceded them. Nineteenth-century Ireland had a rich and varied novelistic tradition, a tradition that has only recently begun to be

---

[1] A good introductory guide to this formation is Liam Harte, ed., *Modern Irish Autobiography: Self, Nation and Society* (Basingstoke: Palgrave Macmillan, 2007). For a considered overview of autobiography as a subject in twentieth-century Ireland, see Elizabeth Grubgeld, 'Life Writing in the Twentieth Century', in John Wilson Foster, ed., *The Cambridge Companion to the Irish Novel* (Cambridge: Cambridge University Press, 2006), 223–37.

[2] For a study of the coming-of-age novel in the Irish context, see Gregory Castle, *Reading the Modernist Bildungsroman* (Gainesville: University of Florida Press, 2006).

recovered, in part because the Revival was so successful in overshadowing its predecessor movements.[3] Recognizing this is important to a reading of the autobiographies of the later period, which do so much to represent their subjects as avatars of bright light shone on the darkness of a dispossessed colonial Ireland. Autobiography can, in this light, be read as the reconstitution of a national body so diminished by the catastrophe of the Famine only a generation before Yeats and Joyce. But if revelation is the Revival's abiding form, then some fiction of disappointment is necessary to the narrative of an emerging and transformative self in the service of Ireland's literary regeneration.

The codes become more complicated when the Revival is read as one of the many cultural movements that blossomed in late nineteenth-century Ireland. The Gaelic League, the Fenian movement and the Gaelic Athletic Association are as important a part of the social panorama as the national theatre movement.[4] Many of these organizations had overlapping memberships, a rich vein for a writer like George Moore to mine in the exposure of each movement's frictions with the other, all in the name of a united Ireland. Autobiography here is a dramatic display of the individual's inability to fit into larger movements, the suggestion being that all such collaborations are based on compromise and hypocrisy. Moore sweetens this observation with comedy, Sean O'Casey with the bitterness of exile in six volumes of memoir that began with *I Knock at the Door* in 1939. The Olympian Yeats set himself above all others, but his marble self-construction was its own sign of weakness, since the lyric reflection of the early poetry had trapped Yeats in a public mode that he later found hard to escape. *Autobiographies* (1926) is a reconstitution of Yeats's public persona and a clearance of the ground before him.

This suggests another dimension to the autobiography and its place in the writer's life, which is the phase at which it appears in an artist's career. The cultural renaissance can be dated loosely from the 1890s to the 1910s and the Literary Revival was over as a movement long before its major figures finished writing. Moore's memoirs capped an already long and distinguished writing life. Yeats's were published in the middle of his, while

---

[3] The study of the nineteenth century has expanded dramatically thanks to recent works such as Emer Nolan's *Catholic Emancipations: Irish Fiction from Thomas Moore to James Joyce* (Syracuse: Syracuse University Press, 2007) and Claire Connolly's *A Cultural History of the Irish Novel, 1790–1829* (Cambridge: Cambridge University Press, 2011), among many others.

[4] For a broad overview of the Revival and its cultural complexity across several movements, see P. J. Matthews, *Revival: The Abbey Theatre, Sinn Féin, the Gaelic League and the Co-operative Movement* (Cork: Cork University Press, 2003).

O'Casey's early poverty was so far from his later success that it seemed the preserve of another person. By the 1920s, the terms of cultural affiliation to any idea of Ireland had changed radically; armed insurrection, a guerrilla war, a civil war and the partition of the island into two unstable and contested jurisdictions complicated ideas of audience, reception and reputation. The early phase of the Revival had taken as its archetype a heroic ideal of character. This pose could be maintained after independence only by an act of enormous imaginative repression, such as O'Casey discovered when the Abbey Theatre erupted in outrage at the performance of *The Plough and the Stars* in 1926.[5] Dissidence took refuge in irony and emerged into public view later and abroad in the drama of Samuel Beckett.

There is one last aspect to consider in the aesthetic construction of the autobiography during the period of the Literary Revival, which is the wider cultural commitment to memorialization that decades of political and commercial culture had inscribed in Irish society at large.[6] By the end of the nineteenth century, the British empire was the world's largest trading aggregate. Its adherents and its enemies were both committed to the exchange of material objects as symbols of loyalty or disaffection, and at the end of this period the Easter Rising caused an explosion of postcards, photographs, trinkets and keepsakes.[7] Literature itself partook of a global market, of which Moore and Yeats were a definite part. Ireland possessed a culture of immediate memory, whereby all events, from the domestic to the national, were capable of capture in scrapbooks, diaries and letters. This impulse took state form in the decades after independence with the creation of the Bureau of Military History and its collection of witness statements from individuals involved in the years of rebellion.[8] This culture requires a particular kind of reading, which in the case of auto-biography extends beyond the usual questions of self and identity towards the collective and the material realms, which take literary form in the life of objects that appear across the literary spectrum from Yeats to Joyce. These objects supply another layer of complexity to writers' reflections on their

---

[5] For more on this, see my chapter on O'Casey and controversy in *Modernism, Ireland and Civil War* (Cambridge: Cambridge University Press, 2003), 42–65.

[6] Roisín Higgins's *Transforming 1916: Meaning, Memory and the Fiftieth Anniversary of the Easter Rising* (Cork: Cork University Press, 2013) is an original and informative account of these various pressures on the public memory of a key historical event like the rebellion.

[7] The material history of these exchanges is uncovered in Lisa Godson and Joanna Brück, eds., *Making 1916: Material and Visual Culture of the Easter Rising* (Liverpool: Liverpool University Press, 2015).

[8] Fearghal McGarry's *Rebels: Voices from the Easter Rising* (London: Penguin, 2012) offers an excellent reading of the political contexts of these statements. An analysis of their importance to cultural history still awaits.

past lives and complicate the idea that to tell the story of the self is to write the narrative of Ireland.[9] Ireland in this context is a contingent assembly of things that come from many places, and their description a declaration that no nation stands alone.

George Moore

Autobiography is arguably one of the most persistently seditious operations of memory in literary form. In a late imperial culture undergoing tremendous disruption, the memoir draws the material outline of a society in transition. The domestic interior that frames the conduct of an individual life becomes a critical indicator of the social life to be, and its variety is a rebuke to the standardization of a new state and a refusal of the demand for Ireland to be one idea alone. This is a signature idea of middle-to-late Yeats and the foundation of a classic passage in the early pages of *Autobiographies*, when he remembers his grandfather, William Pollexfen:

> We knew that he had been in many parts of the world, for there was a great scar on his hand made by a whaling-hook, and in the dining-room was a cabinet with bits of coral in it and a jar of water from the Jordan for the baptizing of his children and Chinese pictures upon rice-paper and an ivory walking-stick from India that came to me after his death.[10]

This pen sketch of a lost world can be read as a symbol of estrangement from the straitening impulse of a national literature and culture. Coral, rice and ivory are symbolic disruptions of a contemporary world that is impoverished by the insular turn of a cultural nationalism formed from a doctrine of self-sufficiency.[11] The jumble of imperial life is connected to the idea of eccentricity, and both are orphan categories in nationalist Ireland. Autobiography reanimates their cultural context and by so doing rebukes the present for its constraint. A richness of character is associated

---

[9] Or, as Eamonn Hughes puts it in '"The Fact of Me-ness": Autobiographical Writing in the Revival Period', *Irish University Review*, 33:1 (2003): 'Autobiographies of the Revival period can be productively read as a series of meditations on and arguments about Ireland and Irishness' (28).

[10] W. B. Yeats, *Autobiographies: Reveries over Childhood and Youth and The Trembling of the Veil* (New York: Macmillan, 1927), 7.

[11] This is the idea parodied in the figure of the Citizen in Joyce's *Ulysses* (London: Penguin, 2000), for example, in which the lists of Ireland's wrongs proceed from the distribution by forceful expatriation of its resources outside the island territory: 'Where are our missing twenty millions of Irish should be here today instead of four, our lost tribes? ... And our wool that was sold in Rome in the time of Juvenal and our flax and our damask from the looms of Antrim and our Limerick lace ... nothing like it in the whole wide world!' (423).

with an excess of things, a connection that was made for Yeats by the high aestheticism of Oscar Wilde.

Similarly, Moore's autobiographical masterpiece, *Hail and Farewell* (1911–14), depends for its existence on its author's financial independence, and the majority of his most cutting comments on Irish life proceed from his representation of its economic incapacity. From the moment he arrives in Dublin he finds it difficult to find a suitable house until George Russell suggests one. The three volumes of *Hail and Farewell* are the single best-known work of autobiography of the Revival. No other work of that period approaches Moore's assembly of memoir, gossip and sly intrigue. Brilliantly funny and flamboyantly self-conscious, *Hail and Farewell* is the making of Moore in the undoing of Ireland. A son of the Catholic gentry in the west of Ireland, Moore was already a famous novelist by the time he published his autobiography.[12] As such he was inheritor to a complex European tradition, which he extended by his early career in Paris, where he made his name first as a painter. This background gave Moore a necessarily wary perspective on the Revival's view of an authentic folk culture in Connacht, which it shared with the Irish language movement. An early exchange has Moore discuss playwrighting with Edward Martyn in London: 'I wish I knew enough Irish to write my plays in Irish,' he said one night, speaking out of himself suddenly. You'd like to write your plays in Irish! I exclaimed. I thought nobody did anything in Irish except bring turf from the bog and say prayers.'[13]

Moore's sentimental education in the idea of Ireland as something other than an attachment to a dying past begins with Martyn and develops into the social circle that he creates in the memoir. *Hail and Farewell* is a study of perspective, with time its subject and its object the characters of Dublin. If Moore's Paris was a new Athens, his Dublin is a comic Florence, full of ambitious pretention and built on the flimsiest of cultural foundations, as when George Russell talks to the ancient gods despite the fact that he cannot speak Irish.[14] Moore trapped the Revival in self-consciousness by incorporating its revelatory mode into the structure of his memoir. Over and again he used its prophetic strategies to undercut its human reality and he did so in the most disarming way, which was to create his own character

---

[12] Adrian Frazier has written a life to equal his subject in *George Moore, 1852–1933* (New Haven: Yale University Press, 2000).
[13] George Moore, *Hail and Farewell: Ave, Salve, Vale*, ed. Richard Allen Cave (Gerrards Cross: Colin Smythe, 1985), 55.
[14] Ibid., 278–79.

as the central fool of the comedy, framing the backdrop to his human theatre with a painter's eye:

> But it is difficult to be angry with Ireland on a May morning when the sun is shining, and through clouds slightly more broken than yesterday's, but full of the same gentle, encouraging light . . . I could see a chimney-stack steeped in rich shadow, touched with light, and beyond it, and under it, upon an illuminated wall, the direct outline of a gable; and at the end of the streets the mountains appeared, veiled in haze, delicate and refined as *The Countess Cathleen*.[15]

Dublin, memorably, is a 'town wandering between mountain and sea'.[16] This stray city reminds Moore of childhood and the time when 'inspired by an uncontrollable desire to break the monotony of infancy, [I] stripped myself of my clothes, and ran naked in front of my nurse or governess, screaming with delight at the embarrassment I was causing her'.[17] All this precedes a reflection on Yeats, which prompts the question of whether Moore's desire to return to Ireland was anything more than 'a desire to break the monotony of my life by stripping myself of my clothes and running ahead a naked Gael, screaming Brian Boru?'[18] This is comic sedition by sly association since one of the undercurrents to *Hail and Farewell* is the disrobing of its subjects' sexual attachments. George Russell's long affair with Susan Mitchell is hinted at, as is Edward Martyn's homosexuality, the irony being that Moore's own affections are much more guarded.[19] His internal life emerges through an aesthetic of sensitivity, which suggests another literary texture to the autobiography: its rendering of the self as a series of suggestive moments, a subtlety in direct contradiction of the Literary Revival's insistence on the solid formation of its cultural nationalism.

There is any amount of personal detail in *Hail and Farewell*, some fabricated, some remembered. All of it is in service to Moore's greater project, which is to use the autobiographical form to build a group portrait of the Literary Revival and its major characters. As Adrian Frazier puts it, Moore's 'highly communal sense of the enterprise of authorship . . . was just what was needed for the start of a literary revival'.[20] The portrait is the assembly of Moore's own talents and the best analogy is to Manet's display of his own work on his wall at home: 'The work of the great artist is

---

[15] Ibid., III.   [16] Ibid.   [17] Ibid.   [18] Ibid.

[19] Frazier writes: 'It was precisely to explode all that goes without saying, the whole system of sub-codes about sex, respectability, religion, sectarianism, and class, that Moore wrote *Hail and Farewell*' (*George Moore, 1852–1933*, 370).

[20] Frazier, *George Moore, 1852–1933*, 281.

himself, and, being one of the greatest painters that ever lived, Manet's Art was all Manet.'[21] In so doing, Moore created a version of the Revival that bound these individuals to a narrative not of their choosing. This generated the anger that greeted his work, just as it secured Moore the role of the artist who staged the picture, which requires a reading of *Hail and Farewell* as autobiography by implication. Moore's character is visible only through its reflection on others, as when he struggles to explain Manet and Monet to Russell. Where Moore sees a peony, a hyacinth, a daffodil, Russell sees a serving girl sewing under a dovecot.[22] Taste is a barrier as deep as class and sensitivity the only means to overcome it. Russell mistakes personal feeling for social motivation and so damns the Revival and its prophets as but one more manifestation of aesthetic decline, for which read the loss of the individual in a world now possessed of so many voices it takes three volumes to capture their babble. This is the lament of *Hail and Farewell*, that the intimate self of the nineteenth century has given way to the public personae of the twentieth. Russell is demagogue, poet and damned by his own words. 'We call it mystery', he says of the art he admires, 'but it is merely stupidity'.[23]

Such flagrant disregard for social convention is a gesture again towards *Hail and Farewell*'s essential autobiographical ambition, which is to establish through memoir the retrospective conditions for a European art in Ireland. It is striking how little of *Hail and Farewell* actually takes place in Ireland, and remarkable, too, to note how much of the Dublin literary scene was energized by characters who came from elsewhere. Moore's literary co-ordinates are Turgenev and Balzac, not the heroic theology of an ancient Ireland summoned to the present by a loose coalition of lapsed Protestants and language revivalists. The one great work he admits to the Revival canon is Synge's *Playboy of the Western World* (1907) and even that is undercut by Moore's acid observation that Synge's death did the popularity of his work much good.[24] Such casual cruelty is easy to read as detachment; it is, however, the logical extension of an aesthetic ideal applied to life and a confirmation that *Hail and Farewell* stands above experience, even as it records it. Moore describes Synge's disappointment in his final hour that he could not see the hills of Wicklow from his hospital window, not having the strength to stand up.[25] The memoir can never be so defeated, written as it is from the eternal moment of literature; 'all my dreams', as Moore puts it, 'frozen into the little space of print'.[26]

[21] Moore, *Hail and Farewell*, 532.   [22] Ibid., 273.   [23] Ibid.   [24] Ibid., 561.   [25] Ibid.
[26] Ibid, 97.

W. B. Yeats

There is remarkable consistency in the idea of the dream as life's motivating principle in autobiographies of the Revival period.[27] Partly this is because of rapid change in the memory of the writers who composed their memoirs, and partly because that change was radical in symbolic intention. The political reality and meaning of the revolution are still matters of debate, but the transformation of the idea of Ireland as a culture capable of self-imagination is undeniable, and is now so self-evident as to be difficult to ever imagine otherwise. Dreams and reverie are relics of a society in transition between one idea of itself and another, and phantom figures populate the autobiographies of the Revival period as memories of what other turns Ireland could have taken, culturally, politically and socially. This is a reminder that all literature is an art of the present and that memoir shapes the past with an eye to the future. There is no better example of this than the episodic prose of Yeats's *Autobiographies*, which is a series of memories drawn into brief chronological fragments that begin with *Reveries over Childhood and Youth* (1916) and trace Yeats's development from early life to his becoming an artist.

The Sligo of Yeats's early imagination is a place of overlapping attachments on the shoulder of Ireland's Atlantic coast, a seaport open to the movement of people and to a world trade in goods and commodities. It was also a gateway to the interior, which Yeats, so unlike Moore, romanticized as the basis of a folk culture whose beliefs were to be the foundation of the Revival's self-image. Yeats's guides to this society were the servants his family employed and his commitment to them in his autobiography is a pledge to the apparent reality of Irish traditional life. His admission that much of the style of his *The Celtic Twilight* (1893) is lifted from the speech of his uncle's servant, Mary Battle, is a testament to Yeats's own role as a writer in Ireland, which was as medium and translator. This returns the reader to the abiding idea of reverie or dream, an idea that takes on the raiment of folklore in Ireland even as it grows from a real, and modern, turbulence in ideas across the imperial world. Yeats, in turn, was fascinated by the idea of illusion in the style and substance of his autobiography. *Reveries* begins with the observation that as a child he remembers looking out two windows, one Irish and one English. The larger volume of which it is a part, *Autobiographies*, is full of Yeats's observations on painting and the

---

[27] Perhaps the greatest single example of this idea of existence as extended reverie is Mary Colum's *Life and the Dream: Memories of a Literary Life in Europe and America* (1947).

art of the pre-Raphaelites, and has a reproduction of Jack B. Yeats's watercolour of Sligo, 'Memory Harbour', in its early pages. The presiding figure in this emblematic phase of Yeats's memory was Oscar Wilde, who encouraged the poet in his early career. Wilde, like Parnell, is a symbol to the writers who followed of the difficulty, and the danger, of embodying social life in the body of the individual.[28] The weight of representation breaks the figure that assumes it, and this again points to Yeats's interest in illusion as a medium of memory, and of literature.

Autobiography is the generation of diverting images, memoir the production of miniature scenes carefully drawn to generate meaning and suggestion. This is in keeping with Yeats's interest in the occult and in secret societies more generally, as with his abiding affection for the Fenian activist John O'Leary. Like Wilde, O'Leary spoke in well-formed sentences, a bond between thought and form that Yeats associates with the disciplined reflection of a passionate mind. If Yeats overplayed the influence O'Leary had on him, it was because of O'Leary's importance to his aesthetic understanding. 'From these debates', he writes, 'from O'Leary's conversation, and from the Irish books he lent or gave me has come all I have set my hand to since.'[29] Aesthetic perception was the gateway to a political motivation that the Literary Revival set itself to master. The summons of the controlling image is the province of the poets and the veiled ambition of any literature that aspired to be national:

> nations, races, and individual men are unified by an image, or bundle of related images, symbolical or evocative of the state of mind, which is of all states of mind not impossible, the most difficult to that man, race, or nation; because only the greatest obstacle that can be contemplated without despair rouses the will to full intensity.[30]

That obstacle in Ireland was, in the mind of Yeats and many of his contemporaries, the suppression of the separatist imagination by the deadening hand of the British empire. It was a suppression felt by Yeats as a young and privileged schoolboy, isolated from his fellows in London and dreaming of some future recognition, a thought caught in his memory of an aunt who told him as a boy: 'You are going to London. Here you are somebody. There you will be nobody at all.'[31] *Autobiographies* situates the

---

[28] Wilde's imprisonment in 1895 stood as a warning to the generation that followed of the catastrophe that could attend the deconstruction of art in a court of law. Wilde's perfect sentences were no defence from legal inquiry and he shared with Parnell a fall determined by a public reaction to private desire. See Richard Ellmann, *Oscar Wilde* (London: Vintage, 1988).

[29] Yeats, *Autobiographies*, 125.   [30] Ibid., 241.   [31] Ibid., 33.

Revival in a phase of late imperial decline, the violence of the period, both symbolic and material, a product of the frictions that represented major changes in Irish society. Yeats's concentration on the early phase of his cultural awakening is a reminder that the major moments of rebellion had their roots deep in the cultural revival. The Easter Rising may have flared unexpectedly to life in wartime Dublin, but the sparks that lit it are scattered through Yeats's multiple autobiographical volumes, from the agitations of O'Leary to the seditious folk dramas of the Abbey Theatre. The Rising was one of a sequence of events that led to the War of Independence, the Irish Civil War and the social constriction of the new state, which Yeats found so loathsome.[32] Yeats drew an arc between these events and his agitation as a young man when he remembered the street fights, the broken windows and the loss of life that attended Queen Victoria's visit to Dublin in 1900: 'I count the links in the chain of responsibility, run them across my fingers, and wonder if any link there is from my workshop.'[33]

Maud Gonne MacBride

Maud Gonne MacBride was Yeats's companion in this period of unpopular agitation for Irish separatism. She figures in his *Autobiographies* as a fleeting figure, despite the long-standing and complicated attachment Yeats had to her throughout his life. Gonne published her own autobiography, *A Servant of the Queen*, in 1938, the year before Yeats died. By this time the two were separated, like many others, by the violent trauma of the Civil War and the gulf between political compromise, represented by the reality of the Irish Free State, and the unyielding pursuit of an independent republic. Executions, imprisonment and marginalization did not deter Gonne from a commitment to full and separate self-government that was born of a messianic belief in Ireland's existence as a spiritual entity. *A Servant of the Queen* applies Revival mysticism to the practice of armed resistance and does so without apology. As Yeats worried over the effect of his words on a rising generation in his 1938 poem 'Man and the Echo',

---

[32] Yeats's signature response to the moral restrictions of the new state, of which he was a privileged member, is signified best in his notorious 1925 speech in the Irish Senate on the subject of a divorce bill. As R. F. Foster points out in *W. B. Yeats: A Life, II: The Arch-Poet 1915–1939* (Oxford: Oxford University Press, 2003): 'Anticipating that "when the iceberg melts [Ireland] will become an exceedingly tolerant country", he went on to instance the monuments in Dublin's streets to Parnell, Nelson, and O'Connell – all, by WBY's definition, adulterers' (297).

[33] Yeats, *Autobiographies*, 452.

Gonne reminded that generation of its responsibility to honour the martyrs who died for Ireland.

This militant philosophy was partly a response to a jumble of difficult experiences that Gonne refined into a way of seeing the world at large. *A Servant of the Queen* is a narrative about agency as much as it is about Ireland, and Gonne's vision of Cathleen ni Houlihan in its early pages can be read as an affirmation of women's centrality to the ideas and practice of Irish nationalism. Histories of the Literary Revival insisted for decades that it was a movement of men. Gonne was significant only as a muse to Yeats, and her role as a militant activist only confirmed a political prejudice from the Civil War that associated republicanism with female hysteria. Culturally, her work with Alice Milligan and a cohort of other women writers was ignored, an omission that is still in the process of being remedied.[34] Yeats was not alone in his objectification of Gonne as a symbol of something other than herself, and the confusion of her beauty and her privileged background with her desire to express herself forcefully in nationalist politics indicates the difficulties she faced in establishing herself as an individual of substance. Gonne was conscious of this pressure and her resistance to it had its own consequences for Yeats and the practice of the Revival as separatist propaganda, as when he wrote *The Countess Cathleen*, first performed in 1899, with Gonne in mind for the lead part, of which she wrote:

> He said he had written the part of the Countess Kathleen for me and I *must* act it. I was severely tempted, for the play fascinated me and I loved acting, but just because I loved the stage so much I had made the stern resolve never to act. I was afraid it would absorb me too much to the detriment of my work. I knew my own weakness, and how, when I got interested in anything, I was capable of forgetting everything else, – house building, evicted tenants, political prisoners, even the fight against the British Empire, might all disappear in the glamour of the stage; it was the only form of self-discipline I consciously practised.[35]

Gonne's particular mix of liberation and restraint was perhaps more Edwardian than might appear. This is no criticism of her commitment to Ireland but an acknowledgement rather that Irish culture, including that of the Revival, was, and remains, an assembly of the local and the global,

---

[34] Catherine Morris's brilliant *Alice Milligan and the Irish Cultural Revival* (Dublin: Four Courts Press, 2012) is a powerful remedy to this history of oversight.

[35] Maud Gonne MacBride, *A Servant of the Queen*, eds. A. Norman Jeffares and Anna MacBride White (Gerrards Cross: Colin Smythe, 1994), 176. Original emphasis.

however nationalism tried to represent it otherwise. There is a beautiful passage in the early pages of *A Servant of the Queen* that illustrates the power of autobiography to represent this, in which the sensory powers of memory undo the bonds of place and time. Her mother dead and her father in mourning, Maud moved with her household to Howth on the north side of Dublin Bay:

> No place has ever seemed to me quite so lovely as Howth was then. Sometimes the sea was as blue as Mama's turquoises, more strikingly blue even than the Mediterranean because so often grey mists made it invisible and mysterious. The little rock pools at the bottom of the high cliffs were very clear and full of wonder-life; sea-anemones which open look like gorgeous flowers with blue and orange spots and, if touched, close up into ugly brown lumps, tiny crabs, pink star-fish, endless varieties of sea-snails, white, green, striped and bright buttercup-yellow.[36]

This passage is worth considering because autobiography tells more than the story of its writer. If the objects that make memory material are important signs of the historical past in literary form, so a rendition of the senses suggests the outer boundaries of a writer's comparative capacity to understand other times and places. This capacity varies with the political contingency of the social moment in which the text is created, so that Gonne's reverie over the bright colours of youth can be read as a revolt against the diminished palette of later life. There can be argument over the practical reality of Gonne's commitment to political revolution in Ireland, but as a work of art *A Servant of the Queen* continues her campaign to disrupt the settlement of ideas into oppressive consensus.[37] Gonne had little interest in securing the reputation of the Literary Revival, or her place in it, but her autobiography shows the movement in a rich context of cultural upheaval, an upheaval that continued long after Yeats's generation gave way to Joyce, Beckett and a modernism that turned away from national construction – a fact in itself that suggests why these later writers left no significant autobiographies, their work being set against any idea of a final constitution of a monumental self.

Such a prescription draws too fine a line, however, between the literary practices of the Revival and the aesthetic innovations of the modernists, the careers of whom so frequently overlapped, as exemplified by Yeats, who

---

[36] Ibid., 17.
[37] Gonne's work as a political activist is an important part of the wider context captured by Margaret Ward in *Unmanageable Revolutionaries: Women and Irish Nationalism* (London: Pluto Press, 1996) and by Liz Gillis in *Women of the Irish Revolution* (Cork: Mercier Press, 2014).

straddled both traditions and can be confined to neither. The remarkable sophistication of the Revival's symbolic self-becoming is a foundation of *A Servant of the Queen* and represents a transnational awareness that is contrary to the idea of Irish cultural nationalism as isolationist because it was separatist. This awareness informs a persistently republican perspective on social history in Gonne's memoir, a perspective that is drawn with varying degrees of subtlety in the text. One early example is the memory of her Aunt Mary, who had married the Comte de la Sizeranne and lived in Paris as a widow. Her aunt's hobby was to launch society beauties and Maud was chosen as her next project, taking her to Guerlin's for perfume and make-up, powders and faces creams, all of which were washed off in favour of her natural appearance:

> She certainly succeeded in getting me spoken of as 'the belle of the season'; enterprising photographers requested me to sit for my photograph; my pictures appeared in society papers; strangers even began asking me to sign autograph albums. Aunt Mary was delighted but it was beginning to get on my nerves, though I was vain enough in some ways.[38]

This passage reveals the poverty of thinking about self-identity in the context of a national literature and points instead to the importance of ephemeral, commercialized moments in the construction of a Revivalist self. Katharine Tynan's memoirs, which stretch across five volumes published between 1913 and 1924, are a classic example of this mode, in which gossip becomes the major material of the autobiography. The past is recounted as a series of vignettes, the collection of which creates a commercial opportunity for the comic memoir, the fictional equivalent of which is Somerville and Ross's *Some Experiences of an Irish R. M.* (1899).

A Servant of the Queen comprises a series of scenes in which the global underpinnings of Irish culture are made visible in the narration of Gonne's revolutionary life. Her establishment upbringing and her radical turn are intimately connected in a culture that is embedded with objects and ideas in constant flow. Part of the Revival's radical strategy had been to use art to create moments of stillness to slow this manic exchange and so disable its imperial machinery. It was so successful that a new literature emerged in which stasis was celebrated as an essential Irish form (it is hard, after all, not to think of the Revival without hearing the drowsy music in the half-light of 'The Lake Isle of Innisfree'). In contrast, *A Servant of the Queen* is

---

[38] The emblematic episode of this aspect of Gonne's experience is her involvement with the socialist James Connolly in the protests that attended Queen Victoria's jubilee visit to Ireland in 1900. See *A Servant of the Queen*, 35.

dramatic and unreconciled, the theatricality of Gonne's subversion a public display of her dissidence.[39]

Conclusion

A Servant of the Queen takes its place beside Yeats's *Autobiographies* and Moore's *Hail and Farewell* as a canonical account of the Irish Literary Revival because, like them, it represents an aesthetic of transformation that is globally inflected by ideas and objects from a range of people and places, the constellation of which draws new boundaries for a movement that did its best to appear island-bound. The ultimate scandal of a work like Moore's was less the revelation of its subjects' vanity than its insistence that Ireland's literary movement, and by extension its cultural imagination, was an inescapably hybrid product of a world closely connected by the movements of its peoples. The Revival itself was one form of adaptation to this migration of ideas. Autobiography was another, a genre that evolved to capture the movement's contradictory complexities.

Further reading

Frazier, Adrian. *George Moore, 1852–1933*. New Haven: Yale University Press, 2000.

Grubgeld, Elizabeth. 'Life Writing in the Twentieth Century', in John Wilson Foster, ed., *The Cambridge Companion to the Irish Novel*. Cambridge: Cambridge University Press, 2006: 223–37.

Harte, Liam, ed. *Modern Irish Autobiography: Self, Nation and Society*. Basingstoke: Palgrave Macmillan, 2007.

Hughes, Eamonn. '"The Fact of Me-ness": Autobiographical Writing in the Revival Period', *Irish University Review*, 33:1 (2003): 28–45.

Matthews, P. J. *Revival: The Abbey Theatre, Sinn Féin, the Gaelic League and the Co-operative Movement*. Cork: Cork University Press, 2003.

McGarry, Fearghal. *Rebels: Voices from the Easter Rising*. London: Penguin, 2012.

---

[39] Gonne MacBride, *A Servant of the Queen*, 217.

CHAPTER II

Irish Literary Autobiography since the Revival

Christina Hunt Mahony

Autobiographical writing by Irish literary figures has proliferated in recent decades, garnering critical acclaim and achieving parity with the authors' creative output. It is worthwhile, then, to remember that the genre has only recently been afforded such respect. Liam Harte dubbed autobiography 'the Cinderella genre' to reflect its overlooked status, and while the sobriquet is apt, it may belie the knowingness of the form.[1] Claire Lynch's related affirmation of the fairy tale allusion includes an awareness of the malleability the genres share. Both feature 'people and things that appear to be one thing only to be revealed as another'.[2] This recognition of inherent duality, and the impossibility of memory retrieving a singular truth about a life, hearkens to George Moore's facetious autobiographical disclaimer in *Hail and Farewell* (1911–14): 'For years I believed myself to be the author of *Hail and Farewell*, whereas I was nothing more than the secretary.'[3] But literary autobiography is not an act of transcription. It is a genre with a tradition as formal as that of the novel. It can be as structured as any poem and, in full autobiographies, have a denouement as crucial as in any successful drama. Even when other elements in the writing give way to experimentation, the familiar autobiographical tropes remain.

Modern literary autobiography in Ireland acquires complexity because it derives from two literary traditions. From mainstream English letters it has acquired the format established in the late nineteenth century, with its greatest exemplars dating from the early decades of the twentieth – Edmund Gosse's *Father and Son* (1907); Henry James's *A Small Boy and Others* (1913), *Notes of a Son and Brother* (1914) and *The Middle Years* (1917);

[1] Liam Harte, 'Introduction: Autobiography and the Irish Cultural Moment', in Liam Harte, ed., *Modern Irish Autobiography: Self, Nation and Society* (New York: Palgrave Macmillan, 2007), 1–13.
[2] Claire Lynch, *Irish Autobiography: Stories of Self in the Narrative of a Nation* (Bern and Oxford: Peter Lang, 2009), 7.
[3] George Moore, *Hail and Farewell: Ave, Salve, Vale*, ed. Richard Allen Cave (Gerrards Cross: Colin Smythe, 1985), 51.

163

and Robert Graves's *Goodbye to All That* (1927). These filial and self-conscious accounts of the lives of great men of letters speak not only to each other, but are also echoed in Irish ur-texts of the genre, such as Yeats's *Reveries over Childhood and Youth* (1916). As the non-fictive equivalent of the *Künstlerroman*, these books often begin in infancy, and their singular aim is to map the journey of the child and youth to the fulfilment of his (early texts are exclusively male) vocation as a writer. The developmental process involves nearly Freudian stages of identification with, and subsequent rejection of, the father or father figures. The second, and indigenous, autobiographical tradition providing a model for Irish writers is that written in the Irish vernacular by inhabitants of the Blasket Islands, notably Tomás Ó Criomhthain, Muiris Ó Súilleabháin and Peig Sayers. Books such as *An tOileánach* (*The Islandman*) (1929), *Fiche Bliain ag Fás* (*Twenty Years A-Growing*) (1933) and *Peig* (1936) track the lives of the authors but are situated within the context of a community and an oral storytelling tradition. These island writers had no models of highly individuated autobiographies and were nurtured in a society in which interdependency was integral to identity formation. From this vernacular and community strain a uniquely Irish form of autobiographical writing has evolved in which the patriarchal transmutes into a nationalist imperative that is noticeably absent in the work of the island writers.[4]

An autobiographical volume that begins at birth, or in infancy, and tracks milestones of personal development to adulthood is only one of many formats available to the literary author. Another is the episodic memoir that features vignettes to illustrate the life as a whole. A writer can also approach literary life-writing by tracing a genealogy or bloodline that situates his or her people in the broad social context, at times to argue for inherited artistic traits. Others sketch a portrait of a literary era or school, a professional parallel to the familial memoir. Whether providing a 'whole' life or a partial glimpse into his or her origins and development as a writer, familiar elements and recurring events will appear predictably. Even *romans à clef*, narrative poems and plays published as fictive works can function as autobiographical narratives.

Since the start of the Literary Revival in Ireland, and especially since the establishment of the state in 1922, autobiographies have been concerned with authenticating a writer's Irishness, especially if that Irishness could be contested. Writers whose heritage was Anglo-Irish and Protestant were among

---

[4] For an apt example, see Máire Cruise O'Brien, *The Same Age as the State* (Dublin: O'Brien Press, 2003).

those whose authenticity was regularly questioned. Beginning with Yeats's account of his early life in *Reveries over Childhood and Youth*, the need to establish national authenticity has become perhaps the most prominent trope in this genre. From the infant Yeats being proudly shown an 'Irish window'[5] in a house previously owned by a family member, to the boy Yeats engaging in punch-ups in a London school where he was forced to defend his nation's honour, Yeats, writing in middle age, sets out to authenticate, retrospectively, his credentials to lead an Irish cultural revival. His early memoir also contains a rather staged incident in which the young Yeats, living in London, longs for a 'sod of earth from some field I knew, something of Sligo to hold in my hand',[6] to better connect him emotionally and physically to his native soil. He makes frequent reference in the book to the unreliability of memory, which is key to our understanding of the genre, but his deft choice of the word reverie in his title places the work on a semi-rational plane of consciousness, somewhere between sleeping and waking.

Boyhood scenes similar to those in Yeats's memoir appear in Louis MacNeice's *The Strings Are False: An Unfinished Autobiography* (1965). MacNeice's father dandles him on his knee and recites the names of towns seen from train windows along the railway line from their home in Carrickfergus to Belfast, thus making the places their own. Later, the school-boy MacNeice admits to playing 'the Wild Irish Boy' at Sherborne pre-paratory school, while archly bemoaning his 'pathetically suburban'[7] upbringing that left him bereft of the riding and poaching skills that could have lent him a genuine Irish panache. The similarity of incidental detail in these works, published almost fifty years apart, is not unusual given that MacNeice had just finished writing his monograph, *The Poetry of W. B. Yeats* (1941), when he undertook to write *The Strings Are False*. Perhaps more surprising is the structural congruity of both books with Joyce's *A Portrait of the Artist as a Young Man* (1916), which, though published and read as a novel, echoes through decades of Irish autobiography, especially in set pieces highlighting the hero's difference from other boys, his moral courage and early fascination with language and the acquisition of language skills – all attributes which mark the nascent writer.[8]

---

[5] W. B. Yeats, *Autobiographies* (London: Macmillan, 1955), 5.   [6] Ibid., 31.

[7] Louis MacNeice, *The Strings Are False: An Unfinished Autobiography* (London: Faber and Faber, 1965), 222.

[8] Joyce's early work differs only, but significantly, in his blatant questioning and rejection of the Irishness his successors work so diligently to establish. See Eve Patten, '"Life Purified and Reprojected": Autobiography and the Modern Irish Novel', in Harte, ed., *Modern Irish Autobiography*, 51–69.

MacNeice, who lived most of his life in England, always identified himself as Irish, and especially with the west of Ireland, where both his parents were born. Living through the Second World War in London, at a time when loyalties were tested, compelled MacNeice to write an auto-biography that established his Irish pedigree, although the book was written on board ship as he returned to Britain voluntarily in late 1940 with the expectation of doing military service. Found unfit to serve, evidence of his continuingly conflicted identity surfaces in his wartime poems, some of which dared to touch upon topics considered unpatriotic, like looting and suicide. The manuscript, which MacNeice gave to his friend and fellow Ulster classicist E. R. Dodds in 1941, remained unfinished and unpublished in the poet's lifetime.

With their boyhood milestones and emphasis on formal schooling – usually the first separation from family – Yeats's and MacNeice's autobio-graphical works adhere to English literary models and their tropes. There is a particular resonance, however, to fostering, an Irish practice with ancient origins, in which boys or young men are given over to others with expertise to develop inherent talent. School (especially boarding school) memoirs provide insights into other formative experiences for those who will become writers. It is here where we often learn what these boys read and witness the begin-nings of language sensitivity. Yeats, who had an erratic education, bemoaned not having simply studied Latin and Greek under his father's tutelage. He also lists books encountered as a boy, either through his father's influence or accidentally – including Shakespeare from an early age, but also early exposure to Shelley, considered risqué by many at the time. His boyhood reading also included the Brothers Grimm and Hans Christian Andersen, followed in young adulthood by Huxley, Darwin, Thoreau and Blake.[9] In vivid contrast to this eclectic start to an intellectual life, MacNeice's list is a perfect example of what a well-bred young man of his era, educated at a public school, would be expected to read: Shakespeare at age eight, but then Dryden and Herrick at nine, Mallory and all of Dante before age fourteen and, by his final year of school, Tolstoy, Dostoievski, Nietzsche, a range of European philosophers and a thorough grounding in Greek.

Boyhood reading matter also features in a pair of autobiographies pub-lished in the 1960s by Cork writers Sean O'Faolain and Frank O'Connor, fated to be forever linked in literary history as they were in life. Like others of their generation, O'Faolain and O'Connor (born respectively in 1900 and 1903) came of age in a country that was not a Yeatsian construct but a

---

[9] Yeats, *Autobiographies*, 47, 57–58.

fledgling polity. Both men fought to secure the future of their new nation and quickly became disillusioned with the reality that evolved after rebellion and civil war. Both undertook significant name changes, thereby adding complexity to their personal and national identities. Sean O'Faolain, who began life as John Whelan, and Frank O'Connor, who was born Michael O'Donovan, were at times friends and colleagues and, at other times, fell out with each other. They shared impoverished urban childhoods and mentoring by nationalist writer and academic Daniel Corkery. Each wrote autobiographical works that became, unusually, bestsellers in Ireland. Many Irish homes had copies of O'Faolain's *Vive Moi!* (1964) and of O'Connor's *An Only Child* (1961) and *My Father's Son* (1968) on their bookshelves, and these titles are well known even today, though the books themselves are less read.

How O'Faolain and O'Connor wrote their life experiences is a study in both comparison and contrast. From the start, with its foreign and exclamatory title, O'Faolain's *Vive Moi!* is an extravagant work, written in a high register. The writer draws a spellbinding portrait of his childhood home on Half-Moon Street, where his mother took in lodgers from the nearby opera house – actors, singers and burlesque artists from various countries, exotic creatures with foreign finery and ways. The strong imagery of the rear door of the opera house gaping open on occasion to allow the boy a glimpse into another life carries throughout the volume. The provincial limitations of Cork city are contrasted with wider and different worlds, be it O'Faolain's initial exposure to the remote, wild stretches of the Gaeltacht beyond Gougane Barra in west Cork or eye-opening experiences of continental travel years later. O'Faolain's tone is emotive, at times rancorous and contradictory, and ceaselessly searching for a satisfactory compromise between Irishness and a cosmopolitan awareness of modern life. As such the book presents an accurate portrait of its author, as contemporary accounts can attest. *Vive Moi!* was reissued in 1993 in an expanded version with information considered too sensitive to include in the earlier printing, especially regarding O'Faolain's extramarital affairs. This later edition was edited and introduced by the author's daughter Julia, a writer of distinction and author of her own memoir, *Trespassers* (2013). Julia O'Faolain's introduction is a rare intervention in the annals of autobiography, including as it does a barbed critique of her father's memoir, penned by a family member with a strong emotional stake in the subject matter.[10]

---

[10] If there is a precedent, it is provided by Elizabeth Nicholson, MacNeice's sister, who appends eight footnotes to the published text of *The Strings Are False*, verifying details and taking issue with one assertion of substance.

Both O'Faolain and O'Connor strengthened the traditions of Irish literary autobiography. Both authenticate their Irishness through detailed portraits, comic or reverential, of real characters from their early lives that bring the rural vernacular tradition into focus. Since the Irish mythos ranks rural life above urban experience, each of these city-born writers is at pains to place himself within a rural continuum. O'Connor chooses the whimsical voice of a child narrator, a diminuendo in contrast to O'Faolain's bravura effort. In *An Only Child*, the child's voice is expertly put to use in the descriptions of his countrified Irish-speaking grandmother, whose coarseness is a source of embarrassment, or so it is portrayed. Numerous country folk, vibrant characters all, populate O'Connor's record of his early life, and serve as prototypes for later fictional characters.

Both autobiographers are acutely aware of, and frequently reference, the titans of previous generations, Yeats and Joyce, and borrow tropes from their work. O'Connor, in *An Only Child*, like Yeats, brings alive a raft of immediate forebears to fill in his genealogy and thus establish his niche in Irish society. In the later *My Father's Son*, O'Connor's final two chapters are largely about Yeats, who predominates as a surrogate paternal figure. A similar level of problematized reverence for Joyce is in evidence in O'Faolain's *Vive Moi!*, along with comparisons of their youthful experiences and attitudes to their native land. That O'Faolain is admiring of Joyce's self-imposed exile in the name of art is apparent from remarks he makes in chapter eight:

> What about Joyce? That one Irish name which will always challenge us stay-at-homes? What heroism, and what martyrdom, that name evokes! He reminds us that there is no end to the dangers of the intellectual adventure, that a man could gamble a whole life on its hazards as surely as a soldier crossing a minefield, that it demands as much moral courage to think as I do, that every man must be lost in admiration of the scholar's persistence and heroic loneliness.[11]

In particular, the autobiographical work of O'Faolain and O'Connor shares with Yeats and Joyce a preoccupation with paternal influence and its ultimate rejection. The world of fathers is in each case depicted, admired, exploited, decried and finally discarded as each man finds his true milieu. While it is true that most autobiographical writing involves such Oedipal separation, in Ireland the process is compounded by nationalist imperatives. This fused rejection of the world of fathers and nation, or

---

[11] Sean O'Faolain, *Vive Moi!* (London: Sinclair-Stevenson, 1993), 114.

aspects of nation, in favour of art, is initially exemplified in Stephen Dedalus's rejection of the improvident Simon Dedalus and of Ireland, its language and religion, in *A Portrait of the Artist*.

O'Connor's autobiographical writing does differ from traditional literary life-writing in one highly significant detail found more commonly in Ireland than elsewhere in the Anglophone world. Because most literary autobiographies concentrate on formal education, the influence of mothers is minimized. They are often omitted from the narrative entirely after the nursery years, when the world of female carers gives way to that of men and boys. This transition usually took place around the age of seven, traditionally considered the age of reason, and often when formal schooling began. In O'Connor's work, for all the emphasis on father-son relations, there is far more about O'Connor's indomitable mother, with whom he often shared a home in adult life and who tolerated her son's unconventional domestic arrangements. (O'Connor had children by four women. At times he lived simultaneously with two of these women and his mother.) O'Connor's doting portrait of Minnie O'Donovan finds an earlier model in Sean O'Casey's six-volume account of his life in which the equally long-suffering Susan Cassidy is fondly remembered.[12] Later Irish writers who, like O'Casey and O'Connor, would choose to work outside the male paradigm include Seamus Deane, Hugo Hamilton and John McGahern, discussed below. These memoirs, which stray from the preferred paternal orientation, share a counter-imperative to reclaim dignity for women who led lives blighted by poverty or domestic abuse or both.

A generation or more after O'Connor and O'Faolain, a pair of writers known for critical rather than creative work and born north of the newly-created border, Denis Donoghue and the aforementioned Deane, seem at first glance to share much biographically. Born in 1928 and 1940 respectively, both men came from the Catholic minority in Northern Ireland, and both became, rather against the odds, eminent academicians. It is perhaps here where obvious parallels end, as Donoghue's father was a member of the Royal Ulster Constabulary. The name of the town where he served long-term as a policeman provides the title of Donoghue's restrained and erudite memoir. *Warrenpoint* (1990) is, perhaps, of all Irish literary autobiographies of its century, the one that is most acutely aware of the English literary tradition from which it originates. Although Donoghue takes time to deride such contrived set pieces as are found in James's *A Small Boy and Others*

---

[12] O'Casey's memoirs were later published in a two-volume edition, *Mirror in the House: The Autobiographies* (1956), and under the single title *Autobiographies* (1963).

(where James gives the impression of being able, as a toddler driven through the streets of Paris, to distinguish architectural styles in passing), the ghost of James hovers, nevertheless, over Donoghue's text.[13] Names of prominent influences on his intellectual life also appear regularly on pages relating a rather ordinary, though disciplined, childhood. As their father was the local sergeant, the Donoghue children were discouraged from mixing with other children in the town, and a suitably aloof quality marks the book's content and style.

Donoghue's autobiography avails of the genealogy trope and reveals an early delight in learning. Like O'Faolain and O'Connor, he also recognizes the Catholic church's crucial role in his early formation. Such accounts by Irish writers note the initial attraction of the Latin mass and the liturgy of other devotions. In unadorned lives, lived in households where there was little that was frivolous, decorative or aesthetically satisfying, the lure of the colour, light, scent, music and exotic language that the church and its rituals provided proved powerful sensory stimulants for a child sensitive enough to become imprinted by early and frequent exposure.

Seamus Deane's award-winning autobiographical novel *Reading in the Dark* (1996) illuminates another world within the boundaries of Northern Ireland. Deane's family, from working-class Derry but with Donegal roots, is wary of the law and its agents within the province. A major thread of this *roman à clef* concerns Deane's fugitive Uncle Eddie and the complex membrane of family loyalties and treacheries that are the backstory for his disappearance. Deane's autobiographical text also contains an unusual feature for any work within the genre. Autobiographies are notorious for eclipsing or eliminating siblings. Yeats's brother and sisters feature minimally; MacNeice had a brother with Down Syndrome as his sole childhood companion after his older sister went to boarding school. Denis Donoghue dedicates *Warrenpoint* to his brother John who died at age four, but his other siblings in the book are sketchily drawn. Frank O'Connor was an only child; Sean O'Faolain refers in passing to a brother halfway through the text. Seamus Deane, unlike all these, and while maintaining the guise of fiction, goes so far as to reproduce on the dust jacket a childhood photograph of himself and one of his brothers. Deane goes on to recount detailed incidents affecting the many children in his family and, like Donoghue, records the death of one of his siblings. This choice gives the strong sense within Deane's book that family solidarity was quintessential to his upbringing. In Northern Ireland, as Seamus Heaney reminded us,

---

[13] Denis Donoghue, *Warrenpoint* (London: Jonathan Cape, 1991), 28–29.

'Whatever you say, say nothing' is a mantra, and became ingrained practice among the impoverished ranks of minority Catholics within Derry's walls. Numerous and complex family alliances give definition and reinforce identity for the evolving writer.

Regarding the formal experience of schooling, *Reading in the Dark* contains one of the fullest, most appreciative and wryest commentaries in print on Catholic education in Ireland during the last century. Deane, a classmate of Heaney's in St Columb's College, a Catholic grammar school in Derry city, sketches the impressive strengths of such formal education, along with its idiosyncrasies and cruelties, all present in cameo form in the chapter entitled 'Maths Class: November, 1951'.[14] Like many scenes in the book, this chapter shares a dynamic with the second chapter of Joyce's *Portrait*, in which a bored and superior Stephen Dedalus silently disparages members of his university cohort, and with the 'Nestor' chapter of *Ulysses* (1922), which depicts Stephen's later experience as a teacher. As in Joyce, the interaction between teacher and students rendered by Deane is not always reverent, but it is razor sharp and as quintessentially Irish as any such account can be.

Memoir (2005), the autobiography of John McGahern, a contemporary of Donoghue and Deane, iterates the normative structures of Irish rural life in the postwar years, and also shines a highly individual light upon the development of writerly consciousness in the mid-twentieth century. McGahern shares the experience of being a policeman's son with Donoghue and Dermot Healy, but exposes a far bleaker portrait of family life lived within strikingly similar parameters. While Sergeant Donoghue of the RUC appears as a highly principled and respected officer, and Garda Healy will appear as a well-loved figure, Sergeant McGahern emerges as a dissatisfied and violent man who lived separately from his growing family for as much of the year as he could. McGahern's autobiography, like O'Connor's, eschews the patriarchal model, offering instead a loving portrait of his poignant relationship with his mother, who died when he was ten years old. Because Susan McGahern was a teacher (who retained her position despite a national ban in the Irish Free State on married women working at jobs in the public service) there is much here about education and learning, and the variance that existed among rural schools. McGahern also turns his lens outside the family home to pen portraits of his wider family connections and the villages where he was reared, thus

[14] Seamus Deane, *Reading in the Dark* (London: Jonathan Cape, 1996), 90–96.

fulfilling the genealogical imperatives of the genre. Kinsmen, neighbours and mentors are formative to the writer he will become.

In both Healy's *The Bend for Home* (1996) and George O'Brien's *The Village of Longing* (1987), family and community form a nearly seamless continuum, the latter being as central to the writer's development as the former. Unlike the island writers whose accounts of community are the essence of their books, neither Healy nor O'Brien remains rooted to the place where he was born. Healy's family moves when his father becomes too ill to work any longer as a garda. O'Brien suffers a similar displacement when, after his mother's death, he is reared by his father's family in their home place. Each child's initial sense of otherness is vividly conveyed. The move to a new place requires authentication or re-authentication – a regional variation on the national impetus and a process embedded in Irish life-writing of the period. When the Healy family leaves the child's beloved village of Finea in Co. Westmeath for Cavan town, his mother's family place, the distraught boy puts himself to sleep by mentally retracing the streets and houses of Finea while trying to find his place in his new surroundings. George O'Brien approached a similar problem as a child, but in reverse. He determined to minimize all elements of his Wexford birthright in his mother's town of Enniscorthy, so as to become a fully-fledged citizen of Lismore in Co. Waterford. Each of these writers, as schoolboys, also escapes into fugitive or unconventional reading. O'Brien's Uncle Geo, himself 'a terror to read', takes the boy weekly to the local library; in an era when there is no such thing as a children's section, the young boy – later sent on occasion to read to an elderly neighbour – is set free to choose whatever books he fancies.[15] Healy, whose secondary school-ing in Cavan meant a more structured regime, still managed unusual choices for a sixteen-year-old boy, clandestinely reading literary texts like *The Vicar of Wakefield* (1766) during science classes.[16] The pleasures of illicit reading appear regularly in Irish literary memoirs, its secrecy a source of recurring relish. It wasn't only Seamus Deane who was reading in the dark.

Authentification through genealogy, religion, education and regional affiliation informs Irish literary autobiography through the decades, and while writers like Donoghue, Deane, Healy and O'Brien emerged from families with less than completely normative backgrounds, each could boast a degree of acceptability within society. For Nuala O'Faolain and

---

[15] George O'Brien, *The Village of Longing and Dancehall Days* (London: Penguin, 1989), 28–32.
[16] Dermot Healy, *The Bend for Home* (London: Harvill, 1996), 220–21.

Hugo Hamilton, who would become friends in later life, a thin layer of surface conformity belied familial dysfunction. In Hamilton's case, the need to authenticate Irishness after the establishment of the Republic in 1949 resulted in his father taking to heart the directives of the new nationalism. As a result, Hamilton (or Ó hUrmoltaigh, in the Irish language) was reared in a home where Irish was spoken to the exclusion of English and he was beaten for any violations of house rules. Hamilton's German mother, who came to Ireland in the wake of the Second World War and appears as a benign presence in her son's memoirs, represented nonetheless another contested arena in the authentication process for her children. *The Speckled People* (2003), Hamilton's first autobiographical volume, is part of a larger project that includes, in differing forms, fiction, non-fiction and theatrical productions.[17] Ironically, so culturally and linguistically isolated from society were Hamilton and his siblings that they considered English-speaking Ireland as the other – an exterior world prohibited by paternal decree – where they were derided because of their 'alien' customs, speech and dress. Ireland lay menacingly outside the Hamilton home. Such continued probing of familial history and its accommodations is not unique in recent Irish autobiographical writing and resembles the multi-generational autobiographical project of Hamilton's contemporary, Sebastian Barry. Barry's work on the stage and page illumines an array of forebears who bear witness to his family's place in Irish history in such works as *The Steward of Christendom* (1995), *Annie Dunne* (2002), *A Long Long Way* (2005), *The Secret Scripture* (2008) and *Days Without End* (2016). Both writers also problematize their relations with family members, questioning the choices made by parents and others and the bearing those decisions had on the writers' own formation.

Nuala O'Faolain (who has no connection with Sean or Julia O'Faolain, discussed above) also writes in this interrogatory mode in *Are You Somebody? The Accidental Memoir of a Dublin Woman* (1996), a record of her search for her own place in Irish society. O'Faolain's home life resembles that of Hamilton in its dysfunctional quotidian reality, which was hidden from others.[18] O'Faolain's father, a well-known journalist

---

[17] *The Speckled People* was followed by *The Sailor in the Wardrobe* (2006), published in the United States as *The Harbor Boys* in the same year. A dramatic version of *The Speckled People* appeared on the stage at Dublin's Gate Theatre in 2011 and was published by Methuen in the same year. *The Mariner*, based on *The Sailor in the Wardrobe*, was also staged at the Gate, in 2014.

[18] As a coda to their autobiographical work and in tribute to his friend's thirst for life, Hugo Hamilton published a novel, *Every Single Minute* (2014), which is a fictionalized version of a trip he and O'Faolain undertook together to Berlin in 2008, when O'Faolain was dying of cancer.

whose *nom de plume* was Terry O'Sullivan, was a beloved figure in Dublin, prominent at a variety of social occasions. Handsome, articulate and gregarious, he was also a womanizer who left his wife and growing number of children at home with insufficient funds for food, clothing and other basics. O'Faolain writes about her mother's painful slide into alcoholism and her own problems with substance abuse and resultant inability to form lasting relations.

O'Faolain's childhood, blighted as it might have been, bears out and elucidates, yet again, the importance and centrality of reading in the early years of these authors. The young Nuala was so delighted when suddenly the mysterious black marks on the page became words that she ran down the street to tell the woman in the local newsagent's that she could read. Reading quickly became her consolation, both at home and later at boarding school. *Are You Somebody?*, with its lists of books the author read at various ages, is a valuable document that gives a rare enough glimpse into female education – in O'Faolain's case, at the highly regarded St Louis Convent in Clones, Co. Monaghan. O'Faolain's account of convent schooling follows on from Kate O'Brien's *Presentation Parlour* (1963), in that both credit the strong influence of nuns in the formation of Irish women for generations. O'Brien's unique contribution is to combine familial history with an account of religious education; three aunts were teaching sisters, one an abbess, and O'Brien, whose mother died when she was five, was fostered within the convent walls. These female accounts of formal Catholic education stand in marked contrast to the early and alternate experiences of writers such as Elizabeth Bowen, who shows in *Seven Winters* (1942) how the world before the Great War in Protestant upper-class Dublin consigned female education to governesses who escorted girls to dancing classes. Bowen's slim volume of her early life is overshadowed by her far better-known genealogical and decidedly patri-archal memoir, *Bowen's Court* (1942), in which she, her father's sole heir, lays territorial claim to her birthright in Co. Cork. Both volumes, pub-lished during the war years, are complex and subtle assertions of Irishness at a time when Bowen's ostensible loyalties were British and she was employed by the British authorities to monitor Irish attitudes towards the war.

The autobiographies discussed above are conventional in format, appearing in single volumes as either memoir or autobiography or a fictionalized account of an individual life. There is also the group memoir form to consider, which in Ireland has included such seminal works as Anthony Cronin's *Dead as Doornails* (1976), which tracks the literary development not only of the author but also of his contemporaries Brendan Behan, Patrick Kavanagh and Brian O'Nolan (aka Flann O'Brien, aka Myles na gCopaleen). Poet John Montague's two autobiographical volumes, *Company: A Chosen Life* (2001) and *The Pear is Ripe* (2007), also place his writing career in relation to Behan's and visiting writers including Doris Lessing, Nelson Algren and Theodore Roethke. Similarly, Richard Murphy's *The Kick* (2002) pinpoints a literary-historical moment in Ireland, with noteworthy encounters with poets Ted Hughes and Sylvia Plath among its highlights. Another captured political and cultural moment features in Michael Longley's elegant and unusual *Tuppenny Stung* (1994), in particular in an essay charting the intricacies of arts administration involving writers and other artists in Northern Ireland during his twenty-year tenure at the Arts Council from 1971.[19] As distinctive and varied as these forms of life-writing are, it is in the recent work of the final two writers considered here that the reader can find genuine innovation within the genre.

Seamus Heaney, who died in 2013 at the age of seventy-four, was considered a formalist poet. His lyric poetry is often intensely autobiographical and the world portrayed, especially of his childhood home in Mossbawn, Co. Derry, gives accurate insight into how rapidly Irish life changed in the later twentieth century. In 2008, Heaney was the subject of, and participated in, an unusual work, *Stepping Stones: Interviews with Seamus Heaney*, an autobiography of sorts, written in interview format. The book was the outcome of a 'conversation' conducted with fellow poet Denis O'Driscoll, in which O'Driscoll submitted biographical and literary questions in writing that Heaney answered by post. Heaney chose this fusion of biography and autobiography, and thus exerted considerable control over the material discussed and the manner and extent to which it was probed. The poet shaped his responses and engaged as writers of autobiographies do, but the questions were initiated by O'Driscoll and often triggered memories that Heaney might never have captured had he not been prompted. Granting interviews in various media (print, video, radio and in person) is not a new method for disclosing autobiographical details, but *Stepping Stones* is an innovative leap in life-writing. It is a new subgenre, conceived and developed by biographer and subject, with ground rules that were both articulated and, at times, tacit.

---

[19] Michael Longley, 'Blackthorn and Bonsai or, A Little Brief Authority', in *Tuppenny Stung: Autobiographical Chapters* (Belfast: Lagan Press, 1994), 43–76.

Novelist Colm Tóibín, a generation younger than Heaney, has also become a recent innovator in the autobiographical format. Tóibín has taken the well-developed trope that writers who write about other writers are self-revelatory in the process and has rung a few changes on what might otherwise be considered overworked territory. As part of the Princeton University Press series *Writers on Writers*, Tóibín's volume, *On Elizabeth Bishop* (2015), is a sensitive and sensible biographical sketch of the American writer and an adroit introduction to her work. *On Elizabeth Bishop* includes some quite unfashionable line-by-line close readings of Bishop's most important poems and, making use of manuscript material, leads readers through drafting stages to reveal the poet's thought processes at work. What distinguishes *On Elizabeth Bishop* in reference to autobiography, however, is Tóibín's choice to interleave the critique with chapters on his own upbringing and travels. Tóibín draws additional comparisons between some of his own life choices and those of Bishop, and triangulates these with references to poet Thom Gunn's life and work. Tóibín's choice is highly risky for a writer who rarely works in the same genre as the others he writes about, and there is an additional risk attendant upon comparing oneself to writers considered among the greats of our time. But *On Elizabeth Bishop* is nothing like a vanity exercise and achieves instead a curious balance of humility and insight into both subject and author. Tóibín's choice of Bishop, and to a lesser extent Gunn, enables him to place his own peripatetic life, familial trauma and acceptance of his gay identity in an autobiographical context outside Ireland, since Irish models of the previous century had not produced a usable template for his personal development as a writer. With Bishop and Gunn he recognizes a bond, that of the wanderer with a scarred childhood, whose otherness finds fruitful expression on the page.

Innovation within a subgenre in literature, such as that undertaken by Seamus Heaney and Colm Tóibín, generally serves to keep the form relevant. It may be that the heyday of the classic volume-length autobiography from great writers is over, a relic enveloped in folds of words that both conceal and reveal the truths about its author. Irish writers have yet to produce anything approaching the radically revelatory project of the Norwegian Karl Ove Knausgård, whose six-volume autobiography, published under the title *Min Kamp* (*My Struggle*) from 2009 to 2011, controversially exposed living family members and friends.[20] But in the

---

[20] An Irish autobiographical novel which quietly entered territory that Knausgård explores, and caused family tension, is Jennifer Johnston's *Truth or Fiction* (2009).

twenty-first century, the blurring of distinctions between and among genres will no doubt continue to intensify, breaking down additional hierarchical literary structures and boundaries to liberate the literary auto-biography for writers and readers of a new generation.

Further reading

Brown, Terence. 'Literary Autobiography in Twentieth-Century Ireland', in Augustine Martin, ed., *The Genius of Irish Prose*. Dublin: Mercier Press, 1985: 89–98.

Buckley, Jerome Hamilton. *The Turning Key: Autobiography and the Subjective Impulse since 1800*. Cambridge, MA: Harvard University Press, 1984.

Deane, Seamus. 'Autobiography and Memoirs 1890–1988', in Seamus Deane, gen. ed., *The Field Day Anthology of Irish Writing*. Derry: Field Day Publications, 1991. Vol. 3: 380–83.

Jolly, Margaretta, ed. *The Encyclopedia of Life Writing: Autobiographical and Biographical Forms*. London: Fitzroy Dearborn, 2001. 2 vols.

Olney, James. *Memory and Narrative: The Weave of Life-Writing*. Chicago: University of Chicago Press, 1998.

Olney, James. *Metaphors of Self: The Meaning of Autobiography*. Princeton: Princeton University Press, 1972.

CHAPTER 12

The Irish Autobiographical Novel

Jonathan Bolton

Autobiographical fiction in Ireland originates close to the moment at which the novel itself begins, with eighteenth-century writers of the privileged and educated classes, such as Laurence Sterne and Thomas Amory, whose experience of Ireland is limited by the social milieu of their class and religion. Although Laurence Sterne went to school in England and remained most of his adult life there, his connections with Ireland, through birth and occasional habitation, and the influence of *The Life and Opinions of Tristram Shandy* (1759–67) on James Joyce, make him a central figure in the history of Irish autobiographical fiction. According to Sterne's biographer, Ian Campbell Ross, his childhood was 'harsh and unsettled, a long series of decampments from one barracks, one country to another',[1] punctuated by the births and deaths of siblings. Although the severity of his family life is largely missing from Tristram's narrative, Sterne's obsessions – patronymic determination, the use of parody to deflect life's misfortunes and the necessity of wit in adapting to 'this scurvy and disastrous world of ours'[2] – anticipate concerns found in later Irish autobiographical fiction. Thomas Amory's *The Life of John Buncle, Esq.* (1756) lacks the influence of *Tristram Shandy*, but it shares Sterne's display of learnedness, if not his wit, and it is notable for its account of religious conflict and exile from Ireland in the eighteenth century. Buncle comes under the influence of a Unitarian tutor, is disinherited by his zealously Trinitarian father and leaves Ireland out of spite. Although Amory's editor, Moyra Haslett, assigns the novel an 'extraordinary inventiveness',[3] *The Life of John Buncle, Esq.* is largely an episodic travel narrative overwhelmed by theology.

Irish Romantic fiction, as Claire Connolly finds, was broadly concerned with 'the politics of representation and the meaning of a national

---

[1] Ian Campbell Ross, *Laurence Sterne: A Life* (Oxford: Oxford University Press, 2001), 21.
[2] Laurence Sterne, *The Life and Opinions of Tristram Shandy* (Basingstoke: Macmillan, 1992), 5.
[3] Moyra Haslett, 'Introduction', in Thomas Amory, *The Life of John Buncle, Esq.*, ed. Moyra Haslett (Dublin: Four Courts Press, 2011), 11.

culture',[4] therefore it was largely preoccupied with formulations of Ireland and quaint Celtic scenes intended for English audiences. These kinds of 'Irish tales', such as F. C. Patrick's *The Irish Heiress* (1797), Lady Morgan's *The Wild Irish Girl* (1806) and John Cummings's *Tales for Cottagers* (1814), proliferated, and few notable works of Irish autobiographical fiction emerged in an era that favoured the expression of sensibility over formative personal experience. A notable exception is Sarah Isdell's *The Irish Recluse* (1809), which offers the author's first-hand accounts of the 1798 and 1803 rebellions and their tragic effect on her life. As the century progressed, Irish novelists continued to avoid using direct autobiographical content. As James H. Murphy notes, the energies of Victorian Irish writers were largely focused on the gothic (Charles Maturin, Sheridan LeFanu and Bram Stoker), religious and historical themes (John Banim, Emily Lawless) and political events such the Land War of 1879–82, which features in Letitia McClintock's *A Boycotted Household* (1881).[5] George Moore's *Confessions of a Young Man* (1888) suggests a renewed interest in the *Bildungsroman*, but Moore's novel reads more as an experiment in fictional autobiography. One notable foray into autobiographical fiction from the Victorian period is the final section of Rosa Mulholland's *Dunmara* (1864), published under the pseudonym of Ruth Murray, in which Mulholland recalls her own attempts to launch a career as a painter in London. The struggles of an Irish woman to establish herself in the London publishing world is the subject of the semi-autobiographical *Molly Carew* (1879) by Elizabeth Casey, who wrote under the *nom de plume* Elizabeth Owens Blackburne.

Two late Victorian works of autobiographical fiction, W. B. Yeats's *John Sherman* (1891) and Hannah Lynch's *The Autobiography of a Child* (1899), are of particular value. *John Sherman* has been regarded mostly as a gloss on Yeats's early poetry, but it contains an extended meditation on the ambivalence of Anglo-Irish allegiance, and his protagonists' conflicts – worldly ambition versus rural seclusion and the squaring of identity – are very much those of Yeats's young adulthood. Sherman's exilic crisis is resolved once he claims his idealized, ancestral homeland. Like Yeats, Lynch's *The Autobiography of a Child* is also concerned with shifting identities and sympathies during the rise of Irish nationalism. Lynch's experience, however, draws on the gothic tradition to form a

---

[4] Claire Connolly, *A Cultural History of the Irish Novel, 1790–1829* (Cambridge: Cambridge University Press, 2012), 1.

[5] See James H. Murphy, *Irish Novelists and the Victorian Age* (Oxford: Oxford University Press, 2011).

gloomier personal narrative. Lynch had an unhappy Catholic upbringing in Dublin and was sent to convent school in Coventry, where she
endured corporal punishment. As Faith Binckes and Kathryn Laing
note, in the novel 'the condition of being Irish in England and a girl in
Ireland is held up for scrutiny by a narrator who revisits the past
through the innocent eyes of her younger self'.[6] Regarded as Irish in
England and English in Ireland, Lynch's heroine fails to assimilate into
either society. Instead, she returns to Ireland after school, takes up the
nationalist cause and cultivates the image of an Irish rebel. When she
fails to feel at home in Ireland, she ends up a restless wanderer. Lynch
herself emigrated to Paris in the 1890s and died there in 1904.

In a manner typical of post-Freudian fiction, with its emphasis on the
interior life, the unconscious and particularly the effects of childhood
experience on individual character and belief, autobiographical fiction
was, as Max Saunders argues, 'central to the modernist project',[7] of
which James Joyce was the visionary architect. In twentieth-century
Ireland, a host of interconnected factors – the violence of colonial conflict;
a war of independence followed by a civil war; the partition of the country;
the manifold pressures of a Catholic theocracy; the hardships of poverty in
an underdeveloped nation; high rates of emigration; the oppression of
women under theocracy – all served to engender personal narrative,
testimony and confession. Moreover, Joyce worked largely with autobiographical material and his fiction served as a blueprint for a kind of life-
writing-as-protest mode, the focus of which was what Seamus Deane aptly
terms the 'squalor, paralysis and servility of Irish life',[8] which would
dominate twentieth-century Irish autobiographical fiction. *A Portrait of
the Artist as a Young Man* (1916) is the prototype for decades of writing in
which protagonists are plagued by cultural imperialism or postcolonial
indeterminacy, by the strict religious imperatives imposed by a Catholic
education and by a culture that inhibits and censors its artists. Some of the
stories in *Dubliners* (1914), such as 'The Sisters', 'An Encounter', 'Araby'
and 'The Dead', as well as Stephen Dedalus's latent quest for a father in
Ulysses (1922), suggest the depth in which psychological problems began to
be treated in fiction. These works also exemplify Joyce's oblique use of

[6] Faith Binckes and Kathryn Laing, 'Irish Autobiographical Fiction and Hannah Lynch's
Autobiography of a Child', *English Literature in Transition, 1880–1920*, 55:2 (2012), 196.
[7] Max Saunders, *Self-Impression: Life-Writing, Autobiographfiction, and the Forms of Modern Literature*
(Oxford: Oxford University Press, 2010), 22.
[8] Seamus Deane, 'Introduction', in James Joyce, *A Portrait of the Artist as a Young Man*, ed. Seamus
Deane (New York: Penguin, 1993), viii.

personal and second-hand experience in his fiction, whether it be his use of 16 June 1904 in *Ulysses* or Nora Joyce's personal history in 'The Dead', which story also addresses tensions Joyce felt between a fidelity to Ireland and the longing for a more cosmopolitan experience. Furthermore, the exilic determination found in *Portrait*, and the conviction that, in order 'to learn what the heart is and feels'[9] the writer must venture outside Ireland, anticipates the outcome of much post-Joycean Irish autobiographical fiction.

Though far less influential than Joyce's fiction, Forrest Reid's *Following Darkness* (1912) offers an impressionistic rendering of genius and its failure to attain its early promise. Reid's novel traces the development of Peter Waring, a precocious schoolboy from Co. Down who comes to maturity in the 1890s. Understandably, the novel stirred interest in Joyce. However, the sources of Waring's alienation – a motherless childhood, a Rousseau-like intensity of feeling and suggestions of repressed homosexuality – are more personal than environmental. Waring's father is devoutly religious in ways that are common but not unique to Protestant Ulster, but the severity of Stephen Dedalus's two masters – the British empire and the Catholic church – and the intense need to escape them do not figure in Reid's account. Moreover, as the novel's prologue states, Waring eventually becomes a minor art critic. *Following Darkness* does end in exile, but Waring leaves Ireland to recover from illness, not for political exigencies or for an earnest need to develop as an artist. Instead, Reid, who returned to Belfast after university and remained there throughout his adult life, retained a romantic attachment to the rural Ulster landscape, to the Mourne Mountains and to the coastal topography and valleys of Co. Down.

In *Two Years* (1930), Liam O'Flaherty also presents himself as an artist in search of a home. Upon his discharge from the British army in 1919, O'Flaherty signed onto a steamer and sailed around the Mediterranean, then worked odd jobs in North and South America. O'Flaherty's narrator sets out with notions of romantic self-determination unhindered by the intrusions of the state and freed by the mechanization of industry from the spiritually deadening activity of labour. By the end of the narrative, however, he has rejected the machine-as-saviour ideal and returns to his native Aran Islands. In nature, he finds an imaginative stimulation superior to that of the factory. The artistic disaffection that runs through Francis Stuart's *Black List, Section H* (1971) is firmly in the tradition of Joyce's *Portrait*, though Stuart claims a literary inheritance that is largely Germanic (Mann, Kafka) and Russian (Dostoevsky and Rozanov). *Black List, Section H*

---

[9] Ibid., 275.

often reads like a travel memoir as it delves into private sexual adventures, from the Irish Civil War to the defeat of Nazi Germany. Despite Stuart's Anglo-Irish upbringing and close connection to the Irish literary establishment through his marriage to Iseult Gonne, daughter of Maud, his protagonist 'believed that nothing short of being utterly cast off from society and its principles could create the inner condition conducive to the new insights that it was the task of the poet to reveal'.[10] The narrative depicts this search for this ideal creative environment and describes a career of contrarian politics and unconventional ways of living, most notably an extended stay with a series of mistresses in Berlin during the rise of Hitler. Stuart controversially claims not to have been a Nazi, but he did feel as though he belonged 'in the company of the guilty' and he seemed to welcome, as the self-designated alienated artist, 'the contempt of the whole healthy world'.[11]

As with Yeats and Lynch before them, autobiographical fiction by mid-twentieth-century Anglo-Irish writers such as Elizabeth Bowen, M. J. Farrell (Molly Keane) and Aidan Higgins continued to be preoccupied with problems related to identity, exile and re-assimilation into post-independence Ireland. Due to the premature death of her father, Bowen's childhood was divided between Dublin, England and the Continent, and she eventually inherited the family estate, Bowen's Court, in Co. Cork. In *The Last September* (1929), Lois Farquar spends her final summer holiday in Ireland. Compelled to marry by class expectations, gender and age, she passively welcomes the attention of a British soldier stationed in Ireland during the War of Independence. One of the most striking things about Bowen's study of Anglo-Irish identity is the indifference with which Lois accepts both her courtship and her undefined sense of national belonging. Bowen herself said she based the novel on 'a period of impatience, frivolity, lassitude and boredom',[12] and this is evident in her portrayal of Lois and Anglo-Irish life more generally. For Molly Keane, Anglo-Irish culture is largely predetermined by sporting traditions and an active, outdoor life; England is, by contrast, urbane, literary and intellectual – an indoors life. In her autobiographical novel *Mad Puppetstown* (1931), Keane fondly represents the leisurely pastimes of Big House living and portrays occasional trips to England to visit family or attend balls as unwelcome interruptions. In *Good Behaviour* (1981), Keane is more critical of the insularity, superficial elegance and philistinism of Big House life.

---

[10] Francis Stuart, *Black List, Section H* (Carbondale: Southern Illinois University Press, 1971), 44.
[11] Ibid., 331, 401.   [12] Elizabeth Bowen, *Bowen's Court* (New York: Ecco Press, 1979), vi.

Although *Good Behaviour* retains something of Keane's early fondness for the sporting pastimes of her class, she generally characterizes the Anglo-Irish as a class in decline, 'lolling helplessly through an objectless, boring life'.[13] Aidan Higgins's *Langrishe, Go Down* (1966), a novel filled with depictions of death, loss and decay, offers perhaps the grimmest account of aristocratic life in terminal decline. Higgins's Ascendency, Catholic-convert background ('the eccentric lapsed convert [child] of lapsed-convert parents'[14]) offers a profound treatment of ambiguous identity and alienation. Higgins's two protagonists, Helen and Imogen Langrishe, are dispossessed of property and alienated from their Catholic peers, who assume they are Protestants, and yet as strict Catholics they examine their consciences unforgivingly. Through inventive temporal shifts in narrative, Higgins presents Imogen's fear of being buried alive as a poignant symbol of the Langrishe sisters' suffocating existence.

For writers who remained in Ireland, the autobiographical content of their fiction often drew attention to the widespread economic hardship of life in the post-independent nation. Ambition and education initially offer a chance of transcendence, but the struggles of the precocious child against the hindrances of environment commonly defeat the hopeful protagonist. Sean O'Faolain's *Bird Alone* (1936), for instance, revisits childhood in a nostalgic manner, celebrating the freedom of youth and praising the beauty of the author's native Cork. Predictably, this idealized childhood ends once his protagonist, Corny Crone, enters the real world of religious sanctimony and political corruption. O'Faolain backdates the narrative timeline so that the fall of Parnell can coincide with his hero's disillusioned coming of age and his failure to find a fruitful environment, which leads to his life becoming solitary and vagrant. A number of Irish autobiographical fictions of this era suggest that a pervasive impoverishment of the intellect and the imagination are more inhibiting and hurtful than poverty itself. Patrick Kavanagh's *Tarry Flynn* (1948), for instance, contains ample evidence of rural poverty and the onerousness of farm labour, but it is primarily a *Künstlerroman* that dramatizes the conflict between a poet attempting to pursue life imaginatively and a mid-century rural Irish community suspicious of such creativity. To make matters worse, Flynn's art is informed by a pagan pantheism that is denounced by his Catholic peers. Amidst the drudgery of farm labour and the pressures of religious practice, Flynn is persistently awestruck by the beauty found in rocks and fields. His inner

---

[13] Molly Keane, *Good Behaviour* (New York: Knopf, 1991), 121.
[14] Aidan Higgins, *Langrishe, Go Down* (London: Calder and Boyers, 1966), 254.

conflict is resolved when Flynn's shiftless uncle advises him to 'do whatever pleases yourself'.[15] Tarry adopts this self-centred philosophy and leaves home, but he does so, in the words of Elmer Kennedy-Andrews, 'not with bitterness or resentment, but out of a desire for a larger imaginative experience'.[16]

Christy Brown's *Down All the Days* (1970) is another novel in which, despite the hardships of poverty and disability, the protagonist's greatest struggle is against an environment inhospitable to writing. Born with a severe form of cerebral palsy and unable to communicate verbally, it was assumed by his family and physicians that Brown was also mentally disabled, and the novel recounts his repeated frustration at being unable to make his intellectual ability evident to his community. Comparing *Down All the Days* to Joyce's *Portrait*, R. Brandon Kershner has observed that 'Brown's protagonist can approximate the modern artist's stance only because of his physical disabilities. They are what motivate his self-efface-ment before the external social world as well as what give credence to his hallucinatory inner life.'[17] Although the novel is autobiographical, Brown writes in the third person and never refers to himself by name, nor do any other characters call him by name. He is either 'the boy' or 'the cripple'. Brown's use of third-person anonymity artfully dramatizes his status as a non-entity in society – a serious writer whom people refuse to take seriously.

In the early decades after independence, Ireland had a largely agricul-tural, export-based economy with little industrial development; thus, there were very few opportunities for class mobility or professional advance-ment.[18] It follows then that Irish writers of this period tend to portray education either as a waste of time because it will not lead to a fruitful career, or as inadequate to the task of preparing one for anything other than a civil service job or a religious vocation. The social status conferred on priests and the esteem accorded a family with a priest in it made a religious vocation one of few careers, along with medicine and the law, to offer the prospect of class mobility. A number of writers after Joyce and Hannah Lynch express frustration over this failed connection between learning and

---

[15] Patrick Kavanagh, *Tarry Flynn* (New York: Devin-Adair, 1939), 249.

[16] Elmer Kennedy-Andrews, 'Life and Work: The Poetry of Sincerity', in Stan Smith, ed., *Patrick Kavanagh* (Dublin: Irish Academic Press, 2009), 29.

[17] R. Brandon Kershner, 'History as Nightmare: Joyce's *Portrait* to Christy Brown', in Mark A. Wollaeger, Victor Luftig and Robert E. Spoo, eds., *Joyce and the Subject of History* (Ann Arbor: University of Michigan Press, 1996), 42.

[18] See Mary Daly, *Industrial Development and Irish National Identity* (Syracuse: Syracuse University Press, 1992), 16–17.

becoming. With Joyce, there was the choice between serving the church or the empire; with his successors, it was a choice between serving the church or state bureaucracy. An interesting example of this form of autobiographical fiction is Oliver St John Gogarty's *Tumbling in the Hay* (1939), which recounts Gogarty's days as a medical student at Trinity College Dublin. Gogarty had come from an affluent family, but his father's untimely death compelled him to set aside his literary ambitions in order to earn a medical degree. Although his protagonist, like Gogarty himself, often squandered his talents in frivolous ways, *Tumbling in the Hay* belongs to a group of novels that illustrates the many ways in which artistic endeavour was discouraged in the new Ireland.

In *The Land of Spices* (1941), Kate O'Brien, through the character of Anna Murphy, recounts with some pleasure the continental educational traditions of her school, Laurel Hill in Limerick. O'Brien is for the most part grateful for the cosmopolitan content of the curriculum, which offered instruction in foreign languages, music and aesthetic appreciation. But at the same time, the novel chronicles how Irish convent schools were threatened and in many ways corrupted by nationalistic efforts to make education serve state ideology. O'Brien does illustrate, however, that state support for education in Ireland offered the opportunity for women to attend university, and her protagonist, despite some family resistance to professional education for women, wins a scholarship to University College Dublin. Whereas *The Land of Spices* credits the quality of an education that encouraged intellectual and literary interests, Benedict Kiely's *There Was an Ancient House* (1955) depicts a less enlightened schooling. Set in a seminary in Co. Laois in the late 1930s, it features many promising young men who were forced into the priesthood without truly feeling a vocation, and this recruitment kept them from professional fulfilment. Kiely's protagonist, Jim McKenna, believes that a monastic life will allow him to write poetry, but is discouraged by Jesuit fathers who, although they encourage scholarship, censor the modernist canon and argue that literary ambition represents a forbidden worldliness. In James Plunkett's *Farewell Companions* (1977), Kate O'Brien's fear of a politicized curriculum taking over becomes reality. At Plunkett's Dublin school, Synge Street Christian Brothers' School, education takes the form of indoctrination: literature by Huxley and Ibsen is banned from classroom and library and the pupils are forced to become 'sturdy champions of the Gaelic mode of life'.[19] Communism and socialism are presented as evil

---

[19] James Plunkett, *Farewell Companions* (New York: Coward, McCann, and Geoghegan, 1977), 38.

doctrines, and teachers denounce the efforts of Plunkett's hero, James Larkin, to unionize Irish labour. Just as O'Brien feared, education in Ireland bows to nationalistic propaganda.

John McGahern's *The Dark* (1965) offers a similarly pessimistic perspective on the destiny of intelligent children in mid-century Ireland, the anonymity of McGahern's protagonist suggesting both typicality and the erasure of identity. In this novel, a bright, studious child excels in school and, because of his intellectual promise, is steered by his teachers towards a religious vocation. After spending a weekend with his cousin, a priest, he learns that the profession he idealizes, the high moral ground upon which he imagined it stood, is actually compromised by the worldly concerns of business and politics. Once McGahern's protagonist abandons the career for which so much of his education had prepared him, he becomes indecisive. His father fails to see the practical value of education and dissuades him from remaining at university, despite his having won a scholarship, thus leaving him few options but to enter the civil service. Like *The Land of Spices*, *The Dark* suggests that a system of national scholarships can enable intelligent young men and women to gain access to a university education, but that familial and financial pressures can still thwart their future prospects. In *The Leavetaking* (1975), McGahern once again mines personal history to disclose the social and family pressures to enter the priesthood. However, his protagonist, Patrick Moran, instead becomes a schoolteacher, a vocation that, under the watchful eye of the bishops, is morally and intellectually restricted.

One of the few positive accounts of education during this period is found in Brendan Behan's *Borstal Boy* (1958), an autobiographical novel that illustrates how a foreign education can counter the nationalistic indoctrination that had led to a criminal life. Behan's early education was founded on Irish fairy lore, balladry and mythology. His family encouraged him to join Fianna Éireann, the purpose of which was to educate Irish youth and protect its nationalist ideals. This education is very much in evidence throughout *Borstal Boy*, as Behan recites an impressive repertoire of revolutionary ballads and songs, and he is well prepared to relate stories of British atrocities in Ireland. Behan recounts how this indoctrination was overcome during a three-year incarceration at Hollesley Bay Prison in Suffolk. As Behan's biographer, Ulick O'Connor, describes it, 'Brendan used to say that his period at Borstal had been one of the happiest of his life', citing his access to books and some faculty members' interest in art.[20] *Borstal Boy* also suggests a love affair with

---

[20] Ulick O'Connor, *Brendan Behan* (London: Hamilton, 1970), 53–54.

a British boy, though its muted presence caused none of the controversy that greeted Edna O'Brien's treatment of female sexuality in her 1960 debut, *The Country Girls*.

Although Kate, the protagonist of O'Brien's semi-autobiographical novel and its sequels, *The Lonely Girl* (1962) and *Girls in their Married Bliss* (1964), is not an aspiring writer, and university never seems to be an option, her educational background is equally stifling, particularly with regard to sexual awareness. O'Brien's heroine is somewhat naïve and pliable compared to her more rebellious friend Baba, who flaunts her sexuality. Despite Baba's assertiveness and autonomy, the mechanisms of sexual and sexist suppression continually hinder and obstruct the desires of O'Brien's characters. The Catholic theocracy never defeats them, however, and their paths continually lead to exile, first from provincial Clare and then from Ireland altogether. Like Edna O'Brien, the fiction of Julia O'Faolain (daughter of Sean) also relates the experiences of first-wave feminist women who, liberated by changing social attitudes towards sexuality, birth control and marriage in the postwar West, come into conflict with an Ireland that is lagging behind the times. Her novel *Godded and Codded* (1970) uses a series of flashbacks in order to contrast the repressiveness of Irish social customs with those of Europe during the sexual revolution. Drawing on her own cosmopolitan experiences, O'Faolain has her heroine, Sally, receive a scholarship to study at the Sorbonne. Determined to have casual love affairs, Sally is nevertheless continually plagued by the inhibitions instilled in her since childhood.

As we near the end of the twentieth century, these kinds of repressive conditions begin to disappear. In Emma Donoghue's *Stir-fry* (1994), for example, a naïve young woman from rural Ireland arrives on a UCD campus that was 'liberal altogether' and deeply invested in 'life, liberty and the pursuit of Guinness'.[21] For the first time, Maria becomes politically active, is able to view foreign films with heterosexual and homosexual content, takes fashion risks by dressing like a punk and agrees to share a flat with a lesbian couple. In works such as *Stir-Fry*, one begins to see the autobiographical novel of education evolving from one of protest against limiting opportunity into a more traditional *Bildungsroman* in which the protagonist assimilates into the culture in a more fulfilling manner. But a more recent coming-of-age queer novel, *The First Verse* (2005) by Barry McCrea, demonstrates that even urban centres like Dublin can still be close-minded and sometimes violently intolerant towards openly gay couples.

[21] Emma Donoghue, *Stir-fry* (New York: HarperCollins, 1994), 16.

Northern Irish autobiographical fiction

Autobiographical fiction from Northern Ireland typically reveals a stronger devotion to place than that from the Republic, often showing a determination to live and survive in, if not reform and improve, a region divided by sectarianism. In *Call My Brother Back* (1939), Michael McLaverty symbolically divides his novel into two sections: the first set on Rathlin Island, the second set in Belfast during the civil strife of the 1920s, at the time of the foundation of the statelet. This division sets up a sharp contrast between two ways of life: one on the non-sectarian Rathlin, an idealized terrain of communal co-operation, agrarian subsistence and monastic seclusion; the other on Belfast's war-torn streets, surrounded by sirens, curfews and police raids. As his protagonist Colm MacNeill points out, Belfast 'was all a terrible mix-up', 'whereas on Rathlin Catholics and Protestants mixed and talked and danced together'.[22] Still, like McLaverty, who became a prominent educator in Belfast, Colm is drawn to the vibrant life and professional opportunity of the city and is determined in the end to forge a life there.

Janet McNeill's work also demonstrates a strong commitment to life in Northern Ireland, her fiction offering a nuanced account of middle-class Protestant life in Belfast before the onset of the Troubles in the late 1960s. Her best-known work, *The Maiden Dinosaur* (1964), presents the lives of several middle-aged Protestant women, who resemble creatures on the verge of extinction, confused and alienated by the changes of the 1960s. McNeill's central protagonist, Sarah Vincent, is a writer who, like McNeill, fails to gain deserved recognition because, as critics saw it, her work lacks the sensational qualities of the Angry Young Man fiction of the day. As Sarah's friend Addie remarks: 'it is widely assumed we never lived. We've only been born and stayed alive for fifty years and been through two world wars and the Troubles and seen our country split in two ... I don't see how we could be expected to write.'[23] Although McNeill retired to England in 1964, her long-time involvement in the Belfast theatre and arts scene attests to her devotion to Northern Irish culture, and her fiction makes a strong case for the viability of all perspectives, particularly those of ordinary women raising children, dealing with marital problems and contending with age.

The better-known Brian Moore, who emigrated to Canada in 1948 aged twenty-seven, used autobiographical fiction to examine what one critic

---

[22] Michael McLaverty, *Call My Brother Back* (Dublin: Alan Figgis, 1970), 170.
[23] Janet McNeill, *The Maiden Dinosaur* (Belfast: Blackstaff Press, 1994), 96.

calls a 'beleaguered Catholicism'[24] in Ireland and elsewhere. This theme figures in a number of novels with protagonists who share Moore's exilic path, such as the eponymous hero of *The Luck of Ginger Coffey* (1960) and Anthony Maloney in *The Great Victorian Collection* (1975). *Fergus* (1970) is more experimental; it is told via a series of ghostly visitations from family members, former teachers, a priest and an ex-girlfriend, who collectively enable Moore to contrast his strict religious upbringing in Belfast with the trappings of a hedonistic California lifestyle. The novel also registers its characters' keen sense of separation from the civil rights campaign in Northern Ireland. *The Emperor of Ice Cream* (1965) is arguably his most autobiographical work, a *Bildungsroman* that focuses on the final years of Moore's late adolescence. This was a period in which, preoccupied with losing his virginity, he struggled in school and rebelled against his father's lofty expectations, all of which coincided with the aerial bombardment of Belfast during the Second World War and led to his resolution to flee Ireland.

A generation after Brian Moore, Bernard MacLaverty also chose to leave Belfast, moving with his wife and four children to Scotland in 1975 to escape the intensifying political violence. However, MacLaverty is less concerned than Moore with the experience of exile and, as Richard Rankin Russell notes, he 'remained rooted in the communal culture and religious Catholicism of the Northern Ireland of his childhood and early adulthood'.[25] As an author committed to reflecting life in Belfast during the Troubles, MacLaverty draws on personal experience to examine sectarianism and the restrictions as well as the consolations of a Catholic upbringing. *The Anatomy School* (2001), his most autobiographical novel, offers a nostalgic look at pre-conflict Belfast, melding memories of his Catholic education, his time as a teacher and his experience of working in the medical laboratory at Queen's University. The fiction of Deirdre Madden, who also left Belfast during the Troubles, is notable for the manner in which it registers the ambivalence of being a Catholic in Northern Ireland. Her work gives voice to the conflict caused by wanting to remain a practising Catholic out of loyalty to one's class, despite the loss of religious faith, and to the tension between a self-protective urge to flee the North and a countervailing desire to stay and join the struggle for civil rights. This ambivalence has been present from the outset of her career, as

---

[24] Jo O'Donoghue, *Brian Moore: A Critical Study* (Montreal and Kingston: McGill-Queen's University Press, 1991), 7.
[25] Richard Rankin Russell, *Bernard MacLaverty* (Lewisburg: Bucknell University Press, 2009), 17.

evidenced by *Hidden Symptoms* (1986), a novel that shifts between the perspectives of Robert, an atheist intellectual who thinks art is above politics, and Teresa, a politically conscious woman whose brother was a casualty of the conflict. The manner in which the two lives overlap suggests that these characters represent something of the competing impulses and desires of the author.

Another notable Northern Irish autobiographical novel is Seamus Deane's *Reading in the Dark* (1996), which offers an intriguing variation on the post-Joycean *Bildungsroman*. Like *Portrait*, Deane's novel begins with childhood perceptions of a fleeting and unstable phenomenal world disturbed by political rivalry, but such childlike confusion is intensified by local mythologies of changelings, ghosts, missing informers, sudden departures and other strange disappearances. The unnamed narrator comes to understand that hauntings are an intrinsic part of Derry life and resolves to leave, twice running away and making it as far as the ferry to Liverpool. He eventually leaves home for university in Belfast, 'glad to be free of the immediate pressures of living there, sorry to have so mishandled everything that I had created a distance between my parents and myself that had become my only way of loving them'.[26] Deane's narrator resolves these conflicts not through a more permanent exile but by returning home, just as the conflict begins to escalate in 1971, to confront and address the climate of violence, suspicion and secrecy from which he had fled.

Glenn Patterson's *Burning Your Own* (1988) also shows a strong attachment to Northern Ireland and a belief that communal solidarity can be created through a focus on a shared regional culture. Set during the eruption of violence in Belfast in 1969, Patterson's novel explores the tribal loyalties and animosities that fuel bigotry and the territorial instincts that make neutrality and compromise extremely difficult. Protestant Mal Martin is nurtured in a culture of virulent anti-Catholicism and, with his skinhead haircut and avid participation in the Twelfth of July bonfires, seems destined for a paramilitary career. But against the narrow mindset of Protestant sectarianism, Mal is exposed to powerful contrary influences and new perspectives. His chance friendship with a charismatic Catholic boy, Francy Hagan, combined with his awareness of internal tensions within the Protestant community and exposure to 1960s British popular culture, nurture more humane impulses.

Not all Northern Irish novelists, however, remain at home to champion and contribute to local culture. David Cavanagh's *Music for Boys* (2003),

---

[26] Seamus Deane, *Reading in the Dark* (New York: Knopf, 1994), 236.

for instance, shares Patterson's love of music and devotion to Belfast culture, but Cavanagh's teenage protagonist's desire to witness a musical renaissance in the city leads instead to disappointment and departure. In the novel, Doug is devoted to a promising local band and tirelessly promotes them, only to see their potential squandered through internal bickering and low effort. He becomes alienated from the band and leaves Belfast to attend university in England, and in the end acknowledges the inferiority of his home city's provincial musical culture. In *Eureka Street* (1996), Robert McLiam Wilson draws on his west Belfast background to show the impoverishing consequences of Catholic disenfranchisement, while also portraying a Northern Ireland that is on the verge of reaching a peace agreement, with friendships stretching across the sectarian divide. The two protagonists in *Eureka Street* survive by working odd jobs, drinking excessively and having sex fairly indiscriminately, all the while using an entrepreneurial inventiveness to attain a better life. And if better opportunities or love lead them elsewhere, they have few reservations about leaving.

More recent autobiographical or semi-autobiographical Northern Irish fiction, such as Nick Laird's *Utterly Monkey* (2005) and Lucy Caldwell's *Where They Were Missed* (2006), also show characters attempting to sever ties with the North, but social connections and regional allegiances prove too strong. Like Laird, Danny, the protagonist of *Utterly Monkey*, leaves rural Ulster for Cambridge, then goes to work for a London law firm and eventually is forced to arbitrate a corporate takeover that would cost Irish workers their jobs. Despite a strong urge to distance himself from home, Danny remains loyal to Northern Ireland. In *Where They Were Missed*, a novel that is reminiscent in some ways of the kind of hauntings and disappearances of *Reading in the Dark*, Caldwell draws on her 1980s Belfast childhood in portraying two young girls, daughters of an RUC officer, who seek refuge in Co. Donegal from the insistent violence of Belfast. The girls struggle to assimilate into rural, small-town life, however, and long to return to their home city.

Conclusion

This chapter offers an inclusive but far from exhaustive account of the rich tradition of autobiographical fiction in Ireland. Despite the incompleteness of this survey, it is evident that autobiographical fiction is an integral part of Ireland's national development. It has offered crucial narratives of personal witness and testimony. It has contributed to public discourse about national identity, education, religion, gender and sexuality. It has chronicled the manifold struggles of growing up in Ireland, protested against prejudice and bigotry, attempted to heal rifts, reform unjust laws and encourage humane governance. It has shown that life in Ireland, north and south, could be, and sometimes has been, impossible to bear. As a genre, Irish autobiographical fiction has helped to form and shape the manner in which Irish lives have been documented.

Further reading

Connolly, Claire. *A Cultural History of the Irish Novel, 1790–1829*. Cambridge: Cambridge University Press, 2012.

Countryman, John and Kelly Matthews, eds. *The Country of the Young: Interpretations of Youth and Childhood in Irish Culture*. Dublin: Four Courts Press, 2013.

Murphy, James H. *Irish Novelists and the Victorian Age*. Oxford: Oxford University Press, 2011.

Patten, Eve. '"Life Purified and Reprojected": Autobiography and the Modern Irish Novel', in Liam Harte, ed., *Modern Irish Autobiography: Self, Nation, and Society*. Basingstoke: Palgrave Macmillan, 2007: 51–69.

Saunders, Max. *Self-Impression: Life-Writing, Autobiographfiction, and the Forms of Modern Literature*. Oxford: Oxford University Press, 2010.

Vance, Norman. *Irish Literature since 1800*. London: Longman, 2002.

CHAPTER 13

Memoirs of Irish Rural Life

George O'Brien

Like the landscapes in which many of them are set, the life-writing and autobiographies of rural Ireland comprise an uneven prospect. The contours of this body of work show the broken land of its historical origins, the ups and downs of its cultural impact and the extensive discursive field of its generic range. Yet, although the personal knowledge and communal insight thereby revealed are considerable, it is difficult to establish a well-grounded critical sense of what has been achieved. Rural autobiography seems to be strangely remote from, or supplemental to, the canon of Irish writing, possibly because the canon consists of so much that draws on the rural (and on the provincial, which is one of the rural's most distinctive components), not only from a representational standpoint but also from that of communal practices, values and experiences. To distinguish between the expressive rural material of the canon and works that belong in the purview of rural autobiography and life-writing risks lending the latter a subsidiary status resulting from its merely local interest, as though the distance of such works' locations is somehow typical also of its beginnings, perspectives and narrative strategies.

Historically, rural Irish autobiography has its roots in letters, journals, day-books, diaries and related forms of documentation, the content of which has received more attention than the nature of the persona or personality accumulating the data. The forms in question tend for the most part to look outward on the world and its immediacies, and consist essentially of a myriad witting and unwitting acts of witnessing. A piece of writing such as *The Diary of Nicholas Peacock 1740–51*, for instance, first published in 2005, hardly strays beyond the concerns of the diarist, a Limerick strong farmer, with land, crops and neighbours. As such, its historical interest is obvious. But its evidentiary value coincides with the fact that 'In the diary, the writer gives no hint of his identity.'[1] The autobiographical dimension is essentially

---

[1] Marie-Louise Legg, ed., *The Diary of Nicholas Peacock 1740–51* (Dublin: Four Courts Press, 2005), 11.

occluded, suggested only when there is 'nothing material'[2] to report, in diary entries that draw attention not only to the absence of the personal but to the type of personality which would consider 'nothing' worth noting. Similarly, *The Diary of Humphrey O'Sullivan*, which recounts the life and contexts of an Irish-speaking schoolmaster and shopkeeper in Callan, Co. Kilkenny between 1827 and 1835, can be thought to owe its significance less to its being a narrative of an individual 'following his own bent' than to its depiction of 'a particularly agitated and important time in Irish history'.[3] And if in Hugh Dorian's 'true historical narrative', composed in 1889–90 but unpublished until 2000, 'it is the pulse of feeling as much as the political analysis' that makes the work 'so compelling',[4] what the pulse animates is the way of life of Famine-era Fánaid in Co. Donegal, not that of the chronicler. Dorian's personality is subsumed by place and people and emerges only in the light of microscopic attention to his tone, language, narrative point of view and related matters.

In each of these three works, place has primacy over person, resulting in much less of the interplay between self and world that is now regarded as an autobiographical staple. The authors' indifference to assuming a persona, to narrative cohesion and to cultural self-consciousness are signs of a general underdevelopment of the technique and poetics of autobiography. Even works that signify an express autobiographical intent – *The Retrospections of Dorothea Herbert* (1929–30), for instance, or *The Memories of William Hanbridge Aged 93* (1939) – also reflect this underdevelopment, although this does not detract from their significance as sources of a more diverse sense of class, gender and religion in rural Ireland during the late eighteenth century, in Herbert's case, and the early nineteenth, in Hanbridge's.[5] Textual underdevelopment also points towards these authors' social and cultural standing. O'Sullivan and Dorian, for instance, exemplify a complicated set of interconnections between subjectivity and being subject. Dorian's embattled relations with a local priest and O'Sullivan's devotion to the Irish language also show them as somewhat eccentric to their locales, while

---

[2] Ibid., 121, where the phrase recurs in entries covering a period of three days.

[3] Tomás de Bhaldraithe, 'Introduction', in Humphrey O'Sullivan, *The Diary of Humphrey O'Sullivan, 1827–1835*, trans. and ed., Tomás de Bhaldraithe (Dublin: Mercier Press, 1979), 11, 13.

[4] Breandán Mac Suibhne and David Dickson, 'Preface to the North American Edition', in Hugh Dorian, *The Outer Edge of Ulster: A Memoir of Social Life in Nineteenth-Century Donegal*, eds., Breandán Mac Suibhne and David Dickson (Notre Dame: University of Notre Dame Press, 2001), xii.

[5] *The Memories of William Hanbridge Aged 93. 1906: An Autobiography* was privately printed by the author's daughter, Mary Ann, 'in very late 1939 or early 1940' (31), according to W. J. McCormack, editor of the revised edition published as William Hanbridge and Mary Ann Hanbridge, *Memories of West Wicklow 1813–1939* (Dublin: UCD Press, 2005).

Herbert's class consciousness and Hanbridge's attitude to the events of 1798 suggest insecurities that are largely shadow-play in their writings. In all cases, there is a strong disinclination to pursue the ideological or cultural implications of their implicitly distinctive positions or to develop a sense of being both related to and distinct from the typicalities of the day. Perhaps the most comprehensive expression of this reluctance is *Sentry Hill: An Ulster Farm and Family* (1981), a documentary history of a south Antrim property which preserves every material and social aspect of the diary of nineteenth-century farmer William McKinney, on which it is based, except a sense of his individuality. In all, these early works' emphasis on conditions and community meet the criteria of life-writing rather than autobiography as such. In *The Annals of Ballitore* (1862), Mary Leadbeater assumed the role of 'annalist',[6] and although this suggests an autobiographical persona, the author's objective seems rather to underwrite a degree of fidelity to her material together with a certain facelessness in transmitting it.

Life-writing, with its inventories, its genealogical information, its knowledge of property and its incidental use of colours and textures, has a clear historiographical appeal. Consolidating this appeal, and relieving the cataloguing effects, these works also feature reactions to historical events of their time, such as Dorothea Herbert's reports of 'parish rebellions'[7] around Carrick-on-Suir in the early 1780s or Tithe War incidents around Humphrey O'Sullivan's *Callain an Chlampair* ('Callan of the Ructions').[8] The experience of being alienated, distressed, outraged or traumatized by episodes of this kind is not beyond the historian's remit. But it cannot be the main focus, so that more intimate and fugitive psychological emphases end up in a discursive no-man's-land, resulting in silences and disregard that impoverish the culture as a whole. Equally, however, autobiographers can invoke historical narratives and documentation to validate their claim to the perspective being brought to their work. Both Elizabeth Bowen's *Bowen's Court* (1942) and David Thomson's *Woodbrook* (1974) – generally acknowledged as the two most noteworthy and accomplished Big House memoirs – make extensive use of such objective sources. These usages contribute to clarifying the kinds of personal claims that the two places in question are being asked to support, so that the emotional and psychological complications of being attached to a

---

[6] Mary Leadbeater, *The Leadbeater Papers: The Annals of Ballitore* (London: Bell and Daldy, 1862), vol. 1, 37.

[7] Dorothea Herbert, *The Retrospections of Dorothea Herbert 1770–1806* (Dublin: Town House, 1988), 86.

[8] O'Sullivan, *The Diary of Humphrey O'Sullivan*, 9.

place are helpfully thrown into relief. The complications of possession, in which distance and affiliation exercise a joint, conflicting appeal, in which love of place is a dimension of other, more impossible involvements – familiar and paternal in *Bowen's Court*, obsessively romantic in the case of Thomson's infatuation with his youthful charge, Phoebe – find an analogue in the twisted strands of the historical record.

History becomes a buttress and a source of validation for structures that over time have grown less assured of their social and cultural standing. The autobiographical persona, isolated and singular, can find authentication and stability by seeing itself not only in the physical space of an inherited house, for instance, but also as a legatee of the past times for which a house can stand. In such ways, autobiography can be read as a stay against abandonment, the cultural value of which is most evident when the way of life in question is eccentric to prevailing conditions. But this iteration of autobiography occurs in works – such as Bowen's and Thomson's – that are later in both a chronological sense and with respect to modernistic developments in the form. Life-writing's interests, on the other hand, consist of witnessing and testifying, and as such are an attempt to maintain a continuum with, and thereby a fidelity to, community and its commonplaces. In most cases, this attempt is essentially rhetorical: a form of words that wishes to overcome a history that is incomplete, that has been amputated from the general course of events – in a word, a Gaelic history. Only a weave of local textures, colourations, lineages and interrelations, with its author in the midst of it articulating his or her awareness of only time and presence without regard to historical conditioning, can achieve a convincing sense of continuum. This rare accomplishment, similar in effect to a so-called primitive painting, is exemplified in Charles McGlinchey's *The Last of the Name* (1986), the 'remembering style' of which 'resists ... external structuring'.[9]

It may be, however, that this resistance has its roots in the work's oral origins. On the one hand, these origins relate it to such significant oral autobiographies as Tomás O'Crohan's *An tOileánach* (*The Islandman*) (1929), Maurice O'Sullivan's *Fiche Bliain ag Fás* (*Twenty Years A-Growing*) (1933) and Peig Sayers's *Peig* (1936), in each of which the rural has a special linguistic and cultural resonance. On the other hand, the originally unsystematic character of McGlinchey's oral recollections bear in print the mark of a shaping editorial hand, a translation of sorts that evokes the authority of

---

[9] Brian Friel, 'Introduction', in Charles McGlinchey, *The Last of the Name* (Nashville: Sanders, 1999), 4.

alternative verbal forms in generating those earlier works' impact and popularity. This authority, however benevolently exercised, may indeed lend these works a context which may be beside the point of these authors' stories and recollections, as is suggested by the well-known testimonial to *Fiche Bliain ag Fás* as 'an account of neolithic civilization from the inside'.[10] Despite exhibiting formulaic tendencies, these oral works also convey a sense of spontaneity and informality, qualities that help distinguish life-writing in general from the more stylized, self-conscious and confessional written autobiography.

Yet, if rural Irish autobiography has its origins in oral tradition, and continues to avail of it as a narrative option, tests of its limits and challenges to its loyalties eventually make their presence known. Such departures are initiated in *The Autobiography of William Carleton* (1896), which the author left unfinished on his death in 1869. This may be regarded as a transitional work, inasmuch as although it is an implicit critique of life-writing, Carleton fails to convince the world that the persona he fashioned for himself could have social agency. Noteworthy for its vivid depiction of the rural community and oral culture of the author's native Tyrone, as well as for his repudiation of the place's lack of opportunity, the work affirms the subject's ambitions and desires while lamenting the outsider status in which they culminate. More revealing than Carleton's awareness of his subjectivity is his belief in its powers, expressed in terms of aspiring social and cultural agency. His pursuit of such aspirations through the authority of schoolteaching and his highly individualized, gender-conscious self-image assert a version of himself as a body of knowledge. This body eventually begets Carleton the writer, although the type of work he is best known for consists of lightly fictionalized portrayals of 'the way it was' rather than further explorations of the inquiry initiated by the *Autobiography* into 'the way I am'. The advice Seamus Heaney imagines Carlton's shade imparting to him in his 1982 collection, *Station Island* – 'Remember everything and keep your head'[11] – expresses the problematic character of independence in the *Autobiography*, where remembering is largely a testament to losses that prove extraordinarily difficult to justify or make good.

Carleton's pursuit of independence and the self-possession that implicitly accompanies it can be seen as a prototype for the next phase of rural Irish

---

[10] E. M. Forster, 'Introductory Note', in Maurice O'Sullivan, *Twenty Years A-Growing* (London: Chatto and Windus, 1936), v.

[11] Seamus Heaney, *Station Island* (London: Faber and Faber, 1984), 66.

autobiography. Not only does independence form an important subtext in the Irish-language oral narratives mentioned above, it is also evident in a memoir like Mary Carbery's *The Farm by Lough Gur* (1937), which in style, class interests and cultural finish is far removed from Blasket Island life. Based largely on reminiscences of an 1870s childhood in a Limerick farmhouse which was not far from Nicholas Peacock's holding, it recapitulates not only that period's social and political ideas of possession but also aligns them with the activity of repossession that memory facilitates. A distinctive sense of place results, anchored in an unobtrusive emphasis on security of tenure, not only with respect to property but also to the adjacent eponymous beauty spot. Lough Gur is a life-enhancing counterpart to 'land, that safe investment',[12] a reservoir of legend and archaeological artefacts providing sustenance that was as rich culturally as the farm was materially. The lake augments feelings of belonging. The child's perception in which these feelings originate are preserved in the autobiographical persona, so that person and place, family life and cultural heritage, attain something like permanent presence, which is unique by virtue of being independent of time and historical contingency.

In contrast to the depth, calm and security projected by *The Farm by Lough Gur*, the kind of independence conveyed by Patrick Gallagher in *My Story* (1939) is concerned with finding remedies to relieve conditions in the impoverished Rosses area of Donegal. Rather than sublimating this community's social and historical contexts by retaining a childhood view of them, Gallagher, who was colloquially known as 'Paddy the Cope', turns them to account through enterprising action and ideological self-consciousness, the latter deriving from identification with the agricultural co-operative movement. His actions result in growth, maturity and worldliness, culminating in the successful elimination from his native place of 'the slave mind'.[13] Economic revival and a change of outlook portray the local transcending the national. In making something of his part of the world, Gallagher makes something of himself, thereby inscribing the triumph of agency which is independence's signature. And in turn, this display of exemplary citizenship entitles him to be regarded as somebody with 'a story to tell which he must tell in his own way'.[14] Yet, Paddy the Cope's saga of overcoming socio-economic constraints notwithstanding,

---

[12] Mary Carbery, *The Farm by Lough Gur: The Story of Mary Fogarty (Sissy O'Brien)* (London: Longmans, Green, 1937), 252.

[13] Patrick Gallagher ('Paddy the Cope'), *My Story* (Dungloe: Templecrone Co-operative Society, n.d. [1945]), 173.

[14] Peadar O'Donnell, 'Introduction', in Patrick Gallagher, *My Story* (London: Jonathan Cape, 1939), 9.

independence can be a troublesome realm for those born to it, particularly independence of mind in an environment which does not welcome it. Such is the case in Patrick Kavanagh's *The Green Fool* (1938), a narrative of being in two minds: 'For years I had been caught between the two stools of security on the land and a rich-scented life on the exotic islands of literature.'[15] The result is a persona embodying a nexus of differences and dissidences worthy of comparison with the character of '"The Idiot" in Dostoevsky's novel', somebody whose experience is that of an outsider in his own place, a lover of nature ill-suited to life on the land, a dreamer amidst 'narrow surveyor[s] of generous hearts'.[16] Loyalty to the local oscillates between praise and critique. The persona of Paddy the Cope's story is emblematic of service to the community. In contrast, Kavanagh's version of himself requires the desiring individual to take precedence over local mores and conditions.

Kavanagh's insecurity and uncertainty are crucial components of his autobiographical self-representation. Their presence in his formation evolved during those years in the early twentieth century when the country as a whole was undergoing a change of identity and, so to speak, self-orientation. Yet, the textures, idiosyncrasies and somewhat meandering narrative of *The Green Fool* implicitly resist the kind of momentum which is characteristic of the national narrative. Kavanagh may be intermittently caught up in the events of the day, but the manner in which he is ends up being yet further confirmation of his basic duality. There is no centre that can hold him. Independence, for him, resides in his own grasp of it. Yet, when he acts on it and, Carleton-like, walks from his rural home to Dublin, the result appears to be further dislocation.[17] But the geographical break with the rural begets imaginative repossession of it. What the autobiographer fashions for himself is not an alternative urban identity but a set of new relations with, and accommodations of, his native place. And the interplay of apartness and recollection on which these relations are structured also provides a prototype for portraits of many other selves whose stories see-saw between the loss and the recuperation of country origins.

[15] Patrick Kavanagh, *The Green Fool* (Harmondsworth: Penguin, 1975), 239. Kavanagh later repudiated this early autobiography, calling it 'a pack of lies', though this repudiation does not invalidate the book's persona. The book was also withdrawn as a result of a 1939 libel action. See Antoinette Quinn, *Patrick Kavanagh: A Biography* (Dublin: Gill and Macmillan, 2003), 112ff., 355.

[16] Ibid., 10, 229.

[17] See George O'Brien, 'The Walk of a Hundred Years: Kavanagh and Carleton', in Peter Kavanagh, ed., *Patrick Kavanagh: Man and Poet* (Orono: National Poetry Foundation, 1986), 351–57.

As though following Kavanagh, the autobiographies of writers with rural backgrounds are particularly marked by the dynamic of valediction and reclamation that *The Green Fool* rehearses.[18] The attempted balancing act – with its implications of retrieval and reconciliation, of being independent yet acknowledging the separation thereby incurred – is to be found throughout all the different subgenres of writing the local. The classic Big House – Bowen's Court, Woodbrook, the Tipperary property of Kevin FitzGerald in *With O'Leary in the Grave* (1986), the Limerick home of Joan de Vere in *In Ruin Reconciled* (1990) – is a structure that stands apart by virtue of its material wealth, political allegiance, cultural significance and historical lineage. Yet in memory these lineaments of power often effectively defer to an intimate matrix of intracommunal relations, mixed attachments and exceptions to and critiques of the image of grandeur and authority that they appear to maintain. This second set of relations tends to be what remains in memory, or what the autobiographer dwells on when the house's historic role has withered away. As in much modernist literature, loss is a precondition of repossession; subjective attachment reinterprets, supplants and outlives outposts of empire; memory satisfies its desires by translating them into landscape; the artifice of autobiography articulates personal and interior realities whose presence is all the more insistent for its lack of persuasive material analogues.

Moreover, such writing's vocabulary of compensation and recovery is haunted by an equally evocative language of loss. If in *Bowen's Court* the author resembles 'an impossibly thwarted Odysseus',[19] it is because she is attempting to reconstitute a heritage while knowing that she has broken with it. The autobiographical impetus derives from an interrupted experience of belonging. And though *Bowen's Court* and *The Green Fool* are poles apart tonally, structurally, culturally and in many other ways, their joint awareness of the reality of the break as a basis for their perspectives make them strange modern bedfellows. In both instances, estrangement provides

---

[18] Permutations and combinations of the dynamic will be found in, for instance, Dervla Murphy, *Wheels Within Wheels* (London: John Murray, 1979); Benedict Kiely, *Drink to the Bird* (London: Methuen, 1991); Aidan Higgins, *Donkey's Years* (London: Secker and Warburg, 1995); Dermot Healy, *The Bend for Home* (London: Harvill, 1996); Hugh Maxton, *Waking: An Irish Protestant Upbringing* (Belfast: Lagan Press, 1997); the opening chapter of Dennis O'Driscoll, *Stepping Stones: Interviews with Seamus Heaney* (London: Faber and Faber, 2008); Cathal O'Searcaigh, *Light on Distant Hills* (London: Simon and Schuster, 2009); Patrick McGinley, *That Unearthly Valley: A Donegal Childhood* (Dublin: New Island Books, 2011); and Edna O'Brien, *Country Girl* (London: Faber and Faber, 2012). This list is not exhaustive. The special case of John McGahern's *Memoir* (London: Faber and Faber, 2005) is discussed in this chapter.

[19] Elizabeth Grubgeld, *Anglo-Irish Autobiography: Class, Gender, and the Forms of Narrative* (Syracuse: Syracuse University Press, 2004), 41.

the ground for imaginative return, the local is prized as the primary world and both questing personae suffer from, and artistically profit by, the incompleteness and discontinuity that inheres in their rural connections. The antinomies that *The Green Fool* and *Bowen's Court* both contend with and embrace portray landlessness as an instructive and perhaps unsuspected form of Irish identity; they also illustrate more generally some of the objectives served by a knowledge of how person and place are in counterpoint.

'Everything interesting begins with one person in one place',[20] no doubt. But in twentieth-century rural Irish autobiography, beginnings are only half the story. The rest consists of discontinuities, of departures for the city or the emigrant boat, of upward social mobility, largely provided by education, and of the seemingly unsystematic but ineluctable erosion of life on the land in all its different hierarchies, settlements and practices. The backward look inspired by these voluntary and involuntary dislocations elevates the local beyond its quotidian reality. Often such highlighting is provided by an author's survey of his or her native ground. The self-consciously geographical overview with which Hugh Dorian opens his narrative is a case in point, as are, in their different veins, the view in *The Green Fool* from 'the tops of the little hills . . . back to the days of St. Patrick and the druids'[21] and the claim in *Bowen's Court* that 'The country conceals its pattern of life, which can only wholly be seen from an aeroplane.'[22] Later iterations of the same approach include Éamon Kelly's declaration in *The Apprentice* (1995) of his fond regard for 'the glorious breasts of the goddess Danu',[23] two mountain peaks in south-eastern Kerry. These perspectives not only distinguish place; they also make the viewer stand out, giving him or her possession of a point of vantage that exercises a command, or sense of privileged apprehension, over his or her territory. This spatial initiative locates the place in the text as it appears in memory, outside of time and also at a distance. The latter feature lends a completeness to what is seen, but it also is a reminder of incompleteness, of being away and in that sense cut off from not only what the view presents but from the life that the viewer has left there.

The most common form of acknowledging and overcoming this sense of severance in Irish rural autobiography is the memoir of childhood. This

---

[20] John McGahern, 'The Local and the Universal', in John McGahern, *Love of the World: Essays*, ed. Stanley van der Ziel (London: Faber and Faber, 2009), 11.
[21] Kavanagh, *The Green Fool*, 8.
[22] Elizabeth Bowen, *Bowen's Court* (London: Vintage, 1999), 5.
[23] Éamon Kelly, *The Apprentice* (Dublin: Marino Books, 1995), 191.

form unites an unimpeachable version of the self with innocent experiences of place, a combination that with regard to Maurice Hayes's *Sweet Killough, Let Go Your Anchor* (1994), for instance, 'surprises by its benignity and its distance from stereotype'.[24] Smallness unites these versions of self and of place. Indeed, size, scope and other measures of extent are recurring features of Irish rural autobiography, from the *Retrospections of Dorothea Herbert*'s 'little world'[25] to *The Farm by Lough Gur*'s 'little colony'[26] to the setting of Florence Mary McDowell's *Other Days Around Me* (1966) in the 'little corner of the Six Mile Valley'.[27] George O'Brien's *The Village of Longing* (1987) portrays 'that small no-place'[28] of Lismore, Co. Waterford; Polly Devlin's *All of Us There* (1983) reports of her Ardboe, Co. Tyrone home that 'We were almost an island.'[29] Ostensible insignificance and, in a peculiar sense, minority status are not confined to space or geography but are also replicated temporally in the rote quality of local life, in the recurring calendar of such activities as hay-making, harvesting and the pattern days of a district's patron saint and in its shooting, fishing, racing, coursing, hurling and bowling seasons. These activities' cyclical aspects are also reproduced in the clerical and school year, where certain fundamental institutional practices reinforce the experience of the reassurances and constraints of a narrow round.

Memory can retrospectively valorize smallness as a source of the fixed, the knowable and the customary. And the source's usually remote location also may be regarded as a cultural form of virtue, gracing the place with uniqueness. These two autobiographical acts of translation, so to speak, also find expression in other subgenres of Irish rural autobiography, small-town remembrances and Travellers' life-writing. And if an individual autobiography 'mixes genres in order to find the most accessible route to link the "strange" past with the present',[30] such a mix will be even more likely when a range of autobiographies is considered. Remoteness in the case of small towns is a relative term. The Lismore of George O'Brien, Dervla Murphy and James Ballantyne is an out-of-the-way place, as are

---

[24] Maurice Hayes, *Sweet Killough, Let Go Your Anchor* (Belfast: Blackstaff Press, 1994), vii.
[25] Herbert, *The Retrospections of Dorothea Herbert*, 455.   [26] Carbery, *The Farm by Lough Gur*, 20.
[27] Florence Mary McDowell, *Other Days Around Me* (Belfast: Blackstaff Press, 1972), 12. The historical value of this work and *Roses and Rainbows* (Belfast: Blackstaff Press, 1972), a companion volume, is noted in J. C. Beckett's foreword to the latter.
[28] George O'Brien, *The Village of Longing* (Gigginstown: Lilliput Press, 1987), 92.
[29] Polly Devlin, *All of Us There* (Belfast: Blackstaff Press, 1994), 13.
[30] Claire Lynch, *Irish Autobiography: Stories of Self in the Narrative of a Nation* (New York: Peter Lang, 2009), 157.

Callan, Co. Kilkenny and Killough, Co. Down.[31] But while that designation may not seem to fit Thurles, Downpatrick, Listowel or Macroom, one
of the relevant aspects of these provincial centres is the ways they are
intimate with, but at the same time face away from, their rural backdrops.
Dennis O'Driscoll's recollection in 'Circling the Square: A Thurles
Prospect' (1989) that 'We spoke of "townies" with some derision but we
weren't quite from the country either'[32] is one variation on the theme of
town and country relations. The uncertain balance it implies between self
and place is also indicated by O'Driscoll's title, as well as by his perspective-
making persona of boyish *flâneur*.

Not quite so playful, but equally evocative, are the father and son Sunday
walks in Maurice Hayes's *Black Puddings with Slim: A Downpatrick Boyhood*
(1996), 'round the Quoile ... down the Saul Road ... up over Irish Street
and Stream Street and out the Vianstown Road'.[33] In neither this instance
nor in the case of O'Driscoll is the countryside an inert tapestry of natural
effects. The possibility of Wordsworthian interludes is occluded – by ruined
abbeys in O'Driscoll's case, by meetings with war veterans in Hayes's.
Experiences of this kind also contribute to the *cachet* of one's place of origin,
enlarging but also consolidating its distinctiveness and interest. This con-
solidation is enhanced when, as Tony O'Malley remembers, 'The country
and town to me were the one.'[34] This fusion produces a sense of the spirit of
place, as though the landscape is teaching the self attending to it, though as
O'Malley reveals (most notably in his celebrated paintings), this degree of
integration is both a matter of direct experience and cultivated perspective,
resulting in an apprehension that 'the landscape, whereas it was always
visible as a physical thing, was really feeling'.[35] In this respect, place is
understood as an image of identity, and something of this type of complicated exchange is also carried out in the backward, recuperative look from
the town of Cavan to his native Finea in Co. Westmeath taken by Dermot
Healy in *The Bend for Home* (1996). The transaction – one more version,

---

[31] Uniquely for a place its size, Lismore is the subject of a three autobiographical works, James
Ballantyne's *Lismore: Autobiography of an Irish Town 1937–1954* (London: The Heap, 2008) com-
plementing Murphy's *Wheels Within Wheels* and O'Brien's *The Village of Longing*.

[32] Dennis O'Driscoll, 'Circling the Square: A Thurles Prospect', in William Corbett and William
Nolan, eds., *Thurles: The Cathedral Town* (Dublin: Geography Publications, 1989), 170.

[33] Maurice Hayes, *Black Puddings with Slim: A Downpatrick Boyhood* (Belfast: Blackstaff Press, 1996),
178ff.

[34] Tony O'Malley, 'Inscape – Life and Landscape in Callan and County Kilkenny', in William Nolan
and Kevin Whelan, eds., *Kilkenny: History and Society* (Dublin: Geography Publications, 1990), 620.

[35] Ibid., 624.

perhaps, of 'the autobiographical pact'[36] – characterizes the occasion of recollection as a tribute the town pays to the country, a compliment that is also complementary, suggesting an awareness that both environments are incomplete and revealing how spiritually enriching (for O'Malley) and personally consoling (for Healy) it is to see each in the other's light.

The value of creating a spirit of place and its significance as an antidote to the more conventional narrative of uprooting and departure is also illustrated by Travellers' autobiographies, although largely by negative means. The experience of failure, the environments of incompleteness, the unavailability of remediation that recur throughout the two principal works in this subgenre – Sean Maher's *The Road to God Knows Where* (1972) and Nan Joyce's *Traveller* (1985) – are all the more vivid because of their authors' attempts to overcome them. Imaginative transmutation alone seems insufficient to heal the various social and other breaches that result from the fact that 'Travellers have traditionally occupied a liminal position in Irish society.'[37] And their traditional standing is confirmed in their many guest appearances in all the other subgenres of Irish rural autobiography, which gives them an air of being part of others' experience without others ever being part of theirs. A view such as Bryan MacMahon's in *The Master* (1992), which highlights 'the vivid and volatile nature of their lives on the road',[38] is not untypical of the distancing exoticism generally applied to these fellow citizens. It is not merely that for the non-itinerant majority Travellers represent a certain tribalism, a form of homelessness, ingrown traditions, obscure resources and, if not exactly a language barrier, a linguistic alternative in which to hide if desired. Settled life, unconsciously perhaps, prides itself on having moved on from, or explicitly broken with, social markers of this kind and with their historical connotations, many of which possess rural colourations and inflections. The autobiographical emphasis of Maher and Joyce falls on the other side, as it were, of that break, the undue frustrations and deprivations that have arisen from maintaining an essentially unchanged way of life. This assertion of independence has resulted in permanent struggle – for self-realization through education in Maher's story, for social justice in Joyce's.

Their stories, however, show Travellers to be closer to the mainstream than their social status indicates. Through their distinctive relationship with the countryside and various other ways of rural, small-town and Big

---

[36] See Philippe Lejeune, *On Autobiography*, trans. Kathleen Leary (Minneapolis: University of Minnesota Press, 1989), 3–30.

[37] Paul Delaney, 'Stories from Below: Sean Maher and Nan Joyce', *Studies*, 93:372 (2004), 462.

[38] Bryan MacMahon, *The Master* (Swords: Poolbeg Press, 1992), 146.

House life, and also because of the complications they bring to the notion of the break and ideas of social development generally, the works of Maher and Joyce become to a certain degree emblematic of the uneven balance between person and place that rural Irish autobiography attempts to negotiate. In their cases, the quest for equilibrium deals with belittlement and security, on the one hand, and with self-respect and resistance on the other. The incomplete outcomes of their particular efforts are indispensable personal testimonies from one of the most remote corners of national life. *Traveller* and *The Road to God Knows Where* also usefully vary conceptions of the local, the communal, the neighbour, the daily round and other structuring elements of narratives of rural life. Moreover, Maher's yearning for settled life – 'I wanted to get away from them, my father in particular'[39] – echoes the Oedipal note which resounds throughout many of the later Irish rural autobiographies and which is one more expression of the play of attachment and detachment that seems central to this subgenre, regardless of location and context.

There was a time when 'The family farm stood at the heart of society, especially in public claims and utterances.'[40] That time has proved to be no more permanent than any other, and individual breaks from rural backgrounds are indicative of larger recent changes in Irish society. From an autobiographical standpoint, however, the father, however configured with respect to his own personality and behaviour, is at the heart of the rural scene and as such is a figure to withstand, circumnavigate, repudiate and surpass. These confrontations occur in various ways, sometimes subliminally, but sometimes too there is a physical component, as in Ross Skelton's *Eden Halt: An Antrim Memoir* (2013), where the child 'became very wary of being near'[41] the father. In other instances, there may be rejection of the land and patrimony that the father stands for, resulting in Sean O'Callaghan's declaration in *Down by the Glenside: Memories of an Irish Boyhood* (1992) that 'Farming was one occupation I detested'[42]; or it may be the great gulf between personalities signified by Denis Sampson in *A Migrant Heart* (2014), who notes that his silent father was 'a farmer who never in his whole lifetime read a book or ... took much interest in the printed word'.[43] The upshot of Oedipal conflict in John O'Donoghue's *In*

[39] Sean Maher, *The Road to God Knows Where* (Dublin: Veritas, 1998), 76.
[40] John McGahern, 'Rural Ireland's Passing', in *Love of the World*, 166.
[41] Ross Skelton, *Eden Halt: An Antrim Memoir* (Dublin: Lilliput Press, 2013), 57.
[42] Sean O'Callaghan, *Down by the Glenside: Memories of an Irish Boyhood* (Cork: Mercier Press, 1992), 88.
[43] Denis Sampson, *A Migrant Heart* (Montreal: Linda Leith, 2014), 11.

a Quiet Land (1957) is that the son runs away from his east Kerry home to the west Kerry coast, where he meets his first love, a handsome young fisherman. But it should also be noted that there are exceptions to these scenarios. Éamon Kelly's precise reconstruction of his father's feats of carpentry and building evoke valuable cultural resonances of making and newness, which makes his autobiography rather more replete with the 'authenticity'[44] attributed to O'Donoghue. In *The Master*, MacMahon, a Listowel school principal, adopts something of the persona of a benign father figure, a resolver of conflicts, who cherishes equally each of the children in his charge. The social connotations of this portrait of the self as a public figure may be usefully compared with the family group depicted in John A. Murphy's 'The Piano in Macroom' (1993), where the town's prevailing political outlook, which adversely affected the father, is offset by the serious domestic business of enjoying 'the enrichment of music'[45] in a triumph of independence over provincialism.

The rural fatherland, like its sons' and daughters' accounts of it, constitutes uneven territory – remote, stony, dangerous, uncharted and every so often sheltering. These characteristics feature in full measure in the most comprehensive and far-reaching narrative of Oedipal conflict in Irish rural autobiography (and, arguably, in Irish literature), John McGahern's *Memoir* (2005). As is well known, this work's material underwent a lengthy gestation in the author's celebrated fiction. In *Memoir*, however, the treatment of the fatherland is even more unsparing, in effect a final stripping-down. At the same time, and in contrast to *Memoir*'s embattled interiors, the rural setting receives a fullness of expression and a symbolic weight that convey a desire to supplant the fatherland with a motherland. The tyrannical policeman father in the stone structure of his barracks is shorn of his authority and of the overplus of *amour propre* which is its spiritual counterpart by recollections of the mother, she who was the teacher, the tutor of sensibility and the liberator of the mind. Her signature is not the badge of office but the wildflower, the status of which for the autobiographer is comparable, despite having a much different commemorative power, to that of the bogland flowers in *The Green Fool*, 'more magical flowers I have not seen since'.[46] Maternal attachment is disrupted by her untimely death, an event which places

44 Sean O'Faolain, 'Foreword', in John O'Donoghue, *In a Quiet Land* (New York: Coward-McCann, 1958), 6.
45 John A. Murphy, 'The Piano in Macroom', in Seán Dunne, ed., *The Cork Anthology* (Cork: Cork University Press, 1993), 235.
46 Kavanagh, *The Green Fool*, 8.

the author in greater proximity to the father and also fortifies the will to break from him and, implicitly, from the image of the state that he represents.[47]

The break and all its freight are of critical importance in *Memoir*. But more significantly, they are not ends in themselves but rather an evidently necessary preliminary to return, a transcending closure of old wounds through a resumption of rural life. The return is to the place of the mother's people, estimable for being 'above all, rooted in their own lives'.[48] Many who have made the break find, like Denis Sampson, that 'in the end, it is not the location of my life that is vital, it is the way in which I have learned to accommodate change'.[49] In *Memoir*, however, McGahern's reattachment and renewal are expressed in terms that suggest an ethos of the rural. This is a sphere comprised not merely of roots and inheritance, but where 'the local and the individual were more powerful than any national identity'.[50] This is a locale where one could be consciously present to an optimal degree in the world of one's own existence, embracing one's own nature in its natural setting. The work's enduring image – the testament to survival that return articulates – is of the child walking with his mother and experiencing 'an extraordinary sense of security, a deep peace, in which I feel that I can live for ever'.[51] This is an image of fusion and belonging that testifies to a spirit of place that is elemental in its simplicity. McGahern's enactment of psychological and material repossession may be used as a lens through which the crosscurrents and multiplicities of rural Irish autobiography can be perceived. For, as one who had more of a right than most to remind us, the relationships between place and personality, between birthright and personhood, between native and citizen, are by no means a matter of 'ending up as your own anthropological specimen'.[52]

Further reading

Bourke, Angela. 'Inner Lives: Creativity and Survival in Irish Rural Life', *Éire-Ireland*, 46: 3–4 (2011): 7–16.
Grubgeld, Elizabeth. *Anglo-Irish Autobiography: Class, Gender, and the Forms of Narrative*. Syracuse: Syracuse University Press, 2004.

---

[47] Conflicting embodiments of the state are an important dimension of the narrative, making *Memoir* a distinguished instance of personal history as a rebuke and supplement to the presumed integrity of the national story.
[48] McGahern, *Memoir*, 43.   [49] Sampson, *A Migrant Heart*, 232.   [50] McGahern, *Memoir*, 211.
[51] Ibid., 4.   [52] O'Driscoll, *Stepping Stones*, 10.

Harte, Liam, ed. *Modern Irish Autobiography: Self, Nation and Society.* Basingstoke: Palgrave Macmillan, 2007.

Lynch, Claire. *Irish Autobiography: Stories of Self in the Narrative of a Nation.* New York: Peter Lang, 2009.

Napier, Taura S. *Seeking a Country: Literary Autobiographies of Twentieth-Century Irishwomen.* Lanham: University Press of America, 2001.

Walsh, Christine. *Postcolonial Borderlands: Orality and Irish Traveller Writing.* Newcastle upon Tyne: Cambridge Scholars, 2008.

CHAPTER 14

The Autobiography of the Irish Working Class

Emmet O'Connor

While the social and discursive activity of writing one's autobiography has many motives, these can broadly be divided into two types, objective and subjective, and there is usually a marked distinction between the two, even if elements of both will always be present. In the case of an autobiographer motivated by an objective or external stimulus, he or she may be inspired by a connection to someone or something that is perceived as being greater than them, be it a heroic figure, an event, an institution, a process or simply the fact of belonging to a collective based on social or economic status. In many such autobiographical works, the author is primarily concerned with this other and has little to say about their own lives or sense of self. Conversely, where the motivation is subjective or centred on the self, the author typically writes from a belief in the intrinsic worth or value of their own story and the resultant narrative may be entirely self-referential. Some define the literary outcome of the more objective approach to recollection as memoir and restrict the use of the term 'autobiography' to works that are more obviously self-centred, but such delineations can be difficult to apply in practice, as will be borne out in the following discussion of written autobiographies by Irish people from working-class backgrounds since the early 1900s. The chapter's main concerns are to evaluate a selection of these works to determine if what we find in them amounts to a coherent self-image and to investigate what these texts reveal about Irish culture and society over time.

However one defines it in literary terms, the narrative act of placing oneself at the centre of events is an act of presumption and self-regard. It requires a measure of education, egotism and even arrogance (not to mention contacts with publishers), traits that were traditionally in shorter supply among the working class than among other groups. In a traditional, authoritarian and conformist society, such as Ireland was for many decades, people are less likely to make that act of presumption. The literary output of the Irish working class has also been curtailed by the country's late industrialization, or more accurately, by its de-industrialization in the nineteenth century and its fragile re-industrialization from the 1930s onwards. Consequently, the growing ubiquity of autobiography by Irish working-class writers had to await the emergence of a more liberal and less deferential culture in the 1960s and 1970s. Meanwhile, few regarded the working class and their culture as being of significance. No matter that this segment of the population sustained a relatively vibrant trade union movement. Exceptionally in Europe, it had no major political expression; the largest party of the left, the Labour Party, averaged about 11 per cent of the national vote in parliamentary elections south of the border from 1922. The Irish proletariat might have amounted to a class *in* itself, but it was not a class *for* itself.[1]

Autobiography and its close relation, oral history, therefore present a somewhat muddled portrait of twentieth-century Ireland as a society with a strong status consciousness and a weak class consciousness. Where it was articulated, class consciousness was commonly caricatured as snobbery or an alien socialist affectation, and the very existence of class, especially the working class, was routinely questioned in Irish social discourse up to the 1970s.[2] Only occasionally did external or objective factors lead individuals to write works of autobiography, and not until modernization took root in the 1960s did subjective motives gain traction beyond the literati. With the revival of labour history in the 1970s, oral history came into wider use and, in recognition of the dearth of working-class recollection, acquired a privileged status in the discipline, comparable with women's history, where it was accorded a similar value for similar reasons. Yet the parameters of the historiography have remained within the confines of a post-1945 'new labour history' paradigm, and a scholarship that has rarely ventured beyond leaders, organizations and politics into the social culture of workers has failed to interrogate autobiography as an investigative and analytical tool.[3]

---

[1] Whether Karl Marx actually made this distinction has been disputed, but the concept is so useful that it is widely used. See Edward Andrew, 'Class in Itself and Class against Capital: Karl Marx and his Classifiers', *Canadian Journal of Political Science*, 16:3 (1983), 577–84.

[2] See Maura Cronin, 'Class and Status in Twentieth-Century Ireland: The Evidence of Oral History', *Saothar*, 32 (2007), 33–43; C. S. Andrews, *Man of No Property: An Autobiography* (Cork: Mercier Press, 1982), 256–57; Diarmaid Ferriter, *The Transformation of Ireland, 1900–2000* (London: Profile Books, 2004), 697.

[3] See Emmet O'Connor and Conor McCabe, 'Ireland', in Joan Allen, Alan Campbell and John McIlroy, eds., *Histories of Labour: National and International Perspectives* (Pontypool: Merlin Press, 2010), 137–63; Fintan Lane, 'Envisaging Labour History: Some Reflections on Irish Historiography and the Working Class', in Francis Devine, Fintan Lane and Niamh Puirséil, eds., *Essays in Irish Labour History: A Festschrift for Elizabeth and John W. Boyle* (Dublin: Irish Academic Press, 2008), 9–25.

The evolution of the subgenre of working-class autobiography in Ireland can be divided into four phases. First comes the classic era, during which autobiography was held to be the prerogative of remarkable people with remarkable stories to tell, or of professional writers and artists. The cultural bias shown towards the writings of such individuals did at least ensure that what was published was of a high literary standard, and some of it shaped the popular image of urban working-class culture. The second phase for the most part features events-focused political memoir. From the 1916 rebellion onwards, the politics of the revolutionary era and the re-emergence of the Irish labour movement provided an objective rationale for veterans of the Citizen Army, the Spanish Civil War and trade union activism to chronicle their life stories. The third phase is more subjective and varied in nature. With the slow and fitful liberalization of Irish society from the 1960s, a number of memoirs and autobiographies, many of them non-political, began to be published by working-class people. These can be divided into two categories, those focused on work and those based on social or ethnographic observation. Broadly speaking, the first category emerged in the 1960s and comprises works written mostly by men. The second category had to await the more substantial secularization trends of the 1970s and later, and contains works that are more likely to be written by women. In each category, there are marked regional differences, notably between Dublin, Belfast and the provinces. Finally, the infamous Celtic Tiger era of the 1990s and early 2000s, and the global exaltation of entrepreneurship of which it was part, produced a fourth phase of auto-biographical writing, which marked the demise of the working class. In what follows, we will examine each of these phases in turn.

The classic era: shaping the public image of the working class

Paradoxically, the first fruits of Irish working-class recollection in book form are associated with two classics of the British labour movement. *Confessions of a Poacher* (1901) by Meath-born Jim Connell is arguably the first Irish working-class autobiography to appear in print. Written by the author of 'The Red Flag', which song became the anthem of the international labour movement, the book is not so much a coherent life story as a collection of episodes in the author's life, from his early rural ramblings in Co. Offaly to his poaching exploits in London, Surrey and Kent. Connell's work, which sold 80,000 copies in two editions, predates and is overshadowed by another bestseller, *The Ragged Trousered Philanthropists* (1914), a socialist autobiographical novel written by

Dublin-born Robert Noonan under the pseudonym of Robert Tressell, and
first published in abridged form three years after his death.[4] In it, Noonan
drew heavily on his grim experiences of underemployment as a house-
painter to produce a work that depicts the lives of a group of working-
class men in Mugsborough, a fictional English town modelled on
Hastings, where Noonan lived from 1902 to 1910. The unexpurgated
edition of the work did not appear until 1955, by which date the novel
had become the most politically influential work of British working-
class culture, although it can also be read as a satire on the deference of
English workers. Both *The Ragged Trousered Philanthropists* and
Confessions of a Poacher were penned primarily for commercial reasons
and were published in London after their authors had settled in
England. This was the norm in an age when London publishing houses
dominated the Irish literary scene and taking the boat-train was very
much a part of Irish working life. Connell and Tressell were therefore
long regarded as belonging to the British labour tradition, although
both have latterly been reclaimed for the Irish canon.

Most other worker-writers of this period were seen as Irish yet had little
impact on the popular consciousness of the nation. Their number includes
Patrick MacGill, who contributed to Jim Larkin's *Irish Worker* in its
halcyon days. MacGill achieved early acclaim (and in some quarters
notoriety) for his somewhat fictionalized autobiography *Children of the
Dead End: The Autobiography of a Navvy* (1914), after which he continued
to mine Irish themes throughout a prolific literary career. Ireland was
marginal commercially in this era and the Irish working class more marginal still. Two comrades of the first Communist Party of Ireland (1921–
24), Liam O'Flaherty and Jim Phelan, wrote autobiographies that covered
the period of their party membership, but treated their political activities as
incidental to jaunty accounts of their adventurous lives. Neither
O'Flaherty's *Shame the Devil* (1934) nor Phelan's *The Name's Phelan: The
First Part of the Autobiography of Jim Phelan* (1948) said much about the
party or their relationship to it. Indeed, O'Flaherty revealed more about
Irish working-class culture in one of his best-known novels, *The Informer*
(1925), the screen adaptation of which is itself symptomatic of the way
social radicalism died of embarrassment after the revolution. The novel has
Gypo Nolan on the run from 'the Revolutionary Organization', a thinly

---

[4] Francis Devine, 'Afterword', in Jim Connell, *Confessions of a Poacher* (Dublin: Lilliput Press, 2004),
161. This, the first Irish edition of the book, was published in association with the Jim Connell
Memorial Committee.

disguised version of the Communist Party, led by Dan Gallagher, a thinly disguised Roddy Connolly. But John Ford's 1935 Academy Award-winning film tellingly transformed Gypo into a renegade Irish Republican Army volunteer. In the 1920s, it was possible to believe that O'Flaherty's significance lay in his communism. 'I think if you eliminate Bolshevism and muck-raking from Liam O'Flaherty', wrote Desmond Fitzgerald, the Irish Free State's first minister for external affairs, 'you have a very unimportant writer.'[5] Subsequently, it became impossible to take Irish communism seriously, even in fiction.

In many respects, the literary characterization of the working class was left to Sean O'Casey and the Behan brothers, Brendan, Brian and Dominic. The process began with O'Casey's dramatic trilogy, especially *Juno and the Paycock* (1924) and *The Plough and the Stars* (1926). If they gave the proletariat a presence on stage, it was not a heroic one. The women are long-suffering and their menfolk feckless rogues or insensitive ideologues. The odd thing about O'Casey, given his strong socialist convictions, is that his stage socialists are negatively drawn, with the exception of his hero, Jim Larkin. O'Casey's autobiographies, which he began to publish in 1939 and which ran to six volumes, are of a different order.[6] Written in the third person, they are about the protagonist, Johnny Casside, first and last. While Johnny evolves through a succession of organizations that were central to the revolutionary era – the Gaelic League, the Irish Republican Brotherhood, the Citizen Army, the Irish Transport and General Workers' Union (ITGWU) – O'Casey's treatment of them is subjective, impressionistic and a treacherous friend to historians. Though not as well known as the plays, and marred by a suspicion that O'Casey exaggerated his proletarian credentials in them, the autobiographies reinforced the association of the working class with Dublin, Larkinism and the notoriously over-crowded inner-city tenements of the early twentieth century.

The Behans were more celebratory of growing up in the Dublin slums and of their 'teeming' social lives, partly because they were humourists writing social and family memoirs rather than strict autobiography and partly because their memories appear to have been genuinely happier.[7] The

---

[5] Quoted in John M. Regan, *The Irish Counter-Revolution, 1921–1936* (Dublin: Gill and Macmillan, 2001), 283.

[6] O'Casey's autobiographical volumes comprise *I Knock at the Door* (1939), *Pictures in the Hallway* (1942), *Drums Under the Windows* (1945), *Inishfallen, Fare Thee Well* (1949), *Rose and Crown* (1952) and *Sunset and Evening Star* (1954).

[7] The Behan family's autobiographical output includes Brendan's *Borstal Boy* (1958) and *Confessions of an Irish Rebel* (1965), Brian's *With Breast Expanded* (1964) and *Mother of All the Behans: The*

young Brian much preferred the intense collectivism of tenement life to the cold 'dog box of a house'[8] in the new suburb of Crumlin, where the family moved during a slum-clearance project in 1937. Brendan's memoirs dealt mainly with his time as a republican activist and a writer, though he was always a living embodiment of the Dublin worker. Brian and Dominic made their mother Kathleen and her brood one of the most famous families in Ireland, with Dominic's autobiographical *Teems of Times and Happy Returns* (1961) being dramatized in ten episodes for RTÉ television in 1977. Politically, the Behans were in the Connolly tradition (the first Irish edition of *Teems of Times* was published by Repsol, the imprint of Sinn Féin the Workers' Party) and differed politically from O'Casey, who treats the linkage of socialism and nationalism as a central problematic in his early work. But the distinction was lost in the public's nostalgic view of the working class as essentially revolving around a Dublin tenement culture of hard lives, warm kinships and, if it came to the crunch, trade-union solidarity. Politics as such did not come into it, and the slums, formerly regarded as a national shame, were easier to acknowledge because they were deemed to be dead and gone by the 1970s. In this regard, there is a revealing contrast between Christy Brown's warm and uplifting auto-biography *My Left Foot* (1954) and his autobiographical novel *Down All the Days* (1970). Conforming to the stereotypes, Brown shifted the setting of the novel away from the big, happy family in working-class Kimmage that he memorialized in the autobiography to a searing, O'Caseyesque version of Dublin in the 1940s and 1950s, complete with an afflicted mother and a brutal father. *Down All the Days* was the better-known work until the Academy Award-winning film adaptation of *My Left Foot* appeared in 1989.

The age of working-class political memoir: keeping a head above water

The revolutionary era witnessed a spike in labour history and inspired two contemporary histories, one of the 1913 Dublin Lockout and one of the Citizen Army, together with numerous pamphlets and the first general history of Irish labour by W. P. Ryan.[9] However, the glory years were soon

Autobiography of Kathleen Behan as told to Brian Behan (1984) and Dominic's *Teems of Times and Happy Returns* (1961) and *Tell Dublin I Miss Her* (1962).

[8] Brian Behan with Aubrey Dillon-Malone, *The Brothers Behan* (Dublin: Ashfield Press, 1998), 7.

[9] Arnold Wright, *Disturbed Dublin: The Story of the Great Strike of 1913–14 with a Description of the Industries of the Irish Capital* (London: Longman's, Green and Co, 1914); P. Ó Cathasaigh (Sean O'Casey), *The Story of the Irish Citizen Army* (Dublin: Maunsel, 1919); W. P. Ryan, *The Irish Labour*

cut short by the economic slump of 1920–21 and a series of strikes from August 1921 to December 1923. Labour was not just defeated; it was eviscerated in what amounted to a triumph of counter-revolution. The five decades that followed were noted for their authoritarianism and emphasis on social conformity, to the detriment of individual liberty. Moreover, embarrassed by their ignominious retreat from 'Red Flag' optimism and exasperated by the civil war within Dublin trade unionism instigated by Larkin in 1923, mainstream labour personalities felt they had little to celebrate. It is surely not a coincidence that the most prolific Irish socialist autobiographer of the era, Peadar O'Donnell, whose works include *The Gates Flew Open* (1932) and *Salud! An Irishman in Spain* (1937), was more in the republican than the labour tradition, or that Paddy 'the Cope' Gallagher, author of *My Story* (1939) and founder of the Templecrone Co-operative Society in Donegal, also stood outside it. When William O'Brien, long-time general secretary of the ITGWU, finally produced a memoir, entitled *Forth the Banners Go* (1969), he refused to write about events that happened later than 1923, though he did not retire until 1946. Numerous literati pressed Jim Larkin for a memoir as he edged into his seventies. He explained humorously to Sean O'Casey in September 1946: 'I am conscious of my obligations that if anything in "Mein Kampf" would be helpful to the present or the future generation I would be compelled to accept.'[10] He was dead within months. Nora was the only one of James Connolly's seven children to publish an autobiography in book form. She, in 1949, and Ina, in 1954, also wrote lengthy witness statements for the Bureau of Military History's archive of first-person accounts by participants in the independence struggle.[11] Son Roddy flatly refused to write an autobiography and the Citizen Army had to wait until 1977 for its sole published memoir of active service, *Under the Starry Plough: Recollections of the Irish Citizen Army* by Frank Robbins. Jack Carney's short memoir of Jim Larkin was written in 1953 to assist the historian Emmet Larkin, who was then a doctoral student and would later become Larkin's first academic biographer.

Movement: From the Twenties to Our Own Day (Dublin: Talbot Press, 1919). For the pamphlets, see the Cork Workers' Club Historical Reprints series.

[10] Cited in Emmet O'Connor, *Big Jim Larkin: Hero or Wrecker?* (Dublin: UCD Press, 2015), 315.

[11] See Nora Connolly O'Brien, *The Unbroken Tradition: An Account of The Irish Rebellion of 1916* (New York: Boni and Liveright, 1918), *Portrait of a Rebel Father* (Dublin: Talbot Press, 1935) and *We Shall Rise Again* (London: Mosquito Press, 1981), all of them autobiographical. See also Ina Heron, Witness Statement 919 and Nora Connolly O'Brien, Witness Statement 286 at www.bureauofmilitaryhistory.ie/ (accessed 22 December 2015).

Out of the 1907–23 period had come an Irish labour movement of various complexions – political and industrial, social democratic and revolutionary – forged by activists who had a confidence in class consciousness. What such activists lacked was the vital ingredient in working-class political memoir: a sense of the relevance of their story. It was mainly commercially minded writers like Phelan, O'Flaherty, O'Donnell and Charles McGuinness, author of *Nomad: Memoirs of an Irish Sailor, Soldier, Pearl-Fisher, Pirate, Gun-Runner, Rum Runner, Rebel and Antarctic Explorer* (1934), who filled the gap. Of the veterans who did provide autobiographical accounts of these years, two were anarchists: Captain Jack White, co-founder of the Citizen Army and author of *Misfit: An Autobiography* (1930), who was with the working class rather than of it, and John Caldwell, author of *Severely Dealt With: Growing Up in Belfast and Glasgow* (1993), who matured politically in Britain.

Liberalization and the rediscovery of labour history in the 1970s turned a key. The Northern Ireland conflict also added to the library in producing a handful of class-conscious recollections, though their tiny number in the much bigger and very politically driven corpus of Troubles autobiography speaks volumes, literally, about the nature of the conflict.[12] The most dramatic unpacking of the past concerned the Spanish Civil War. Virtually unspoken of before 1980, the fiftieth anniversary in 1986 of Franco's revolt marked a turning point. A stream of publications began to flow, including biographies, local and general histories, poems, plays and songs. Unfortunately, it was too late for all but five short autobiographical memoirs to be penned: *With the Reds in Andalusia* (1985) by Joe Monks; *La Niña Bonita agus an Róisín Dubh: Cuimhní Cinn ar Chogadh Cathartha na Spáinne* (*Nina Bonita and Róisín Dubh: Recollections of the Spanish Civil War*) (1986) by Eoghan Ó Duinnín, better known as Eugene Downing; *A Soldier of Liberty: Recollections of a Socialist and Anti-Fascist Fighter* (1996) by Peter O'Connor; and *Memorias de un Rebelde sin Pausa* (*Memories of a Rebel without a Pause*) (2002) and *Brigadista: An Irishman's Fight Against Fascism* (2006) by Bob Doyle. All went into print as a contribution to the history of political radicalism, most at the prompting of young admirers with a romantic view of Spain. All four autobiographers

---

[12]　For autobiographies that deal with social class, see especially Bernadette Devlin, *The Price of My Soul* (London: Pan Books, 1969) and Eamonn McCann, *War and an Irish Town* (Harmondsworth: Penguin, 1974). Stephen Hopkins's otherwise comprehensive *The Politics of Memoir and the Northern Ireland Conflict* (Liverpool: Liverpool University Press, 2013) does not contain a section on labour or social class.

were communists to the end, apart from Ó Duinnín. Possibly because he left the party for activism 'in an individual kind of way',[13] or possibly because he wrote in Irish, his second language, which distanced most readers from the text, Ó Duinnín offered the most candid account, peppered with anecdotes showing comrades to be more human than the stainless heroes of legend. To this small corpus can be added oral history interviews with Frank Edwards and Michael O'Riordan carried out by Uinseann MacEoin.[14]

A similar unpacking of history led to the publication of hitherto forgotten recollections by Belfast mill-girl Nellie Gordon, a trade union memoir by Gilbert Lynch and oral history interviews with communists Betty Sinclair, Joe Deasy and Andy Barr, and with veteran trade union leaders Jack Macgougan, John Freeman and Stephen McGonagle.[15] Gordon, an apolitical doffing mistress, would never have imagined writing her story, nor might it ever have been published, had she not met James Connolly. The appearance of such publications reflected the emergence of memoir as an increasingly popular genre on the political left and in the trade union movement, though the autobiographies of retired senior political figures were still more commonplace than those of union leaders.[16] The limits of class consciousness were delineated by the fact that the simple reality of

---

[13] Michael McInerney, *Peadar O'Donnell: Irish Social Rebel* (Dublin: O'Brien Press, 1974), 181.

[14] See 'Frank Edwards', in Uinseann MacEoin, ed., *Survivors: The Story of Ireland's Struggle as Told Through Some of Her Outstanding Living People* (Dublin: Argenta, 1980), 1–20 and 'Michael O'Riordan of Cork City and the International Brigade', in Uinseann MacEoin, *The IRA in the Twilight Years, 1923–1948* (Dublin: Argenta, 1997), 751–66. O'Riordan was also interviewed by newspapers and wrote for communist journals on Spain.

[15] National Library of Ireland, Dublin (NLI), Ellen Grimley papers, MS.13.096; Helga Woggon, ed., *Ellen Grimley (Nellie Gordon): Reminiscences of Her Work with James Connolly in Belfast* (Dublin: SIPTU, 2000); Gilbert Lynch, *The Life and Times of Gilbert Lynch*, ed. Aindrias Ó Cathasaigh (Dublin: Irish Labour History Society, 2011); Betty Sinclair, 'A Woman's Fight for Socialism, 1910–80', *Saothar*, 9 (1983), 121–32; Joe Deasy, 'The Evolution of an Irish Marxist, 1941–50', *Saothar*, 13 (1988), 112–19; Andy Barr, 'An Undiminished Dream: Andy Barr, Communist Trade Unionist', *Saothar*, 16 (1991), 95–111; Jack Macgougan, 'Letting Labour Lead: Jack Macgougan and the Pursuit of Unity, 1913–1958', *Saothar*, 14 (1989), 113–24; Peter Collins, 'John Freeman: A Life on the Left', *Saothar*, 24 (1999), 129–38; Stephen McGonagle, 'Navigating a Lone Channel: Stephen McGonagle, Trade Unionism and Labour Politics in Derry, 1914–1997', *Saothar*, 22 (1997), 139–52.

[16] See, for example, Noël Browne, *Against the Tide* (Dublin: Gill and Macmillan, 1986); Paddy Devlin, *Straight Left: An Autobiography* (Belfast: Blackstaff Press, 1993); Barry Desmond, *Finally and in Conclusion: A Political Memoir* (Dublin: New Island Books, 2000) and *No Workers' Republic!: Reflections on Labour and Ireland, 1913–1967* (Dublin: Watchword, 2009); and Matt Merrigan, *Eggs and Rashers: Irish Socialist Memories*, ed. D. R. O'Connor Lysaght (Dublin: Umiskin Press, 2014).

being a worker was never deemed an adequate justification for writing a political memoir.[17]

Non-political working-class memoir: work, life and society

Non-political working-class memoir has developed steadily in Ireland since the 1960s. In retrospect, and in light of accelerated technological change, it seems that books about the experience of work itself were a passing phase, the product of that overlapping period when manual labour was still significant and readers were becoming interested in the labour process. Unusually, the pioneering figures in this field are two Irish-language writers, Micí Mac Gabhann and Dónall Mac Amhlaigh, for whom work and earning a living were synonymous with emigration. Mac Amhlaigh was also unusual in that he needed no prompting from social 'superiors' to become a writer. Born in Galway in 1926, he compiled fifty-three volumes of diaries and literary notebooks and, though an active socialist, was not a political writer.[18] Such was the novelty of his rather mundane *Dialann Deoraí* (1960) that it was translated into English by Valentin Iremonger as *An Irish Navvy: The Diary of an Exile* and published in London in 1964. Mac Amhlaigh himself later took aim at 'the irritating simplicity'[19] of the book in his hilarious self-parody *Schnitzer Ó Sé* (1974), the English translation of which appeared in 1985. The dull style of *An Irish Navvy* reflected the fact that Mac Amhlaigh was not a native Irish speaker. His importance as a prolific social commentator on 'the middle nation',[20] as he called the Irish in Britain, is beyond question, however. Donegal-born Mac Gabhann, who had less of the social analyst about him, laboured on the farms of Scotland in the 1880s before emigrating to America, where he worked in the mines of Montana before being lured by the Klondike gold rush of the late 1890s. Mac Gabhann dictated his sole work, the unsentimental *Rotha Mór an tSaoil* (1959), which was translated into English as *The Hard Road to Klondike* in 1962, to his son-in-law, the folklore collector Seán Ó hEochaidh, back in Donegal before his death in 1948.

---

[17] One measure of this is the fact that a rare autobiography by a Dublin worker, written around 1970, still awaits a publisher. See Patrick Cunningham, 'Draft Autobiography of a Dublin Worker, 1900–1930', NLI, microfilm n.6205 (*c.* 1970).
[18] NLI, Collection List No. 59, diaries and notebooks of Domhall [sic] Mac Amhlaigh, MS. 32,596/1–53.
[19] Dónall Mac Amhlaigh, *Schnitzer O'Shea* (Dingle: Brandon Press, 1985), 145.
[20] See Dónall Mac Amhlaigh, 'The Middle Nation', *Irish Times*, 14 October 1970.

Reflecting the industrial make-up of Ireland for much of the twentieth century, the remainder of this slim corpus of non-political autobiographical writing is dominated by contributions from the north of the country on life in working-class Belfast and from the south on agricultural labour.[21] That few such workers realized the importance of their story is demonstrated by the fate of two manuscripts that lay neglected for years in the Public Record Office of Northern Ireland. The curmudgeonly Robert McElborough, who was born in 1884, began his memoirs in 1946, motivated by a desire to expose the poor treatment of Belfast gas workers by their trade union.[22] In focus and content, his memoirs wandered and presented to editors a problem common to the genre, that of reconciling personal recollection with historical fact. As a result, McElborough's published autobiography is considerably shorter than the manuscripts on it which it is based; nevertheless, it provides valuable subjective insights into the city's labour history between 1907 and 1945. Belfast linen-worker William Topping, who was a contemporary of McElborough, wrote his memoirs between January 1971 and early 1972, in response to an inquiry from Betty Messenger, an American academic researching the folklore of the Ulster textile industry. With chapters entitled 'First Days at Work' and 'Apprenticeship', Topping's *A Life in Linenopolis* (1992) is a work-centred narrative in which there are few references to family or married life.[23] Sadly, a funereal thread runs through these and other recollections of working lives, as the authors are often memorializing the end of the occupation in question and, by extension, the passing of a way of life.

---

[21] There is relatively little autobiographical writing that deals with the Southern Irish experience of urban, industrial work, a deficiency that is being mitigated by the upsurge in oral history. See the occasional features in *Saothar*, the journal of the Irish Labour History Society, especially Cronin, 'Class and Status in Twentieth-Century Ireland'. See also Kevin C. Kearns, *Dublin Tenement Life: An Oral History* (Dublin: Gill and Macmillan, 1994) and *Dublin Pub Life and Lore: An Oral History* (Dublin: Gill and Macmillan, 1996). Local history journals are also a fruitful source. For an account of farming life in Cork, see Liam O'Donnell, *The Days of the Servant Boy* (Cork: Mercier Press, 1997).

[22] Robert McElborough, *Loyalism and Labour in Belfast: The Autobiography of Robert McElborough, 1884–1952*, eds. Emmet O'Connor and Trevor Parkhill (Cork: Cork University Press, 2002). Despite the title, imposed by the publishers, the narrative is not primarily about politics. The McElborough archive in the Public Record Office of Northern Ireland includes four manuscript volumes and correspondence.

[23] William Topping, *A Life in Linenopolis: The Memoirs of William Topping, Belfast Damask Weaver, 1903–56*, eds. Emmet O'Connor and Trevor Parkhill (Belfast: Ulster Historical Foundation, 1992); Betty Messenger, *Picking Up the Linen Threads: A Study in Industrial Folklore* (Austin: University of Texas Press, 1978).

A second, ubiquitous trend within recent Irish working-class autobiography has been for writers to move the narrative away from the workplace to focus on domestic, adolescent and family life. Arguably, the class dimension is incidental to these stories that tell of struggle and hardship on a wider plane and which are usually upbeat in tone and laced with humour. Perhaps the best-known examples are those about 'darlin' Dublin' in the 'rare oul' times', written in what might be called a 'Behan-lite' style and idiom, such as the autobiographies of Bill Kelly and Éamonn MacThomáis.[24] Of course, an upbeat tone does not necessarily mar the literary quality of such works. Lily O'Connor's *Can Lily O'Shea Come Out to Play?* (2000), which was serialized on RTÉ radio, managed to be both optimistic and vivid in its description of the poverty endured by Dubliners during the de Valera era. Written from a Protestant working-class perspective, it has the added distinction of being one of the few autobiographies by women who grew up poor during the 1930s and 1940s. A sequel, *Dreams of Hope* (2006), dealt with O'Connor's emigration to England and Australia in the 1950s.

Rare too are memoirs of working-class lives in the Dublin suburbs or the windswept new housing estates beyond the canals. Was childhood so dull outside the urban bustle of the tenements and the Liberties? Evidently not, according to Phil O'Keeffe's *Down Cobbled Streets: A Liberties Childhood* (1995) and Gene Kerrigan's *Another Country: Growing Up in '50s Ireland* (1998), which spoke to a generation that was familiar with suburban conformity, a heightened clericalism and the subsequent advent of pop culture in the 1960s. The characters in *Another Country* are a world away from the quirky inner-city tenement dwellers who populated the working-class autobiographies of earlier eras. Since the 1960s, the northside suburbs of Dublin have displaced the slums as the quintessence of working-class Ireland, with the southside being similarly caricatured as its middle-class polar opposite. The residents of the northside estates have been given a voice in the fiction of Dermot Bolger and Roddy Doyle, both of whom infuse their work with a political agenda based on anti-nationalism and modernization theory, but the dysfunctional tower blocks and dreary sprawl of avenues, drives and crescents have failed to generate anything to rival the autobiographical power of the now-vanished tenements.

[24] Bill Kelly, *Me Darlin' Dublin's Dead and Gone* (Dublin: Poolbeg Press, 1983); Éamonn MacThomáis, *Gur Cake and Coal Blocks* (Dublin: O'Brien Press, 1976) and *The Labour and the Royal* (Dublin: O'Brien Press, 1978). MacThomáis also wrote popular public histories of Dublin. See http://copac.jisc.ac.uk/search?author=eamonn%20macthomais&rn=1 (accessed 22 December 2015).

In all of this, geography matters. Postwar Belfast had the critical population mass needed to foster urban memoirs. Gerald Dawe's *My Mother-City* (2008) recounts the city's fragile cosmopolitanism in the 1960s, and in the same decade Robert Harbinson Bryans, who wrote under the *noms de plume* Robert Harbinson and Robin Bryans, was billed as 'the first working class [sic] Ulster Protestant writer to be published to international acclaim', a coveted accolade to a people on the 'cultural cringe'.[25] Coming from the heavy-industry heartland of East Belfast, Bryans's homosexuality led him to be befriended by Welsh poet and aristocrat Evan Morgan and set on a prolific writing career. Bryans composed no less than a quadrilogy of autobiographies – *No Surrender* (1960), *Song of Erne* (1960), *Up Spake the Cabin Boy* (1961) and *The Protégé* (1963) – that covers his time as a child and wartime evacuee in Fermanagh, a shipyard worker and a cabin boy on a Belfast mudboat. It is unfortunate that the achievement of Bryans and other Belfast autobiographers such as John Boyd, who got 'out of his class' through a scholarship to the Royal Belfast Academical Institute, has been obscured by the Troubles.[26] Nor is it clear why Boyd, like many Protestants, decided to self-identify as an Irish writer.

Inevitably, the problems of Northern Ireland weigh heavily on its artists. The frivolity possible in a late twentieth-century Dublin memoir is unimaginable in its Belfast counterpart, even in the humorous tales of Sam 'Soda-bread' McAughtry.[27] There is, too, an awkwardness about handling the sectarian divisions – or is the unease in the eye of the beholder? The importance of locality is even more pronounced in other provincial Irish working-class memoirs, many of which have emerged as a by-product of the flowering of interest in local history and amount to a nostalgic celebration of growing up in days of yore, with incidental social observation and commentary. Outside of Dublin and Belfast, only Cork (which was also a magnet for a cluster of Waterford writers that included Thomas McCarthy and Seán Dunne) and the lost world of labour-intensive agriculture might make a claim to a vigorous tradition of working-class autobiography and memoir. Even then, it is rare to encounter the class anger one finds in the autobiographical trilogy by Cork poet, playwright and lifelong outsider

[25] Cited at www.culturenorthernireland.org/features/literature/obituary-robert-harbinson-robin-bryans (accessed 22 December 2015).

[26] John Boyd, *Out of My Class* (Belfast: Blackstaff Press, 1985) and *In the Middle of My Journey* (Belfast: Blackstaff Press, 1990).

[27] Sam McAughtry, *Play It Again Sam* (Belfast: Blackstaff Press, 1978); *McAughtry's War* (Belfast: Blackstaff Press, 1985); *Hillman Street High Roller: Tales from a Belfast Boyhood* (Belfast: Appletree Press, 1994); *On the Outside Looking In: A Memoir* (Belfast: Blackstaff Press, 2003).

Patrick Galvin, author of *The Raggy Boy Trilogy* (2002). As a rule, the smaller the town, the cosier the recollection.

Goodbye to all that

The final phase of autobiography to be considered here is one that implicitly bids farewell to the Irish working class and its culture. The best known of this corpus is Frank McCourt's Pulitzer Prize-winning *Angela's Ashes* (1996), which appeared when an economically uplifted Republic was congratulating itself on having forever eliminated the grinding poverty of McCourt's Limerick childhood. McCourt saw no echoes of the positivity of O'Casey or the Behans in his recollection of his miserable 1940s youth, only destitution and a drunken father who abandoned his family. As soon as he could, McCourt returned to New York, the city of his nativity. A very different approach was taken by Bill Cullen, one of the Celtic Tiger's celebrity cubs. Between 2008 and 2012 he hosted the Irish version of *The Apprentice*, the reality television show so illustrative of the contemporary pornography of capitalism, where viewers can vicariously enjoy seeing cash-strapped would-be entrepreneurs realize their dreams or have them crushed. Published at a time when the Irish economy seemed invincible, and graced by a foreword by Taoiseach Bertie Ahern, *It's a Long Way from Penny Apples* (2001) is very much a heart-warming rags-to-riches story that tells of Cullen's loving upbringing in the Dublin tenements, his mother's fruit-selling activities and his leaving school at thirteen to work his way through various dead-end jobs before becoming a millionaire in the motor trade and a philanthropist.[28] The book was a bestseller, despite being unendowed with literary flair. Cullen himself, among many others, compared his memoir to *Angela's Ashes*, suggesting that positivity was itself the secret of his publishing success, and his work came to be celebrated as the perfect antidote to the bleakness of McCourt's memoir. No one needed to observe that both books were a way of exorcizing an unwanted past. That was taken for granted.

Working-class autobiography will survive in some form as long as there are working-class people. The Behan tradition, for example, is alive and well in the work of Peter Sheridan, author of the trilogy *44: A Dublin Memoir* (1999), *Forty Seven Roses* (2001) and *Break a Leg: A Memoir* (2012). But the 'purer' version of the subgenre, written by workers for workers to explain how class works and to advance the political cause of

---

[28] In 2005, Cullen released his second book, *Golden Apples: Six Simple Steps to Success*.

labour, is as dead as the brothers Behan themselves. Even the working-class political memoir – as distinct from the former politician's memoir recounting a glorious parliamentary career – has all but disappeared. It was never very common in Ireland in the first place. Only in relation to the Spanish Civil War, or sporadically in trade unionism, can one detect a synergy between recollection and social or political agitation. Autobiographers as icons of the left are few, being limited to veterans of the Connolly Column, Sean O'Casey, Brendan Behan and, on the republican wing, Peadar O'Donnell.

Conclusion

Broadly speaking, working-class autobiography and memoir corroborate oral history accounts of working lives in suggesting that nineteenth- and twentieth-century Irish society had a strong grade distinction but a weak class consciousness among those at the lower end of the spectrum. It is striking that so many memoirs were written at the bidding of middle-class people. It is curious too that those who grew up in the Dublin slums always had something good to say about them and found the experience educational. Also notable is the gender imbalance, although women memoirists have begun to feature in more recent non-political or non-occupation-based publications. For the most part, however, class was simply part of the writer's social context, associated with poverty, oppression and disempowerment, and therefore something to escape from. Stripped of its collectivism in high-density, inner-city housing as a result of its dispersal to atomized suburbia in the postwar years, the working class, as a class for itself, lost confidence and lapsed into relative silence.

The shift in attitudes to the subgenre of working-class autobiography in the course of the past century reflects structural as well as ideological change. In twentieth-century Ireland's authoritarian, collectivist and conformist society, autobiography was regarded as an act of presumption and therefore justified only in exceptional circumstances. The more recent growth in working-class autobiography had to await the emergence of a more liberal society after the 1960s and the expansion of publishing opportunities. Ironically, the blossoming, such as it was, of writing by working-class people in these later decades was dependent on the disintegration of the collectivism which was a pillar of social class in earlier eras. It remains to be seen how the genre will evolve in the twenty-first century, as technology produces a new working class, disaggregated and without an agreed political future.

Further reading

Engel, Susan. *Context is Everything: The Nature of Memory*. New York: W. H. Freeman, 1999.

Foster, R. F. *The Irish Story: Telling Tales and Making It Up in Ireland*. London: Allen Lane/Penguin, 2001.

Harte, Liam, ed. *Modern Irish Autobiography, Self, Nation and Society*. Basingstoke: Palgrave Macmillan, 2007.

Kenneally, Michael. 'The Autobiographical Imagination and Irish Literary Autobiographies', in Michael Allen and Angela Wilcox, eds., *Critical Approaches to Anglo-Irish Literature*. Gerrards Cross: Colin Smythe, 1989: 111–31.

Lynch, Claire. *Irish Autobiography: Stories of Self in the Narrative of a Nation*. Bern and Oxford: Peter Lang, 2009.

Marcus, Laura. *Auto/biographical Discourses*. Manchester: Manchester University Press, 1994.

CHAPTER 15

Irish-Language Autobiography

Bríona Nic Dhiarmada

The history of autobiography in the Irish language, which is a post-1900 phenomenon, has been marked from the outset by the debates provoked by the language revival movement during the early years of the twentieth century and the contested role of the language as a cultural signifier in the newly independent Irish state. The specificities of the sociolinguistic and political contexts of literary production in the Irish language have to be acknowledged, therefore, if we wish to understand the reasons for the prominence of this genre in Irish-language letters. Indeed, to describe it as a genre is itself a contested act, given the myriad subgenres that flourish under the sign of life-writing in Irish. There is also a larger generic problem to consider. Within Anglophone criticism, scholars distinguish between autobiography, generally understood as a chronological retrospective account by the author/subject from childhood to the time of composition, and memoir, conceived as a more episodic narrative dealing with a specific era, event or relationship. As G. Thomas Couser explains, 'autobiography is more comprehensive, memoir more limited, in scope', and he goes on to note the significance of the recent preference for the latter term to describe self-referential non-fiction writing: 'The rise of the term *memoir* has in part to do with the contemporary trend away from comprehensive scope toward narrower focus – either in time span or in "thickness."'[1] Historian and essayist Perry Anderson couches the distinction in different terms, however, focusing on the degree of self-reflective interiority on display: 'a memoir can re-create a world lavishly peopled with others, while saying very little about the author himself. An autobiography, on the other hand, may take the form of a pure portrait of the self; the world and others featuring only as *mise en scene* for the inner adventures of the narrator.'[2]

---

[1] See G. Thomas Couser, *Memoir: An Introduction* (Oxford: Oxford University Press, 2012), 23.

[2] Quoted in George O'Brien, 'Memoirs of an Autobiographer', in Liam Harte, ed., *Modern Irish Autobiography: Self, Nation and Society* (Basingstoke: Palgrave Macmillan, 2007), 222.

If one were to accept Anderson's thesis, most Irish-language works would find it difficult to fit into his conception of autobiography, including one of the earliest and the most famous of all, *An tOileánach* (*The Islandman*) (1929) by Tomás Ó Criomhthain (Tomás O'Crohan), a fisherman from the tiny Irish-speaking Great Blasket Island situated off the west coast of Kerry, which tells the story of his life there. In fact, Seán Ó Tuama, the leading Irish-language critic of his time, remarked of Ó Criomhthain's book: '*An tOileánach* is more the biography of an island community than of a single islander.'[3] Ó Criomhthain himself, in a much-quoted paragraph in his final chapter, explains his own purpose in writing his life story, articulating a view that combines elements of personal voice and communal reportage, and which appears to move between the modalities of autobiography and memoir, as commonly understood in Anglophone criticism:

> Do scríobhas go mion-chruinn ar a lán dár gcúrsaí d'fhonn go mbeadh cuimhne i mball éigin ortha agus thugas iarracht ar mheon na ndaoine bhí im'thimcheall a chur síos chun go mbeadh ár dtuairisc 'ár ndiaidh, mar ná beadh ár leithéidí arís ann. . . . Ó lasadh an chéad teine insan oileán so níor scríobh aenne a bheatha ná a shaoghal ann. Adhbhar maoidhimh domh-sa mo scéal féin is scéal mo chomharsan a chur síos. 'Neosfaidh an scríbhinn seo conus mar bhí na hoileánaigh ag déanamh sa tseanaimsir.[4]

> I have written minutely of much that we did, for it was my wish that somewhere there should be a memorial of it all, and I have done my best to set down the character of the people about me so that some record of us might live after us, for the like of us will never be again. . . . Since the first fire was kindled in this island none has written of his life and his world. I am proud to set down my story and the story of my neighbours. This writing will tell how the Islanders lived in the old days.[5]

Yet while the Irish-language terms *dírbheathaisnéis* and *cuimhní cinn* correspond to 'autobiography' and 'memoir' respectively, this differentiation has not been much in evidence within Irish-language criticism and has rarely if ever been employed as an analytic prism to read life narratives in Irish. Instead, critics working in this field have created their own taxonomy which better serves and reflects ideological approaches such as the postcolonial and the ethnographic, which are seen to have particular

---

[3] Seán Ó Tuama, *Repossessions: Selected Essays on the Irish Literary Heritage* (Cork: Cork University Press, 1995), 205.
[4] Tomás Ó Criomhthain, *An tOileánach*, ed. Pádraig Ó Siochradha (Baile Átha Cliath: Oifig an tSoláthair, 1929), 265–66.
[5] Tomás O'Crohan, *The Islandman*, trans. Robin Flower (Oxford: Oxford University Press, 2000), 244–45.

relevance to Irish-language texts.[6] One of the foremost of these critics, Máirín Nic Eoin, has asserted: 'While accepting the theoretical usefulness of differentiating various forms of life writing – memoir, travel journal, diary, autobiography, auto-ethnography and so on ... the mode of production of much Irish-language autobiography has often resulted in the confusion of such generic categories.'[7] Nic Eoin goes on to differentiate two main strands in Irish-language life-writing, that written in the Irish Gaeltacht, which she characterizes as 'autobiography as *lieu de mémoire*', and non-Gaeltacht life-writing, which she categorizes as 'autobiography as self-invention'.[8] Yet as she herself acknowledges, her inclusion under the latter heading of Seosamh Mac Grianna, a writer from the Donegal Gaeltacht, due to his subversion of 'the conventions of Gaeltacht autobiography',[9] shows the difficulty if not the impossibility of confining works to a particular category.

The fact is that much of life-writing in Irish defies single or stable generic classification. Take the example of Colm Ó Gaora's *Mise* (*Myself*) (1943). This is certainly a Gaeltacht autobiography, one of the relatively few from Connemara in Co. Galway. Yet it is also and equally a political and historical memoir comparable to those written by non-Gaeltacht writers such as Séamas Ó Maoileoin, author of *B'Fhiú an Braon Fola* (*It was Worth the Spilling of Blood*) (1958), and to English-language autobiographies covering the same revolutionary period, such as Dan Breen's *My Fight for Irish Freedom* (1924) and Ernie O'Malley's *On Another Man's Wound* (1936). So while there is a certain critical usefulness in dividing life-writing into thematic subgenres, this can be undermined if we forget the porousness of the boundaries between them and the inevitability that some works will fit more than one category.

The complexity of the issues surrounding the categorization and subcategorization of Irish-language autobiography informs the analysis of this chapter, which examines the development of the form from its beginnings in 1915, and in the process questions some of the prevailing critical frameworks and interpretations. Like the literatures of other peoples with a

---

[6] See Máirín Nic Eoin, 'Twentieth-Century Gaelic Autobiography: From *Lieux de Mémoire* to Narratives of Self-Invention', in Harte ed., *Modern Irish Autobiography*, 132–55; John Eastlake, 'Orality and Agency: Reading an Irish Autobiography from the Great Blasket Island', *Oral Tradition*, 24:1 (2009), 125–41; Breandán Ó Conaire, ed., *Tomás an Bhlascaoid* (Indreabhán: Cló Iar-Chonnacht, 1992); Cathal Ó Háinle, 'Aspects of Autobiography in Modern Irish', in Ronald Black, William Gillies and Roibeard Ó Maolalaigh, eds., *Celtic Connections: Proceedings of the 10th International Congress of Celtic Studies* (Linton: Tuckwell Press), 360–76.
[7] Nic Eoin, 'Twentieth-Century Gaelic Autobiography', 132. [8] Ibid., 132ff., 145ff. [9] Ibid., 145.

history of colonialism, Irish-language autobiography provides a means of self-expression for speakers of a minority language which is also a national language, at once symbolically central and culturally peripheral. Although barely a century old, this tradition encompasses a diverse set of texts, as we shall see. It has brought forth the voices of many individuals whose gender and class usually leave them outside literary discourse, voices which assert their cultural difference and their subjectivity while insisting upon their common humanity. My main focus here will be on Gaeltacht life-writing and in particular the remarkable and highly influential corpus of autobiographical writing produced by the inhabitants of the Great Blasket Island in Co. Kerry. Non-Gaeltacht autobiography will also be attended to, particularly those works that are centred on the struggle for Irish independence, several of which have suffered a notable degree of critical neglect.

The genesis of Gaeltacht life-writing

Mo Sgéal Féin (*My Own Story*) (1915) by An tAthair Peadar Ua Laoghaire (Father Peter O'Leary) was the first autobiographical work to be published in book form in Modern Irish.[10] Father O'Leary, or An tAthair Peadar as he was commonly known, was a native speaker of Irish from the Muskerry district in west Cork and had been to the fore in the language revival movement since the 1890s. In a sometimes bitter debate among the revivalists of the Gaelic League, he was the leading proponent of the argument that a modern literature and literary standard for Irish had to be based on *caint na ndaoine* ('speech of the people'), the living language as spoken by the remaining native speakers. Others believed that those writing in Irish should return to the classical language as practised by Seathrún Céitinn (Geoffrey Keating) in the seventeenth century. That proponents of *caint na ndaoine* won the day was in no small part due to the exemplary literary efforts of An tAthair Peadar himself.[11]

In *Mo Sgéal Féin*, Ua Laoghaire uses his native Muskerry dialect to give an account of the turbulent sociopolitical events he had witnessed during his life, including the Great Famine of the 1840s, when he was a small boy, and the turbulence of the Land War (1879–82), from the perspective of the indigenous rural Irish-speaking farmer class to which Ua Laoghaire himself belonged. One of the few native speakers literate in Irish – it is unclear

[10] An tAthair Peadar Ua Laoghaire, *Mo Sgéal Féin* (Baile Átha Cliath: Brun and Ó Nualláin, 1915). The book has been republished as *Mo Scéal Féin* in modern spelling.
[11] See Philip O'Leary, *The Prose Literature of the Gaelic Revival, 1881–1921* (Pennsylvania: Pennsylvania State University Press, 1994).

whether he learned to read and write in Irish in his youth or when he was training to be a priest in Maynooth seminary in the 1860s – he was equally adept in English and therefore made a conscious choice to tell his story in a language which, while in a precarious state, was beginning to arrest its decline. Ua Laoghaire's choice of linguistic medium was remarkable enough to elicit a comment from Bishop Ó Domhnaill of the diocese of Raphoe, who noted in his English preface to the original 1915 edition:

> He was bilingual from the cradle. Not his knowledge of Irish, much less his knowledge of English, has made him what he is, but his knowledge of both, and his long acquaintance with the classics of Greece and Rome. Irish is the dominant factor. The rest served as helps to draw out Irish in dignified literature from a cultivated mind. But he could have been famous in English also, had he turned to it with Irish as an aid.[12]

Of course, Father O'Leary's choice of his native tongue and idiom for *Mo Sgéal Féin* was a political and cultural one, in keeping with his role as a language activist and ardent nationalist during the revolutionary years that heralded the birth of the Irish Free State. In many ways, *Mo Sgéal Féin*, which was a staple of the Irish secondary school curriculum for several decades after independence, stands as the first in the subgenre of Gaeltacht autobiography. Like many later works, Ua Laoghaire's has been lauded for its capturing of a communal voice and for its recovery and recording of what in today's terms might be described as subalternized discourses. As one critic observes:

> Where this work does come into its own is in the depiction of life in the nineteenth century. As most native speakers of Irish in the nineteenth century were illiterate, most accounts of Ireland in this period are by English-speaking Irishmen (or by outsiders, including Englishmen). *Mo Sgéal Féin* allows the voices of the rural, Irish-speaking areas to be heard.[13]

This positive appraisal of *Mo Sgéal Féin* is accompanied by criticisms of its dearth of biographical detail and perceived lack of self-reflexivity, such that it 'hardly seems to be an autobiography'[14] at all. This critique of Ua Laoghaire's book arises from the traditional idea of autobiography in post-enlightenment Western culture as, in the words of French theorist Phillipe Lejeune, 'the retrospective narrative in prose that someone makes of his

---

[12] An tAthair Padraic Ó Domhnaill, 'Preface', in Ua Laoghaire, *Mo Sgéal Féin*, vii.
[13] Unattributed preface to an edition of *Mo Scéal Féin* published by Muskerry Critical Editions. Available online at https://corkirish.files.wordpress.com/2014/11/msf-full-draft.pdf (accessed 20 January 2017).
[14] Ibid.

own existence when he puts the principal accent upon his life, especially upon the story of his own personality'.[15] Although Nic Eoin describes *Mo Sgéal Féin* as the earliest Irish-language autobiography, she does not consider it as an 'autobiography of Gaeltacht life' and does not include it in her discussion proper of Gaeltacht autobiography, which begins with *An tOileánach*, published some fourteen years after *Mo Sgéal Féin* and generally recognized as 'the most significant work of autobiography to have been written in Irish'.[16] The question arises, then, as to why *Mo Sgéal Féin* has not been acknowledged fully as a Gaeltacht autobiography, given that Ua Laoghaire was a native Irish speaker and his book displays a number of characteristics – lack of interiority and self-reflection on the one hand and a wealth of ethnographic and historical detail on the other, combined with a richness of language and idiom – that have been synonymous with most Gaeltacht autobiographies, especially those emanating from the Blasket Islands. Before attempting an explanation, let us turn our attention to the works of these islanders, which so unquestionably belong to the category of Gaeltacht autobiography as to be a *bona fide* literary phenomenon.

The Great Blasket phenomenon and its legacy

Although it is his most renowned work, *An tOileánach* was not Tomás Ó Criomhthain's first autobiographical publication; that distinction belongs to *Allagar na hInise* (*Island-Cross Talk*), which appeared in 1928. The books are quite dissimilar in style, although they shared the same editor, Kerry-born Pádraig Ó Siochradha, known in literary and cultural circles as *An Seabhac* ('The Hawk'). *Allagar na hInise* contains anecdotes of island life and lore, presented in diary form with much use of dialogue. *An tOileánach*, published when Ó Criomhthain was sixty-six years old, is a more straightforward-seeming autobiographical narrative, although it draws extensively on the uniqueness of island life. Together, these two works inaugurated a truly remarkable spate of autobiographical writing that emanated from this miniscule island in the twenty-five-year period that preceded its evacuation and abandonment in 1953.

Having learned to read and write in English in the island school as a boy, Ó Criomhthain only became literate in Irish in middle age. In the

---

[15] Cited in Robert Folkenflik, 'Introduction: The Institution of Autobiography', in Robert Folkenflik, ed., *The Culture of Autobiography: Constructions of Self-Representation* (Stanford: Stanford University Press, 1993), 13.
[16] Nic Eoin, 'Twentieth-Century Gaelic Autobiography', 132.

early 1900s, he became involved with a number of scholarly visitors to the Blaskets who were drawn by the purity of the Irish language spoken there and their view of the islands as an unsullied remnant of a premodern Homeric way of life, long vanished in other parts of Europe. There is no doubt that neither *An tOileánach* nor *Allagar na hInise* would exist were it not for the inspiration, support and indeed the collaborative skills these intrepid individuals provided. One of the most important of these visitors was a young man from Killarney, Briain Ó Ceallaigh, who introduced Ó Criomhthain to the work of Maxim Gorky and Pierre Loti and encouraged him to take pen to paper himself to write his own life story. Ó Ceallaigh had gone to the Blaskets to learn Irish on the advice of Ó Siochfradha, his mentor, who would eventually take over from the younger man and edit both of Ó Criomhthain's autobiographical compositions. Another hugely influential figure was Robin Flower, an English scholar and writer who was Keeper of Manuscripts at the British Museum. A lifelong visitor to the Blaskets, where he was affectionately known as *Bláithín* ('little flower') by the islanders, he too was to the fore in encouraging Ó Criomhthain in his literary endeavours. Flower's translation of *An tOileánach* first appeared in a Talbot Press edition in 1934 and was disseminated to a global readership in the Oxford University Press edition of 1951, by which time Flower had published his own memoir, *The Western Island* (1944).

The publication of *An tOileánach* was followed in 1933 by another autobiography by a much younger islander, Muiris Ó Súilleabháin (Maurice O'Sullivan), author of *Fiche Bliain ag Fás* (*Twenty Years A-Growing*). Born on the Great Blasket in 1904, Ó Súilleabháin was removed to the orphanage in Dingle on the mainland as an infant, following the death of his mother, but returned to the island when he was seven. The book tells of his upbringing by his grandfather, father and siblings and ends shortly after his departure to join An Garda Síochána, the Irish police force. Posted to Connemara, Ó Súilleabháin was tragically killed in a drowning accident in Galway at the age of forty-six. His second book was refused for publication and was subsequently lost. Much as Ó Criomhthain's writing had been encouraged by Ó Ceallaigh and Flower, the English philosopher and classicist George Thompson was instrumental in bringing Ó Súilleabháin's text to publication and in producing an English translation, which appeared in the same year as the Irish-language version.

The third book to come from the Blaskets was entitled *Peig .i. A Scéal Fein* (1936), a first-person account of the life of Peig Sayers, who was born

on the Kerry mainland in 1892 and married into the island as a young
woman. Sayers was a renowned storyteller and acknowledged as such not
only by her peers but by the many language and folklore students and
professionals who visited the Great Blasket in the first half of the twentieth
century. Robin Flower said of her: 'she is a natural orator, with so keen a
sense of the turn of phrase and the lilting rhythm appropriate to Irish that
her words could be written down as they leave her lips, and they would
have the effect of literature with no savour of the artificiality of composition'.[17] If Ó Criomhthain had Ó Ceallaigh and Flower as muse and Ó
Suilleabháin George Thompson, Sayers's life narrative also had midwives
at hand to bring it to the page. Interestingly, it was two women who
encouraged Sayers to write her memoir, Máire Ní Chinnéide, an Irish-
language activist and playwright from Dublin, and Léan Ní Chonalláin,
another cultural visitor to the islands. Although highly polished in the oral
tradition, as confirmed by Flower among others, Peig was herself illiterate
in Irish. She had learned to read and write in English at school but claimed
to have forgotten most of this knowledge. At Ní Chinnéide's suggestion,
Peig dictated her story to her son Mícheál Ó Guithín, known locally as An
File ('The Poet'), who wrote it down. The manuscript was then sent to Ní
Chinnéide who copied and edited it for publication. Peig was to be a
permanent presence in the Irish school curriculum for well over fifty years.

A further collaboration between Peig, Ó Guithín and Ní Chinnéide
ensued, resulting in the publication of Machnamh Seanmhná (An Old
Woman's Reflections) in 1939, in which we encounter a much more episodic
life story than the continuous chronological narrative of Peig. Machnamh
Seanmhná contains stories taken from Peig's immense store of folklore, as
in the chapter entitled 'A Man who was Clean in the Sight of People but
Unclean in the Sight of God'; reminiscences of island life, contained in 'An
Ass, A Bag of Potatoes and Geese; Mackerel Shoaling'; and accounts of
historical events she experienced, recorded in 'The News of the 1916
Revolution: The Black-and-Tans' Visit' and the penultimate chapter,
'I am Seeking the Widows' Pension: I am in a Motor-Car'. What shines
through all of the chapters is a very strong sense of Peig's humanity. She
emerges as a woman who fully inhabits her voice and creates a powerful
impression of one who had a lively sense of humour, an earthy presence
and an empathetic disposition. The mode of remembrance in this book,
with its interweaving of personal narratives with stories from the oral
tradition, allows us to see Peig as a narrator at the crossroads of competing

[17] Robin Flower, The Western Island (Oxford: Oxford University Press, 1978), 49.

narrative modes; in this, she bears resemblance to the contemporary Native American author Leslie Marmon Silko, whose autobiographical practice is to juxtapose 'a dominant modern mode and an alternative indigenous mode'.[18]

The exceptional nature of this outpouring of autobiographies from the Great Blasket Island in the late 1920s and 1930s was recognized nationally and internationally. The works were immediately acclaimed on first publication in Irish and would achieve worldwide recognition in translation.[19] Indeed, this phenomenon continued into a second and third generation of autobiographers, including those who had moved to the mainland following the evacuation of the Great Blasket in 1953. Books followed from Seán Ó Criomhthain, the son of Tomás – *Lá Dár Saol* (*A Day in Our Life*), published in 1969 – and Peig's son Mícheál Ó Guithín – *Is Truagh ná Fanann an Óige* (*A Pity Youth Does Not Last*), published in 1953. Ó Criomhthain's grandson, Pádraig Ua Maoileoin, continued the family tradition, most interestingly in *Na hAird O Thuaidh* (*The Northern Heights*) (1960). Originally written as a series of radio talks, it provides a different perspective on the dynamic between the oral and the literary modes that is at play in the work of the first generation of Blasket autobiographers, whose works not only encouraged and inspired their own descendants, now fully literate, but also led to the pre-eminence in Gaeltacht letters of auto-ethnography, to use the term employed by Nic Eoin in her discussion of former islander Máire Ní Ghaoithín's *An tOileán a Bhí* (*The Island that Was*) (1978) and *Bean an Oileáin* (*Island Woman*) (1986).[20]

Although writers of Blasket descent continued to be prolific, the genre also exercised a hold in the other Gaeltacht regions, although Munster could still claim a pre-eminence. The Ulster writer Seosamh Mac Grianna published a memoir in 1940, *Mo Bhealach Féin* (*My Own Way*), which broke strikingly with the sensibility and tone of the Munster autobiographies. Unlike the elegiac nostalgia of much Gaeltacht autobiography, Mac Grianna's text expresses and inhabits both stylistically and thematically the dislocation of someone trapped between the rural and the urban, between tradition and modernity. As Philip O'Leary succinctly puts it: 'Perverse,

---

[18] Sidonie Smith and Julia Watson, *Reading Autobiography: A Guide for Interpreting Life Narratives*, 2nd edn. (Minneapolis: University of Minnesota Press, 2010), 23.

[19] Oxford University Press published seven books in total from the Blasket Islands, all of which have been in print since their first publication. They are: *Island Cross-Talk* (Tomás O'Crohan); *The Islandman* (Tomás O'Crohan); *Twenty Years A-Growing* (Maurice O'Sullivan); *An Old Woman's Reflections* (Peig Sayers); *The Western Island* (Robin Flower); *A Pity Youth Does Not Last* (Mícheál O'Guiheen); and *A Day in Our Life* (Seán O'Crohan).

[20] Nic Eoin, 'Twentieth-Century Gaelic Autobiography', 142.

paranoid, prophetic and exasperating, Mac Grianna's is a startlingly modern if frequently discordant voice in the chorus of Gaelic writing in his time.'[21]

Another discordant Gaeltacht voice – albeit a fictional one created by a writer who was not born in the Gaeltacht – was heard in 1940 in the form of Brian Ó Nualláin's hilarious but excoriating parody, *An Béal Bocht* (*The Poor Mouth*), which mercilessly lampooned the idealized pieties of the Gaelic way of life, as portrayed in Ó Criomhthain and his followers. Ó Nualláin's faux memoir did little to stem the tide of sincere personal testimonies, however. Notable contemporaneous works from the Donegal Gaeltacht include the volumes *Nuair a bhí Mé Óg* (*When I was Young*) (1942) and *Saoghal Corrach* (*Troubled Times*) (1945) by Seosamh Mac Grianna's brother, the prolific Séamus Ó Grianna, who wrote under the pen name of Máire. More recent Donegal autobiographies include *Róise Rua* (1988), the life story of Róise Rua Mhic Grianna, a woman from Arranmore Island, which was written in autobiographical form by Pádraig Ua Cnáimhsí, an Arranmore schoolteacher and language enthusiast, under whose authorial name the book appears. This work departs from the convention established in earlier dictated life narratives, most famously in *Peig* but also in works such as Mící Mac Gabhann's *Rotha Mór an tSaoil* (*The Hard Road to Klondike*) (1959), where the subject speaking in the first person is credited as author. Despite the undoubtedly benign intentions of Ua Cnáimhsí in wishing to pass on Roise's memories of a hard but fruitful life, this claim of authorship of another's life story – in this instance by a literate man of that of an unlettered woman – raises thorny questions about ethics, agency and appropriation.

Contemporary autobiographies from Connemara have been fewer in number than those from the other Gaeltacht regions, one notable example being *Saol Scolóige* (*A Smallholder's Life*) (1993) by Seán Ó Conghaola, which combines memoir with folklore and the social history of Connemara. The immense contemporary popularity of sporting memoir is reflected in *Lá an Phaoraigh* (*Power's Day*) (2007), in which former Galway All-Ireland-winning footballer from Connemara, Seán Óg de Paor, in conjunction with his sister Aoife, recounts his glory days on the field.

Autobiography or ethnography?

Apart from the inherent fascination of the texts themselves, one of the most interesting aspects of autobiographies from Gaeltacht regions is their

---

[21] Philip O'Leary, *Gaelic Prose in the Irish Free State* (Pennsylvania: Pennsylvania State University Press, 2004), 233.

critical reception and categorization as a discrete genre. The work of the big three, so to speak – Ó Criomhthain, Ó Súilleabháin and Sayers – is often seen and treated as the ur-template. Their early supporters revered these authors' works as unique artefacts, free of all artifice, akin to the 'egg of a sea-bird – lovely, perfect, and laid this very morning',[22] to quote E. M. Forster's laudation of *Twenty Years A-Growing*. Later critics emphasized the texts' lack of reflexive interiority, finding them closer to ethnography than literature, while praising them for giving readers an important insight into social customs in a vanished or vanishing world.[23] Critics such as Cathal Ó Háinle and Irene Lucchitti have provided a corrective to such readings by pointing out the inherent literary nature of the Blasket auto-biographies, Lucchitti in particular going against the grain of most depictions of Ó Criomhthain by drawing attention to 'his identity as a man of letters'[24] and his assertion of a literary persona. Such attempts to situate the Blasket autobiographies within literary paradigms have been in the minority, however. Much recent scholarship reflects a critical turn to compositional processes and modes of production. Nic Eoin, for example, speaks of 'the critical dilemma posed by the mode of production of most Gaeltacht autobiographies, which makes them fall more easily into the category of autoethnography than that of modern autobiography'.[25] More recently, John Eastlake has focused attention on the literary and editorial processes that led to the publication of the 'collaboratively produced'[26] Blasket autobiographies, which he compares to Native American autobiographies, thus echoing a comparison previously made by Ó Tuama, although the two scholars approach the subject from very different ideological and critical perspectives.[27] Eastlake identifies three roles, that of native, editor and translator, whose interaction 'during the process of producing a collaborative text is what distinguishes native autobiography from other acts of self-representation'.[28] Nic Eoin, writing in 2006, also identified a number of roles in what she described as a collaboration between 'a native "author" and an external editor, redactor or mentor, often a priest, a teacher

---

[22] E. M. Forster, 'Introductory Note', in Maurice O'Sullivan, *Twenty Years A-Growing* (Oxford: Oxford University Press, 1983), vi.

[23] See Nic Eoin, 'Twentieth-Century Gaelic Autobiography', 135–39; Ó Tuama, *Repossessions*, 205.

[24] Irene Lucchitti, *The Islandman: The Hidden Life of Tomás O'Crohan* (Bern and Oxford: Peter Lang, 2009), 183.

[25] Nic Eoin, 'Twentieth-Century Gaelic Autobiography', 136.

[26] Eastlake, 'Orality and Agency', 126.   [27] Ó Tuama, *Repossessions*, 203.

[28] Eastlake, 'Orality and Agency', 126.

or a folklore collector',[29] and in a later essay described these Gaeltacht autobiographies as 'a collaborative effort involving an unlettered "author" and various intermediaries'.[30]

In my view, this emphasis on process in a supposed transition from an oral to a literary mode of self-narration is one of the reasons why certain scholars have been reluctant to accept *Mo Sgéal Féin* into the canon of Gaeltacht autobiography. An tAthair Peadar Ua Laoghaire was far from unlettered, so it appears that it is his status as a literate author that excludes his work from this canon. But Ua Laoghaire also had an editor, Norma Borthwick. Can we say that her role was any less important than those of Pádraig Ó Siochradha and Máire Ní Chinnéide, for example? While the recent critical attention devoted to the processes of literary production provides a necessary corrective to blinkered views of what a life narrative should consist of, I would argue that if we place undue emphasis on these processes, and on autobiography's ethnographic value, we diminish the usefulness of any such classification. As Couser reminds us:

> categorizing works is not the *end* of genre analysis but its starting point. The goal is not to *classify* works but to *clarify* them. We can't fully understand what a particular author or story is doing without some sense of the operative conventions, which are a function of its genre. Especially in life writing, then, genre is not about mere literary form; it's about force – what a narrative's purpose is, what impact it seeks to have on the world.[31]

Focusing on the means of textual production, then, dilutes the force and impact of much life-writing in Irish. It draws attention away from the materiality of the text, as well as unnecessarily dividing the earlier Blasket texts and other dictated narratives from *Mo Sgéal Féin* and the memoirs of Seán Ó Criomhthain and Mícheál Ó Guithín, for example. A number of other texts, such as Ó Gaora's aforementioned *Mise*, muddy the waters of generic categorization further. *Mise* was well received and appeared shortly after another account of the War of Independence in Connemara, Tomás Ó Máille's *An tIomaire Ruadh* (*The Redtopped Ridge*) (1939). Apart from these two personal accounts of republican activism and the aforementioned *B'Fhiú an Braon Fola* by Séamas Ó Maoileoin, which includes a searingly honest account of the IRA's guerrilla campaign in east Limerick, there are a

---

[29] Máirín Nic Eoin, 'Contemporary Prose and Drama in Irish', in Margaret Kelleher and Philip O'Leary, eds., *The Cambridge History of Irish Literature, Volume II: 1890–2000* (Cambridge: Cambridge University Press, 2006), 280.

[30] Nic Eoin, 'Twentieth-Century Gaelic Autobiography', 132.

[31] Couser, *Memoir*, 9. Original emphasis.

number of other Irish-language memoirs from the mid-twentieth century by non-Gaeltacht writers which deserve much more critical attention. The Chief among these is *Cuimhní Cinn* (*Reminiscences*) (1951) by Liam Ó Briain, who was professor of romance languages at University College Galway and a major figure in the tumultuous events of the period, fighting with the Citizen Army during the Easter Rising and standing as a Sinn Féin candidate in the 1918 general election. The book, which predates the rise of Irish historical revisionism by several years, not only gives us a compelling account of the period but is also marked throughout by introspection and an exploration of the rights and wrongs of armed rebellion without an electoral mandate. Equally overlooked is Earnán de Blaghd's (Ernest Blyth) autobiographical trilogy, *Trasna na Bóinne* (*Across the Boyne*) (1957), *Slán le hUltaibh* (*Farewell to Ulster*) (1969) and *Gaeil á Múscailt* (*The Wakening of the Gaels*) (1973). De Blaghd was a hugely important and indeed controversial figure in the cultural and political life of Ireland both before and after independence. His memoirs, together with those of 1916 activist, government minister and second Irish president Seán T. Ó Ceallaigh (Seán T. O'Kelly), simply entitled *Seán T.* (1963), act as political counterweights to the more quotidian Gaeltacht autobiographies, however exotic the latter might appear to an urban readership.

One of the reasons why these and other non-Gaeltacht memoirs of the revolutionary period have attracted comparatively little critical attention, either as literary works or as historical documents, may lie in the wish of critics to decouple the Irish language from political nationalism and militant republicanism.[32] Critics acting under the influence of postcolonial theory since the late 1980s have been more inclined to search for subaltern voices in the self-narratives of indigenous residents of the Gaeltacht than in those of IRA volunteers, especially in the context of the Troubles and subsequent peace process in Northern Ireland. This backdrop created the conditions whereby previously unquestioned cultural manifestations of political nationalism, including revolutionary memoirs in Irish and in English, were consigned to a state of official and unofficial amnesia. A further complication was the fact that several of the ex-revolutionary autobiographers in question, such as O'Kelly and Blythe, had risen to influential positions in the postcolonial Irish state, and could therefore no

---

[32] For a discussion of some of these issues, see Bríona Nic Dhiarmada, 'Irish-Language Literature in the New Millennium', in Kelleher and O'Leary, eds., *The Cambridge History of Irish Literature: Volume II*, 613–15.

longer pose as oppositional voices, despite writing in Irish, which itself increasingly came to be seen as a recuperative and symbolic act.

In general, however, the slippery and mercurial nature of Irish-language life-writing and its refusal of easy categorization would be difficult to overstate. Such generic elusiveness finds a thematic echo in works that are concerned with invented or appropriated identities, the ethics of which are much discussed in contemporary autobiography studies. One notable example is provided by the autobiographies of Tarlach Ó hUid, who was born Augustus Walter Hood in London in 1917 and who, despite having no known Irish connections, recreated himself as an Irish-speaking republican activist in the 1930s. His first memoir, *Ar Thóir mo Shealbha* (*In Search of What was Mine*) (1960), is based on an entire fabrication and has echoes of more recent controversies about sincerity and impersonation in the world of Anglophone autobiography. His second, *Faoi Ghlas* (*Under Lock and Key*) (1985), gives an account of his time spent in various prisons in the North of Ireland for IRA activities in the 1940s. Another practitioner of the art of autobiographical self-reinvention was Mícheál Mac Liammóir, author of autobiographical volumes in English – *All for Hecuba* (1946) – and Irish – *Ceo Meala Lá Seaca* (*Honey Dew on a Frosty Day*) (1952). Born Alfred Willmore in London in 1899, he fabricated a Cork identity for himself and became one of the most feted Irish theatre personalities of his time and a hugely important figure in Irish-language literature. Another singular work of self-invention, notable in the main for its odious and hateful apologia for racism and fascism, is Róisín Ní Mheara's *Cé hí seo Amuigh* (*Who is This Outside?*) (1992), which drew a chorus of condemnation from many quarters. Written in an overwrought nativist style and stuffed with stereotypical Gaelicisms, the book gives an account of the author's life up to and including her sojourn in Nazi Germany. The autobiographical style is mostly a veneer for the unreconstructed anti-Semitic and pro-Nazi views of Ní Mheara, whose authorial identity is itself a concoction. Róisín Ní Mheara was born Rosaleen James and was the adopted daughter of a British general, Sir Ian Hamilton, and his wife Lady Hamilton.

Allied to such instances of radical self-invention are the cases of authors who, though non-native Irish speakers, choose to write in a minority language that is marginalized within Ireland itself, while at the same time occupying a high symbolic status in the ideology of the state. For many of these writers, Irish-language writing was not a sleight of hand but a logical cultural and linguistic choice. A recent example of a memoir of this kind is *Titim agus Eirí* (*Rise and Fall*) (2012) by Diarmaid Breathnach, who is best known for his collaboration with Máire Ní Mhurchú on a nine-volume biographical dictionary of Irish-language writers, scholars and activists, which is itself a monumental contribution to Irish-language scholarship. In *Titim agus Eirí*, he retraces his early life in Co. Wicklow, the seminal event of which was the untimely death of his father, before moving on to document his career as a librarian and his growing attraction to the Irish language and culture in which he became immersed.

Conclusion

As we have seen, a recurring issue within Irish-language literary criticism, and one which impinges on our reading of Irish-language autobiography and memoir, is the nature of the relationship between the oral and the literary. It is important to remember that the authors of the earliest and most feted life narratives, notably the triumvirate of Ó Criomhthain, Ó Súilleabháin and Sayers, inhabited a space that encompassed both a traditional oral culture and a culture that was attuned to the literary, insofar as it enabled individuals to become authors of their own life stories.[33] The reason this is important is because much of the analysis and evaluation of Irish-language life-writing, and in particular that which has become known as Gaeltacht autobiography, has tended to rely strongly on extra-textual criteria. Often, this has led to works being read primarily as social documents and assessed through the prism of their ethnographic authenticity, while their 'literariness' has been questioned or found lacking because of assumptions about subjectivity and orality. It has been my intention here to question such binary readings and to posit a location for these texts that is more intermediary in character, in keeping with my view of Irish-language autobiography as the product of 'a set of shifting self-referential practices that, in engaging the past, reflect on identity in the present'.[34]

Further reading

Coughlan, Patricia. 'Rereading Peig Sayers: Women's Autobiography, Social History and Narrative Art', in Patricia Boyle Haberstroh and Christine St. Peter, eds.,

---

[33] It important to remember also that the culture of the Blasket Islands and Irish-language culture generally cannot be regarded as a genuinely primary oral culture. For a discussion of these matters, see Bo Almqvist, 'The Mysterious Micheál Ó Gaoithín, Boccaccio and the Blasket Tradition', *Béaloideas*, 58 (1990), 75–140.

[34] Smith and Watson, *Reading Autobiography*, 1.

Opening the Field: Irish Women, Texts and Contexts. Cork: Cork University Press 2007: 58–73.

Eastlake, John. '*The* (Original) *Islandman?*: Examining the Origin in Blasket Autobiography', in Nessa Cronin, Seán Crosson and John Eastlake, eds., *Anáil an Bhéil Bheo: Orality and Modern Irish Culture*. Newcastle upon Tyne: Cambridge Scholars, 2009: 236–49.

Lucchitti, Irene. *The Islandman: The Hidden Life of Tomás O'Crohan*. Bern and Oxford: Peter Lang, 2009.

Nic Eoin, Máirín. 'Twentieth-Century Gaelic Autobiography: From *Lieux de Mémoire* to Narratives of Self-Invention', in Liam Harte, ed., *Modern Irish Autobiography: Self, Nation and Society*. Basingstoke: Palgrave Macmillan, 2007: 132–55.

Ó Háinle, Cathal. 'Aspects of Autobiography in Modern Irish', in Ronald Black, William Gillies and Roibeard Ó Maolalaigh, eds., *Celtic Connections: Proceedings of the 10th International Congress of Celtic Studies*. Linton: Tuckwell Press: 360–76.

O'Leary, Philip. *Gaelic Prose in the Irish Free State, 1922–1939*. Pennsylvania: Pennsylvania State University Press 2004.

CHAPTER 16

Orality and Life-Writing in Modern Ireland

Kelly Fitzgerald and Mary Muldowney

Despite disparities between them, the collection and analysis of folklore and the practice of oral history have many shared concerns, chief among which is the centrality of people's life histories and memories to both fields of study. Folklorists study the verbal transmission of traditions, beliefs, customs and other forms of knowledge across generations; oral historians collect, preserve, interpret and retell people's stories about their pasts, thereby capturing individual voices, memories and histories that might otherwise remain unrecorded. The ability to recognize the autobiographical in folkloric accounts goes hand in hand with the ethnographic collecting process; the exposition of a single life is fundamental to the oral history interview. Both investigative modes rely on the establishment of a trusting relationship between the collector/oral historian and the informant/narrator, on focused questioning and on thoughtful, empathetic listening. It has been argued that because orality is so central to the methodologies and approaches of both disciplines that it is difficult to identify distinctions between folklore and oral history.[1] However, we believe that there are some crucial differences between the two fields and therefore will discuss them separately in this chapter, which will consider the evolution of folklore studies and oral history as academic disciplines in post-partition Ireland, with reference to the particular kinds of autobiographical expression they contain. The first section will examine the cultural recovery work of Irish folklorists; the second will concentrate on a subfield of oral history studies, political oral history, using as case studies two major projects that examined, respectively, Ireland's revolutionary period (1913–21) and the Northern Ireland Troubles (1969–98) through the personal testimony of veterans and participants.

The institutional study of oral narrative and the verbal arts in the Republic of Ireland was developed under the much broader discipline of

---

[1] See, for example, Helen P. Harrison, ed., *Audiovisual Archives: A Practical Reader* (Paris: UNESCO, 1997).

folklore studies or folkloristics. Its history as a distinct academic discipline began in 1971 with the creation of a Department of Irish Folklore in University College Dublin under Bo Almqvist. The Department acted as custodian of the recently disbanded Irish Folklore Commission and introduced undergraduate and postgraduate courses in the subject, which were informed by an interdisciplinary ethos that blended literary, ethnographic and anthropological approaches. The recognition of fieldwork was paramount, as was a knowledge of medieval and classical literature. In 1977, courses in folklore and oral tradition, initiated by Gearóid Ó Crualaoich, began to be taught at University College Cork under the auspices of the Department of History, which eventually led to the setting up of a separate Department of Folklore and Ethnology.

Oral history has been described as 'an established form for actively making memories' which 'both reflects and shapes collective or public memory'.[2] It is not simply a means of giving voice to the unheard, although that is a vital element of the practice, but an interpretative tool that explores *why* people remember as much as *what* they recall. In oral history, the historian takes a direct part in creating a record of the past but this does not mean simply turning on a recorder and inviting the interviewee to speak. Oral history is produced through an exchange between interviewer and interviewee. While the oral historian structures the narrative through the questions he or she selects, the interview itself is largely shaped by the rapport that develops (or fails to develop) between two (or sometimes more) people. The issues of mutual trust and respect are therefore keys to successful oral history interviewing, especially when exploring emotionally or politically sensitive issues, and this trust must extend to the area of informed consent: until the informant has given informed consent to the use of an interview, whether it is a transcript, an audio recording or a video, they should retain complete ownership of their testimony.[3] It can often take a great deal of time and patience on the part of the interviewer to build a working relationship that allows the interviewee to open up. Sometimes, a trusting relationship between the two participants may already be in place but this does not necessarily make it any easier to elicit the kind of reflective storytelling that

---

[2] Paula Hamilton and Linda Shopes, 'Introduction: Building Partnerships between Oral History and Memory Studies', in Paula Hamilton and Linda Shopes, eds., *Oral History and Public Memories* (Philadelphia: Temple University Press, 2008), viii.

[3] The practice of asking an interviewee to sign a consent form at the conclusion of their interview may compromise the interviewee's capacity to alter or edit what is subsequently made public. See Oral History Society (UK), 'Is Your Oral History Legal and Ethical?' Available at www.ohs.org.uk/ethics.php (accessed 20 August 2015).

goes beyond a bare narrative. In this regard, consciousness of the cultural and social processes that shape the telling of stories is crucial. In his influential study *A Shared Authority: Essays on the Craft and Meaning of Oral and Public History* (1990), Michael Frisch argues for an oral history practice based on a partnership between interviewer and interviewee from the beginning to the end of the process. While it can be difficult to achieve, this kind of partnership has produced some of the best explorations of undocumented histories in recent decades because it both challenges the orthodox view of events and foregrounds how the past is shaped, evaluated and mediated.

Folklore collecting: history, ethos, practice

Recording the thoughts and words of the ordinary person in order to learn about their life was not the norm in Western Europe until the twentieth century. There are important precursors, of course, such as Charles Perrault, author of the two-volume *Les Hommes illustres qui ont paru en France pendant ce siècle* (1696–1700), who elicited tales from his servants and introduced these to his social circles in seventeenth-century Paris. Perrault did so not to hear about his servants' lives as much as to collect their stories from them. Work in this area was further developed by the German linguists and lexicographers Jacob and Wilhelm Grimm in the early decades of the nineteenth century. The rise of nationalism in Europe and the corresponding growth of industrialized capitalism prompted many scholars to search for the sources of cultural authenticity away from the burgeoning metropolitan centres and to identify the purest form of culture with the life and outlook of the peasant, who was often seen in isolation from his social and economic context. This development began to manifest itself with particular force in Europe's most westerly island in the late 1800s, under the aegis of a cultural movement that would redefine Irishness for generations to come.

In nineteenth-century Ireland, interest in the lives of ordinary people as spoken in their own words and in folk tradition and storytelling as untapped reservoirs of cultural expression was cultivated by the Wexford-born antiquarian Patrick Kennedy, author of four volumes of Irish folklore, the most notable of which are *Legendary Fictions of the Irish Celts* (1866) and *The Fireside Stories of Ireland* (1870). Considered the 'Irish Grimm' by English folklorist Joseph Jacobs, Kennedy believed in the national and international importance of recording oral lore that was on the cusp of being lost forever. Thus, he provided the educated reader with extensive notes and glossaries and sometimes included his informants' names in his published versions of a folk tale or legend.[4] Whereas Kennedy concentrated on the English-speaking peasantry of his native county, the American collector, scholar and linguist Jeremiah Curtin was one of the first to collect material in Irish-speaking districts of the country, albeit with the assistance of a translator, and to publish his findings in English in volumes such as *Myths and Folklore of Ireland* (1890). The first to collect and publish oral material in Irish was Douglas Hyde (Dubhghlas de hÍde), first professor of modern Irish at UCD and later Ireland's first president, whose pioneering *Leabhar Sgeulaigheachta (Book of Storytelling)* (1889) and *Beside the Fire* (1890) comprise folk tales, rhymes and stories collected from Irish speakers in the west of Ireland. The collection of vernacular stories by Hyde and others, such as William Larminie, had particular merit in cultural revivalist terms, not only because the documenting of oral traditions captured information about dying customs and ways of life but also because this oral material helped cement the basis on which a new national culture and consciousness were being forged by artists and writers led by W. B. Yeats. Yeats himself was steeped in contemporary folklore scholarship and deeply in thrall to the folk beliefs of Connacht from a young age, as evidenced by his first anthology, *Fairy and Folk Tales of the Irish Peasantry* (1888). Unlike Hyde, however, he was not an Irish speaker and did not collect folklore himself.

It was not until twenty-six of Ireland's thirty-two counties became self-governing in 1922 that an institutional framework was put in place to enable the systematic archiving and cataloguing of the country's folk heritage. The establishment of the Irish Folklore Commission (*Coimisiún Béaloideasa Éireann*) in 1935 gave state recognition to the importance of collecting, indexing and preserving vernacular culture and documenting the individual voice. The Commission professionalized the voluntary work of collecting oral traditions by appointing a number of full-time and part-time folklore collectors throughout the country, who were expected to have a strong knowledge of their designated area. The person largely responsible for the founding of the Commission was Séamus Ó Duilearga (James Delargy), who was to become professor of Irish folklore at UCD, where he began as an assistant to Hyde, and editor (from 1928 to 1970) of *Béaloideas*, the journal of the Folklore of Ireland Society, which was formally established in 1927. Ó Duilearga was inspired by his contact with figures such as Séan Ó Conaill in Ballinskelligs in Co. Kerry, where he went to improve his Irish in the 1920s. He also received important training in fieldwork and folkloristics in

---

[4] See Diarmuid Ó Gio lláin, *Locating Irish Folklore: Tradition, Modernity, Identity* (Cork: Cork University Press, 2000), 103–04.

Scandinavia, Estonia and Germany in 1928, which would later inform his proposed remit of the newly formed Commission. Part of this remit involved a folklore survey, the objectives of which were as follows:

(a) Systematic co-ordination and arrangement of the existing literary material (i.e. printed oral tradition).

(b) Systematic collection of the unrecorded oral traditions with a view to

(c) The eventual co-ordination and treatment of the whole material thus obtained and its linking up with a culture of the other Celtic nations, in order to clarify its position in the shaping of a distinct Irish nationality and its interrelations with European civilisation in general.[5]

The need for the Commission's collecting work to centre on the story-teller's life and social environment was emphasized by Ó Duilearga's friend and mentor, the Swedish folklorist Carl Wilhelm von Sydow, whose tutelage continued after Ó Duilearga's time in Sweden through correspondence. In one of his letters, von Sydow advised:

> You should stress the importance of a collector living among the people and the opportunity this gives you to get to know the people at close quarters and to study living tradition. It is not a question, however, of just collecting as many tale types as possible, but of learning as much as possible from that exercise and also of learning as much as possible from the people themselves.[6]

One consequence of this approach is that contextual information in the collected oral material ceases to be mere illumination and instead becomes an integral part of the storytelling process. As the Commission's work evolved, this emphasis on the context of folkloric performance intensified and was underpinned by the belief that 'the memoirs of tradition bearers are of the utmost value'.[7] Von Sydow wished that a memoir be created for every informant, not merely the best-known storytellers, and implored the Commission's archivist,

---

[5] Séamus Ó Duilearga, 'Collection of Oral Tradition in Ireland', cited in Mícheál Briody, *The Irish Folklore Commission, 1935–1970: History, Ideology, Methodology* (Helsinki: Finnish Literature Society, 2007), 109. See also Séamus Ó Catháin, *Formation of a Folklorist: The Visit of James Hamilton Delargy (Séamus Ó Duilearga) to Scandinavia, Finland, Estonia and Germany 1 April–29 September 1928* (Dublin: Comhairle Bhéaloideas Éireann, 2008).

[6] Letter from Carl von Sydow to Séamus Ó Duilearga, 24 March 1936, cited in Ríonach Uí Ógáin, 'Some Comments on Context, Text and Subtext in Irish Folklore', in Lauri Honko, ed., *Thick Corpus, Organic Variation and Textuality in Oral Tradition* (Helsinki: Finnish Literature Society, 2000), 161.

[7] Letter from Carl von Sydow to Seán Ó Súilleabháin, 1945, translated from the Swedish and held in the National Folklore Collection, UCD. For more on the importance of memoir, see James H. Delargy, 'The Gaelic Story-Teller, with Some Notes on Gaelic Folk-Tales', *Proceedings of the British Academy*, 31 (1945), 177–221 and Séamus Ó Duilearga, *Leabhar Sheáin Í Chonaill* (Dublin: An Cumann le Béaloideas Éireann, 1948).

Seán Ó Súilleabháin (Sean O'Sullivan), to see to it that this was carried out as comprehensively as possible. Ó Suilleabháin spent several months in Uppsala, where he adapted the Swedish system of folklore classification for Irish use to produce *An Lámhleabhar Béaloideasa* (1937), an expanded version of which was published as *A Handbook of Irish Folklore* in 1942, which became the bible of the Commission's developing archive.

From the outset the new organization concentrated on Irish and English material. However, due to the rapid decline of Irish-speaking areas, the focus of collecting activity became the western seaboard of Ireland. The emphasis of ethnographic fieldwork in the early days of the Commission was on the storytelling traditions of international folk tales in Irish.[8] Full-time collectors were recruited, all of whom were male, and many were provided with sound-recording equipment for use in the field. In keeping with technological progress, sound recordings were made on ediphone cylinders and acetate discs, and, in the later years of the Commission, with tape recorders. Collectors transcribed their fieldwork findings into note-books, which they then posted along with the sound recordings to the head office in Dublin. It is these transcriptions, imprinted with the voice of the informant, that form the core archival material in the National Folklore Collection at UCD, Ireland's primary repository of traditional vernacular culture. Collectors were also encouraged to take photographs of the story-tellers, their houses and aspects of vernacular tradition and architecture. Ethnologist Caoimhín Ó Danachair (Kevin Danaher) played a pioneering role in the establishment of the photographic and sound archives that resulted from this activity.

Full-time collectors were required to keep a diary or daily journal which was intended to be both a professional and a personal record.[9] As we can see from the published field diaries of Séamus Ennis, strong personal bonds could develop between collector and informant. Here, for example, is Ennis describing his experiences in Co. Galway in June 1945:

> She [Maidhcil Sheáin Pheadair Ó Caodháin's mother] is a tall, thin woman, 73 years old now, and is still strong. She welcomed me heartily and was very kind to me. She is a Gannon from Caladh Mhaínse, the first townland east of Roisín na Mainiach, and she learned the song there as a young girl ['Scilléidín Mheargait']. But she gave me all the details of her personal life,

---

[8] A folk tale is designated international if it can be catalogued according to the taxonomy outlined in Hans-Jörg Uther's *The Types of International Folktales: A Classification and Bibliography Based on the System of Antti Aarne and Stith Thompson* (Helsinki: Academia Scientiarum Fennica, 2004).

[9] See Mícheál Briody, 'The Collectors' Diaries of the Irish Folklore Commission: A Complex Genesis', *Sinsear*, 9 (2006), 27–45.

in a simple chatty fashion. I thanked her and went to Colm Ó Caodháin. He wanted me to write a letter to the people in charge of the dole in Galway – they do not believe that scallop fishing has finished. When I had written it on his behalf, I started reading and correcting his text with him.[10]

An interview conducted by James Delaney with Bill Egan in Co. Offaly in September 1969 shows how a skilled folklore collector could capture not only the intimate details of local customs – in this example, domestic preparations for Christmas – but also the idiomatic speech of his interlocutor:

DELANEY   What would ye put across the chimney?

EGAN   Across the chimney then, ye had what we call a winnin' [i.e. winnowing JD] sheet ... (They used to have them for corn business at the aul' horse-powers an' at the thrashin's, with the thrashin mills.) Ye had to put that across in the front o' the chimney [i.e. cover the whole of the open fire place JD]. The way none o' this aul dust or stuff id g'out around the house.

            Well, you had to stand inside o' that [winnowing sheet which acts as a screen JD]. Ye might have li'l' short ladder that ye'd be up a bit in the chimney. An' ye had an aul bag, then, turned down – med a 'v' of it, turned down on your head, to keep the soot from goin' into your mouth an' eyes. An' ye'd scrape it down, th' aul' chimney, then.

            Some used to g' up in them. Some has a big arch, that they can g' up to the very top in it, an' work. An' ye can clant it with a hoe. It's wud a hoe I always clane it.

DELANEY   I see.[11]

In a similar vein, the work of the Urban Folklore Project (1979–80), described as 'a sophisticated exercise in collecting the unofficial history of Dublin',[12] shows how a collector (here, the folklorist and writer Éilís Ní Dhuibhne) could prompt an informant (a Mrs Lily O'Reilly of Donnybrook in Dublin) to disclose details of political activism that were hitherto unrecorded:

NÍ DHUIBHNE   And tell me, were you a member of Cumann na mBan?

O'REILLY   Well, I was, yes.

NÍ DHUIBHNE   And tell me how you joined up.

---

[10] Ríonach Uí Ógáin ed., *Going to the Well for Water: The Séamus Ennis Field Diary 1942–46* (Cork: Cork University Press, 2009), 249.

[11] National Folklore Collection, MS 299:1796–97. This excerpt is taken from a long interview by Delaney in which he elicits details of annual calendar customs in the Irish midlands.

[12] Éilís Ní Dhuibhne, '"They Made Me Tea and Gave Me a Lift Home": Urban Folklore Collecting 1979–80', *Béaloideas*, 73 (2005), 66.

O'REILLY	I was only going up and down to them. I wasn't really a member. I was too young.
NÍ DHUIBHNE	You were too young.
O'REILLY	And we were arrested and put into Kilmainham.
NÍ DHUIBHNE	Tell me about that.
O'REILLY	One Friday I came home to my mother to my dinner.
NÍ DHUIBHNE	And how old were you at this stage?
O'REILLY	I was thirteen.
NÍ DHUIBHNE	Which was around 1920?
O'REILLY	Twenty-three.
NÍ DHUIBHNE	1923, yes.
O'REILLY	And I came home to my dinner and of course I put up my nose to fish, I didn't want it and my mother said: 'I'll see the day that you'll be glad to eat the head of a fish let alone anything else.' And I was arrested that day. The boy next door, he's dead now, he gave away. He said I was in it [Cumann na mBan]. I was doing their work for them. I used to carry messages and all that for my brother-in-law. There was a price on his head. Cripps, Joe Cripps was his name. C-R-I-P-P-S. And they're dead now. The Lord have mercy on them all. And when I came to Kilmainham, wasn't pals of mine in there after being arrested and weren't they in Kilmainham so I wasn't too lonely I needn't tell you.[13]

These three excerpts illustrate the nature of folklore collecting and how autobiographical accounts emerge in the process. The fact that all three exemplify the recording of practices or activities that would otherwise be lost to history, not least because the informants evidently did not deem them significant enough to document in any other form, testifies to the vital role folklorists can play in establishing the legitimacy of memory as a source of historical knowledge. These excerpts also foreground the fact that, at its core, fieldwork involves witnessing and working with an oral performance. The fieldworker records the voice of the individual informant and the autobiographical context gives validation to the recorded text. From a folklorist's point of view, this voice embodies numerous threads of vernacular tradition about society, community and, not least of all, the individual. The transformation of the spoken word into written form must not lose sight of this or be regarded as the marginalization of the embodied voice, any more than it should lead us to construct a false polarity between spoken and written discourse. Yet while care must be taken over the transcription of voice

---

[13] O'Reilly was recorded by Ní Dhuibhne in Dublin in 1980. The Urban Folklore Project is now part of the National Folklore Collection.

recordings, in folkloristic terms, recordings and transcriptions are ultimately secondary to the live, interactive performance itself.

Political oral history: challenges, protocols, ethics

Oral history interviewing in a political context is a practice that has become intrinsic to the peace and reconciliation processes in many post-conflict situations.[14] Well-conducted interviews can be used to prompt political reflection and to compensate for deficiencies in mainstream historical sources. While it is true that public history is open to political manipulation and people are often reluctant to speak candidly about their roles in highly contentious events, understandings of divisive and traumatic episodes can benefit significantly from the interventions of oral historians, as Ronald Fraser's work on the Spanish Civil War shows.[15] One of the first such projects in Ireland was the collection of personal accounts by participants in the struggle for political independence from Britain. After years of discussion and false starts, the Bureau of Military History was set up in January 1947, its stated aim being to 'assemble and co-ordinate material to form the basis for the compilation of the history of the movement for independence from the formation of the Irish Volunteers on 25 November 1913 to the [signing of the Truce on] 11 July 1921'.[16] Despite its name, the Bureau was not solely interested in military activities but 'in every contributory factor or development, reaching back in many cases to the beginning of the twentieth century'.[17] The terms of reference set for the Bureau cannot be separated from the political contexts and considerations that informed them.[18] The chronological parameters of the Bureau would seem to have been dictated by the wish to avoid references to the Irish Civil War, which began in June 1922, probably because so many of the actors were still on the public stage and the

---

[14] Among the conflict resolution situations in which oral history has been employed as a healing and learning tool are the Truth and Reconciliation Commission in South Africa, the Iraqi Oral History Project and the cross-community Healing Through Remembering Project in Northern Ireland.

[15] Fraser's *Blood of Spain: The Experience of Civil War 1936–1939* (1979) was based on interviews with participants on both sides of the conflict and is celebrated for its emphasis on the experience of so-called ordinary people rather than the leaders.

[16] Report of the Director, 1957, quoted in Jennifer Doyle, Frances Clarke, Eibhlis Connaughton and Orna Somerville, *An Introduction to the Bureau of Military History, 1913–1921* (Dublin: Military Archives, 2002), 1.

[17] Ibid., 6.

[18] For an account of the Bureau's formation, see Eve Morrison, 'Bureau of Military History Witness Statements as Sources for the Irish Revolution', n. d. Available at http://bureauofmili taryhistory.ie/files/Bureau_of_Military_witness_statements%20as_sources%20for_the_Irish %20Revolution.pdf (accessed 17 August 2015).

wounds opened up by the conflict were still tender. If this decision was meant to depoliticize the project or lessen its contentiousness, it had only limited success. Many opponents of the treaty that ended the War of Independence did not give witness statements to the Bureau and other activists chose not to participate for a variety of reasons, including political distrust, concerns about the possible uses of their testimonies and a wish to write their own memoirs. As is the case in so many oral history projects, those who took part in the initiative were self-selecting.

As many combatants of the 1913–21 period had died in the years prior to the formation of the Bureau, it was decided to focus on interviewing the surviving officers of divisions, brigades, battalions and companies that had seen active service. Media appeals for volunteers attracted a broad range of responses which led to former members of the Irish Volunteers, Cumann na mBan, the Irish Republican Brotherhood, Sinn Féin, the Irish Citizen Army, relatives of deceased individuals and people not associated with any organization contributing statements about how they had been affected by the independence struggle. Many of these witnesses were people whose involvement at a local or national level was often crucial to the outcome of the campaign but whose later political quietism resulted in their contributions being forgotten or deliberately omitted from the historical record. The scarcity of written records about the experiences of 'ordinary' political activists is one reason why oral history is so valuable in facilitating the restoration of marginalized or neglected accounts to the historical record, thereby challenging what E. P. Thompson termed 'the condescension of posterity'.[19]

Since the original impetus for the Bureau came from the Irish army, 'which was considered a natural choice to collect material and administer such a project',[20] the investigators were mainly military men who were instructed to gather statements that were as detailed as possible and to deter interviewees from indulging in fantasy and political point-scoring. Unlike contemporary oral history practitioners, these men were less concerned with preserving the witnesses' actual words than with capturing the substance of their evidence. While some witnesses wrote their own statements, many others told their stories to the investigators, who then composed them into coherent documents for signature by the participants. Consequently, we cannot be certain whether the language used in any given statement is that of the witness or the investigator, or whether this makes a significant difference to the testimony. After much debate about contributor confidentiality, it was

[19] E. P. Thompson, *The Making of the English Working Class* (New York: Random House, 1966), 12.
[20] Morrison, 'Bureau of Military History Witness Statements', 2.

decided not to make the testimonies available to the public during the Bureau's lifetime, though no official decision was made on how long the embargo should last after the Bureau's work was terminated in December 1957. Eventually, it was agreed that the material in the collection would be made publicly accessible when the last recipients of the military service pension had died. This meant that it was 2003 before the archive was opened to researchers and a further nine years before the 1,773 witness statements in the collection were digitized and made freely available online.[21]

Despite its growth in the latter decades of the twentieth century, oral history practice continued to be viewed with suspicion within the conservative culture of Irish academia, where a research bias towards official archival sources, coupled with concerns about the validity and reliability of memory-based oral testimony, made it a minority pursuit.[22] Such concerns were partly justified by the discrepancies and inaccuracies in some of the Bureau witness statements, not least because of the passage of time between the recording of the testimonies and the events they recall. However, such inherent imperfections do not necessarily invalidate the value of the information elicited in oral history interviews, whereby a 'memory narrative is actively created in the moment'.[23] As Guy Beiner appositely points out: 'By including error, imagination, and desire, oral sources reveal not only the history of what happened, but the history of what it meant.'[24] Moreover, as Eve Morrison reminds us: 'Retrospective testimony of any kind ... has to be consulted in conjunction with contemporary sources and, where available, other interviews.'[25]

Over fifty years after its formation, the Bureau of Military History provided a model for an oral history initiative conducted by researchers at Boston College in Massachusetts. Known as the Belfast Project and launched in 2001, it set out to interview a number of participants in the Northern Ireland conflict to ensure that their own recollections and analyses of their activities were captured in their lifetimes. Because of the political and legal sensitivities surrounding such testimonies, the project researchers were adamant that cast-iron guarantees of confidentiality must be given to interviewees. Thus, the project participants signed contracts with Boston College, which assured them that their interview material, collected between 2001

---

[21] The Bureau of Military History website (www.bureauofmilitaryhistory.ie/) gives searchable access to the witness statements and a collection of other contemporaneous documents and photographs.

[22] Guy Beiner, '*Bodhaire Uí Laoire*: Oral History and Contemporary Irish Historiography'. Available at http://www.ucd.ie/pages/99/articles/beiner.html (accessed 17 August 2015).

[23] Lynn Abrams, *Oral History Theory* (London: Routledge, 2010), 23.

[24] Beiner, '*Bodhaire Uí Laoire*'.

[25] Morrison, 'Bureau of Military History Witness Statements', 5.

and 2006, would be stored safely in the Burns Library and that the ultimate power of release would rest with the interviewees until their deaths. Anthony McIntyre, lead researcher on the project, said of it:

> Distilled down, the overriding purpose of the Belfast Project was to ulti-mately enhance public understanding. This was to be achieved through collating and sealing for a time within academia the perspective of those who were combatants or people who had insights that would add to societal knowledge of the conflict.[26]

In 2010, journalist Ed Moloney who, with Robert K. O'Neill, was the prime mover behind the Belfast Project, published *Voices from the Grave*. The book featured interviews with Brendan Hughes and David Ervine, both of whom had died in the intervening period. Hughes had been an IRA activist and leader of the 1980 hunger strike in the Maze prison; Ervine, a UVF member who became leader of the Progressive Unionist Party. The book was quickly adapted as a film documentary and widely distributed.[27] Former IRA volunteer Dolours Price was also a participant in the project. In February 2010, she told an *Irish News* journalist about her involvement in several high-profile abductions, which she claims had been carried out under orders from her IRA commander at the time, Gerry Adams, who went on to become president of Sinn Féin.[28] Because Price was being treated for depression at the time she gave her testimony, the newspaper amended the scope of the story. A short time later, however, a *Sunday Life* journalist wrote that Price had previously admitted her role in the abductions in her archived Boston College interview. On foot of this information, British government officials asked the US Department of Justice to issue a subpoena under the Mutual Legal Assistance Treaty for the production of the Hughes and Price record-ings, thus triggering a long legal battle by the College to protect the con-fidentiality of its archive. Some recordings were released to the British authorities, including that of Price, who died in 2013, while the rest of the material remains locked in the Burns Library. The researchers have argued that the participants should be given the opportunity to take back their contributions but this has not yet happened.

The fate that befell the Belfast Project underlines the need to under-stand that oral history interviewing, whether political or otherwise, is

---

[26] Anthony McIntyre, 'The Belfast Project and the Boston College Subpoena Case'. Paper presented at Oral History Network of Ireland second annual conference, Ennis, Co. Clare, 29 September 2012.

[27] Written by Ed Moloney and Patrick Farrelly, and directed by Kate O'Callaghan and Patrick Farrelly, *Voices from the Grave* was broadcast by RTÉ television on 26 October 2010.

[28] Allison Morris, 'Interview with Dolours Price', *Irish News*, 18 February 2010, 1–3.

not just a matter of turning on a recorder and letting the informant speak. If interviews are to be of research value, then it is vital to establish and follow best practice guidelines, central to which are the researcher's obligations to ensure that interviewees are fully informed about how and where their testimony will be made public and to think through the potential consequences of any breach of agreement. The most important lesson of the project is that making recordings available for research and other use should only happen within a legal and ethical framework which protects the interests of the interviewees. As Ted Palys and John Lowman argue:

> Pragmatically, pledging and maintaining strict confidentiality provides the foundation of trust and rapport that allows researchers to gather valid data to promote understanding of the human condition, and provide the basis for rational social policy. In some cases, information shared with a researcher may be so sensitive – and its disclosure so potentially damaging – that the fate of the individual may literally rest in the researcher's hands. In such situations, both the researcher's ethical obligations and the need for a solid bond of trust are clear. If people do not trust researchers, they will not share sensitive information, and the value of research to society will diminish.[29]

The Belfast Project was not the only contemporary oral history initiative to be centred on post-conflict Northern Ireland. The Peace Process Layers of Meaning Project was carried out by researchers from Queen Mary University of London, Trinity College Dublin and the Dundalk Institute of Technology between 2010 and 2013. The aims of this EU-funded project included the collection of one hundred heritage interviews intended to preserve the testimony of key figures in the peace process, the provision of an oral history training programme for participants from both main communities in the North and the development of online resources.[30] A defining feature of the project was its explicit attention to the personal testimony of individuals whose private and professional lives were touched by sectarian violence in different ways. As the lead researchers explain:

> Looking beyond the formal and organised history of conflict resolution we acknowledged that peace-making has many layers, extending far beyond the narrow confines of high politics. At the level of personal recollection there are many individuals crying out to be heard and enduring the painful

---

[29] Ted Palys and John Lowman, 'Protecting Research Confidentiality: Towards a Research-Participant Shield Law', *Canadian Journal of Law and Society/Revue Canadienne Droit et Société*, 21:1 (2000), 163.

[30] The fact that the confidentiality of the interviews is to be protected by an embargo of forty years should prevent a recurrence of the debacle that overtook the Belfast Project.

frustration of being ignored. These extend across every strata of society and include private citizens as well as members of the emergency services, hospital staff, public servants etc. In torn communities peace must mean the reformation of everyday relations in places of education, work and recreation – indeed everywhere that nuance and acute awareness of the 'other' guide interactions and transactions.[31]

Conclusion

The collection and preservation of personal testimony is central to both folklore studies and oral history practice, and the nature of such testimony can be as varied as the subjects from whom it is elicited. Memory is an intrinsic element of each practice, whether it is the recall of personal stories or the transmission of collectively recollected experience. Both fields of historical inquiry use similar equipment and must deal with the practicalities of reconciling advances in technology with the imperative to archive material securely and sustainably. Creating an atmosphere of trust between the collector/historian and the interviewee/narrator is essential to the working practices of both disciplines, and the establishment of robust ethical and legal measures is also crucial to ensuring that this trust is not misplaced.

The recognition of personal agency in the creation of history is as important as understanding that the fallibility of memory does not necessarily detract from the value of autobiographical testimony. In each of the major projects discussed in this chapter, whether they were inspired by political, cultural or institutional agenda, personal and communal memories are at the heart of the collecting and investigative work. Learning from personal experience has been fundamental to the researchers' methodology in each case, with techniques and protocols being refined over time. There has been an evolution, too, in the nature of the interaction between collector/historian and interviewee/narrator, which is no longer characterized in starkly active/passive terms. This development reflects the increasing recognition of the role of storytelling in the remaking of history and in the healing of historical divisions, as exemplified by the case of contemporary Northern Ireland, where oral testimony has become an important part of the ongoing efforts to reform a society devastated by many years of sectarian strife.

If these developments signify anything, it is that the voice of the individual citizen has come into its own in understandings of Irish culture

---

[31] Available at www.peaceprocesshistory.org/ (accessed 15 August 2015).

in the twenty-first century. Whereas in earlier times the voices of ordinary people were consulted in order to preserve what appeared to be the vestiges of disappearing traditions, today's folklorists and oral historians place a much wider cultural value on the documentation of vernacular culture and on voices that speak autobiographically. Scholars and practitioners also recognize that it is not enough to hear from those at the top of the social hierarchy; the voices of those without cultural power must also be amplified and preserved if we are to create a more inclusive social history. The challenge of making sense of the Irish past demands that we continue to make room in the historical record for the multiplicity of individual and group experiences that emerge from the collection of folklore and the fieldwork of oral historians.

Further reading

Briody, Mícheál. *The Irish Folklore Commission, 1935–1970: History, Ideology, Methodology.* Helsinki: Finnish Literature Society, 2007.

Dawson, Graham. *Making Peace with the Past? Memory, Trauma and the Irish Troubles.* Manchester: Manchester University Press, 2007.

Hamilton, Paula and Shopes, Linda, eds. *Oral History and Public Memories.* Philadelphia: Temple University Press, 2008.

Moloney, Ed. *Voices from the Grave: Two Men's War in Ireland.* London: Faber and Faber, 2010.

Murphy, Michael J. *Tyrone Folk Quest.* Belfast: Blackstaff Press, 1973.

Ó Giolláin, Diarmuid. *Locating Irish Folklore: Tradition, Modernity, Identity.* Cork: Cork University Press, 2000.

CHAPTER 17

Southern Irish Protestant Autobiography since Partition

Robert Tobin

Introducing his memoirs in 2005, the Anglo-Irish writer Kildare Dobbs observed that 'my story is that of a man raised in an already obsolete tradition, and educated for a role that no longer existed, who nevertheless managed to become a different sort of person, better adapted to the tempestuous times in which he found himself'.[1] Born in 1923, shortly after the Irish Civil War, Dobbs was the son of an Indian civil servant and grandson of the former archbishop of Dublin, John Henry Bernard. He was raised on the family estate in Co. Kilkenny and educated at St Columba's College, before enlisting in the Royal Navy during the Second World War. In contrast to his Anglo-Irish forbears, however, Dobbs concluded there was no place for him in an independent Ireland, and after the war he made his life in Canada.

At one level, this biographical arc confirms the wider phenomenon of the Ascendancy's retreat from power and place, a key ingredient in the popular narrative about Ireland's struggle for self-determination and the achievement of the Irish Free State. Yet as Dobbs's comments about his personal evolution also make clear, life carried on for him and other Southern Irish Protestants, even after their allotted part in the Irish story was deemed to have finished.[2] The autobiographical writings produced by members of this community since partition testify to their efforts to survive and reinvent themselves under the new dispensation, be it at home or abroad, as individuals or collectively. These works also serve as a reminder of the diversity of conditions and perspectives within the minority community itself, an entity frequently presumed to be socially homogenous. Perhaps unsurprisingly, what the authors nearly all have in common is a

---

[1] Kildare Dobbs, *Running the Rapids: A Writer's Life* (Dublin: Lilliput Press, 2005), 7.
[2] For a demographic analysis of the Protestant community during this period, see Malcolm Macourt, *Counting the People of God? The Census of Population and the Church of Ireland* (Dublin: Church of Ireland Publishing, 2008), 65ff.

sensitivity to questions about their own Irishness and the associated challenges of belonging and participating in a culture that often found their
continuing presence inconvenient. As a result, many display a strong sense
of contingency, an appreciation of the way public events can dictate and
shape the course of private lives.[3] Taken together, then, these post-partition autobiographies bear witness to an overlooked reality in modern Irish
culture, that of Southern Protestants seeking to construct workable identities for a future free of sectarian constraint and the tyrannies of history.

Admittedly, grasping this reality has not been made any easier by the
readiness with which certain Protestant writers have exploited the imagery and language of extinction for their own ends. Not least, the trope of
Anglo-Irish ruin was to be central in the later career of W. B. Yeats, who
refashioned himself as an elegist for the whole tradition and thereby lent
credibility to a deeply limiting structure for conveying the Protestant
story.[4] This approach Ian d'Alton has aptly termed the 'grand tragedy'
model of historical interpretation, one whose dramatic proportions and
foregone conclusions have made it perennially appealing to the Irish
literary imagination.[5] In almost always resorting to either the rotting or
burning Big House for its setting, this narrative form has produced some
good fiction but proved a poor guide to the daily lives of most Protestants
south of the border.[6] Only a limited proportion of the minority population inhabited this milieu in the first place, so to generalize about their
experience on the basis of what happened to members of the landed
classes is to indulge in a kind of Yeatsian myth-making. Even those who
have opted to emphasize the futility of this rarefied world in its post-
partition form have done so more with self-deprecation than pretension.

In her memoir *In Ruin Reconciled* (1990), for instance, Joan de Vere
records how at sixteen she returned to Co. Limerick after her father's
various colonial postings abroad, only to realize that the 'county

---

[3] Michael Kenneally, 'The Autobiographical Imagination and Irish Literary Autobiographies', in
Michael Allen and Angela Wilcox, eds., *Critical Approaches to Anglo-Irish Literature* (Gerrards
Cross: Colin Smythe, 1989), 112–13.

[4] G. J. Watson, *Irish Identity and the Literary Revival* (Washington, DC: Catholic University of
America Press, 1994), 149–50; R. F. Foster, *W. B. Yeats: A Life, II: The Arch-Poet 1915–1939*
(Oxford: Oxford University Press, 2003), 620.

[5] Ian d'Alton, 'A Perspective upon Historical Process: The Case of Southern Irish Protestantism', in
F. B. Smith, ed., *Ireland, England and Australia: Essays in Honour of Oliver MacDonagh* (Canberra:
Australian National University Press, 1990), 82–84.

[6] Fascination with life in and around the Big House has spawned an entire subgenre of fiction. See
Otto Rauchbauer, ed., *Ancestral Voices: The Big House in Anglo-Irish Literature* (Hildesheim: George
Olms, 1992) and Vera Kreilkamp, *The Anglo-Irish Novel and the Big House* (Syracuse: Syracuse
University Press, 1998).

society'[7] her parents had idealized was now hopelessly stultifying and irrelevant. Even more direct in its portrayal of Anglo-Irish deterioration is Jesse Hoare's *The Road to Glenanore* (1975), in which she tells of going to live with an aged relative in rural Cork. She is not long settled before she realizes her curmudgeonly cousin Ned is slowly going bankrupt due to his own incompetence and routine embezzlement by his employees.[8] Yet nowhere is the theme of decay more assiduously pursued than in Annabel Davis-Goff's *Walled Gardens: Scenes from an Anglo-Irish Childhood* (1990), a book in which self-deprecation gives way to self-loathing. In it, virtually everything embarrassing, depressing or inexplicable about Davis-Goff's upbringing becomes emblematic of a hereditary Anglo-Irish incapacity for living properly.[9] With genteel failure the only course open to them in both practical matters and personal relationships, the Protestants depicted here can never emerge as three-dimensional human beings, as the author's own grievance precludes the possibility of deeper insight.

One prominent Anglo-Irish figure whose autobiographical writings have been too often appropriated in the service of this decline narrative is the novelist Elizabeth Bowen. While undoubtedly she made repeated use of the theme of ruin in her fiction, Bowen's own life reveals an ongoing commitment to Ireland and the possibility of Protestant participation in its future.[10] Her 1942 family history, *Bowen's Court*, in particular demonstrates a firm belief in the continuing legitimacy of her Anglo-Irish inheritance. And even after she found it necessary in the 1950s to sell the house for which the book was named, and then watched helplessly as it was demolished by the new owner, Bowen refused to consider her personal difficulties an indictment of the whole tradition. 'My family, though notably "unhistoric", had their part in a drama outside themselves', she insists in the afterword to the 1963 edition. 'Their assertions, their compliances, their refusals as men and women went, year by year, generation by generation, to give history direction, as well as colour and stuff. Each of the family, in

[7] Joan de Vere, *In Ruin Reconciled: A Memoir of Anglo-Ireland* (Dublin: Lilliput Press, 1990), 69.
[8] M. Jesse Hoare, *The Road to Glenanore* (London: Howard Baker, 1975), 98ff.
[9] Annabel Davis-Goff, *Walled Gardens: Scenes from an Anglo-Irish Childhood* (London: Picador, 1990), 21–38.
[10] See, for example, Elizabeth Bowen, 'The Big House', *The Bell*, 1:1 (1940), 71–77. See also George O'Brien, 'The Strangeness of Elizabeth Bowen', *Dublin Review*, 20 (2005), 70 and Robert Tobin, 'Between the Old World and the New: The Postwar Travels of Elizabeth Bowen', *Irish Review*, 48 (2014), 60–64.

their different manners, were more than their time's products; they were its agents.'[11]

Another product of the gentry still more eager to combat the notion of Anglo-Irish irrelevance was the essayist Hubert Butler. In *Escape from the Anthill* (1985), he is quick to disavow any claim to grand ancestry, yet he upholds the general principle that, by virtue of Protestants' historical relationship to Ireland, individuals like himself have both the right and responsibility to participate in the nation's development. 'Though we have long been unimportant people, the Butlers, of whom my family is a junior branch, had ruled the neighbourhood since the fourteenth century', he says in recounting why he was always determined to stay put in the family home, adding that 'there is scarcely a parish in Tipperary or Kilkenny that does not bear some trace of our sometimes arrogant, sometimes kindly interference. Could I not interfere too?'[12] The localist ethos that Butler would develop over the course of half a century proceeded from this initial conviction that, for good or for ill, his caste could not be parted from its heritage.[13]

Given that the authenticity of their community's Irishness was to be repeatedly questioned and sometimes derided under the new dispensation, Bowen's and Butler's assertion of genealogical credentials is by no means unusual among Southern Protestant writers.[14] In *The Brimming River* (1961), for example, Raymond F. Brooke reasons that since his family arrived in Ireland during the reign of Elizabeth I and had been resident ever since, 'I think I may claim to be Irish – though I know there are many who would not admit the claim in one of English descent.'[15] Others show an awareness that recounting their ancestry might appear as so much special pleading and assume an attitude of ironical detachment towards the family lore they relate, but this does not prevent them rehearsing it.[16] Thus L. A. G. Strong reports that 'my mother was continually impressing upon my sister and me that we came of a high lineage. We can find no evidence of this. It was an ancient lineage, certainly, on my father's side,

---

[11] Elizabeth Bowen, *Bowen's Court* (Cork: Collins Press, 1998), 452.

[12] Hubert Butler, *Escape from the Anthill* (Mullingar: Lilliput Press, 1985), 1.

[13] Robert Tobin, *The Minority Voice: Hubert Butler and Southern Irish Protestantism, 1900–91* (Oxford: Oxford University Press, 2012), 83–115. Another Southern Protestant determined to stay home was writer Arland Ussher, who explains in *Spanish Mercy* (London: Victor Gollancz, 1959) that 'whether from cowardice or lethargy, I spent the best years of my life . . . on a remote family estate' (34).

[14] Elizabeth Grubgeld, 'Anglo-Irish Autobiography and the Genealogical Mandate', *Éire-Ireland*, 33:1–2 (1998), 104.

[15] R. F. Brooke, *The Brimming River* (Dublin: Allen Figgis, 1961), 11.

[16] As poet Richard Murphy concedes when rehearsing his own lineage in *The Kick* (London: Granta, 2002): 'genealogical speculation may prove nothing more than the inclinations of the speculator, but the legends that arise out of speculation often influence our minds and actions' (25).

but nothing to make a fuss about.'[17] Similarly, son of the manse W. B. Stanford remembers how he and his siblings, if ever they felt patronized when playing with wealthier Protestant children, would 'comfort ourselves by referring to our associates as "Cromwellians" and recalling our remote kinship with Lord Edward Fitzgerald and Bonnie Prince Charlie'.[18] But Stanford then hastens to add that 'we had enough sense, however, to keep these pretensions to ourselves'.[19] Another clergyman's son, Lionel Fleming, opens his *Head or Harp* (1965) with a lengthy account of his forebears in Co. Cork, in whom he takes evident pride, not least because they purchased rather than seized their lands in the eighteenth century.[20] To a country as obsessed with the past as Ireland, longevity, however undistinguished or dubious its vehicle, would seem to bestow a certain moral authority that is impossible to dismiss entirely. So Benedict Anderson, armed with an elaborate family tree supplied by a friend expert in genealogy, managed as a young man to persuade Dublin officials to grant him an Irish passport; this he did, he explains wryly, despite the fact that neither he nor his parents had actually been born in the country.[21]

Continuing after independence in 1922 to live alongside the Anglo-Irish remnant but distinct from it were the 'plain' Protestants, those working farmers, tradesmen, shopkeepers and others scattered across the countryside and provincial towns. In *Excursions in the Real World* (1993), novelist William Trevor associates himself with this stratum, which he refers to as 'smalltime Protestant stock'.[22] As a teenager, Trevor writes, he assumed that his future 'lay in some form of commerce, serving in a grocer's shop or a draper's, or as a bank clerk'.[23] Another autobiographer from this background is Victor Griffin, later dean of St Patrick's Cathedral in Dublin. Born to a farming family in Co. Wicklow, Griffin remembers that during the 1930s and 1940s, class distinctions within the minority community continued to shape social relations: 'Protestant and Roman Catholic were looked on and looked down on with equal dispassion' by the Anglo-Irish gentry, he notes, such that 'no special degree of intimacy was extended to Protestants'.[24] Someone else who later became prominent in Irish life yet remained conscious of his plain Protestant roots is art historian Homan Potterton. Although his father was a farmer and businessman from an old

[17] L. A. G. Strong, *Green Memory* (London: Methuen, 1961), 9.
[18] W. B. Stanford, *Memoirs* (Dublin: Hinds, 2001), 50.   [19] Ibid.
[20] Lionel Fleming, *Head or Harp* (London: Barrie and Rockliff, 1965), 7–14, 17.
[21] Benedict Anderson, 'Selective Kinship', *Dublin Review*, 10 (2003), 12.
[22] William Trevor, *Excursions in the Real World* (London: Penguin, 1993), xiii.   [23] Ibid., xv.
[24] Victor Griffin, *Mark of Protest* (Dublin: Gill and Macmillan, 1993), 23, 27–28.

Meath family, Potterton insists in *Rathcormick: A Childhood Recalled* (2001) that the family was always characterized by 'low-key, low-profile, and above all low-church'[25] tendencies. Declaring that 'we were almost as different to the true Anglo-Irish as we were to Catholics', he argues that the dissimilarity was fundamentally cultural: unlike the Anglo-Irish, the Pottertons had no family or educational links with England, nor did they have a history of British army service.[26] Potterton's remarks, like those of Trevor and Griffin, suggest a form of Southern Protestantism possessing an integrity all its own because rooted in the daily observances and occupations of working life.[27] As such, these Protestants also appear comparatively less troubled by the legacy of dual loyalty so often preoccupying their Anglo-Irish counterparts.

The interplay between religious affiliation and social standing becomes still more significant when considering memoirs written by Southern Protestants from an inner-city, working-class background. Contrary to the image of the typical Protestant as a country squire, the minority community during most of its history has been an economically mixed, urban phenomenon.[28] The writers whose families continued to inhabit this working-class environment tend to exhibit a more immediate and nuanced understanding of their non-Protestant neighbours than do their rural or suburban cousins. In *Speaking Volumes: A Dublin Childhood* (2000), for example, Edith Newman Devlin relates her experiences growing up in the poor part of Dublin surrounding St Patrick's Hospital for the mentally ill, where her father worked as the lodge-keeper. Though always conscious of her otherness because of her religion, Devlin recounts with fondness the warmth and kindness of the poor Catholics among whom she was raised. A source of much greater anxiety in retrospect was to be her sense of inadequacy among wealthier classmates when attending Protestant schools.[29] Analogously, Hugh Maxton in his memoir records the details of his upbringing in the Dublin district of Harold's Cross, punctuated by

---

[25] Homan Potterton, *Rathcormick: A Childhood Recalled* (Dublin: New Island Books, 2001), 28.

[26] Ibid., 132.   [27] Risteárd Ó Glaisne, *To Irish Protestants* (Dublin: Ara, 1991), 44.

[28] Toby Barnard, *A New Anatomy of Ireland: The Irish Protestants, 1649–1770* (New Haven: Yale University Press, 2003), 328. The greatest numerical losses suffered by the Protestant population after partition took place among its poorer strata, and less for political reasons than as a result of unemployment and inter-marriage. See Martin Maguire, 'The Church of Ireland and the Problem of the Protestant Working-Class of Dublin, 1870s–1930s', in Alan Ford, James Maguire and Kenneth Milne, eds., *As by Law Established: The Church of Ireland Since the Reformation* (Dublin: Lilliput Press, 1995), 202.

[29] Edith Newman Devlin, *Speaking Volumes: A Dublin Childhood* (Belfast: Blackstaff Press, 2000), 113–15, 134, 190–91.

visits to his mother's family farm near Aughrim, Co. Wicklow.
Throughout, Maxton subtly evokes memories of the modest but essentially
happy home life he enjoyed, summed up by his observation that 'My father
was not a great conversationalist any more than he was a great singer. But
things held together.'[30] It is only when, like Devlin, his academic ability
propels Maxton into the company of more affluent Protestants that he
becomes attuned to markers of class and status, such as from which shop
one's school blazer had been purchased: 'A slight difference in the colour of
the material betrayed the Goravan customer from the Nicholls customer,
with discernible if unstated social implications.'[31] Such seemingly minor
details abide in the memory as epiphanies, capturing for certain Protestants
the sense of being simultaneously included in and marginalized by the
community that is their birthright.

A final group adding to the story of latter-day Southern Protestantism is
the offspring of those professionals who continued to occupy the fashionable squares and leafy suburbs of Dublin and Cork after 1922.[32] A notable
pattern in the memoirs of these people is the recollection of just how little
their lives were disturbed by the establishment of the Irish Free State. Peter
Somerville-Large, whose father had a successful practice as a surgeon in
Dublin in the 1930s, recalls that Protestant doctors and lawyers 'continued
to have keys to the park in Fitzwilliam Square and share a quiet prosper-
ity'.[33] Randal Sadleir confirms the point when recounting the anachronistic
career of his father Thomas, who, in running the office of the Ulster King-
of-Arms at Dublin Castle, carried on anomalously in the crown's service
until 1943. Of his father's unusual routine, Sadleir candidly explains that it
all seemed normal because it took place within 'the cloistered world of the
castle, Trinity College, St. Patrick's Cathedral and the Kildare Street
Club'.[34] Likewise, Brian Inglis in *West Briton* (1962) describes the way
Protestants in suburban Malahide carried on after independence as though
nothing had changed, observing that

> like passengers on a ship seized by mutineers, the members of old
> Ascendancy families continued to behave in the way they had always

---

[30] Hugh Maxton, *Waking: An Irish Protestant Upbringing* (Belfast: Lagan Press, 1997), 23.
[31] Ibid., 154.
[32] Ian d'Alton, '"A Vestigial Population"? Perspectives on Southern Irish Protestants in the Twentieth
Century', *Éire-Ireland*, 44:3–4 (2009), 13–14.
[33] Peter Somerville-Large, *An Irish Childhood* (London: Constable, 2002), 3–4.
[34] Randal Sadleir, *Tanzania: Journey to Republic* (London: Radcliffe Press, 1999), 6. See also Susan
Hood, *Royal Roots, Republican Inheritance: The Survival of the Office of Arms* (Dublin: Woodfield
Press, 2002), 103–64.

behaved – as if determined to give an example to the lascars who had come from the bilges to take over the ship, and who might otherwise disgrace themselves by panic or excess.[35]

Inglis says he began to understand that his social enclave had managed to sustain this peculiar lifestyle because 'from nursery days . . . to formal dinners a decade later, with the men lingering over brown sherry after dinner, everything was ordered; not tyrannical – a measure of independence, even of eccentricity, was acceptable – but safe'.[36] At least part of what lends these retrospective evocations their power is the writers' knowledge that a far more complicated future awaits them in their own adulthood.

Southern Protestant memoirists are of course hardly unique in their urge to romanticize the past, but striking nonetheless has been their readiness to employ pastoral motifs to conflate the innocence of an individual childhood with a reimagined prelapsarian Ireland that has since disappeared.[37] Seamus Deane has identified this narrative device in Irish autobiography as the 'Edenic resource',[38] noting that it establishes a fixed basis on which all subsequent discontinuities and alienations in the writer's personal and public life can be judged. Why this should be particularly appealing to Anglo-Irish writers since partition must be obvious.[39] In his memoir *Five Arches* (1980), scholar T. R. Henn devotes considerable space to reminiscing about the open-air adventures he had at his mother's home in Clare, which was called, appropriately enough, Paradise. Henn relates that before his expulsion from this Eden to attend prep school at Fermoy, he enjoyed the free run of the 'self-contained and quasi-feudal world'[40] of which the household was the centre. In like fashion, Anita Leslie, Sheila Wingfield, Mary Pakenham, Violet Powell, Kildare Dobbs, Christopher Fitz-Simon and Joseph Hone, among others, all register memories of a carefree existence in an Irish countryside they experienced as impervious to the demands of wider society.[41]

[35] Brian Inglis, *West Briton* (London: Faber and Faber, 1962), 13.   [36] Ibid., 21.

[37] Grubgeld, 'Anglo-Irish Autobiography and the Genealogical Mandate', 108.

[38] Seamus Deane, 'Autobiography and Memoirs 1890–1988', in Seamus Deane, gen. ed., *The Field Day Anthology of Irish Writing* (Derry: Field Day Publications, 1991), vol. 3, 382.

[39] In *The Irish Story: Telling Tales and Making It Up in Ireland* (London: Allen Lane/Penguin, 2001), Roy Foster notes that 'the idea of both Ireland and the writer's youth as adjacent and interdependent lost demesnes can appeal at all social levels', but he concedes that 'it is most readily associated with a crumbling Big House' (164).

[40] T. R. Henn, *Five Arches* (Gerrards Cross: Colin Smythe, 1980), 53.

[41] Anita Leslie, *The Gilt and the Gingerbread: An Autobiography* (London: Hutchinson, 1981), 82; Sheila Wingfield, *Real People* (London: Cresset Press, 1952), 1–6; Mary Pakenham, *Brought Up and Brought Out* (London: Cobden-Sanderson, 1938), 9–13; Violet Powell, *Five Out of Six: An Autobiography* (London, 1960), 22; Kildare Dobbs, *Running to Paradise* (Toronto: Oxford University Press, 1962), 18; Christopher Fitz-Simon, *Eleven Houses: A Memoir of Childhood*

For adults and children alike, it was the Second World War that often marked the end of these cosseted circumstances. Whether they actively supported Britain or identified more strongly with neutral Ireland, few Protestant memoirists would claim their personal trajectory was unaffected by the events of 1939–45.[42] Among the most profound memoirs produced by any Irishman about the war is Denis Johnston's *Nine Rivers from Jordan* (1953), which charts the ways his minority identity both informed and was informed by his experiences as a journalist for the BBC. Initially, Johnston assumes a posture of cynical detachment as a self-proclaimed neutral reporting from the sidelines, but as the narrative progresses he is increasingly driven to embrace some more active role amidst the suffering and destruction he is witnessing. One side effect of this deepening engagement is a sense of disgust with the complacency and pietism of his compatriots when he visits Dublin on leave.[43] Meanwhile, those Protestants who had opted to remain in Ireland during 'the Emergency' struggled with the sense of isolation their choice brought with it. Scholar W. B. Stanford later judged that neutrality had 'made us all too much inclined to brood on our own insular ills and fears. The mood of the religious minority in the South seemed to have become dangerously despondent. Many of those who might have advocated more dynamic policies had joined the allied forces.'[44] A clear exception to this tendency was Hubert Butler, who believed that neutrality offered Irish people a unique opportunity to develop greater self-reliance and mutual understanding. Looking back on one notable literary initiative of those years, he recalls that 'we remnants of the Anglo-Irish "intelligentsia" would have been nobody's children, had Sean O'Faolain's *The Bell* not taken us under its wing'.[45] He then proceeds to list those Protestants – 'all of us rather odd and not finding it easy to put Ireland first'[46] – who, in spite of all contrary pressures, persisted throughout the war in focusing their energies upon the promotion of a positive Irish identity.

If the Emergency challenged Protestants in the South to make common cause with their Roman Catholic neighbours, it also served to exacerbate their sense of otherness from their Northern co-religionists. Very much at war, the latter were frequently bitter over what they considered the soft

(Dublin: Penguin, 2007), 154–77; and Joseph Hone, *Wicked Little Joe: A Tale of Childhood and Youth* (Dublin: Lilliput Press, 2009), 54–55, 240–41.
[42] Among other examples, see Patricia Cockburn, *Figure of Eight* (London: Chatto and Windus/ Hogarth, 1985), 161.
[43] Denis Johnston, *Nine Rivers from Jordan* (London: Derek Verschoyle, 1953), 372–73.
[44] Stanford, *Memoir*, 105.   [45] Butler, *Escape from the Anthill*, 148.   [46] Ibid., 149–50.

option taken by their fellows in Éire, to whom one Ulsterwoman would refer derisively in 1943 as 'just Southerners' who 'hadn't the decency to evacuate'.[47] Of course, a sense of cultural difference between Northern and Southern Protestants was nothing new. Edith Devlin, the daughter of a Church of Ireland mother from west Cork and a Presbyterian father from Co. Down, notes that even before partition Protestants themselves recognized 'that the north-east of the country was very different in mentality from the relaxed and sleepy south-west, and was inhabited by very different people'.[48] Less diplomatically, Sheila Wingfield confesses in *Sun Too Fast* (1974), published under her married name, that she always felt 'a massive mental barrier' between herself and Northerners, finding their mores and attitudes 'emotionally offensive'.[49] Having served Church of Ireland parishes on both sides of the border, Victor Griffin by contrast grew to appreciate the Ulster Protestants' perspective, not least their anxiety about suffering a fate akin to that of the minority in the twenty-six counties. In *Mark of Protest* (1993), he says of them: 'They looked on the Southern Protestants as a dying breed, nice, respectable, quiet people who, having lost the instinct for survival, gracefully waited for the undertaker.'[50] Particularly sensitive to this charge was Hubert Butler, who even after the Troubles erupted in the late 1960s continued to insist not only that the Northern and Southern Protestant communities were inextricably linked but that both were in fact essential components to any lasting peace and unity on the island.[51]

Notwithstanding the robust idealism of activists like Butler, though, Southern Protestant autobiographers have tended to portray the postwar years in the Republic as a time of sectarian isolation. With Cold War discourse serving to exacerbate Catholic nationalist sensibilities, relations with members of the majority religion remained largely cordial but distant. Norman Ruddock, who grew up in the 1940s as the son of a Carlow shopkeeper, remembers that 'we lived in a kind of ghetto community with little contact with our Catholic neighbours ... We kept our heads down and almost apologised for not being "papists"! There was dreadful

---

[47] Harry Craig, 'A Protestant Visits Belfast', *The Bell*, 7:3 (1943), 242. In fact, large numbers of Southern Irishmen, Protestant and Catholic, enlisted in the British forces. See Richard Doherty, *Irish Men and Women in the Second World War* (Dublin: Four Courts Press, 1999), 27–54.

[48] Devlin, *Speaking Volumes*, 16.

[49] Sheila Powerscourt, *Sun Too Fast* (London: Geoffrey Bles, 1974), 270–71.

[50] Victor Griffin, *Mark of Protest*, 90. See Dennis Kennedy, *The Widening Gulf: Northern Attitudes to the Independent Irish State 1919–49* (Belfast: Blackstaff Press, 1988).

[51] Hubert Butler, *The Appleman and the Poet* (Dublin: Lilliput Press, 2014), 156–63.

religious apartheid.'[52] Ruddock later found himself embroiled in the events surrounding the notorious Fethard-on-Sea boycott of 1957, when, as a young cleric, he was charged with keeping the faltering Protestant school going amidst the crisis.[53] In keeping with Ruddock's characterization is the explanation offered by Brian Wilson of why his Southern Protestant family settled in Northern Ireland after the war. Grandson of the formidable archbishop of Armagh, J. A. F. Gregg, Wilson recalls that his father expended considerable effort seeking a suitable appointment as a surgeon but was appalled by the interference of the Catholic hierarchy in matters of health and welfare policy. Unwilling to acquiesce in such clerical domination, Wilson's father eventually accepted a post as a senior consultant surgeon in Lisburn instead.[54] Trinity classicist W. B. Stanford also remembers becoming more and more disturbed by signs of exclusion during this period, as manifested by the 'special position' accorded the Catholic church in the Irish Constitution and the chauvinistic activities of groups like the Legion of Mary, the Catholic Truth Society and the Knights of Columbanus.[55] But what brings their sense of vulnerability into boldest relief for minority writers is the issue of mixed marriage. With the enforcement of the *Ne Temere* decree, which mandated that any children from mixed marriages must be raised in the Catholic faith, Protestants were, in Homan Potterton's words, 'incensed and shaken'[56] by this interference in private matters but also confirmed in their broader view of Roman Catholicism as an oppressive presence in Irish life. Thus, when reflecting on his activities as a Protestant nationalist over a span of forty years in *To Irish Protestants* (1991), Risteárd Ó Glaisne maintains a dubious tone about mixed marriage, even though *Ne Temere* by that point had long since ceased to be enforced.[57]

Besides the Church of Ireland, two prominent institutions that remained closely aligned with Southern Protestant culture after partition were Trinity College and the *Irish Times*. A number of memoirists, in

---

[52] Norman Ruddock, *The Rambling Rector* (Dublin: Columba Press, 2005), 23.

[53] Ibid., 57–66. This boycott was launched against Protestant shops and businesses in a small Wexford town at the urging of the local Catholic clergy. For a full account of the episode, see Tim Fanning, *The Fethard-on-Sea Boycott* (Cork: Collins Press, 2010).

[54] Brian W. J. G. Wilson, *Experience is an Arch* (Weardale, Durham: Memoir Club, 2007), 19–20. Another Protestant who had earlier struggled to find his place in the Free State medical establishment was paediatric specialist Robert Collis. See Robert Collis, *To Be a Pilgrim* (London: Secker and Warburg, 1975), 68ff.

[55] Stanford, *Memoirs*, 78–80, 108.

[56] Potterton, *Rathcormick*, 177. See also Devlin, *Speaking Volumes*, 118 and Butler, *The Appleman and the Poet*, 135–42.

[57] Ó Glaisne, *To Irish Protestants*, 103–06.

chronicling their personal evolution, also capture something of the texture and mood of these places during the postwar period. Niall Rudd's *Pale Green, Light Orange* (1994), for example, evokes the lively insularity of Trinity, where figures such as Stanford, Owen Sheehy-Skeffington, David Webb and R. B. McDowell combined learning with wit. At Trinity, Rudd concludes, 'you didn't have to be particularly *good* at anything; it was all part of education'.[58] In the recollections of Edith Devlin, however, the pleasures of Trinity life were still largely denied to its women students, who were treated as interlopers in this traditionally all-male preserve and scarcely tolerated. It was only in the late 1960s that Trinity became a truly open place, receptive to the wider society in which it was situated.[59] Similarly, journalists Brian Inglis, Lionel Fleming and Tony Gray attest to the changes the *Irish Times* underwent during the same time, recalling the ways larger-than-life editor R. M. Smyllie gradually transformed this traditional mouthpiece of the Ascendancy into a serious news source for all educated Irish people.[60] Yet both Fleming and Inglis end their accounts with a departure for Fleet Street, and in *West Briton* the latter expresses scepticism as to whether even the most well-meaning Protestant can ever truly hope to 'absorb Irishness' or achieve 'full acceptance'.[61] Inglis's eloquent but ultimately defeatist portrayal of his attempts to integrate into the larger society aroused irritation in Hubert Butler, who in a review remarked of *West Briton* that it is 'as cheering to the remnant that still hangs on in its native land as a nice cup of Ovaltine to the victim of disseminated sclerosis'.[62]

At the heart of the disagreement between Inglis and Butler lies the question T. R. Henn poses when accounting for his own life choices: 'how far can the acceptance of nationalistic ideals and politics be seen as capable of redeeming the misfortune of religion and birth?'[63] For Butler, the error committed by too many of his co-religionists was sharing Henn's appraisal of their religion and birth as misfortunes in the first place; rather, meaningful embrace of Irish nationalism by Protestants

---

[58] Niall Rudd, *Pale Green, Light Orange: A Portrait of Bourgeois Ireland, 1930–1950* (Dublin: Lilliput Press, 1994), 143–65. Original emphasis.

[59] Devlin, *Speaking Volumes*, 208–09; Stanford, *Memoirs*, 60ff.

[60] Fleming, *Head or Harp*, 117ff; Brian Inglis, *Downstart* (London: Chatto and Windus, 1990), 88ff; Tony Gray, *Mr Smyllie, Sir!* (Dublin: Gill and Macmillan, 1991).

[61] Inglis, *West Briton*, 105, 148.

[62] Hubert Butler, *Grandmother and Wolfe Tone* (Dublin: Lilliput Press, 1990), 138.

[63] T. R. Henn, *Last Essays* (Gerrards Cross: Colin Smythe, 1976), 28–29. The classicist E. R. Dodds was another Protestant whose academic ambitions pushed him reluctantly but inexorably towards England. See E. R. Dodds, *Missing Persons: An Autobiography* (Oxford: Clarendon Press, 1977), 70ff.

must derive from a conviction that they had a unique and necessary role in its success. While he acknowledges that 'there is a rich crop of slights and misunderstandings to be harvested' while building good relations with Catholics, his writings continually emphasize the power of local initiatives in dispelling inherited antipathies.[64] Another Protestant committed to promoting non-sectarian communal structures was Chalmers 'Terry' Trench, son of Professor W. F. Trench of Trinity College. Educated at Repton and Cambridge in the late 1920s, Trench returned to Ireland while still a young man. In 1931, he was instrumental in the creation of the Irish Youth Hostel Association, *An Óige*, based on models he had observed on the Continent. Trench's two memoirs document his efforts to expand this organization across the country over the next half-century.[65] Someone who, by contrast, did not return to Ireland to settle was Kildare Dobbs, an old family friend of Hubert Butler. Recalling a visit he made to Butler in Kilkenny after he had emigrated to Canada, Dobbs says that Butler 'gave me, in his gentle way, a hard time. He thought I should have stayed home and argued for the liberties I believed in. I sensed that he thought I was in pursuit of the dollar when all I was seeking was a livelihood.'[66] The exchange cited here is a poignant one, capturing the divergence of perception between two men with similar backgrounds who have nonetheless taken remarkably different paths in life. It speaks in microcosm to the larger tangle of personal needs and corporate responsibilities with which their whole community has had to contend since independence.

Apart from recounting the details of particular lives, arguably these autobiographies serve as a collective appraisal of what Southern Protestants should seek to preserve about their shared history in order to construct a viable future.[67] A strong sense of contingency is what finally binds together all save the most predetermined of them, a tacit recognition that history consists primarily of individuals willing and able to engage with the

---

[64] Butler, *Grandmother and Wolfe Tone*, 138. See also Edna Longley, *The Living Stream: Literature and Revisionism in Ireland* (Newcastle upon Tyne: Bloodaxe Books, 1994), 140–41.

[65] Chalmers [Terry] Trench, *Nearly Ninety: Reminiscences* (Ballivor, Co. Meath: Hannon Press, 1996), 5–25, 109–18; Terry Trench, *Fifty Years Young: The Story of An Óige* (Dublin: An Óige/Irish Youth Hostel Association, 1981), 9–10.

[66] Dobbs, *Running the Rapids*, 36–38.

[67] Barry Sloan, '"Drawing the Line and Making the Tot": Aspects of Irish Protestant Life Writing', in Liam Harte, ed., *Modern Irish Autobiography: Self, Nation and Society* (Basingstoke: Palgrave Macmillan, 2007), 174.

circumstances in which they find themselves.[68] Even those who seek to return to their roots or who register a certain nostalgia for the simpler past nonetheless accept that such a past is irrecoverable. During their absence, the Eden they once knew has disappeared forever.[69] What remains is the legacy of memory itself, the testimony to variousness during a period in Irish life when such complexity was the thing least wanted. In the process, the very act of memoir writing becomes an assertion of continuing vitality, a kind of Protestant dissent from majority narratives that would blithely sweep away the good with the bad. It also serves as a record among Southern Protestants of their own internal diversity, a reminder that social and economic distinctions among them have been more determinative of their varied fortunes than some have been wont to acknowledge.[70] In short, these post-partition autobiographies stand as an affirmation of Irishness as an identity transcending any one point of view, forever expanding out of the past to accommodate new experiences. Or, as Joseph Hone concludes: 'Memory lane doesn't need to be a cul-de-sac, but a road to an undiscovered country, suggesting exits, not ends.'[71]

Further reading

Crawford, Heather. *Outside the Glow: Protestants and Irishness in Independent Ireland*. Dublin: UCD Press, 2010.

Foster, R. F. *The Irish Story: Telling Tales and Making It Up in Ireland*. London: Allen Lane/Penguin, 2001.

Grubgeld, Elizabeth. *Anglo-Irish Autobiography: Class, Gender, and the Forms of Narrative*. Syracuse: Syracuse University Press, 2004.

Sloan, Barry. '"Drawing the Line and Making the Tot": Aspects of Irish Protestant Life Writing', in Liam Harte, ed., *Modern Irish Autobiography: Self, Nation and Society*. New York: Palgrave Macmillan, 2007: 156–75.

Tobin, Robert, *The Minority Voice: Hubert Butler and Southern Irish Protestantism, 1900–91*. Oxford: Oxford University Press, 2012.

Wills, Clair, *That Neutral Island: A Cultural History of Ireland during the Second World War*. London: Faber and Faber, 2007.

---

[68] David G. Wright, *Yeats's Myth of Self: The Autobiographical Prose* (Dublin: Gill and Macmillan, 1987), 9.

[69] Cockburn, *Figure of Eight*, 243; Henn, *Five Arches*, 215.

[70] Martin Maguire, '"Remembering Who We Are": Identity and Class in Protestant Dublin and Belfast, 1868–1905', in Francis Devine, Fintan Lane and Niamh Puirséil, eds., *Essays in Irish Labour History: A Festschrift for Elizabeth and John W. Boyle* (Dublin: Irish Academic Press, 2008), 63–64.

[71] Joseph Hone, *Duck Soup in the Black Sea* (London: Hamish Hamilton, 1988), 240.

CHAPTER 18

Northern Irish Autobiography since 1960

Barry Sloan

The proliferation of autobiography is a marked feature of Northern Irish writing in recent decades. While it may be true that the 'strength and vitality' of many of these works 'stems in part from the pressure of extraordinary circumstances on ordinary women and men, from the desire to bear witness, and from a desire to contest or collaborate with the mainstream media versions of the conflict'[1] that shaped so much of the period since the late 1960s, those 'extraordinary circumstances' themselves need to be understood within a wider framework of reference. The inclusion of a chapter in this *History* specifically devoted to Northern Irish autobiography implies that it is distinctive from autobiographical writing produced elsewhere in Ireland, or shaped by different factors. Foremost among such considerations is the impact of the Government of Ireland Act, which created the politically engineered state of Northern Ireland in 1921 as the compromise to enable British withdrawal from the country without facing civil war in the northeast. This Act conceded to the religious and economic difference of the region, with its unique concentration of Protestants, many of Scottish Presbyterian descent, and its nineteenth-century heritage of industrial development. It made provisions that guaranteed perpetual government by the Protestant majority as long as the respective political affiliations of Catholics and Protestants were defined by religion, and thereby encouraged the demonization of the minority. Partition left many Northern Catholics not only feeling politically disenfranchised and marginalized within a state predicated upon its allegiance to Britain, and to the monarchy in particular, but also the victims of an injustice secured by Protestant militancy which left them cut off from their natural links with the rest of Ireland at the very time it gained independence. However, if the survival of the Northern state

---

[1] Anne Crilly, Hazel Gordon and Eilish Rooney, 'Women in the North of Ireland 1969–2000', in Angela Bourke et al., eds., *The Field Day Anthology of Irish Writing, Volume V: Irish Women's Writings and Traditions* (Cork: Cork University Press in association with Field Day, 2002), 1481.

without serious challenge for almost fifty years seemed to confirm its resilience, the rapidity and completeness with which it collapsed after 1968 exposed its actual precariousness and how much it had depended on containing Catholic aspirations and influence. In the unprecedentedly prolonged political conflict that followed, questions of identity and belonging – of what it is to be Irish or British, Protestant or Catholic in Northern Ireland – and about the relationships between the Northern state, the Irish Republic and the United Kingdom, became important and pressing both for individuals and for the society as a whole.

This was very different from the early twentieth-century world of Florence Mary McDowell, who was born in 1888 and published two volumes of autobiography in 1966 and 1972 respectively. Recalling the 'swarry' presented by the pupils of Cogry Mills National School in Co. Antrim, where she was a trainee teacher, McDowell observes that although most of the children were 'Orange to the backbone', both the Irish and the British songs and recitations they performed 'belonged utterly' to them: 'They knew they were Irish. They knew they were British. They knew they were Ulster. They had not the slightest difficulty in being all three.'[2] But that was before the politics of partition coerced Northern identities into narrow and often mutually exclusive channels of orange and green. Since many Northern autobiographies published since 1960 focus extensively on the writers' formative years in the decades immediately following partition, this chapter shows how its cultural, social and political consequences are repeatedly reflected in their life stories. It is against this background, too, that the autobiographies which span the years of the Troubles must also be read because, as Claire Lynch has noted, there is a frequent 'correlation between national and personal history'[3] in Irish autobiography, and this has nowhere been more evident than in the contested world of the North.

Many Catholic Irish autobiographies have explored the relationship between the individual and the church and the formative influence of church-controlled education on personal development. Northern writers prove no exception. However, not only was Catholicism the religion of the disadvantaged minority in Northern Ireland, the Catholic church was one of their strongest links to people in the rest of Ireland and to aspects of Irish life and culture which received little encouragement or recognition from the Northern state. Catholic schools promoted Irish history, language and

---

[2] Florence Mary McDowell, *Roses and Rainbows* (Belfast: Blackstaff Press, 1972), 104. McDowell's earlier autobiography is entitled *Other Days Around Me* (1966). 'Swarry' is a humorous corruption of soirée.

[3] Claire Lynch, *Irish Autobiography: Stories of Self in the Narrative of a Nation* (Bern and Oxford: Peter Lang, 2009), 9.

literature alongside the public examination curricula, in contrast to the secular state schools attended by most Protestant children, which usually taught only British history and English literature. For this reason the Catholic church 'provided a badge of identity, a stake in the community, for people who needed some guiding system they could fit into, to make sense of their lives', as Patricia Craig puts it in her memoir *Asking for Trouble* (2007).[4] Her recollection that 'Convents, nuns, priests, the Mass, indeed everything to do with Catholicism, were part of the social fabric of that time and utterly taken for granted'[5] echoes Polly Devlin's evocation of the all-embracing character of religion in her remote community of Ardboe on the edge of Lough Neagh: 'The myths, the secrecies, the pulls of history and our strivings to get free of any or all of it were surrounded by the biggest, most pervasive myth of all – our church and our religion.'[6]

The fortifying power of Catholicism against social and cultural isolation is particularly prominent in Denis Donoghue's *Warrenpoint* (1990), his account of his boyhood between 1930 and 1944, when his father was an RUC police sergeant in the eponymous Co. Down town. In this complex and self-reflexive text, Donoghue merges his own alienation with that of his father, who is the overarching figure in his austere life. This estrangement is grounded in the unwanted circumstances of Sergeant Donoghue's relocation from the South and his awkward position in 'an obviously Protestant organization' whose 'chief aim' was 'to keep Catholics in check'.[7] This sense of apartness was reinforced by the family's own determination to minimize contacts with local Protestants and by a conviction that it was a 'social necessity' to be able tell a Protestant from a Catholic, even when locally there was 'no enmity' between them.[8] Within this negatively conceived environment, Donoghue saw in his father – 'Physically upright, morally upright: he walked the streets as he walked through life, straight ahead, knowing at any moment where he was going and why'[9] – the embodiment of many of the securities and assurances he also found in Catholicism. In a remarkable summative passage, he declares:

> I felt that my father was not only a strong man but the source of strength for me. Not strength to be developed in me by conflict. He was to me an

---

[4] Patricia Craig, *Asking for Trouble: The Story of an Escapade with Disproportionate Consequences* (Belfast: Blackstaff Press, 2007), 57.
[5] Ibid., 47.   [6] Polly Devlin, *All of Us There* (Belfast: Blackstaff Press, 1994), 23.
[7] Denis Donoghue, *Warrenpoint* (London: Jonathan Cape, 1991), 10.
[8] Ibid., 46–47. Patricia Craig expresses incomprehension at Donoghue's complete sense of estrangement from Protestants. See *Asking for Trouble*, 68.
[9] Ibid., 83.

example, an image; it was sufficient that I contemplated it, and not at all necessary for me to vie with his power. Merely by looking at him or by watching him as he crossed the square, I saw that it was possible to be fearlessly large in the world. I imitated him, as a devout Christian lives by imitating Christ, not by challenging his authority or strutting in his presence.[10]

Reverence and respect are perhaps more evident here than love or even affection, and these feelings also characterize the author's disposition towards the doctrines and teachings of the Catholic church, which he was not inclined to question or challenge. 'The dogmatic character of the Church was what most fully satisfied me', he declares, precisely because it 'did not consult my interests', and he acknowledges his 'exotic pleasure' in the very words of the Mass although he did not comprehend them.[11] Thus Donoghue reconstructs his dependence on unquestioning belief in the verities represented by his father and embodied in the church, to counterbalance all that was unsatisfactory about life in Warrenpoint. 'Mine', he adds, 'was the intelligence that comes after.'[12]

That 'intelligence' enters the book in the numerous reflections on literature, religion, philosophy and history which make *Warrenpoint* much more than an account of boyhood. Furthermore, given its composition during the Troubles, and its pointed commentary on them, it is particularly pertinent to bear in mind Susan Engel's contention that 'The remembering self is always a person in a specific situation, remembering for a particular reason.'[13] The roots of Donoghue's hostility to the 'artifice' of Northern Ireland may lie in his family, but it was reinforced at school by the Christian Brothers, who 'encouraged us to be spiritually and silently insurgent', 'to maintain a sense of Ireland' and 'above all to keep alive the great consanguinity between Ireland and the Catholic Church'.[14] While he accepts that such teaching is potentially inflammatory, Donoghue is much more critical of late twentieth-century revisionist readings of Irish history and literature: 'Social history is an attempt to remove from Irish history the glamour of its sacrifices and martyrdoms. Revisionism is a project of slow history, or confounding the drama, thwarting the narrative. Unfortunately, Ireland without its story is merely a member of the EC, the begging bowl our symbol.'[15] From a nationalist perspective, that 'story' remains unfinished while Ireland remains divided. In this context, therefore, it must be inferred that the *Irish Times*

---

[10] Ibid., 187–88. [11] Ibid., 63, 121, 70. [12] Ibid., 121.
[13] Susan Engel, *Context Is Everything: The Nature of Memory* (New York: W. H. Freeman, 1999), 86.
[14] Donoghue, *Warrenpoint*, 172, 151, 157. [15] Ibid., 172.

reports on a murderous Provisional IRA ambush of British soldiers beside Carlingford Lough in 1979 and a bomb attack aimed at Warrenpoint's heavily fortified police station in 1989, which are included without comment on the last two pages of the memoir, are Donoghue's final testimony to the failure of partition.

In *Voices and the Sound of Drums* (1981), Patrick Shea, who was also the son of a Southern Royal Irish Constabulary officer who moved north of the border, developed a very different view of Anglo-Irish and North-South relations. This is prefigured in his discrepant memories of the celebrations in the military town of Athlone when the Home Rule Bill was passed in 1914 and his family's detachment from the events that marked the establishment of the Irish Free State in 1922: 'Those who were putting up decorations, marching behind bands, waving green, white and orange tricolours represented something in which we had no part.'[16] Shea's strong belief that political violence is 'sinful and wrong' and religious intolerance unchristian came from his father. It shaped his view of the 1916 Rising and War of Independence, during which he feared for his father's safety, and made him 'an uncompromising, unapologetic West Briton'.[17] What perplexed him, therefore, when the family moved to the Protestant town of Rathfriland in Co. Down was the 'tribal feudalism' which made him feel 'out of harmony with those with whom I had come to make common cause' against republicanism.[18] Through his resistance to the conflation of religion and politics, and his rejection of the sectarian dimension of unionism resulting from its connection with the Orange Order, Shea challenges the 'divisive influence'[19] of religious prejudice, which he identifies as the bane of public and private life in Northern Ireland. In the same spirit, he refuses to view his own advancement in the civil service as 'a Catholic victory in a Protestant world',[20] seeing it instead as a recognition of merit, even though for many years his promotion to very senior positions was frustrated by the sectarianism of government ministers.

---

[16] Patrick Shea, *Voices and the Sound of Drums: An Irish Autobiography* (Belfast: Blackstaff Press, 1981), 74.

[17] Ibid., 31, 37.   [18] Ibid., 56.   [19] Ibid., 141.

[20] Ibid. Shea ended his career as only the second Catholic to achieve the rank of permanent secretary in the Northern Ireland civil service. In his penultimate chapter, he reproduces a memorandum he wrote in 1972, summarizing 'some of the issues which seemed to me to be important to an understanding of what have been called the two communities'. He contends that the unionists' failure of generosity in the postwar period forfeited Catholic goodwill, and is deeply critical of the influence of Orangeism on unionist party politics. With characteristic even-handedness, he is equally critical of Catholic suspicion and rejection of people like himself who were regarded as having gone over to the 'other side' by joining the civil service. See *Voices and the Sound of Drums*, 192–98.

The formative moral and social influence of Catholicism is particularly problematic for female autobiographers. *Asking for Trouble*, Patricia Craig's 'story of an escapade with disproportionate consequences', centres on the injustice of her expulsion from her Belfast convent school for allegedly provoking 'some previously chaste girls to assume an uncharacteristic licentiousness' at an Irish language school in Co. Donegal by circulating a copy of the novel *Peyton Place*.[21] Far from being rebellious or promiscuous, Craig humorously describes her prudish disincentives to the amorous advances of Donegal locals, prompted by her religiously inscribed fears of sex and disgrace. (Her contemporary, Derry-born Nell McCafferty, who also attended the Rannafast summer school, shared none of these anxieties and exuberantly records 'being danced off my feet every night by a boy, and the face kissed off me later in bed, by a girl'.[22]) Craig's perplexity at the readiness with which her guilt was assumed and judgement passed precipitates her interrogation of the moral and religious ethos of the church and of Catholic education in the 1950s. As she puts it:

> I am merely trying, I think, to get to grips, however partially, with a complex web of religious pressure, social expectation, nationalist truism, anti-feminist fabrication and all the rest of it – all the bits and pieces of a system which, at some deep level, placed us all in a faulty relation to nature and natural forces.[23]

Laura Marcus has written of the importance not only of 'Narrative, in the sense of recounting stories and the drive to narrate' in childhood autobiographies, but also of 'the charge attached to images and memories which stand out against the backdrop of the past'.[24] The undiminished 'charge' of Craig's memories decades later is self-evident, but time, maturity and experience now inform her attempts to articulate, comprehend and contextualize them. Yet the tentativeness and degree of hesitancy in some of the phrasing in the quotation above suggest that she is still circling her memories and seeking to clarify her purpose through what she calls 'deflected autobiography'.[25] Later in the text she is more assertive. She castigates the infantilizing power of the 'church fathers' who 'reserved to themselves the right to make judgements about what was, or was not,

---

[21] Craig, *Asking for Trouble*, vii.
[22] Nell McCafferty, *Nell: A Disorderly Woman* (Dublin: Penguin Ireland, 2005), 67. Lynch notes that McCafferty's account 'subvert[s] the stereotype of Gaeltacht holidays' associated with 'the promotion of traditional Irish values' (*Irish Autobiography*, 166).
[23] Craig, *Asking for Trouble*, 101.
[24] Laura Marcus, *Auto/biographical Discourses* (Manchester: Manchester University Press, 1994), 214.
[25] Craig, *Asking for Trouble*, 213.

suitable fodder for their dependents', and laments the fate of Northern children in the Catholic education system of the 1950s, who 'were at the mercy of educators who'd inherited the Church's whole package of pietistic hogwash' by which she herself was condemned.[26] However, even this re-evaluation is modified in Craig's final acknowledgement that her 'attitude to the puritan ethic' is 'less straightforward' than she had supposed, and that as a 'means of fending off anarchy it is not to be deplored'.[27] If this seems unexpected, it is also symptomatic of her surviving Catholic legacy of 'abundant anxieties' about sex and morality acquired in her childhood.[28]

Polly Devlin also interrogates the past she evokes in her recuperative account of childhood in countryside still almost untouched by modernity in the 1950s. She begins by suggesting the complexity of memory itself in a description of how 'a photograph held in my imagination' of the seven children in her family reveals itself to her in different ways. At first the children's expressions seem 'appealing, appeasing and eager', but then, as if altered by 'double exposure of the imagination', 'A look of travail seeps out from under those placatory expressions ... as though they had perceived already what the world had in store.'[29] This cross-fading of the innocence of the first vision into the premature experience of the second anticipates the various ways in which Devlin weighs recollections and thoughts against each other to enlarge her understanding of herself, her family and her community. So, for example, her initial feeling that formal studio portraits of the children show them in their 'most unfamiliar aspects' yields to a recognition that they disclose her mother's longing for her 'lost urban world' of social aspiration in Newry and Warrenpoint and 'a proper and conventional life' from which marriage into the 'left-over atavistic world' of Ardboe had removed her; and that insight in turn illuminates the strained dynamics of her parents' relationship and the burden of the children's undefined anxieties.[30]

As one of six sisters, Devlin is particularly exercised by the debilitating impact of the all-pervading conservative Catholic culture upon women. 'Effacement and quietness became equated with goodness', she writes; chastity was the supreme virtue, questions or challenges to authority were

---

[26] Ibid., 178, 179.   [27] Ibid., 213.

[28] For another view of this, see McCafferty's comment on her feelings before the publication of *Nell*, in which she discusses her lesbian orientation: 'I was astonished to realise that the curse put upon me in the womb in 1944, by all religions and all societies worldwide then, had gone deep into me and not been exorcised' (425). The subtitle of her book wittily appropriates the Catholic church's designation of lesbians and homosexuals as 'intrinsically disordered'.

[29] Devlin, *All of Us There*, 9.   [30] Ibid., 18, 22.

discouraged, and the image of Mary at the foot of the cross waiting to receive the body of Christ was presented as 'the perfect role-model'.[31] In this oppressively anti-feminist environment, Devlin read the yearbooks which the family received from a relative in an American convent school as 'despatches from a dream world': here were lives characterized by opportunity, encouragement, self-assurance and self-confident sexuality, utterly unlike her own 'life-diminishing' education, but somehow still Catholic.[32] Yet just as she doubted the reality of the yearbooks, Devlin is wary of the bias and selectivity of memory itself, which threatens the reliability of any autobiographical project because it 'bolster[s] the idea you need to have to retain your current idea of yourself, distorting incidents to give your past the particular significance you have already endowed it with, as an explanation for your sense of grievance, your reactions, your strange ways of love and especially perhaps your search for consolation'.[33]

The specific influence of the church is much less evident in most Protestant life-writing, partly owing to the multiplicity of denominations and sects in the North and partly to the secular education of most Protestant children. Beyond this, however, Northern Protestantism is often equated with a particular version of history that valorizes the defence of liberty of conscience against Catholic authoritarianism rather than with a set of religious beliefs. John Boyd, for example, in *Out of My Class* (1985) questions why his maternal grandfather, 'a stalwart Protestant'[34] and an Orangeman who impressed upon him how King William III had saved Protestants from popery, rarely attended church; and Robert Greacen in *The Sash My Father Wore* (1997) tells how 'History meant Protestant history. Suffering and heroism meant that undergone by Protestants. There was never a whisper of the sixth-century Derry that had become a great centre of missionary zeal, long before we Scots-Irish settled there.'[35] The austerity of Presbyterianism led Walter Ellis to complain in *The Beginning of the End* (2006) about the lack of a sense of mystery, while the exciting combination of theatricality, sensation, rhetorical preaching and dramatic personal testimony in evangelical Protestantism captured the attention of John Young Simms, author of *Farewell to the Hammer: A Shankill Boyhood* (1992) and Robert Harbinson Bryans, author of the autobiographical quartet *No Surrender: An Ulster Childhood* (1960), *Song of Erne* (1960), *Up Spake the Cabin Boy* (1961) and *The Protégé* (1963), which he published under the name Robert Harbinson.

[31] Ibid., 130–31.   [32] Ibid., 148.   [33] Ibid., 152.
[34] John Boyd, *Out of My Class* (Belfast: Blackstaff Press, 1985), 19.
[35] Robert Greacen, *The Sash My Father Wore* (Edinburgh: Mainstream Publishing, 1997), 10.

Harbinson's expansive account of his youthful involvement with evangelical groups in both Ireland and Britain is an idiosyncratic blend of self-
mockery and self-fascination with his own immersion in gospel hall
religion and mission preaching. Through such immersion this only son
of a widowed mother in a poor part of east Belfast discovered a sense of
identity, belonging and status. So, for example, wearing the uniform of the
Church Lads' Brigade, he remembers how 'such smart clothes carrying at
once a sense of power and superiority and expressing the feelings of
belonging to a body corporate, could not fail to raise my strongest emotions'.[36] The rhetoric and atmosphere when individuals were called to
salvation fed those emotions further, encouraging Harbinson himself to
begin preaching. Through the crowded and increasingly bizarre events that
follow, he represents the growth of his precocious self-importance and
dogmatic arrogance, and of his manipulative, hypocritical and self-deceiv-
ing behaviour, which was often motivated by sexual desire. The resulting
text is a hybrid mix of confessional autobiography and picaresque adventure, but another story underlies and complicates Harbinson's flamboyant
reconstruction of his early life: that of a poorly educated, vulnerable boy
raised on the narrow myths of Protestantism and an anti-Catholicism
absorbed from Orange songs and slogans, living turbulently and largely
unsupported by adults through his adolescent years, and profoundly
affected by his wartime evacuation to a denominationally mixed rural
community in Co. Fermanagh, where he discovered that Catholics were
not the 'incarnate devils'[37] he had imagined. Furthermore, his multi-
volume autobiography covers less than twenty years and ends with the
author severing his church relationships and departing for Canada. By
implication, this also marks his rejection of the identity he had constructed
for himself within evangelicalism and gives no indication of what will
replace it. 'At seventeen I could never resist the opportunity of investing life
with a dramatic value it did not possess in reality',[38] he observes. Such
judgements give his autobiography its colourful narrative vitality, but,
more tellingly, they show the retrospective critical self-knowledge that
saves it from its own extravagance.

If Harbinson's future sense of identity is uncertain, Geoffrey Beattie's
Protestant Boy (2004) follows an opposite trajectory. Beattie grew up in a
working-class area of north Belfast known as the murder triangle during

---

[36] Robert Harbinson, *No Surrender: An Ulster Childhood* (London: Faber and Faber, 1960), 58.
[37] Robert Harbinson, *Song of Erne* (London: Faber and Faber, 1960), 194.
[38] Robert Harbinson, *The Protégé* (London: Faber and Faber, 1963), 129.

the Troubles. Unlike many of his boyhood friends, he avoided the lure of paramilitarism by gaining a place at grammar school and going to university in England, where he has since had a distinguished academic career. In his autobiography, his visits home to his widowed and increasingly frail mother make him reflect on how his family and working-class background have shaped his life, but it is her accusation that he has 'turned into one of those English snobs'[39] that prompts his exploration of Protestant identity. 'I have always felt myself to be an Ulsterman, a Protestant Ulsterman', he writes. 'But this, I must say, is a private, slightly vague feeling rather than a conscious and clear sense of identity.'[40] Beattie regards his own vagueness as symptomatic of the wider uncertainties of Protestants in the context of the Troubles, and contrasts Catholics' apparent certainty about their national identity with 'we Protestants', who 'just wanted the status quo, . . . to stay British'.[41] His quest is therefore both personal and social, and this is reflected in the book's structure.

Beattie uses his own memories and discoveries about previous generations of his family to construct a history of his ancestors and their lives in Ulster, which he juxtaposes with a record of the Battle of the Somme and reflections on its emotional and psychological legacy. For those who survived, it was an unspeakable memory, but for their Ulster Protestant descendants it has become the defining example of courageous patriotic sacrifice, appropriated by the latter-day Ulster Volunteer Force 'in order to sanction their own actions in a very different sort of combat'[42] and invoked by those who protested annually against the banning of an Orange march to the church at Drumcree in the 1990s. These personal and public explorations of Protestant history synthesize in the 'iconic' sight of three elderly Orangemen on parade:

> There was a look of quiet pride and determination on their faces. It was the dignity of the look as much as anything that affected me emotionally . . . It said something about thrift and hard work and self-reliance, something about strength and resilience. It was the Somme all over again, right in my face, and a memory of a family in the 1960s living in a damp, condemned house in North Belfast, a family who just got on with life without excuses and without any help from anyone else, and a mother who went to Ewart's

---

[39] Geoffrey Beattie, *Protestant Boy* (London: Granta, 2005), 6.   [40] Ibid., 9.

[41] Ibid., 9, 10. Protestant loyalty is to Britain and the monarchy, not to England. Beattie's mother is insulting him when she says he has become English. Walter Ellis makes a similar point in *The Beginning of the End*, noting that his parents did not visit England until he was a teenager, and were distrustful of its foreignness and possible degeneracy. In contrast, they regarded the Irish Republic as their natural hinterland and regularly holidayed there.

[42] Ibid., 126.

Mill every day for her children, without making a song and dance about it, to make things better. And I was just immensely proud for that moment. I simply felt tremendously privileged to be who I was. Not English, not Scottish, not even Irish. Just an Ulster Prod.[43]

This secular vision grounds Ulster Protestant identity in attributes of character and a proudly self-sufficient attitude in the face of life's hardships and sufferings. Beattie recognizes that these are equally embodied in the Orangemen who resolutely defy age and infirmity to commemorate a legacy of courage and sacrifice, and in people like his own mother whose family stories of hard work and stoical resourcefulness are inseparable from the larger history of Ulster. This realization satisfies his personal quest for a confident understanding of his Ulster Protestant identity, but it begs the question of how it affects his perception of the relationship between the two Northern communities.

Unsurprisingly, many recent Northern political autobiographies foreground their authors' involvement in events associated with the Troubles. Michael Kenneally has argued that political autobiographies 'would more accurately be described as memoirs' because they record the individual's public life, whereas autobiographies are 'ultimately focused inward to subjective states and feelings, to one's past relationship with reality, and, now, to one's contemporary conception of those former selves'.[44] Paddy Devlin's *Straight Left: An Autobiography* (1993), Maurice Hayes's *Minority Verdict: Experiences of a Catholic Public Servant* (1995) and Austin Currie's *All Hell Will Break Loose* (2004) exemplify Kenneally's conception of memoir.[45] Hayes's record of his career in public service offers a highly individual commentary on many leading personalities and events in the government of Northern Ireland, particularly from the late 1960s until his retirement in 1993.[46] Currie and Devlin began from rural nationalist and urban Labour backgrounds respectively. They became founder members of the Social Democratic and Labour Party, which formed the parliamentary opposition to the governing Unionist Party until the Stormont parliament

---

[43] Ibid., 223.

[44] Michael Kenneally, 'The Autobiographical Imagination and Irish Literary Autobiographies', in Michael Allen and Angela Wilcox, eds., *Critical Approaches to Anglo-Irish Literature* (Gerrards Cross: Colin Smythe, 1989), 112–13.

[45] Hayes has also published two volumes of autobiography which give highly evocative accounts of life in Killough and Downpatrick in the 1930s and early 1940s: *Sweet Killough, Let Go Your Anchor* (Belfast: Blackstaff Press, 1994) and *Black Puddings with Slim: A Downpatrick Boyhood* (Belfast: Blackstaff Press, 1996).

[46] This contrasts with Patrick Shea's *Voices and Drums*, which combines personal history and self-reflection with an account of the author's experiences in the civil service.

was prorogued in March 1972 and direct rule imposed from Westminster, and went on to participate in the ill-fated power-sharing executive of 1974. Both wrote after their active political lives had ended, but their aim, which is perhaps common to all political autobiographies, was not only to provide insight and personal testimony for future students of the period but also to influence the judgements that will be made of their parts in it. However, the sheer volume of detail they include about their political activities leaves little room for them to develop their powerful embryonic stories of the immense personal dangers, courage and costs to family they endured in the exceptional circumstances of the time. Susan Engel's observation that 'It is the experience of lives we want to know about more than the facts of the life'[47] highlights a problem with this kind of autobiographical writing and identifies what one misses most in the accounts of Currie and Devlin.

This issue presents itself in another way in the work of Gerry Adams. Unlike the post hoc accounts of Currie and Devlin, Adams wrote while he was shaping both his own future and that of his party, Sinn Féin, as it moved towards participation in constitutional politics. Again, there are multiple accounts of meetings, alliances, disagreements, work done to assist beleaguered families, brutality inflicted by police and army, violent deaths and so on, but as Roy Foster has argued, the evasions and lacunae surrounding the subject himself are problematic.[48] Attempts to introduce a personal or human dimension through reconstructed conversations (with family, between rioters, with members of the security forces), anecdotes and excerpts from his earlier fiction are 'made to serve as a means of validating a particular ideology'[49] and seem merely contrived or clichéd. Thus, for example, during an army house search accompanied by screaming soldiers and gunfire, Adams whispers to his girlfriend, Colette McArdle: 'If we get out of this, I'm going to marry you.'[50] Meanwhile the silence surrounding the key question of the relationship between the Provisional IRA and Sinn Féin, and Adams's own role in it, might seem to follow Peter Lombard's advice to Hugh O'Neill in Brian Friel's 1989 play *Making History*, on the political value of telling a selective version of events: 'People think they just

[47] Engel, *Context is Everything*, 98.
[48] R. F. Foster, 'Selling Irish Childhoods: Frank McCourt and Gerry Adams', in *The Irish Story: Telling Tales and Making It Up in Ireland* (London: Allen Lane/Penguin, 2001), 164–86. See also, Stephen Hopkins, 'Fighting Without Guns?: Political Autobiography in Contemporary Northern Ireland', in Liam Harte, ed., *Modern Irish Autobiography: Self, Nation and Society* (Basingstoke: Palgrave Macmillan, 2007), 176–96.
[49] Liam Harte, 'Introduction: Autobiography and the Irish Cultural Moment', in Harte, ed., *Modern Irish Autobiography*, 11.
[50] Gerry Adams, *Before the Dawn: An Autobiography* (Dingle: Brandon Press, 1996), 158.

want to know the "facts"; they think they believe in some sort of empirical truth, but what they really want is a story.'[51]

There is no such calculated cautiousness in Bernadette Devlin's *The Price of My Soul*, published in 1969, months after her election to the House of Commons at the age of twenty-one, which attracted international attention. The briskness with which she announces her aims – 'to explain how the complex of economic, social, and political problems of Northern Ireland threw up the phenomenon of Bernadette Devlin' and to 'put the real flesh-and-blood Bernadette on record'[52] – shows her overt political purpose. Because of her youth, Devlin's experience before 1968 was largely defined by her strong family relationships and in particular by the impact of the premature deaths of both her parents, which left her caring for younger siblings while she was a student at university in Belfast. She conveys the realities of having little money and limited employment opportunities, especially for someone like her father who had to work in England because he had been classified as a political suspect. The tensions with her forceful grandmother, who believed her equally strong-willed daughter had married beneath her, introduced her also to the divisiveness of class prejudice. In these circumstances, Devlin forms the view that 'If it hadn't been for the fact that I had an essentially Christian background from my mother, poverty would have made me bitter rather than socialist, and what I knew of politics would have made me a mad Republican.'[53] Her socialism was reinforced by an early realization that poor Protestants and Catholics were in an equally parlous situation, and that unionist and nationalist politicians alike used 'religion to divide and rule the working class',[54] a perception that led to her later disagreements with the Civil Rights Association, which she accused of foregrounding Catholic deprivation. Above all, it is the phenomenon of Devlin's precociously rapid political education and radicalization, from her participation in the first civil rights march in August 1968 to the 'Battle of the Bogside' twelve months later, that energizes her autobiography and invests it with personal experiential interest. This energy is vividly present in Devlin's sweeping claims, naïve confidence and intermittent arrogance, as illustrated by her comment on the fighting in Derry in August 1969: 'In fifty hours we brought a government to its knees, and we gave back to a downtrodden

[51] Brian Friel, *Making History* (London: Faber and Faber, 1989), 66.
[52] Bernadette Devlin, *The Price of My Soul* (London: André Deutsch and Pan Books, 1969), unpaginated foreword.
[53] Ibid., 29.   [54] Ibid., 57.

people their pride and the strength of their convictions.'[55] However over-simplified this seems, Devlin generates an unusually powerful sense of how things looked to her at a specific moment, unqualified by the complications of hindsight and the second thoughts that characterize most political autobiographies.

Near the conclusion of *The Beginning of the End*, Walter Ellis suggests that although he was not personally abused as a child, 'the entire society in which I grew up was abused, causing me, like everyone else, to see life through a jagged and peculiar prism'.[56] Recent autobiography from Northern Ireland gives wide support to this claim. Although most of the books under consideration here centre on periods before the onset of the Troubles in the late 1960s, many were written against that background. All of them reveal the extent to which Catholics and Protestants lived separate lives in which mutual ignorance and suspicion were commonplace and where interdenominational friendships rarely formed part of childhood experience. These weaknesses in Northern society were underpinned by partition and exacerbated by their calculated exploitation within both Protestant and Catholic communities by vested interests and competing political agendas. This in itself was an abuse for, as Polly Devlin observes: 'All children born in segregated places are born with a dark soul, a web of ambiguities around them, from which it is difficult to struggle free.'[57] Paradoxically, it is that struggle to be free, whether from the religious, moral, political or cultural legacies and prejudices that have bedevilled life in Northern Ireland, which empowers the region's best autobiographical writing.

Further reading

Engel, Susan. *Context is Everything: The Nature of Memory*. New York: W. H. Freeman, 1999.

Foster, R. F. *The Irish Story: Telling Tales and Making It Up in Ireland*. London: Allen Lane/Penguin, 2001.

Harte, Liam, ed. *Modern Irish Autobiography: Self, Nation and Society*. Basingstoke: Palgrave Macmillan, 2007.

---

[55] Ibid., 205. Devlin's comment finds an echo in Nell McCafferty's observation that in the fighting in the Bogside in 1968, in which she was a participant, 'Generations of pent-up humiliation were unleashed in a show of rage that night. It felt completely, inexplicably right. I felt completely at home' (*Nell*, 124).

[56] Walter Ellis, *The Beginning of the End: The Crippling Disadvantage of a Happy Irish Childhood* (Edinburgh: Mainstream Publishing, 2006), 239.

[57] Devlin, *All of Us There*, 161.

Kenneally, Michael. 'The Autobiographical Imagination and Irish Literary Autobiographies', in Michael Allen and Angela Wilcox, eds., *Critical Approaches to Anglo-Irish Literature*. Gerrards Cross: Colin Smythe, 1989: 111–31.

Lynch, Claire. *Irish Autobiography: Stories of Self in the Narrative of a Nation*. Bern and Oxford: Peter Lang, 2009.

Marcus, Laura. *Auto/biographical Discourses*. Manchester: Manchester University Press, 1994.

CHAPTER 19

The Irish Travel Memoir I
Journeys within Ireland

Glenn Hooper

Defined as a hybrid literary form, the travel narrative has long been identified as a blend of journalism, ethnography and memoir. In a time of increasing literary experimentation and demands from readers for more diverse, open-ended forms of writing, the integration of disparate forms has proved to be one of its greatest strengths. In the stir of its woven elements, in the interface between the narrative threads it commonly employs, lies an appeal that for many readers remains undiminished. However, while a good deal of the popularity of travel writing resides in the supple nature of its composition, much of its specific appeal is surely found in the autobiographical, in those digressionary textual moments when the author discloses a sense of self, whether discomfited, watchful, divided, traumatized or liberated. In an era of globalization and no-frills air travel, when many of us in the West are well enough travelled to know about the vicissitudes of coping with alterity, and when dedicated news coverage is instantly and universally available, we might say that the testimony of the traveller compels more than that of the ethnographer or journalist. For all the interesting cultural and topographical detail in works such as Ted Simon's *Jupiter's Travels* (1979), William Least Heat-Moon's *Blue Highways* (1982) or Jonathan Raban's *Coasting* (1987), it is their narrators' inner disclosures that are the most engaging, even when the stories they tell are of failed or troubled relationships, of selves fractured and dissolving amidst a world of strangers. Even in this era of ubiquitous social media we seem more drawn to the lives of others than ever before. The television programmes that feed off a hunger for revelation and display or a passion for local history, heritage and genealogical data – not to mention the proliferation of autobiography, memoir and life-writing – are an implicit response to, as well as a reflection of, this evolving process. To the question, 'who do you think you are?' we might truthfully answer: 'I don't know, but does it really matter?'

Although it is tempting to begin a discussion of the autobiographical strain within Irish-centric travel writing with a landmark modern text such as Sean O'Faolain's *An Irish Journey* (1940), an examination of earlier writings, especially those that sought to understand Ireland and explain it to others, reaps rich dividends. John Gamble's *A View of Society and Manners in the North of Ireland in the Summer and Autumn of 1812* (1813), for example, specifically addressed the English reader 'by hasty sketch, by short tale, and brief dialogue, rather than formal dissertation ... to make better known to the inhabitants of England a people well deserving to be known'.[1] A free-thinking Presbyterian and medic from Co. Tyrone, Gamble based himself around his home town of Strabane, from where he made several sorties into neighbouring towns and villages, occasionally interacted with his Irish-speaking Catholic compatriots and hinted at a simmering political disquiet. Writing in the shadow of the 1798 uprising, Gamble chose the ordinary over the picturesque and focused on a part of Ireland where evidence pointed to inequality, division and unrest. Gamble was no cheerleader for Catholicism, yet a common decency and honesty (qualities not always in evidence among travel writers) readily prevailed and led him to question why 'the feelings of the Catholics [should] be tortured, and their pride wounded, by seeing all greatness in the hands of rivals, who form so inconsiderate a part of the population'.[2] In his second instalment, dated 1819, Gamble suggests that autobiographical revelation can bring the characteristics of the wider community into view when he explains that he knows no better way to describe his countrymen 'than by an unreserved display of my own feelings, and by shewing myself as I am'.[3] Any attempt to eradicate subjective opinion in the name of a putative objectivity is therefore rejected. The very nature of the travel format, and the close affinity it facilitates between the writing self and the observed other, makes 'some interminglement of self ... unavoidable'.[4]

If Gamble was a relatively straightforward figure, imbued with a sense of duty to convey the complexities of Ireland's north-west to an English readership, then Caesar Otway was an altogether more contentious observer in the context of nineteenth-century Ireland. Associated with the evangelical wing of the Church of Ireland, a friend of William Carleton

---

[1] John Gamble, *A View of Society and Manners in the North of Ireland in the Summer and Autumn of 1812* (London: C. Cradock and W. Joy, 1813), v.
[2] Ibid., 394.
[3] John Gamble, *Views of Society and Manners in the North of Ireland, in a Series of Letters Written in the Year 1818* (London: Longman, Hurst, Rees, Orme and Brown, 1819), v.
[4] Ibid.

and a brusque and difficult narrator, Tipperary-born Otway travelled to the west and north-west of Ireland less for its scenic attractions than for comic relief and political advantage. In Donegal, a place even now associated with a certain earthy and dishevelled charm, he was moved to praise and compassion at the site of a village 'composed entirely of Protestants . . . a fine race of men, a fair family of women, decently clad, sufficiently fed'.[5] The neighbouring Catholic community, however, represent 'a most bigoted and superstitious race, given up to will-worship and saint adoration', and produce only trenchant and loathsome disavowal.[6] It is not just that representations such as these must have appeared clumsy even to early nineteenth-century readers, but that the reiteration of long-held and apparently intractable views of the native Irish has made it all but impossible to consider them in any meaningful way. Fixed and known, Catholics are here presented as an unchanging category of people that requires no further thought or evaluation. So whereas Gamble registers a degree of complexity and is conscious of competing ideologies and the need to preserve balance, Otway wavers only between hostility and dismissal. And where Gamble's sense of self is at times tenuous, marked by a heightened sense of vulnerability and a need for deeper understanding of his compatriots, Otway's subjectivity is robustly constructed and seemingly unconcerned with ecumenical and ethnographic niceties.

It might be said of Otway that the more he contemplated Irish Catholicism the more certain he became of his own Protestant identity, a confirmation that demanded even greater corroboration of his sense of authority. For example, in his *A Tour in Connaught* (1839), he describes himself as not only a 'native' but as someone who has 'made the history, antiquities, traditionary lore, and social relations of the island, his study'.[7] Here is a narrator who presents himself as being confidently at the centre of Irish life, to whom the reader can turn for definitive commentary. Ireland might be less exotic and easier to access, admits Otway, but the fashion for continental travel as the epitome of sophisticated self-discovery is overstated. Moreover, the anthropological potential of Ireland lends texture of a sort not always found elsewhere in the British Isles. But if the Irish are a known entity to Otway, others are less secure in their pronouncements. When we look to Gamble we are struck by an air of ambivalence and a

---

[5] Caesar Otway, *Sketches in Ireland: Descriptive of Interesting, and Hitherto Unnoticed Districts, in the North and South* (Dublin: W. Curry, 1827), 100.

[6] Ibid., 101.

[7] Caesar Otway, *A Tour in Connaught: Comprising Sketches of Clonmacnoise, Joyce Country, and Achill* (Dublin: W. Curry, 1839), vi.

distinct lack of fixity, especially when it comes to matters of ethnic identity. In his *Views of Society and Manners in the North of Ireland, in a Series of Letters Written in the Year 1818* (1819), Gamble wrote of the differences then existing in Ulster, where the Irish and the Scots were 'in some degree intermingled', where 'Irish vivacity [had] enlivened Scotch gravity' and where 'Irish generosity [had] blended with Scotch frugality' to form 'a third character', which he says is not necessarily 'better than either, but certainly different from both'.[8] Neither one thing nor another, the Northerner is here described as the very embodiment of hybridity, the ethnically and culturally mixed product of very specific social and historical circumstances.

Accounts of travel within Ireland by Irish Protestants continued throughout the nineteenth century; whether this was because of a greater acceptance of a form of witness or testimonial writing among Protestant authors or because of a heritage that positioned them as Irish yet somewhat removed from the Irishness of the majority Catholic population is difficult to say. Amidst the turmoil of agrarian unrest and politically motivated violence in the 1870s and 1880s stand figures such as William O'Connor Morris, a landlord and county court judge, who from his estate in Tipperary produced *Letters on the Land Question of Ireland* (1870). Moving around the country, usually by train, O'Connor Morris proves a thoughtful and intelligent narrator and, unlike many who theorized about Irish difficulties, displays a keen sense of duty and an understanding of land-related issues, including its usage, variability and potential for reform. But more than the scrupulous agricultural gaze he turned upon the land-scape there emerges from his text a demonstrative sense of self. Indeed, no one is more confident of his abilities or of the importance attached to his self-appointed role than the author himself, as his insistent egoism attests ('I venture to make . . .', 'I have long managed . . .', 'I have endeavoured to see . . .'[9]). It is hardly surprising that he later committed himself to a formal autobiography, *Memories and Thoughts of a Life* (1895), in which his views about the country are set against a protracted and exhaustive discussion of his ancestry, upbringing and professional calling, all of which, as in *Letters on the Land Question of Ireland*, allowed for an existential and historical reappraisal, periodically played out in the form of a tottering and one-sided dialogue:

---

[8] Gamble, *Views of Society and Manners in the North of Ireland*, iv.

[9] William O'Connor Morris, *Letters on the Land Question of Ireland* (London: Longmans, 1870), viii.

'Ireland', Mr. Parnell has said, 'is a nation;' 'Ireland', Mr. Gladstone chimes in, has 'a right to satisfy her national aspirations and hopes;' and on these grounds there must be an Irish Parliament, and an Irish executive dependent on it. But Ireland is in no sense 'a nation;' Ireland has no 'national aspirations and hopes,' as every real student of history knows; and the assumption, therefore, completely fails, on which the demand for Home Rule is preferred.[10]

What every real student should also know is that Irish history, in particular, is all too easily shaped to a political agenda, and it is unhelpful to insist that historical understanding be based upon personal experience or memory, for we know that the latter is unreliable and provides only impressionistic traces. Not only do we remember what we wish to remember, but as often as not the memories we most cherish are subjectively captured, cropped and augmented. Therefore, any attempt to make memory more dependable, to ensure a greater degree of accuracy, has only a modest chance of success. Moreover, if both travel writing and autobiography are notoriously unreliable, and memory, the very thing necessary for their composition, a precarious construct, how then does the travel memoir, a non-fictional work seemingly aligned to 'truth', succeed at all? More specifically, how did it win over the nineteenth-century observer who, unlike contemporary readers with their educated awareness of blended and malleable literary forms, read in the expectation of honest and accurate representation? We have seen that Caesar Otway indulged in a form of caustic-cum-comic narration, despite his simultaneous demand to be taken seriously as a commentator on Irish affairs. The more balanced writings of Gamble and O'Connor Morris might have had greater appeal, especially to British readers who would have seen them as possessing privileged local knowledge. But what about the production of Irish travel writing in the late nineteenth and early twentieth centuries, a time of increasing levels of mobility and of great political and social change? What challenges did Ireland pose to the new generation of travel writers? And did the implied (English) reader remain as before?

Late nineteenth-century Irish travel writing was situated in relation to a number of national and transnational influences. On the one hand, the late 1880s and 1890s saw European powers dramatically extend and consolidate their colonial operations in Africa, facilitated by the Berlin Conference of 1884–85, which led to an increased interest in exploration, greater levels of transcontinental mobility and a public appetite for colonial writing,

---

[10] William O'Connor Morris, *Memories and Thoughts of a Life* (London: George Allen, 1895), 306.

including travelogues, guidebooks and diaries. On the other hand, Ireland was itself undergoing significant cultural change; there was growing nationalist sentiment, a renewed interest in Irish art and folklore and a drive to revivify the Irish language, then as now most widely spoken along the Atlantic seaboard. This was also a time in which travellers' interest in the country was strengthened by burgeoning cultural organizations such as the Irish Literary Society (founded 1892), the Gaelic League (founded 1893) and the Irish Literary Theatre (founded 1899), each of which helped to position Ireland as culturally important and distinctive from the rest of Britain. The prospect of encountering a different language, heritage and culture only hours from British shores proved attractive to many and had the added effect of increasing the demand for writings about the country, as visitors sought first-hand accounts of the finest Irish attractions, when to visit them and how to get there.

Three early twentieth-century texts, produced within five years of each other, helped define intranational travel writing about Ireland. William Bulfin's *Rambles in Eirinn* (1907), John Millington Synge's *The Aran Islands* (1907) and Robert Lynd's *Rambles in Ireland* (1912) did more than describe topographical features and archaeological sites; they brought the Irish themselves centre stage and gave validation and context to their lives. This ethnographic turn in Irish travel writing was particularly significant because it was produced at a time of increasing nationalist feeling and self-confidence, and so provided approval, if not outright legitimacy, for renascent cultural values. This is not to suggest that ethnographic portraiture, or a version of it, had not materialized in Ireland before the late nineteenth century. There were in fact many texts, including those by the likes of Otway, which wove into their coverage descriptions of native customs and religious beliefs. Insofar as some of these contained a crude proto-anthropological discourse, they echoed the derogatory assumptions of travel narratives produced under the aegis of late nineteenth-century European imperialism.[11] By contrast, Synge, Bulfin and Lynd were driven by a sympathetic curiosity towards their fellow countrymen and women.

One of the principal achievements of *The Aran Islands*, which Synge completed in 1901 but did not publish until April 1907, three months after the riot-provoking Abbey Theatre production of *The Playboy of the Western World*, lies in its capturing of a highly complex society at

---

[11] See Joan Pau Rubiés, 'Travel Writing and Ethnography', in Peter Hulme and Tim Youngs, eds., *The Cambridge Companion to Travel Writing* (Cambridge: Cambridge University Press, 2002), 242–60.

an auspicious moment in its development. Perched on the edge of Ireland, at the most westerly point of Europe, and splintered across islands with a singular and unforgiving landscape, the islanders shared ambitions very similar to those of today. Curious about the outside world and new technologies, and increasingly mobile and adaptive, they displayed a remarkable facility for accommodating themselves to the agents and forces of modernity. Indeed, despite his continuing interest in folklore, prehistoric ruins and the simplicity of island life, Synge was as much an agent of modernity as he was a celebrant of the primitive, and it is to his credit that he presented the islanders as singular, complex beings rather than ethnographic curiosities. Moreover, like all good modernists, Synge's self-presentation was one in which flux and uncertainty abounded. An ethnographer and sometime resident of the Continent, he also appeared to the islanders as a photographer, translator and stenographer, as well as a traveller and bringer of news from the Transvaal, Rome, Paris and Mainz. The opening pages of *The Aran Islands* do more than connect the reader to the world beyond the islands, however. Synge – a student Irish speaker from Wicklow, Protestant and educated – uses language as a way of infusing his narrative with a sense of the exotic. Unlike Bulfin's *Rambles in Eirinn*, where the native voice rarely intervenes and is subordinate to accounts of depopulated landscapes, language in *The Aran Islands* conveys the entirety of all that is unique about Synge's islanders. Indeed, no greater example of authenticity exists than in the mouths of others: 'I am in Aranmor, sitting over a turf fire, listening to the murmur of Gaelic that is rising from a little public-house under my room.'[12] Identified in the very first line of the text as being linguistically distinct, the islanders are all the more alluring for being citizens of the United Kingdom, only hours from Dublin, the second city of empire in the British Isles.

The emphasis placed upon the Irish language by Robert Lynd in his *Rambles in Ireland* serves a somewhat different purpose. Urbane and witty, Lynd was an Irish-speaking Belfast Protestant whose text, illustrated by Jack B. Yeats, celebrated the boisterous and lively scenes of provincial life to be found at the Galway races, the Lisdoonvarna matchmaking festival in Clare and the Puck Fair festival in Kilorglin in Kerry. However, Lynd was astute enough to know that a delicate balance had to be maintained between capturing change and recording the timeless uniqueness of

[12] J. M. Synge, *The Aran Islands* (London: Allen and Unwin, 1934), 1.

particular regions. What he therefore offered the reader was a more rounded version of Ireland than that found in many other texts. And for all the theatricality, fun and entertainment of certain of his portrayals, such as 'the boisterous and hospitable welcome'[13] that greeted him in Lisdoonvarna, there was a serious side to his analysis. A mere five pages into the text we find him not only speaking Irish with a hotel owner but establishing his political credentials as a Gaelic Leaguer. Later, he would prove dismissive of tourists in Kerry and foreground his religious identity – 'I am a Protestant of Protestants myself, and suspicious of any but simple services' – while at the same time warmly anticipating political independence: 'Dublin today is only leading a bath-chair existence compared to the leaping energy of life that will be hers when she is a capital in liberties and duties as well as in name. When the Irish Parliament is re-opened.'[14]

Thus, where Synge focuses on the minutiae of the Aran islanders' lives, from their food and clothing to their mythologies and ballads, Lynd paints in broader strokes, while preserving the ethnographic flavour that was so intrinsic to the Wicklow writer, in whose work quiet introspection and thoughtful contemplation of anticipated social change are to the fore. Whereas Synge focuses on linguistic distinctiveness to better understand his compatriots, Lynd accentuates it to advance a cultural and political agenda. But whatever the differences in emphasis, both writers employed a largely ethnographic analysis because it validated an emergent political and cultural philosophy to which they were aligned, because it allowed them to see native culture from the inside and because it enabled them, as Protestants, to feel a greater sense of self-identification with the country and its people. William Bulfin, a Catholic from the Irish midlands who returned in 1902 from an eighteen-year stay in Argentina, was probably better placed to feel confidence in his ability and right to speak for and about the 'ordinary' Irish. However, Bulfin's intense association with the Irish landscape also became a vehicle for settling scores and setting the story straight. No uneducated rustic shirking a challenge, Bulfin dismissed the commonplace and touristic in favour of byroads and lanes, his eye caught by the everyday and the apparently unremarkable.

The 1930s was a markedly productive era for travel writing, with 1936 setting a particularly high standard. Graham Greene, Robert Byron, Evelyn Waugh, W. H. Auden and Louis MacNeice all produced travel narratives that year, thus helping to position the form at the forefront of contemporary prose writing. There were other, more practical reasons for

---

[13] Robert Lynd, *Rambles in Ireland* (London: Mills and Boon, 1912), 179.   [14] Ibid., 271, 105.

the form's growing popularity, among them the technological changes that were transforming sea and air transport into glamorous enterprises and, more importantly, making travel to the farther reaches of the globe more realizable. It may appear somewhat surprising then that just as foreign travel was becoming easier and more enjoyable, the 'home tour' should develop so emphatically and successfully throughout the interwar period. For all the tales of exotic travel to the Far East and sub-Saharan Africa, an emerging interest in the local and the regional prevailed throughout these years and led many readers to acquaint or reacquaint themselves personally with parts of Britain and Ireland, a trend consolidated by texts such as H. V. Morton's *In Search of Scotland* (1929), J. B. Priestley's *English Journey* (1934) and George Orwell's *The Road to Wigan Pier* (1937). This increased affinity for, and accessibility of, home locales allowed many to respond in terms of self-exploration and a sharper engagement with the specificities of place, identity and home.

As a culture emphatically rooted in a sense of place, where regional distinctions were frequently pronounced and local loyalties loudly proclaimed, one wonders how Ireland fared during the 1930s and 1940s. Recently at war with Britain and with itself, and now partitioned and faced with the challenge of forging a new and inclusive identity, was the country still of interest to the twentieth-century traveller? Had the changes it had undergone made it a more compelling place to visit? More importantly, if it had historically proved to be something of a conundrum to many a British visitor, what did the Irish themselves now make of their country in such altered circumstances?

The new Ireland could be many things to many people: a partitioned island within the Atlantic archipelago; a recently independent nation state; a member of the British Commonwealth; an assemblage of regional identities. Rather like the memoir and the travelogue, this shifting entity required considerable readerly resources, not to mention imagination and patience, for it to cohere. Indeed, it might be argued that paraliterary forms such as memoir, autobiography and travel writing were ideally suited to the task of capturing the inconsistencies and disparities inherent in notions of self and nation. Certainly, Cork-born John Whelan knew a thing or two about the art of self-invention. The son of a Royal Irish Constabulary officer, Whelan was active in the IRA before he found literary fame in the 1930s as Sean O'Faolain. Already an established novelist and biographer, O'Faolain published an impressionistic travelogue in 1940 entitled *An Irish Journey*. The book's appearance coincided with his founding of *The Bell*, a literary and cultural journal, and with the early stages of a world war in which the Southern Irish state remained neutral. In the company of Belfast-born artist Paul Henry, O'Faolain travelled around the island, stopping to ruminate on topics such as the culture of tourism in Killarney and the industrial resources of Northern Ireland, all the while hoping 'to rediscover that simpler, more racy Ireland of the people'.[15] As this phrase suggests, his journey was shadowed by a tension between clashing versions of subjectivity and nationhood, a tension captured in his less than convincing claim to be no longer in thrall to the mystique of a mythic racial identity:

> I know that not for years and years did I get free of this heavenly bond of an ancient, lyrical, permanent, continuous, immemorial self, symbolized by the lonely mountains, the virginal lakes, the traditional language, the simple, certain, uncomplex modes of life, that world of the lost childhood of my race where I, too, became for a while eternally young.[16]

Over the past thirty years or so, travel writing has often been situated in relation to ideologies of European imperialism, and many critics, from Edward Said onwards, have looked to highlight and deconstruct the form's complicity in colonial discourse. Other critics such as Carl Thompson have viewed the form as inherently conservative and nostalgic, one that offers 'consoling, self-congratulatory' reassurances to its readership and typically seeks 'not to reflect or explore contemporary realities, but rather to escape them'.[17] While this may be true in the context of overseas travel, where ethnic and racial difference is more acute, the case is harder to make in relation to domestic travel. Without a clear sense of 'us' and 'them', and denied the creative and narrative possibilities that might be said to arise naturally from opposition and alterity, the writer must look elsewhere.

That several writers who covered the Northern Irish conflict chose the travel narrative as a way of engaging with the realities of violence, civil disturbance, sectarianism and collusion says much about the flexibility of the form. The 1950s and 1960s were rather dead decades for the Irish travel memoir, but from the mid-1970s, starting with Richard Howard Brown's *I Am of Ireland: An American's Journey of Discovery in a Troubled Land* (1974), there was a resurgence of interest, much of it centring on the North. Brown, an Irish-American who came to Northern Ireland in the aftermath of Bloody Sunday in January 1972, wrote about the trauma of the conflict as it was played out across the province. But reflections on

---

[15] Sean O'Faolain, *An Irish Journey* (London: Longman, Green, 1941), 13.   [16] Ibid, 136.
[17] Carl Thompson, *Travel Writing* (London: Routledge, 2011), 5.

subjectivity and affinity, and questions about the author's role as a reporter and witness, are also very much to the fore. 'The formation of an Irish identity, or perhaps better said, the identification of myself as Irish, was a gradual thing',[18] Brown admits, and became a shaping influence on his role as observer-cum-anthropologist amid the deprivation and despair of Derry. The 'discovery' that is referred to in Brown's subtitle is therefore as much metaphysical as literal, the turmoil on the streets paralleling his own internal struggle for identification and belonging: 'I'm Irish because of these people, a tenuous connection perhaps, but one that matters to me.'[19] These diasporic voices add greatly to the Irish travelogue tradition in terms of the personal experiences they reveal and because of the differently accented perspectives they bring to bear upon the country.

After Brown, most of the travel memoirists who chose to roam the Northern landscape were from the Republic. Irish but not Northern Irish, they were, in John Hewitt's words, 'not native here'[20] yet not fully foreign either. This outsider-insider status afforded them a distinctive perspective on the boarded-up houses and pervasive paranoia, but more importantly it allowed them the flexibility to distance themselves in the event of a crisis or challenge. In Dervla Murphy's *A Place Apart* (1978), which despite the passage of time still reads as a truly despairing narrative, we find one of the fairest and most detailed of all these texts. Murphy produced a work that was brave, at times foolhardy, yet always honest and driven by a conspicuous effort to understand the place and its people: 'Leaving the restaurant, I wondered why I was so pleased to be back in Belfast ... I realized then that respect is at the root of my affection for this least popular city in the British Isles.'[21] Her attempts to fathom the North fail, however. The only certainty to emerge from her travels is that the complexities of the place are not only incomprehensible but also seemingly intractable: 'At one stage I had hoped to be able to clarify the present Northern Irish turmoil for the ordinary citizens of Britain and the Republic. But the more time I spent up North the less capable I felt of doing any such thing.'[22] An equally despairing note is audible in Peter Somerville-Large's *The Grand Irish Tour* (1982), especially when the author visits Derry's Church of Ireland cathedral and the village of Eglinton on the city's outskirts, where he happens upon

[18] Richard Howard Brown, *I Am of Ireland: An American's Journey of Discovery in a Troubled Land* (Colorado: Rinehart, 1995), 17.
[19] Ibid., 26.
[20] John Hewitt, *The Collected Poems of John Hewitt*, ed. Frank Ormsby (Belfast: Blackstaff Press, 1991), 58.
[21] Dervla Murphy, *A Place Apart* (London: Penguin, 1979), 239.   [22] Ibid., 11.

ancestral memories. Whereas Murphy tries to delve beneath the topsoil of sectarianism in an attempt to comprehend peoples' fears and anxieties, Somerville-Large – who is seemingly more comfortable in the metaphorical company of earlier literary tourists such as Richard Pococke and William Makepeace Thackeray – appears to succumb to hopelessness: 'I retired to a cafe in Ship [sic] Street darkened by steel grilles before going down below the Diamond and the city walls to the bus station. Two small boys were inside a bus breaking up the seats.'[23]

This pervasive sense of bafflement and ironical disregard on the part of Southern Irish writers, which Dervla Murphy prophesized in the 1970s, is amplified in some travel memoirs of the 1980s. 'In Ireland, during recent years, many Southerners have been voicing anti-Northern sentiments with increasing vehemence and frequency', wrote Murphy, only two years after the Republic's Broadcasting Act was amended to ban the airing of interviews with spokespeople for named organizations linked to political violence. 'Some such outbursts may be excused on the grounds of frustration and despair but most, I fear, are symptoms of a spreading infection.'[24] The virus that Murphy identified, which was yet to morph into the phenomenon known as historiographical revisionism, would eventually find its way into much public discourse, though not everybody saw it in the same terms as Murphy. For a writer such as Colm Tóibín, author of *Walking Along the Border* (1987), this trend, which was reinforced and legitimized by academic debates and television documentaries, signalled a welcome change. Perhaps the North was too far gone for Tóibín to care or be fully disturbed by it. His sense of self seems to be more physically than metaphysically challenged on Northern soil: 'I bought a pamphlet with the Union Jack on the front of it, but I still felt that I looked like an outsider. I edged in against the wall, and stood with my back to a shop window.'[25] The immersive intensity of Murphy's inquiry, complete with sources, interviews and bibliography, is here replaced by a curiously detached persona. As Conor McCarthy suggests, what we find here is 'a mode of writing ... that aspires to neutrality or innocence, even. This is a highly debateable approach, since neither the context nor the narrative mode, nor space itself, are innocent or neutral.'[26]

[23] Peter Somerville-Large, *The Grand Irish Tour* (London: Hamish Hamilton, 1982), 253.
[24] Murphy, *A Place Apart*, 239, 11–12.
[25] Colm Tóibín, *Walking Along the Border* (London: Macdonald and Co, 1987), 100. This book was reissued as *Bad Blood: A Walk Along the Irish Border* in 1994.
[26] Conor McCarthy, 'Geographies of Liberalism: The Politics of Space in Colm Toibin's *Bad Blood: A Walk Along the Irish Border* and *The Heather Blazing*', in Glenn Hooper, ed., *Landscape and Empire, 1770–2000* (Aldershot: Ashgate, 2005), 210.

Like Somerville-Large, Rosita Boland's commitment in *Sea Legs: Hitch-Hiking the Coast of Ireland Alone* (1992) is to the whole island of Ireland, though the forty pages allocated to the North (which includes a two-page entry for the city of Derry, where, we are told, 'it rained and rained and rained'[27]) suggest that geopolitical and commercial considerations took precedence over a deep and sustained engagement with people and place. But it is ideology as much as form that aligns Boland with her mentor Tóibín, whom she thanks for reading her manuscript in full. There is a revealing mirroring of their respective journeys, particularly where geography and politics intersect. Whereas Tóibín encircles the North from its southern end by travelling along the border that separates it from the Republic, Boland navigates its northern flank, taking a coastal path that minimized the opportunities for human interaction. The perspective is the same, however. Seen as self-contained, hysterical and incoherent, the North appears as a no-go area. Despite the putative objectives of Tóibín and Boland, this is a place to be kept at a distance, one framed as a gothic nightmare that seems beyond understanding:

> As I passed a small bungalow which was just beside the road, a woman stood at the window with her back to me. There were no curtains on the window and I could see her clearly. As she turned she suddenly caught sight of me from the side of her eye and then with her full vision, she screamed at the top of her voice.[28]

That the Irish travel narrative-cum-memoir has been resuscitated in recent years is due in large part to the work of English-born second-generation Irish writers, many of whom are drawn to this impure form because of the greater latitude it gives them to probe the complexities of transnational belonging. Just as second-generation Irish people in Britain were in the vanguard of revitalizing indie music in the 1980s and alternative comedy in the 1990s, they also injected fresh vigour into a paraliterary form that has often thrived on controversy and irreverence. Behind the chatty humour of Pete McCarthy's *McCarthy's Bar: A Journey of Discovery in the West of Ireland* (2000), for example, lies a more profound engagement with notions of Englishness and Irishness, place and belonging, as when McCarthy's archaeological forays around west Cork prompt him to reflect: 'In the land of my birth I feel detached: an outsider, an observer, in some way

[27] Rosita Boland, *Sea Legs: Hitch-Hiking the Irish Coast Alone* (Dublin: New Island Books, 1992), 134.
[28] Tóibín, *Walking Along the Border*, 31.

passing through. But as soon as I hit the tarmac or the quayside over there, I feel involved, engaged – as if I've come home, even though I've never actually lived there.'[29] John Walsh explores similar thematic territory in *The Falling Angels: An Irish Romance* (1999), a memoir that subjects the meanings of 'home' for the second-generation Irish person to sustained interrogation.

In her critical discussion of women's life-writing, Victoria Stewart observes that while 'autobiography necessarily rests on the presumption that there is a coherent self which can be narrated',[30] such beliefs are seriously misguided. Roger Porter, in a suasive essay on the author's broader needs, argues that the principal aim of the autobiographer is to construct 'the self in the act of writing about it',[31] while John Barbour suggests that an 'important motivation for writing an autobiography is a person's need for further "self-invention"'.[32] Read in the light of these remarks, the second-generation Irish travel memoirist can be seen to be less involved in a speculative search for a sense of self derived from philosophically fashionable theories of agency than in an unassuageable quest for connection, for a sense of home. As Stanley Price writes at the end of *Somewhere to Hang My Hat: An Irish-Jewish Journey* (2002), reflecting on his own emigration and the 'endless departures' that Dublin Bay has witnessed:

> Now, when I am on the boat, sailing out through the open end of that horseshoe, I have the strange sensation of both going home and leaving home at the same time. My parents must have felt that way too on the countless times they passed this way. It is the divided self that haunts all expatriates and exiles. I seem to have inherited it. Even though my mother always said you must have somewhere to hang your hat, she herself ended up with at least two places. As for my own hat problem, I have finally resolved it, at least officially, by having two passports.[33]

If travel writing is indeed a set of paraliterary and social scientific discourses rather than a distinct literary category, then the travel memoir, as a strain within it, is no less contested or troubled. Described by Mary Jacobus as a

[29] Pete McCarthy, *McCarthy's Bar: A Journey of Discovery in the West of Ireland* (London: Hodder, 2000), 10.
[30] Victoria Stewart, *Women's Autobiography: War and Trauma* (London: Palgrave Macmillan, 2003), 21.
[31] Roger Porter, *Self-Same Songs: Autobiographical Performances and Reflections* (Lincoln: University of Nebraska Press, 2002), xiv.
[32] John Barbour, *The Conscience of the Autobiographer: Ethical and Religious Dimensions of Autobiography* (London: Macmillan, 1992), 9.
[33] Stanley Price, *Somewhere to Hang My Hat: An Irish-Jewish Journey* (Dublin: New Island Books, 2002), 237.

'mixed and transgressive genre', and regarded by Barbara Johnson as a 'monstrosity', autobiography, like the travelogue, sometimes struggles for critical acceptance.[34] However, as James Olney has argued, 'autobiography, in spite of – or more likely because of – its literary impurity and instability, has in recent years, become, paradoxically, something like the paradigmatic literary form'.[35] From this brief overview of some two hundred years of Irish travel memoir we can see that while certain key elements recur, the form has become increasingly engaged with the challenges of transculturation and living with otherness and difference. Brown, McCarthy and Price collectively engage with the specificities of being Irish, yet they do so from a removed perspective. So too does Annie Caulfield, author of *Irish Blood, English Heart, Ulster Fry: Return Journeys to Ireland* (2005). Aged four when she left Northern Ireland for England, Caulfield see-saws between jurisdictions, communities and religions, seeking through autobiography a route to increased, though never definitive, self-understanding: 'Geography. The world goes round, people move around and before they know it, time has passed and the place they left may no longer be a place they can go back to.'[36] It is arguably in its capacity to accommodate sustained reflection on such spatial and spiritual shifts that the greatest strength of the travel memoir resides.

Further reading

Colbert, Ben, ed. *Travel Writing and Tourism in Britain and Ireland*. Basingstoke: Palgrave Macmillan, 2012.

Harte, Liam, ed. *Modern Irish Autobiography: Self, Nation and Society*. Basingstoke: Palgrave Macmillan, 2007.

Hooper, Glenn and Leon Litvack, eds. *Ireland in the Nineteenth Century: Regional Identity*. Dublin: Four Courts Press, 2000.

Hulme, Peter and Tim Youngs, eds. *The Cambridge Companion to Travel Writing*. Cambridge: Cambridge University Press, 2002.

Noonan, James, ed. *Biography and Autobiography: Essays on Irish and Canadian History and Literature*. Ottawa: Carleton University Press, 1993.

Thompson, Carl. *Travel Writing*. London: Routledge, 2011.

---

[34] The views of Jacobus and Johnson are cited in Laura Marcus, 'Theories of Autobiography', in Julia Swindells, ed., *The Uses of Autobiography* (London: Routledge, 1995), 14.

[35] James Olney, 'On the Nature of Autobiography', in James Noonan, ed., *Biography and Autobiography: Essays on Irish and Canadian History and Literature* (Ottawa: Carleton University Press, 1993), 109.

[36] Annie Caulfield, *Irish Blood, English Heart, Ulster Fry: Return Journeys to Ireland* (London: Viking, 2005), 14.

CHAPTER 20

The Irish Travel Memoir II
Journeys beyond Ireland

Michael Cronin

Life as a journey is a standard trope of writing from the trials of Ulysses to the shipwreck of Crusoe. Departure, trials and return are convenient signposts of decision and transformation. Not surprisingly, the influential monotheisms in Western culture have had wanderers as leaders – Moses, Jesus and Mahomet. The spiritual journey of the pilgrim will in time morph into the secular odyssey of the traveller. In Ireland, the tradition of the *immrama* ('voyages'), the travel narrative that provides a vehicle for the adventures of pagan heroes and Christian saints, points to an indigenous template for the topic of travel as a mode of discovery and medium of metamorphosis. If the memoir tracks the shifting versions of self, it is only to be expected that travel accounts will figure prominently in the attempts by Irish selves over the centuries to capture what happens when the subject sets out on a journey to lands both known and unknown. Travels through the inner psychic landscapes of memory and recall parallel the travellers' recurrent discovery and, on occasions, reinvention of self as they come into contact with realities that challenge their sense of who they are and where they come from.

Immrama: early voyage narratives

The *immrama* provide an early example of the travel trope to describe a process of change. The most notable accounts are *Immram Brain maic Febail* ('Voyage of Bran son of Febal'), *Navigatio Sancti Brendani Abbatis* ('Voyage of St Brendan'; composed in Latin) and *Immram Curaig Máele Dúin* ('Voyage of the Curragh of Máel Dúin'). Although basically Christian in outlook, they combine elements from pre-Christian belief systems. For Bran, son of Febal, voyage becomes synonymous with promise after a strangely attired woman appears in his house in Dún Brain and begins to sing to him of an otherworld where there is no knowledge of death or decay.

On an island supported by four feet of white bronze and inhabited by 'many thousands of variegated women',[1] music fills the air and there is no gloom, sorrow or treachery. Bran sets off with a company of twenty-seven companions and eventually reaches the island of the women. Although initially reluctant to disembark, Bran and his fellow sailors are eventually brought to the island where they live a life of uninterrupted pleasure until one of their number, Nechtán mac Ala-Brain, becomes homesick. Ignoring the warnings of the women of the island that they should not set foot in Ireland, Bran and his comrades return to the island of their birth. They eventually come to Srúb Brain in Lough Foyle where, on being asked to identify themselves by the people assembled there, Bran is informed that he is only known to them because the 'voyage of Bran is in our ancient lore'.[2] When Nechtán is put ashore, he immediately turns to ashes. Several centuries have passed and the fate of Nechtán is the natural fate of any human in the normal passage of time. Bran remains in his boat to recite the account of his journey, then bids the company farewell and vanishes forever.

Bran's journey is not simply a trip into the unknown, with its catalogue of mishaps and marvels; it is also the uncovering of a bitter truth, that of mortality itself. Nechtán's demise is a graphic snapshot of a journey's end that is the one that awaits all human travellers. What the travellers pursue – the absence of death or decay – is what humans flee – gloom, sorrow, treachery. The escape is, of course, temporary as the closure of return unsettles the pieties of utopian longing. As Bran stands in his boat reciting the chronicle of his wanderings, the ashes of Nechtán are there to remind him that he cannot elude the hold of time. The *immram*, anticipating a classic trope of post-Romantic disappointment, brings the self back to the frontiers of the all too human. Insofar as memoir and memory are tightly bound, *Immram Brain maic Febail* suggests that if travel may be about wanting to forget, at journey's end the traveller will be reminded of what it is he or she wanted to leave behind, even if that means being remembered for failing to remember.

In *Immram Curaig Máele Dúin*, unusually for an early Irish prose tale, there is a statement regarding both authorship and the purpose of writing: 'Áed Find, chief sage of Ireland, arranged that story as it is here so that it might give mental pleasure to the kings and people of Ireland after him.'[3] If the story of Máel Dúin is about an attempt to avenge the circumstances

---

[1] Séamus Mac Mathúna, ed. and trans., *Immram Brain: Bran's Voyage to the Land of Women* (Tübingen: Niemeyer, 1985), 36.

[2] Ibid., 45.

[3] H. P. A. Oskamp, ed. and trans., *The Voyage of Mael Dúin* (Groningen: Wolters-Noordhoff, 1970), 178.

of the troubled birth of the eponymous hero, the resolution is not a dramatic bloodbath but an act of reconciliation and mercy. The primary purpose, however, is not moral instruction but, as the chief sage promises, entertainment. In other words, the thirty separate adventures recounted in the *immram* are justified in terms of their narrative appeal for a broad audience ('kings and people of Ireland'). The assertion of authorship and the stress on memorability ('after him') suggest even at this very early stage that travel can be both personalized (the account comes from the pen of a particular writer) and impersonalized (the journey told here can continue on in the minds of others long after the writer is dead and his journey over).

The *Navigatio Sancti Brendani Abbatis*, composed in Latin in the eighth century, either in Ireland or by an Irish monk on the European Continent, is a travel narrative that has enjoyed considerable success in both the original and in translation into a number of European languages. In recounting the epic voyage of Brendan to the 'land of promise of the saints',[4] the *Navigatio* firmly links the fate of the Kerry monk to the destiny of all Christians who set out on the journey of faith. The incident-strewn voyage is a spiritualized autobiography where Brendan is the archetypal Christian faced with a familiar mix of entitlement and entrapment. The narrative does not make the reader systematically privy to an internal psychological life of Brendan in the post-Romantic sense but he is clearly the focus of the account. Brendan is constantly addressing and reassuring his monk companions who are not quite as sanguine as their spiritual father in the face of the perils of the open sea and the unknown. When in one episode he meets an elderly hermit, 'Paul the Spiritual', clothed uniquely in the hair of his body and 'white as snow from old age', the narrator comments:

> St Brendan, observing this, was moved to grief, and heaving many sighs, said within himself, 'Woe is me, a poor sinner, who wears a monk's habit, and who rules over many monks, when I here see a man of angelic condition, dwelling still in the flesh, yet unmolested by the vices of the flesh'.[5]

Brendan has an emotional response to events on the trip ('heaving many sighs') and has an inner life ('said within himself') which reveals the tensions and self-examination brought on by his travel encounters. If the monks at the end give praise for the safe return of their patron to his monastery, they will also learn from Brendan 'all which he had seen or

---

[4] Carl Selmer, ed., *Navigatio Sancti Brendani Abbatis: From Early Latin Manuscripts* (Notre Dame: University of Notre Dame Press, 1959), 29.
[5] Ibid.

heard during his voyage'.[6] Though highly codified by the canons of Christian belief, the *Navigatio* nonetheless offers an important glimpse into the travel account as an early Irish parable of self-exploration.

Travel and conquest

The travel memoir as more conventionally understood emerged in the seventeenth century with the composition of Tadhg Ó Cianáin's diary account of the Flight of the Earls. Ó Cianáin was one of a select group of writers before the late nineteenth-century Literary Revival who kept diaries in the Irish language, the others being Tarlach Ó Mealláin, whose diary covers the years from 1641 to 1647, Cathal Ó Conchubhair (kept from 1736 to 1748) and Amhlaoibh Ó Súilleabháin (kept from 1827 to 1835). Ó Cianáin was from a learned Fermanagh family who were *ollamhs* ('masters') in history to the Maguires of Fermanagh. He entered the service of Hugh O'Neill, the second Earl of Tyrone, and became close to him. Not surprisingly, he joined O'Neill and Ruaidhrí O'Donnell, Earl of Tyrconnell, and Cú Chonnacht Maguire when they and an estimated ninety-six followers left Ireland in September 1607 to seek military assistance on the European Continent. The diary begins nine days before the flight and covers O'Neill's journey from the Pale to Tyrone and on to Rathmullan on Lough Swilly. It details the adventures of the exiled Irish in France, Spain and Italy, and mainly covers the period from September 1607 to November 1608. For Ó Cianáin, the journey is not so much an exercise in spiritual reckoning as an act of personal and national self-definition. He deliberately avoids using the term *Gael* throughout the diary; in his description of himself and his fellow Irish men and women meeting the subjects of different countries he uses the term *Éireannach*. This term will later feature prominently in Geoffrey Keating's plea for a common cause between the native Irish and the Anglo-Norman settlers, and indicates the extent to which Ó Cianáin in the intimate form of the travel diary began to define himself as part of a new polity that was not beholden to older ethnic divisions, even if it will embrace newer religious ones.

Central to Ó Cianáin's account is a recurrent status anxiety about his own standing (he was a wealthy man when he left Ireland) and that of his companions in the changed political circumstances of the time. The kingdom of France proves not to be as welcoming as anticipated and he records with evident relief the generous reception once they cross over into

---

[6] Ibid., 127.

Spanish-held territory in Arras. The journey through various territories in search of assistance becomes at times a painful experience in the loss of self-worth, which will be exacerbated at the end of the journey in Rome when O'Donnell dies in July 1608 and Maguire the following month. In recording meetings with the leading luminaries of the Irish colleges in Europe, men such as Flaithrí Ó Maoil Chonaire and Roibeárd Mac Artúir, Ó Cianáin is conscious of a transnational connectedness located around religion, language and culture. Yet he is equally sensitive to the personal vulnerability of a group of exiles who are dependent on the kindness (or more properly, the political calculations) of strangers. The sense of the 'personal' in the diary is more a question of witness than grammar. Ó Cianáin describes the lavish receptions that were laid on for the Irish in Spanish Flanders and shares vicariously in the implicit acknowledgement of the distinct identity and position of the Irish but he does not use first-person constructions to pick out his unique vantage point.

If travel revealed to Ó Cianáin the precariousness of his new-found identity as an *Éireannach*, his compatriot, William James MacNevin, almost two centuries later would also see the travel memoir as a way of teasing out the complexities of personal identity and political belonging. MacNevin was born near Aughrim, Co. Galway in 1763 and went on to study in Prague and Vienna before returning to Dublin as a qualified doctor in the 1790s. He became a member of the United Irishmen in 1796 but was arrested in 1798 and after his release in June 1802 was forbidden to return to Ireland. That same year he went on a walking tour of Switzerland, his account of which was published as *A Ramble through Swisserland in the Summer and Autumn of 1802* (1803). MacNevin firmly situates himself as the source of the narrative, which is mediated through his own set of experiences and political beliefs. Switzerland emerges as a country whose political freedom, despite complicated relationships with its French and German neighbours, is exemplary in the degree of popular assent it commands. As he travels through the country, he is in dutiful thrall to the sublime effects of Alpine landscapes but is equally beguiled by the sturdy freedoms of the Swiss peasantry. He notes that they universally possess arms and concludes: 'Though they suffered much injustice where they were subjects, because they never understood how to unite for a general purpose, yet the rigour of government had near limits towards a brave people with arms in their hands: it was not expedient to drive such men to despair.'[7]

---

[7] William James MacNevin, *A Ramble through Swisserland in the Summer and Autumn of 1802* (Dublin: J. Stockdale, 1803), 224.

MacNevin's recent experience of armed insurrection and the sombre spectacle of sectarian disunity at home ('never understood how to unite for a general purpose') is obviously preying on him, such that he uses Switzerland as an elaborate geographical metaphor for his personal and political experience of the 1798 rebellion. In his account, there is a constant oscillation between the 'modes and manners' approach to travel experience, evidenced by his item-ization of the costs of food and hotel accommodation, and a more 'senti-mental' evocation of subjective experience that for modern readers seems to be more securely in the realm of the autobiographical. He describes in detail the personal experience of walking and the 'great beauty' of the waterfall in Lauffen, though he confesses in an air of quiet chauvinism that 'the waterfall of Powerscourt is superior to any thing of the same nature in Swisserland'.[8] MacNevin is much more to the fore than Ó Cianáin in registering the emotional impact of sights on his consciousness but shares with the Ulsterman a strong sense of the autobiographical as being nested in a larger narrative of politicized identity.

The Irish Grand Tour

The new political order in eighteenth-century Ireland ushered in a differ-ent breed of traveller, one who was a member of the emergent landowning Ascendancy class or the Protestant professional middle class and attuned to the values and fashions of the wider English-speaking polity. Travel was considered central to the education of the social and political elite of the period. The formation of self was only complete if the subject read in the great book of the world. The scientific revolution of the seventeenth century had put a premium on the evidence of what you saw rather than what you had been told, so to know the world was to see it. Despite the fetishization of objectivity in the language of science, the self was core to this new project of knowing.

In 1802, Catherine Wilmot, who was born in Drogheda in 1773, went on a Grand Tour of the European Continent with the family of Lord Mount Cashel. The account of her tour was published in 1920 as *An Irish Peer on the Continent, 1801–1803*. Though the peer is in the title, the narration is firmly in the hands of Wilmot. The account is notable for the extent to which the traveller or travel writer becomes a dramatic character in her own right. For example, in Pavia she stays with the Mount Cashells in a 'miserable wild dismantled looking house, with all the air in the world of

---

[8] Ibid., 13.

being haunted'.[9] Wilmot describes going to the upstairs room of the inn where she is greeted by the sight of 'everything inside in frightful disorder, the long deal table overturn'd and cut and slash'd with dinner knives upon the surface; a picture of Jesus Christ revers'd upon its peg and warnings scrawl'd with blood and charcoal against the wall'.[10] Wilmot goes on to describe a night of gothic sleeplessness, with the wind 'roaring a hurricane, and the rain pattering frightfully against the windows'.[11] The highly coloured writing, which is more reminiscent of narrative prose fiction, points to a dual shift in the travel memoir, a shift that owes its origins in both instances to the writings of Wilmot's compatriots. Edmund Burke's precocious *A Philosophical Enquiry into the Origin of Our Ideas of the Sublime and the Beautiful* (1757) will place the category of the sublime – that which is awe-inspiring, compelling and potentially destructive – at the heart of the Romantic reaction against the perceived aesthetic orderliness of the classical world. Though the basic template for the Grand Tour is the dutiful trek through the sites associated with classical antiquity, Wilmot's travel account shows the deep influence of the Burkean sublime on the evocation of the mundane detail of travel itself, notably the familiar trinity of travel, accommodation and weather.

Alongside the new value placed on heightened emotional response, there is the move away from the impersonal narrator of the seventeenth century, who typically gave details of physical features and shipping tonnages, to a more writerly investment in subjective presence. A crucial precedent here is the work of another Irishman, Laurence Sterne's *A Sentimental Journey through France and Italy* (1768). The book, which is presented as a novel, has the traveller emerge as a person with opinions, emotions and reactions, so that the focus shifts from the traveller-narrator as a source of authority on classical erudition to the traveller as primarily shaped by his or her own personal responses to the sights they see and the events that befall them. In the sentimental mode, travel becomes inextricably bound up with the autobiographical, as the journey becomes as much about the traveller as the places visited. When Lady Morgan in *France* (1817), for example, talks of the fallen state of a labourer she meets, she is careful to set the scene by framing it through her presence and mediating it through her sensibility:

> I was one morning, in the summer of 1816, walking under the venerable towers of Château la Grange, and leaning on the arm of its illustrious

---

[9] Catherine Wilmot, *An Irish Peer on the Continent, 1801–1803*, ed. T. U. Sadleir (London: Williams and Northgate, 1920), 117.
[10] Ibid., 27.   [11] Ibid., 119.

master, general the marquis de la Fayette (and who would not boast of being supported by that arm, which raised the standard of independence in America and placed her banner above the dungeons of France?).[12]

The pre-determined itinerary of the Grand Tour, then, consecrated by classical precedent, gives way to the more idiosyncratic roaming of the senti-mental traveller who is guided more by personal inclination than scholarly duty. As Thomas Colley Grattan puts it in *High-ways and By-ways* (1823): 'Travelling, as I always do, without guide or compass, it is no merit of mine if I sometimes light on passing scenes, or mix with interesting people.'[13] There may, of course, be structural constraints on these personal inclinations. Part of the growing self-reflexivity of the travel writing genre is a more explicit awareness of the conditions of travel and, more particularly, of how fixed gender roles can undermine utopian fantasies of free movement. Melesina Trench, who kept a journal of her travels to Germany in 1799 and 1800, noted bleakly: 'It grieves me to find travelling contributes so little to the improvement of my mind. A variety of causes operates to prevent the possibility of a woman reaping much benefit from a journey through Germany, unless she totally gives up the world.'[14] Trench finds that not only her gender but also her social class mean that contact is frequently confined by 'the bounds of custom, of associating with any but noblesse'.[15] The democratic promise of travel and the potential for self-discovery in the company of foreign others are cruelly undercut by the restrictive social and sexual norms ('the bounds of custom') which police conduct and restrict connection.

Tourism and the rise of the Irish middle class

The nineteenth century, particularly in the years following the Catholic Emancipation Act of 1829, sees the emergence of a new kind of Irish traveller: the middle-class Catholic. Contrary to received wisdom, Irish travelling prac-tices in this century bear witness not to a model of arrested development but to the emergence of a modern consumerist culture where leisure practices feature prominently in the construction of personal identity. From the 1860s onwards, new modes of transport, new routes to the Continent and the organization of guided tours from Dublin by Thomas Cook meant that travel became

---

[12] Lady Morgan, *France* (London: Henry Colburn, 1817), vol. 1, 19.
[13] Thomas Colley Grattan, *High-Ways and By-Ways; or Tales of the Roadside* (London: Whittaker, 1823), 3.
[14] Melesina Trench, *Journal Kept During a Visit to Germany in 1799, 1800*, ed. the Dean of Westminster (London: Savill and Edwards, 1861), 36–37.
[15] Ibid., 37.

accessible to a wider group of people, more especially from the majority population. Notable accounts from this period include Martin Haverty's *Wandering in Spain in 1843* (1844), Julia Kavanagh's *A Summer and Winter in the Two Sicilies* (1858), James Roderick O'Flanagan's *Through North Wales with my Wife: An Arcadian Tour* (1884) and Eugene Davis's *Souvenirs of Irish Footprints over Europe* (1889).

What is apparent in these accounts as the century progresses is that both religion and nationality come to feature prominently both in the self-presentation of the writers and the choice of destination. Starting with the latter element, it is evident that these writers map out a different Europe from their aristocratic predecessors and are primarily attracted to Catholic spaces where they find a sense of collective solidarity with their co-religionists on the European Continent. There is a sense in which taking possession of the personal nature of the travel memoir becomes a way of affirming a growing ethnic, religious and class self-confidence. Kavanagh, for example, starts *A Summer and Winter in the Two Sicilies* with a confession of her initial reluctance to publish yet another travel book on Italy, not only because the country had been so often the subject of travel accounts but also because 'in a personal narrative, the unfortunate pronoun "I" must occur oftener than I cared to use it, being more accustomed to speak to the public through the medium of imaginary beings than in my own person'.[16] If Kavanagh invokes a formal property of the post-Romantic travel account, the prominence of the narrative subject, it is less to disavow it than to prepare her reader for the presence of a writer who draws on her national and religious background to create a specific identity. Part of this specificity lies in an increased interest in demarcation. As English speakers and products of a country that was still part of the British empire, many Irish travellers of the period are increasingly anxious about what they feel are the pitfalls of misattribution. They want to distinguish themselves from their fellow British Anglophones. There is a sense in which they feel that an important element of self is obscured if they are taken for what they no longer feel themselves to be.

This argument is particularly explicit in Eugene Davis's *Souvenirs of Irish Footprints over Europe*, in which he mixes autobiographical accounts of time he spent in Paris and Louvain with references to places on the Continent associated with Irish travellers. For Davis, it is the very ability of the Irish to travel and flourish in different circumstances that makes

---

[16] Julia Kavanagh, *A Summer and Winter in the Two Sicilies* (London: Hurst and Blackett, 1858), vol. i, v–vi.

arguments against Irish self-government untenable: 'the absurdity of the proposition that a people whose children could reach the highest rung of the social ladder and could rule and govern abroad are unworthy of ruling and governing at home'.[17] Davis deliberately seeks out destinations (Douai, Louvain, St Omer) that would not be on traditional tourist routes because of their association with Irish exiles. Whereas he castigates the boorish cockney who shouts in English for a cup of tea in a Louvain inn, seeing him as a hapless victim of national prejudice, Davis regards nationality as an enabling condition in the case of the Irish. This is not simply because what is of interest to them lies off the beaten track but that their way of getting there is also different. Underlying his critique of modern modes of transportation is Davis's more general association of 'Britishers' with utilitarianism. Thus, at a moment when he is addressing the rising Irish Catholic middle class whose sense of themselves is increasingly bound up with forms of conspicuous consumption, including travel,[18] Davis needs to reassure them that their sense of self is not compromised by these leisure activities. They can most be themselves when they are most like the other Irish who have gone before them, even if he rather conveniently elides the difference between the short stay and the permanent residency. For many Irish travellers of the period, the travel memoir offers the dual attraction of the construction of self at a subjective level through the use of personal forms of address and a broader identity construction at the level of class, ethnicity and religion through the comparison between Irish experiences and those of other nations. Cultural relativism becomes less an exercise in self-abnegation than in self-definition.

Post-independence Ireland

The outbreak of the First World War, followed by the Easter Rising and War of Independence, which led to the eventual formation of an Irish Free State, meant that Irish travel memoirs would be written in dramatically altered circumstances. Whether it was the role of religion, language, the burden of history or the dearth of economic opportunity, travel to foreign lands for many Irish writers from the 1920s to the 1960s became a forum for the working out of anxieties and dilemmas that haunted the self in post-independence Ireland. The onset of the Northern Troubles in 1968 added a

---

[17] Eugene Davis, *Souvenirs of Irish Footprints over Europe* (Dublin: The Freeman's Journal, 1889), 180.
[18] See Stephanie Rains, *Commodity Culture and Social Class in Dublin 1850–1916* (Dublin: Irish Academic Press, 2010).

contemporary urgency to these ruminations, such that the travel memoir often plays the role of a 'fifth province' of speculative personal and political imagination. From Kate O'Brien's *Farewell Spain* (1937) and Monk Gibbon's *Swiss Enchantment* (1950) to Sean O'Faolain's *An Autumn in Italy* (1953) and Colm Tóibín's *The Sign of the Cross: Travels in Catholic Europe* (1994), the travel memoir becomes a way of trying to situate the self in relation to the dominant understandings of what identity was assumed to be in an independent Ireland.

Part of that effort can consist of trying to retrieve a sense of individual selfhood which risks becoming obliterated by larger, collective forms of identification. Kate O'Brien, for example, in *Farewell Spain* defends her decision to write and publish the book at a very difficult time for Spain, stating: 'Let us praise personal memory, personal love.'[19] Although O'Brien is not above some sweeping generalizations, particularly about the influence of the 'Moorish' element on Spanish life, she sees the strength of the travel memoir lying in its attention to particulars, its devotion to the description of individual lives and personal encounters. Only the fine detail of the generally unremarked can save people from the reductive stereotypes of hatred. Indeed, this a more general feature of Irish travel accounts in the post-independence period: a reluctance to engage in sightseeing around conventional sites of interest and a repeated engagement with the individual stories of people met along the way, as if the travel genre itself was an overt form of collective autobiography. This is also a period where language itself becomes an issue for the writer, with the commitment of the new state to promote the restoration of the Irish language. Travel writing, indeed, becomes one of the most popular genres of writing in Irish, with writers from Liam Ó Rinn to Gabriel Rosenstock penning accounts of their travels elsewhere. Not surprisingly, a recurrent theme in these accounts is how the majority or minority status of a language can have a decisive impact on how the self will interpret or experience otherness.[20]

One way of capturing otherness is through comedy or satire, and a persistent strain in the Irish travel memoir from Sterne onwards is comic self-deprecation. In Sean O'Faolain's *An Autumn in Italy*, he gives an account of the various misfortunes that befall one of his Sicilian guides and comments: 'He was the kindest man I met in Italy, and one of the most

[19] Kate O'Brien, *Farewell Spain* (New York: Doubleday, 1937), 12.
[20] See Michael Cronin, *Across the Lines: Travel, Language, Translation* (Cork: Cork University Press, 2000).

cultivated, and, having in the past often been wounded for the honour of Ireland, I understood, sympathised and thought him just as absurd as I had often been myself. One can love one's country too much.'[21] By assuming the dual identity of spectator and victim, O'Faolain defuses the supercilious censoriousness that can often inform the presentation of the lives of others as pure vaudeville. The self that is on display is uncertain, prone to self-doubt, and any pretensions to superiority are swiftly ridiculed. In the sobering reality of an independent Ireland, there is less room for idealized versions of self and a certain circumspect modesty becomes the signature disposition of the postcolonial traveller.

This is notably the case in the many travel accounts of Dervla Murphy, the best-known Irish travel writer of the twentieth century, who saw the straitened circumstances of her upbringing as the best possible preparation for the rigours of travel. How these circumstances might impinge on the wider world becomes more pressing as, from the late 1960s onwards, the country experienced almost three decades of armed conflict with the loss of thousands of lives. The travel memoir, from Murphy's *A Place Apart* (1978) to Colm Tóibín's *Walking Along the Border* (1987), becomes a vehicle both for the interrogation of the inherited prejudices of self and an examination of lives lived in extremely trying conditions. The mixture of autobiographical reminiscence and the emphasis on highly personalized encounters give these accounts a depth and a complexity that are clearly at odds with the brutal polarities of the sectarian. However, the gaze inward is not always in opposition to the gaze outward. In *The Sign of the Cross*, Tóibín tries to come to terms with the Catholicism of his childhood by travelling to other lands where the religion is practised. Unlike his nineteenth-century predecessors, he is not seeking the complicity of mutual recognition but a way of understanding how he has been shaped by particular forces in Irish life. After visiting Lourdes, he describes how he had felt 'something of the power of the place, the amount of hope and spirit which had been let loose within these walls all over the years. I was confused by this mixture of hatred and fear of the Church's authority with my susceptibility to its rituals and its sheer force.'[22] As Tóibín observes the practices of others, he charts the changes in his own life and beliefs, giving voice once more to the old dictum that the shortest road to Tara is through Holyhead.

[21] Sean O'Faolain, *An Autumn in Italy* (New York: Devin-Adair, 1953), 125.
[22] Colm Tóibín, *The Sign of the Cross: Travels in Catholic Europe* (London: Cape, 1994), 16.

The Ryanair generation

The ending of protectionist economic policies in the 1960s and the accession of Ireland to the European Economic Community in 1973 set the country on a path that eventually led to its becoming one of the most globalized and open economies in the developed world by the turn of the millennium. The deregulation of air transport and the emergence of low-cost airlines such as Ryanair had a dramatic effect on Irish mobility. In 2015, for example, there were almost seven million trips taken abroad by Irish residents.[23] Globalization and hypermobility have been central features of the Irish experience in the early part of the twenty-first century. Being on the make means almost invariably being on the move.

In *Ruinair* (2008), his account of travelling to a number of destinations served by Ryanair, Paul Kilduff notes:

> We are the Ruinair generation who take flights abroad in the way that our parents took bus trips into town. Ruinair takes us from A to somewhere remotely near B: from Aarhus to Zaragoza (Pyrenees). They fly to every hamlet in Europe: Altenburg, Billund, Brno, Lamezia, Pau, Vaxjo, ... Weeze, Zadar; places that I doubt even exist.[24]

What is noticeable in Kilduff's memoir is the change of scale, the repositioning of Irish travel and sense of self in a global context. He notes of 'our own *Eireflot*' that 'This is no longer a little Irish airline. It's an epidemic of global proportions.'[25] If much of Kilduff's account is taken up with the mode of travel itself – the experience of flying with Ryanair – the focus is firmly autobiographical in that it is through the personal experience of the author that we see the shaping of the neoliberal Irish subject in a world of deregulated services. By making the mode of travel central to the account, the writer constantly reminds the reader not only of the impact of increased mobility on their perception of the outer world but also of how Ireland is no longer peripheral but central to European histories of mobility. The airline's destinations ('every hamlet in Europe') may often be peripheral but the overall operation is not.

As time-space compression and price wars make foreign destinations increasingly accessible, definitions of Irish selfhood need to fold in this nomadic dimension to the lives of many people in the contemporary

---

[23] Central Statistics Office. Available at www.cso.ie/en/ (accessed 26 February 2016).
[24] Paul Kilduff, *Ruinair: How to Be Treated Like Shite in 15 Different Countries ... and Still Quite Like It* (Dublin: Gill and Macmillan, 2008), 3.
[25] Ibid.

moment. Paying attention to travel memoirs is also a way of responding to the shift from extrinsic alterity to intrinsic alterity in Irish society. This shift reflects the demographic change in Ireland itself, where a country with the highest net emigration rate in the EEC in the 1980s found itself with the highest net immigration rate in the EU by the early 2000s.[26] The foreign is no longer over there or beyond the waves (extrinsic alterity) but next door, across the street, in the local corner shop (intrinsic alterity). A crucial body of writing in reflecting on the development of intrinsic alterity and the implications for self-understanding and self-representation is the largely neglected corpus of Irish travel memoirs which thematise travel abroad.

The American critic Paul Fussell has written of the diasporic conditions of interwar literary modernism and the rootlessness of many English-speaking writers: 'This diaspora seems one of the signals of literary modernism, as we can infer from virtually no modern writers remaining where he's "supposed" to be except perhaps Proust – we think of Pound in London, Paris and Italy; Eliot in London; Joyce in Trieste and Paris; Mann ultimately in the United States.'[27] For Fussell, literary modernism and twentieth-century travel writing owe their common origin to this unhousedness, this compulsive desire to be elsewhere. It is of course the permanency of being elsewhere that underscores the drama of exile, the condition of a Joyce or a Beckett on the European Continent. Travel, however, defines itself in the moment of return, in the sighting of Ithaca after the trials of difference. This dimension of Irish nomadic experience, which has clear consequences for an understanding and representation of the self throughout history, has, however, been curiously disregarded. Travel writing about Ireland, whether by Irish or foreign authors, has been the focus of critical attention; commentary on travel writing by Irish people travelling elsewhere in the modern period has been relatively sparse. The oversight is significant and points to a danger in Irish cultural criticism whereby only certain forms of movement are privileged in analysis. The permanent move to Canada but not the sojourn in Sicily, the emigrants' letters home from Australia but not the visit to Berlin, become objects of critical inquiry. Irrevocability risks becoming a talisman of authenticity – real travel (exile) versus superficial travel (tourism) – and concentration on the Irish in North America, Britain and Australia may

---

[26] See Martin Ruhs, 'Emerging Trends and Patterns in the Immigration and Employment of Non-EU Nationals: What the Data Reveal' (2003). Available at www.tcd.ie/policy-institute/publications / (accessed 23 January 2016).

[27] Paul Fussell, *Abroad: British Literary Travelling Between the Wars* (Oxford: Oxford University Press, 1980), 11.

narrow the world to encounters with varieties of Anglophone Irishness and neglect individual Irish experiences of a multilingual and multicultural planet.

Conclusion

In considering the role of the Irish travel memoir in the evolution of Irish autobiography, the emphasis in this chapter has been on journeys undertaken outside of Ireland. The purpose has been partly to engage in a shift away from a disproportionately diasporic emphasis in Anglophone Irish Studies to what might be termed diffusive perspectives on Irish self-representation. What is intended by the term 'diffusive' is a way of capturing the interaction between Irish cultural activity and strategies of self-representation with the different literatures, languages and polities of the world outside of the increasingly well-documented networks of an Irish Anglophone diaspora. If there has been much focus on how others have seen the Irish, it is equally important to see how the Irish have seen themselves through others, a task that is all the more relevant as the others have now come to live among the Irish.

The future of travel may not be one of continued growth. There are no ecological low costs associated with air travel. In an era of climate change, the inhabitants of an island nation may need to think again about how they are to remain in touch with the rest of the world. Central to this rethinking will be work of Irish writers who, from the *Navigatio* to *Ruinair*, have defined their sense of self not so much through the fact of being here as of being elsewhere.

Further reading

Cronin, Michael and Barbara O'Connor, eds. *Tourism in Ireland: A Critical Analysis*. Cork: Cork University Press, 1993.
Hulme, Peter and Tim Youngs, eds. *The Cambridge Companion to Travel Writing*. Cambridge: Cambridge University Press, 2002.
Share, Bernard, ed. *Far Green Fields: Fifteen Hundred Years of Irish Travel Writing*. Belfast: Blackstaff Press, 2002.
Smyth, Gerry. *Space and the Irish Cultural Imagination*. Basingstoke: Palgrave Macmillan, 2001.
Wondrich, Roberta Gefter. 'Exilic Returns: Self and History Outside Ireland in Recent Irish Fiction', *Irish University Review*, 30:1 (2000): 1–16.
Wooding, Jonathan M., ed. *The Otherworld Voyage in Early Irish Literature: An Anthology of Criticism*. Dublin: Four Courts Press, 2000.

CHAPTER 21

Life-Writing and Diaspora I
The Autobiographical Writings of the Irish in the USA and Latin America

Laura P. Z. Izarra and James Silas Rogers

Few nations have been so keenly aware of their own diaspora as Ireland, the descendants of which are estimated to number as many as seventy million people worldwide.[1] The calibration and interpretation of this massive out-migration and its generational legacies have long been central concerns of demographers, historians, sociologists and writers of different kinds. This last category includes diasporic memoirists and autobiographers, in whose work Irish ethnicity sometimes features as a cherished heirloom but more often functions as a figure in the carpet, indelible but inconspicuous, its contours indistinct and shifting. Tracing these fugitive designs in the fabric of two distinctly different bodies of autobiographical writing will be the main work of this chapter. The first section will focus on Irish-American memoirs and autobiographies since the 1920s, excluding from this category works of fiction and emigrant letters and diaries, on which excellent scholarship already exists. The second will survey autobiographical works by writers of Irish birth or descent in Latin America since the earliest times, a corpus that is much smaller, more fragmentary and less studied than its American equivalent. The criteria for inclusion has therefore been made more elastic to accommodate travelogues, diaries and fictionalized autobiographies.

A similarly flexible approach governs the critical frames within which these two literatures will be read. The first section draws in part on Kathleen Brogan's distinction between 'ethnographers' and 'heirs' to elucidate some of the signature themes of Irish-American life-writing.[2] As we

---

[1] Though estimates vary, this figure has been cited by successive Irish politicians from President Mary Robinson in 1990 to Minister Jimmy Deenihan in 2014. See www.dfa.ie/news-and-media /speeches/speeches-archive/2014/october/global-forum-on-diaspora-and-development/ (accessed 24 April 2016).
[2] Kathleen Brogan, *Cultural Haunting: Ghosts and Ethnicity in Recent American Literature* (Charlottesville: University Press of Virginia, 1998).

shall see, autobiographers from the early part of our chosen period tend to be ethnographically minded insofar as they anatomize manners and mores and register the processes of immigrant adaptation, assimilation and integration, whereas more recent writers are more drawn to the effects of transplantation and cross-cultural encounter on individual and collective self-understanding, thus following the 'heirs' model. This critical template is also applicable to aspects of the autobiography of the Irish in Latin America, though it will help our understanding to combine it with Patrick O'Sullivan's proposition (borrowed from Gerda Lerner's categorization of women's history) that diasporic histories tend to be written as stories of oppression, compensation and contribution.[3]

Before turning to the texts themselves, brief acknowledgement must be made of the manifold markers of difference that separate these two bodies of writing and their social and cultural contexts. For much of the past three hundred years, the American colonies and, later, the United States have been a primary destination for Irish emigrants, such that they (and their descendants) have advanced and assimilated across the full spectrum of American society, helped by the absence of language barriers. In Latin America, which presents a more recent experience of colonialism than the United States, cultural assimilation and upward social mobility have also occurred, but here the volume of Irish immigration was smaller, settlement patterns more sporadic and the levels of re-emigration to other destinations higher. Irish settlement in Latin America has also been more geographically confined than in the United States, Argentina and a handful of Caribbean islands being the chief sites where Irish communities took root and endured, even as the visible signs of ethnic difference faded. Consequently, the life-writings of the Irish in Latin America are much more individualistic and heterogeneous in character, unlike the autobiographies of writers of Irish birth or heritage in United States, where a powerful assimilationist ideology worked to undermine literary expressions of separateness among many immigrant communities. Certainly, the Irish in Latin America did not experience the same politics of transfiguration that Irish immigrants strove for in the nineteenth-century United States, where they used labour unions, the Catholic church and the Democratic Party to become part of the 'white republic'. Yet neither were they

---

[3] Patrick O'Sullivan, 'General Introduction to the Series', in Patrick O'Sullivan, ed., *The Irish World Wide: History, Heritage, Identity. Volume 1: Patterns of Migration* (London: Leicester University Press, 1992), xviii–xx. The first category refers to narratives of victimization, the second to histories that focus on exceptionally accomplished individuals and the third to those who have made a positive difference to their host society or culture.

identified as 'black Europeans'. Paradoxically, the Irish were frequently viewed as English (sometimes willingly so) due to the language they spoke, and in some parts of Latin America they at first profited from this identification by getting better jobs than the natives when English and American companies settled in these non-Anglophone countries during their respective periods of modernization.

The autobiographical writings of the Irish in the USA

Major interpretive histories and numerous regional studies have moved the study of Irish-American ethnicity forwards by astonishing leaps, though as elsewhere in Irish literary studies, autobiography has seldom been given significant attention. A notable exception is John Duffy Ibson's *Will the World Break Your Heart? Dimensions and Consequences of Irish-American Assimilation* (1990), a quirky and highly original study that draws heavily on autobiographical material. Oddly, the spotlight now being shone on Irish diasporic ethnicity arrives at a time when the distinctiveness of the Irish in America has largely become a matter of what the sociologist Herbert J. Gans termed 'symbolic ethnicity'.[4] According to Gans, by the fourth generation after emigration, the assimilation of white ethnics is nearly complete; ethnic memory becomes relegated to such things as food, jokes, pictures on the wall, occasional written materials and a few familial words in a now disused heritage language. In the United States, Irish ethnic and religious out-marriage has become the norm since early in the twentieth century. The Irish have not formed a meaningful voting bloc for almost as long, and all but a few of the urban neighbourhoods that had sustained Irish ethnicity were abandoned for the homogeneity of the suburbs after the Second World War.

Where, then, do autobiography and memoir fit into our understanding of this attenuated ethnic consciousness? One useful approach is suggested by the distinctions that Kathleen Brogan makes in her study of 'cultural haunting' in late twentieth-century American ethnic literature, in which she identifies two types of ethnic writers, ethnographers and heirs. Brogan argues that autobiographers in the ethnographer mode record the elements of an Irish identity in the New World, with direct or indirect accounts of what it was like to live and work, or to be a child, in an Irish-American context. The heirs model, which may or may not take the form of a search

---

[4] Herbert J. Gans, 'Symbolic Ethnicity: The Future of Ethnic Groups and Cultures in America', *Ethnic and Racial Studies*, 2:1 (1979), 1.

for ancestral roots, is a more recent development and one that calls for greater interiority and reflection. Thus, many Irish-American memoirists are 'certain that being Irish in America conveys something distinctive – even if they are not always clear what that distinctiveness is, nor necessarily pleased when they find out'.[5]

In the ethnographer model, autobiographers confirm, refute or complicate a number of received opinions about the elements of Irish identity in America. The first such element is the experience of emigration itself, including the Atlantic crossing and the adaptation to a new culture. Second, that adaptation has necessarily engaged with the ideology of the American Dream. Third, the Irish in America have come to be defined by attachments to specific urban neighbourhoods, at the heart of which lay a fourth cornerstone of their ethnicity, a resolute Catholicism, or at the least a perception that Irishness and Catholicism were synonymous. The fifth such theme is the century-long evolution of Irish-American nationalism, an especially forceful presence well into the 1920s, and one which re-emerged after 1970. A sixth element is the large role that this immigrant group played in the Democratic Party, and especially in its labour wing. Finally, Irish-American identity has long been associated with a sentimental affection for ancestral places in Ireland.

As Kerby Miller has shown, the Irish experience of emigration to the United States before the introduction of immigrant quotas in the 1920s was well recorded in correspondence and diaries; it is far less accessible in the published autobiographical record.[6] Silence and forgetfulness pervade the autobiographical literature, and nowhere more so than in the matter of emigration itself. For instance, David S. Lawlor's *The Life and Struggles of an Irish Boy in America* (1936) records his 1872 crossing in this terse paragraph: 'The voyage lasted nine days and I had a happy and hungry time. I was always hungry, all the other boys being hungry too. I remember my mother giving her two potatoes to a couple of boys she had tucked under her wing.'[7] Lawlor's memoir follows the rags-to-riches model in almost every particular, charting his rise from toil in the textile mills of Fall River, Massachusetts to eventual success in journalism and advertising,

---

[5] James Silas Rogers, 'Introduction', in *Extended Family: Essays on Being Irish American from 'New Hibernia Review'* (Chester Springs: Dufour Editions, 2013), 12.

[6] See Kerby A. Miller, et al., eds., *Irish Immigrants in the Land of Canaan: Letters and Memoirs from Colonial and Revolutionary America, 1675–1815* (New York: Oxford University Press, 2003). Miller's earlier *Emigrants and Exiles: Ireland and the Irish Exodus to North America* (New York: Oxford University Press, 1985) also draws heavily on letters and diaries.

[7] David S. Lawlor, *The Life and Struggles of an Irish Boy in America: An Autobiography* (Newton: Carroll Publishing Company, 1936), 23.

success that he portrays as the result of hard work, education and faith. It could have been written by Benjamin Franklin. Yet for all his embrace of the American Dream, and his soft-pedalling of his childhood in Co. Tipperary, the fact remains that Lawlor invokes his ethnicity in the title of his autobiography. In this, he displays one of the most persisting patterns among Irish-American memoirists: a self-conscious declaration of Irishness, coupled with a reluctance to explore the real-world difference that such Irishness entailed.

Although Irish Americans rank among the most financially and professionally successful of American ethnic groups, their autobiographies include many accounts of missing out on the American Dream. A prominent example is Frank McCourt's *Angela's Ashes: A Memoir* (1996). Most of the book takes place in Limerick, but it opens with the family fleeing New York city as victims of the Depression. In *The Hard Road to Klondike* (1962), first published in Irish in 1959, Michael MacGowan is left behind to freeze to death on his way to the Alaskan gold fields in 1899. Jim Tully's nostalgia for the gutter is the subject of *Beggars of Life* (1924) and *Shanty Irish* (1928), the latter highlighting his ditch-digger grandfather in rural Ohio. Two memoirs that provide insight into the enduring anomaly of South Boston – a neighbourhood that embodies Irish-American shortfall – are *Life Is My Adventure* (1937) by Barbara Mullen and *All Souls: A Family Story from Southie* (1999) by Michael Patrick MacDonald. The former is the story of a young woman trying to break out of poverty in Prohibition-era Boston by becoming a professional Irish dancer; the latter, an account of the racial unrest in the 1970s sparked by court-ordered school integration and the exclusion of the author's poor neighbourhood from any larger civic life.

The political and economic outsiderhood that lies at the heart of Irish-American radicalism has given us a number of lively autobiographies. Irish-born Mary Harris 'Mother' Jones, a labour heroine in mining camps across America, published a 1925 autobiography that is nearly as uninformative about her young emigration as Lawlor's. She sums up her origins and her complicated balancing of national identities in these brief sentences, with which her book begins:

> My people were poor. For generations they had fought for Ireland's free-dom. Many of my folks have died in that struggle. My father, Richard Harris, came to America in 1835, and as soon as he had become an American citizen he sent for his family . . . Of that citizenship I have ever been proud.[8]

---

[8] Mary Harris Jones, *The Autobiography of Mother Jones* (Chicago: Charles H. Kerr, 1925), 1.

In *I Speak My Own Piece: Autobiography of 'The Rebel Girl'* (1955), Elizabeth Gurley Flynn asserts a direct connection between her Irish heritage and her later radical convictions, whereas a more conventional story of labour activism is contained in Margaret A. Haley's *Battleground*, posthumously published in 1983 (Haley died in 1939). The figure of the Irish-American schoolteacher is almost a stereotype; Haley's account gives a thoughtful picture of their actual working conditions.

Conventional political life has given rise to numerous Irish-American autobiographies. The vast majority are political life-and-times stories and some are nakedly self-serving. *I'd Do It Again: A Record of All My Uproarious Years* (1957), the highly anecdotal memoir by Boston's flamboyant mayor James Michael Curley, takes this to extremes. More measured books, such as *Counsel for the Defense* (1979), the recollections of the New York liberal attorney Paul O'Dwyer, and *Man of the House* (1987) by congressional leader Thomas 'Tip' O'Neill, provide little in the way of interiority. This should not surprise: reflection is the engine that drives memoir and political life rarely fosters reflection. One political memoir that does afford a glimpse into the heart of its author is Abigail McCarthy's *Private Faces, Public Places* (1972). McCarthy's book is a fine portrait of the '*Commonweal* Catholics', a group that took its name from the influential periodical that denotes an intellectual Catholicism that is open and pluralistic. McCarthy herself was a long-time columnist for *Commonweal*, where most of her colleagues were the children and grandchildren of Irish immigrants.

The Irish diasporic community kept a close eye on events at home in the days of the Fenians, the Home Rule movement and on through independence, but generally did so in polemical rather than personal writing. Two later memoirs that touch on interest in Irish politics are Richard Howard Brown's surprisingly sophisticated excursion into the early years of the Northern Ireland Troubles, *I Am of Ireland: An American's Journey of Discovery in a Troubled Land* (1974), and *Irish on the Inside: A Search for the Soul of Irish America* (2001) by Tom Hayden. Despite its extremely programmatic politics – Irishness as a mandate for radicalism – Hayden's linkages of the traumas of emigration and famine to the sterility of his Midwestern suburban childhood does read compellingly. Indeed, some of the best Irish-American memoir of recent years has been precisely this sort of work, in which authors trace the larger sweeps of history in their own lives. Although not precisely an autobiography, Richard White's *Remembering Ahanagran: Storytelling in a Family's Past* (1998) set the gold standard for such writing. An excellent short example is Caroline Ramsay's 'The Need to Feed', collected in *Motherland: Writings by Irish American*

Women about Mothers and Daughters (1999), which persuasively traces the legacy of the Famine to diasporic food ways – the Sunday pot roast as an archaeology of hunger.

There is a kind of 'deep Irishness' at work when an author draws on their knowledge of Irish history and culture to inform their understanding of personal experience. This is especially true in discussing the engagement of Irish-American autobiographers with the Catholic church, vividly demonstrated in William Gibson's *A Mass for the Dead* (1968), which is structured in alignment with the Latin Mass. The language, images and patterns of Catholicism give shape to Gibson's experiences in chapters bearing such titles as 'Credo' and 'Introibo'. Among Irish-American Catholics, the group that was most fully invested in their religious identity, the clergy, has been almost silent, autobiographically speaking. Given the importance of vocations to the Irish-American family (the stereotypical mother giving her pride and joy to God), the extraordinary social and political influence of priests on Irish-American life and the fact that virtually all of these priests were educated, literate men, we might expect a large body of confessional writing by priests. In fact, very few such works, and even fewer by nuns, were written until after the Second Vatican Council of the 1960s. Catholic autobiography has tended to limit itself to the authors' intellectual journeys and often deliberately avoids self-disclosure. An unusual priest's memoir in this regard is Donald Hayne's *Batter My Heart* (1963). Born in 1908 in Albany, New York, Haynes was in and out of seminaries and various dioceses all his life. At times guarded and tediously cerebral, *Batter My Heart* nonetheless portrays the family dynamics of this young Irish Catholic, whose father was a criminal and whose mother came from a starchily respectable Irish family. Most remarkable, given its publication date, is Haynes's openness about his homosexuality.

If anything, the autobiographical charting of Catholic Irish America has largely been the province of those who leave the church. For example, the ex-priest James Carroll's *An American Requiem: God, My Father and the War That Came Between Us* (1996) reprises the familiar battle with authoritarianism and conscience, with Vietnam as the flashpoint. But arguably the most famous account of leaving the church is Mary McCarthy's *Memories of a Catholic Girlhood* (1957). The leading woman intellectual of mid-twentieth-century America, McCarthy spent an utterly miserable childhood in an Irish Catholic enclave in Minneapolis. When both her parents died in the 1918 flu epidemic, Mary was thrust into the care of a cruel aunt and uncle. At age ten, she won a statewide essay contest for a piece on 'The Irish in America', after which her guardians stole the prize money and beat her. Understandably bitter, *Memories of a Catholic Girlhood* concedes that her youthful Catholicism was in some ways enlarging and openly declares gratitude to the nuns who taught her. Before it is an intellectual journey, however, McCarthy's memoir is emphatically a memoir of a place, a rendering of the sights, faces and rituals of her girlhood. It is in the highly developed rendering of their American places of origin that diasporic memoirists most effectively take on the approach of an heir rather than an ethnographer – that is, where the authors begin to ask 'what does it mean to be Irish?' Patrick Sheeran asserted that it is 'well-nigh a truism that Irishness and a sense of place go together'[9]; the autobiographical record suggests that this linkage strongly persists in the diaspora, especially in urban neighbourhoods.

Naturally, not all Irish-American memoirs are urban. The under-recognized life of the farming Irish finds a memorable record in two books by Charles B. Driscoll, *Kansas Irish* (1943) and *Country Jake* (1946). Although the point has been debated, Driscoll's books at least confirm the conventional wisdom that the Irish were ill-suited to farming on the American prairies. City life has defined Irish America, however. The defeat of Alfred Smith in the presidential election of 1928 has often been identified as a repudiation by mainstream America of the urban Irish Catholic. Smith's sometimes charming autobiography, *Up To Now* (1929), displays his unabashed affection for New York, the city he governed. The journalist Pete Hamill's recovery narrative, *A Drinking Life* (1993), memorably evokes the Irish neighbourhoods of his native Brooklyn, as well as the saloons where his Belfast-born father modelled the alcohol dependency that would later dominate Hamill himself. The picture of urban Irish America in recent memoir is frequently tinged with regret. Joe Queenan's *Closing Time: A Memoir* (2009), for instance, savages the insularity of the Philadelphia neighbourhood in which he grew up, while two fine recent accounts of Irish-American childhoods in New York city – Michael Pearson's *Dreaming of Columbus: A Bronx Childhood* (1999) and Maureen Waters' *Crossing Highbridge: A Memoir of Irish America* (2001) – call out street names as demarcators of class and confinement. Waters charts the psychic costs of living in a claustrophobic Irish urban village, saying that her parents 'remained displaced persons, never fully at home on these expedient shores'.[10]

---

[9] Patrick Sheeran, 'Genius Fabulae: The Irish Sense of Place', *Irish University Review*, 18:2 (1988), 191.
[10] Maureen Waters, *Crossing Highbridge: A Memoir of Irish America* (Syracuse: Syracuse University Press, 2001), 41.

In contrast to these portraits, the autobiographical literature of Irish America abounds with works in which neighbourhoods and communities are depicted as nurturing, intimate environments. Charles Fanning, the pre-eminent scholar of Irish-American literature and author of *Mapping Norwood: An Irish American Memoir* (2010), has written that 'Ingrained reverence for the spirit of place accompanied the many thousands of immigrants who left homes in post-Famine Ireland for new lives in urban America.'[11] Place is at the centre of his story of coming of age in a Boston suburb. Of the idiosyncratic 'mapping' of his home town, Fanning remarks that he and his Irish-American friends were 'participating in the ongoing, universal human project of making necessary surveyor's maps of the places where we lived'.[12] An even more forceful statement of the power of place comes at the end of Monica Wood's superb account of a girlhood in a working-class New England town, *When We Were the Kennedys: A Memoir from Mexico, Maine* (2012). Under the town's smokestacks, Wood writes that she 'experienced the shock of loss, the solace of family, the consolation of friendship, the power of words, the comfort of place'.[13] 'Place', she says bluntly, 'means us.'[14] In a similar vein, Dan Barry's *Pull Me Up: A Memoir* (2004) provides a valuable window on the processes by which place – even in a nondescript postwar suburb – creates meaning. The book opens with Barry's Irish immigrant mother dying 'deep in the living room couch that had been her place all those years'[15] and closes with Barry himself, having recovered from cancer, standing on a pier in Ireland, feeling utterly at home.

Perhaps owing to the ease of present-day travel, the notion of return has become a key element in recent diasporic autobiographies. A plethora of books involving stories of transplantation or resettlement has been written by Americans who decide as adults to relocate to Ireland permanently. Although these works almost inevitably tend towards the comic, tales of the 'returned Yank' are not always funny. For example, in *'Tis* (1999), Frank McCourt's follow-up to *Angela's Ashes*, the author comes back to Limerick in his GI's uniform expecting to be treated as a glamorous exotic, only to find that the locals ignore him. In the end, however, the image of

---

[11] Charles Fanning, *Mapping Norwood: An Irish American Memoir* (Amherst and Boston: University of Massachusetts Press, 2010), 32.

[12] Ibid.

[13] Monica Wood, *When We Were the Kennedys: A Memoir from Mexico, Maine* (New York: Houghton Mifflin Harcourt, 2012), 230.

[14] Ibid., 220.

[15] Dan Barry, *Pull Me Up: A Memoir* (New York: W. W. Norton and Company, 2004), 9.

Ireland that Dan Barry draws at the close of *Pull Me Up* appears to be becoming the most resonant theme in Irish-American memoir. For Barry and other heirs, Ireland and Irishness can be enigmatic, but, like lodestones, they exert an enduring pull. However improbably, the old country can still function as a landscape of origins and of healing in which the subterranean dimensions of identity are to be mined. In the absence of an ethnic identity that reaches deeper than the symbolic, future contributors to the tradition of Irish-American autobiography and memoir will surely continue this process.

The autobiographical writings of the Irish in Latin America

Despite its not being an English-speaking territory, Latin America received various waves of Irish immigrants from the mid-1500s onwards. Many of the earliest Irish settlers in countries such as Brazil, Argentina, Paraguay and Mexico were members of Catholic families displaced by colonial warfare at home. The first recorded Irish settler in Brazil was a Limerick-born Jesuit priest, Thomas Field, who arrived in 1577 and spent three years in São Paulo before moving to Paraguay. The expansion of European commercial and colonial enterprises in the Amazon basin in the early 1600s brought Irish adventurers to the region, along with English, French and Dutch pioneers. Among them was Bernard O'Brien, a tobacco planter from Co. Clare who, along with Irish brothers Philip and James Purcell, established trading settlements on the lower Amazon in the 1620s. O'Brien's written record of his experiences, simply entitled 'Bernard O'Brien's Account of Irish Activities in the Amazon, 1621–1624', constitutes the first known autobiographical testimony by an Irishman in Latin America, though it can hardly be said to have inaugurated anything so grand as a literary tradition. Instead, what we find are individual autobiographical voices cropping up in different territories at different times, many of them belonging to travellers or temporary residents rather than to settlers *per se*.

One such voice is that of Richard Flecknoe, a Catholic priest, poet and playwright who may have been Irish-born, and whose *A Relation of Ten Years' Travels in Europe, Asia, Affrique and America* (c. 1656) is considered to be the first book by an English-speaking traveller to Brazil. In it, he tells of his voyage from Lisbon to Pernambuco and onwards to Rio de Janeiro, where he spent most of 1649, chronicling his impressions of the climate, vegetation, animals, commodities and 'savage' natives. Ethnographic descriptions of the landscape and urban environment of Rio de Janeiro also feature in *An Account of a Voyage to Establish a Colony at Port Philip* (1805) by Cork-born naval officer James Tuckey, who spent twenty days in the city en route to Australia in 1803 and recorded his observations on its commercial and civic life, which include remarks about women and the practice of abortion. An acute insight into the plight of some recently arrived Irish immigrants in 1820s Brazil is provided by Robert Walsh, a Waterford-born Anglican clergyman and historian who was appointed chaplain to the British embassy in Rio de Janeiro in 1828. In *Notices of Brazil in 1828 and 1829* (1830), Walsh describes the fate that befell almost 3,000 Munster men and their families who were recruited by William Cotter, an Irishman serving in the Brazilian army, to fight against Argentina in the Cisplatine War. Instead of the rewards promised by Cotter, they were met by squalid living conditions and hostility from enslaved Africans in Rio, who denigrated the newcomers as 'white slaves, "escravos brancos"'.[16] After a brief but bloody mutiny, the majority of these transplanted people were repatriated to Cork where, Walsh reports, 'there is not one, perhaps, who is not now enduring want and misery'.[17]

Other first-person accounts from this period reveal that some migrants suffered as much discrimination in their new life in Latin America as they had under British rule at home. In the Spanish Caribbean islands, stories are recorded of Irish navvies who were recruited by the Cuban Railroad Commission, which oversaw the building of the island's first railway in the mid-1830s. Harsh working conditions and maltreatment led them to mount a workers' strike, the first on record in Cuba's history, which was ruthlessly suppressed by the Spanish authorities. Irish migrants are also represented in the narratives of Cuba's planter elite in the context of labour relations in a slave-based sugar plantation economy. None of these have left a literary trace, however. The closest we get to autobiographical testimony in this period is *The Mambi-land, or Adventures of a Herald Correspondent in Cuba* (1874) by Fenian conspirator James J. O'Kelly, which is a richly detailed first-person account of Cuba during the Ten Years' War, written from behind insurgent lines.[18]

In the late eighteenth and early nineteenth centuries, an unknown number of Irishmen arrived in Argentina as conscripted British army soldiers. Many subsequently deserted from the army and settled in the

---

[16] Robert Walsh, *Notices of Brazil in 1828 and 1829* (London: Frederick Westley and A. H. Davis, 1830), 283.

[17] Ibid., 299.

[18] O'Kelly appears as a character in Tomás Mac Síomóin's Irish-language novel *Ceallaigh: Scéal ón mBlárcatha* (2010), part of which dramatizes Cuba's nineteenth-century independence struggle.

country, with some reviving their military activities in the armies of the two great liberators of Spanish South America, José de San Martín and Simón Bolívar. Bolívar employed a succession of Irish *aides-de-camp*, the most notable of whom was Cork-born Daniel Florencio O'Leary, who accompanied Bolívar on his epic march across the Andes in 1819 and who was also with him in 1825, when his march to Upper Peru led to the creation of the republic of Bolivia. By the time of his death in 1854, O'Leary had completed a draft of his memoirs, written in English and Spanish. His son Simón edited and published these as *Memorias del General O'Leary publicados por su hijo Simón B. O'Leary* in thirty-two volumes between 1879 and 1888, though only three volumes of this monumental work relate to O'Leary's own life, the other twenty-nine being devoted to the activities and correspondence of Bolívar. Another Corkman, Francisco Burdett O'Connor, who came from Protestant stock, served as a commander in Bolívar's campaign to liberate Venezuela from Spanish rule and was later feted as a liberator of Bolivia alongside Bolívar and Antonio José de Sucre, who became the country's first president in 1826. The following year, O'Connor issued a proclamation to the 'People of Ireland' as he made an abortive attempt to establish an Irish colony called New Erin in the southern Bolivian province of Tarija, where he died in 1871. His diary, *Independencia Americana: Recuerdos de Francisco Burdett O'Connor*, which includes detailed observations on the South American wars of independence, was published by his grandson Tomás O'Connor d'Arlach in 1895. As figures whose achievements brought them more honour and glory in their adopted homeland than in Ireland, O'Connor and O'Leary clearly fit the mould of contribution history and their memoirs continue to be much valued for their documentary insights.

Irish emigration to Argentina increased substantially during the period from the 1840s to 1870s. Some of these newcomers swelled the Irish-*porteño* ('people of the port') community in Buenos Aires, while many others established themselves as rural ranchers or *estancieros* in Buenos Aires province. If the immigrant Irish found farming life on the US prairies inimical, many of their counterparts in Argentina prospered in the rich grasslands of the humid pampas. Some became wealthy landowners and helped to promote chain migration from Ireland, while others worked as farm hands, shepherds and servants. Yet only a tiny handful of these settlers left accounts of their experiences, none of which were published in their lifetimes. John Brabazon, a Westmeath Protestant who settled in Argentina in the early 1840s, chronicled events in his life from 1845 to 1864, including the barbarous murder of his first wife, in a diary entitled 'The

Customs and Habits of the Country of Buenos Ayres from the year 1845',
which has been described as having 'the atmosphere of a *Bildungsroman*'.[19]
Another unpublished narrative that belongs to 'the sphere of intimacy'[20] is
'The Memoirs of Edward Robbins 1800–1853', a short work written in the
form of a diary, with annual entries ranging in length from a single
sentence to a paragraph. Robbins, an Offaly farmer of considerable
means, travelled with his second wife and eleven children to Buenos
Aires in 1849, a gruelling journey that exacted a heavy personal toll, as he
recorded in a matter-of-fact style:

> On the 21st of August my wife died and was buried in the Recoleta. On the
> 29th of same month my son Bernard died, and on the 4th of September my
> adopted daughter Mary Ann Coffy died. I could muster hard on £80 when I
> landed, but when the dead were buried and the sick recovered and arranged,
> I was some 5 or 600 dollars in debt.[21]

'The Memoirs of Tom Garrahan 1864–1912', which is a somewhat more
expansive work, contains the perspective of an industrious second-generation Irishman whose family affirmed its right over a 'conquered' territory.
The narrative is replete with details of the family's agricultural entrepreneurship, as they expanded their share of land, livestock and capital over
several decades to become respected members of the rancher class.
Garrahan's transformed sense of belonging is symbolized by his naming
his *estancia* in Lobos 'New Home' and it was here that he composed his
memoirs in the late 1920s or early 1930s.[22] Lobos was also the birthplace in
1855 of Roberto Murphy, the son of another Offaly immigrant who became
a successful *estanciero*. From 1887 until his death in 1934, Murphy maintained a diary in which he recorded his thoughts and observations about
family, social and business life.[23] Both Garrahan and Murphy epitomize
the type of Irish settler whom we glimpse in the pages of two lively travel
memoirs, *Two Thousand Miles' Ride Through the Argentine Provinces* (1853)
by William MacCann, who may or may not have been Irish-born, and *A
Search for Fortune: The Autobiography of a Younger Son* (1878) by Hamilton

---

[19] Juan José Delaney, 'Irish-Porteño Literature', in Micheál Ó hAodha and Máirtín Ó Catháin, eds.,
New Perspectives on the Irish Abroad: The Silent People? (Lanham: Lexington Books, 2014), 148. The
original diary remains unpublished. A Spanish translation, edited by Eduardo Coghlan, was
published as *Andanzas de un Irlandés en el Campo Porteño (1845–1864)* in 1981.

[20] Edmundo Murray, *Becoming Irlandés: Private Narratives of the Irish Emigration to Argentina, 1844–
1912* (Buenos Aires: L.O.L.A., Literature of Latin America, 2006), xvii. Murray's book contains
annotated editions of the memoirs of Robbins and Tom Garrahan respectively.

[21] Ibid., 35.   [22] Ibid., 115.

[23] A digital scan of the diary can be found at www.irlandeses.org/inicial.html (accessed 24 April 2016).

Lindsay-Bucknall, in which he recorded his positive impressions of Argentina and Brazil in the 1870s. A rare insight into the life of an Anglo-Irish *estanciero* is provided by *Work and Play in the Argentine* (1925), a memoir by Dublin Protestant and British army captain John Macnie, which betrays the Anglocentric cultural prejudices of his class. Autobiographical testimonies by Irish-born professionals in Latin America are scarcer still, a rare instance being the memoirs of Kildare-born Arthur Pageitt Greene, which details his years as the only doctor in a remote area of the pampas and then as a physician at the British Hospital in Buenos Aires.[24]

In 1858, a young Dubliner called Michael Mulhall went to Argentina, where his brother Edward was already working as a sheep farmer. By 1861, the brothers, who considered themselves British, had established a printing house in Buenos Aires from which they published *The Standard and River Plate News*, the first English-language newspaper in South America (the title was shortened to *The Standard* in 1882). In 1863, the Mulhall brothers published a *Handbook of the River Plate* in which they mapped the most fertile regions and their economy, with the aim of encouraging European immigration to the region. Michael went on to document his extensive travels in South America in works such as *The Cotton Fields of Paraguay and Corrientes* (1864) and *Journey to Matto Grosso, September 1876* (1879). This latter volume was preceded by *From Europe to Paraguay and Matto Grosso* (1877) written by Marion McMurrough Mulhall, Michael's Irish-born wife and travelling companion, who portrayed herself as a courageous English woman facing the wilderness of the unknown country. Marion later published *Between the Amazon and Andes, or Ten Years of a Lady's Travels in the Pampas, Gran Chaco, Paraguay and Matto Grosso* (1881), which includes observations on Irish settlers in these areas. Although her book presents itself as history, Mulhall has in fact a mythical, ahistorical vision of the places she describes.

The Mulhall brothers were not the only Irish press pioneers in Buenos Aires at this time. In 1875, a Galway priest, Patrick J. Dillon, founded *The Southern Cross*, a weekly English-language newspaper to which *The Standard* eventually lost market share. Among its contributors was William Bulfin, who emigrated from Co. Offaly in 1884 and remained for twenty-five years, during which time he did much to nurture a sense of Irishness among his exiled compatriots. His tales of the pampas and

---

[24] Greene's memoirs were edited and published in 2015 by his great-great-niece Susan Wilkinson under the title *Recollections of an Irish-Born Doctor in Nineteenth-Century Argentina*.

'Sketches of Buenos Aires', published under the pen name 'Che Buono', chronicle his first-hand impressions of rural and urban life in the country, including the lives of his fellow countrymen who worked on the *estancias*. Under Bulfin's editorship in the 1890s, *The Southern Cross* sought to bind exiles to the old country more firmly through its regular coverage of Irish political and cultural affairs and promotion of the activities of the Gaelic League branch in Buenos Aires, which was established in 1899. In *Tales of the Pampas* (1900), his collection of humorous short stories set among *gauchos* and nomadic workers, Bulfin captures the effects of displacement on Irish settlers' attempts to sustain an ethnic identity in a new land.

Among Bulfin's circle of friends in Buenos Aires were Tom and Catherine Nevin, who had followed a similar emigrant route from the Irish midlands in the 1880s. Although neither was literary-minded, one of their daughters, Kathleen, wrote a fictionalized autobiography based on her mother's journey to South America and her first experiences in Buenos Aires. Entitled *You'll Never Go Back*, the book was completed after Kathleen's death by her sister Winnie and published in Boston in 1946. The plot revolves around three young Irish women who travel to Buenos Aires hoping to find work as teachers, save money and eventually return to Ireland. However, the Spanish language acts as a barrier to their social interaction with, and empathetic understanding of, the native people and immigrants from other cultures. Although written in the first person, *You'll Never Go Back* struggles to conjure up autonomous fictional identities and is closer in tone to an ethnographic study of the host society and culture. By contrast, Dublin-born Barbara Peart adopts a novelistic narratorial style in her memoir *Tia Barbarita* (1933), confessing that she could be 'much more revealing under the faint disguise of the third personal pronoun'.[25] At first conveying the freedom she felt after moving to Argentina in the 1870s with her new *estanciero* husband and his brothers, *Tia Barbarita* soon changes tone. Peart's illusions about the land of exile vanish once she settles in and faces the difficulties of isolation and learning a new language. She describes how, after many vicissitudes, she and her family thought of returning to Ireland before eventually deciding to move to Texas, thence to Mexico City and finally to Monterey.

If diasporas 'always leave a trail of collective memory about another place and time and create new maps of desire and attachment',[26] then

---

[25] Barbara Peart, *Tia Barbarita: Memories of Barbara Peart* (London: Faber and Faber, 1933), unpaginated foreword.

[26] Arjun Appadurai and Carol Breckenridge, 'Editors' Comments: On Moving Targets', in Steven Vertovec and Robin Cohen, eds., *Migration, Diasporas and Transnationalism* (Cheltenham: Edward Elgar Publishing, 1999), 484.

contemporary Irish-themed Latin American memoirs and autobiographies are keeping the past alive. In 1990, María Elena Walsh, an Irish-Argentine poet and children's songwriter, published a memoir entitled *Novios de Antaño (Old Fashioned Sweethearts)*, which contains autobiographical fragments of the first decade of her life. The final section, 'Grandmother Agnes', consists of a collection of family letters narrating the life of both Irish and British immigrants in Buenos Aires during the 1880s. Agnes states that the Irish who made a lot of money as sheep traders behaved like aristocrats and exploited some of their countrymen. More recently, fourth-generation Irish writer Juan José Delaney, who defines himself as Irish-*Porteño*, published *Moira Sullivan* (1999), a novel written in the form of a memoir of an elderly Irish-American woman, a former silent movie actress and scriptwriter who moved with her second husband to live in the Argentinean capital. In *Memoria de Theophilus Flynn (The Memoir of Theophilus Flynn)* (2012), Delaney narrates the turning points in the eponymous protagonist's life from multiple points of view and gives shape to the various imaginings of Ireland in the minds of the immigrant characters we encounter. Drawing on the technique of *bricolage*, Delaney rewrites the experiences of lives taken from historical sources, letters and even postcards published in *The Southern Cross*. As an exercise in ethnic reinvention, *Memoria de Theophilus Flynn* is as much a story of cultural haunting as anything written by contemporary Irish-American memoirists. Like several of the memoirs discussed in this chapter, it testifies to the persistence of the desire among autobiographers of dual heritage to find ways of giving an account of the self that is not one story but many.

Further reading

Ibson, John Duffy. *Will the World Break Your Heart? Dimensions and Consequences of Irish-American Assimilation*. New York: Garland Publishing, 1990.

Izarra, Laura P. Z. *Narrativas de la diáspora irlandesa bajo la Cruz del Sur*. Buenos Aires: Corregidor, 2010.

Kelly, Helen. *Irish 'Ingleses': The Irish Immigrant Experience in Argentina, 1840–1920*. Dublin: Irish Academic Press, 2009.

Murray, Edmundo. *Becoming Irlandés. Private Narratives of the Irish Emigration to Argentina, 1844–1912*. Buenos Aires: L.O.L.A., Literature of Latin America, 2006.

Rogers, James Silas, ed. *Extended Family: Essays on Being Irish American from 'New Hibernia Review'*. Chester Springs: Dufour Editions, 2013.

Rogers, James Silas. *Irish-American Autobiography: The Divided Hearts of Athletes, Priests, Pilgrims, and More*. Washington, DC: Catholic University of America Press, 2017.

CHAPTER 22

Life-Writing and Diaspora II
The Autobiographical Writings of the Irish in Britain and Australia

Patrick Buckridge and Liam Harte

There is no more common Irish journey than that made by generations of people 'across the water' to Great Britain. A complex set of factors, from the countries' geographical proximity to the colonial nature of their historical relationship, combine to ensure that Irish migration to Britain 'comprises a very large, very special case'.[1] Australia, too, has claims to exceptionalism as a receptor of Irish migrants. Oliver MacDonagh proposes three respects in which the Irish-Australian diaspora differs from its counterparts in Britain and North America: its historically high percentage of the total population of the new country, its very even demographic distribution and the somewhat special status of the Irish as a 'founding people', arriving in Australia – mainly as convicts and soldiers – at the beginning of its European colonization, thereby exercising a potentially stronger influence over the shape and destiny of the new nation than the other Irish emigrations could hope to achieve.[2] Although points of commonality co-exist with these markers of difference – particularly for Catholic Irish migrants, who have a shared historical experience of being a denigrated out-group in both countries – any joint examination of the autobiographical writings of the Irish in Britain and Australia must expect the contrasts to eclipse the correspondences. Yet, as this chapter will show, despite being shaped by highly distinctive diasporic histories and sociocultural conditions, these respective literary corpuses reveal certain narrative preoccupations that illuminate the shifting meanings of home and belonging for those whose identities are forged across boundaries and heritages.

[1] Donald Harman Akenson, *The Irish Diaspora: A Primer* (Toronto: P. D. Meany, 1996), 192.
[2] Oliver MacDonagh, 'The Irish in Australia: A General View', in Oliver MacDonagh and W. F. Mandle, eds., *Ireland and Irish-Australia* (London: Croom Helm, 1986), 155–72.

The plural subjectivities of the Irish in Britain

At the fountainhead of the tradition of Irish life-writing in Britain stands a woman of Protestant Anglo-Irish stock whose autobiographical writings disclose experiences, preoccupations and representational strategies that were to be revisited and reworked by many of the writers who came after her. Of Mary Davys we know pitifully little apart from the merest biographical details, which show that she was born in 1674 and died fifty-eight years later in Cambridge, having been resident in England since about the year 1700. The place of Davys's birth is a matter of uncertainty. In *The Fugitive; Or, The Country Ramble* (1705), she explains that she was taken to Ireland by her mother at the age of six. Two decades later, in *The Merry Wanderer* (1725), a rewriting of *The Fugitive* in which Davys recounts her travels in England and Wales, she flatly contradicts this assertion by claiming Irish birth. One reason for such inconsistency may lie in 'a fear that her place of origin may discredit her' in an England where 'distrust and disparagement of the Irish was both an established comic trope and a matter of contemporary concern'.[3] As an impecunious woman abroad, who was determined to make a living from her writing, Davys would have had to negotiate a plethora of cultural prejudices and social stigmas in early eighteenth-century England, chief among which was the equation of female authorship with sexual promiscuity and prostitution. Proclaiming her nationality could therefore only worsen her predicament, as she was not only an outsider but also a widow, the loss of her clergyman husband in 1698 having left her vulnerable to reputational as much as physical injury.

Not that Mary Davys could unequivocally lay claim to an Irish identity in the first place, even we accept that she was born in the country. As a Protestant Anglo-Irish woman she belonged to a settler colonial community that, as its hyphenated designation indicates, was on intimate terms with duality, ambivalence and insecurity. Yet in *The Merry Wanderer,* Davys conceals any identity crisis she may have experienced in Ireland behind an amusing and sophisticated game of identity role-play, which she acts out in order to mock her English hosts' racial prejudice and misogyny. Stigmatized as one of the 'wild Irish' by the first Englishman she meets, Davys plays up to the stereotype by pretending to be a once barbarous native Irish woman who was civilized by the English in Ireland during her childhood. Her repudiation of the ideology that racialized the indigenous

---

[3] Martha F. Bowden, 'Mary Davys: Self-Representation and the Woman Writer's Reputation in the Early Eighteenth Century', *Women's Writing*, 3:1 (1996), 24, 19.

Irish as inferior others explicitly invokes the satiric genius of Jonathan Swift, yet silently masks the inconvenient truth that the power and privilege of the Protestant elite in early modern Ireland depended upon the territorial expropriation and political disenfranchisement of the majority Catholic population. Thus, the early autobiographical evidence suggests that the journey from Ireland to England called for a certain nimbleness of wit as well as of foot.

This resort to play-acting and code-switching to negotiate the intricacies of national affiliation or deflect the arrows of bigotry is a traceable thread in the work of later Anglo-Irish autobiographers who ventured into Britain. One such was the educationalist and engineer Richard Lovell Edgeworth. Although his forebears owned land in Ireland since Elizabethan times, Edgeworth himself was born in Bath and moved his family back to the ancestral estate in Co. Longford in 1782. Punctuated by journeys back and forth across the Irish Sea, Edgeworth's *Memoirs* (1820), which was posthumously completed by his novelist daughter Maria, contains a fleeting insight into his becoming a cultural chameleon at an early age, capable of switching between an Irish brogue and an English accent as circumstances required. The pleasure Edgeworth takes in reporting that he 'never was taken for an Irishman'[4] when in English company would doubtless have amused the culturally and sexually ambiguous Oscar Wilde, whose artistic career and public persona in late Victorian London were built upon the strategic performance of otherness as a means of subverting moral hierarchies and the stereotyping of temperament. Wilde's affinity for the mask and the pose were such that W. B. Yeats formed the impression that he 'perpetually performed a play which was in all things the opposite of all that he had known in childhood and early youth'.[5]

As critics have observed, Wilde's persona-switching reflected his belief that identities were not amenable to stable and secure iteration, since 'in being true to a single self, a sincere man may be false to half a dozen other selves'.[6] Such determined openness to plural subjectivities is also an underlying thematic in the art of Elizabeth Bowen and Louis MacNeice, paradigmatic literary exemplars of modern(ist) Anglo-Irish bifurcation. All three of these writers produced partial autobiographies in which the drive to chronicle or confess is in tension with the impulse to refashion the self or explore imagined or imaginary selves. Wilde's expurgatory love

[4] Richard Lovell Edgeworth, *Memoirs of Richard Lovell Edgeworth* (London: R. Hunter, 1820), vol. 1, 63.
[5] W. B. Yeats, *Autobiographies* (London: Papermac, 1980), 138.
[6] Declan Kiberd, *Inventing Ireland: The Literature of the Modern Nation* (London: Jonathan Cape, 1995), 38.

letter, *De Profundis*, written in 1897 and first published in edited form in 1905, is a hybrid, divided text in which he alternates between the roles of hero and victim; Bowen's short, episodic *Seven Winters* (1942) is poised between her realization 'that I was I' and her 'comprehension of life as being other than mine'[7]; and MacNeice's *The Strings Are False: An Unfinished Autobiography* (1965) sets out to test a hypothesis of relational subjectivity: 'Maybe, if I look back, I shall find that my life is not just mine, that it mirrors the lives of the others – or shall I say the Life of the Other?'[8]

If these autobiographers' exploration of the narrative possibilities of performance and performativity earns them a certain typicality as writers of no singular identity, their class background and literary genius set them apart from the majority of Irish immigrants that left autobiographical accounts of their experiences in Britain, a majority that itself constitutes a tiny fraction of the sustained exodus that saw over eight million people leave Ireland between 1800 and 1922.[9] Although the impoverished Irish were frequently denigrated as a malign influence, the social, economic and industrial transformation of nineteenth-century Britain would not have been possible without this 'proletarian diaspora – largely unskilled, highly localized and with little money'.[10] Economic need was a perennial driver of this migratory stream, such that 'by the 1830s emigration was more than an economic necessity; it had become part of the Irish people's culture'.[11] It was to remain so throughout the post-Famine era, fluctuations in the levels and patterns of emigration notwithstanding. It should not surprise us, then, to find that experiences of work and employment are recurring concerns and common structuring devices in the autobiographies of the poorer class of Irish people in post-1800 Britain. This is evident from the titles of some the earliest autobiographical accounts of working-class Irishmen in Victorian England, such as 'Life of an Irish Tailor, Written by Himself' (1857) by Antrim-born J. E. and 'Fifty Years' Experience of an Irish Shoemaker in London' (1869) by John O'Neill, both of which chronicle the authors' search for regular employment against a backdrop of economic adversity and personal misfortune. Despite living through the spectacular changes

---

[7] Elizabeth Bowen, *Seven Winters and Afterthoughts* (New York: Alfred A. Knopf, 1962), 15, 55.

[8] Louis MacNeice, *The Strings Are False: An Unfinished Autobiography* (London: Faber and Faber, 1965), 35.

[9] Enda Delaney, *The Irish in Post-War Britain* (Oxford: Oxford University Press, 2007), 11.

[10] John Hutchinson, 'Diaspora Dilemmas and Shifting Allegiances: The Irish in London between Nationalism, Catholicism and Labourism (1900–22)', *Studies in Ethnicity and Nationalism*, 10:1 (2010), 122.

[11] Donald M. MacRaild, *Irish Migrants in Modern Britain, 1750–1922* (Basingstoke: Macmillan, 1999), 41.

wrought by the British industrial revolution, neither worker speaks the language of political radicalism or class struggle; both instead accentuate the benefits of diligence, thrift, abstinence and piety, thus implicitly combating pejorative associations of the immigrant Irish with moral degradation and fecklessness.

Involvement in radical politics does feature in Ulster-born James Dawson Burn's *The Autobiography of a Beggar Boy* (1855), which was published anonymously and went through four editions in the 1850s. Yet it too strikes a morally improving note, even though the book is centrally concerned with the chronically rootless author's desire to overcome his feelings of existential alienation, acquire self-knowledge and become a respected member of society. Although usually classified as a British memoir (perhaps because of Burn's vagueness about his origins and failure to self-identify as Irish), *The Autobiography of a Beggar Boy* is an important precursor text in the male-dominated tradition of life-writing by tramps and unskilled Irish migratory workers in Britain who found themselves in low-status jobs. Witty, moving and reflective, Burn's memoir anticipates Patrick MacGill's semi-fictional *Children of the Dead End* (1914), whose rare and vivid recreation of the social habits and mindsets of tramp navvies gripped the Edwardian imagination as intensely as Burn's testimony did the Victorian. MacGill's landmark work proved highly inspirational for later literary-minded migrants, especially those from impoverished rural backgrounds, notably Thomas Skelton, who recollects his navvying experiences in interwar England and Scotland in *Clay Under Clover* (1949); Dónall Mac Amhlaigh, whose *Dialann Deoraí* (1960), translated as *An Irish Navvy: The Diary of an Exile* in 1964, gives voice to the homesickness and resilience of the postwar Irish labourer in England; and John Neary, author of the conversationally narrated and privately published *Memories of the Long Distance Kiddies* (1994), which powerfully conveys the unforgiving social environment of nomadic labourers in 1930s England.

This corpus of navvy life-writing is further augmented by the autobiographies of workers whose lives were shaped by an Irish economic system that had institutionalized seasonal migration to Britain in the decades before and after the establishment of the Irish Free State in 1922. The most significant of these are Patrick Gallagher's *My Story* (1939), Micí Mac Gabhann's *Rotha Mór an tSaoil* (1959), translated as *The Hard Road to Klondike* in 1962 and Sean Ó Ciaráin's *Farewell to Mayo: An Emigrant's Memoirs of Ireland and Scotland* (1991), which is dedicated to Mac Amhlaigh. These works are manifestly the testimonies of unassimilated outsiders, cultural strangers who, as one of their number remarked, 'regarded themselves as a race apart'[12] and whose sense of belonging was breached by continual travel back and forth across the Irish Sea. Each developed their own strategy for coping with displacement and report on the shifting accommodations of others to similarly bilocated lives. Emotionally anchored in Ireland, few intended to make Britain their home, even those, such as Mac Amhlaigh, who expressed a frustrated contempt for the Irish governments and politicians that made them economic refugees in the first place. While the narrative uses to which the life is put varies with the writer, the fact that most of these dislocated figures share a desire to 'set down the inside story of our experiences as a document to those who come after us'[13] makes them compelling observers of the working lives of impoverished rural Irish men in England and Scotland between the 1880s and the 1950s.

The perspectives of these proletarian memoirists are complemented by the insights of better-educated migrants whose self-positioning is more overtly intercultural and whose interweaving of personal history and socio-cultural commentary is more pronounced. These include Oxford-educated John Stewart Collis, author of *An Irishman's England* (1937), an autoethno-graphic portrait infused by a deep fascination and regard for the English character, and Mairin Mitchell and Nesca Robb, authors of *Back to England* (1941) and *An Ulsterwoman in England, 1924–1941* (1942) respec-tively. Both women profess a 'deep, if not wholly uncritical, affection'[14] for the English as 'the most civilised people in the world',[15] sentiments that were strongly coloured by their experiences of wartime London. The early 1940s witnessed a spike in the number of Irish workers emigrating to Britain, among whom were many women destined for work in munitions factories, hospitals and private houses. The sombre mood of this exodus is recalled in *Three Villages* (1977) by Dónal Foley, who likens the British Railways ship on which he sailed in 1944 to 'a travelling Irish town' from which 'a long dark crocodile of people' emerged on its arrival at Holyhead, to the 'dread sound' of an air raid siren.[16] Although few in number, female autobiographical perspectives on this period show how emigration could be a catalyst for a more emotionally fulfilling existence than the one left behind. Both Mauyen Keane's *Hello, Is It All Over?* (1984) and Elaine

---

[12] Dónal Foley, *Three Villages: An Autobiography* (Dublin: Egotist Press, 1977), 59.
[13] Sean Ó Ciaráin, *Farewell to Mayo: An Emigrant's Memoirs of Ireland and Scotland* (Dublin: Brookside, 1991), unpaginated preface.
[14] Nesca Robb, *An Ulsterwoman in England, 1924–1941* (Cambridge: Cambridge University Press, 1942), vii.
[15] Mairin Mitchell, *Back to England* (London: Frederick Muller, 1941), 179.
[16] Foley, *Three Villages*, 53, 54.

Crowley's *Technical Virgins* (1998) depict the blossoming of young women's lives away from an Ireland that Crowley condemns as claustrophobically pious, while *A Restless Life* (2008) by Leland Bardwell, who fled to Birmingham in 1944 as a pregnant teenager, provides a synoptic portrait of this generation's longer-term fate: 'Ingenuous Irish girls. What did we know? Fodder for the English war. Without qualifications. One by one we melted into this foreign atmosphere. Got to like it, even, the freedom, the anonymity.'[17]

Foley's assertion that, for these first-generation emigrants, '"Being Irish" was not a term that was exactly defined for anybody'[18] took on a much sharper significance for many of their sons and daughters, for whom the articulation of an identity that reflected their sense of cultural specificity and hyphenation has seldom been straightforward. If the categories of 'British' or 'English' are problematic because they presuppose assimilation and silence difference, then, as Marc Scully observes, 'claiming Irishness in an English accent is fraught with difficulty and possible rejection, as the two identities tend to be seen as incompatible. Indicative of this perceived incompatibility is the fact that no widespread "English-Irish" *national* equivalent of the "Irish-American" identity label exists.'[19] Hence the use of the pejorative term 'plastic Paddy' to exclude from the circle of 'authentic' Irishness those who were not born in Ireland and return them to the discursive terrain of Britishness, where they exist as 'a buried presence', as writer Moy McCrory explains:

> I remember how 'we' were brought up dreaming of somewhere else. We grew up dreaming history ... We were not immigrants in the proper way, we did not come up on official forms as a minority group, but in those places we had settled, we were a problem to be solved. We were not expected to achieve. We were to be pitied.[20]

The governing preoccupations of second-generation Irish autobiography, then, are dilemmas of identification and belonging, intergenerational tensions, the complications of 'home' and the gap between myth and

---

[17] Leland Bardwell, *A Restless Life* (Dublin: Liberties Press, 2008), 147–48.
[18] Foley, *Three Villages*, 60.
[19] Marc Scully, '"Plastic and Proud"? Discourses of Authenticity among Second-Generation Irish in England', *Psychology and Society*, 2:2 (2009), 126. Original emphasis. Interestingly, the Colchester-born broadcaster Dermot O'Leary begins his memoir, *The Soundtrack of My Life* (London: Hodder and Stoughton, 2014), by announcing his Irishness in a very familiar English accent: 'OK, to kick things off, I'm Irish. I know I don't sound it, but I am' (1).
[20] Moy McCrory, '"This Time and Now": Identity and Belonging in the Irish Diaspora: The Irish in Britain and Second-Generation Silence', in Christine Berberich, Neil Campbell and Robert Hudson, eds., *Land and Identity: Theory, Memory, and Practice* (Amsterdam: Rodopi, 2012), 172.

reality. More often than not, these themes are explored within working-class contexts, through the lens of childhood experience. Ingrained poverty and inequality frame early renditions of the intimate paradoxes of growing up Irish in Britain in Joseph Keating's *My Struggle for Life* (1916), Tom Barclay's *Memoirs and Medleys: The Autobiography of a Bottle-Washer* (1934) and Pat O'Mara's *The Autobiography of a Liverpool Irish Slummy* (1934). Brian Keaney's *Don't Hang About* (1985), which is explicitly pitched at 'children of immigrant parents', light-heartedly describes 'what it feels like to be growing up slightly at odds with your surroundings' in an Irish working-class family in 1970s Walthamstow.[21] Kentish Town of the late 1940s and 1950s is the setting for the far more harrowing childhood scenes of John Healy's *The Grass Arena* (1988), which include the protagonist's early experiences of being the butt of anti-Irish prejudice in London and of Anglophobic hostility during holidays in Sligo. The psychic legacies of a poor second-generation upbringing in which the vestigial pull of a putatively Arcadian parental homeland destabilizes the child's mundane here-and-now are explored in Bill Naughton's *On the Pig's Back* (1987) and *Saintly Billy* (1988), John Boyle's *Galloway Street: Growing Up Irish in Scotland* (2001) and John Bird's *Some Luck* (2002). But the most sustained investigation of the perplexities of inherited homesickness is to be found in *The Falling Angels: An Irish Romance* (1999), journalist John Walsh's memoir of his middle-class London Irish upbringing. Walsh's account of how the years he spent 'being both English and Irish' transformed him into 'a cultural chameleon' not only returns us to the tropes of play-acting and code-switching in the Anglo-Irish autobiographies of earlier eras, albeit with added self-reflexivity.[22] It also holds in counterpoint the inescapability of the second-generation desire for a form of 'homecoming' that would satisfy the ache to belong and the impossibility of this desire ever being more than a 'romance'.

The Irish-Australian Odyssey

Much has been claimed for the role of the Irish in Australia's national development. Patrick O'Farrell, for example, argued that 'until very recently, the Irish have been the dynamic factor in Australian history, that is, the galvanizing force at the centre of the evolution of our national

---

[21] Brian Keaney, *Don't Hang About* (Oxford: Oxford University Press, 1985), 104–05.
[22] John Walsh, *The Falling Angels: An Irish Romance* (London: Flamingo, 2000), 30, 225.

character'.[23] Such claims are not inconsistent with a recognition of the contempt, distrust and prejudice to which people of Irish birth and descent in Australia – and particularly the Catholic Irish – were subjected by the dominant English culture for several generations; indeed, O'Farrell saw these as empowering. But the combination of demographic strength and cultural subordination made for ambivalence and instability in the way Irishness was regarded, not least by the Irish themselves, whose individual responses to their own ethnicity might range from proud celebration to outright denial, with everything in between.

Life-writing is the literary form *par excellence* in which the complexity of these responses can be registered and explored. Indeed, an Irish connection, however mediated, displaced or minimized, might well exert a distinctive pressure on the work of self-understanding and self-construction that shapes and animates the form. To see how this works in particular instances, this discussion will propose a general pattern or template for the ways in which Irish-Australian writers have tended to articulate their self-narratives. It is a pattern that hints at the felt importance, even the *inescapability*, of the Irish connection, enacting it even when the surface of the text ignores or denies it. A shorthand term for the pattern might be 'Odyssean', since it involves a moment of departure from 'home' (Ireland/Ithaca) and a moment of return, more or less delayed, which is also a moment of rediscovery. Departure and return are often not physical journeys but journeys of the mind or heart; but the persistence of the pattern, even when the two movements are psychic rather than physical, is of some significance.

William Ievers' *Fifty Years After, or Old Scenes Revisited* (1890) provides a useful *entrée* to the form, if only because its Odyssean pattern is so clearly delineated. Ievers was born in Limerick in 1818 and emigrated with his wife and six children to Melbourne in 1855, where he became a wealthy and prominent estate agent. *Fifty Years After* is not a full autobiography but a detailed memoir of an extended world tour he undertook with his eldest son in 1890, of which the central section describes their three-month stay in Ireland. The accounts of Limerick and its surroundings are disarmingly direct in their wistful sorrow at old places now changed, old friends gone and hospitable but unfamiliar kinsfolk. There is also – perhaps unexpectedly, given the author's distance and estrangement from the country of his youth – a sense of serious (and partisan) engagement with, and almost ownership of, Ireland's great national issue, Home Rule, with Ievers warning that the wealthy classes opposing it risk exclusion from a future Ireland.

---

[23] Patrick O'Farrell, *The Irish in Australia* (Sydney: University of New South Wales Press, 1987), 10.

Ievers' memoir points us towards other Odyssean instances that yield at least partial comparisons. Sir James Duhig, Catholic archbishop of Brisbane from 1917 to 1965, was born near Limerick in 1871 and emigrated to Brisbane with his family at the age of thirteen. Duhig returned to Ireland twice, in 1909 and 1922, both times as extensions to his episcopal *ad limina* visits to Rome. His memoir *Crowded Years* (1947) describes both visits rather ceremoniously, in terms of public figures and momentous historic events. Where Duhig's attachment to Ireland shines out is in the light-hearted and often humorous anecdotes and characters of Irish-Catholic Australia, such as the two parish priests whose 'good, clean Irish wit, like the knife of the skilled surgeon, cut deep without leaving any jagged edges'.[24] Unlike the militant Irish republican Daniel Mannix, archbishop of Melbourne from 1917 to 1963, Duhig was a conciliator, more interested in what the Irish contributed to Australian Catholic culture than in what Irish-Australians might do for the emerging Irish nation. His memoir ends, accordingly, on a note of gratitude 'to Australia that took me to its arms as a child, that became my adopted country, and that afforded me opportunities which I might have looked for in vain elsewhere'.[25]

The bushranger Ned Kelly's parting verdict on the world – 'Such is life!' – inspired Joseph Furphy's fictional masterpiece of that name. But Ned himself also wrote (or, rather, dictated) what could fairly be regarded as a memoir, the famous 'Jerilderie Letter' of 1879, a 'testament' of over 8,000 words in which he gives an unpunctuated but eloquent account of the events of the last ten years of his short life, inveighing against police corruption and defending his criminal actions as a response to the cruel treatment meted out by police and government officials to his own and other Irish-Australian families. Kelly was born in rural Victoria in 1855, but his parents were from Tipperary and Antrim (his father a transportee), and Ned's family and most of those in the surrounding district were strongly Irish and Catholic. In that figurative sense, Ned's point of departure was indeed Ireland, even though his life was lived in Australia. Furthermore, the 'Letter', written within a year of his death, marks an emphatic return, not only to the Irish culture of his family and community, but to an idea of Ireland itself as a nation with a long history of colonial suffering and injustice analogous with his own.[26]

---

[24] James Duhig, *Crowded Years* (Sydney: Angus and Robertson, 1947), 11.   [25] Ibid., 138.
[26] The manuscript of the 'Letter' is available on the National Museum of Australia website, www .nma.gov.au/collections/collection_interactives/jerilderie_letter (accessed 1 February 2016).

Some of the police involved in Kelly's pursuit and capture were themselves Irish, as were four of the gang's police victims. Superintendent John Sadleir, born in Tipperary in 1833, the man in charge of the famous siege at Glenrowan, wrote a fuller and rather more conventional memoir, *Recollections of a Victorian Police Officer* (1913). It is a modest and dispassionate narrative, of which some sixty pages are devoted to the Kelly gang, compared with a mere two pages on Sadleir's own life in Ireland before he emigrated to Melbourne, at the age of nineteen, with two brothers. Sadleir is no exile from Erin and no Odyssean return to Tipperary is either undertaken or even imagined by him. Irishness is simply not a valued component of his professional identity; his only reference to it is made when he blames his failure to prevent a riot between Orangemen and Catholics in Brunswick on his informant, an Irish Catholic priest, 'speaking inaccurately, as my countrymen are apt to do'.[27]

Similar demeaning – if perhaps also affectionate – stereotypes are invoked by Martin Cash, who published an autobiography, *Martin Cash, the Bushranger of Van Diemen's Land in 1843–4*, in 1870. Like Sadleir, Cash, a Wexford boy, gives a quite brief account of his life in Ireland prior to his transportation for house-breaking, also at the age of nineteen. His story comprises long periods of hardship and danger which he survives by a strict self-discipline only occasionally derailed by moments of passion or rebelliousness, and these are nearly always marked as regrettable irruptions of Irishness. Cash's use of his ethnicity – at least in autobiographical retrospect – as an instrument of self-fashioning is echoed in the memoirs of the writer James Dwyer, born in New South Wales in 1874 to working-class parents from Cork. From the age of twenty-five, he served three years for counterfeiting in the notorious Goulburn Jail, an ordeal which he also survived by recognizing and restraining his Irish inheritance: 'I determined to put a clutch on the rebellious traits that came from an Irish-bred Australian and see the days through with patience.'[28] That constructive 'departure' was followed, however, by a later redemptive return to his ethnicity, proudly embracing his parents' Irish heritage. Easily the most prominent of all Australia's Irish prisoners was the great colonial statesman Sir Charles Gavan Duffy, born in Monaghan in 1816 and imprisoned for his leading role in the Young Irelander rebellion of 1848. Duffy emigrated to Melbourne in 1855 and spent fourteen turbulent years in Victorian politics before retiring to the south of France. Duffy explained the nature and purpose of his two-volume

---

[27] John Sadleir, *Recollections of a Victorian Police Officer* (Melbourne: George Robertson and Co., 1913), 259.
[28] J. F. Dwyer, *Leg-Irons on Wings* (Melbourne: Georgian House, 1949), 61.

autobiography as 'authentic history',[29] both Irish and Australian. Accordingly, he endeavoured 'to make the story as impersonal as such a narrative can ever become'.[30] He succeeded only too well: his is indeed a very 'public' life story, ending in 1880, the year when he retired from the speakership of the Victorian parliament, wearied by sectarian accusations of a loyalty divided between the public interest and the pope.

Other Irish-Australian politicians also wrote extended memoirs. Some, like Simon Hickey and Sir Arthur Fadden, grounded their identities, affectively and intellectually, in the history and legends of Australia rather than Ireland, calling on their Irish backgrounds mainly as a source of sentiment and humour. Hickey, a successful manufacturer, a Catholic and a Labor member of the New South Wales parliament during the 1920s and 1930s, wrote a funny and erudite book of reminiscences, *Travelled Roads* (1951), in which he suggested that Irish immigrants like his father 'were mostly "characters" and contributed something to the infrequent humour of pioneering days'.[31] Fadden was Australian Federal Treasurer through the 1950s. In his memoir *They Called Me Artie* (1969), he mentions his parents' origins in Galway and Tyrone on the first page and never alludes to Ireland again. Like many Irish-Australians, Hickey and Fadden clearly did not find their Irish heritage inescapable or even perhaps especially interesting in itself, though both men were probably formed by it – in their humour, their gregariousness and their love of a good story – in ways they declined to scrutinize.

Not so Arthur Lynch, one of the most remarkable individuals to claim the hyphenated identity. Classified in the *Australian Dictionary of Biography* as a 'rebel and polymath',[32] Lynch was the fourth of fourteen children born to an Irish father and a Scottish mother in Smythesdale, Victoria in 1861. By the age of twenty-six, he had gained degrees in civil engineering, mathematics and moral philosophy at the University of Melbourne (where he was also a champion athlete) before departing for Europe, where he continued his studies. Along the way he found time to write nearly thirty books, among them his autobiography, *My Life Story* (1924). In the late 1890s, he travelled to South Africa as a war correspondent, but ended up forming and commanding an Irish brigade to fight with the

[29] Sir Charles Gavan Duffy, *My Life in Two Hemispheres* (London: T. Fisher Unwin, 1898), vol. 1, 1.
[30] Ibid., 2.   [31] Simon Hickey, *Travelled Roads* (Melbourne: Cheshire, 1951), 3.
[32] Geoffrey Serle, 'Lynch, Arthur Alfred (1861–1934)', *Australian Dictionary of Biography*, http://adb.anu.edu.au/biography/lynch-arthur-alfred-7270/text12599 (accessed 11 February 2016). Patrick Buckridge is indebted to the *Australian Dictionary of Biography* for information about many of the writers discussed in this chapter.

Boers against the British. On his return to England in 1902 he was arrested, tried and sentenced to death for treason, but released after a year by royal intervention and later pardoned following mass petitions. Thereupon he entered parliament and retained a seat (later West Clare) until 1918, after conducting an energetic campaign of Irish recruitment for the British army. In recognition of this war service, the Australian prime minister Billy Hughes saw fit to 'forgive' Lynch's earlier crimes against the empire and would have welcomed him back in Australia. But he never did return and was to die in London in 1934. Lynch's journey to Ireland after a childhood spent under the influence of a strong and revered Irish Catholic father bears a superficial resemblance to the Odyssean pattern, but his emotional and intellectual affiliations actually suggest an inversion of the pattern. A return to Australia would have completed his homecoming, for Australia, not Ireland, was Lynch's 'native land',[33] even though he realized, as a young man, that it could never accommodate his ambitions.

Published autobiographies by Irish-Australian women, while disappointingly few in number, also exhibit the varied ways in which the two nations can figure in the dynamic of narrative self-construction. One female memoirist with a more direct connection to Australian politics than Arthur Lynch was Ada Kidgell, the radical liberal wife of William Holman, the first Labor premier of New South Wales. Born in 1869, Ada Holman worked as a literary and political journalist before her marriage, and attributed her passion for politics to her Irish-born mother Agnes Martin, 'the descendant of a brave rebel Irish family'.[34] Her *Memoirs of a Premier's Wife* (1948), however, is largely a series of remembered anecdotes about the famous people she met during her travels with her brilliant and controversial husband. They include the Irish parliamentarian and journalist T. P. O'Connor, who, in passing on greetings from her cousins in Ireland, addresses her 'in a rich voice with just the right touch of brogue'.[35] The phrase aestheticizes and sentimentalizes Irishness, separating it from her real family connections; such cultural distancing is a common characteristic of colonial diasporas.[36]

For Catherine 'Caddie' Edmonds, author of *Caddie: The Autobiography of a Sydney Barmaid* (1953), the brogue has an interestingly different

[33] Arthur Lynch, *My Life Story* (London: John Long, 1924), 68.
[34] Ada Holman, *Memoirs of a Premier's Wife* (Sydney: Angus and Robertson, 1948), 1.
[35] Ibid., 68.
[36] A similar phenomenon can be noted among members of the Scottish diaspora in Australia. See Patrick Buckridge, 'Robert Burns in Colonial Queensland: Sentiment, Scottishness and Universal Appeal', *Queensland Review*, 16.1 (2009), 69–78.

function, as a token of personal deliverance. Born in 1900 in Penrith, New South Wales to an Irish-born railway fettler, Caddie was raised in poverty and regularly abused by her drunken father. Hers is a story of fierce independence and individual survival, but she sometimes receives unexpected help, and on two of those occasions – when an old woman, Mrs Sweeney, appears out of nowhere to mind her children while she works in the bar, and again when she is offered a job as a bookie by one Paddy Maher – her benefactors are Irish. Touchingly, Mrs Sweeney's brogue, which thickens as she reminisces, comes to signify the parental love and security Caddie had been denied by her own Irish parents. Again, the circularity of the Irish-Australian odyssey is hinted at, though Irishness as such is barely thematized here at all.

The brogue makes a fleeting appearance again, this time as a Victorian-era patriarch's medium of 'withering scorn'[37] for his daughter's social lapses, in a memoir that could hardly be more different from Caddie's in ambience and sensibility. Kathleen Fitzpatrick, née Pitt, an academic historian at the University of Melbourne from the 1930s to the 1960s, had upper-middle-class Irish Catholic grandparents on both sides. Her memoir, *Solid Bluestone Foundations* (1983), tells the story of her first twenty-five years, ending just a few years before her brief marriage to the radical historian Brian Fitzpatrick. Even though her Irish point of departure was thus two generations old, her closeness both to her maternal grandmother's family, the O'Briens, and to her paternal grandfather's, the Pitts, made the two families' different styles of Irishness and Catholicism surprisingly central to her sense of her own individual formation. In writing her much later account of those early years in Melbourne and Oxford, Fitzpatrick is constantly drawn to 'Irish indices' – the brogue is one – as keys to understanding herself and the other people in her life: her cousin's 'Irish-looking . . . dark hair and dark blue eyes'; her father's 'verbal play, and . . . dry, stinging Irish wit'; her own 'gift of the gab, very common among people with Irish blood'; and the 'black Irish pride' that enabled her to cope with academic setbacks with dignity.[38] It is as if, in seeking to make sense of her youthful experiences, Fitzpatrick – in a kind of imaginative 'homecoming' – has adopted received national stereotypes and uses them as intellectual tools to investigate the complexities in her own and her family's past lives.

---

[37] Kathleen Fitzpatrick, *Solid Bluestone Foundations and Other Memories of a Melbourne Girlhood, 1908–1928* (Melbourne: Macmillan, 1983), 38.
[38] Ibid., 12–14, 57, 140, 188.

Like Fitzpatrick, Vincent Buckley draws on a rich Irish typology in *Cutting Green Hay* (1983), the first of his two books of memoirs, but makes no attempt to analyse himself in these terms. Like Duffy, he believed 'the self of the narrator does not need stressing, for it can be deduced, or seen in silhouette, as the light falls on the places where he lived with others'.[39] One such place was Buckley's 'home country' around Shepparton in Victoria, to which most of his forebears had come from Tipperary and Cork during the Famine years. Once here, he insists, though they built a strong and durable sense of Irish Catholic identity in the new country, 'there was little sense of connected history ... little keeping of a lifeline to Ireland by direct tapping of an historical or mythopoeic memory'.[40] Buckley's complex critique of Celtic memory is persuasive in his own Australian context: at least for the working-class Catholic majority of the post-Famine period, Irishness was a badge of affiliation with others in the same situation rather than a substantive inheritance from another time and place. And though homesickness was surely a sad reality for many of the migrants themselves, the overriding imperative was to keep the past in its place and get on with the job of becoming Australians. Buckley's own preoccupation with Irish politics in his second memoir, *Memory Ireland* (1985), was a spiritual homecoming of sorts, to what he called his 'source country';[41] but it was also (as for Odysseus) a dispiriting revelation of Ireland's less admirable contemporary realities. His more lyrical responses he reserved for his poetry.

Thomas Keneally, a novelist of international repute, is also one of the most familiarly Irish of Irish-Australians. This is partly because of his well-known Irish Catholic background and his public advocacy for an Australian republic on the Irish model. Keneally's directly autobiographical writing, like Buckley's, is divided between two books, of which the later one, *Homebush Boy* (1995), deals with his home life, his schooling and his decision, in his sixteenth year, to enter the Catholic priesthood (an ambition he abandoned before ordination). Four years prior to this book, however, Keneally had published another memoir, *Now and in Time to Be* (1991), the Yeatsian title of which reflects the intense interest in Ireland and its history that has characterized his later years, and which thus conforms – part metaphorically – to the Odyssean pattern of departure and homecoming. If Buckley's engagement with modern Ireland was intellectual and political, Keneally's is social, emotional and geographical; indeed, the book is structured as a composite

---

[39] Vincent Buckley, *Cutting Green Hay: Friendships, Movements and Cultural Conflicts in Australia's Great Decades* (Ringwood, Victoria: Penguin, 1983), xii.
[40] Ibid., 10–12.   [41] Vincent Buckley, 'Looking at Ireland', *Helix*, 5–6 (1980), 105–06.

tour of Ireland and is packed with physical descriptions and place-specific historical anecdotes. It is also permeated by a nagging awareness that 'sentiment is the malaise of the returning pilgrim of Irish connection. The sensible native Irish are offended by it.'[42] At every stage of his journey, wrong assumptions and misrecognitions threaten the possibility of acceptance, even for the eager Irish-Australian. Immersed in Irish history, landscape and the ordinary people he happens upon, Keneally is more focused on his immediate experiences, and the passing meditations they evoke, than on the larger meaning of it all, either for him or for Ireland. To some extent, it is a process of positive disenchantment – 'the returning visitor to Ireland always thinks according to the iconography of rebellion'[43] – but one that leads to the very writerly conclusion that storytelling and myth-making are still at the heart of the Irish character.

Neither Buckley nor Keneally have much to say about their grandparents' experience of leaving Ireland or of arriving and settling in Australia. This is partly through lack of information, but there is also a sense that both authors understand and approve their forebears' determination to start life afresh in the new country, in a largely compliant if not assimilated relation to its dominant culture: 'Britishness prevailed, and even the Irish-Australian working class were part of that Britishness.'[44] To the extent that a group identity was embraced, it was Catholicism rather than Irishness that provided both the external separation and the internal coherence of the group. For Gerard Windsor, whose three books of memoirs span the 1990s, the situation was different. Having known two of his grandparents well – his Irish paternal grandfather and Irish-Australian maternal grandmother – he can portray them as complex individuals, while at the same time seeing their respective careers as doctor and shopkeeper as exemplary realizations of the opportunities available to ambitious middle-class Irish Catholics in early twentieth-century Australia. These are the central themes and characters of the first book, *I'll Just Tell You This* (1999), which was initially published as a collection of stories and sketches called *Family Lore* in 1990. The second, *Heaven Where the Bachelors Sit* (1996), deals with the author's seven years in the Society of Jesus, and the third, *I Asked Cathleen to Dance* (1999), with his several visits to Ireland. The trilogy as a whole is thus yet another instance of the Odyssean pattern.

The third volume is entirely devoted to Windsor's direct experience of Ireland. The metaphor of 'entering' the eponymous Cathleen as an act of

---

[42] Ibid. 3.   [43] Ibid., 13.
[44] Thomas Keneally, *Homebush Boy: A Memoir* (Melbourne: William Heinemann Australia, 1995), 25.

sexual penetration reflects and parallels the author's own belated entry into sexual experience. The emphasis throughout, however, falls on the ambiguity, impenetrability and opacity of the social and sexual culture he encounters, and on the diversity and unpredictability of Irish people, places and events. There is very little sense of his Irish sojourns as an Ithacan 'homecoming' – and this despite the fact that, unlike Buckley or Keneally, he does in fact find relatives there. Places and people change between visits, and the carefully achronological and recursive structure of the narrative militates against any obvious sense of growing familiarity with, let alone understanding of, the country. Windsor's confrontations with the 'real' Ireland, nonetheless, are deeply personal, indeed *person-forming*, in ways that none of the other Irish-Australian encounters recorded in these autobiographies seem to be. Whether or not, in the end, the myth of an Odyssean circularity can usefully contain or illuminate the Irish-Australian subject's vexed and varied negotiations with the idea of Ireland – and there are plainly outliers – there is a striking historical irony in the fact that the 'outsider' status imposed on many of the earliest Irish immigrants to Australia has also been experienced by some, at least, of the more recent Irish-Australian 'homecomers' to Ireland.

Further reading

Delaney, Enda. *The Irish in Post-War Britain.* Oxford: Oxford University Press, 2007.

Fitzpatrick, David. *Oceans of Consolation: Personal Accounts of Irish Migration to Australia.* Ithaca: Cornell University Press, 1994.

Harte, Liam, ed. *The Literature of the Irish in Britain: Autobiography and Memoir, 1725–2001.* Basingstoke: Palgrave Macmillan, 2009.

Reid, Richard and Brendon Kelson. *Sinners, Saints and Settlers: A Journey though Irish Australia.* Canberra: National Museum of Australia Press, 2010.

Simmonds, Kathleen. 'Irish Cultural Memory in Australian Writing since World War II', in Tadhg Foley and Fiona Bateman, eds., *Irish-Australian Studies: Papers Delivered at the Ninth Irish-Australian Conference, Galway, April 1997.* Sydney: Crossing Press, 2000: 224–32.

Wills, Clair. *The Best are Leaving: Emigration and Post-War Irish Culture* (Cambridge: Cambridge University Press, 2015).

CHAPTER 23

The Irish Abuse Survival Memoir

Moira J. Maguire

In the late 1990s, the Irish government was rocked by a growing number of allegations about the abuse and neglect of children in state-funded institutions. This culminated in 1999 with the airing on RTÉ television of a documentary series entitled *States of Fear*, written, produced and directed by journalist Mary Raftery, which confronted viewers with graphic evidence of the widespread physical, emotional and sexual abuse of children, spanning several decades, in the country's extensive network of industrial and reform schools.[1] The public outcry provoked by the series led Taoiseach Bertie Ahern to issue a formal apology to the survivors of such institutions and to set up the Laffoy (later Ryan) Commission to investigate the extent and effects of childhood abuse in the period since 1936. Although some former industrial school residents had begun sharing their experiences of abuse and neglect prior to 1999, the broadcast of *States of Fear* opened the floodgates for a torrent of autobiographical testimony to emerge in different forms. Further documentaries followed, and newspapers and other media featured numerous stories of horrific acts perpetrated on young children in care by members of the male and female religious orders who oversaw the industrial school regime. Suddenly, it seemed, Ireland had taken centre stage in the global phenomenon of the 'paedophile priest', forcing church and state to launch protracted inquiries into the nature, extent and handling of sexual abuse complaints at a diocesan and national level.[2] The cumulative effect of these developments was to embolden some of those who had spent their lives in silent shame, fear and trauma to commit their stories to print, where they fed a growing

---

[1] Raftery's watershed series was preceded by an equally important documentary, Louis Lentin's *Dear Daughter* (1996), which told the story of Christine Buckley, including the harsh, abusive regime she endured in St Vincent's Industrial School in Goldenbridge, Dublin.

[2] The two most well-known reports into clerical sexual abuse in Ireland are the 2009 Murphy Report and the 2005 Ferns Report.

public appetite for first-hand accounts of how this hidden institutional subculture was allowed to persist for so many years.

While the abuse of children in industrial schools and by paedophile priests have received the lion's share of media attention over the past twenty years, there have also been those noteworthy (or media-worthy) cases of children who were victimized by their own parents. One of the earliest semi-autobiographical narratives of this sort was *The Kilkenny Incest Case* (1993), Alison Cooper's account (co-authored with journalist Kieron Wood) of the chronic sexual and physical maltreatment she suffered at the hands of her father. More recently, Barbara Naughton in *Why Can't I Speak?* (2007) and Audrey Delaney in *Innocent: The Story of a Shattered Childhood* (2008) have written about the sexual and physical damage inflicted by their fathers, their efforts to hold their abusers accountable and the varying responses of other family members. The anecdotal evidence provided by these and other abuse memoirs discussed here reinforces the notion that there was an extraordinary level of violence inflicted on Irish children, at least until the 1960s.[3] The bulk of these works address the violation and neglect of children in institutional settings; a handful of others address the physical abuse of boys by priests and the brutalization of girls by their parents (usually fathers). Research also shows that Irish children experienced a high level of physical violence at school and in their own homes during the middle decades of the last century. Corporal punishment was a common feature of daily school life for many pupils and parents' unfettered right to chastise their children physically was upheld by the courts.[4] In other words, these autobiographical accounts are part of a broader history of church and state in an independent Ireland that purported to cherish its children, but which in reality allowed the most vulnerable of its citizens, especially the children of the poor, to be subjected to a level of violence that by contemporary standards would be regarded as not only immoral but criminal.

Memoirs of institutional abuse

While the majority of autobiographical accounts of abusive childhood in Ireland have been published since the broadcast of *States of Fear*, a significant minority of men and women spoke out earlier, risking the censure and scepticism of family, friends and wider society to chronicle the pain and humiliation they suffered in the nation's industrial and reformatory

---

[3] See Séamus Ó Cinnéide and Moira J. Maguire, '"A Good Beating Never Hurt Anyone": The Abuse and Punishment of Children in Twentieth Century Ireland', *Journal of Social History*, 38:3 (2005), 635–52.
[4] Ibid.

schools. Christina Noble's *Bridge Across My Sorrows* (1994), for example, documents her life both before and after she and her siblings were committed to industrial schools in 1950s Dublin. Although the book's primary focus is on her work with Vietnamese street children, Noble writes candidly about her experiences as an inmate of St Joseph's Industrial School for Girls and Junior Boys in Clifden, Co. Galway in the late 1950s, 'at that time reckoned the worst place in all of Ireland for a girl. This was where Ireland hid its illegitimate daughters and its orphans, as well as young girls who were sent there by the courts. I felt like a criminal.'[5] But the true pioneers of the Irish abuse survival memoir are Gerard Mannix Flynn, author of *Nothing to Say* (1983), which is cast as fictionalized autobiography, and Paddy Doyle, who in *The God Squad* (1988) powerfully testified to the savage treatment he received from the age of four in St Michael's Industrial School in Cappoquin, Co. Waterford. In his foreword to the revised 2003 edition of *Nothing to Say*, which the jacket describes as a 'modern Irish classic', Flynn recalls how he was incited to write it by a chance encounter with a homeless Traveller whom he had known when they were children in St Joseph's Industrial School in Letterfrack, Co. Galway. Although subsequently lauded for his bravery, Flynn recalls that his overriding emotion was one of fear:

> Writing the story was frightening: I knew that certain sections of Irish society would reject the notion that the Christian Brothers could do anything wrong. As for the sexual abuse, well, that word was just not heard anywhere in Ireland. Strange, because they all knew that children were being sexually abused by those in authority; the government knew, the police knew, the clergy and religious knew, yet nobody could name it. They were afraid of their own shame, and conspired to deny and hide it.[6]

Doyle echoes these remarks, speaking of 'the chill running through my body as I wrote', before going on to present himself as a representative witness:

> This book is not an attempt to point the finger, to blame, or even to criticize any individual or group of people. Neither is it intended to make a judgement on what happened to me. It is about a society's abdication of responsibility to a child. The fact that I was that child, and that the book is about my life is largely irrelevant. The probability is that there were, and still are, thousands of 'mes'.[7]

[5] Christina Noble with Robert Coram, *Bridge Across My Sorrows: The Christina Noble Story* (London: Corgi Books, 1995), 121.
[6] Gerard Mannix Flynn, *Nothing to Say* (Dublin: Lilliput Press, 2003), 5–6.
[7] Paddy Doyle, *The God Squad* (London: Corgi Books, 1989), 10–11.

Nothing to Say and *The God Squad*, then, are the founding texts of a subgenre that, by the early 2000s, had become a ubiquitous fixture in the country's bookshops. In breaching the collective amnesia that suppressed the voices of the victimized, Flynn and Doyle highlight the centrality of religious judgementalism and class prejudice to the inhumane treatment of the children who were consigned to the industrial schools system. What happened to them and to countless others happened in large part because a hyper-moralistic and intolerant society had difficulty coping with parents and children from working-class backgrounds who did not fit the middle-class ideal of 'appropriate' or 'normal' family life. The dozens of autobiographical accounts that have been published since then add to our understanding of this episode in Irish history and illuminate the culture of violence against children that existed in mid-twentieth-century Ireland.

A number of common themes pervade these memoirs. Most of the accounts of life in boys' industrial schools document sexual abuse coupled with a degree of physical violence that was vast in scale and degree. Former female residents relate a similar litany of physical and psychological pain and humiliation, as well as semi-starvation, inadequate clothing, lack of education and an absence of love and affection. Substance abuse and relationship dysfunction also are common themes; many ex-inmates turned to drugs and alcohol to help them cope with the traumas they experienced while in care, while others reported being institutionalized to such a degree that they were subsequently incapable of relating in normal ways to other people and found intimate relationships particularly problematic. Feelings of abandonment also feature prominently in these narratives: several former residents were anxious to find their families or at least arrive at an explanation for why they ended up in institutions in the first place. Most telling of all, perhaps, is the fact that so many of these testimonies express profound anger at a state and society that turned a blind eye to the suffering of poor, neglected and abused children over a prolonged period of time.

Perhaps unsurprisingly, then, the overarching theme of many of these accounts of abusive childhoods is the hypocrisy of church, state, family and community in allowing violence and brutality to be inflicted on vulnerable, defenceless children. One such account is *Childhood Interrupted* (2005) by Kathleen O'Malley, who was confined to an industrial school as a result of a sexual assault when she was eight. Kathleen's own mother had a difficult upbringing, starting life in an orphanage and ending up boarded out at the age of six. Although her foster family initially treated her well, when Kathleen's mother got pregnant with her older sister at the age of sixteen they threw her out. The family's fortunes rose and fell over the years and it was not long before Kathleen's mother came to the notice of the National Society for the Prevention of Cruelty to Children (NSPCC). In September 1947, Kathleen and her older sister were committed to St Vincent's in Goldenbridge in Dublin. Their younger sister Lydia was not committed; Kathleen believed this was because Lydia was the only one of the three who was not born outside marriage. Kathleen's mother successfully petitioned the courts in 1948 for their release from Goldenbridge. However, several months later, following a sexual assault on Kathleen by a neighbour, all three sisters were sent to Moate Industrial School in Co. Westmeath.

O'Malley felt acutely that she and her sisters were singled out while in care because she was a victim of sexual assault and therefore seen as morally 'tainted'. Their mother sent letters and gifts regularly, and visited when she could, but none of this prevented the girls from being physically and verbally abused by the nuns. Meanwhile, in Kathleen's mind, other girls, whose parents were married and where there was no suggestion of sexual interference, were treated well, even if the girls' parents did not write or visit. O'Malley's account suggests that the same hierarchies and prejudices that existed in Irish society were replicated within the industrial school system, among both the nuns and the children themselves. O'Malley, like so many others, was critical of a society that placed a high premium on outward displays of Catholic piety while allowing deeply unchristian practices and behaviour to flourish behind walls. Her memoir, like those of Doyle and Flynn, also highlights the class biases and moral assumptions that underpinned the care system. Poor children, illegitimate children and children who had no family safety net seem to have fared much worse in industrial schools than their less disadvantaged peers.

The motivations of authors of abuse survival memoirs are often explicitly stated or easy to infer from the works themselves. Most write out of a desire to purge their souls, have their voices heard or bear witness to the suffering of others. The goal of Goldenbridge survivor Bernadette Fahy's *Freedom of Angels* (1999) is to tell a story that 'may help people understand the long struggle involved in shedding the heritage offered by a confused, dysfunctional family situation and a cold, impersonal, cruel institution'.[8] Lily O'Brien, in *The Girl Nobody Wants* (2012), highlights the chemical dependency, dysfunctional relationships and seemingly high rates of suicide experienced by some former industrial school residents. O'Brien

---

[8] Bernadette Fahy, *Freedom of Angels: Surviving Goldenbridge Orphanage* (Dublin: O'Brien Press, 1999), 210.

dedicates her book to fellow survivors, especially 'those who took their own lives later in life as a way to escape from the torment that never left them alone',[9] her younger brother among them. Patrick Touher's agenda in *Fear of the Collar* (1991) is to expose not only the brutality of 'those bastards who wore a collar under the cloak of a Christian Brother'[10] but also, and perhaps more importantly, to highlight the inhumanity of a state regime that disposed of unwanted children without a thought for their future well-being. Touher was born to a single mother who died not long after his birth. Prior to her death, when she became too ill to care for him, she turned Patrick over the nuns at St Brigid's Orphanage in Dublin. They in turn boarded him out to a family named Doyle, who loved him and treated him like one of their own; Touher remembers being very happy in the Doyle home. However, for reasons that were never explained to him or to the Doyles, he was removed at the age of eight and sent to Artane Industrial School, where his suffering began.[11]

Joe Dunne shares Touher's anger at a putatively Christian society that allowed church and state to rip poor children from good homes and place them in institutions where they were abused and neglected. In *The Stolen Child* (2003), he writes:

> That such extreme piety and religious observance – which was displayed before the world in those days – should exist hand in hand with such covert cruelty and injustice, and on so large a scale, was surely the ultimate hypocrisy. A militant, intense form of Catholicism was everywhere observed – and how! But true Christianity was little known, or practised.[12]

Dunne's title reflects the sense of betrayal he feels about what happened to him. Yet his account is unusual in that he does not appear to be angry with the religious orders that ran the industrial schools. On the contrary, he asserts that while the regime was harsh, his religious custodians sacrificed their own comfort and freedom to care for the children.[13] But while Dunne is grateful that Irish society has become more enlightened in its treatment of its most marginalized members, he keeps before us nonetheless the shame of an earlier era in which vulnerable children were consigned to an institutional existence that stripped them of their dignity and humanity.

---

[9] Lily O'Brien, *The Girl Nobody Wants: A Shocking True Story of Child Abuse in Ireland* (Leicester: Matador, 2012), unpaginated dedication.

[10] Patrick Touher, *Fear of the Collar: Artane Industrial School* (Dublin: O'Brien Press, 1991), 66.

[11] In all likelihood, Touher was sent to an industrial school because the orphanage would have stopped paying his maintenance allowance once he reached the age of eight years.

[12] Joe Dunne, *The Stolen Child* (Cork: Marino Books, 2003), 11.   [13] Ibid., 218.

Many of the children who ended up in industrial schools came from troubled or unsettled backgrounds that contributed in some way to their committal. In *The Boy at the Gate* (2012), Dubliner Danny Ellis recalls the circumstances that led to his detention in Artane between 1955 and 1963. The Ellis family was destitute and his father emigrated to the United States to find work. While he was away, Ellis's mother became pregnant by another man, which brought the family to the notice of neighbours and child protection agencies. By the time he was six, Ellis was already getting into trouble with the authorities. Indeed, one of the more tragic ironies of his life is that his mother would sometimes threaten to send him to Artane when frustrated by his behaviour. At the time Ellis wrote his memoir he was a singer-songwriter and musician living in the United States, where news reached him of the arrest on charges of sexual abuse of some Christian Brothers who once worked in Artane. Gradually, he began to use his music to work through his feelings about his past, recording a cathartic, highly autobiographical album, *800 Voices* (2008), in which he sought to give voice to his own pain and that of the countless survivors of the Irish industrial school system who did not have his gift for self-expression.

Like Ellis, Mickey Finn, author of *In My Own Words (Still Running)* (2011), experienced a tumultuous early life. At the age of ten or eleven he was charged with stealing a twenty-pound note from a delivery man, after which he continued on the path of juvenile delinquency and was eventually committed to St Joseph's in Letterfrack in 1964. Finn is vehement in his condemnation of the Christian Brothers-run regime that existed there:

> They were nothing but an assemblage of sick perverts only too quick to abuse the power they held and to turn a blind eye; cover up for their accomplices in sin ... It has been said that not all of the brothers were wicked; there must have been some good ones who were driven by the ideals of their calling. This was not based on my experience.[14]

Finn depicts a regimented environment defined by cyclical brutality – violence inflicted by the Brothers on the boys and violence inflicted by the boys on each other. The constant tension and volatility were so palpable that the smallest perceived slight was met with aggression. Finn describes how he spent most of his three years in Letterfrack trying to protect himself from sexual abuse at the hands of the Brothers. Like Dunne, he directs his strongest anger at the hypocrisy of those who masqueraded as moral guardians while callously violating young people,

---

[14] Mickey Finn, *In My Own Words (Still Running)* (Bloomington: AuthorHouse, 2011), 57.

and at a knowing local community that did nothing to stop the wickedness that was happening in its midst.

All Irish memoirs of abusive childhoods are sobering in their own right, but those that chronicle the degree of sexual abuse perpetrated in boys' industrial schools are particularly troubling. In some schools, competition appears to have existed between the Brothers for the attentions and affections of particular boys. This is borne out by Michael Clemenger's *Everybody Knew* (2012), the subtitle of which – *A Boy, Two Brothers, A Stolen Childhood* – lays bare the utterly dysfunctional and unregulated culture that flourished within the system.[15] Clemenger's account exposes a sexually charged environment where boys and Brothers alike knew the unwritten and unspoken rules about 'relationships', and where jealousies between two or more Brothers could lead to even greater misery for those inmates unfortunate enough to be caught in such perverted 'love triangles'. Clemenger began planning his memoir after returning to Ireland from the UK in 1996 and noticing the increasing media attention being paid to the historical treatment of children in state-run institutions. In April 1999, he learned that two Brothers who had been his tormenters at St Joseph's Industrial School in Tralee, Co. Kerry, which closed in 1970, were being charged with physical and sexual abuse. Like other memoirists before him, Clemenger was angry with the hypocrisy in Irish people's reactions to these charges: 'What upset me most, however, was the jeering of the angry mob that stood outside the court. Where were these brave men and women back in the fifties and sixties, when their voices would have made a big difference?'[16] As the pain he had suppressed for forty-five years began to resurface, Clemenger turned to autobiography, a decision influenced by his reading of the memoirs of other men, including Touher, who survived degrading institutional childhoods. Through autobiography Clemenger hoped to achieve a measure of catharsis for himself and to honour the memory of all those whose lives were so scarred by their experiences that they had little hope of living normally or speaking for themselves:

> Many of them, I am sure, were unfit for the vicissitudes of life outside those walls, slipping quietly into lonely mediocrity never to be heard of again. Many died filled with rage, unable to form close physical relationships with the opposite sex, have families of their own or find fulfilment in their lives.[17]

---

[15] Clemenger's memoir was originally published in Ireland under the title *Holy Terrors* in 2009.
[16] Michael Clemenger, *Everybody Knew: A Boy, Two Brothers, A Stolen Childhood* (London: Ebury, 2012), 355–56.
[17] Ibid., 358.

Given the degree of ruthless violence and injury that was inflicted by the male religious in charge of the more notorious single-sex industrial schools, such as those in Artane and Letterfrack, perhaps it is not surprising that sexual abuse was also perpetrated by some of the older boys on the younger ones. Patrick J. Fahy, author of *Child of Sorrow* (2008), spent almost his entire childhood in two institutions, the junior boys' school in Kilkenny and the senior boys' school in Upton, Co. Cork. When Fahy arrived in Upton he discovered, in effect, a two-tiered system, with the boys who had families on the outside often being put into positions of authority over the boys who did not. The former cohort sometimes abused their positions and in some cases molested those deemed to be their subordinates.

Irish autobiographical accounts of institutional abuse, then, are similar not only in their depiction of the physical, emotional and sexual cruelty and suffering that were perpetrated by the Catholic religious orders who ran these so-called schools but also in their denunciation of a state and society that allowed professed Christians to treat children with such brutality. Perhaps the most important work in this subgenre is *Founded on Fear* (2006) by Peter Tyrrell. Born into poverty in Co. Galway in 1916, Tyrrell spent eight years of his childhood in Letterfrack, where he was subjected to the same kind of harrowing brutality described by others who were sent there. What is noteworthy about Tyrrell, however, is that in 1958 he came to the notice of Senator Owen Sheehy-Skeffington, who two years earlier had delivered a series of scathing indictments of corporal punishment in Ireland's schools from the floor of the Irish Senate. Tyrrell wrote to Skeffington, who encouraged him to write his life story, which he did in 1959, posting it in instalments over a five-month period, though it remained unpublished until long after both men were dead. The two men carried on an intermittent correspondence until, in 1968, Sheehy-Skeffington was notified of Tyrrell's suicide by self-immolation on Hampstead Heath in London, his charred remains eventually having been identified by police. *Founded on Fear* is important not only because it epitomizes the brutality and callous indifference of the industrial school regime but also because of the stark warning it issues about the long-term ramifications of systematic cruelty and suffering: 'The child who is beaten by someone bigger and stronger than himself, will very often grow up bitter and full of hatred of society. He will want to get his own back. He may one day hit back. *I warn society against the child who has been hurt.*'[18]

---

[18] Peter Tyrrell, *Founded on Fear*, ed. Diarmuid Whelan (Dublin: Irish Academic Press, 2006), 1. Original emphasis.

Memoirs of abuse within the home

In March 1993, Kilkenny-man Michael Cooper was sentenced to six-and-a-half years in prison on multiple counts of incest, rape and assault committed against his daughter Alison, then aged twenty-seven, over a span of more than fifteen years. Instances of fathers being charged with incest are not unique in twentieth-century Ireland. What made the Cooper case exceptional and transformative was the decision of the victim to agree to be interviewed on national television and then to narrate her experiences to journalist Kieron Wood, which led to the publication of the co-authored *The Kilkenny Incest Case* later that same year. The case was so shocking not only because of the chronic nature of Cooper's abuse but also because Alison had been hospitalized multiple times over the years and had given birth to a child fathered by her abuser. In other words, what went on in the Cooper household was not the dark secret that incest is often portrayed to be. People knew and said nothing; this would become a recurring theme in subsequent autobiographical accounts of child sexual abuse within Irish families. A key part of the rationale for *The Kilkenny Incest Case*, therefore, lies in Michael Cooper's defence attorney's indictment of medics and social workers for failing to act on their knowledge of Alison's systematic victimization. But Wood himself goes further in his foreword, arguing that such criticism is 'pointless' unless it leads to meaningful change: 'The response to Alison's sufferings should not be a witchhunt, but a balanced and considered programme of changes to the law and proper funding for a range of improvements to facilities for the victims of violence.'[19]

By the time the recollections of Audrey Delaney and Barbara Naughton appeared in the 2000s, the memoir of family sexual abuse had become a recognized Irish autobiographical subgenre. The experiences of the two women are in some ways similar but in others very different. Both suffered appalling levels of paternal violence before eventually deciding to come forward and tell their stories, with markedly different consequences. Delaney's family were supportive, Naughton's disbelieving to the point where her aunt tried to influence the outcome of Patrick Naughton's trial by calling on a government minister to intercede on his behalf. So whereas the vindication Delaney felt following her father's prosecution and four-year jail sentence emboldened her to speak out on behalf of herself and the numerous victims of his abuse who chose not to come forward, Barbara Naughton writes

[19] Kieron Wood and Alison Cooper, *The Kilkenny Incest Case* (Dublin: Poolbeg Press, 1993), i–ii. The Cooper case led to the first major child abuse inquiry in Ireland, the recommendations of which contributed significantly to the legal reform of child protection services.

out of a disillusionment that was deepened by her discovery that the only support service available to her was a drop-in centre for institutional abuse victims who themselves were far from healed:

> I was constantly reminded of the negativity that surrounds the subject matter of abuse. The poor souls in this centre were constantly comparing the level of abuse they had suffered. It was like a competition to establish who had suffered the most. It became apparent to me at an early stage that such a centre had little chance of rehabilitating victims of such experiences.[20]

Naughton was reluctant to relive her ordeal as she contemplated writing her memoir, yet her frustration at the absence of state support for victims of domestic abuse was one of the factors that compelled her to use her story to raise awareness of the plight of victims.

In at least one case, that of Kathy O'Beirne, physical and sexual abuse experienced in the home and its environs led to a child being incarcerated in a series of state-run institutions. *Kathy's Story* (2005), O'Beirne's account of the experiences that led to her spending half a lifetime in institutional care, is not only harrowing but also reflective of the reluctance to interfere in 'private' family matters in post-independence Ireland. Outwardly, O'Beirne's father was a successful and loving parent; in private, he was physically, verbally and emotionally abusive and his children grew up in fear and torment. This abuse, coupled with Kathy's sexual molestation by local boys from the age of five, contributed to the psychological trauma that led in turn to her being diagnosed at the age of eight as a 'child with a troublesome mind'.[21] As O'Beirne points out, however, dismissing her behaviour as merely troublesome represented 'a simple way of describing my condition without requiring any investigation into why or how I arrived at that state. Nobody was going to bother attempting to find out what had been going on.'[22] Her father tired of her behavioural issues and sent her to an industrial school; from there she went to a psychiatric hospital and ultimately to a Magdalen laundry, religious-run workhouses in which women deemed to be morally suspect were indefinitely confined. O'Beirne reports that she was physically and psychologically abused at every stage on her grim journey. As it became more acceptable to speak openly about the horrors that occurred in Ireland's correctional

---

[20] Barbara Naughton, *Why Can't I Speak?* (Milton Keynes: AuthorHouse, 2007), 235.
[21] Kathy O'Beirne, *Kathy's Story: The True Story of a Childhood Hell Inside Ireland's Magdalen Laundries* (Vancouver: Greystone Books, 2006), 36.
[22] Ibid.

institutions, O'Beirne became more determined to tell her story so that people would be aware of the evils inflicted on young children. This led to her version of events being strenuously challenged by family members, who denied both that she had been abused and that she had spent significant portions of her childhood in institutional care. These denials, which were linked to a battle over a family inheritance, were forceful enough to derail plans for a sequel to *Kathy's Story*, though the controversy itself became the subject of a book by a journalist.[23]

O'Beirne's case is compelling, then, not only because it illustrates the link between family abuse and the industrial school system, at least until the 1970s, but also because it raises in very overt ways the challenges to memory and veracity that surround the autobiographical testimony of abuse survivors. Many of the earliest authors of abuse survival memoirs were disbelieved because their accounts contradicted what respectable Irish society thought it knew about the role of religious orders in caring for underprivileged or unruly children. Today, there is the corresponding challenge of giving credence to accounts of abusive childhood that have been produced many years after the fact, without substantiating evidence. In light of this, one can only wonder what might have become of Cooper, Naughton and Delaney had they lived just a decade or two earlier. Would they too have ended up in industrial schools when their parents tired of their resistance or rebellion? Would they have been believed or would – should – they have been required to provide documentary evidence to support their abuse claims?

The autobiographical accounts of women like Alison Cooper, Barbara Naughton and Audrey Delaney suggest that into the last decades of the twentieth century there existed a 'don't ask, don't tell' mentality when it came to child abuse in Ireland, especially when it occurred within families. When placed within the broader context of cases such as those of Ann Lovett, Lavinia Kerwick, Sophia McColgan and indeed Kathy O'Beirne herself, we see a clear pattern of family members, medical professionals, teachers and others shying away from or deliberately ignoring behaviour within families that could be cordoned off as 'private'. The emergence of the family sexual abuse memoir over the last twenty years or so has belatedly given a voice to a generation of women in particular, women who were silenced by church, state and society precisely at the time when they most needed to be listened to.

---

[23] Hermann Kelly, *Kathy's Real Story: A Culture of False Allegations Exposed* (Dunleer: Prefect Press, 2007).

Memoirs of clerical sexual abuse

As already intimated, over the past two decades dozens of Irish diocesan priests have been exposed as paedophiles; so many, indeed, that the public has almost become inured to the seemingly endless litany of allegations and revelations, a litany that has inflicted deep damage on the Catholic church's moral credibility. Three of the most notorious offenders were Ivan Payne, Seán Fortune and Brendan Smyth, whose crimes are the subject of memoirs by Andrew Madden, Colm O'Gorman and Brendan Boland respectively.

Madden was one of the first people to go public with his account of being sexually abuse by a priest in *Altar Boy* (2003). For three years he was preyed upon by Father Payne, until he stopped serving as an altar boy and the priest no longer had regular access to him. About a year after the abuse ended Madden confided in a teacher, who reported the matter to diocesan officials. He was later told that Payne admitted to the abuse and that he would be dealt with. However, Madden is convinced that his reporting of the abuse haunted him later in life. He had planned to be a priest but was told at his interview that he was not a suitable candidate. The second half of the book chronicles his descent into alcohol addiction and his efforts to reclaim his life and come to terms not only with his homosexuality but also with the legacies of his childhood violation. The book ends with Madden looking back in anger – 'I regret that I wasted my entire youth on a vocation that was never realized, on a Church which turned me away and shielded evil' – while moving forwards with a sense of having conquered his demons, in part through the act of autobiography: 'I feel better for having gone public and spoken out. And writing everything down has helped me more than I thought it could . . . Although I still carry many of the effects of child abuse, I no longer consider myself a victim. I've done something about it. I've turned it around.'[24]

Brendan Boland, author of *Sworn to Silence* (2014), was abused by Father Brendan Smyth over a span of several years in the 1970s. His autobiographical testimony provides evidence that the church authorities were aware as early as 1975 (and perhaps earlier) of Smyth's activities and took steps to cover them up. They interviewed Boland, who was then a teenager, without his parents being present and compelled him to sign a statement vowing never to reveal what had happened to him. Boland's parents were not made aware of this 'settlement' and in fact believed that another priest, Father Oliver

---

[24] Andrew Madden, *Altar Boy: A Story of Life After Abuse* (Dublin: Penguin Ireland, 2003), 195–96.

McShane, to whom they reported the abuse had informed the police about the matter. They were later devastated to learn that McShane had informed only the church authorities and that Smyth was subsequently moved from one parish to another, where he was free to commit further sexual crimes. It was only after Boland watched a 1994 documentary about Smyth, who was eventually found guilty in 1997 by a Dublin court of seventy-four charges of sexual violence against children, that he realized the extent of the paedophile's crimes against other boys in the period since 1975.

Perhaps the most noteworthy contemporary narrative of clerical abuse survival is *Beyond Belief* (2009) by Colm O'Gorman, who was terrorized by Father Seán Fortune as a child in 1980s Wexford. While many victims of abuse have written their memoirs as a way to heal or have their voices heard, O'Gorman's was published after he had taken significant action to bring his abuser to justice. In 1998, he sued the bishop of Ferns, Brendan Comiskey, and the Dublin papal nuncio, actions that led to the resignation of the bishop and the establishment of the Ferns Inquiry, one of the first official investigations into the extent of clerical sexual abuse in Ireland and the Catholic church's handling of it. *Beyond Belief* is significant, therefore, not only for the further insights it provides into the way trust was exploited by paedophile priests and the difficulty of victims being believed in a climate where the church was above reproach; the memoir is also important because it chronicles the author's efforts to hold that church accountable. O'Gorman, perhaps more than any other individual, was instrumental in forcing the institutional church to answer for the way it responded to allegations of criminal wrongdoing and for knowingly covering up what would become an international scandal. O'Gorman has used his voice to campaign for justice for all abuse survivors and, as executive director of Amnesty International Ireland, has since extended his advocacy to include victims of all forms of abuse.

Conclusion

Born of the scandals and revelations that have shaken the country's patriarchal structures and religious- and state-run institutions, Irish abuse survival memoirs give the lie to any claims that the post-independence state cherished all its children equally. This body of writing depicts a culture and society that was self-righteous, punitive, prejudiced against the poor, intolerant of transgressions of prevailing moral and social norms and hypocritical in its practice and promulgation of Christianity. The autobiographical narratives discussed here chronicle an appalling level of physical, sexual and psychological violence inflicted on the most vulnerable of individuals by their putative guardians and protectors. The history of these memoirs' reception is itself significant, since in it we can plot a telling evolution from an era of collective incredulity, denial and protectiveness towards the Catholic church to a time in which abuse victims can disclose their experiences in an empathic climate, and in the process begin, perhaps, to heal without fear of ridicule or repercussion.

Further reading

Arnold, Bruce. *The Irish Gulag*. Dublin: Gill and Macmillan, 2009.

Ferriter, Diarmaid. 'Suffer Little Children? The Historical Validity of Memoirs of Irish Childhood', in Joseph Dunne and James Kelly, eds., *Childhood and Its Discontents*. Dublin: Liffey Press, 2003: 69–106.

Maguire, Moira J. *Precarious Childhood in Post-Independence Ireland*. Manchester: Manchester University Press, 2009.

Molino, Michael R. 'The "House of a Hundred Windows": Industrial Schools in Irish Writing', *New Hibernia Review*, 5:1 (2001): 33–52.

Ó Cinnéide, Séamus and Moira J. Maguire. '"A Good Beating Never Hurt Anyone": The Punishment and Abuse of Children in Twentieth Century Ireland', *Journal of Social History*, 38:3 (2005): 635–52.

O'Sullivan, Eoin and Ian O'Donnell. *Coercive Confinement in Ireland: Patients, Prisoners and Penitents*. Manchester: Manchester University Press, 2012.

CHAPTER 24

Irish Celebrity Autobiography

Anthony P. McIntyre and Diane Negra

The celebrity memoir can lay claim to being the most influential subgenre of Irish autobiography on the basis of its commercial ubiquity, its popular appeal and its democratic accessibility, as evidenced by the wide cross-section of society it represents in terms of class, ethnicity, gender and sexuality. While this chapter will consider early examples of the celebrity memoir from the 1960s, disproportionate attention will be paid to works by more contemporary figures, whose fame in the era of neoliberal capitalism coincides with transformations in notions of individuality and achievement that bear crucially on the production and consumption of autobiographical texts. Considerations of Irish autobiography, particularly of the literary variety, tend to stress the writer's identification against a powerful other, which typically appears in a colonial or patriarchal guise.[1] In the case of celebrity authors, however, such negotiations tend to be displaced by engagements with powerful cultural and media institutions, many of which are non-Irish, that facilitate the public visibility upon which this form of heightened individuality depends.

The roughly chronological development of this chapter allows us to assay changes in Irish textual subjectivities from the 1960s to the present. While the profound changes that have shaped Irish society over this period are no doubt manifold and highly complex, the increasing ubiquity of celebrity discourses is tied to technological developments in the infrastructure of Irish and global media. Ireland's somewhat belated entry into television broadcasting in the early 1960s meant that the discursive and institutional structures that comprise stardom and celebrity were imported from elsewhere, along with the expertise needed to set up a domestic television service. As Gay Byrne, the country's first celebrity chat show host, explained: 'Those in charge of the fledgling RTE television had come

---

[1] See Taura S. Napier, *Seeking a Country: Literary Autobiographies of Twentieth-Century Irishwomen* (Lanham: University Press of America, 2001), 1–17.

from star systems in Britain and America, and for the first time, stars were born in Irish broadcasting.'[2] Thus, from its first indigenous incarnation Irish celebrity was a globalized form of heightened individualism that eventually came to appropriate the fame and notoriety that were previously the reserve of Irish poets, dramatists and artists.

During the period covered by this chapter, the media landscape has changed dramatically in many respects, not least of which is the marked cultural turn towards self-promotion as a feature of citizenship and social life, and it is within these contexts that twenty-first-century celebrity memoirs must be situated. One figure who emblematizes the interaction between celebrity and a changing mediascape is drag queen and gay rights campaigner Rory O'Neill (aka Panti Bliss), author of *Woman in the Making* (2014), who, in becoming the public face of the successful Yes campaign in the Republic's same-sex marriage referendum of 2015, high-lighted the sway such emanations of heightened individualism increasingly hold in the public sphere. Another memoirist, Niall Breslin, author of *Me and My Mate Jeffrey* (2015), has used his celebrity to become an advocate for anxiety disorder awareness, while former Miss World Rosanna Davison sparked controversy in 2015 when promoting her semi-autobiographical *Eat Yourself Beautiful*, when she was understood to be advocating a gluten-free diet as a means of avoiding a range of illnesses, including autism. Thus, in Ireland as elsewhere, the cultural capital and authority of many celeb-rities derive solely from their public personae and are often bound up with their involvement with, or attitudes towards, wider societal issues.

Founding fathers: Eamonn Andrews and Gay Byrne

The claim of Eamonn Andrews's *This is My Life* (1963) to be considered the first Irish celebrity autobiography rests not only on its date of publication but also on its having established many of the rhetorical and ideological features common to the subgenre in this era. Thus, the memoir extols the rewards of hard work and perseverance, presents the author as an uxorious husband and dedicated family man, stresses the likability and down-to-earth nature of others and avoids salacious content in relating anecdotes about famous figures. Having risen to prominence as one of the most popular BBC presenters (a move emulated by later emigrant broadcasters such as Terry Wogan and Graham Norton), Andrews's fame was established

---

[2] Gay Byrne with Deirdre Purcell, *The Time of My Life: An Autobiography* (Dublin: Gill and Macmillan, 1989), 228.

when broadcasting in Ireland was in its infancy and a national television service had yet to be established. The Dubliner can therefore unproblematically reconcile his love for his native land with the necessity of leaving it to fulfil his broadcasting ambitions in Britain. In his autobiography, he stresses, like Gay Byrne after him, the degree of perseverance and risk this entailed. Both men display the entrepreneurial zeal that would become naturalized in later celebrity autobiographies, as they recall taking on multiple engagements across Ireland and the UK and running their own media businesses, while at the same time fulfilling their commitments to the BBC and RTÉ respectively.

Towards the end of *This Is My Life*, Andrews casts himself in the role of the successful returning son, having been appointed in 1960 as chairman of the body established to oversee the introduction of a national Irish television service. Like many of the celebrities discussed in this chapter, and in keeping with the Irish cultural preference for understatement, Andrews is careful not to overplay the significance of his accomplishments. This is evidenced by his recollection of an encounter with Lord John Reith, the first director general of the BBC and a man renowned for his somewhat didactic approach to broadcasting (Reith's view that the BBC existed to provide educational and entertaining high-quality programming was echoed by President Éamon de Valera when he launched RTÉ television in December 1961). Andrews recalls an occasion on which Reith publicly slighted him, after which he muses that, to Reith, he may have 'represented much of what was frivolous and worthless, by his great standards, on radio and television'.[3] Andrews can thus be seen, in part, as positioning himself as a populist antidote to culturally elitist views of public service broadcasting that were vying for control of the airwaves in the early days of television in both the UK and Ireland. The comment is also somewhat prescient in its evaluation of how celebrity – and, indeed, the lucrative genre of celebrity autobiography – is generally perceived as shallow and insignificant despite, or perhaps because of, its broad popular appeal.

Gay Byrne's broadcasting career was, by his own admission, profoundly influenced by Andrews and, with the exception of his wife, no other individual gets mentioned as much as his 'idol'[4] in his 1989 autobiography. Byrne's memoir closely follows the pattern set by Andrews by tracing

[3] Eamonn Andrews, *This Is My Life* (London, Macdonald, 1963), 247.
[4] Byrne, *The Time of My Life*, 82.

a similar trajectory from working-class Dublin roots to hard-won professional success, the one difference being the slightly defensive tone Byrne adopts when narrating his various achievements. The pair's career paths were in fact remarkably similar: both progressed from part-time announcing posts in Dublin, which they combined with day jobs in insurance, to more lucrative BBC and ITV engagements which they had to fit in around their contractual obligations with RTÉ. Whereas Andrews eventually moved to the UK permanently and became one of the BBC's most recognized presenters, Byrne, after moving from Manchester's Granada TV to a less fulfilling position with the BBC, ended up returning to Ireland, where he would become in time the most influential broadcaster of his generation. This status was in part due to his long-standing role as presenter of *The Late Late Show*, which he fronted from 1962 to 1999. Perhaps inevitably, given its longevity, this flagship programme has changed from being a forum for the debate of weighty and often controversial public issues in its early decades to its more recent incarnation as a conservative, worthy, though somewhat dated cultural institution – a description that could equally fit Byrne himself, now the grand old man of Irish broadcasting.

Hollywood Irish: Maureen O'Hara and Gabriel Byrne

Whereas for figures such as Andrews and Byrne, a fluid traversal of British and Irish institutional assignments was characteristic, and indeed necessary, for a career in broadcasting, Irish-born actors who achieved success in the United States tend to be more concerned in their memoirs with amplifying the contrast between the quaintness of old-world Ireland and the globalized consumer capitalism epitomized by Hollywood. Two brief case studies must suffice here. Maureen O'Hara's *'Tis Herself* (2004) is in many ways a stock Hollywood memoir and her invocations of Irishness in the book are of the sort that underpinned the actress's persona as a combative but ultimately compliant female subject of mid-twentieth-century Hollywood dramas and comedies. The book invokes an 'Irish' moral clarity that not only puts expatriates in good stead when contending with Hollywood 'decadence' but is also notably sexual in nature. Whereas O'Hara shows herself to be relatively tolerant of violence, she is protective of her sexual probity, which is sourced in her Irishness. For example, when abused on set and even struck by directors (notably by Irish-American filmmaker John Ford), O'Hara says nothing, yet recoils when producer George Jessel massages her shoulders and is enraged when accused of having had an abortion. 'I was also from a very conservative country', she reflects, 'which compared to Hollywood, was a completely different world'.[5]

A disquieting feature of O'Hara's autobiography is the disjunction between her self-representation as a 'tough dame' and her near total inability to make sound personal decisions or extricate herself from abusive relationships. What stands out in the book is O'Hara's reverence for male authority figures and her (sometimes tortured) struggles to lionize them in the face of their perverse, cruel and sometimes sadistic conduct. Patriarchy, the Hollywood film industry, the US military and other institutions are stabilizing entities in O'Hara's worldview and she clings to them. To a great extent this conservatism is linked to the cultural formations of O'Hara's motherland, and indeed Ireland itself is persistently gendered in *'Tis Herself*, with a typical passage rhapsodizing the country's soothing tranquillity:

> The cares of the world seemed to vanish overnight and a feeling of peace and serenity overtook me as my plane reached the coast of Ireland and closed in on Shannon Airport. If you have never had the chance to visit her in the summertime, then you must. She is simply glorious.[6]

With its propensity for 'tortured artist' photography, stream-of-consciousness style and flowery prose, Gabriel Byrne's *Pictures in My Head* (1994) evidently wishes to be taken quite seriously as an account of the author's life story and subjectivity. From its opening pages, the book accentuates the inherent theatricality of everyday Irish life. The Dublin of Byrne's early childhood is populated by quirky characters who speak in vivid aphorisms. Brendan Behan shows up on the 50B bus and nuns appear to be in a rage one minute and kind the next. Such depictions position Ireland as a wellspring of creativity and verbosity and in this way seek to source Byrne's craft in very specific forms of cultural authenticity. As he becomes a Hollywood star, Byrne presents himself as still being in possession of an 'Irish' common sense that causes him to be disinterested in drugs or plastic surgery when they are suggested to him. Other Irish people in his narrative display a similar down-to-earthness. Byrne recounts how he found Liam Neeson doing the dishes during a party at his Hollywood home, while his own mother is heard to exclaim on glimpsing a woman (inferred to be Nancy

---

[5] Maureen O'Hara with John Nicoletti, *'Tis Herself: An Autobiography* (New York: Simon and Schuster, 2005), 74.
[6] Ibid., 157.

Reagan) at a Hollywood restaurant: 'Skin and bone, she could do with a good plate of spuds.'[7]

Pictures in My Head also manifests a recurrent emphasis on the emotional dysfunction of fame culture, with Byrne observing rather plaintively of Los Angeles: 'Although the freeways are called arteries, it is the only city I know without a heart.'[8] By contrast, he summons up a lyrical, restorative Ireland and in a chapter entitled 'Return of the Quiet Man' describes his retreat to a cottage in the west where he reacquaints himself with nature: 'I realise that these sounds have become alien to me, and I must learn to listen again.'[9] The book closes with reveries of the actor's childhood and a chapter that recounts the life story (and mimics the voice) of an Irish Traveller with whom Byrne worked on the 1992 film *Into the West*, gestures that seemingly seek to up the ante on a purified Irishness that the author retains as ballast as he makes his way amidst corrupt and corrupting international media industries.

The moral economies of contemporary female celebrity memoirs

If, in the Hollywood Irish autobiographies discussed above, Irishness is imbued with a moral purity and restorative authenticity that rhetorically secures conservative national affiliations, then a substrand of female-authored celebrity memoir demonstrates how the symbolically overdetermined categories of femininity, motherhood and religion are configured rather more ambivalently. Derry-raised singer and sometime politician Dana (born Rosemary Brown and now known by the name Dana Rosemary Scallon) has written two autobiographies, *Dana* (1985) and *All Kinds of Everything* (2007). In both, the singer, like O'Hara and Gabriel Byrne, situates her authenticity in her Irishness. In Dana's case, this is primarily done through recounting the wholesome and communal atmosphere of a prelapsarian Derry prior to the outbreak of the Northern Troubles in the late 1960s, where, although material poverty was rife, 'music was the one thing which made it bearable'.[10] The conflict, which was intensifying when the young singer shot to fame on winning the 1970 Eurovision Song Contest for Ireland, is only lightly touched on in her 1985 memoir. Conspicuously, though perhaps unsurprisingly, there is no mention of one of the defining events of the conflict, Bloody Sunday, when

[7] Gabriel Byrne, *Pictures in My Head* (Boulder: Roberts Rinehart Publishers, 1995), 116.
[8] Ibid., 119.   [9] Ibid., 135.
[10] Dana with Lucy Elphinstone, *Dana: An Autobiography* (London: Hodder and Stoughton Religious, 1985), 8.

British troops killed fourteen unarmed protestors in the Bogside area of her native city in January 1972. This omission is rectified in *All Kinds of Everything*, a move that can be read as indicative of the singer's career transition from music to politics.

Like other female celebrity memoirists analysed here, Dana shows the music business to be a fractious and unwholesome environment, with the teenage star finding her personal agency curtailed in numerous ways. Significantly, the narrative builds upon descriptions of the difficulties Dana encountered over the years, leading to the singer's own Damascene moment at an evangelical prayer meeting she attended with her husband-to-be, at which she came to the realization that 'God loves me and cares for me. He gives me what I need. More than that, He gives me what is *best* for me, at the *time* that it is best for me.'[11] Assessments of this kind bespeak the targeting of Dana's memoirs at the avowedly Christian audience she increasingly courted through her music, a shift in approach that culminated in a lucrative career rejuvenation in the United States in the 1990s, her account of which features prominently in *All Kinds of Everything*.

Dana's religiously inflected memoirs are precursors to the autobiography of boxing champion Katie Taylor, whose *My Olympic Dream* (2012) similarly credits her achievements to a devout Irish Catholicism. Professions of religious faith recur throughout the text and constitute its most consistent discursive keynote, closely followed by descriptions of her closeness to family and expressions of patriotism. *My Olympic Dream* also adheres to the durable convention of praising the natural beauty of the homeland ('Of all the places I have been around the world, there is nowhere more beautiful than Ireland on a blue-sky, summer's day'[12]) and emphasizes Taylor's appreciation (with perhaps a trace of bemusement) of her avid Irish fan base. But her staunchest commitment is to the articulation of her religious belief: 'My Olympic dream began first in the heart of God before it ever began in me – this was my God-given destiny!'[13] Her autobiography, which is a glossy, pictorial production, closes with a dedication to her grandmother, Nanny Kathleen, and a full reprint of Psalm 18. Thus, the book holds in place a public image of Taylor as devout, modest, family-centred and unthreatening in her advocacy of women's sport. Notably, the coincidence of Taylor's peak celebrity with some of the worst years of the post-2008 Irish economic recession imbues *My Olympic Dream* with an additional cultural significance, allowing

---

[11] Ibid., 117. Original emphasis.
[12] Katie Taylor and Johnny Watterson, *My Olympic Dream* (London: Simon and Schuster, 2012), 172.
[13] Ibid., 3.

it to be read as the testimony of a woman who embodies groundbreaking international success, traditional national values and, crucially, a resilient self-sufficiency. As Marcus Free astutely observes:

> In an age of post-'Celtic Tiger' economic austerity in Ireland, driven by the logic of neoliberalism, but conjoined with the rhetoric of conservative cultural nationalism, the 'Katie Taylor' of Irish media representation was presented as a model of frugality and self-reliance as a national 'icon' – though one who, with her male amateur Irish boxing counterparts, succeeded with minimal material support from the State.[14]

Raised in a Church of Ireland family in Portadown in Northern Ireland, broadcaster Gloria Hunniford, like both Dana and Taylor, sees religious belief as performing an organizing and defining role in her celebrity. Hunniford eschews strong institutional affiliations in favour of a more personal reliance on faith and, more controversially, espouses a new-age belief in angelic intervention. Her first autobiography, *Gloria* (1994), depicts her as determined to make it in a man's world, and although early chapters provide a somewhat bucolic and sentimental portrait of her mid-Ulster upbringing, she also gives a measured view of the sectarian divisions that marked Northern Ireland in those years, notably in her description of her father's refusal to attend her wedding to a Catholic. Hunniford's religious beliefs are foregrounded in her later memoirs, *Next to You* (2006) and *Always with You* (2008), which detail her struggle to come to terms with the death of her television-presenter daughter Caron Keating in 2004, after a long battle with breast cancer. Arguably, this event has somewhat overshadowed Hunniford's significant broadcasting achievements, yet the popularity of these memoirs attests to the cultural resonance of an autobiographical mode that accentuates both the pains and pleasures of the maternal bond, while simultaneously promising to deliver a toolkit for emotional self-help in an unforgiving world.

In contrast to the preceding autobiographies, Coleen Nolan's *Upfront and Personal* (2009) casts its author as both loosely affiliated with and estranged from Irishness. Her references to Ireland are rather scant, predictably enough for a woman who has lived and worked in the UK all her life. The emigrant Irishness with which the musical Nolan family was associated in their heyday is on the whole lightly worn, being vaguely associated with a tribal family outlook and a trouper mindset on the road. Irishness is also equated with long-suffering and abiding maternalism,

---

[14] Marcus Free, '"He is my Strength and my Shield": The Antimonies of Katie Taylor as Female Sporting Celebrity in Twenty-First-Century Ireland', *Sport in Society*, 18:10 (2015), 2.

exemplified by a passage in which Nolan accounts for her mother's choice to sleep on a couch to accommodate her large family by remarking: 'that's an Irish woman thing, isn't it? No sacrifice is ever too big in the name of hospitality.'[15] Like the autobiographies of Maureen O'Hara and Dana, *Upfront and Personal* presents its author as navigating the perils of early media celebrity with wholesomeness, naivety and an endearing lack of guile. However, Nolan's narrative diverges from the others considered here when, later in the text, these qualities give way rather dramatically to revelations of abortion (this seems to have been a particular selling point for a book promoted as providing 'explosive new material' on its dust jacket), depression, weight struggles and the kind of hard-won emotional knowledge that anchored her appearances as a panellist on the television chat show *Loose Women*, where she often featured alongside Hunniford. Religion, notably, offers no salvation from these travails. Unlike the auto-biographical accounts of Dana, Taylor and Hunniford, which emphasize how obstacles can be overcome by placing one's faith in God, Nolan's memoir stresses female emotional resilience and the rewards as well as the tribulations of family life.

The Celtic Tiger celebrity memoir

The massive expansion of the Irish celebrity export market in the 1990s meant that the development of a full-fledged indigenous celebrity economy became a marked feature of the later years of the Celtic Tiger era in the early 2000s. Arguably for the first time, a set of home-grown (sometimes emphatically so) media personalities emerged whose talents were not necessarily a strong explanatory feature of their renown. The rise of the Irish boy band in this period offers perhaps the most ready case study of this phenomenon. As Noel McLaughlin and Martin McLoone note, one can easily 'draw parallels between the rise of the boy band form in Ireland and the emergence of the Celtic Tiger and the crass commercial imperatives and neoliberal economics that this represented'.[16] In Moynagh Sullivan's assessment, groups like Boyzone and Westlife appear 'innocently apolitical' but 'they implicitly perform not only the new-found success of Celtic Tiger Ireland, but also the reasons for that

---

[15] Coleen Nolan, *Upfront and Personal* (London: Pan Books, 2009), 7.
[16] Noel McLaughlin and Martin McLoone, 'From Men to Boys: Masculinity, Politics and the Irish Boy Band', in Conn Holohan and Tony Tracy, eds., *Masculinity and Irish Popular Culture: Tiger's Tales* (Basingstoke: Palgrave Macmillan, 2014), 62–63.

success'.[17] The activities of music promoter Louis Walsh are pertinent here, as is the emergence of girl bands like B*Witched and twin singers Jedward. In all such cases, promotional zeal outweighs and outsignifies musical talent. As Patricia Neville and Teresa Neville aptly note of Eurovision contestants Jedward, the pair were 'noted more for their chaotic dynamism than their innate musical prowess'.[18] This shift was accompanied by a turn away from a previously respectful and at times even reverential public regard for celebrity towards a more critical consumptive mode. The invention of pseudocelebrities like Ross O'Carroll-Kelly and novelty act Dustin the Turkey further exemplifies this trend, as does the domestic dethroning of global superstar Bono, towards whom public antipathy seemed to surge in this era, earning him the mocking moniker 'St Bono'.

This repositioning of celebrity status in Irish culture significantly parallels the intensified neoliberalism of Irish public life. People's increasingly deconstructive relationship to celebrity and their readiness to exhibit a heightened *schadenfreude* over the misfortunes of individual media personalities obliquely articulate a deeper disenchantment with the logic of national economic strategies in the aftermath of the boom years. As Steve Cross and Jo Littler have persuasively argued, such *schadenfreude* can work to express 'a reaction to the blocks "ordinary" people face in relation to social mobility and recognition and the forms of inequality which are rightly perceived to constitute the celebrity economy'.[19] Heavy tabloid coverage of perceived Celtic Tiger casualties like broadcaster Gerry Ryan and model Katy French came to provide a platform for the expression of anger at the inequalities that an officially euphoric national economic narrative sought to obscure. Indeed, the premature deaths of both Ryan and French can be read as unravelling their celebrity narratives about the new virtues of intense individual self-promotion and multi-platform leveraging. As Anne Sexton observes, French in particular became the subject of a paradox: 'While the contemporary media offers rewards to subordinate celebrity women prepared to trade on their sexuality, Irish society reads such women ambivalently at best; although their entrepreneurial zeal is

[17] Moynagh Sullivan, 'Boyz to Men: Irish Boy Bands and Mothering the Nation', in Wanda Balzano, Anne Mulhall and Moynagh Sullivan, eds., *Irish Postmodernisms and Popular Culture* (Basingstoke: Palgrave Macmillan, 2007), 184.

[18] Patricia Neville and Teresa Neville, 'The Spectacle of Twinship in Jedward', *Celebrity Studies*, 4:1 (2013), 97.

[19] Steve Cross and Jo Littler, 'Celebrity and *Schadenfreude*', *Cultural Studies*, 24:3 (2010), 412.

lauded, they are also severely judged for violating traditionalist norms of femininity.'[20]

Of all the Irish celebrity autobiographies published during this time, it is Ryan's which best captures the contradictions of the era. Both in terms of its financial inception and its content, *Would the Real Gerry Ryan Please Stand Up* (2008) acts as a metaphoric encapsulation of the excesses and wilful self-delusion of a country that in hindsight had, as the commonly used Irish idiom puts it, lost the run of itself. Ryan, a high-profile broadcaster on RTÉ radio and television, received a €100,000 advance from Penguin Ireland for his memoir, a figure unprecedented in Irish publishing. It is highly doubtful whether Penguin ever recouped its investment and it is tempting to see in the deal a correlation between the overvaluing of celebrity and the famously extortionate Dublin property market that defined the era. The content of Ryan's book also exemplifies the delusions of grandeur that prevailed at this time. For instance, he memorably describes the restaurant of Dublin's upmarket Four Seasons Hotel as his 'canteen' where he held meetings and, in a characteristic piece of namedropping, adds: 'I know Louis Walsh does the same thing.'[21] Ryan's descriptions of his love of fine cigars, rare single malt whiskies and first-class transatlantic trips are somewhat surprising given the posthumous revelations regarding the huge debts he had accrued by this time, debts that were themselves revealed to be a major incentive for him to write the book. Indeed, the posthumous speculation generated by the discovery of cocaine in Ryan's system at the time of his death (a habit never mentioned in his autobiography) led to his public dethroning and also facilitated a (limited) venting of public disenchantment with an elite class whose risk-taking with the money of others is still having profound effects on Irish society.

Queering the nation: Graham Norton and Rory O'Neill

Apparent in both Graham Norton's and Rory O'Neill's memoirs is a disaffiliation with conventional signifiers and reference points of Irishness, although, in Norton's case at least, this does not necessarily entail a complete break with the romantic discourses of cultural identity so prominent in the autobiographies of Gabriel Byrne and Maureen O'Hara. *The Life and Loves of a He Devil* (2014), the sequel to *So Me*

---

[20] Anne Sexton, 'Katy French: National Identity, Postfeminism and the Life and Death of a Celtic Tiger Cub', *Television and New Media*, 14:3 (2013), 219.

[21] Gerry Ryan, *Would the Real Gerry Ryan Please Stand Up* (Dublin: Penguin Ireland, 2008), 54.

(2004), comprises Norton's mid-life ruminations on selected topics, one of which is Ireland, a place he reveals he has 'fallen back in love with'[22] early in the narrative, citing as reasons the humour, parental tough love, communal values and the idiosyncrasies of Irish commerce. As he sees it, the country is steadfastly immune to celebrity – 'small-town Ireland makes a nonsense' of it – though it does sponsor a natural loquaciousness, talking being 'something we in Ireland are especially gifted at'.[23] What attracts him more, however, is the country's growing modernization, liberalism and sexual tolerance, all of which developments make it a place where he chooses to spend holiday time on his country estate in Cork. This maturation is presented as being equivalent to Norton's own: 'While I've become more comfortable in my own skin, Ireland too has grown in confidence. It seems to have realised it can embrace the modern world without losing its identity or what makes it such a special place.'[24]

Norton's Ireland, then, reflects his own balancing act as a media-savvy cosmopolitan who interviews the world's biggest celebrities on national television and is seldom overawed, while still being tied in important ways to an unpretentious rural heritage. Yet despite reminding us of his alternate cultural positioning as a Southern Protestant, and making occasional cursory attempts to dispel stereotypes, as when he states that 'whatever you may imagine being raised in Ireland was like, I never suckled Guinness or whiskey from a baby's bottle',[25] Norton is generally at pains to validate popular associations of Irishness with conviviality and 'the craic'. In doing so, he sources his own identity as chat show host and comedian in a wellspring of national authenticity. The attributes of Irish culture that he highlights are precisely those that make him good at his job. In this way, Irishness is figured as a credential of sociality and upward mobility throughout his autobiography.

A similar ambivalence with regard to notions of Irishness is apparent in O'Neill's memoir. In 'Popeular', the opening chapter of *Woman in the Making*, he presents Pope John Paul II's visit to Ireland in 1979, which marked the high point of the Catholic church's power and popular appeal in late twentieth-century Ireland, as the occasion when, as an eleven-year-old boy, he experienced 'an epiphany of sorts'.[26] Whereas for Dana the pontiff's visit is lauded as a cultural landmark to be celebrated, O'Neill bathetically recalls standing in the rain and murk in Knock, Co. Mayo and

[22] Graham Norton, *The Life and Loves of a He Devil* (London: Hodder and Stoughton, 2014), 3.
[23] Ibid., 68, 69.   [24] Ibid., 70.   [25] Ibid., 172.
[26] Rory O'Neill, *Woman in the Making: A Memoir* (Dublin: Hachette Books Ireland, 2014), 9.

realizing that 'I didn't belong there ... I felt no joy. I felt afraid ... The Pope's visit unhooked me from the dead weight of religion and pushed me into the stream of my own consciousness. It gave me a mind of my own.'[27] However, while somewhat self-consciously setting himself up as a voice of a new Ireland and jettisoning Catholicism as a key reference point for national identity, O'Neill occasionally reappropriates select moments from Irish history, as when he celebrates the fact that his home town of Ballinrobe gave the world the word 'boycott' as a result of the towns-people's actions in resisting a particularly unpopular nineteenth-century agent for absentee landlords. At such moments, O'Neill obliquely aligns his own actions on behalf of LGBTQ people in contemporary Ireland with an anti-colonial enterprise in the Irish past.

O'Neill's autobiography traces a number of key stages in the performer's life, including a period during the Celtic Tiger years when, as Panti Bliss, he became a countercultural mainstay due to his involvement in promot-ing a Dublin fetish club called G.A.G. and the Alternative Miss Ireland pageant for drag queens, which 'in its own small way [was] an attempt to redefine Irishness, to queerify Irishness'.[28] O'Neill's descriptions of this time are the most colourful in the book and openly challenge traditional notions of Irishness and their attendant conservative sexual politics. Panti's outlandish performative displays at the inaugural G.A.G. club night, as narrated by O'Neill, stand out as particularly subversive actions that would have been unthinkable even a decade earlier. Like Norton, O'Neill describes in almost wholly positive terms an Ireland, or more specifically a Dublin, undergoing profound social and economic changes in the mid-to-late 1990s:

> There was a sense of possibility about the place and a confidence we'd never had before. The city was changing before our eyes ... The mad rush to get off the island had stopped because, for the first time, we actually believed it was as good as anywhere else. We stopped looking across the water at London or Barcelona or New York, and stopped apologising for being from Dublin. Sure wasn't the whole world Riverdancing.[29]

With the return of large-scale youth emigration in the wake of the 2008 financial crash, it is hard not to detect a melancholy note in this description of boomtime Dublin which, unwittingly or not, plays into the 'we all partied' narrative that has since come to define this contentious era.[30]

---

[27] Ibid.   [28] Ibid., 141.   [29] Ibid., 126–27.
[30] With its flamboyant descriptions of outré events and hedonistic living, *Woman in the Making* counterbalances the other prominent recent autobiography by a gay Irish celebrity, *Come What May*

It was the media and legal storm created by an incident in 2014, dubbed Pantigate, and its knock-on effect on the 2015 marriage equality referendum, that proved to be the making of O'Neill as a culturally significant figure who exemplifies new ways of imagining Irish citizenship and subjectivity after the economic crisis.[31] The episode started somewhat innocuously on RTÉ television's *Saturday Night Show* when O'Neill, being interviewed as himself, commented that the only places where it was acceptable to express homophobic views in Ireland were on the internet and in newspaper opinion pieces. Pressed to say which people he was referring to, O'Neill named journalists Breda O'Brien and John Waters and the Iona Institute, a conservative Catholic lobby group. When threatened with litigation, RTÉ removed the programme from its online player, issued a public apology to the journalists concerned and paid out a settlement of €85,000, actions that led many to question whether the national broadcaster was allowing itself to be censored and effectively shirking its public service remit. Others took to social media to voice their outrage. A few weeks later Panti made a speech at the Abbey Theatre which went viral on YouTube and gained global coverage for the issues of LGBTQ rights and homophobia in Irish society.

The so-called Pantigate episode reinforced the sense that state-backed media institutions which had for so long shaped and defined Irish public discourse were being increasingly outflanked by emerging technological platforms. It also demonstrated the bottom-up characteristics that have come to define emerging norms of social media engagement, and attested to the profound impact such nascent technologies have had in the realm of celebrity culture and on wider social issues such as the rights of minority groups within the state. O'Neill himself emerges from all of this as a shrewd media operator capable of utilizing a variety of media platforms to advocate for equality and diversity as defining values of a new Ireland. In addition to *Woman in the Making* and O'Neill's significant social media presence, the largely crowd-funded and widely celebrated documentary *The Queen of Ireland* (2015) brought Panti's story to the big screen, further boosting his political and economic capital.

(2009) by Cork hurler Dónal Óg Cusack. The overly 'straight' narrative at the centre of Cusack's book contrasts markedly with the provocations of *A Woman in the Making* and suggests a bifurcation inherent to popular narratives of gay experience in Ireland.

[31] Although *A Woman in the Making* was initially published in the period between Pantigate and the referendum, the paperback edition contains a foreword written days after the Yes vote prevailed, thus reinforcing the perception of O'Neill as being pivotal to the victory.

Conclusion

When read in the context of a national culture that for complex reasons has often found it difficult to generate fully indigenous notions and narratives of success, Irish celebrity autobiographies negotiate cultural boundaries, register social changes and exemplify shifting subjectivities in illuminating ways. In particular, they show how an evolving acceptance of claims to individual agency is becoming more pronounced, as the deflected autobiographical mode, in which subjects self-deprecatingly foreground their interactions with significant figures other than themselves, gives way to a more subject-centric approach that complies with neoliberal norms of commercial self-promotion. Another way of characterizing this shift is in terms of the subjectivity of labour: whereas earlier celebrity accounts tend to stress the subject's affiliation (however qualified or problematic) with stable or even fixed institutional and national categories, more recent texts cast their narrators as entrepreneurial citizens of a nation that is changed and changing, and whose institutions are rickety and flawed. In this sense, these recent works are consistent with what Imre Szeman identifies as 'a now general and increasingly widely accepted rule: the entrepreneur has become a model of how to be and behave, and not only in the world of business ... *We are all entrepreneurs now.*'[32]

A defining aspect of recent celebrity autobiographies, therefore, is their relation to new, more narcissistic and self-promoting forms of Irish citizenship. Given the return of mass emigration, the prevalence of offshore economic arrangements and the regularization of precarity and mobility, the very newest of these memoirists also speak from/to/of a profoundly undecided moment in the life of the Republic and its associated concepts of national identity. As Carmen Leah Kuhling puts it: 'Nationalism, Catholicism and now Neoliberalism have all proven to be deeply problematic, and no new collective signifiers of self-identity have emerged in their wake.'[33] The contemporary Irish celebrity autobiography, then, with its focus on the narration of exemplary selfhood, plays a role in brokering the complexities and contradictions of a post-Celtic Tiger and, for some, post-recession era. Whereas earlier autobiographers tended to want to hold in place the stabilizing power of institutions, this feature is conspicuously absent from the works of the newer generation, in whose memoirs we can discern

---

[32] Imre Szeman, 'Entrepreneurialism as the New Common Sense', *South Atlantic Quarterly*, 114:3 (2015), 472. Original emphasis.
[33] Carmen Leah Kuhling, 'Zombie Banks, Zombie Politics and the "Walking Zombie Movement": Liminality and the Post-Crisis Irish Imaginary', *European Journal of Cultural Studies* 20:4 (2017), 407.

an overt embrace of actions and attitudes that would once have been deemed shamefully self-serving and culturally gauche. In these and numerous other ways, the celebrity autobiography offers a window onto changing relations between self and society in an Ireland marked by high rates of emigration, no-questions-asked hospitality to transnational capital, the fraying of social ties and institutions, deep political disenchantment – and a still tenacious investment in contemplating and celebrating what it is to be Irish.

Further reading

Barton, Ruth. *Acting Irish in Hollywood: From Fitzgerald to Farrell.* Dublin: Irish Academic Press, 2006.

Dyer, Richard. *Heavenly Bodies: Film Stars and Society.* New York: St. Martin's Press, 1986.

Freeman, Traci. 'Celebrity Autobiography', in Margaretta Jolly, ed., *The Encyclopedia of Life Writing: Autobiographical and Biographical Forms.* London: Fitzroy Dearborn, 2001. Vol. I: 188–90.

Holmes, Su and Diane Negra, eds. *In the Limelight and Under the Microscope: Forms and Functions of Female Celebrity.* New York: Continuum, 2011.

Lee, Katja. 'Reading Celebrity Autobiographies', *Celebrity Studies*, 5:1–2 (2014): 87–89.

Marshall, P. David. *Celebrity and Power: Fame in Contemporary Culture.* Minneapolis: University of Minnesota Press, 1997.

CHAPTER 25

Irish Life-Writing in the Digital Era

Claire Lynch

Autobiography is difficult, perhaps even impossible. As Patrick Kavanagh makes clear, 'talking' or writing about the self is both uncomfortable and unreliable; for every revealing anecdote included, another is edited out: 'I dislike talking about myself in a direct way. The self is only interesting as an illustration. For some reason, whenever we talk about our personal lives they turn out to be both irrelevant and untrue – even when the facts are right, the mood is wrong.'[1] Simply writing about memory is to acknowledge how much we forget. It is partly for this reason that literary scholars are so often preoccupied with the matter of what is and is not autobiography. Memoir, diaries, letters, *Bildungsromane* and other narrative forms all retain a clear family resemblance to autobiography in the way they reflect upon and portray the self. In the so-called digital era, blogs, apps, personal websites, emails, social networks, online dating and professional networking profiles have become the ubiquitous genres through which people respond to the autobiographical impulse. These digital manifestations of life-writing differ most clearly from their printed predecessors in their relationship to time. One of the foundational assumptions about life-writing is that it is retrospective, or at least 'recursive in the sense that it refers back to and draws upon the life that it narrates'.[2] Whether the autobiographer looks to the past with nostalgic warmth or triumphant rejection, the narrative is, inevitably, of the life already lived. Yet in the very act of reflecting on the past, autobiographers write to the future, projecting the life story beyond their own lifetime.

In the digital era, our long-established perceptions of time and geographical distance have been disrupted. Life-writing, like so many other aspects of contemporary culture in the Global North, has evolved alongside the

---

[1] Patrick Kavanagh, *Self Portrait* (Dublin: Dolmen Press, 1964), 7.
[2] Kate O'Riordan, 'Writing Biodigital Life: Personal Genomes and Digital Media', *Biography*, 34:1 (2011), 128.

expectation that previously unimaginable quantities of information are instantly accessible and that intimate human relationships might flourish without physical proximity. In simple terms, family histories stretch out beyond the limits of memory because digital census returns and online archives are so accessible. Similarly, the instant publication experienced by users of Twitter and Facebook allows the most recent past to be narrated in real time. In this chapter, these phenomena will be understood as a mutation of the grammar of Irish autobiography. The examples discussed here cluster around the past, present and future tenses of Irish life-writing in the digital era.

Irish people's adoption of online technology for the purposes of leisure, education and increased productivity has led Gerry Smyth to proclaim that 'Few countries embraced the IT-sponsored information revolution with as much alacrity as Ireland.'[3] In recent decades, periods of economic instability and increased political activism have been among the motivations for Irish men and women to make the private self public. This chapter will therefore also consider a number of the prevailing narratives and literary conventions in digital Irish autobiography. Starting with those who seek to understand themselves by looking to the past, the chapter will explore family history research and projects designed to reconnect the diaspora with contemporary Ireland through the framework of life stories. This will then be followed by a discussion of Irish life-writing rooted in the present via the collective narration of the @Ireland Twitter initiative. Finally, the chapter considers the production of an online archive of the life stories of those who arrive into and leave the Republic, as curated by the *Irish Times* projects 'Generation Emigration' and 'New to the Parish' respectively.

Past tense

In Sebastian Barry's *The Secret Scripture* (2008), a novel bound up in family secrets and the archival detective work needed to unpick them, the elderly Roseanne McNulty remarks:

> It is funny, but it strikes me that a person without anecdotes that they nurse while they live, and that survive them, is more likely to be utterly lost not only to history but the family following them. Of course that is the fate of most

[3] Gerry Smyth, 'Tiger–Theory–Technology: A Meditation on the Development of Modern Irish Literary Criticism', *Irish Studies Review*, 15:2 (2007), 126.

souls, reducing entire lives, no matter how vivid and wonderful, to those sad black names on withering family trees, with half a date dangling after and a question mark.[4]

It is an act of self-memorialization, then, which prompts Roseanne to write her life narrative, a 'brittle and honest-minded history of myself'.[5] Barry's novel provides a useful starting point here by reminding us that life-writing is not about impossibly neutral reportage but self-conscious narrating; life stories must be told in order to 'survive'. Roseanne writes out her life in her own words precisely because 'withering family trees' appear to be such an inadequate form of capturing memories, experiences and legacies. In the digital era, in which so many people have access to so much information, it is perhaps odd that these rigid and rather sparse textual diagrams have thrived to the extent that family history research accounts for the 'second largest use of the internet'.[6] Material practices have become digital with relatively little controversy, large scrolls of paper conveniently replaced with software that models family trees and hours of pencil transcription in national archives substituted with home access to digitized census records. However they are gathered and presented, family trees are usefully thought of in the digital era as a network diagram. Fed and watered on official 'evidence' such as death certificates and parish registers, the family tree betrays a core belief that people are 'defined by who and where we are "from"'.[7]

Constructing one's own sense of self through the lives and locations of Irish ancestors has become a well-established hobby for people all over the world. The oft-cited statistics of the '70 million people throughout the globe who can claim Irish ancestry'[8] can be understood anew alongside the proliferation of online chat rooms, genealogy websites and digital resources targeting the Irish diaspora.[9] Former President of Ireland Mary McAleese's equally famous reference to the 'global Irish family' is pertinent here and is, perhaps, partially responsible for the boom in gathering 'sad black names' on family trees in recent decades. This, after all, is a

---

[4] Sebastian Barry, *The Secret Scripture* (London: Faber and Faber, 2008), 15.   [5] Ibid., 8.

[6] Paul Basu, *Highland Homecomings: Genealogy and Heritage Tourism in the Scottish Diaspora* (Oxford: Routledge, 2007), 261. The largest use of the internet is pornography.

[7] Julia Watson, 'Ordering the Family: Genealogy as Autobiographical Pedigree', in Sidonie Smith and Julia Watson, eds., *Getting a Life: Everyday Uses of Autobiography* (Minneapolis: University of Minnesota Press, 1996), 297.

[8] Brian Walker, 'The Lost Tribes of Ireland', *Irish Studies Review*, 15:3 (2007), 267.

[9] For more on these resources see Ashley Barnwell, 'The Genealogy Craze: Authoring an Authentic Identity through Family History Research', *Life Writing*, 10:3 (2013), 261–75. As Barnwell writes: 'These websites are among tens of thousands of personal pages and blogs devoted to family trees, surnames, clans, tribes, local histories, genetic genealogies and celebrity descendants' (262).

narrative that also draws on the irresistible idea of the network, linking up nodes distanced by time and space. More recently, large-scale events such as the Irish Tourist Board's The Gathering have worked hard to connect lives present and past, near and far.[10] A particularly interesting aspect of The Gathering was the project's relationship with 'Ireland Reaching Out'. A reverse genealogy organization and online resource, 'Ireland Reaching Out' aims to reconnect people with places by inviting members of the Irish diaspora to visit the towns and villages of their ancestors during 'Weeks of Welcome'.[11] While traditional genealogy relies on the individual tracing his or her origins back to a place, the 'Ireland Reaching Out' approach sees the place trace the person.

While several factors have contributed to the recent growth in family history research, online access to public records, maps, census transcripts and cultural history archives has clearly led to 'something approaching a democracy of knowledge'.[12] It is revealing then that for all of the material newly available, the inevitably reductive narrative form of the family tree retains prominence. The family tree hints at profound self-definition but it also obscures it. For all of the valuable information they curate, family trees are also narratives of absence. Relationships not sanctioned by church or state and children unacknowledged by structures of legitimacy perch unseen on the branches; those who 'don't or can't find their way in that story – the queers, the single, the something else – can become so easily unimaginable'.[13] Whatever else it represents, the family tree is more blank space than text. When life narratives depend upon a privileging of archives in this way, be they digital or material, real people and their stories are displaced by documents. As Catherine Nash so eloquently explains, this involves a combination of 'empirical detective work' and 'the imaginative work of constructing always incomplete family histories from evocative names and

---

[10] The Gathering was a 2013 government-led tourism initiative, devised by Failté Ireland and Tourism Ireland. The central objectives of The Gathering were to strengthen relationships with the diaspora and to mobilize the Irish abroad and people of Irish descent in the work of economic recovery in Ireland. The latter of these aims led to significant controversy and the satirizing of the project as The Grabbing. A full report on the findings and recommendations from The Gathering is available at www.thegatheringireland.com/ (accessed 18 June 2013).

[11] See http://www.irelandxo.com/ (accessed 18 June 2013).

[12] Simon Schama, 'Television and the Trouble with History', in David Cannadine, ed., *History and the Media* (Basingstoke: Palgrave Macmillan, 2004), 27. The increased popularity of online family history research takes place alongside the surge in genealogical television programmes, magazines and community projects.

[13] Lauren Berlant, 'Intimacy: A Special Issue', *Critical Inquiry*, 24:2 (1998), 286. On 22 May 2015, Irish voters supported the thirty-fourth constitutional amendment, permitting lawful marriage 'by two persons without distinction to their sex'. Couples in same-sex relationships who choose to marry will, as a consequence, have their relationship recorded by the state.

dates, fragmentary memories, sketchy stories, and nameless figures in old family photographs, the affective artefacts of family history'.[14]

While online research might excavate names and dates, the very process threatens a never-ending collection of data in place of the intended result: an increased understanding of the self. Family trees, and the acorns of egocentrism from which they grow, provide, at best, a framework in which one life may be positioned among many. In this we see the tension between the reflective first-person narratives typically thought of as autobiography and the more summative outputs of family history research. While family history researchers dedicate countless hours to online chat rooms and digitized archives, autobiographers remain bonded to a narrative built on 'memory'. It is here that the forms typically part ways, since 'What autobiography celebrates as the fruitful variety of remembered human constructions of events is suspect to the genealogist.'[15] In the simplest terms, while the contemporary family historian gazes out to the expanse of the web, the autobiographer still looks within.

As Dr Grene recalls in *The Secret Scripture*, modern Ireland's personal and national history rests upon the burning of 'almost every civil record to ashes, births, deaths, marriages, and other documents beyond price, wiping out the records of the very nation they were trying to give new life to, actually burning memory in its boxes'.[16] Contrary perhaps to many lay expectations, digital records and documents are even more precarious than their paper equivalents. Formats change, hardware is upgraded and components become irreplaceable, meaning that, if personal archives are not backed up as institutional ones are, there is a genuine risk of our own time becoming the 'forgotten century'.[17] Indeed, the very concept of memory has shifted from something that 'lives' within the brain to something that describes the power of computers. Even as we consider the very essence of what it is to narrate a life, we outsource some of our memory work to our machines. In doing so we offload some of the burden of remembering, relying 'more than ever on computer memory to enhance our human capabilities to remember and recall information, both institutional and

---

[14] Catherine Nash, *Of Irish Descent: Origin Stories, Genealogy, and the Politics of Belonging* (Syracuse: Syracuse University Press, 2008), 17.

[15] Watson, 'Ordering the Family', 303.

[16] Barry, *The Secret Scripture*, 214. In 1922, the Four Courts building in Dublin, site of the Public Record Office, was severely damaged by shelling. Numerous irreplaceable documents were destroyed as a consequence. It is to this event that Dr Grene is referring.

[17] Google vice president Vinton Cerf, cited in Paul Longley Arthur, 'Material Memory and the Digital', *Life Writing*, 12:2 (2015), 190.

personal'.[18] There are important comparisons to be made between the now digitized official documents traditionally used to produce family trees, such as birth and marriage certificates, and the typically paper-based love letters, postcards or teenage diaries that capture the anecdotal life. There is a temptation to think of the perishable paper version of a life as the more ephemeral, whereas in fact digital traces are typically more precarious. As Paul Longley Arthur explains: 'We speak about the digital "dark ages" as being the 1990s, but much personal data faces exactly the same risks today.'[19]

Present tense

Perhaps the most significant shift in the evolution between print and digital modes of Irish life-writing is that towards an explicitly participatory readership. Digital life-writing is a form of mutual voyeurism shaped around 'passive' observation and public commentary. While diary writers and traditional prose autobiographers wrote with an imagined or anticipated future audience in mind, their digital counterparts receive tangible real-time endorsements through 'likes', 'comments' and 'favourites'. Never before have life-writers operated with the expectation of such an immediate response. The frequency too has clearly changed; the digital age has witnessed millions of people producing mouthfuls of life narrative several times a day, regurgitated onto social media at their leisure. Recent statistics indicate that 26 per cent of the Irish population has a Twitter account.[20] Both as a series of fragmented texts and as collated narratives, these new forms of life-writing represent a wealth of material for future scholars of Irish writing, history, culture and society. A particularly noteworthy example is the @Ireland account set up in March 2012. The @Ireland Twitter account operates by a process of 'shared-curation', rotating to a different user each week.[21] The principle is to disrupt the idea that any individual can be a spokesperson for a whole nation. Instead, by sharing in the experiences and observations of many different people, readers or 'followers', might come to a greater understanding of the diversity of the nation. As the organizers explain: '@Ireland can help to further connect

---

[18] Ibid.,189. [19] Ibid., 197.
[20] Shane O'Leary, 'The Irish Digital Consumer Report 2015', http://shaneoleary.me/blog/index.php/the-irish-digital-consumer-report-2015/ (accessed 22 November 2015).
[21] See https://twitter.com/ireland (accessed 10 October 2014).

Ireland to the world and the world to Ireland through the different voices that curate the account each week.'[22] There is something appealing, admirable even, in this attempt to deconstruct the myth of a singular national identity, even if it is necessarily limited to those with Twitter accounts.

The @Ireland account takes its inspiration from the @Sweden campaign, an initiative established by the National Board for the Promotion of Sweden. There, Swedish people were appointed 'Curators of Sweden' with the express purpose of contributing to the country's international reputation in the weighty matters of 'political objectives, trade, investments, visitors, exchange of talent and creativity'.[23] @Sweden was widely admired for changing the landscape for digital media and tourism, winning multiple awards and inspiring clone projects such as @netherlanders and @denmarktweets which similarly hope to dispel stereotypes or extol national virtues. It was not without problems, however. When the Swedish account rotated to a person who expressed anti-Semitic views, many saw the freedom awarded to curators backfiring. Interestingly, it was precisely the way the @Sweden account handled this episode which was taken to be its greatest success. Rather than suppress the account and censor the rogue contributor, the project allowed other Twitter users to engage in debate and express counter-arguments. For many commentators, this demonstrated a welcome willingness to treat social media problems in a social media context.[24]

Since the @Ireland account changes from week to week with each curator, followers might be challenged to think about high-profile themes such as climate change, environmental activism and gender politics, as well as aspects of popular culture, including sport, music and television. Whatever the topics, the weekly curator makes him or herself vulnerable to the views of thousands of followers. While the sensitive and well-informed discussion of a new topic can attract admiration, curators are also subject to mockery or criticism when they fail to recognize that followers are not the same as actual friends. When a mature student from Dublin tweeted a detailed account of having had an abortion as a young woman, the potential of the project became clear. The curator's narrative formed part of the wider discussion of reproductive rights in Ireland and, arguably, was

[22] See www.irishcentral.com/roots/what-is-the-ireland-twitter-feed-223955441–237781181.html (accessed 22 November 2014).
[23] See www.curatorsofsweden.com/about/ (accessed 19 November 2014).
[24] Several accounts can be read online, for example, www.tnooz.com/article/the-sweden-twitter-scandal-did-tourism-officials-handle-it-correctly/ (accessed 24 November 2014).

only made possible because of the technology that allows personal experience to become public record. Although largely ignored by the mainstream media in Ireland, the @Ireland curator's Twitter testimony was taken up by online news sites and internationally distributed. Aside from the relevance of this to the current calls to repeal the Eighth Amendment of the Constitution, this extract of a life story speaks to a wider theme. Irish Studies has long grappled with the idea that an individual (real or symbolic) can stand in for the nation. While widely admired by many for her bravery and eloquence, the @Ireland curator was also attacked by those who saw her as manipulating the account for the purposes of propaganda. Comments, criticism and censure directed towards this autobiographical narrative, both via Twitter during the original event and subsequently on blogs and opinion pieces, are telling. For all of the potential afforded by new technologies for self-narration, precisely who speaks 'for' or 'as' Ireland, and what they are permitted to say, remains highly contested.

One of the challenges of working with Twitter as a form of digital life narrative is its incompleteness. For now, we read these expressions of life-writing serially, hour by hour, in the present moment. In this way, Twitter profiles provide a drip-feed of textual self-portraiture. Each user constructs a cumulative narrative, each tweet contributing to a portrayal of the individual as politically motivated, perhaps, or emotionally incontinent. In the future, however, there is a very real potential that these fragments of life will be read as a complete narrative, as several years' worth of observations, reflections and commentary are collated. Furthermore, tweets, along with other forms of digital narrative, require specific reading practices. They are, for example, dialogic as well as highly contextual. Concurrent sociopolitical events, trends in popular culture and even the time of day are all relevant in parsing a tweet. Hashtags are similarly important, both as a mode of organizing material into thematic conversations and as marking a linguistic innovation. So while it would be easy to dismiss this form of writing as self-absorbed and vacuous, it is equally clear that it has the power to inspire, educate and memorialize.

In his final words of comfort to his wife, Nobel laureate Seamus Heaney produced, however inadvertently, a micro-autobiography which encapsulates Irish life-writing in the digital age. The two-word text message, '*Noli timere*', sent on 30 August 2013, was shared with the congregation by son Michael at Heaney's funeral, and thus with the world's media. Typed into a mobile phone, read on a screen and finally proclaimed from the pulpit, this text message soon became global news, reproduced in newspapers and on television. But it was online, notably through Twitter, that Heaney's imperative not to fear became the hub of a global network of disparate lives. Concise and compelling, the poet's 'last words' appeared in the world as a ready-made tweet, seemingly composed that it might be forwarded and shared between the computers and mobile devices of millions of people. Even after the initial media attention had passed, sharing the once private message became a public tribute, an act of communal condolence and vicarious stoicism. While the words of the message were much discussed and admired, the fact that they were transmitted by text message was either overlooked or taken as an anomaly. Even as Heaney's message was being analysed and admired on blogs, news websites and social networks, it was also being appropriated. Taken up as an online battle cry against any and all obstacles, sending and receiving a facsimile of Heaney's message allowed people to absorb the poet's imperative into their own devices and lives. As discussed above, a family tree is as much a record of death as of life. So too this short private message positioned Heaney's death within the lives of innumerable others but its global dissemination produced a wholly different network diagram: a bloated and misshapen family tree on which people with no biological or legal relationship link themselves to a singular life.

Such connections subvert the hierarchical, chronological structure of the straight-lined, right-angled family tree. This is a reflection of the age we live in, since, in both content and form, digital life narratives privilege the anecdotal and the personal. Mainstream social networks have increased the number of life narratives we are exposed to and with that our expectations of what a life should be. Even when we understand that a Facebook profile or Pinterest board is the height of artifice, online as in print, life narratives are highly performative, contrived, mediated and influential. Both the @Ireland account and Seamus Heaney's final text message form part of this innovation but they also remain tied to a core assumption of Irish autobiography, that individual lives are never fully separated from the communal story of the nation.

Future tense

Discussing Colm Tóibín's novel *Brooklyn* (2009) and Edna O'Brien's *The Light of the Evening* (2006), Eve Walsh Stoddard asserts: 'At least in literature, there is a sense that once an Irish person moved to America or Australia, though not to Britain, an attempt to return would be disruptive to the Irish place whence they migrated.'[25] As Stoddard observes,

---

[25] Eve Walsh Stoddard, 'Home and Belonging among Irish Migrants: Transnational versus Placed Identities in *The Light of Evening* and *Brooklyn: A Novel*', *Éire-Ireland*, 47:1 (2012), 157.

geographical proximity differentiates Britain from destinations like America and Australia, which are seemingly 'more different' not only in terms of space but also time. Since return is eminently possible from Britain, it is often expected, not least in times of celebration or crisis. The advent of low-cost air travel led commentators to coin the terms 'Ryanair generation' and 'semigrant' to indicate the cohort of Irish people able, and arguably then obliged, to travel back and forth to Ireland from other European countries and, in particular, from Britain. More recently, this trend for bilocation has been displaced by the so-called 'Skype generation', a term used to describe Irish emigrants who are 'not really gone because they are always in touch'.[26] Certainly, new technologies and affordable air travel have undermined the idea that emigration is unidirectional. As Piaras Mac Éinrí explains: 'The notion of the finality of the act of emigration has been replaced by a much more fluid reality of sojourners, circular migration, and transnational experiences and identities.'[27]

Nevertheless, Irish emigration remains a hugely emotive topic. For some, it is a cyclical national tragedy; for others, evidence of innate youthful ambition. The most recent 'wave' took place against the backdrop of the economic crash of 2008, resulting in what Breda Gray describes as 'the familiar response of emigration'.[28] Although socially and economically significant, as Gray points out, 'the emigration of Irish nationals remains well below that of the late 1980s when more than 70,000 people left in one year'.[29] The quantitative facts relating to the latest period of outward migration – in particular, the details of exactly *who* is leaving – are often displaced by the long-held anxiety that Irish emigration is evidence of collective cultural and economic failure. It is in this context that stories of young, successful emigrants achieve such an obvious currency.

On 21 October 2011, the *Irish Times* launched the 'Generation Emigration' project, with the explicit aim of depicting 'how the internet has made the world a smaller, cosier place for emigrants'.[30] Featured in the print and online editions of the newspaper, as well as via dedicated social media accounts, 'Generation Emigration' proclaimed itself a 'contributor-sourced web-centered discussion' that aimed to 'create an archive of resources on contemporary emigration'.[31] The series opened with familiar language, referring to the 'mass exodus of Irish citizens', yet it had a clear

---

[26] Breda Gray, '"Generation Emigration": The Politics of (Trans)National Social Reproduction in Twenty-First-Century Ireland', *Irish Studies Review*, 21:1 (2013), 21.

[27] Piaras Mac Éinrí and Tina O'Toole, 'Editors' Introduction: New Approaches to Irish Migration', *Éire-Ireland*, 47:1–2 (2012), 10.

[28] Gray, '"Generation Emigration"', 20.   [29] Ibid.   [30] Ibid., 22.   [31] Ibid., 26.

longitudinal aim: to consider emigration in terms of its 'lasting impact on their lives, on the lives of those they've left behind, and our society and economy'.[32] 'Generation Emigration' was also rooted in new technologies from the start, being focused on the 'current generation of mobile Irish citizens'.[33] So while the emigrants featured share their experiences and offer advice to others with an awareness of the evolving economic and political climate, the project has a far grander aim in its ambition to become a digital archive of Irish emigration for the future. To some degree this ambition has already been achieved, with online archives on the newspaper's website reflecting several years' worth of blog postings by the latest generation of emigrants.

The short, first-person blog posts that comprise the 'Generation Emigration' archive are significant precisely because they are so familiar. The young graduate who describes himself as an economic migrant, having left for Britain days after finishing college, is all too typical, viewing the event as 'a natural (almost expected) progression rather than an option'.[34] Versions of his story proliferate in the archive and are placed into historical perspective by academic contributors who note the undeniable echo of 'single young people in the late teens and early 20s' leaving, as well as the irresistible difference for this new generation: technology. As Enda Delaney observes: 'An emigrant who left in the middle of the 19th century was unlikely to see friends and family ever again. Today it is a very different world with instantaneous communication.'[35] Taking this much further, writer Belinda McKeon builds on the ubiquity of web technology to claim:

> This is how we do emigration these days. Online, of course; that goes without saying. Not that we emigrate to the internet (although, on second thoughts, maybe we do); rather, that we emigrate with a few clicks of the mouse – the destination researched, the forum joined, the visa sought, the flight booked. Then, once away, we click our way back into Ireland: status updates. Twitter streams.[36]

[32] Ciara Kenny, 'Generation Emigration: What's it all About?', *Irish Times*, 20 October 2011, www.irishtimes.com (accessed 6 September 2015). In its updated format, 'Generation Emigration' also acts as a forum for those who may emigrate in the future, offering destination guides, case studies and practical advice.

[33] Ibid.

[34] Diarmaid O'Neill, 'Current Generation is Gone, Act now to Save the Next', *Irish Times*, 20 October 2011, www.irishtimes.com (accessed 6 September 2015).

[35] Enda Delaney, 'Traditions of Emigration: The Irish Habit of Going Away', *Irish Times*, 2 November 2011, www.irishtimes.com (accessed 6 September 2015).

[36] Belinda McKeon, 'Hashtag Homesick: Our House', *Irish Times*, 7 June 2012, www.irishtimes.com (accessed 6 September 2015).

If McKeon is characteristically attentive to the symbolic, other contributors are resolutely practical. Louise O'Sullivan, quoted in an article by Alan Keane, goes so far as to say: 'Social media makes it easier to leave. Knowing I can communicate with family and friends is a huge reassurance. I would definitely not be as quick to leave if the likes of Skype and Facebook didn't exist.'[37]

This sense in which technology permits Irish emigrants to stay 'in touch' applies to the political as much as the personal. One of the tributary victories of the marriage equality referendum of 2015 was surely a transformed sense of the collective power of the Irish diaspora. Through their 'We're Coming Back' campaign, David Burns and Connor O'Neill drew attention to the frustration of Irish people living abroad, the great majority of whom are unable to vote in Irish elections and referenda. Such individuals were depicted in 'Generation Emigration' as only able to 'stand by and watch the news in a forced, frustrated quiet as a decision that may affect their future is made without their input'.[38] As marriage equality campaigners came to recognize, in line with Gray's analysis, the putative connectivity of communication technology 'does not deliver when "being there" is required and can in fact create a heightened sense of separation and personal failure'.[39] In the event, many Irish people living overseas did return for the referendum, their journeys and testimonies captured across social media via #hometovote. Their commitment to the cause and access to funds to travel further reinforced the idea that these were a new breed of Irish emigrant, open-minded, well-educated, technologically astute.

For the most part, these are the types of lives on display at 'Generation Emigration'. Barry McKinley's blog post, by contrast, does not describe the corporate opportunities in Dubai or food culture in Korea; rather, he is 'one of the other guys'.[40] As he writes about returning to New York in what he views as a second period of forced economic migration, McKinley observes that all of the concern for Irish 'cleverness trickling away' might have obscured the equally significant 'muscle wastage', as those who 'wash windows and sweep floors on construction sites' also leave.[41] For McKinley, the Skype generation of Irish emigrants is a source of suspicion

---

[37] Alan Keane, 'Emigrant Friends Compare Lives around the World on Facebook', *Irish Times*, 20 March 2012, www.irishtimes.com (accessed 6 September 2015).

[38] David Burns and Connor O'Neill, 'Emigrants Want to Vote in Marriage Equality Referendum', *Irish Times*, 22 August 2014, www.irishtimes.com (accessed 6 September 2015).

[39] Gray, "'Generation Emigration'", 26.

[40] Barry McKinley, 'Off to New York with the iPaddies', *Irish Times*, 30 March 2012, www.irishtimes.com (accessed 6 September 2015).

[41] Ibid.

(and indeed derision), being seen as inauthentic virtual Irish men and women: 'These are not the emigrants of your father's generation; these kids have seen the world before they even get there, through Facebook and MySpace and LinkedIn. They network, and they work the Net. These aren't just Paddies, these are iPaddies.'[42]

As a future archive of Irish emigrant experience, 'Generation Emigration' continues its effort to represent the diversity of the contemporary experience. More recently, the *Irish Times* has built on the success of the project with a companion series, 'New to the Parish', which reports on the experiences of people who have moved to Ireland in the past decade. Following a similar model to 'Generation Emigration', contributors to 'New to the Parish' provide a potted life history, describing how and why they came to Ireland, what their first impressions were, what they observed, felt, wondered. These mini-autobiographies appear online, often supplemented with a short video. Although references to extreme hardship and trauma are inevitably present, for the most part these are upbeat stories of innovation and perseverance. By their nature, the stories featured on 'New to the Parish' often involve people overcoming obstacles or falling in love. The subjects include a charismatic fashion designer and businesswoman from Nigeria and an earnest, softly spoken Swedish barman – who wouldn't welcome such people? Rhetorically and politically, it is hugely significant that those arriving are portrayed as at least as interesting and talented as those who leave. Rather than the intellectual and cultural deficit implied by the 'depressingly, long-existent cliché terms' such as brain drain, the lives curated in 'New to the Parish' suggest an equal exchange of cleverness, capability and creativity.[43] If the lives captured by 'Generation Emigration' offer up new versions of the oldest of Irish stories, those in 'New to the Parish' are an essential reminder that those who arrive, like those who depart, have stories of their own, with reasons, motivations and dreams; things to run away from and things to run towards.

Conclusion

In her 1997 inauguration speech, President Mary McAleese thanked the emigrants of the 'global Irish family', noting, somewhat romantically, that they had 'kept their love of Ireland, its traditions and its culture deep in their hearts'.[44] For the most recent, twenty-first-century wave of

---

[42] Ibid.   [43] O'Neill, 'Current Generation is Gone, Act now to Save the Next'.
[44] Mary McAleese, 'Inauguration Speech', http://gos.sbc.edu/m/mcaleese.html (accessed 6 September 2015).

emigrants, it might be more accurate to say that they have kept a love for Ireland deep in their pockets, on the smart phones which allow them to stay in touch with friends and family. These evolutions in technology simply remind us that both the scattering out and indeed the gathering back in of Irish people is a process not only of physical relocation but also of flights of the imagination. It seems somewhat redundant, then, to claim that Irish life narratives, the manifold forms in which Irish people attempt to express what it is to live a life, have been altered in response to digital modes and capacities. At the very least, it is clear that digital life narratives have moved beyond the literary formalities which distinguish between autobiography, biography, memoir, the diary, ego documents and so on. It is also clear that the long-form prose narratives of the nineteenth and twentieth centuries are no longer the only model for Irish autobiographers. Arguably, the clearest day-to-day manifestation of this is the move away from predominantly textual iterations of a life narrative, culminating in that most obvious derivation of the self-portrait, the selfie. Equally significant is the way digital life-writing is rarely just writing but also a bricolage of media, shared videos and filtered and doctored images.

This chapter opened with family historians and their search for documented, tangible connections to the lives of their ancestors, an activity which might easily be seen in parallel to the contemporary need to be perpetually connected to the people of the present via social networks. Collating a family tree produces a narrative in which the past informs and defines the present. In many digital iterations of life narrative, by contrast, the present is shaped to construct the future. A witty tweet or carefully posed Instagram picture is precisely curated in order to draw comment and approval in the very near future. Contemporary Irish emigrants are a case in point: physically distanced, technologically connected and subject to a social media which throws 'connections at us like so many spindly-branched family trees'.[45] These changing technologies of identity expect – even demand – that we engage with one another in an unending cycle of self-narration and social commentary. Rarely, though, do we think of such narratives as the archives of our own lives on which future generations may draw. Pause now to think about your own social media profiles or archived hard drives; it's hard not to pity any unfortunate descendants who might one day trawl through the various webpages you have shared, or the ubiquitous pictures of snowy days or restaurant meals unnecessarily and dully photographed. Like most people, these fragments and clichés

---

[45] McKeon, 'Hashtag Homesick'.

which constitute an online life will say so much about you and, of course, say nothing much at all.

Further Reading

Arthur, Paul Longley. 'Digital Biography: Capturing Lives Online', *a/b: Auto/ Biography Studies*, 24:1 (2009): 74–92.

Kenny, Ciara, ed. *Ireland and Me: Reflections by Emigrants.* Dublin: Irish Times Books, 2015.

Lillington, Karlin. 'Ireland, Technology and the Language of the Future', *Irish Review*, 31 (2004): 66–73.

Lynch, Claire. *Cyber Ireland: Text, Image, Culture.* Basingstoke: Palgrave Macmillan, 2014.

O'Sullivan, James, Órla Murphy and Shawn Day. 'The Emergence of the Digital Humanities in Ireland', *Breac: A Digital Journal of Irish Studies* (October 2015).

Poletti, Anna and Julie Rak, eds. *Identity Technologies: Constructing the Self Online.* Madison: University of Wisconsin Press, 2014.

Index